The Media in Your Life

The Media in Your Life

An Introduction to Mass Communication

THIRD EDITION

Jean Folkerts
George Washington University

Stephen Lacy
Michigan State University

PEARSON

Boston • New York • San Francisco
Mexico City • Montreal • Toronto • London • Madrid • Munich • Paris
Hong Kong • Singapore • Tokyo • Cape Town • Sydney

Executive Editor: Karon Bowers
Series Editor: Molly Taylor
Senior Developmental Editor: Carol Alper
Editorial Assistant: Michael Kish
Senior Marketing Manager: Mandee Eckersley
Composition and Prepress Buyer: Linda Cox
Manufacturing Buyer: Megan Cochran
Cover Administrator: Linda Knowles
Editorial–Production Service: Omegatype Typography, Inc.
Interior Designer: Carol Somberg
Cover Designer: Susan Paradise
Photo Research: Laura Frankenthaler
Illustrations: Omegatype Typography, Inc.
Electronic Composition: Omegatype Typography, Inc.

For related titles and support materials, visit our online catalog at www.ablongman.com.

Between the time Website information is gathered and then published, it is not unusual for some sites to have closed. Also, the transcription of URLs can result in typographical errors. The publisher would appreciate notification where these errors occur so that they may be corrected in subsequent editions.

Library of Congress Cataloging-in-Publication Data

Folkerts, Jean.
    The media in your life : an introduction to mass communication / Jean Folkerts,
Stephen Lacy.—3rd ed.
        p.   cm.
    Includes bibliographical references and index.
    ISBN 0-205-38701-2
    1. Mass media.   I. Lacy, Stephen.   II. Title.
P90.F628   2004
302.23—dc21   2003044423

Printed in the United States of America

10   9   8   7   6   5   4   3   2   1   VHP   08   07   06   05   04   03

For Leroy and Jenny Towns and Sean Lange

For Leslie, Katie, and Laurie Lacy

BRIEF CONTENTS

CONTENTS

chapter 3

Public Relations
56

chapter 4

Advertising
86

PART TWO: Media Industries — 112

chapter 5

Books — 112

chapter 6

Newspapers

chapter 7

Magazines

chapter 8

The Movies
188

chapter 9

Radio
220

chapter 10

Television 248

chapter 11

Music and the Recording Industry 284

chapter 12

Computers and the Internet 314

PART THREE: Media Issues   340

chapter **13**

Ethics   340

chapter **14**

Regulation   366

chapter 15

Mass Communication Research: From Content to Effects 398

FEATURES at a GLANCE

■ MEDIA IN YOUR LIFE

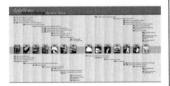

■ DATELINE

■ CULTURAL IMPACT

■ GLOBAL IMPACT

■ MEDIA CONVERGENCE

■ PROFILE

■ DISCUSSING TRENDS

■ NAVIGATING THE WEB

PREFACE

How should we evaluate media and media products we see in our everyday lives? Media exert an enormous impact on our lives through their global economic power as large corporations, such as Disney and Comcast. But these media companies are more than large economic entities. They produce media content. People's perception of media content influences the way they understand the world and react to other people. As a result, media content can have a powerful impact on individuals. Should we consider content as simple works of art? Popular culture entertainment? Symbolic representations of power and ideology in society? Are they reflections of media as a corporate institution? Perhaps they can be all of these.

Thinking about these questions as teachers and scholars more than a decade ago led us to develop the themes for *The Media in Your Life*. This book emphasizes economics, technological convergence, globalization, and cultural change within the context of history. As teachers, we could not find a text that covered all these topics and issues to the degree we think students need and want. As a media economist and a historian, we wanted more context for our students. Context is essential to viewing mass media in the modern world. Context is what enables us to perceive technological change over time and to see similarities and differences. It keeps us from either overemphasizing or discounting developments such as the Internet. To further emphasize the importance of context, we have incorporated a historical perspective into each chapter rather than including a separate chapter on history.

Even though we have continued with the basic concepts behind the first and second editions, the third edition is a very different book. We have restructured the order of chapters to emphasize the basic functions of media—to inform, to entertain, and to persuade. In doing so, we added a general chapter about journalism. To enhance student interaction, we added a section at the end of each chapter to stimulate discussion of evolving trends. We also have followed the advice of many of our colleagues in revising the third edition to shift emphasis on a particular topic or to clarify key points. Examples are updated. Tables and statistics and the discussions of their significance reflect the changing pace of the media world. Pages have been redesigned to make information more accessible. The result is a book that serves as an up-to-date guide to the world of media literacy and practice.

As with earlier editions, we benefited from discussions in our classes about how audiences interpret and incorporate the media into worldviews and lifestyles. What we came to consider important for students to discover is how media products and their impact on audiences have important societal functions that influence and interact with the industry that generated them. Media products have social, economic, and political roles that need to be examined along with their immediate role for consumer audiences and producer industries.

Media in a Student's Life

As teachers of mass communication, we have developed a text that guides students on how to view and interpret media messages. This book moves students beyond the "gee-whiz" level of interpretation of media to evaluating how media influence our personal and professional lives. Organizational and pedagogical aids in the text help students enjoy the study of media and understand its influence and day-to-day relevance. We have therefore retained the title of the earlier editions: *The Media in Your Life: An Introduction to Mass Communication.*

The book's scope is geared to a broader audience than many introductory texts for mass media courses. It is appropriate for majors in journalism and mass communication programs as well as for nonmajors who seek a general education course in media literacy. With this wide audience in mind, the book can best be characterized as having a liberal arts approach—an approach that is consistent with the needs of nonmajors, but an approach that, nevertheless, also meets accreditation standards of the Accrediting Council in Journalism and Mass Communication. Although a large amount of information as to how the media work is provided for those planning to become professional journalists, the book is relevant for general communicators as well.

Goals for This Book

Our goals for this edition include an attempt to show current and historic examples of media as an institution of life in the United States. This emphasis and the examples we chose encouraged us to ask students to seek explanations for the way media function within society, rather than limiting them to a microscopic examination of the day-to-day operations of media organizations.

We especially believe students will benefit from a text that examines the professional and cultural aspects of media within an economic framework. Only when the media assume their true place as an institution that interacts systematically with other institutions such as churches, governments, and schools can media study be relevant. Students need a systemwide perspective of the media's functions on a day-to-day basis rather than a projection of the media's negative social consequences.

The commerce of media is discussed from the assumption that, collectively, media organizations form an institution that ranks with government and religion in impact on U.S. society. Because of this power, the U.S. media system should be understood for what it is: a collection of primarily commercial organizations that influence people and society in both positive and negative ways. A key part of this understanding is a neutral discussion of how the media operate within the U.S. economic system and its member organizations.

Seeing the Media as a Coherent Story

We believe that an understanding of the media in contemporary society is based on an understanding of the history of media: Key segments of the media create stories that make sense. Too often the economic, political, social, and cultural strands of the media have been seen as single threads in a tapestry to be examined individually or in small sections. But seeing the full effect of the media tapestry requires that one view all the threads as a whole, which presents a coherent story over time. Because many schools no longer require a separate media history course, this complete picture may be unavailable, even to media majors. *The Media in Your Life* offers its chapters as complete stories of how each element of our media system evolved, what its issues and elements are, and where it seems to be headed.

As part of the ongoing story of media within society, the development of technology is woven into this book. Since the original conceptualization of this book, communication technology has expanded and changed with incredible speed. The impact has been tremendous, but not always as strong as or in the direction some have predicted. Many who hyped changing technology saw it as a gold mine for generating money, but that has not happened. Computer-based technology has yet to replace existing media, but its simple use for e-mail and instant messaging has dramatically reshaped how people interact. But despite developing communication technology's failure to live up to previous hype, it continues to promise amazing transformations in society and communication. This promise will develop as media experiment and blend, and so the book stresses the concept of media convergence to highlight important overlapping and blending in media functions as technology changes. Because media technology and the technology industries are constantly changing, we stress the effects of evolving technology as part of media's social, economic, and cultural roles.

The Plan of This Book

The book has been reorganized for the third edition. The first four chapters deal with the process and functions of mediated communication. Media companies produce content to inform, to entertain, and to persuade. When media inform, they provide content that helps people understand their lives and helps them make decisions about their world. That is why people read and watch news. When media entertain, the content brings enjoyment to people in a variety of ways. That explains why people go to movies and watch television. Organizations and people use media to try to convince someone to believe certain things or act in certain ways. Advertisements and editorials aim to do this.

These three uses cover almost all content in media. In addition, a particular element of content may be used in more than one way. A well-written book can entertain and inform. All three uses can take place in any medium, although some media work better at these uses than others. The authors reorganized the book to emphasize these uses and to provide an understanding of what motivates the creators of content and why people pay attention to media content.

To emphasize the three main uses, a new chapter about journalism was added to the chapters about advertising and public relations that appeared in earlier editions. The material in the first and second chapters of the second edition was combined into a new first chapter, which discusses the basic process of communication. Although somewhat abstract, the material in the first chapter can be used to analyze the rest of the book.

Chapters 5 through 12 are about particular media and media industries. These include books, magazines, newspapers, television, movies, music and recordings, computers, and radio. Despite efforts to converge media, the communication businesses continue to use the familiar categories of media. As long as this is the case, this is one way, but not the only way, of understanding media in your life.

The third section of the book, Chapters 13 through 15, includes chapters from the second edition that address issues and processes that cut across media. These include chapters about ethics, regulation, and communication research. These affect all media in a variety of ways, and because of this, they are presented after students study media industries.

Starting with Chapter 2, each chapter has a similar organization. An introductory vignette leads into a "Media in Your Life" feature, which helps readers develop an awareness of the chapter's ongoing issues. Each chapter begins with a historical

narrative that discusses media's impact on U.S. life. The chapter moves on to "Today's Market Structure," which thoroughly describes economic and institutional processes that affect each segment of the media, including production. The "Trends" section concerns ongoing developments affecting the particular medium, use, or process. These trends have the potential to reshape media, but their outcomes remain unclear. A new section called "Discussing Trends" has been added in the third edition to stimulate discussion of the trends. This section provides questions specifically related to the trends and provides a basis of discussion and research by the class.

Guidance for Learning Important Ideas, Concepts, and Terms

The third edition of *The Media in Your Life* continues its unique learning system with the "Key Concepts" listed at the beginning of each chapter. These key concepts reappear along with definitions or explanations throughout the chapter in relevant sections. The ideas encapsulated under the key concepts are central to the media topic in each chapter and are highlighted as guideposts to students when reviewing main ideas. The key concepts, along with the issues posed in the chapter introduction, are designed to help students focus on main ideas and terms to make sense of the media story and to follow the thread of each chapter. In addition to these learning guides, distinctive **media terms** within the chapter text are boldfaced and featured with glossary definitions in the margin. Although these media terms function to ensure that students absorb the unique terminology of the media without confusing their grasp of larger concepts, they can also be used by individual instructors as the focus of learning goals for a more technical understanding of each of the media formats. Finally, after students have completed the chapter and are ready to review, they will find the issues listed in the introductory section reinforced at the end of the chapter with "Questions for Review" and "Issues to Think About."

Special Features to Focus Interest and Learning

A number of special features have been retained and updated in the text at appropriate intervals to highlight key ideas and to serve as the focus of special instructional units.

Chapter Opening Vignette ✦ Each chapter begins with a vignette and accompanying photo to help the reader put the content of the chapter into a real-life context.

Media in Your Life ✦ The introductory vignette of each chapter concludes with an interactive "Media in Your Life" feature, which alerts readers to how their everyday media behavior relates to forthcoming issues in the chapter. This feature is not a quiz or learning check; it is a chance for readers to take note of their own media awareness and to relate issues in the chapter to their own media attitudes and behavior.

Datelines ✦ A graphic continuum, "Dateline," spreads out major media events across time, which helps students relate events and sequences in the media story with historic events that may be familiar to them.

Impact Features ✦ Three special-feature boxes throughout the chapters are presented to illustrate key social and technical influences that intersect with the media. To focus attention on key

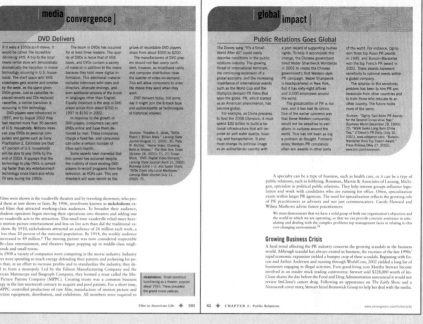

concepts and themes, the text includes the following boxed features: "Cultural Impact" (highlighting the ways the media influence and represent American culture), "Media Convergence" (stressing the continuing overlapping and blending of media functions as technologies develop), and "Global Impact" (calling attention to international influences in key areas).

Profiles ✦
A prominent person in each medium is highlighted with a special portrait to focus attention on key roles of typical and influential players. This feature provides a miniature case study of a career that can be analyzed in assignments.

Graphic Charts, Diagrams, and Photos ✦
An array of illustrative material in each chapter provides supplementary data, useful charts illustrating key ideas, and historical and current photos that provide visual examples of concepts presented in the text.

Navigating the Web ✦
Each chapter has a special section listing web sites that pertain to the material in the chapter. These sites provide information about the topic of the chapter and can be consulted for special projects, collaborative discussions, or term papers.

Supplements for the Instructor

Instructor's Manual/Test Bank ✦
The Instructor's Manual, by Randall Pugh of Montana State University, features a wide variety of student activities, Internet exercises, chapter summaries, chapter outlines, and questions to spark classroom discussions. The Test Bank, by Kenya McCullum, includes 1,200 multiple choice, true/false, matching, fill-in-the-blank, short answer, and essay questions.

Computerized Test Bank ✦ The printed test questions are also available electronically through our computerized testing system, TestGen EQ. The fully networkable test generating software is now available in a multiplatform CD-ROM. The user-friendly interface enables instructors to view, edit, and add questions, transfer questions to tests, and print tests in a variety of fonts. Search and sort features allow instructors to locate questions quickly and arrange them in a preferred order.

PowerPoint™ Package ✦ Available at http://suppscentral.ablongman.com, this presentation package, prepared by Richard Caplan, University of Akron, provides slides combining graphic and text images in modular units to accompany each chapter. The package is compatible with Windows and Macintosh systems.

The Allyn & Bacon Interactive Video Program and User's Guide ✦ Our video program brings media issues to life in your classroom! Encompassing a wide range of media issues and problems, this supplement features specially selected news segments complete with commentary and on-screen critical thinking questions. A printed guide will help you integrate the video program into your curriculum effectively. Some restrictions apply.

Allyn & Bacon Communication Studies Digital Media Archive, Version 2.0 ✦ This archive is available on CD-ROM and offers more than two hundred still images, video excerpts, and PowerPoint™ slides that can be used to enliven classroom presentations.

Blockbuster Video Guide for Introductory Mass Communication Classes ✦ This guide, prepared by Deborah Petersen-Perlman of the University of Minnesota, Duluth, assists teachers in reaching today's students through film and video to convey basic media concepts, illustrate complex interrelationships, and present historical facts.

The A&B Mass Communication Video Library and the Movie Library ✦ Adopters of this text have access to two rich libraries: (1) a set of videos about the media, created through Insight Media and Films for the Humanities; and (2) the *Movie Library*, featuring popular entertainment movies that can be used to illustrate key media topics and issues. Some restrictions apply.

Supplements for the Student

Companion Website with Online Practice Tests ✦ Prepared by Andris Straumis, University of Wisconsin–Eau Claire, and expanded and enhanced for the current edition, this site's in-depth coverage of hot topics and personalities in mass communication is sure to benefit your study of mass communication. It also features convergence case studies and Internet-linked dateline charts. Find it at www.ablongman.com/folkerts3e.

Research Navigator Guide for Mass Communication ✦ This reference guide, by Ronald Roat of Southern Indiana University, includes tips, resources, activities, and URLs to help students. The first part introduces students to the basics of the Internet and the World Wide Web. Part two includes more than thirty Internet activities that tie into the content of the text. Part three lists hundreds of web resources for mass communication. The guide also includes information on how to correctly cite research and a guide to building an online glossary. In addition, the Research Navigator Guide booklet contains a student access code for the Research Navigator database, offering students free, unlimited access to a collection of more than 25,000 discipline-specific articles from top-tier academic publications and peer-reviewed journals, as well as popular news publications such as the *New York Times*. It is available packaged with new copies of the text.

Media Literacy Guide ✦ This activity guide, prepared by Ralph Carmode of Jacksonville State University, helps you use critical thinking skills to develop an awareness and understanding of how and why the media and their messages affect us.

Acknowledgments

This text has evolved over time and through experience in teaching at two major mass media programs at George Washington University and at Michigan State University. We offer a special thank-you to Lucinda Davenport of Michigan State University, who helped conceptualize and write the first edition. We also thank Pamela Laucella and Keith Kincaid for their contributions to the public relations and advertising chapters. We wish to thank our other colleagues at these schools who encouraged us to shape an introductory course in the direction that this book has taken. In particular, we thank Leslie Lacy and Leroy Towns of the Michigan State University staff, and Maria George, executive aide, and Tracy Cook Pannozzo, communications director, in the School of Media and Public Affairs at George Washington University. We would also like to thank Dwight Teeter, whose advice across the years has been thoughtful and sustaining and whose great joy in being an administrator has been invaluable in helping others along their way.

At Allyn & Bacon, many editors and marketing people have helped bring this book to a level that best expresses our approach to the course. In particular, Allen Workman, the development editor for the first edition, motivated us to complete the project and systematically helped conceptualize the pedagogical elements of the text. For the second and third editions, Carol Alper, the development editor, kept us on course. We also thank Robert Howerton of Omegatype Typography, Inc., for his dedication to this project. For the first and second editions, Karon Bowers, our acquisitions editor, provided support and guidance. We thank Molly Taylor, series editor, for her commitment to and work on the third edition.

For all three editions, a number of our colleagues have provided helpful manuscript reviews at each stage of development. We hope they feel the book has benefited from their comments and advice. We wish to thank the following reviewers:

Edward Adams, Angelo State University
Tom Buckner, McClennan Community College
Larry Campbell, University of Alaska, Anchorage
Richard E. Caplan, University of Akron
David W. D'Alessio, University of Connecticut, Stamford
Bill Dean, Texas Tech University
Thomas Draper, University of Nebraska, Kearney
Donald G. Godfrey, Arizona State University
Colin Gromatzky, New Mexico State University
James L. Hoyt, University of Wisconsin
Jack Keever, Seton Hall University
Kenneth J. Levine, Illinois State University
Carol M. Liebler, Syracuse University
Rebecca Ann Lind, University of Illinois, Chicago
William M. Lingle, Linfield College
Toni J. Morris, University of Indianapolis
Jack A. Nelson, Brigham Young University
Fred Owens, Youngstown State University
Elizabeth M. Perse, University of Delaware
Evelyn Plummer, Seton Hall University
Randall K. Pugh, Montana State University at Billings

Ronald C. Roat, University of Southern Indiana
Jeanne Rollberg, University of Arkansas at Little Rock
Marshel Rossow, Mankato State University
Kim A. Smith, Iowa State University
Roger Soenksen, James Madison University
Andris Straumanis, University of Wisconsin, Eau Claire
Hazel Warlaumont, California State University, Fullerton
Sandra Wertz, The University of South Carolina

In addition to those who specifically read chapters and provided comments during the writing and revision of this text, we wish to thank all those who worked with us on research and teaching projects over the years, whose guidance led us to incorporate our knowledge—and much of theirs—into this text. These individuals include:

David Coulson, University of Nevada–Reno
Wayne Danielson, University of Texas at Austin
Carolyn Dyer, University of Iowa
Douglas Gomery, University of Maryland
Owen Johnson, Indiana University
Peter M. McGrath, The George Washington University
Robert Picard, Turku School of Economics
Shirley Quate
Stephen Reese, University of Texas at Austin
Dan Riffe, Ohio University
Mary Alice Shaver, Michigan State University
Pamela Shoemaker, Syracuse University
Todd Simon, Kansas State University
Jeffery Smith, University of Wisconsin–Milwaukee
Ardyth Sohn
Christopher Sterling, The George Washington University
Jim Tankard, University of Texas at Austin

The Media in Your Life

We the People

Media and Communication

On April 8, 2002, the *New York Times* was awarded an unprecedented seven Pulitzer Prizes for its news coverage and commentary during 2001—a year that was itself without precedent.

In the shattered calm of a clear September day, history was forever altered. Events unfolded with an almost unimaginable speed, in myriad directions—and across countless lives. Covering these events and their aftermath was, and continues to be, a heartbreaking obligation to fulfill. But we will continue to work to the best of our ability to assure the depth and breadth of our coverage—in print, and online.

—*New York Times* Institutional Advertisement in the *Columbia Journalism Review*, May/June 2002 (inside cover)

After terrorists flew jetliners into the World Trade Center and the Pentagon, most American adults turned to the three major networks to follow the story. There was no measurement of the daytime television audience on September 11, 2001, but that night, at least 80 million Americans were watching ABC,

CBS, or NBC throughout prime time (8–11 P.M.). Before the terrorist attacks, 20–25 million people watched the three evening news shows each night.

—Leonard Downie Jr. and Robert G. Kaiser, *The News about the News: American Journalism in Peril*

With the cable news networks attracting a significantly higher share of people using television after 9/11, combined ratings for these outlets have surged from year-ago levels. Although all of the networks have shown hefty percent increases, CNN, Fox News Channel and MSNBC have garnered the largest point gains.

—McCann-Erickson WorldGroup Press Release, www.mccann.com/news/pr19.html, accessed June 26, 2002

Internet news sites have sustained significant traffic increases since the events of September 11. As compared to the week ending September 9, page views for the week ending September 30 were up 70.0% at ABCNEWS.com, 78.0% at MSNBC.com, 69.2% at NYTimes.com, 31.2% at USATODAY.com and 47.8% at Washingtonpost.com. In addition, average daily unique visitors were up 65.1% at ABCNEWS.com, 63.3% at MSNBC.com, 69.2% at NYTimes.com and 39.7% at USATODAY.com for the same period. Average daily unique visitors at Slate.com increased 76.6% for that period, as well. Many local sites also showed significant gains. For example, Knight Ridder Digital's Miami.com was up 67% in average daily unique visitors, according to Media Metrix, and DetroitFreePress.com was up 98%.

—Knight Ridder News Release, www.knightridderdigital.com/press/releases/p10112001b.htm, accessed June 26, 2002

The events of September 11, 2001, and the unfolding news stories that followed reinforced a long-held belief: Communication media are a defining characteristic of the U.S. political, social, and cultural systems. In this particular instance, as a reader can discern from the quotations at the beginning of this chapter, Americans "tuned in" in large numbers to newspapers, network news, cable

This chapter provides a set of definitions and concepts to help you understand how media affect your life. These concepts have been developed from a few simple questions:

◆ How do people communicate?

◆ How did the media system in the United States evolve and how is it structured today?

◆ What are the converging technological, regulatory, and content issues that affect our ability to communicate?

◆ What are the implications of changing media for a democratic society?

◆ How do media affect cultural and social change?

◆ What is meant by media literacy?

◆ How does the globalization of media affect communication among citizens of the world?

◆ What are the specific functions of mass media?

◆ How do individuals and groups use media in their lives?

Communication *in Your Life*

Interacting with Others and Using Media

This chapter discusses some of the differences between interpersonal communication and mediated communication. It also explains how mass media systems work. Think about the role of communication in your life. As you read this chapter, think about the following questions. Your answers will help you better understand how media affect your life.

- Can you describe a recent experience that involved both the use of media and interaction with another person?
- How was the interpersonal interaction different from your experience using a particular mediated communication?
- How was the media product (program, newscast, advertisement) designed to affect you and others?
- How did you use the media product, and how did you share your experience with others?

broadcasts, magazines, and the Internet. These quotations also demonstrate some of the issues media face today. These issues have to do with the functions of media and with the political impact, economics, cultural force, internationalism, and convergence of today's media.

Communication media are intertwined with the country's historical emphasis on voter participation in popular elections, with a society that has emphasized market values and consumerism, and with a cultural system that faces continuous tensions between the promotion of diversity and the maintenance of social stability. Most important, media are a direct outgrowth of the right to freedom of expression in a democratic society.

Media now are global. Many media companies operate throughout the world in a variety of conditions. About 3,300 newspapers are online worldwide.[1]

Young adults consume media at high levels. They listen to radio an average of six hours a day, they read textbooks and novels, and they watch television (TV sets are turned on in the average household in the United States for seven and a half hours each day). Many spend hours on the Internet in chat groups or use various forms of e-mail. They also read newspapers and magazines. Music, tell-all talk shows, soap operas, situation comedies, and infotainment shows are popular.

All of these communication forms share certain characteristics, but they also differ. People share their experiences and impressions through language, which is a collection of symbols. Communication requires the exchange of information with at least one other person. The exchange can be face-to-face with no intervening technology, or it can be mediated, which requires some mechanism, such as television or the Internet, to communicate these symbols. Mediated communication directed at a large audience is called mass communication.

The role, structure, and economic nature of the system of mass communication in the United States are all concepts that affect our everyday lives. These elements characterize media as an institution, similar to the institutions of government, education, and religion.

In this book, we trace the history of the media because we believe the context in which different forms of mass media emerged significantly affected their role in modern life. Content is affected by economic structure as well as by the cultural values of consumerism. The key to understanding media is to understand such relationships. Thus we have chosen the following media markers—the context of history, economic structure, cultural change, globalization, and technological development/convergence—as the structural elements for this book.

HOW DO PEOPLE COMMUNICATE?

Emily nervously typed her notes into the computer, trying to recall what she had seen and heard at the campuswide discussion session convened to talk about the aftermath of September 11, 2001. She had never dreamed she would find herself covering such a confusing event during her first year working for the campus online news service. As she typed her notes into the computer, she tried to recall what she had seen and heard. She thought she had heard two groups of students arguing about who was responsible for the attacks on Washington, D.C., and New York; but the groups were relatively diffuse, and she wasn't sure what points they were making or whom the people represented.

As Emily typed, Sharon, her editor, approached and sat down. "How are you doing?"

"I feel so emotional about all of this," Emily replied, "but I'm okay. I couldn't always understand what I saw out there."

"Yeah, I remember my instructors talking about covering the Vietnam War demonstrations for their campus newspapers," Sharon said. "Confusing, to say the least. After you finish with your notes, go back to see how people responded to National Guard troops on their campuses during the Vietnam conflict. Some campuses, particularly in New York and Washington, D.C., may be facing similar situations. Some comparisons might make a good sidebar."

After saving her notes, Emily checked into the newspaper's electronic library and entered the words *campus unrest*. She had a hard time narrowing the search, but an hour later, Emily finished her eight-inch story and sent it to the copy desk for a headline and page placement. She leaned back in her chair and thought about what she had seen and how people would react to the stories she and her colleagues had written for the web site and tomorrow's newspaper.

Communicating with other people about events and experiences involves a complex process that has become even more complicated with the communication revolution of the past twenty years. We communicate face-to-face, as Sharon and Emily did, and through electronic media. Emily and the other journalists also communicated their experiences at the campus meeting to thousands of readers through the newspaper.

Mediated Communication

The communication process is sometimes described through models. One well-known **model**, devised by scholars Claude E. Shannon and Warren Weaver, illustrates aspects of the *mediated communication* process.[2] See Figure 1.1.

In Shannon and Weaver's model, the sender translates an idea into symbols, such as words, drawings, or gestures. The symbols create a message that is communicated across a **channel**, or system, that physically transfers the message from the sender to another person or group of people. A telephone, a television set, and the human voice are all channels. The person or people who get the message are receivers. The receiver translates the message from the channel into a mental image. One can assess the accuracy of the process by asking whether the mental image of the receiver corresponds to the idea of the sender. This process can be applied to all human communication.

However, the process of sending and receiving a message is not as simple as it may seem. **Channel noise** (technical or physical interference) or **semantic noise** (the interference created by language or interpretation) can disrupt or distort the message. If Emily's readers could not access her story online because of heavy Web traffic, they would have experienced channel noise, just as if they had been trying to study and their roommates were playing the radio loudly. Sometimes channel noise can be solved rather simply by increasing the capacity or the quality of the technology. Historically, technological improvements have solved many problems of channel noise, such as radio static.

Semantic noise, however, is less easily reduced or ended because it involves underlying meaning. For example, when a word has more than one meaning, readers or listeners may be confused. Readers don't know whether they're invited to a feeding

Figure 1.1

The Communication Process (modified Shannon–Weaver model)

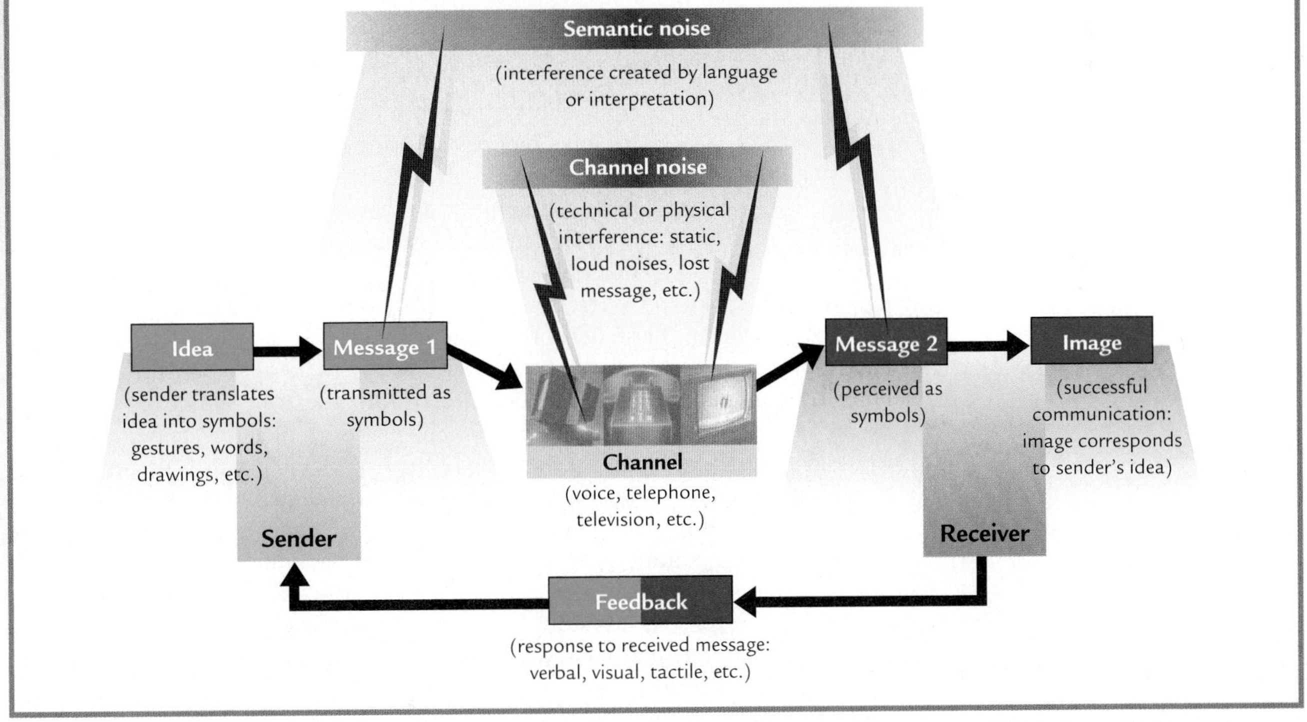

Semantic noise
(interference created by language or interpretation)

Channel noise
(technical or physical interference: static, loud noises, lost message, etc.)

Idea
(sender translates idea into symbols: gestures, words, drawings, etc.)

Message 1
(transmitted as symbols)

Channel
(voice, telephone, television, etc.)

Message 2
(perceived as symbols)

Image
(successful communication: image corresponds to sender's idea)

Sender

Receiver

Feedback
(response to received message: verbal, visual, tactile, etc.)

Source: Claude Shannon and Warren Weaver, *The Mathematical Theory of Communication* (Urbana: University of Illinois Press, 1949), p. 98.

frenzy or being fed spot news when they read the *Washington Post* headline "H. Robert Heller to Be Fed Nominee."[3] Careful crafting of the message by the sender reduces semantic noise.

Another element in the model, **feedback,** also helps reduce semantic noise. Feedback usually starts from the receiver in response to a message, but a series of messages may generate many feedback messages. If Emily remarks to her roommate that "the room is a mess," implying by her tone that the roommate made the mess, the roommate might reply, "What do you mean by that remark?" The fastidious Emily could reply, "You live like a pig, and I want you to pick up your mess." In this situation, feedback has eliminated the semantic noise, although it may not have improved the relationship between the two students.

Feedback can take many forms: verbal, visual, and tactile. In *interpersonal communication,* a simple nod or a quiet "uh-huh" provides feedback that the message is understood. Because mediated communication requires a technological channel, it limits feedback and increases the possibility of mistakes in communication. Receivers of mass mediated messages struggle to create effective responses to an impersonal medium.

Mass Communication

Mass communication involves sharing ideas across a large audience either at a given point or through an extended time frame and usually involves a professional communicator. Most people agree that **mass media** include newspapers, magazines, books, films, television, radio, and recordings. In this book, the Internet is treated as a mass medium, although some scholars believe that its interactivity distinguishes it from traditional mass media. Direct mail, telemarketing, and outdoor advertising may also qualify as mass media even though the particular medium involved may not be considered "mass" by most people.

Although Shannon and Weaver's communication model accounts for mediation—voice, telephone, or other electronic device—it does not account for the intervention of a professional communicator. Most media companies employ professionals to construct, organize, and deliver messages, whether the messages be journalistic, entertaining, or persuasive. Emily was acting as a **professional communicator** when she wrote the story for the student online news service.

Emily's experience can be compared to that of a professional reporter covering another aspect of the same event. Both involve a professional communicator, an aspect of mass communication that is illustrated in the model in Figure 1.2, a modified version of the Westley–MacLean model first published in 1957.[4] On September 20, 2001, President George W. Bush spoke to Congress—and to the nation—to outline his plan for combating terrorism in the aftermath of the September 11 attacks. The model shows how information such as Bush's speech flows as a message to an audience through a mass medium. The communicator in the model selects information that she sees or views from the event and that she obtains from sources. She processes them for delivery to an audience, sometimes interpreting the meaning of the source and events. The communicator thus becomes a determining factor in the accuracy and quality of the message.

The communicator's role can be defined as that of a *gatekeeper of information,* a term defined by a communication theorist, David Manning White, in 1950.[5] He said that journalists tend the gates that control the flow of information; they select what others will receive as news. In the years since the original study, the term *gatekeeper* has come to mean anyone who controls information; the term is applied to the source as well as to the communicator.

The importance of sources is also illustrated in Figure 1.2. Sometimes the source is also the communicator, but more often professionals take over this role. In mak-

Figure 1.2

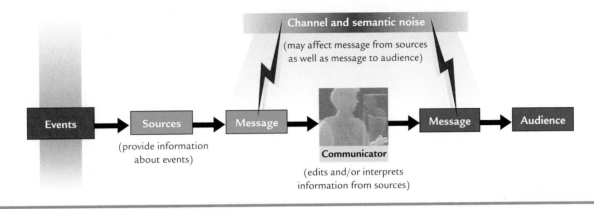

The Mediated Communication Process (modified Westley–MacLean model)

Unlike the simple communication process, mediation requires a communicator to carry the message from a source or sources to an audience. The source provides information to a communicator, such as a journalist, and the communicator analyzes the information and passes on a version of it to the audience. Both steps are subject to semantic and channel noise.

Channel and semantic noise

(may affect message from sources as well as message to audience)

Events → Sources → Message → Communicator → Message → Audience

(provide information about events)

Communicator

(edits and/or interprets information from sources)

Source: Bruce H. Westley and Malcolm S. MacLean Jr., "A Conceptual Model for Communication Research," *Journalism Quarterly* 34 (1957): 31–38.

ing a speech on television, President Bush is a communicator. In other instances in which journalists interview Bush, he becomes a source. Journalists sometimes witness events and report on them, as they did when viewing the Bush speech, but they often rely on sources to interpret events—to expand what the journalist can witness—or to explain issues. Sources in government office can influence news coverage by treating certain reporters more favorably than others and expecting favorable treatment in return. However, more often sources provide information for a story because they believe the story will have a positive effect on an issue they believe in. Reporters need to weigh this information by relying on a variety of sources.

The mass communication process faces the same problems as the interpersonal communication process. Channel noise and semantic noise both affect how well audience members understand the message they receive. Two steps of interpretation occur during mass communication: The semantic noise that occurs when the communicator interprets the message and when the audience interprets it helps to explain media inaccuracy. Journalists and sources sometimes disagree about the meaning of what the source said, and audience members always interpret the meaning of mediated messages in light of their own experiences.

President George W. Bush, seen at a 2002 press conference in Washington, is the source of information. The journalists gathered in the hall will become the communicators who will interpret the information for the mass audience. When Bush speaks directly to the nation via television, he acts as both source and communicator.

Power to the People

During the 1930s, communications researchers were convinced that media had tremendous power. In fact, they believed the power of media was so great that it acted like a "magic bullet"—instantly penetrating the human mind. Although researchers have altered their view of media impact, almost all researchers, media critics, and philosophers believe that media have the power to shape society, at least in some ways.

Critics argue that a small number of gatekeepers—reporters, editors, and producers—determine which information the audience sees or hears. With the advent of the computer information network—the Internet, as well as commercial online services—gatekeepers can be avoided. The possibility of avoiding gatekeepers could have a radical impact on the politics of our society. Howard Rheingold wrote in *The Daily Telegraph*, "Philosophers such as John Locke and pamphleteers such as Tom Paine proposed the radical notion that, if people are educated and free enough to discuss issues among themselves, then citizens would be able to govern themselves, not only by electing repre- sentatives by secret ballot, but by discussing the issues that affect them. This notion has been called the 'public sphere.'"

Rheingold further argued that television had converted the public sphere into a "commodity that could be bought and sold. Reasoned argument lost ground to riveting images and emotional soundbites." Rheingold believes that computer technologies can revitalize the public sphere by creating a new "forum for free speech."

Source: Howard Rheingold, "Switching on the World," *The Daily Telegraph*, May 11, 1994, p. 17.

Media Literacy

Because media have become such an integral part of society, scholars often refer to the need for *media literacy.* Media literacy involves understanding the impact of communication—from advertising, to ideas, to technology.

Browsing the *Media Literacy Review* online gives a reader an understanding of the full scope of issues that fall under this category of media literacy. The commercialization of society through advertising, discerning honest advertising from fraudulent forms, and the distortion of content through media images all fall into the category of media literacy.

The goal of media literacy scholars and educators is to educate the public about how media deliver messages and also to help parents avoid "media tricks." One article in the *Media Literacy Review,* for example, encourages parents to bake cookies with their children in lieu of encouraging them to play with media-related toys. Sometimes the issues addressed are larger societal issues. In 1982, for example, one statement put out by UNESCO (United Nations Educational, Scientific, and Cultural Organization) was, "We must prepare young people for living in a world of powerful images, words, and sounds." Elementary and secondary curricula now include segments on media literacy, and web sites on media literacy resources are numerous.

EVOLUTION OF MASS MEDIA IN THE UNITED STATES

Men and women have always sought ways to communicate with one another and with groups of people. As the groups grew larger, the necessity for technology increased. From listening to the lectures of Socrates in ancient Greece to hearing the beating of drums in Africa, individuals have recognized the importance of information to personal survival and to the development of civilization. As long ago as two thousand years before the birth of Christ, Mediterranean civilizations used technology to create a system of movable type by pressing signs into clay. Carvings in stone and hand printing on thin paper made from the papyrus plant are historical remnants of attempts to communicate. In about 1041, the Chinese printer Pi Sheng printed books using movable type made of hundreds of clay blocks bearing Chinese ideograms. That printing technique was introduced to Europe when Marco Polo returned from his travels in China in 1295. However, the development of movable metal type in the Western world by Johannes Gutenberg in the fifteenth century paved the way for the expansion of a print culture. Gutenberg first carved wood so that letters stood in relief on tiny blocks that could be rearranged into different words; he then inked the blocks so multiple copies of documents could be made. The wood blocks made fuzzy letters, but Gutenberg's assistant, Peter Schöffer, soon realized that metal could be used instead of wood to produce a cleaner type. He used this method to print the English Bible in 1455.[6]

A flatbed press from the Gutenberg era.

Technological development altered types of communication and social and business relationships; it affected the adoption of cultural norms. In medieval Europe before Gutenberg's invention, religious elites controlled information, and the Catholic Church acted as an early gatekeeper of information by dominating the dissemination of official notices. Books were copied laboriously by hand by monks secreted away from the world of trade; official notices also were hand copied and carried as letters or posted where those who could read could see them and pass on the information to those who could not.

Even then, informal networks spread alternative messages and challenged ideas, transmitting a social heritage with a greater dimension than that conveyed by official proclamations. After Gutenberg's invention, the economics of distribution affected the marketplace of ideas. This intellectual marketplace became a commodity market in which books containing a variety of ideas were bought and sold. The mass production of books not only loosened the church's grip on information, but it also created new relationships between the church and the entrepreneur or merchant. Soon merchants began to produce and sell books, providing an outlet for ideas and values that had been kept out of print and confined to oral transmission. The public eagerly sought the histories, religious books, travelogues, and romances that were traded on the open market. Some books that offended the official gatekeepers were prohibited by the church, but they still were sold on the black market. Once printing was available, it was not easily controlled despite the best efforts of kings and church officials.[7]

Communication Networks in North America

The English model of printing was carried to North America, but the lack of a transportation system kept the colonies relatively isolated from one another. Ships from Europe brought letters, newspapers, and books for elite colonists about the government and church in their homelands. In the absence of widely distributed printed forms of information, ministers acted as a powerful elite, conveying official information and moral instruction from the pulpit. Such communication was supplemented, but not replaced, by the first printing press, which was established by Elizabeth Glover in 1638 in Cambridge, Massachusetts. Mrs. Glover's press issued *The Freeman's Oath*, a formal contract of behavioral rules that citizens in the colony were required to sign, and the *Bay Psalm Book*. Those books and documents were intended not for casual reading but for creating standards for the public life of the community. Religious elites used information channels to promote prosocial values such as keeping one's word, keeping the faith in public worship, and advancing literacy.

Once postal routes were established, information became a commercial as well as a political and social commodity. Newspapers circulated first in local communities and then along some of the more popular trade routes, which also served as the delivery system for books.

From the 1830s through the end of the nineteenth century, communication industries expanded. Advanced technology in transportation systems and printing presses allowed for communication systems to serve new audiences and increased the number and type of products available. As railway lines spread throughout the massive geographic area that was to define the United States, products were marketed nationally. The new transportation lines provided new circulation routes for newspapers and fledgling magazines, and national marketing ensured a wide advertising base for at least the mainstream publications. Circulations expanded, and the distribution of newspapers, magazines, and books spread throughout the country. The introduction of rotary printing presses meant that a printer, with the same number of motions required to print a single page on a flatbed press, could feed a roll of paper through the press and produce enormous numbers of printed pages. Whereas in the late 1700s a circulation of 2,500 was considered excellent, by the 1890s newspapers such as the *New York World* reached a million people.

Technology, Transportation, and Communication

In the beginning, communication was linked to transportation because information could travel only as fast as a horse and rider. Information traveled along trade routes along with other commodities.

The Telegraph ✦ The link between communication and transportation was broken in 1844 when Samuel Morse opened the nation's first telegraph line with the question, "What hath God wrought?" No longer was the speed of communication dependent on how fast a horse could gallop; information could travel instantaneously by means of wires from its point of origin to a publisher's desk.

By 1846, newspapers in upstate New York were using the wires to transmit news between the state capital of Albany and other New York cities. In 1848, a group of New York newspapers, including the *Courier and Enquirer, Sun, Herald, Journal of Commerce, Tribune,* and *Express,* hired a steamer to retrieve news from the major port of Halifax, Nova Scotia. The group also negotiated a joint arrangement to use telegraph lines to transmit news from Boston to New York. Those ventures resulted in the establishment of the Associated Press, a **wire service** that dominated delivery of national and international information until the early 1900s.[8]

Radio Revolution ✦ By the early twentieth century, the advent of radio had broken a second link between transportation and communication: Not only could news

wire service: Organizations that collect and distribute news and information to media outlets. Referred to as "wire" because before computer transmission, these services relied on use of the telegraph wires.

Communication via telegraph depends on an infrastructure of telegraph poles and wires. During the Civil War, wires were often cut, and soldiers had to restring them to establish connections with the rest of the country.

travel from its source to an editor's desk as fast as the wires could carry it, but news also could travel from the editor or commentator to the public as fast as it could travel across the air waves.

Radio technology played an important role in World War I in ship-to-shore communications and was regulated by the U.S. Navy. Amateurs also enjoyed building and using radio sets, but few had conceived of it as a broadcasting—or mass communication—tool. At the end of the war, the U.S. Navy strongly opposed returning the rights to the British-owned Marconi Company, which had a monopoly on radio parts. With what historian Christopher Sterling labeled "tacit government approval," Owen D. Young, chairman of the board for General Electric Co., organized a new corporation to hold all U.S. patents. General Electric, together with American Telephone and Telegraph, United Fruit, and Westinghouse Electric, formed the Radio Corporation of America (RCA) and bought out American Marconi for $2.5 million.[9] The companies operated together until 1926. That arrangement set the stage for further radio development organized and controlled by big business and government.

Farm families heard news of the world, as well as classical music and comedy shows, over their radios. For the first time, the distribution of information was not tied to the speed of transportation.

As Westinghouse, General Electric, and RCA established stations in the early 1920s, radio became so popular that RCA sold $11 million worth of receivers in 1922 alone. By 1927, seven hundred U.S. stations were operating, and in 1929, $135 million worth of sets was sold. In 1923, only 7 percent of U.S. households owned a radio set; by 1930, almost 35 percent owned sets.

Motion Pictures and Television ◆ The motion picture industry was well under way by the beginning of World War I, and experimentation with television began in the 1930s. The movies were a popular form of entertainment during the financial depression of the 1930s because people sought an escape from the harsh realities of daily life. Television arrived after World War II in the midst of an expanding consumer society. The prosperity of the post–World War II era and the new technology together began to shape media as a basis for creating a consumer culture. The media attracted mass audiences, and the information provided by the media helped homogenize the audience, stripping it of regional characteristics, dialects, and mores.

Computers and Communication ◆ Computers entered the mass media as typesetting machines during the late 1960s, but computer technology had a more powerful impact on mass media with the development of the home personal computer, or PC. Although traditional media such as newspapers benefit from computer-based technology, such new technologies also create forms of information exchange that were not possible with the old styles of production and distribution.

Communication by means of the computer began in the late 1960s, when the U.S. government connected four computers in Utah and California. The goal was to develop the framework for an emergency communication system by sending information across special high-speed telephone lines. After the mid-1970s, smaller networks such as that used by the National Science Foundation (NSFnet) decided to work together—to internetwork. Today, the Internet links millions of academic, governmental, and commercial sites. No one owns the Internet. Rather, it is a loose collection of computer networks whose users pass along information and share files.[10] Costs are shared rather informally by a variety of institutions.

It is the Internet that allows students to e-mail their professors and allows researchers to exchange ideas worldwide. Students regularly communicate through sophisticated software programs based on the Internet and designed specifically for the classroom. Programs such as Blackboard allow professors to create automatic e-mail lists, to construct electronic grade books, to give students assignments, to create interchanges among students, and to provide feedback. No longer is access to a professor limited to two class periods a week and a few office hours. Messages can be sent, received, and answered in a matter of minutes.

Technology: New and Convergent

In every generation, there are old media and new media. During the colonial period, books and newspapers were old media and magazines were new media. Today, we use the term *new media* to refer to media forms and media content that are created and shaped by changes in technology. Thus the **Internet** became one of the new media of the twentieth century. The term continues to be used because the Internet still represents the dominant new technology, although CD-ROMs and DVDs could also be considered new media. Because the content of the Internet is still very much in flux, the term *new media* is also used to refer to changes in content. As new media evolve, old ones change forms. Consumers may spend additional time using media when new media arrive, or they may simply shift their patterns of use from one medium to another. As the following chapters reveal, there are many historical shifts that document these claims. When radio news redefined timeliness, newspapers knew they couldn't beat the speed of that new technology. So newspapers were forced to become more interpretive. When television's pictures outdistanced radio news, radio turned to music formats. As portable CD-ROM technology provided increased quality of music, radio incorporated talk formats. Now news, talk, and music formats attract listeners on the move. As new media include concepts such as "virtual reality" and "artificial intelligence," forms and content will continue to change.

As new technologies appear, media forms and technologies come together, an action referred to as *media convergence.* For example, newspapers (old media, old technology) go online (new media, new technology). But the content of the old media is apparent in the new format. Consumers today confront old media in their old forms, new media in their new forms, and converged media, which represent a merging of content, distribution systems, and other elements of the media mix.

Developments during the past twenty years have created a technological convergence that blends technologies to deliver a message. In May 1994, the *New York Times* signaled the shift with a headline, "I Wonder What's on the PC Tonight."[11] The headline suggested the way in which media were combining. For example, newspapers regularly offer a variety of online services, including high school sports scores and stock prices.

In the 1990s, many industry analysts viewed the struggle for the control of technology as a mere battle for profit, but the implications of the struggle are much broader.

key concept

New Media New media are media forms and content that are created and shaped by changes in technology.

key concept

Media Convergence Media convergence refers to different forms of media converging. This may reflect the convergence of types of content, such as advertising that is incorporated within the story line of a motion picture. Sometimes this term also is used to mean technological convergence.

Internet: A linkage of thousands of academic, government, and commercial computer sites created when the U.S. government saw the need for an emergency communication system. Computers are tied together through special high-speed telephone lines.

Although the convergence of media has changed the way journalists work and how content is created and distributed, the more enduring issues of access to information and freedom of expression remain constant.

As the editors of the *Media Studies Journal* wrote, "The more enduring issues have to do with access to information, the quality of news and entertainment, the diversity of media in the marketplace and, most important, freedom of expression itself."[12]

Convergence has implications not only for content but also for *media regulation* and policy. By 1996 the evolution of technology had created conditions that required major policy changes for the first time in sixty years. The Telecommunications Act of 1996 changed existing media ownership rules, deregulated cable television, and required television makers to install a computer chip in new TV sets that allows people to block shows that are electronically labeled for violence and other objectionable content.[13]

key concept

Media Regulation Governments enforce rules and regulations to promote social stability and mediate social conflicts. Because the media and the public "space" they occupy can affect many members of society, the government has always been particularly concerned with regulation of the media.

THE MEDIA SYSTEM IN THE UNITED STATES

The United States, like every country, has a communication system that coordinates its activities. Highly industrialized countries have complex systems and depend on sophisticated computer technology. Oral tradition, print media, and radio dominate the communication systems of less industrialized countries. Most media systems can be defined as *market* or *nonmarket systems.* In market systems, consumers demand information and media companies supply it. Media companies in market systems supply the types and amounts of information for which people will pay. Nonmarket systems supply information based on what some institution, usually a government, decides people should have.

In market systems, such as the one found in the United States, profit—the difference between revenue and costs—plays a motivating role. Media organizations consider many factors when they set **profit margins,** the amount of "extra" revenue

key concept

Market and Nonmarket Media Systems In a free-market society, mass communication can be described as a system that produces information on the basis of the interaction between two forces: audience demand and the ability of media companies to supply content. Media companies produce what someone will pay for. In a highly structured nonmarket or authoritarian society, mass communication may function as a system in which content is decided by an institution, usually a government. In such societies, the media produce not what the public will pay for, but what the authorities want the public to know.

profit margins: The difference between revenue and expenses.

they intend to seek. Profit does not play a role in nonmarket systems. The institution that controls information pursues other goals, which often include maintaining power. This basic difference in market and nonmarket systems has a profound impact on how the systems function within societies. However, as the world becomes a global village and as satellite delivery crosses national boundaries, the line between the two systems becomes less defined.

Figure 1.3, which we refer to throughout this chapter, explains how a market system works. The center of the diagram shows the individuals and groups who participate in the mass communication system. They include almost all people in the United States—anyone who sees a movie, reads a newspaper, listens to the radio, or watches a television show. People have different information needs and wants, which come from their psychological states and from their interactions in groups. Those needs and wants translate into a demand for information and ideas.

Figure 1.3

The Mass Media Market System

The U.S. mass media market system is cyclical, with people at the center. People have needs and wants, which they take to the three types of markets in the system (consumer, advertising, and the marketplace of ideas). These wants and needs become demand for information, advertising space and time, and ideas to help society function properly. The media companies observe the demand and supply content to the three markets to satisfy the wants and needs. At the same time people are exercising their demand, they also act as sources of information for the media organizations. This mass media system is not isolated from the rest of the world. It serves the demand from other countries by sending content to them. At the same time, other countries supply content to the U.S. system based on demand from that system.

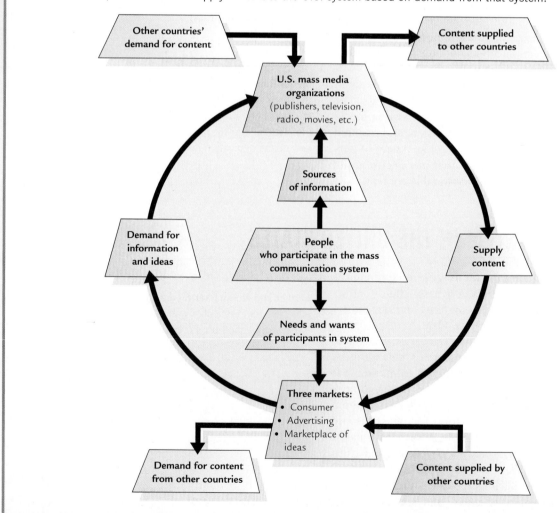

Not only do individuals and groups fulfill wants and needs through the mass communication system, but they also act as sources for that system. When a newspaper runs a story about a fire, for example, sources of information may include a neighbor who called the fire department or firefighters who fought the blaze.

Three Communication Markets

When we look at mass communication as a market system, we see that people seek information, and businesses either sell or give information through communication markets. People can use the information for a variety of purposes, but as in all markets, exchange takes place. A consumer might buy a book or a recording, thus exchanging money for information or entertainment. In another instance, a business might buy an advertisement, thus exchanging money for access to public attention. Further, people might exchange ideas in a political debate—the marketplace of ideas. Three markets emerge in this view of the U.S. system: the consumer market, the advertising market, and the marketplace of ideas.

People use the two commercial markets—consumer and advertising—to satisfy their individual needs (e.g., surveillance, decision making, social and cultural interaction, self-understanding, diversion). Communities use the marketplace of ideas to find ways to satisfy their information needs (e.g., correlating group actions, transmitting heritage).

The users of mediated content by individuals and groups (receivers) may not be consistent with the goals of the suppliers (senders). Suppliers create content with three purposes in mind: to inform, entertain, and persuade.

Consumer and Advertising Markets ✦ People use the *consumer market* most often. In this market, the media deliver information to readers, viewers, and listeners. The purpose of the information varies from entertainment to persuasion to education. Those who acquire information pay with either money or the attention they give to advertisements. People buy newspapers, watch television, and listen to recordings in this market. The consumer, not the originator, of the information determines how a particular bit of information is used.

> ### key concept
> **The Media as a Consumer Market** The mass media can be described as operating in a market that sells useful information to readers, viewers, and listeners.

The *advertising market* involves selling the attention of readers, viewers, and listeners to advertisers. Businesses and other groups buy time or space in this market to influence what people buy or believe. An organization that advertises wants people to buy some good or service. Images of Tiger Woods wearing Nike apparel entice golfers to buy Nike products. Dancers wearing khaki try to persuade young people to buy jeans from the Gap.

> ### key concept
> **The Media as an Advertising Market** The mass media can be described as operating in a market that sells the attention of readers, viewers, and listeners to product advertisers.

Assigning transactions to one of the two commercial markets is easier from the media company's perspective than from the consumer's perspective. Media organizations have different departments that serve the advertising and consumer markets. Often, media organizations label advertising to separate it from news and editorial content. However, readers, listeners, and viewers do not necessarily make the distinction between markets. When people want to buy a car, they may consult *Consumer Reports'* guide to cars on the Internet, check local prices in newspaper advertisements, and watch the Jeep Grand Cherokee climb an off-road hill in a television advertisement. Just how much each of these influences a particular buyer depends on the individual. Because people seek information from both advertising and news and often don't distinguish between the two, some advertisers deliberately create ads that masquerade as news.

The Marketplace of Ideas ✦ The consumer and advertising markets are both commercial markets. An identifiable exchange of money takes place between supplier and user. The *marketplace of ideas* does not require money. In this market, ideas compete for acceptance by society and its subgroups. People and groups seek to influence this exchange of ideas because the arguments made in the marketplace of ideas may help create laws and norms for behavior.

Efforts to develop a national health-care policy is an example of how the marketplace of ideas works. Politicians make speeches, newspapers publish editorials, and radio stations accept listener call-ins with comments about health care. Eventually, Congress holds public hearings, drafts legislation, and votes on a health-care bill. The president signs or vetoes the bill. All the steps include communication, much of it through mass media. The ideas compete in the marketplace of ideas for final acceptance as official policy.

Although the three markets are distinct, information produced for one can be used in another. Political candidates try to influence the marketplace of ideas by purchasing advertisements. When Walt Disney portrayed Donald Duck rushing to the mailbox to pay his taxes on time during World War II, he used his Hollywood reputation to influence the marketplace of ideas by building patriotic spirit. In the same period, movies provided diversion in the consumer market by entertaining viewers with stories that emphasized cultural stereotypes of the enemy. Advertisers such as Benetton often use cultural ideas in the consumer market to promote their products in the advertising market.

Role of Media Organizations in the Marketplace

The needs and wants that people take to the three communication markets result in a demand for information and ideas. Media organizations in a market system supply that demand with media content, which flows into the three markets. Some needs and wants are fulfilled, and the cycle starts again. In that circular process, media organizations must (1) evaluate the demand for information and ideas in the three markets, (2) draw on people as sources in the system, and (3) supply content to fulfill the demand.

Media organizations take a variety of forms. Individual television stations, newspapers, or magazine and book publishers are media organizations. But the term also can be applied to corporations that own and/or manage several newspapers, television stations, or magazines. Most media organizations are part of larger conglomerates, or groups, that own varied types of media.

Table 1.1 shows some of these multimedia groups and their holdings. In 2002, Gannett owned ninety-four daily newspapers with a circulation of 7.7 million (up from seventy-four in 1999), including *USA Today;* a variety of nondaily publications; and twenty-two television stations covering 17.7 percent of U.S. households. Gannett also has more than one hundred web sites in the United States and United Kingdom. Other operations include Gannett News Service; Gannett Retail Advertising Group;

Table 1.1

Types of Media Outlets by Multimedia Groups

GROUP	DAILY NEWSPAPERS	TELEVISION STATIONS	RADIO STATIONS
Freedom Newspapers	28	8	0
Gannett	94	22	0
Lee Enterprises	45	0	0
New York Times Co.	18	8	2
Media General	25	26	0
Scripps Howard	21	10	0

Sources: Company web sites.

Gannett TeleMarketing, Inc.; Gannett New Business and Product Development; Gannett Direct Marketing Services; Gannett Offset, a commercial printing operation; Gannett Media Technologies International; and Telematch, a database marketing company.

The groups can be owned either publicly or privately. Under public ownership, the corporation sells stock to the public. Anyone who has enough money to buy stock can become part owner of the public corporation. Under private ownership, a person or group of people owns all the company stock. Ownership type has a significant impact on organizations. For example, the higher the percentage of stock owned by the public, the less likely the company is to reinvest its profits in the company. This happens because the profit is returned to investors in order to keep the stock prices high.[14] The danger in this policy is the potential lowering of content quality.

Demand for Information and Ideas

Demand in the U.S. mass communication system reflects social and economic changes. Today, an increase in disposable income and leisure time provides viewers with more time and money to buy new technology that can supply needs for entertainment and information. In addition, the population is nationally—even internationally—oriented as the role of the federal rather than state and local government dominates decision making that affects our lives. Further, incidents such as those that occurred on September 11, 2001, create an audience realization that life is affected by international behavior, which further shifts the audience focus to an international perspective.

Demand for information and ideas comes from individual needs and wants. Media organizations cannot meet individual demands one person at a time because media can supply information and ideas only at the market level. Demand structure determines the nature of the aggregate demand and has three characteristics: audience similarity, the geographic nature of the market, and available technology.

Audience similarity can be charted on a continuum ranging from everyone being exactly alike to everyone being entirely different. Members of any audience share characteristics, but those members also are different in many ways. For example, readers of the *Tuscola County* (MI) *Advertiser* share more similarities than do readers of the *Washington Post*. Tuscola County is an agricultural area populated primarily by people who were born and raised there. Washington, D.C., is a giant metropolis populated by people from all over the world. Because the audience of the *Post* is more diverse, it costs more to provide the diversity of content needed to appeal to the broader group.

In addition to audience similarity, geography also defines demand structure. Information helps define communities, sometimes through audience similarity, as in the women's suffrage movement of the early twentieth century, and other times through geography. The success of *USA Today*'s page of short, informational blurbs about individual states capitalizes on people's identification with their home states. Geography also affects demand because geographic features such as lakes, rivers, and mountains determine the history, economy, and culture of people in a given market. Those factors in turn affect the type of information and advertising the audience demands. Whereas Kansas farmers might pay attention to fertilizer ads on television, such ads would be wasted on a Los Angeles, California, audience.

The final determinant of demand structure is technology, a factor that can make geography less important. Just as the telegraph expanded mass media audiences in the mid-nineteenth century, now cable and satellite technology have expanded the political, social, and economic range of those who have access to television. In addition, satellites transmit newspaper content to printing plants across the United States, making a local or regional daily newspaper available throughout the country. The expansion of national and international media distribution reduces the distinctions among separate cultures. In the process, some cultures may join to share common ideas, and some local or minority cultures may be overwhelmed.

The convergence of technology will continue to give consumers more choice, opening up new avenues of distribution for print media and fostering interactive communication in television and other electronic media. In late 1999, two information companies, Autonomy and breathe.net, combined to introduce a new personalized information system in Europe. The new service takes information from the Web, e-mail, phone calls, faxes, and voice mail; categorizes it; adds hyperlinks to related material; and delivers it through a laptop, mobile phone, radio, or interactive television. Travelers in Europe can access information packages personalized for them anywhere and anytime they want.[15]

Demand in the Consumer Market ✦ Consumer demand for media content varies considerably depending partly on household decisions about **media mixes.** For example, one person might mix media by watching an hour of television a day and reading a couple of newspapers. Another person might watch television and not read newspapers or magazines. A person's mix represents his or her wants and needs. However, other factors such as price and accessibility also affect demand. Generally, as the price of a media commodity increases, some consumers will substitute different content or media. The ability to read or to use a computer also will affect media choices.

Demand in the Advertising Market ✦ Demand in the advertising market is straightforward compared to demand in the consumer market. Advertisers want to pay the lowest possible price to send their message to the highest possible percentage of potential customers. To do this, the advertiser must identify the location of potential customers and the best medium for reaching those customers. In most cases, advertisers use a combination of media to target the media mixes used by their audience.

Advertisers choose between mass and **targeted advertising,** depending on the size and type of audience they want to reach. A local department store uses mass advertising aimed at a diverse group because individuals with different levels of income or different interests will all buy products from its store. However, a Mercedes Benz dealership targets only those with a large enough income to buy its cars.

Demand in the Marketplace of Ideas ✦ Demand in the marketplace of ideas is more complex than transactions in the two commercial communication markets. Transactions in this market involve no money. The demand is for ideas, information, and reinforcement of cultural values that allow society to maintain and improve itself. The demand is diffuse and difficult to quantify because not all members of society agree on how to maintain and improve society.

In the United States, society uses the marketplace of ideas to form majority views about government and social norms. People and groups compete—often through media—to have their ideas accepted. Media coverage of an issue can help it gain political attention, but the U.S. system of government ensures, for better or worse, that political change is evolutionary rather than rapid. The right of a woman to choose whether to have an abortion has been a political and social issue for many decades. Abortion continues to gain media attention as a political and social issue because people are divided. *Roe v. Wade* established the right of women to choose and maintained that right for nearly twenty years, but subsequent legislation and court decisions have chipped away at that position. The marketplace of ideas continues to entertain varying points of view.

Access to the marketplace of ideas varies from country to country. A dictatorship allows very little influence from the outside world. Dictators want to retain power, which becomes difficult if people have open access to outside information and ideas. When a dictator is able to control the marketplace of ideas, the country may suffer economic and social harm. For example, Fidel Castro's dictatorship of Cuba has succeeded in controlling that country's marketplace of ideas since 1959, but the country's economy has crumbled, and most people live in poverty.

As national economies become more international through growing exports and imports, a global marketplace of ideas will increase in importance. Beginning in 1996, the British Broadcasting Corporation (BBC) broadcast directly into Germany,

media mix: Consumers' use of a variety of media, such as newspapers, television, and the World Wide Web.

targeted advertising: Trying to sell a product or service to a particular group of people.

trying to attract German viewers with a twenty-four-hour English news service. Although BBC broadcasts had been available by way of cable and satellite, that marked the first commercial over-the-air television signal aimed at attracting viewers in another country. International television is likely to continue its growth with remarkable implications. How extensively will the cultures of different countries affect one another once "free" television is available across boundaries? What control should and can a government exercise over the broadcasts into its nation? These and other questions will be debated in the global marketplace of ideas.

Supply of Content

As shown in Figure 1.3, mass media organizations supply content to the three communication markets to meet demand. In order to do this, every mass media organization must go through six processes:

1. Media organizations must *generate content*. Sometimes organizations create original content, and sometimes they buy content from other sources.
2. Once the organization generates content, it must *produce and reproduce content in quantity*. That is how media become mass media. Content must be replicated many times over to serve large audiences. The replication comes about because a printing press prints thousands of copies or because a million television sets change electronic pulses into pictures and sound.
3. Content must be *delivered to users*. Once it has been reproduced, the content must somehow reach users. A delivery person might throw a newspaper onto a porch, or a cable may carry electronic pulses into living rooms.
4. Mass media must *generate financial support*. Most mass media organizations either sell information to users or sell space and time to advertisers. However, other forms of financing are available. The selling of information and advertisements reflects the commercial nature of U.S. economic, social, and political systems. Some media organizations, such as public television and radio, are supported by grants, donations, and even the government.
5. The products of the organization must be *promoted*. Because so many media options are available today, an organization cannot assume that potential users will even know its product exists. Advertising and public-relations activities inform and persuade people to buy or use their products.
6. The first five processes must be *managed*. The generation, reproduction, delivery, financing, and promotion of mass media must be coordinated so that certain activities are accomplished in specific periods of time.

Effective strategies for carrying out these processes differ according to the size and complexity of each organization. At a weekly newspaper with a circulation of five thousand, the editor and one or two reporters write stories, take pictures, and compose headlines. A computer produces plates that go on a printing press. When the newspaper copies are printed, someone, often the editor, picks up the copies and returns to the newspaper office. After address labels are placed on subscribers' copies, most of the newspapers are delivered by mail. Promotion for the weekly paper might include annually delivering a paper containing a subscription flier to every household in town. Advertising salespeople collect money from advertisers; subscription fees are paid by mail. The editor and publisher manage the newspaper processes. A weekly paper can often be managed by only four to six full-time employees and three to six part-time employees.

In contrast, a metropolitan daily with circulation of 350,000 has a department for each process. The newsroom and advertising department create the content. A metropolitan daily owns its own presses. The circulation department places copies in news racks and delivers newspapers to customers' doorsteps. The promotion department buys advertising on radio, television, and billboards, as well as running telemarketing campaigns. The accounting office bills advertisers and collects subscription money. The publisher, department heads, and dozens of assistant managers coordinate the activities, which might involve five hundred or more people.

Interaction of Supply and Demand

Interaction between supply and demand in the consumer and advertising markets determines the amount and nature of media products and how financial resources are distributed among media companies. Consumers demand information to help them live. Mass media companies provide the content to make money. Ideally, consumers will get useful information, advertisers will get effective advertisements, and media companies will make a reasonable profit. However, market interactions often fail to achieve this ideal.

key concept

Interaction between Supply and Demand The interaction of media organizations' supply and consumers' and advertisers' demand determines the type of information and ideas available in a media market system. This interaction involves media organization managers researching what people demand and finding ways to supply it. The reaction of individuals to the supply determines the content that media companies produce in the future.

Three important factors create interaction problems: the level of competition for consumers, an organization's understanding of its customers, and the organization's goals. All three affect the responsiveness of media organizations to consumer and advertiser demand.

Competition moves power from producers to consumers. If some readers do not like *Time,* they can subscribe to *Newsweek.* Competition allows for choice, and choice forces companies to respond to consumer demand. Typically, media companies respond to competition for consumers by keeping the price of their product low, by increasing spending on content, and by trying to improve the usefulness of the information to the consumer. The goal of these responses is to provide a better product at a lower price than the competition.

A similar effect results from competition in the advertising market. If an advertiser does not like the price that one television station charges for advertising time, it can buy time from another. Competition holds down advertising prices and improves service to advertisers.

Although competition serves the consumer and the advertiser, it costs the media company. It is more expensive to produce and deliver information in competitive markets than in monopoly markets. The result of higher cost is lower profit. If media managers are given a choice, most will pick a less competitive market.

Even though competition forces media companies to respond to consumer demand, it does not guarantee that the company managers will accurately understand the customer's needs. The increased spending and lower price that results from competition will benefit the consumer only if companies produce more useful information or more attractive content. The managers of media organizations must predict, through intuition, experience, and research, what type of information would be useful to the consumer.

The final factor affecting the outcome of market interaction is organizational goals. Most mass media organizations seek profits, but some aspire to higher profits than others. To increase profits, media organizations must either lower their expenses or raise their revenues. Efforts to increase revenues are risky, but cutting costs is not, at least in the short term. As a result, the local daily newspaper, which is usually the only one in town and thus has little direct competition, may get by with fewer reporters than it might be expected to have in order to cover news well. Similarly, organizations with higher profit goals will keep a closer watch on advertising prices to make sure they are getting the best price possible. Over time, however, efforts to cut costs and hike prices often result in lower quality and fewer customers.

The profit goal is basic to the market system, but the impact of that goal differs depending on whether managers take a short-term or long-term approach. Profit goals motivate some media businesses to invest in long-term quality, which usually increases long-term profits because many consumers are attracted to quality information. Profit goals motivate others to cut costs to the bone for short-term profits. Over time new technology usually allows more companies to enter a market, and the effect of more companies is to reduce the ability of individual companies to squeeze profits from consumers and advertisers during the short term.

Media systems are cyclical. That is, each cycle allows media organizations to adjust to the changing demands of consumers, advertisers, and society itself. The nature of many of the cycles varies, but some are consistent. For instance, the broadcast television networks in the United States traditionally have a yearly cycle. Every fall networks drop some programs and add new ones designed to attract more viewers. The more successful a network was the previous year, the fewer changes it makes.

Interaction: Media and Society ✦ Often the interaction of supply and demand in a market system reflects a level of tension between societal values and pushing the cultural boundaries. Although critical discussions of media have been ongoing since the mass production of books, modern media criticism and concerns about the impact of media on society began in the 1920s with the introduction of radio and intensified in the 1930s with the advent of feature-length sound films. Critics worried that radio would corrupt traditional values. They believed that adolescents, watching movies in a dark theater, would be influenced by sexual content, and that teenagers might adopt screen behaviors that did not conform to traditional standards. Critics also believed that media influences would make it more difficult for parents to maintain control over their children.

Through the years, researchers have looked at the social effects of the media, particularly the effects of television, that ubiquitous screen that brightens nearly every living room or family room in the United States. Many studies have focused on the effects of television on individuals and on societal norms. In the aftermath of the rash of school shootings, particularly that in 1999 at Columbine High School in Littleton, Colorado, critics began to search for causes of the violent behavior of some students. Many political figures were quick to conclude that repeated exposure to violent TV programming might increase individual violence. We now know that media do have effects—both negative and positive—on individuals and that the effects are a complicated result of not only media influence but also family and societal behavior. Many of society's and individuals' images come from the media. However, those perceptions are supplemented by other factors, such as interpersonal communication or conversations. Knowledge gained from experience and education often enhances the images and ideas suggested by television or other media forms. With the advent of computer-exchanged information, critics and consumers once more are concerned about what kind of information they, their children, and their society will acquire.

Interaction of Supply and Demand Internationally ✦ Internationalism can be looked at in three separate ways: (1) multinational ownership of media companies; (2) production of content in various regions of the world; and (3) styles and regulation of reporting ideas and information.

Media increasingly are run by multinational corporations. Books and films are produced for foreign as well as domestic consumers. Internet technology allows professors, students, and other consumers of online services to communicate electronically

Some researchers believe that tragic events, such as the school shooting in Littleton, Colorado, may be connected to repeated exposure of young people to violence in the media.

profile

Marshall McLuhan

Marshall McLuhan argued that the "medium is the message." McLuhan believed that the nature of technology was as important as its content.

His ideas were so controversial for the time and had so much influence on scholars of mass media that the term *McLuhanism* appears in the *Oxford English Dictionary*. The dictionary distills his entire work into a statement that the introduction of mass media deadens the critical faculties of individuals.

Herbert Marshall McLuhan was born in Edmonton, Alberta, Canada, on July 21, 1911, to a Protestant family of Scottish-Irish descent. His mother, Elsie, was an actress, and his father, Herbert, was a salesman.

He went to the University of Manitoba to become an engineer but switched his major to English literature. He graduated with a bachelor of arts degree in 1933 and earned a master's degree the following year. He then studied literature at Cambridge University in England, where he obtained a B.A. in 1936 and a doctorate in 1942. McLuhan married Corrine Keller, a Texan who studied drama at the Pasadena Playhouse in California.

McLuhan established his teaching and scholarly career at the University of Toronto, where he was influenced by Harold Innis, a pioneer in communication studies. In 1963, McLuhan was appointed director of the University of Toronto's Marshall McLuhan Center for Culture and Technology, where he worked for fourteen years before retiring.

McLuhan wrote more than fifteen books, including *The Mechanical Bride: Folklore of Industrial Man*, published in 1951. That book was his first attempt to examine the effects of mass culture and "the pressures set up around us today by the mechanical agencies of the press, radio, movies, and advertising." He made a greater impact with his second book, *The Gutenberg Galaxy,* written in 1961, which discusses the effect of movable type on western European culture in the fifteenth century.

In 1964, McLuhan earned popular acclaim with *Understanding Media: The Extensions of Man,* in which he contends that the introduction of electronic circuitry made behavior less isolated and more conformist than before. He expands on his concept of the "global village," arguing that media bring different cultures closer together. Another popular book, *The Medium Is the Massage,* published in 1967, illustrated McLuhan's ideas of "hot" and "cold" media. His objective was to show that a medium is not neutral, but rather it transforms life.

McLuhan earned praise as the media guru of the 1960s, but he also was the target of criticism from scholars. He received many honors, awards, and medals, including citations from the British and Italian governments. McLuhan died on December 31, 1980, at the age of sixty-nine.

Sources: Alden Whitman, "Marshall McLuhan, Author, Dies," *The New York Times* (January 1, 1981), sec. 1, p. 1; Alan M. Kriegsman, "Marshall McLuhan Dies," *The Washington Post* (January 1, 1981), sec. C, p. 16.

---

both within the United States and across national borders to and from Europe, Australia, Africa, South America, and Asia. This technology has reduced or eliminated the boundaries of space, time, and politics in ways that no other technology has done.

During the 1960s, Canadian professor of English literature and media guru Marshall McLuhan popularized the concept that electronic media were key players in public affairs and argued that media power could bring about a better world. McLuhan envisioned a "global village," in which humankind could be liberated from the linear thinking of print, a vision both "tribal and collective."[16] But critics are more pessimistic and argue that the explosion of information and the economic costs that go with it will continue to divide underdeveloped countries from those that are more advanced.

Most multinational companies are Western based and dominate the production of information that is distributed throughout the less-developed world. The flow of information raises concerns about *cultural imperialism.* Will superior production quality and media economic systems allow the West to dominate the cultures of less-developed countries? By 1984, for example, Latin America imported 42 percent of its media programs; the United States imported only 2 percent.

key concept

Cultural Imperialism Media products and political and business practices of one culture may have important influences on another culture. These influences can be considered "imperialistic" if they impose patterns and values that ignore or denigrate local customs.

Some of that imbalance may be changing, however. As non-U.S.-based media develop and expand to address audiences that live within the United States as well as in other countries, a variety of views that do not fall within the latitude of accepted political discussion penetrate the airwaves. During the aftermath of the 2001 terrorism attacks, for example, the television network Al-Jazeera featured interviews and stories clearly designed for consumption by anti-Western audiences but presented them through the standard formats known to the West, thereby giving them an appearance of objectivity.

A third issue is the ability to collect news across national boundaries. Western countries, particularly the United States, have operated under different principles from those adopted in most parts of the world. After World War II, U.S. reporters and editors worked in cooperation with the U.S. government to try to ensure a flow of information across national boundaries through an open system similar to that of the United States. In the 1970s, UNESCO took up the communication controversy. Governments in many less-developed countries expressed concern about Western values that were being beamed into their countries. The United States argued that it had promoted a complex communication system that benefited all parts of the world through improved educational, social, and technological services.[17] The UNESCO debate was never resolved, and the United States ultimately withdrew from the organization. In 2002 there was discussion of the United States once again becoming a member of UNESCO.

Cell phone technology may be a less expensive option than poles and wires for the development of a modern telecommunication system in places such as China, where the existing land line system is not adequate.

But today the issue of collecting news across national boundaries has become more personalized. In 2001 nine journalists died in Afghanistan. In 2002 *Wall Street Journal* reporter Daniel Pearl was killed in Pakistan. Increasingly, journalists, photographers, and television crews covering the Israeli–Palestinian conflict are being attacked. Michael Parks, former editor of the *Los Angeles Times* and director of the School of Journalism at the University of Southern California, says that news executives must deal not only with the safety of their journalists but also with the "more fundamental question of when a story is too dangerous to cover."

USE AND FUNCTIONS OF MEDIA IN THE MARKETPLACE

In 1948 Harold Lasswell, a political scientist who is considered one of the founders of communication research, formulated a statement of the "functions" of mass communication in society, with the idea of illustrating how media perform essential tasks for the maintenance of society. Lasswell argued that media performed three functions: (1) surveillance of the environment; (2) correlation of the parts of the society; and (3) transmission of culture. Looking at function in a slightly different way, some media scholars have identified the individual "uses" involved when people seek information to fulfill their needs and wants. Those uses fall into five types: surveillance, decision making, social and cultural interaction, diversion, and self-understanding.[18]

Surveillance involves monitoring one's environment. It occurs in two types of situations: everyday surveillance, such as checking baseball scores or stock prices, and extraordinary surveillance, such as keeping up with events during a war or natural disaster. Surveillance keeps people in touch with environmental and other social and political changes that are crucial to their lives. When people watched CNN at the height of the U.S. military action in Afghanistan, they were surveilling, or monitoring, their environment. Surveillance also helps people decide how to use information for decision making, social and cultural interaction, and diversion.

Decision making involves collecting information in order to select among options. The decision may be as minor as which TV program to watch or as important as for which presidential candidate to vote. Use of information for decision making is purposeful and specific. Surveillance and decision making overlap because surveillance often determines what types of decisions need to be made.

Social and cultural interaction involves using information that defines, identifies, and maintains membership in a group. All groups define themselves with information, which allows individuals to hold and demonstrate membership in the group. The group may be as large as a country or as small as a household. Sometimes people get information formally, such as through classes for people who want to become U.S. citizens. Other times information passes informally through conversations among group members, such as in discussions during fraternity and sorority rushes.

Diversion involves using information for entertainment and enjoyment. Watching football on television or reading a short story may make a person feel sad, happy, or even horrified. Individuals seek different types of diversion, which is why some people prefer films by Spike Lee and others prefer films by Steven Spielberg.

Self-understanding requires that people use media to gain insight into their own behaviors and attitudes. A person feeling alone and isolated might gain solace from listening to a song about loneliness. A college student reading a news story about the consequences of binge drinking might seek to avoid excessive alcohol consumption.

The five distinct individual uses of information often are related. The seemingly simple process of selecting a movie to go to includes checking the newspaper to find out what is showing (surveillance), asking friends about the two or three films you are considering (social and cultural interaction), picking one (decision making), and going to see the movie (diversion).

The same information can be used in more than one way. For example, people may see a movie for entertainment. The next day they may discuss it with people at work (social and cultural interaction). The following year, they may remember how much they enjoyed a particular actor and decide to see a new movie starring the same person (decision making). The more different uses a person has for a given message, the more utility that message has.

Although individual members of a group may use mass communication to create social and cultural interaction, communication also may serve a group by correlating actions of its members and by transmitting its social and cultural heritage. Groups vary in size from a small group of friends to a tribe to an entire society, but they all involve member interactions and a common culture and heritage.

Large groups such as societies follow economic, political, and social agendas. *Economic actions* involve the exchange of goods, services, and money. News, as well as advertising, can affect economic actions. If Mary intends to buy an imported car, she might postpone her purchase if she reads a newspaper article that suggests Congress might cut import taxes, which could increase the cost of cars from other countries.

Media correlate *political actions* by providing information about politicians and the political process. John and Catherine might watch the television coverage of presidential debates either to make up their minds about a candidate or to reinforce their closely held beliefs. An irate property owner might write a letter to the newspaper editor complaining about the actions of a city council member. In countries where citizens have a great deal of political power, the media gain importance because of their role in the political process. The need to correlate political activities forms the basis for the First Amendment to the Constitution. Without a free flow of information, people in a democracy cannot decide who should run their country.

Media correlate social activities and actions. The correlation may be as simple as helping a community to coordinate and attend a Memorial Day parade, local club activities, or school events. Or media may help correlate a national march in support of integration—an act that is both political and social. The media's coverage of the 1963 March on Washington helped convince Congress and the population that civil rights legislation was needed to promote equality in the United States.

In addition to correlating a society's activities, fostering the transmission of social heritage is another important function of mass communication. Societies are defined by their common heritage. Although education plays the most important role in this transmission, media often contribute to the common understanding of social and cultural heritage. People who say they are Americans recognize a common history with others who claim the same label. History can be shared at the local, regional, national, or international level. The 1996 Olympic Games in Atlanta gave the South an opportunity to transmit its social heritage to the world. The closing ceremonies included a concert that featured jazz, blues, Latino music, and country music—all part of the southern and American heritage.

This book is organized to incorporate the role or functions of the media into descriptions of the various types of media and uses of communication. You will note that the book is organized into three parts: (1) Media Processes and Functions; (2) Media Industries; and (3) Media Research, Regulation, and Restrictions. In the first section, you will read about how the media functions of informing and persuading are incorporated into the basic activities of journalists and advertising and public relations professionals. In Part II, you will see how these functions, along with entertainment, are incorporated into the various media. And in Part III, you will see how regulation, ethics, and research shape the media landscape.

summary

- ✦ Content and behavior of media are closely tied to the development of technology and the economics of big business. Media operate within a context of political behavior, social and cultural development, and globalization.
- ✦ The communication process involves transmitting information and ideas to one person or to a large group of people.
- ✦ Successful communication of information from a sender to a receiver depends on eliminating semantic noise and channel noise.
- ✦ Typically, media include newspapers, magazines, television, radio, books, recordings, and movies. The authors here include the Internet, although some scholars argue that its interactivity makes it different.
- ✦ The convergence of technologies is ongoing. In the past, as new technologies developed, old ones adapted. New technologies, alone and in combination with older forms of media, have an impact on our daily lives, but no one can predict the exact impact of each technology.
- ✦ Media companies have experimented with converging technologies by combining news functions in a single newsroom, but they continue to use various distribution systems such as newspapers, broadcasts, and online delivery.
- ✦ The U.S. media system involves a circular process through which people and groups turn their information wants and needs into demand for content.

- ✦ Demand occurs in the consumer market, the advertising market, and the marketplace of ideas.
- ✦ As suppliers of content, all media organizations carry out six processes. Content must be generated, reproduced, and delivered; those three processes must be financed, promoted, and managed.
- ✦ Supplying the consumer market involves selling or giving information to people in exchange for their potential attention to advertising.
- ✦ Supplying the advertising market means selling space and time primarily to businesses and other organizations so they can transmit messages that influence the behavior of their audience.
- ✦ Supplying the marketplace of ideas involves contributing ideas and information to political leaders and other citizens.
- ✦ Individuals use mass communication for surveillance, decision making, social and cultural interaction, diversion, and self-understanding.
- ✦ Groups use mass communication to coordinate the political, economic, and social activities of their members and to transmit their social and cultural heritage.
- ✦ No media system can be isolated from other systems in the world. The U.S. system supplies and demands information and ideas from systems in other countries.

navigating the web | Communication on the Web

Media institutions and industries use World Wide Web sites to generate interest in their activities and to provide information about business ventures. At the other end of the spectrum are research sites that provide critical information about media as institutions.

Veronis, Suhler & Associates
www.veronissuhler.com

This site contains financial and economic data about all types of media, such as television, newspapers, and books. VS&A is a communication investment banking organization that also provides annual industry-level data about communication. More detailed information is made available through books published annually.

Media Communications Studies
www.aber.ac.uk/media

The Media Communication Studies site was established by Daniel Chandler at the University of Wales, Abery-stwyth. Included among its numerous pages is one about media institutions. It also provides other links and materials by Ben Bagdikian and Noam Chomsky about media institutions and society.

Media Literacy Review
http://interact.uoregon.edu/medialit/mlr/readings/contents/advertising.html

The *Media Literacy Review* site is a Media Literacy Online Project established by the Center for Advanced Technology in Education, University of Oregon–Eugene. It is the goal of the *Media Literacy Review* to make available to educators, producers, students, and parents information and resources related to the influence of media in the lives of children, youth, and adults.

questions for review

1. Why was Gutenberg's invention of movable type important?
2. What does *technological convergence* mean?
3. What is channel noise? Semantic noise?
4. Explain the difference between interpersonal, mediated, and mass communication.
5. How do social groups use mass media?
6. What are the differences between market and nonmarket communication systems?
7. What are the three communication markets described in this chapter?
8. What is meant by demand for information and ideas?

issues to think about

1. How will the convergence of technologies affect your life?
2. What are some of the problems of applying advertising models to online and other computer information services?
3. How do television images dominate our views of society at home and abroad?
4. What are the positive and negative impacts on society of market and nonmarket systems of communication?
5. How important is interactivity in a media system to the development of individuals and of society?
6. If you were the president of a developing country and you wanted to create a market system of communication, what modifications in the U.S. system would you seek to make?
7. What are the primary functions of media in a democratic society?

suggested readings

Altschull, J. Herbert. *Agents of Power: The Media and Public Policy*, 2nd ed. (White Plains, NY: Longman, 1995).

Bagdikian, Ben H. *The Information Machines: Their Impact on Men and Media* (New York: Harper & Row, 1971).

Blumler, Jay, and Elihu Katz, eds. *The Uses of Mass Communication* (Beverly Hills, CA: Sage, 1974).

Bogart, Leo. *Commercial Culture: The Media System and the Public Interest* (New York: Oxford University Press, 1995).

Kovach, Bill, and Tom Rosenstiel. *Warp Speed: America in the Age of Mixed Media* (New York: The Century Foundation Press, 1999).

McChesney, Robert. *Corporate Media and the Threat to Democracy* (New York: Seven Stories Press, 1997).

Schiller, Herbert I. *Culture, Inc.* (New York: Oxford University Press, 1989).

Journalism

Information and Society

Champagne corks popped as Eric Freedman and Jim Mitzelfeld hugged each other in the *Detroit News* newsroom. They had just learned they had won the 1994 Pulitzer Prize for beat reporting for uncovering corruption in the Michigan legislature.

Similar scenes occur at a handful of U.S. newspapers each year as the top awards in journalism are announced. These celebrations often mask the huge effort that goes into winning a Pulitzer. Many of the topics that win might even seem boring to some readers, but the results help make democracy work. The Michigan legislative story, for example, involved more than one hundred stories over a two-year period. As a result, ten people were convicted of felonies, including a state legislator, and Michigan now requires that all legislative agencies meet in public and issue public reports.

Journalism—reporting on government, politics, policies, economics, and other news and issues—has become a cornerstone of American life. The United States was founded on the assumption that a populace could govern if it was well informed. President James Madison wrote that "knowledge will forever govern ignorance, and a people who mean to be their own governors, must arm themselves with the power knowledge gives. A **popular government** without popular information or the means of acquiring it is but a prologue to a farce or a tragedy or perhaps both."[1]

From almost the beginning of the history of the United States, newspaper editors and printers sought to inform the people about the happenings of the day. In a January 16, 1787, letter to Colonel Edward Carrington, Thomas Jefferson wrote, "Were it left to me to decide whether we should have a government without newspapers, or newspapers without government, I should not hesitate a moment to prefer the latter." But his next sentence is less widely quoted: "But I should mean that every [person] should receive those papers and be capable of reading them."[2]

As late as 1945, Supreme Court Justice Hugo Black reaffirmed the importance of information in American society, noting that the First Amendment guarantee of a free press "rests upon the assumption that the widest possible dissemination of information from diverse and antagonistic sources is essential to the well-being of the public."[3]

Although the history of journalism is often confused with the history of the newspaper because newspapers were one of the earliest and most common methods of distribution of information about public life, the two are separate and distinct. Newspapers are a delivery system. Today the delivery systems for journalism include radio, television, magazines, books, and sites online. Some people define journalism as an act—a method and art of collecting and presenting information that ultimately is distributed through various channels; others describe it as a ritual—a way of sustaining, enriching, and challenging societal norms; still others see it as the mere dissemination of information.

Journalism has a changing face. As we continue our adventure into the twenty-first century, these issues will need to be addressed:

◆ How will journalists maintain their credibility in the face of infotainment—a combination of news and entertainment designed to win profits for media companies?

◆ How does journalism foster the values of a society?

◆ What has been the impact of the twenty-four-hour news cycle on the thoughtful delivery of news?

◆ How does the role of the journalist change as she or he adapts to a variety of delivery systems including print, radio, television, cable, and online?

Journalism *in Your Life*

Information and Credibility

Most of us trust that journalists' goal is to provide news and information that helps us to adapt to our society and to make informed judgments about political and economic choices. What journalistic venues do you trust?

JOURNALISTIC VENUES	TRUSTWORTHINESS (Rate from One to Five, with Five Being the Most Trustworthy)	REGULARITY OF USE (Rate as Daily, Several Times a Week, or Weekly)	TYPE OF INFORMATION (Rate as Breaking News, Analysis, or Entertaining News)
Network television news			
Cable television news			
Local television news			
Online news from newspapers			
Online news from national web sites (CNN, MSNBC, etc.)			
Newspapers			
Magazines of information and opinion			
Radio news			

JOURNALISM IN AMERICAN LIFE

Throughout U.S. history, *journalism* has helped make the government a government "of" and "by" the people. *Political journalism* has helped guard against secrecy and governmental power. Thus journalism's primary purpose has been to inform. But in different periods, it also has been a powerful persuasive tool. And from the earliest times, it has sought to entertain by providing information about unusual happenings and humorous incidents. In recent years, a move by many media industries toward **infotainment,** a blur of information and entertainment, has caused many journalists to worry about redefining the essence of journalism.

key concept

Journalism Reporting on government, politics, policies, economics, and other news and issues.

key concept

Political Journalism Reporting on the political process, including campaigns and elections, Congress, the presidency, and other government and political entities.

popular government: Government that is controlled by the citizenry rather than an elite cadre of officials.

infotainment: A blend of information and entertainment. Critics believe such treatments masquerade as journalism and deceive the public.

Challenges to Elite Authority

During the early colonial period, journalists were not a separate occupational group; they were editors, postmasters, and elite businessmen who sought to earn a living by printing information and who wanted to play a role in the founding of a new country. These writers were citizens first and intellectuals or commentators second. This point is important because freedom of expression is not granted to an elite cadre of

1600s. Journalists double as printers and editors.

1700s. Journalists covering Congress act as recorders of debate.

1733. Zenger attacks establishment.

1794. Senate opens press gallery.

1790–1830. Journalists debate values of competing parties.

1820s. Journalistic reports extend recording debate to reporting.

1830s. Occupational role of journalist develops.

1861–1865. Young reporters come to Washington, D.C., to cover war.

1890s. Journalists cover sports, social events, theater. Development of muckraking.

1920. Photojournalists take advantage of new technology.

1922. First noontime news broadcast

1932. Radio reporters cover Hoover–Roosevelt presidential race.

1400–1700	1800	1860	1880	1900	1920	1930

1620. Pilgrims land at Plymouth Rock.

1690. *Publick Occurrences* is published in Boston.

1741. First magazine is published in America.

1776–1783. American Revolution

1830s. The penny press becomes the first truly mass medium in the United States.

1861–1865. American Civil War

1892. Thomas Edison's lab develops the kinetoscope.

1914–1918. World War I

1915. *The Birth of a Nation* marks the start of the modern movie industry.

1920. KDKA in Pittsburgh gets the first commercial radio license.

1930s. The Great Depression

1939. TV is demonstrated at the New York World's Fair.

1939–1945. World War II

---

journalists—it is granted to citizens of the United States. Thus journalists do not have rights that ordinary citizens do not have.

Scholars debate how courageous journalists were during the colonial period. Some argue that journalists were quite cautious, rarely challenging the status quo. Others point out that despite the fact that governors in the colonies did not like criticism of themselves or the British government, journalists still spoke out.[4]

For example, in 1733, John Peter Zenger, printing the *New York Weekly Journal* for a radical attorney named James Alexander, was charged with **seditious libel** for openly criticizing the royal governor of New York. At that time, the law allowed a jury to determine only whether a printer had actually published specific material, not whether the material was true or was, indeed, seditious. After a highly publicized trial and an eloquent defense by Andrew Hamilton, the jury acquitted Zenger, thereby establishing a political, although not a legal, **precedent** for the right to criticize government. Hamilton argued that truth should be a defense in any seditious libel trial and that a jury should be able to judge not only whether an accused printer actually printed the material, but also whether it was libelous. He appealed to the

seditious libel: Criticism of the government. In colonial times, such criticism was considered libelous even if it was true.

precedent: A legal decision that sets a standard for how subsequent cases are decided.

1940s. Edward R. Murrow broadcasts from Europe.

1960s. Journalists experiment with writing styles.

1963. Evening news television broadcasts expand from 15 to 30 minutes.

1968. Journalists adapt to television newsmagazine format.

1980s. Reporters use computers to assist work.

1990s. Journalists report for combined systems—Internet, print, broadcast.

2000. Journalists struggle to fill continuous air time with election coverage.

2001. Reporters strive to balance patriotism with critical reporting.

2002. Demand for 24-hour news increases.

1940	1950	1960	1970	1980	1990	2000

1949. First electronic computer is produced.

Early 1950s. Rock 'n' roll begins.

1969. First person lands on the moon.

1970s. VCR is developed.

1989–1991. Cold War ends and the USSR is dissolved.

Late 1980s. National Science Foundation creates the basis of the Internet.

1996. Telecommunications Act

2000. Presidential election nearly tied

2001. Terrorist attacks on New York and Washington, D.C.

The acquittal of printer John Peter Zenger on charges of seditious libel made media history because it set a precedent for truth (as a defense for libel) in journalism.

colonists' dislike of arbitrary power, an aversion that would become even stronger as colonists began to consider independence.[5]

Independence and the Marketplace of Ideas

Journalists played an important role during the late-eighteenth-century struggle for independence. They not only recounted events but also presented competing ideologies for discussion in the marketplace of ideas. During the mid-eighteenth century—especially after the French and Indian War, which required colonists to contribute to what they considered a British cause—colonists began to entertain the idea of increased independence from Britain. Many of the imported books, local newspapers, and pamphlets read by the colonists spread the ideas of the Enlightenment, a philosophical movement during the seventeenth and eighteenth centuries that generated new ideas about scientific reasoning, democracy, rule by consent of the governed, and free criticism of government. These ideas challenged authoritarian control and championed individual rights and democratic participation.

Chief among intellectuals and editors who challenged British authority was Benjamin Franklin. He established a prominent newspaper in Philadelphia, ran a bookshop, printed a newspaper and various pamphlets, attempted publication of a magazine, and helped found a public library system. He extended his printing network to the southern colonies by financing printers so they could start bookshops and printing establishments in growing cities. He gained fame for both the lightning rod experiments that later earned him a place in elementary school science books and the "Join or Die" snake, a graphic representation of the need for the colonies to stick together in their fight against England or else undergo separate deaths.

When the British Parliament passed the Stamp Act, which assessed a tax on paper, newspaper publishers rebelled. The tax was designed to help pay for the French and Indian War, which started in 1756. The colonists argued that they had no say in whether or how the war should be fought and therefore should not have to pay the tax. In protest some of the newspaper publishers printed woodcuts with skull-and-crossbones emblems; other ceased publishing and refused to pay the tax. By the time of the Revolution, most printers were notoriously patriotic. A lack of tolerance for diversity of political opinion characterized most communities, and printers who remained loyal to the British Crown were quickly exiled. Despite protests against British control of the press, colonists readily exercised their own control of public opinion by suppressing unpopular opinions. The resistance to free expression for everyone during times of stress became a characteristic of American media during the next two centuries, and the media often felt free to demonize and stereotype America's enemies in times of social strife or war.

Newspaper editors and pamphleteers such as Thomas Paine cheered the colonists onward. During the struggle for independence, when George Washington's troops were mired in winter snows in Trenton, New Jersey, Paine offered eloquent pleas for steadfastness, such as, "These are the times that try men's souls."

The Fight for Political Dominance

Although the states ratified the Constitution with no provision for a free press, within three years (in 1791) a Bill of Rights was added to ensure civil liberties: among others, the right to assemble, to choose a religion, to speak and write freely, and to be tried fairly. Chief among the Bill of Rights was the First Amendment:

> Congress shall make no law respecting an establishment of religion, or prohibiting the free exercise thereof; or abridging the freedom of speech, or of the press; or the right of the public peaceably to assemble, and to petition the government for a redress of grievances.

From 1790 to 1830, during the constitutional debates and the establishment of political parties, most editors and commentators argued vociferously on one side. Eighteenth-century political writers did not value objectivity as an ideal. Journalists, often members of the social elite and appointed by a politician, helped establish the function of the press in a newly created democratic society.[6] They sometimes overstepped the boundaries of good taste, but they established the right of journalists to comment on political competition, a right that has fueled the political process ever since. These commentators sided with either the Federalists, who wanted a strong central government, or the Anti-Federalists, who argued to preserve the powers of the states.

The period of rabid political rhetoric has been labeled the **Dark Ages** of American journalism by many historians. Anti-Federalist Benjamin Franklin Bache, the grandson of Benjamin Franklin, accused the revered George Washington of having "debauched" the nation and argued that "the masque of patriotism may be worn to conceal the foulest designs against the liberties of a people." Bache was so outrageous that even his friends at times turned against him. But he stuck to his political principles, "in which he said that government officers were fallible, the Constitution good but not obviously 'stampt with the seal of perfection,' and that a free press was 'one of the first safeguards of Liberty.'"[7] A vituperative editor on the Federalist side, William Cobbett, called Bache black-hearted, seditious, sleepy-eyed, vile, and perverted.

Despite the First Amendment, a Federalist Congress in 1798 passed the restrictive Naturalization, Enemy Alien, and Sedition Acts. These laws, commonly called the **Alien and Sedition Acts,** made it possible to indict those who "shall write, print, utter, or publish . . . false, scandalous and malicious writing or writings against the Government of the United States, or the President of the United States, or either house of the Congress . . . with intent to defame . . . or to bring them into contempt or disrepute." Those who were convicted could be punished by a fine of not more than $2,000 and could be imprisoned for two years. Anti-Federalist editors across the land were indicted and jailed, and only when Thomas Jefferson took office as president of the United States in 1801 were those editors released. The Alien and Sedition Acts indeed marked a low point, with their restrictions against the criticism of government in a time of peace. Because those acts were passed but not renewed, such restrictions generally have been reserved for times of war.

History of Press Responsibility

When the First Amendment was written, idealists adhered to the *Enlightenment philosophy* that all individuals are born equal to learn, improve, and make proper decisions from which to lead productive lives. The government was thought to exist only as an extension of the people. It was the responsibility of the press to provide information to individuals, who were considered rational beings who could discern truth from falsehood. The founders of the United States believed that if a variety of people contributed ideas to the discussion, a free marketplace of ideas would be created and the truth would emerge. For the marketplace of ideas to succeed, the market needs to provide free access for those who would contribute.

By the twentieth century, the Industrial Revolution had changed society and the press. Individuals became more interdependent, and national media developed as radio and television expanded. During the Great Depression, Franklin Delano Roosevelt introduced federal programs based on the concept that government has the responsibility to make sure people live in acceptable conditions. In addition, with the implementation of compulsory education, people gave government the responsibility of educating the children. To some degree, U.S. society had exchanged individualism for protectionism and collectivism. With that change came renewed calls for offering individuals information that would allow them to put events and issues into context.

In 1947 a commission chaired by Robert Hutchins expressed the change in society's expectations of the press system. The **Hutchins Commission,** funded primarily by Henry Luce, founder of *Time* and *Life,* said that the great influence of media and the concentration of ownership required that media be socially responsible. The commission, after reviewing press behavior, decried the state of American journalism.

The commission listed five "ideal demands of society for the communication of news and ideas":

1. A truthful, comprehensive, and intelligent account of the day's events in a context that gives them meaning
2. A forum for the exchange of comment and criticism
3. The projection of a representative picture of the constituent groups in society
4. The presentation and clarification of the goals and values of society
5. Full access to the day's intelligence

After evaluating the press in light of its ideal demands, the commission found freedom of the press in the United States to be in danger because of the monopolistic nature of the press. Concentration meant, the commission noted, that fewer people had access to communication channels and that those in charge had not provided a service adequate to society's needs.

Concerned with the potential of new technology to be developed for either good or evil, the commission discussed guidelines for regulation of new technology and international communications systems.[8] The commission chose, however, to assign the press the responsibility of "accountability," rather than recommending increased government regulation. The commission suggested that retraction or restatement might better serve victims of libel rather than suits for damages, and it recommended repeal of state syndicalism acts and the Alien Registration Act of 1940, saying they were of "dubious constitutionality." The commission also suggested that the government assume responsibility for disseminating its own news, through either private channels or channels of its own.

The commission suggested that the press should accept the responsibility of being a "common carrier" of information and discussion rather than assuming that ownership meant dissemination of a personal viewpoint. It encouraged owners to experiment with new activities, especially in areas in which profits were not necessarily assured. The commission also encouraged vigorous mutual criticism by members of the press and increased competence of news staffs. It also chided the radio industry for giving away control to soap sponsors and recommended the industry take control of its programs by treating advertisers the way the "best" newspapers treated them.

Focusing on freedom as "bound up intrinsically in the collective good of life in society," the commission further suggested that the public had a social responsibility to ensure continued freedom of the press, requesting that nonprofit institutions help supply variety and quality to press service. It requested that educational centers be created for advanced research about communications and emphasized the importance of the liberal arts in journalistic training.[9]

Renewing the discussion of the importance of a free and accessible press to a democratic society, the Hutchins Commission finally recommended that an independent agency be established to appraise and report annually on the performance of the press. The commission worried, however, that too much emphasis was being placed on that recommendation. Nevertheless, it seemed to be the only solution commissioners could agree on, after acknowledging that the concept of laissez-faire, not government control, would eliminate the effects of monopoly.[10]

Needless to say, the owners of the agencies of mass communication reacted negatively. Many members of the press were critical because no one from its ranks was included on the commission. Responding to the criticism, the American Society of Newspaper Editors (ASNE) in 1950 appointed ten newspapermen and educators to investigate self-improvement possibilities. The editors' findings reaffirmed the concept of laissez-faire and rejected the commission's recommendations, claiming that improvement of U.S. newspapers depended on "the character of American newspapermen" and their "acceptance of the great responsibilities imposed by freedom of the press." The ASNE study suggested that reporters and editors might be more willing to profit by the "intelligent criticism of the newspaper-reading public" than they would by suggestions made by a commission over which they had no control.[11]

Social Responsibility ✦ During the twentieth century, **social responsibility** has become the dominant theoretical model for media. As coauthor of *Four Theories of the Press*, Theodore Peterson wrote, "freedom carries concomitant obligations; and the press, which enjoys a privileged position under our government, is obliged to be responsible to society for carrying out certain essential functions of mass communications in contemporary society." In addition, media should continue to be free from government in order to watch over government.

Although most journalists and media critics accept social responsibility in some form, not all do. Communication scholars John Merrill and Jack Odell have written about the hazards of the social responsibility approach:

> We simply (1) cannot understand exactly what is meant by a *theory* of social responsibility, and (2) cannot help feeling that a growing emphasis on such a theory will lead a nation's press system away from freedom toward authoritarianism. In the eyes of individual persons in *any* society various media at times will perform what they see as irresponsible actions; for irresponsibility, like beauty, is in the eye of the beholder.
>
> Some critics see social responsibility as self-censorship that could deprive the marketplace of ideas of potentially beneficial information. They also fear that standards of responsibility will come from the powerful and not from ordinary citizens.[12]

Emergence of the Reporter

The shift from editor/printer/intellectual to reporter/editor came with the advent of the penny press in the 1830s. As you will read in the chapter on newspapers, urban editors wanted to expand circulations, hoping that revenues would follow. In doing so, they recognized that strong political affiliations with parties would jeopardize the expansion of their readership. They began to rely more strongly on advertising and sought to report news that would be of interest to all. With this strategy in mind, Benjamin Day of the *New York Sun* hired a reporter—a person who collects information and presents it in a readable fashion to a wide range of readers.

Day hired George W. Wisner, a young reporter, and paid him four dollars a week to rise at four in the morning to cover daily police court sessions. Wisner turned police court charges of spousal assault and petty debt into action and drama for the *Sun*'s news pages. Crime stories reinforced the social values of the day by showing what happened to those who broke the rules, but they also appealed to an interest in "bad people." Wisner was an ardent abolitionist, so he used his position to try to sneak antislavery editorials into the *Sun* along with his police reports.

When Wisner left New York for Michigan, Day hired Richard Adams Locke, an educated man who was interested in scientific discovery. Locke is famous in journalism history for his 1835 series of articles exploiting the discoveries of Sir John Frederick William Herschel, the greatest astronomer of his time, who had established an observatory near Cape Town, South Africa. Locke's story illustrates that entertainment, along with information, was considered a journalistic goal. Locke reported that Herschel, through the use of a new telescope, had discovered planets in other solar systems and had seen the surface of the moon with vegetation, animals, and winged creatures that resembled men and women. Locke cited the *Edinburgh Journal of Science* as his source and managed to fool not only the general public but the scientific community as well.

The *Sun* defended the **hoax,** saying that it was useful in diverting the public mind from such worrisome issues as the abolition of slavery. The Moon Hoax, as it came to be called, is often used to illustrate

> **social responsibility theory:** As applied to freedom of the press, a philosophy that states that with freedom comes responsibility to the social good.
>
> **hoax:** An act or story intended to deceive; a tall tale; a practical joke or serious fraud.

The *New York Sun* fascinated its readers in the 1830s with stories of observations of winged creatures on the moon. The stories and the illustrations turned out to be fakes.

the claim that penny editors were less concerned with fact and objectivity than with entertaining their public. Sometimes a little fiction was useful in building circulation. Some critics speculate that Locke was trying to upstage the staid, political papers of New York City, which had rejected the penny press as sensationalistic. These papers could not ignore Locke's story, and most of them printed it. When the hoax was revealed, the papers had little argument with which to defend themselves against the penny press upstarts.

The reporter thus became established as a fixture in American journalism. Fictional accounts of reporters in the late nineteenth and early twentieth centuries depict them as semieducated "tough guys" who were out to expose corrupt businessmen and government officials. Women, though they began to enter the ranks, are relatively invisible in the fictional accounts. The intellectual role of the newspaper was relegated to the editorial page, and editors who often were heavily involved in politics made editorial decisions. The editors continued to separate themselves financially from political parties, but most editors strongly supported a particular party.

The Reporter and Social Conscience

◆ During the mid-1800s, newspaper journalists began to expose the wrongdoings of city officials and to focus on city services and politics. During the late 1800s, reporters established the form of reporting called **muckraking**, unearthing corporate greed and exposing it to the masses. The food and drug industry had expanded quickly without regulation, and reporters found that many commercial food-handling situations were dangerous to the consumer. Although the articles were often labeled sensational, they were boring by today's standards. Filled with detail, they dutifully chronicled industry violations of safety and health standards. But they were sensational at the time because to that date no one had written publicly about the issues being discussed. People were shocked to see the material. Much of the material was in the same vein as the social documentary, which found a place in books and, after the turn of the century, to some degree in newsreels. Muckrakers established the *journalism of exposure* as a basic tenet of American journalism.

Photojournalism. As the Kodak box camera began to revolutionize public photography after 1900, the development of the 35-millimeter camera and fast film created new opportunities for photojournalism, which was an extension of the type of photography social reformers had used between 1880 and 1915 to document the negative social effects of the Industrial Revolution.

This heart-wrenching example of photojournalist Jacob A. Riis's work as a social reformer shows street children in New York City in 1889.

Some journalists tried to expose these problems through heavy use of illustration. Jacob A. Riis and Lewis W. Hine photographed the plight of the poor and homeless to show what can happen to unskilled workers in an unregulated capitalist economic system. In the 1920s, social documentary photography was greatly enhanced with the introduction of the small Leica camera, made by E. Leitz of Germany. With the Leica, a photographer could work unnoticed while recording a scene. Film that could be quickly exposed and new printing techniques contributed to the development of picture magazines in Germany, England, and the United States. By the 1960s, *Life* and *Look* became showcase magazines for the work of photographers. However, television quickly eclipsed the magazines, and current visual images that moved captivated the public.

JOURNALISM ON RADIO AND TELEVISION

Print journalism—and print and wire reporters—dominated journalism through the first third of the twentieth century. At first radio was merely a voice for the newspaper; newspaper copy fashioned by print journalists was read across the air. Later, reporters developed specific styles oriented toward listeners and viewers. In July 1922, the *Norfolk* [Nebraska] *Daily News* started the first regularly broadcast noon news program. In 1932, radio reporters covered the Roosevelt–Hoover presidential race and launched radio news. They also started a major industry battle between newspapers and radio, and publishers sought to keep radio from competing with them by limiting radio access to news from the major wire services. Newspapers could not stop radio, however, and by the late 1930s radio news was becoming a standard feature.

Radio and World War II

Radio journalists became popular sources of news with their dramatic and complete coverage of World War II. Before radio, war news took hours, days, or even weeks to reach the general public. Radio was instantaneous. Furthermore, print could never match the immediacy of Edward R. Murrow broadcasting from London as German bombs ripped through the city. Murrow developed a radio style, an intimate conversation with his listeners.

During the 1938 coverage of Germany's invasion of Austria, Murrow set up the first simultaneous broadcast with reporters in Vienna, London, Paris, Berlin, and Rome. By the time Hitler invaded Poland in 1939, CBS and NBC had placed experienced reporters throughout Europe. By 1943, the amount of radio news in the networks' evening programming had tripled, and a majority of people in the United States rated radio as more accurate than newspapers in war coverage.

Television Journalism

Newsreels, shown in movie houses, and television offered the first electronic visual journalism. Although some experimentation with television news occurred as early as 1940, development of news programming was delayed until after World War II; the half-hour television network news shows did not appear until the 1960s.

In 1945, NBC set up an organization for production of news film. In 1948, the network presented *NBC Newsroom*, a program produced by radio journalists and broadcast from the NBC radio newsroom. Critics argued that pictures of a man reading the news did not add much to an understanding of world affairs, but ratings were sufficient to keep the program on the air and attract competitors. The current evening newscast format dates to NBC's *Camel News Caravan*, a fifteen-minute nightly program starring John Cameron Swayze. CBS inaugurated a similar program, *Douglas Edwards with the News. Camel News Caravan* solidified NBC's news operation for the short term. By May 1951, forty stations carried the program, which mixed newsreel footage with visual reading of the news. NBC Television News established bureaus

profile

Edward R. Murrow

Long before the publicity machine peppered U.S. society with one-name idols such as Madonna and Eminem, people earned that sort of recognition through a lifetime of accomplishments. Of these career icons, perhaps the most influential journalist was Edward R. Murrow, who shaped journalism in radio and television. Although it seems that much of broadcast news has fallen into sensationalism and pandering, current standards for good public service journalism can be traced directly to Murrow.

Murrow was born in North Carolina in 1908 and moved to Washington State at age six. During his youth, he worked as a farmhand, a bus driver, and a logger. While attending Washington State College, where he changed his first name from Egbert to Edward, Murrow participated in campus politics; he graduated in 1930.

During the five years between graduation and the beginning of his twenty-six-year career with the Columbia Broadcasting System (CBS), Murrow worked with educational organizations and traveled throughout Europe. He started work for CBS in 1935 and was promoted to CBS representative in Europe two years later. It was in Europe that he shaped the values of radio news and trained a group of broadcast journalists who would guide both radio and TV news for a generation.

From Europe, Murrow covered the steady expansion of Hitler's power. His broadcasts from London during World War II, which started with the statement "This is London," allowed Americans to experience war as they had never before experienced it. Murrow said that during the war Winston Churchill "mobilized the English language and sent it into battle." This could be applied accurately to Murrow's reporting efforts.

Murrow did more than simply report. He trained other journalists such as Howard K. Smith, Charles C. Collingwood, Eric Sevareid, and Richard Hottelet. These colleagues would help define radio news and establish television news a decade later.

Following the war, Murrow became an executive with CBS before returning to journalism on television.

Two of his programs, *See It Now* and *Person to Person*, helped shape the public's expectations of TV journalists. The high point of his TV journalism career came in 1954 when he attacked Senator Joseph R. McCarthy on *See It Now* for creating a witch-hunt in the name of anticommunism. McCarthy attacked people from the floor of the Senate and caused many to lose their jobs; some even committed suicide. Few people had been willing to do battle with such a powerful senator. But Murrow used his thirty-minute program to criticize McCarthy with McCarthy's own words and images. He said of McCarthy's attacks, "We must not confuse dissent with disloyalty," and added, "We will not be driven by fear into an age of unreason if we remember that we are not descended from fearful men, men who fear to write, to speak, to associate and to defend causes, which were, for the moment, unpopular."

Murrow continued at CBS until 1961, when President John F. Kennedy appointed him director of the United States Information Agency (USIA). The USIA's mission was to spread information about the U.S. government and culture around the world. He served as director until 1963 and died in 1965.

During his career, Murrow grew to understand the power and potential of broadcasting. On October 15, 1965, he spoke at the convention of the Radio–Television News Directors Association and said of television: "This instrument can teach, it can illuminate, and yes it can inspire. But it can do so only to the extent that humans are determined to use it to those ends. Otherwise, it is nothing but wires and lights in a box."

Sources: "Edward R. Murrow," *Compton's Encyclopedia Online,* www.optonline.com/compton/ceo/03310-A.html, accessed in October 1999; "Edward R. Murrow: A WWW Information Source," Washington State University, www.wsu.edu/Communications/_ERM/index.html, accessed in October 1999; Jean Folkerts and Dwight L. Teeter Jr., *Voices of a Nation: A History of Media in the United States* (New York: Macmillan, 1989).

---

in New York, Chicago, Washington, D.C., Cleveland, Los Angeles, Dallas, and San Francisco. It recruited **stringers** from abroad, hired camera crews and photographers, and signed exchange agreements with affiliate stations for news film. Initially, this meant additional jobs for journalists, but in 1952/1953, as production costs increased and NBC's news programs encountered financial difficulty, the network dramatically reduced its news division.

Meanwhile, CBS also expanded its news operations. William Paley, along with his second-in-command, Frank Stanton, shaped CBS into a leader in entertainment and news programming. Paley solidified CBS's financing, then demonstrated an uncanny skill for negotiating with affiliates and with celebrities. He was willing to allocate resources to programming, and it didn't take Paley long to ensure that CBS would surpass NBC as a leader in news and information programming.

stringers: Reporters, often at a location remote from the newspaper, who sell occasional pieces at "space rates," or by the column inch.

Veteran news reporters remember the Edward R. Murrow days as the Golden Age of Television News, when money flowed through CBS newsrooms and news shaped the reputation of the individual network. Murrow, famous for his radio news broadcasts during World War II, debuted in television in 1951 with the first network public affairs series, *See It Now.* In later years, Murrow made CBS famous for its **documentaries,** such as *Harvest of Shame,* which depicted the plight of migrant farmworkers.

Political Reporting on Television ✦ Just as television restructured U.S. entertainment patterns and the process through which people got their news, so it also reshaped the process of reporting on government officials. Television combined with expanding education, increasing mobility, participatory democratic legislation, and sophisticated research methods during the 1950s and 1960s to weaken political parties in the United States and increase the role of the media in selecting leaders.

Network journalists covered the presidential campaign of 1952, a race between the popular General Dwight D. Eisenhower, a hero of World War II, and Illinois Governor Adlai Stevenson, one of the nation's foremost intellectuals. During this race, politics began to conform to the requirements of television. Stevenson's long commentaries bored too many of his listeners; Eisenhower, although anything but a polished television star, at least learned the value of short spots.

Soon after being named Eisenhower's running mate, Richard Nixon was accused of being the beneficiary of a secret trust fund set up by wealthy businessmen. The public was scandalized. Fearing that Eisenhower would drop him from the Republican ticket, Nixon chose television as the medium for his defense. It was through television that Richard Nixon was able to bypass journalists. Television provided this politician the opportunity to present himself in public without editing by journalists. In what became known as "the Checkers speech," Nixon detailed his financial condition and vowed that, though his children's dog Checkers had been donated by an admirer, the family loved the dog and "regardless of what they say, we're going to keep it." This personalized use of television built on what Franklin Delano Roosevelt had accomplished with his "Fireside Chats" over radio before and during World War II. Politicians began to go directly to the public, rather than having information first sifted through reporters and editors for newspapers and magazines.

The Image ✦ Image has always played a role in U.S. politics. Image helps to define candidates for voters. Television, with its strong visual impact, enhanced the ability of media and politicians to manipulate political images.

John Kennedy used presidential debates and press conferences to shape his image. His ready wit and handsome smile made him a natural for the cameras. In the first ***televised presidential debate*** between Kennedy and Richard Nixon in 1960, Kennedy established himself as a man with a vision for leadership and placed Nixon in the position of defending the status quo. The role of image was demonstrated further by the reaction of people who listened to the debate on the radio: The majority of radio listeners believed Nixon won the debate.

The Kennedy–Nixon debates set a precedent for future presidential campaigns. Debates are now an expected part of the campaign process, and their effectiveness or lack of it is controversial and thus interesting to voters. In the 1992 elections, the questioning of candidates in a town hall format, with citizens rather than journalists asking questions, gained more attention than did the formal debates. However, as the 2000 election debates showed, formal encounters continue to be a significant part of presidential campaigning.

In 1968 Richard Nixon hired people who understood the art of television advertising, and paid media became a significant force in political campaigning. Nixon's people knew how to research public taste and to create advertising. Although disarray in the Democratic Party in 1968 aided Nixon's victory, some critics charge that without the mastery of the television image devised by his advisors, Nixon might never have become president.

key concept

Televised Presidential Debates Debates between candidates in front of TV cameras or audiences have become significant factors in presidential elections. Televised debates for primary candidates in key states, as well as in national elections, can earn respectable TV ratings and appear to be an important way for the public to see candidates interact and talk about issues.

documentaries: Film or video investigations. Based on the term documents—these accounts document the details of a historical or current event. Often used as a term that implies investigative reporting.

The precedent for televised presidential campaigns was set in 1960 as Americans sat riveted around their television sets for the Kennedy and Nixon presidential debates.

Today, political candidates work hard to control their images through advertising and by making arranged appearances. Many candidates limit their exposure to journalists, preferring to display a crafted image rather than respond to impromptu questions. Whenever candidates do respond to the press, their spin doctors work to get the candidate's interpretation of an event or issue into journalists' stories. The promotion of image rather than issues and substance is also fostered by some of the current production values of television. News values that promote higher ratings through ever shorter **sound bites** allow candidates to shape a planned, desirable television image, no matter what their actual political history.

Expanded Television News ✦ In 1963, only a few weeks before the assassination of President John F. Kennedy, whose funeral made television history, NBC expanded its evening news coverage from a mere fifteen minutes to a thirty-minute newscast featuring the anchor team of Chet Huntley and David Brinkley. CBS followed suit with a news program anchored by Walter Cronkite. ABC, whose newscasts were at best a fledgling operation, didn't expand to a half hour until 1967. Since the 1960s, the networks have often explored expanding their evening newscasts to an hour. However, the affiliated stations continue to run their own profitable local newscasts in the lead-in time slot (usually 5:00 to 6:30 or 7:00 P.M. EST) and retain the time slot following the network news for profit-making syndicated shows such as *Wheel of Fortune* and *Jeopardy*.

By the end of the 1960s, television had become the country's dominant medium for the visual display of social controversy. The civil rights movement, the war in Vietnam, environmental damage, and women's demands for equality were the big stories of the decade. Television covered them all. In 1969 even Vice President Spiro Agnew, who despised and feared the power of television, admitted that

> [t]he networks have made "hunger" and "black lung disease" national issues overnight. The TV networks have done what no other medium could have done in terms of dramatizing the horrors of war. The networks have tackled our most difficult social problems with a directness and immediacy that is the gift of their medium. They have focused the nation's attention on its environmental abuses . . . on pollution in the Great Lakes and the threatened ecology of the Everglades.[13]

sound bites: A short quotation used on radio or television to express an idea.

newsmagazines: Fifteen- to twenty-minute news segments put together to form hourlong electronic magazines such as *60 Minutes* or *Dateline*. These programs combine soft features with hard-hitting investigative reporting.

Expansion of network news came not in the prestigious and expensive evening hours but in morning news, in which a softer format appealed to audiences with shows such as *Good Morning America*. The definition of news also expanded to include **newsmagazines** such as *60 Minutes*, which began in 1968 but did not achieve a permanent slot on the weekly schedule until the late 1970s. The expansion also includes late-night news programs such as Ted Koppel's *Nightline*, which ABC intro-

The nighttime slot provides journalists with enough time to cover stories in depth. In this 2002 taping of *Nightline*'s "Town Meeting" at the Church of Notre Dame in Jerusalem, Ted Koppel listens while chief Palestinian negotiator Saeb Erekat makes a point and Israeli Foreign Minister Shimon Peres looks on.

duced in 1979 during the height of the crisis arising from Iranian militants' seizure of hostages in the U.S. embassy in Tehran. In the late 1980s, the number of newsmagazines in prime time grew. By 2000, ABC, NBC, and CBS were producing as many as a dozen newsmagazines a week.

OBJECTIVITY AND STORYTELLING

American journalism has emerged from two separate traditions, that of *objectivity* and that of storytelling, or the *narrative tradition.* Modern journalism exhibits a tension between these traditions, with many editors and station managers arguing that objectivity is the golden norm of journalism, while others struggle to retain and understand the narrative tradition and its importance.

We know that impartiality or objectivity was a criterion used as early as the colonial days. Benjamin Franklin speaks of being an "impartial printer." During the Civil War, J. Thrasher, head of the Press Association in the Confederate states, tells editors to be "objective." When Adolph Ochs strives to make the *New York Times* a newspaper of record in the mid-1800s, he speaks of "objectivity."

Traditionally, objectivity has included five components: detachment from the object of the story, nonpartisanship, a reliance on facts, a sense of balance, and use of the inverted pyramid style of writing.[14] However, many journalists believe it is impossible to be totally objective. In fact, journalists have dropped the word *objectivity* from such documents as the Society for Professional Journalists' code. Whereas Walter Cronkite, the renowned anchor of the CBS evening news from 1962 to 1981, ended his newscast saying, "And that's the way it is," Dan Rather ends his with the words, "And that's part of our world." The strive for objectivity has been replaced by use of the words *truthfulness, accuracy,* and *comprehensiveness.* However, journalists often endorse objectivity as a principal tenet. Leonard Downie, managing editor of the *Washington Post,* reveres the concept to the degree that he claims he does not vote because doing so would force him to take sides and make him less objective.

The tradition of narrative journalism has remained strong. Telling stories was a component of colonial and frontier newspapers. Sometimes they were totally factual;

key concept

Objectivity Looking at a story as though through a perfect lens uncolored by a reporter's thoughts about a subject; trying to view a story from a neutral perspective. Some critics believe pure objectivity is impossible and that fairness and balance are more important.

key concept

Narrative Tradition Journalism as story. Many writers employ fictional techniques in writing nonfiction material.

at other times, they were representations of reality. Narrative journalism, or "literary journalism," was controversial as early as the 1880s, when it threatened literature, whose predominant form during the period was realism. The controversies centered on some themes that are still heard today: the conflict between "high" and "low" culture and the blending of fiction and fact. Many narrative journalists actually aspired to be novelists.[15]

During the late 1960s, when a young generation of journalists evaluated the role of journalism in the social change brought about by civil rights and Vietnam activities and debates, they turned to what they labeled "new journalism" as a way of expressing the social context of political arguments. Some of these young reporters abandoned the objective, straightforward approach of "Who? What? When? Where? and Why?" The demands of interpretation and the political and cultural context of the decade demanded new techniques, new language, and incorporation of styles that had distinguished alternative media for many years. Everette Dennis, in the *Magic Writing Machine,* divided **new journalism** into five types: (1) the new nonfiction, also called "reportage" and "parajournalism"; (2) alternative journalism, also called "modern muckraking"; (3) advocacy journalism; (4) underground journalism; and (5) precision journalism. David Halberstam wrote a journalistic account of Vietnam (new nonfiction); the *Village Voice* advocated political positions on issues such as free love (alternative and advocacy, which sometimes blend); underground newspapers were printed and distributed without acknowledgment of authorship; and precision journalists used new statistical methods to prove points.

Today, narrative journalism appears in books by journalists such as Mark Bowden, whose account of the disastrous U.S. intervention in Somalia is chronicled in *Black Hawk Down.* Controversy about the method still abounds, especially in relation to books such as *Midnight in the Garden of Good and Evil,* a supposedly nonfiction account of a high-profile murder in Savannah, Georgia. Many critics contend that although the basic structure is nonfiction, the narrative is embellished considerably with fictional constructs.

TODAY'S MARKET STRUCTURE

Today's journalists operate in a highly competitive marketplace. Both the objective and the narrative traditions are used in reporting news for newspapers, radio, television, and the Internet. However, the marketplace has become increasingly competitive, and media companies have "gone public," or begun to sell stock on the markets, thereby creating a need to pay dividends to those individuals who buy the stocks. This has increased the attention paid to ratings of television and radio news, as well as to the circulation numbers of newspapers and to the numbers of hits on Internet sites. Entertainment has assumed more importance.

Although journalism has always been a business, during the last thirty-five years it has evolved into big business. Whether television, radio, newspapers, or online, the corporations that increasingly own large news outlets require ever-higher profit margins to please the stock analysts and mutual fund managers. The results have varied. In some cases, publicly owned companies such as the *New York Times* produce award-winning journalism. In other cases, such as that of Thomson newspapers, the journalism got so bad that companies lost large numbers of readers. Thomson eventually sold its newspaper holdings.[16] When newspapers seek profit levels that exceed those of most other industries, the result is often a reduction in the number of journalists and a corresponding decline in local, quality coverage.[17]

Despite these problems, journalism today is supported by thousands of devoted journalists in all media who aim to serve the public and society. The quality of journalism often rests on the initiative of the individuals who put in extra time just to get the story right. However, the tension between profit and quality journalism will continue as long as journalism is a commercial enterprise.

new journalism: Used at different times in the history of journalism. In the 1890s, it defined sensationalism. In the 1960s, the term was used to describe experimentation in reporting strategies and writing styles.

AUDIENCE DEMAND IN JOURNALISM MARKETS

An often debated question in newsrooms is whether the journalist should give the people what they "need" or whether the journalist should provide the material that audiences "want." Such an argument assumes that the journalist and editor know what people need to read. The public certainly does not agree and through its purchasing power does make its own decisions about what kinds of information it needs and wants.

The marketplace of ideas assumes that all ideas should be discussed in the open. The more ideas, the better. Only when ideas (even those thought radical) gain access to the public forum can social change occur. Women fought for almost a century before gaining the right to vote through a constitutional amendment adopted in 1920. Their ideas were considered radical by many men—and women.

The marketplace of ideas involves social discourse, and social discourse can lead to policy formation. For example, the state of Oregon adopted strict recycling standards for its population by the early 1970s, ten to twenty years before most other states did the same. Oregon's marketplace of ideas considered the recycling issue important, and the discussion in that marketplace led to policy changes that other states eventually adopted.

The audience demands information that it can discuss; thus journalism provides the discussion points that help to create the marketplace of ideas. Through the marketplace, the public—individually and in groups—makes political, social, and economic decisions.

Who Uses Journalism?

Because information available through new technology requires that someone purchase a technological device, the possibility exists for a society divided into information-poor and information-rich segments. In such a society, information is the golden key to success, and the information is available only to those with money. Research has consistently shown that those with already high levels of information gain even more information as they begin to use new technologies, and even if information-poor consumers become more knowledgeable, they continually fall behind in the socioinformation struggle. Therefore, the *knowledge gap,* the distance between those who use information technologies at the highest levels and those usually with lower socioeconomic status who do not, increases rather than decreases.[18]

The creation of a knowledge gap is of concern for many reasons. A 1972 study showed that information distribution inequities in a society could be directly related to inequities in the distribution of other elements of social life such as education, affluence, and exposure to communication channels. The United States has long succeeded as a democracy at least in part because of its high literacy rates and its emphasis on maintaining a solid middle class; democracies are known to survive longest in countries with a strong middle class. If class begins to be defined not only by education and social status but also by access to and possession of information, the creation of a knowledge gap may signify the weakening of the middle class.

> ### key concept
>
> **Knowledge Gap** A division of people within a society by their amount of knowledge. With an increasing delivery of news by means of computers, some individuals will not have access to the information. Studies show that those with information and access to technology are more likely to increase their knowledge more rapidly than those without access. Technological delivery of information, therefore, can increase the gap between those with information and those without.

SUPPLYING THE AUDIENCE'S DEMAND

The supply for the marketplace of ideas comes from all sources of information, including individuals, newspapers, movies, television, recordings, and radio. Consumers, journalists, lobbyists, public-relations personnel, and government officials determine, both as individuals and as groups, what content has use in the marketplace of ideas. Because people are both information sources and information consumers, they make the mass communication system an important part of the political and social process. Media serve as *agenda setters:* the content of media helps determine which topics and issues society considers important. Who gets to comment affects the information we all receive, so if only one political party were permitted to comment, content presented by the media would not reflect the social and political world we all must deal with. Likewise, if social issues were presented from only one point of view, such as that of the businessperson, the social context of those on welfare, of working single parents, or of educators would be excluded from the picture. When the agenda setters fairly present all points of view, society is best served.

key concept

Agenda-Setting Research Media research that seeks to understand the relationship between readers' determination of important issues and politicians' and press's treatment of them. The research focuses not on how media cover an issue but on how they set an agenda through the choice of the issues they cover.

Consumers want varying kinds of news. The bulk of nonadvertising information is news. News can be soft, hard, or deep. Soft news includes a variety of feature stories, such as the story of the first woman to serve as drum major of a university band or the story of the birth of a Siberian tiger at the local zoo. Soft news also includes advice columns, such as "Dear Abby." Hard news focuses on current events that have serious effects on people, such as crime, politics, and disasters. If a child dies in a house fire, the story is hard news. In-depth news requires the story to go beyond breaking stories to incorporate background details and trends. Investigative articles often fall into this category. A series of stories about the impact of changing federal regulations on student loans is an example.

News in newspapers comes from three sources: the newspaper staff, wire and news services, and feature syndicates. Staff and news service reporters share similar standards for selecting which events and issues become news. These standards are called *news values,* and their application to particular stories is called "news judgment." Over time, several news values have evolved. The following values are usually cited as the reasons behind news selection and are even taught in reporting courses in journalism school:

key concept

News Values Newspaper editors and owners try to develop standards of value for determining which events and issues are newsworthy—that is, deserving of being given space in the paper.

- Impact applies when a large number of people are affected by an event or issue or when a small number of individuals are intensely affected. A car accident that kills three people has a greater impact than one that causes a small cut on one person's forehead.
- Proximity deals with the geographic location of an event. The more local the event, the more news value it has. A story that shuts off electricity for eight hours in Lansing, Michigan, will be reported in the *Lansing State Journal* but not in the *Detroit Free Press* because the *Journal* is proximate to Lansing readers.
- Prominence concerns how notable or famous a person is. Politicians, sports figures, and entertainment stars are prominent figures. An illicit affair by a shoe store clerk would not be news, but President Clinton's affair was because of prominence.
- Timeliness deals with recency of an event or issue. A bank robbery that happened yesterday has more news value than one twenty years ago. The focus is on breaking stories.
- Conflict relates to disagreement among people. The conflict can be physical, as in crime and war, but it need not be. Much political news involves conflict in the marketplace of ideas.
- Disaster includes both natural calamities such as earthquakes and human-caused catastrophes such as an oil spill in the ocean.
- Human interest relates to personal details that intrigue readers. The story of an eighty-year-old woman who drives a school bus and is called "Grandma" by elementary students has human interest.

News values may change as society changes. The penny press, for example, emphasized crime news, which contained conflict and impact. A more recent type of news

The disintegration of the space shuttle Columbia in 2003 as it returned to Earth gained worldwide attention and news coverage because the event exhibited several news values: disaster, timeliness, impact to society, and prominence of the seven astronauts who died. Here, U.S. Senator and former space shuttle astronaut Bill Nelson speaks with reporters at an impromptu press conference at the Kennedy Space Center.

is called "coping information." Life in the United States has grown more complicated. More readers want information that will help them live more efficiently. Articles about how to stay healthy through better eating and exercise help people cope with daily stress.

A story can have more than one news value. The more of these values in a story, the more likely it is that people will read it. In addition, some values are more important than others. Because newspapers tend to emphasize local news, proximity is important for most staff-prepared stories.

Journalists don't sit with a checklist of news values when picking events to be covered. Rather, they internalize these values and judge whether stories will be of interest to their readers. As the audience changes, however, the match between the journalists' and the audience's news values can change. Coping information emerged because readers wanted it.

Many readers criticize newspapers for emphasizing too much *bad news*, another term for conflict and disaster. Journalists counter that some bad news is important and must be understood if people are to be effective citizens. Many readers grew tired of reading about the Clinton and Lewinsky controversy. The debate centered not only on the amount of coverage but also on the nature of the coverage. Readers and journalists can agree on a story having news value but disagree on how that story should be presented to readers.

Specialized Supply in the Marketplace

Information can be supplied in many forms through many different media. Listed in the following sections are some of the ways that information has been gathered and delivered in recent decades.

Computer-Assisted Reporting ◆ A major trend in journalism is the use of computers for reporting. Computers have altered the way newspapers produce and print news, and they have allowed newspapers to distribute news electronically. People can access news from computers, through newspaper, broadcast, and specific online web sites. The computer, however, has also affected the way news is gathered and written. *Computer-assisted reporting* (CAR) is an umbrella term for several uses of computers in reporting. CAR activities range from finding addresses and phone numbers online, to accessing government databases, to using programs that manipulate data to create new interpretations of old data.

key concept

Computer-Assisted Reporting (CAR) The use of computer technology to gather and analyze information for news articles includes the use of the Internet, spreadsheets, and databases.

Convergence can affect both the distribution and creation of journalism. Computer-assisted reporting allows reporters to access and analyze large databases from government agencies and other organizations in order to produce more accurate and complete news.

Initially, only investigative reporters at large newspaper organizations practiced CAR because it involved more computer and database skills than most journalists possessed. As journalists gained better computer skills and governments put databases online, CAR use increased. It remains a complex and expensive tool, but it increasingly plays a significant role in helping reporters understand everything from economic reports to census numbers.

The Public Journalism Controversy ✦ The development of *public journalism* as a theoretical and practical approach to reporting has created a great deal of controversy. Newspapers and local broadcast news reports have always served communities.

But during the mid-twentieth century, many reporters strived not to enter community journalism, because they viewed working for big papers such as the *New York Times*, *Chicago Tribune*, and *Washington Post*, or for network news, as the road to professional advancement and career success. On a smaller scale, journalists left the small towns for papers in the state capitals. Urban journalists could adopt the professional values of being detached, objective, tough, and critical. They stood apart from the communities they served.

As their audience and their competition changed, newspaper organizations found themselves with diminishing circulations and a lack of connection with their communities. Seeking to reestablish their identities, some newspaper editors, as well as academicians, began to explore a philosophy of public journalism. Many local newspapers partnered with broadcast stations in public journalism efforts. Many of these efforts also included online components of newsgathering and dissemination. The *American Journalism Review* lists five components of public journalism:

> asking readers to help decide what the paper covers and how it covers it; becoming a more active player and less an observer; lobbying for change on the news pages; finding sources whose voices are often unheard; and, above all, dramatically strengthening the bonds between newspaper and community. At its heart is the assumption that a newspaper should act as a catalyst for change.[19]

Words such as *involvement* invoke specters of political corruption from the past, and editors feared that trying to influence the outcome of public action would affect newspapers' credibility. In addition, some editors saw the new approach as a loss of control of their own product. Marvin Kalb, director of the Washington Office of the Joan Shorenstein Center on the Press, Politics and Public Policy at Harvard University, while acknowledging that the public journalism movement "is not a flash in the pan phenomenon," urged caution: "A journalist who becomes an actor, in my view, is overstepping the bounds of . . . traditional responsibility."[20]

The Pew Center for Civic Journalism has funded many journalism projects involving newspapers, television, and radio stations. The *Portland Press Herald* and the *Maine Sunday Telegram* in Portland, Maine, used the money to allow teenagers to work with the news staff to publish news and features online. The *Savannah Morning News* in Georgia studied and wrote about the effects of an aging population on taxes, lifestyles, and services in the region. However, Pew start-up funding is ending, and the question is whether public journalism survives through other infusions of funding or because news organizations adopt it as an essential element of news coverage.

The debate over public journalism centers on three main questions: (1) What is public journalism? (2) Does public journalism increase circulation and viewing and improve attitudes toward the media? (3) What should be the role of readers in determining journalistic content? The first question seems easy to answer, but critics maintain that public journalism represents the worst of media marketing—giving readers what they say they want just to sell newspapers or gain viewers. Supporters say journalists cannot recognize all the issues that audiences need to know about without communicating with those readers.

INTERNATIONAL JOURNALISM

Media organizations are becoming increasingly global. Multinational companies own media outlets in multiple countries. Ownership ultimately has an impact on journalism. In World War II and in Vietnam, for the most part U.S. citizens covered the war and reported on it in U.S. media for U.S. consumers. Other countries relied on various systems for gaining information. Some of that information was U.S. based, such as international news broadcasts by Voice of America, the government-owned information service.

Today, however, CNN employs news reporters from around the world. They may or may not be U.S. citizens. This means that the view of reporters in regard to international incidents may vary considerably more than reporter views varied during earlier international conflicts. CNN executives also are searching for audiences

global impact

Journalists at Risk

Journalism can be a deadly activity. During the last decade (1991–2001), according to the Committee to Protect Journalists (CPJ), 389 journalists were killed while carrying out their work. By October 2002, eleven journalists had been killed during that year alone. The vast majority do not die in cross fire, but rather are hunted down and killed, often in direct reprisal for their reporting. According to CPJ statistics, only 62 journalists died in cross fire, while 298 were murdered. The others died while covering violent street demonstrations or in other similar activities.

Since 1992 only twenty of these cases have been resolved with the person or group ordering the murder of the journalist being arrested. CPJ notes this disturbing fact: that "those who murder journalists do so with impunity." Journalists are killed for a variety of reasons, including trying to prevent them from reporting on corruption or human rights abuses.

Photographers seem to be the most likely to be killed in cross fire, but they, just like reporters, also have been deliberately murdered. Others, such as Daniel Pearl (2002), were killed after being kidnapped.

Radio reporters also are at risk, in part because radio is an important vehicle worldwide for disseminating information, particularly in poor, isolated countries.

Although American journalists are extremely visible while working abroad and tend to be employed by powerful news outlets, deaths are relatively rare. During the last decade (through 2001), only fourteen of the 389 journalists killed were American.

Source: Committee to Protect Journalists, www.cpj.org/killed/Ten_Year_Killed/Intro.html, accessed October 14, 2002.

In our global economy, news is gathered all around the world and fed to various media organizations. Here, Anti-Qaida commander Haji Zahir holds a press conference from the back of a pick-up truck in Agom, Afghanistan.

around the world. An example of this was apparent during the spring and summer of June 2002, when many Israeli groups charged CNN with biased coverage of the Palestinian–Israeli conflict. Media watch groups charged that CNN humanized Palestinians and merely noted the number of dead in Israel. Ted Turner's comments to the *London Guardian* didn't help: "The Israelis, they've got the most powerful military machines in the world. The Palestinians have nothing," Mr. Turner told the London-based *Guardian*. "So who are the terrorists? I would make a case that both sides are engaged in terrorism."

Here is the *Washington Times*'s account of the apology that followed:

"AOL Time Warner understands and takes seriously the feelings of those offended by Mr. Turner's statements on Israel," AOL Time Warner spokesman Ed Adler said in a statement. "Mr. Turner has no operational or editorial involvement at CNN. Mr. Turner's comments are his own and do not reflect the views of our company in any way."

Another executive rued the loss of convivial relations between CNN and other broadcast companies in the troubled region.[21] Global ownership of media companies does affect content, as can be seen from this example. This raises new questions about the role of a reporter as a citizen, as an employee, and as an objective journalist.

TRENDS

Throughout history, journalistic trends have come and gone. Sometimes they involve technology and delivery of news, and other times they involve the impact of business and journalistic practices on what people receive as news. Currently, four major trends are shaping journalism: issues of credibility, journalism and political participation, the future of journalism online, and the impact of profits on journalism.

Credibility

Journalists have come on hard times—their credibility with the public has taken a nosedive. In an attempt to address these issues, several associations and "think groups" have studied the credibility issue. A study conducted by *Time* magazine in 1998 found that newspaper credibility had sunk to a level at which only 21 percent of Americans believed all or most of the content in the local newspaper, representing a decline from 28 percent in 1985.

The American Society of Newspaper Editors (ASNE) began a $1 million project to improve credibility. They discovered that the public finds too many factual and spelling/grammar errors in newspapers, too little respect for and knowledge about their communities, too much influence of reporters' biases on what is covered and how it is reported, too much sensationalism to increase sales, and too much concern with profit.

In 1997, a group of twenty-five distinguished journalists came together at Harvard University to discuss the profession. They created the Committee of Concerned Journalists. The committee conducted public forums, did interviews and surveys, and studied the content of news reporting. Bill Kovach, former curator of the Nieman Foundation, and Tom Rosenstiel, director of the Project for Excellence in Journalism, used information gathered through the committee and from other sources to write a book titled *The Elements of Journalism*. In this book, they seek to reestablish the important principles of journalism. During the summer of 2001, the *Nieman Reports* was dedicated to articles addressing these elements. Kovach and Rosenstiel identified the following principles:

1. Journalism's first obligation is to tell the truth.
2. Journalism's first loyalty is to citizens.
3. The essence of journalism is a discipline of verification.
4. Journalists must maintain an independence from those they cover.
5. Journalists must serve as an independent monitor of power.
6. Journalism must provide a forum for public criticism and comment.
7. Journalists must make the significant interesting and relevant.
8. Journalists should keep the news in proportion and make it comprehensive.
9. Journalists have an obligation to personal conscience.

These principles are not exactly new. They closely parallel codes of ethics by such organizations as The Society for Professional Journalists. However, they point to a significant trend—and to an important issue. The trend is actually twofold: (1) Journalism has declined in credibility and the public doesn't believe journalists; and (2) critics and journalists are striving to address the issue because they believe credibility to be important not only to their profession but also to the society in which they live. The issue is whether journalistic principles can survive in the modern-day cacophony of entertainment noise and profit-seeking values.

Interaction: Journalism and Political Participation

Being able to participate in the selection of political leaders is one of the characteristics of a democracy. However, in the United States declining percentages of eligible voters participate in the process. In 1964, 69.3 percent of people of voting age actually cast a ballot. That number has declined until in 2000 it fell just short of 55 percent. In 2000, because of large immigration numbers, the Census Bureau reported the statistics slightly differently. It reported the percentage of voters of eligible age and eligible citizenship who voted. Using that population, the percentage of eligible voters actually casting a ballot rose to 60 percent, up 2 percent from 1996. Only 64 percent of those eligible to vote registered to do so.[22]

You might ask, "Isn't that a political issue? Is that an issue for journalism?" It is an issue for journalism because journalists deliver most political messages to U.S. voters. And when an election is so close that journalists cannot adequately report it—indeed, the vote counters cannot accurately count the votes—the role of journalists in the political process becomes even more apparent. The election of 2000 caused many reporters, editors, and managers to rethink how they cover elections.

In addition, journalists and political critics have become increasingly concerned about the reliance on popular culture media for political news and about the trend toward increased political advertising and decreased political coverage. In 1992, President Clinton appeared on the *Arsenio Hall Show* and on *Donahue,* in addition to responding to journalists on traditional political shows such as *Meet the Press* and the *MacNeil-Lehrer NewsHour.* He played his saxophone in an effort to establish a link with the American public. He participated in a new style of debate in Richmond, Virginia, responding to questions from the audience rather than to questions from journalists. By 1996, this type of media behavior did not seem unusual. In the 1998

Covering Politics, Campaigns, and the Elections

The election cycle of 2000 was an "important laboratory" for the Internet, a new medium used to cover politics. Salon.com and Slate.com, newly organized news organizations, used irreverent, opinionated coverage to compete with more established media.

Mainstream media organizations also experimented with the Internet. Dan Balz, a *Washington Post* political reporter, was followed by a two-person video crew from Washingtonpost.com. The goal was to "record their thoughts while covering the election." With *Slate* and another, now defunct publication, Washingtonpost.com used young staffers and freelancers to produce stories for their Net Election series. These stories included tradi-

tional themes of political trickery and campaign money raising. A new theme emerged as well—tracking web sites of politicians and evaluating them for accuracy.

Broadcasters and print journalists formed partnerships to cover the election. Nationally, the *Post* and NBC news partnered through MSNBC.com. The *New York Times* and ABC News also produced a daily fifteen-minute webcast called "Political Points," which appeared on each organization's site. Campaign reporters and commentators discussed the campaign. It was the news about the news.

Mark Halperin, political director for ABC News, and Michael Oreskes, who in 2000 was the Washington

bureau chief for the *New York Times,* said the production taught them the pitfalls of converged media. They learned that audio worked better than video, especially on the typically slow connections of 2000, and that they had underestimated the time and cost of producing video.

The Pew Research Center for the People and the Press found that one-fifth of Americans had gone online for news, but most had relied on traditional news organizations such as CNN.com rather than on upstart dot-coms or candidate web sites.

Source: A. L. May, *The Virtual Trail: Political Journalism on the Internet,* Graduate School of Political Management, George Washington University, pp. 8–9.

midterm elections, the major television networks carried 73 percent fewer stories about the elections than they did in the 1994 midterm elections. Political advertising on broadcast television alone amounted to over $400 million dollars in 1996; in 2000, it reached $606 million.[23] However, television stations billed $531 million in political advertising, the highest election billing year ever.

Michael Kelly, in a *New York Times Magazine* article, argued that "the conversation of politics now is carried on in the vernacular of advertising. The big sell, the television sell, appears to be the only way to sell. Increasingly, and especially in Washington, how well one does on television has come to determine how well one does in life." Kelly describes Washington, D.C., as a national capital where increasingly the "distinction between reality and fantasy has been lost. . . . Movie stars show up with their press agents and their bodyguards to 'testify' before Congress. Politicians and reporters make cameo appearances as movie stars, playing themselves in fictional scenes about politics and reporting."[24]

The effectiveness of the marketplace of ideas in different societies varies with the type of government and with the extent of commercialism in each country. In authoritarian countries, the government often limits access to the public forum. In a country where ordinary citizens participate in governance, extensive participation in the marketplace of ideas is crucial for effective government. In the United States, media critics recently have become concerned about the quality of political participation because of the commercialization of the political process through TV advertisements and the sensationalism of quasi-entertainment political talk shows.

Some argue that television has corrupted the marketplace of ideas into a showplace for images rather than a public forum for issues and that it has destroyed any possibility for rational political discourse. Others argue that popularization of politics through television and other avenues has brought—and will continue to bring—more individuals into the political process.

Journalism and the Internet

Old-line media companies are meeting new media companies on the Web. Many newspapers have a presence on the Web. However, too often their presence amounts to searchable classified advertising and news content that experts call "shovelware." That is, the newspapers simply post their paper content on a web site with a few graphics and pictures.

New media companies, however, value the interactivity of the Web and seek to provide content unique to the new medium. Chip Brown, in an article aptly titled "Fear.Com," writes in *American Journalism Review* that the "Web may usurp" the role of newspapers as

> agenda-setters and news filters. The Web puts a cornucopia of primary sources within everyone's reach, and makes the stuff of which news is made available to anyone, raw and unprocessed, minus the contributions of reporters and editors, minus their judicious evaluation and careful fact-checking, but also minus their "family newspaper" euphemisms, their pack-mentality blind spots and their sometimes patronizing determinations about what is in the "public interest."[25]

Brown says the problem with newspapers on the Web is that there is other information available that is more informative, interesting, and playful.

Many media companies are creating news sites rather than shoveling newspaper content onto the Web. Web news has some advantages over paper: Contents can be searchable, they can be updated frequently, and they can link to sites outside their own. Web news is interactive, with instant e-mail feedback, online chatrooms, or live interviews. For instance, washingtonpost.com offers several hours of live chat and other programs featuring *Post* reporters. Restaurant critic Phyllis Richman's show attracts many questions. Even the late Katharine Graham, publisher of the *Post*, signed on for interactive sessions with the public.

Some analysts note that the release of special prosecutor Kenneth Starr's report on the Clinton–Lewinsky issue marked a "defining moment" for the Web. Many newspapers elected to print short excerpts with a notation that their web sites carried the full text. PilotOnline, the web site for the *Virginia-Pilot*, beat its print edition by twelve hours. The Web is a natural enhancement for newspapers and broadcast units involved in civic journalism. Traditional civic journalism usually involves a media organization acting as a catalyst to get a community to talk about issues, suggest solutions for problems, and be involved in specific news projects. New Hampshire Public Radio used the Internet as a mechanism for people to discuss a series of reports about an airport access road construction project. Jan Schaffer, former executive director of the Pew Center for Civic Journalism, says that although there can be a "civic space in a town hall meeting . . . there also can be a civic space on the Internet where people can share ideas and have a discussion."[26]

A. L. May, associate professor in the School of Media and Public Affairs at George Washington University, found that journalists use campaign finance web databases freely. Other uses are more "haphazard." Some reporters are interviewing sources online, but more often they use the Internet to find sources and set up interviews. Journalists complain about e-mail overdose.[27]

Traditional media organizations are quick to criticize Internet journalism and to blame the ills of the profession—valuing speed over accuracy, sensationalism, and arrogance—on web journalists operating without traditional editing and control. And in truth, web journalists say that the constant deadlines spur them to quick decision making that may lead to inaccuracy. However, vast differences in web sites may well be recognized by the public. Just as readers distinguish between the *Washington Post* and the *National Enquirer*, so they can distinguish between Matt Drudge's undocumented reports and *Slate*, a credible online magazine.

Business and Journalism

Providing meaningful journalism is expensive. Reporters, editors, designers, artists, and photographers must be paid. As a result, the vast majority of U.S. newspapers are

discussing trends

The information in this chapter leads to the conclusion that journalists are concerned about their lack of credibility and about the encroachment of entertainment into the world of news and information. We know that accurate information that interprets and explains society is important to the functioning of democracy. Some questions that must be answered include:

■ How much profit enough profit?

■ When should profits be poured back into producing a quality product?

■ What can journalists do to change the entertainment climate?

■ What interactions between journalists and owners can productively meet the needs of both?

commercial enterprises. They sell advertising and in some cases charge for the news. Of the revenue generated from advertising and selling news, most goes to support the news organization, but some goes to the owners as profit. It is the distribution of revenues between these two areas that determines how good journalism will be in a community.

During the last forty years, two business trends have shaped news organizations. First, media companies that own newspapers, newsmagazines, and television news operations have started to sell their stock to the public. Stock shares are ownership shares. As the public has increased its ownership of news organizations, the demand has grown for these news organizations to make higher-than-normal profits. Many newspaper companies try to give 20 percent or more of their revenues to stockholders as profit. Television networks aim for even higher profit rates.

Second, as these profit expectations have grown, the number of companies competing for the advertising revenue also has grown. Economic theory explains that as competition increases, average profits for individual companies will decrease. At a time when news organizations face more competition, they need more profit. Therefore, to keep high profits while advertising revenues are level or declining, news organizations will have to cut the number of journalists they employ. The outcome will be a long-term decline in the quality of journalism, which in turn will probably reduce the number of viewers, listeners, and readers.

News organizations will face a trade-off between high short-term profits and high long-term profits. To keep one, they must sacrifice the other as competition for advertising revenue grows. Of course, which choice is made will depend on who owns the news organization and the goals of the owners. The decision by owners will vary from company to company, but the outcome of the decisions will affect the quality of journalism within communities throughout the United States.

summary

- ◆ The U.S. government is based on an assumption that information will be disseminated freely and that the people will be well informed.
- ◆ The primary purpose of journalism is to inform, but it also often entertains and sometimes seeks to persuade.
- ◆ The business of reporting developed as editors sought to achieve mass audiences.
- ◆ The philosophy of the Enlightenment was used by American colonists to defend civil liberties.
- ◆ Televised politics has changed the nature of political campaigning.

- ◆ Reporters have sought through the years to expose the corrupt dealings of business and of government. This activity is called muckraking.
- ◆ Journalism has two traditions: one is the objective analysis of the facts at hand and the other is a narrative tradition, or storytelling.
- ◆ Journalists have lost credibility during an era of infotainment.
- ◆ The move of news companies to sell stock publicly has affected the level of profits sought by such companies.

navigating the web | Journalism on the Web

Columbia Journalism Review
www.cjr.org

The *Columbia Journalism Review*, published in conjunction with the Columbia School of Journalism, is a critique of modern media, but it offers excellent information for journalists about the business and about how to make ethical decisions. A similar publication, the *American Journalism Review*, can be accessed at www.wjr.org.

Poynter Institute
www.poynter.org

The Poynter Organization's site claims it has "[e]verything you need to be a better journalist." The Poynter Institute is a school dedicated to "teaching and inspiring journalists and media leaders. It promotes excellence and integrity in the practice of craft and in the practical leadership of successful businesses. It stands for a journalism that informs citizens and enlightens public discourse. It carries forward Nelson Poynter's belief in the value of independent journalism." Nelson Poynter is a former editor of the *St. Petersburg Times*.

Fox News Channel
www.foxnews.com
CNN
www.cnn.com

For up-to-the-minute national and international news, Fox News Channel and CNN are excellent sites. Major newspaper sites also provide good national and international news.

questions for review

1. What is the importance of the John Peter Zenger case?
2. What is the Bill of Rights?
3. What does the First Amendment protect?
4. What factors contributed to the development of the reporter?
5. Why is image important to politicians?

issues to think about

1. Try to imagine a society without the free dissemination of information. How would your life be different from the way it is today?
2. Should journalism be used to persuade and to entertain as well as to inform?
3. Explore the relationship of Enlightenment philosophy to the development of independent journalism in the United States.
4. What are the fundamental differences between print and broadcast reporting?
5. Name several news values and critique them.
6. Critique the concept of public journalism.
7. Discuss the occupation of journalist. What is attractive about it? What is not so attractive?

suggested readings

Downie, Leonard Jr., and Robert Kaiser, *The News about the News: American Journalism in Peril* (New York: Knopf, 2002).

Glasser, Theodore L., and James L. Ettema, *Custodians of Conscience* (New York: Columbia University Press, 1998).

Kovach, Bill, and Tom Rosenstiel, *The Elements of Journalism: What Newspeople Should Know and the Public Should Expect* (NY: Three Rivers Press, 2001).

Mindich, David T., *Just the Facts: How "Objectivity" Came to Define American Journalism* (New York: New York University Press, 2000).

Pavlik, John Vernon, and Seymour Topping, *Journalism and New Media* (New York: Columbia University Press, 2001).

Public Relations

For more than three weeks, Montgomery County Police Chief Charles Moose faced the crowd of cameras and reporters. He talked about the thirteen people who had been shot. He explained leads in the case. He criticized reporters for publicizing information, and he became emotional speaking of the thirteen-year-old schoolboy who was shot by a sniper.

Holding press conferences in the midst of a criminal crisis is a trying job, but it is a job that has to be done. In addition to communicating with the killers through the media, Moose informed the public about events in one of the worst cases of serial killings in U.S. history, and he reassured the public that police were working to stop the shooting spree. Most people might not think of these activities as public relations, but they are. Promoting calm and helping people understand tragic events are central to crisis management. Although Moose could have used the police department spokesperson to address the press, he understood that an important part of crisis communication involves making the top decision makers available to the press and public at large.

Getting out an organization's message during a crisis is only part of the field called public relations (PR). PR also includes activities such as writing newsletters and magazines for a company's employees, influencing legislation, staging events to raise money for charities, and writing press releases about sports teams. The great variety of PR activities prevents any one definition from being inclusive.

Edward L. Bernays, one of public relations' instrumental pioneers, defined PR as "the science of creating circumstances, mounting events that are calculated to stand out as genuine, unstaged and 'newsworthy.'" Both Bernays and journalist Walter Lippmann asserted the need for an elite group of opinion leaders who engage in perception management and the manufacturing of consent. Public relations' reach has infinitely broadened since Bernays uttered this statement, and it now exerts influence on audiences as vast as venture capitalists and prospective employees.[1]

However, public relations can be defined adequately as "planned and sustained unpaid communication between an organization and the publics that are essential to its success."[2]

An examination of the terms in this definition help clarify it. First, public relations usually involves *organizations*. Although some individuals such as actors and musicians might hire a PR firm to create and promote an image, these are exceptions. Second, public relations differs from advertising because companies pay for advertising messages; they do not pay for media content that is generated by public relations activity. Advertising and public relations both fall

Understanding public relations is essential to navigating through public life in the United States today. The pervasiveness of information generated through PR efforts poses many issues such as the following:

◆ What is the role of public relations in a complex, postindustrial, democratic society?

◆ What are the inevitable tensions for public relations practitioners whose commitment is to an organization but also to ethical standards of fairness and accuracy?

◆ What role does the Internet play in public relations?

◆ How does increased specialization affect public relations activities?

Public Relations *in Your Life*

Do You Know It When You See It?

Sometimes it is difficult to decide what information comes from public relations sources and what constitutes news and entertainment.

Think about some recent public events that you consider to be examples of PR and events you consider to be non-PR-generated news or entertainment. Considering these events, develop your own definition of public relations material.

PR-GENERATED EVENTS	NON-PR-GENERATED NEWS/ENTERTAINMENT
Local radio station's sponsorship of a charity walkathon	Natural disaster, such as a flood

under the heading of promotion, which is part of marketing, but PR is fundamentally different from advertising. Public relations practitioners hope that their materials will be used or will generate interest and news stories. Advertising practitioners simply buy time or space to advance the exact message they want to promote.

Some organizations define public relations as a consistently positive force. For example, in 1978 the International Public Relations Association adopted as a definition of public relations "the art and science of analyzing trends, predicting their consequences, counseling organization leaders, and implementing planned programs of action which will serve both the organization's and the public's interest." However, James Grunig, prominent public relations scholar, notes, "not all public relations is done responsibly; neither is all medicine or law or journalism." Public relations also can be defined as the "management of communication between an organization and its publics."[3]

Publics—the people and organizations that the company deals with—constitute the audience for PR practitioners. Consumers are a public for a department store because their purchases determine whether a store will make a profit. Television station owners consider the government to be one of their publics because the Federal Communications Commission licenses stations. Good public relations involves knowledge of publics and monitoring of their messages.

In addition to sending out messages and monitoring feedback from various publics, organizations plan and sustain their PR activities. **Strategic planning** helps companies avoid the possibility of officers making off-the-cuff remarks that can be damaging to a company's image.

PUBLIC RELATIONS IN AMERICAN LIFE

Although communication between organizations and publics has occurred for thousands of years, public relations was perfected as an art and practice in the United States. In ancient Athens, orators in public forums provided information and persuaded people about public policy. Some historians describe Samuel Adams as the first American PR practitioner. Adams was a radical patriot in Massachusetts who helped bring about the American Revolution. His goal was to whip up the fervor for rebellion and keep the public's ire sustained so that they would act, not just protest, against England. He used a variety of media, created an activist organization, employed symbols and slogans, created **pseudo-events** such as the Boston Tea Party, orchestrated conflict, and recognized the need for a sustained saturation campaign.[4] However, only in modern times have professional public relations people been paid to represent organizations through planned and sustained public relations activities.

Public relations history can be viewed from two perspectives. It can be understood as the evolution of professional public relations practice, and it can be recognized as a type of communication that evolved to serve specific social needs.

key concept

Practice of Public Relations Public relations—systematic, planned communication with an organization's publics—helps explain complex information and shape news agenda. It can also be used to mislead if practitioners do not adhere to ethical standards.

publics: The various groups to whom PR professionals address messages. They may be internal or external to the organization.

strategic planning: Planning that includes elements designed to work toward a goal.

pseudo-event: An event created solely for the purposes of public relations to gain favorable notice for an organization.

Public Relations in Social Context

The *practice of public relations* developed from people's desire to hold political power and to profit from entertainment and business. As the United States grew and diversified during the early 1800s, Andrew Jackson sponsored a Kentucky editor named Amos Kendall, who supported Jackson's candidacy. Kendall wrote speeches and advised Jackson, while "Old Hickory" capitalized on his military image to become president.[5] Although sponsored through government printing contracts rather than being paid directly, Kendall functioned as an early political PR consultant.

Jackson's use of PR to gain political office suggests a social condition in the United States that generated a need for public relations: the dispersion of power. Voters hold the power to choose from all available ideas. Strong monarchies and dictatorships can coerce; governments that hold less power rely on persuasion. Voters in a democracy have the power to influence their government, but they need information on which to base decisions. Ideally, the information is provided by knowledgeable, unbiased sources. However, when there is an information gap, it can be filled by those seeking office. Jackson, along with other government officials, used the power of persuasion to influence the voters (a significant public in U.S. society) to choose him. Political advertising, news, entertainment, and public relations efforts all crowd the marketplace of ideas.

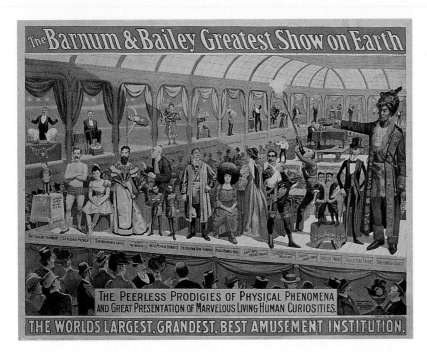

P. T. Barnum, who provoked curiosity for a variety of circus sideshows, was a genius at using publicity techniques to arouse expectations.

Press Agents and Entertainment ✦ *Early press agents* hawked their wares and worked doggedly with entertainment businesses to get publicity in newspapers. The first master of publicity was P. T. Barnum. In the late 1830s, he toured the eastern United States with an African American woman, Joice Heth, who claimed to be the 160-year-old nurse of George Washington. With a combination of advertising and **publicity** in newspapers, Barnum drew large crowds. When attendance slumped in Boston, he wrote a letter to a local newspaper claiming that Heth was an early form of robot run by springs. Attendance grew as people checked out the fraudulent story.[6] An autopsy of Heth after her death revealed that she was about half her announced age. Meanwhile, Barnum had been collecting about $1,500 a week from people who wanted a look at the pipe-smoking old woman.

When Barnum formed the Barnum and Bailey Circus with James A. Bailey, he hired his own press agent, Richard Hamilton. With the increased business responsibilities of running a company of 800 employees, Barnum could no longer afford to do what he did best—get people into the tent. The world's greatest press agent had to hire a press agent.

Press Agentry and Business ✦ In the mid-1800s, businesses began to experiment with similar press agentry techniques. However, in addition to publicity they also hired press agents to persuade government officials to serve their cause. During the 1850s, capitalizing on fears of a coming civil war, the Illinois Central Railroad organized a public relations campaign to get the government to construct a north–south railway that would bind the country together. This successful campaign for federal funds altered a historic pattern of local funding for railroad development. Other railroads used similar persuasion techniques. They argued that building railroads served the public, and Congress responded by giving forty grants to railroads between 1852 and 1857. Railroad companies continued to use lobbying and press relations throughout the nineteenth century, eventually influencing the Interstate Commerce Act of 1886 in their favor.[7]

Railroad executives were vulnerable public targets because they were viewed as land grabbers who had little regard for local communities. To create more positive public images, railroad officials became masters of early press relations. They offered editors appealing tours through various parts of the country in return for free advertising. At the turn of the century, most editors carried free railway passes in their wallets.

publicity: The dissemination of information to attract public interest.

The Committee on Public Information helped develop a variety of public relations techniques during World War I. This Liberty Bond poster resembles many designed by the committee and those who supported its efforts.

Emerging Professionalism ✦ During the last half of the 1800s, big business became a target of citizen anger as the public began to perceive it as a greedy octopus that grabbed power and money and worried little about the common person. Efforts to break up large steel, oil, and railroad monopolies increased as the twentieth century began. The muckrakers from *McClure's* magazine began to expose the excesses of wealthy industrialists such as J. P. Morgan, Cornelius Vanderbilt, and John D. Rockefeller. Recognizing that they needed a better public image, the captains of industry turned to public relations experts.

Ivy Ledbetter Lee emerged during this period as the model for public relations practitioners. Lee worked as a newspaper reporter for three years before becoming a PR counselor for a number of corporations. Lee advocated honest communication between his clients and their publics. John D. Rockefeller sought Lee's advice after two women and eleven children were killed during a strike at his Colorado coal mines in an incident known as the Ludlow Massacre. Lee replied that "the first and most important feature of any plan of publicity should be its absolute frankness; that there should be no devious ways employed."[8] Rockefeller hired Lee to tell his side of the labor war that had developed.

Not everyone believed that Lee lived up to his own words. Poet Carl Sandburg attacked Lee for his role in publicity following the Ludlow Massacre. In his 1919 book on the press, *The Brass Check*, Upton Sinclair gave Lee the nickname "Poison Ivy."[9] Nevertheless, Lee's admonition to public relations practitioners to avoid deceit remains the basis of the professional approach to PR.

Public Relations and War ✦ During the early part of the twentieth century, much of the U.S. public did not believe that the country should take an active part in European affairs. To promote U.S. participation in World War I, President Woodrow Wilson set up the Committee for Public Information run by George Creel. Creel, a former newspaper editor, successfully ran a **propaganda** campaign that generated support for U.S. involvement and created hatred of Germans. The committee's efforts cost $4.5 million. It mailed 6,000 news releases that generated about 20,000 columns of newsprint each week. The committee developed cartoons, created posters, and issued war photographs to the schools. Part of the appeal was based on fear, and Germans were depicted as without morals. Many of those who worked for the Creel Committee took the techniques they learned with them and moved into the modern, postwar world of business and government public relations, in which they successfully blended *propaganda and public relations.* Edward Bernays, who worked on the Committee for Public Information, wrote the first book about public relations in 1923. *Crystallizing Public Opinion* received mixed reviews, but it introduced hundreds of thousands of people to the activities of public relations.[10]

Bernays's career in public relations lasted more than five decades. He argued that public relations should be a profession in which social science principles are applied and consideration for the public takes precedence over profit:

> The standards of the public relations counsel are his own standards, and he will not accept a client whose standards do not come up to them. While he is not called upon to judge the merits of his case any more than a lawyer is called upon to judge his client's case, nevertheless he must judge the results which his work would accomplish from an ethical point of view.[11]

propaganda: The art of persuasion. Material disseminated by a group or cause to persuade another group of the validity of its own position.

Public relations activities expanded during the 1930s, though most people in the United States were unaware of PR techniques until after World War II. The Office of War Information (OWI), created in June 1942, handled propaganda and absorbed the Office of Government Reports, the Office of the Coordinator of Information, the Office of Facts and Figures, and several smaller agencies. Elmer Davis, former *New York Times* staffer, directed the operation.

Edward L. Bernays wrote the first book on public relations and taught the first public relations class at a major university. In 1989, *Life* magazine named him one of the most important Americans in the twentieth century.

The nephew of Sigmund Freud, Bernays sold the public on everything from presidents to Ivory soap. Clients whose images and products he promoted included singer Enrico Caruso, automobile manufacturer Henry Ford, inventor Thomas Edison, moviemaker Sam Goldwyn, and first lady Eleanor Roosevelt. Bernays worked for every president from Calvin Coolidge in 1925 to Dwight D. Eisenhower in the late 1950s. He is said to have turned down Adolf Hitler and Generalissimo Francisco Franco of Spain.

Bernays was born in Vienna, Austria, in 1891 and was brought to New York a year later. He received his bachelor's degree from Cornell University in 1912. During World War I, he worked for the War Department as a government propagandist, learning how to mold public opinion. He used this experience as a foundation when he opened his public relations business with Doris Fleishman in 1919.

Three years later, he married Fleishman. She kept her maiden name and was the first American woman to maintain it on her passport. Bernays and Fleishman

Edward L. Bernays

ran their business together until she died in 1980.

In 1923, Bernays wrote *Crystallizing Public Opinion*, the first book on public relations. In this book, he moved from using mass communication to reach one large public to targeting specific audiences. He stressed that clients had different relations with different publics.

Bernays wrote fourteen books in all. In his 1965 autobiography, *Biography of an Idea*, he wrote that public relations had moved "from a one-way street of information and persuasion from client to public" to a two-way interaction between client and public. However, he was unsuccessful in his drive to have public relations practitioners licensed, an attempt to legitimize the field.

Bernays had about 350 clients, ranging from federal government departments to labor unions and from individuals to large corporations. He continued giving speeches until a few years before his death at age 103, on March 9, 1995, in his home in Cambridge, Massachusetts.

Sources: Harvey Smith, "The Original Persuader," *The Guardian*, (March 24, 1995), the Guardian Features Page section, p. T21; "Edward Bernays," *The Boston Herald* (March 10, 1995), Obituary section, p. 61.

OWI's domestic and foreign operations in May 1945 at the peak of activity required the services of 9,600 persons, and the budget was $132,500,000 for the three years of operation.[12] Three experienced editors and publishers directed the domestic operation: Gardner Cowles Jr. of the *Des Moines Register and Tribune*, the *Minneapolis Star-Journal* and *Tribune*, and *Look* magazine; E. Palmer Hoyt, editor and publisher of the *Portland Oregonian*; and George W. Healy Jr., publisher of the *New Orleans Times-Picayune*. The government controlled the broadcasting facilities of five companies that had been disseminating shortwave programs from the United States, including CBS and NBC. News and other programs broadcast through these facilities to a variety of enemy and allied countries became known as the Voice of America, an operation still in existence. The Voice of America and related overseas activity constituted 85 percent of the total OWI budget.

Information and Persuasion

The *process of public relations* consists of PR activities as communication. Public relations specialists act as senders who encode messages and send them to receivers (the organizatios publics). Because these messages are planned, they have purposes. The exact purpose may vary, but public relations messages usually aim either to inform or to persuade.

Informational messages make the receiver aware of some event or issue that the sending organization considers important. A public information director at a local community college sends course catalogs to residents of

key concept

Process of Public Relations Public relations messages, which can be informational or persuasive, are created by interacting with the publics addressed. The continuous process involves surveying and monitoring publics, creating messages, and evaluating feedback.

the community to inform them which classes are available. A sports information director mails pregame press releases to tell sportswriters about the importance of an upcoming basketball game. Publics cannot make effective decisions without information, so organizations must inform their publics.

Persuasion causes people to change their beliefs or to act in certain ways. The environmental lobbyist who talks with a senator over lunch tries to persuade the senator to vote for a bill that will protect an endangered species. The press release about a new department store aims to get a newspaper to publish an informational story about the grand opening.

Ultimately, whether PR practitioners use an informational or a persuasive model, they want to persuade their publics that the company's position is accurate, complete, and justified. However, effective public relations relies on accurate information. Consumers who do not trust a company's communication, or reporters who cannot trust a PR practitioner, will not be persuaded by communication from those organizations and people. Publics may be fooled a few times, but sustained PR efforts will falter without accurate information.

Public relations activities constitute a process. An organization and its publics are *interdependent*. Because of differences in exposure, attention, perception, and retention, people experience the same events in many different ways. Public relations communicates the organization's perspective on the events and, in doing so, tries to alter the results of consumers' selective processes. Hospital PR departments call patients after discharge to see how they feel about their stays. If the patients have a negative perception of the hospital, the PR specialists will talk with them or send them some printed material to change that perception. Perceptions of service, people, and products determine success.

Under some situations, such as special events, the PR process also will entertain. However, efforts to entertain primarily aim to attract an audience that can be informed or persuaded.

Internal Public Relations

Unlike **external PR,** which has been around in some form for almost 200 years, **internal PR** is relatively new. The study of communication in organizations progressed "from a footnote mention in pre–World War II days" to an entire area of study in the 1990s.[13] Before 1930, managers thought of employees as pieces of a big industrial machine. They did their work, got paid, and went home. However, in the process of studying the impact of lighting and environment on productivity, researchers at the Western Electric plants in Cicero, Illinois, discovered that relationships among employees were as important as technological working conditions. People who enjoyed their work performed better. Managers began to think in terms of the *human dimension* and recognized that employee well-being and effective communication increased productivity.

In 1938, Chester Barnard, the former president of the New Jersey Bell Telephone Company, wrote in *Functions of the Executive* that three elements were essential to the existence of all organizations: a purpose, people willing to pursue that purpose, and communication to coordinate the pursuit.[14] As companies consolidated and increased in size, they also became more bureaucratic. Layers of management often acted as blocks to communication, spurring the development of departments of internal communication during the last half of the twentieth century. Internal public relations then developed as a process of planned and sustained communication between the organizational leadership and its employees.

Internal public relations remains a phenomenon of developed countries such as Japan and the United States. But the concept of human relations is still unheard of in most other parts of the world. Women in developing countries often receive less than subsistence wages for sixty to one hundred hours of work a week.[15]

external PR: Messages directed at publics external to the organization.

internal PR: Communication within the various units and between individuals of the organization.

The Greening of PR

It has been more than thirty years since the first Earth Day celebration in 1970, and since then most people have adopted environmental concern as a basic value. Today, more than half of all households in the United States recycle on a regular basis; in 1970, only a small percentage of people even knew what the word *recycle* meant.

As public concern about the environment grows around the world, companies have begun to promote themselves as environmentally friendly. The introduction in 1990 of Origins, a cosmetic and personal care brand that is part of the Estee Lauder Companies, shows how environmentally conscious PR can be. The botanically based line includes skin care products made from plant extracts and packaged in recyclable materials. Origins was introduced with public relations campaigns aimed at consumers, department stores, and the media. The company had press conferences and sponsored events such as "Run for Earth" to gain attention. Origins and the public relations efforts behind

the launch worked. Within a month, sales were 70 percent higher than expected.

By 2000, most cosmetic companies the world over were emphasizing the importance of ecological awareness. In 2002, two Swedish multinational companies, Alfa Laval and Haldex, joined to make diesel engine gases clean. That same year the British nuclear energy industry announced: "Safe operations and environmental performance remain at the heart of all we do."

But the greening of business has not eliminated ethical problems for PR professionals. Some companies claim their products are environmentally safe even though they are not. Some critics say that public relations firms are co-opting some environmental organizations such as Greenpeace by donating money and hiring former members of those groups. The environmental organizations defend their cooperation with PR firms and various companies as efforts to find solutions to environmental problems rather than just criticizing polluters.

In the long run, efforts to fool the public could backfire if consumers decide they cannot trust green claims by companies. The ethics of individual PR professionals will affect the level of trust.

Sources: John Baran, "Every Day Is Earth Day," *Public Relations Journal* (April 1991): 22–23; "Public Relations, Store Tie-Ins Launch Green Cosmetic Line," *Public Relations Journal* (April 1991): 24–25; "Burson-Marsteller Hires a Green 'Cash Cow,' " *PR Watch* 9:1 (2002), www.prwatch.org/prwissues; Sharon Beder, "From Green Warriors to Greenwashers," *PR Watch* 6:3 (1999), www.prwatch.org/prwissues; "Government's White Paper Paves the Way for 'New BNFL,' " *PR Newswire for Journalists*, www.prnewswire.com, accessed on July 4, 2002.

SOCIAL AND CULTURAL IMPACT

Ethics and integrity within public relations practice are continuing issues. Journalists deride public relations as a profession not related to journalism and claim that PR people present only their employers' side of the story. However, public relations education is often included in journalism schools, and many journalists eventually become PR professionals. Since the time of Ivy Lee, PR practitioners have argued that honesty and accuracy must be the ethical foundation of the profession. Another ethical value of journalism—objectivity—does not apply to professional public relations. No one, journalist or ordinary citizen, expects public relations experts to present multiple

1700s. Mercantile newspapers serve public relations goals.

1773. Boston Tea Party is early PR event.

Early 1800s. Amos Kendall helps elect Andrew Jackson president.

Mid-1800s. P. T. Barnum uses public relations techniques.

1850s. Railroad companies use public relations to influence Congress.

1900s. Ivy Ledbetter Lee improves John D. Rockefeller's image.

1917–1918. CPI handles PR during World War I.

1919. Upton Sinclair attacks PR practitioners in *The Brass Check*.

1923. Edward L. Bernays writes *Crystallizing Public Opinion*.

1924–1932. Hawthorne studies lead to human relations management.

1941–1945. OWI handles propaganda during World War II.

1948. Public Relations Society of America starts.

1400–1700	1800	1880	1900	1920	1930	1940

1620. Pilgrims land at Plymouth Rock.

1690. *Publik Occurrences* is published in Boston.

1741. First magazine is published in America.

1776–1783. American Revolution

1830s. The penny press becomes the first truly mass medium in the United States.

1861–1865. American Civil War

1892. Thomas Edison's lab develops the kinetoscope.

1914–1918. World War I

1915. *The Birth of a Nation* marks the start of the modern movie industry.

1920. KDKA in Pittsburgh gets the first commercial radio license.

1930s. The Great Depression

1939. TV is demonstrated at the New York World's Fair.

1939–1945. World War II

1949. First commercial electronic computer is produced.

views. The public relations view is one piece of information within the marketplace of ideas. Often it is a powerful message generated by sophisticated communication techniques and supported by power and money.

Public relations practitioners organized after World War II to emphasize skill development and ethical applications. Growth in public relations education accompanied the quest for a more professional standing. In 1961 the American Public Relations Association, begun in 1944, merged with the Public Relations Society of America (PRSA), organized in 1948. PRSA is the most prestigious public relations professional group today.[16]

The degree of professionalism found in public relations is higher now than it was fifty years ago, but ethical problems remain. The heart of the professional approach to PR concerns openness between the organization and its publics. Advocates of professional PR, such as Bernays, argue that public relations practitioners should advise their clients to be honest with those affected by their business.

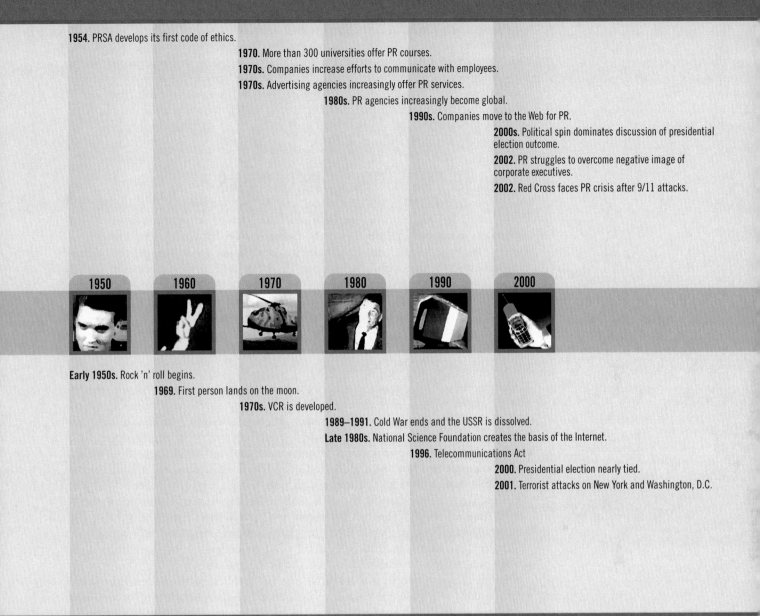

1954. PRSA develops its first code of ethics.

1970. More than 300 universities offer PR courses.

1970s. Companies increase efforts to communicate with employees.

1970s. Advertising agencies increasingly offer PR services.

1980s. PR agencies increasingly become global.

1990s. Companies move to the Web for PR.

2000s. Political spin dominates discussion of presidential election outcome.

2002. PR struggles to overcome negative image of corporate executives.

2002. Red Cross faces PR crisis after 9/11 attacks.

1950 1960 1970 1980 1990 2000

Early 1950s. Rock 'n' roll begins.

1969. First person lands on the moon.

1970s. VCR is developed.

1989–1991. Cold War ends and the USSR is dissolved.

Late 1980s. National Science Foundation creates the basis of the Internet.

1996. Telecommunications Act

2000. Presidential election nearly tied.

2001. Terrorist attacks on New York and Washington, D.C.

One of the classic cases in ethical public relations is that of Johnson & Johnson, a company that reacted with concern for the public after cyanide was discovered in some Extra-Strength Tylenol capsules in 1982. Seven people died in and around Chicago. Johnson & Johnson immediately stopped production and recalled all of its Tylenol capsules. The company contacted the media and federal government. Johnson & Johnson did not try to hide anything that had happened. Its first response involved protecting and warning the public. Instead of a knee-jerk reaction aimed at short-term results (keeping Tylenol on the shelves), Johnson & Johnson considered long-term goals and the importance of its credibility to continuing its business success. As a result, the company lived up to its business credo of public responsibility and regained its share of the market within a year. This strategy has been adopted by many companies, particularly those dealing with pharmaceuticals.[17]

In contrast to Johnson & Johnson, the Augusta National Golf Club, home of the Masters Tournament, created a public relations nightmare when the National Council of Women (NCW) asked in June 2002 that the club allow women to join. William Johnson, chairman of Augusta, replied that Augusta would not be forced into changing its rules. After Martha Burk, chairwoman of NCW, said that the group would ask companies to withdraw advertising from the 2003 Masters Tournament, Johnson declared that the tournament would go on without advertisers. During the controversy that followed, some of the 300 members of Augusta promised to work to admit women, and Tiger Woods said both sides are right.[18] It seems inevitable that women will join Augusta, but the negative publicity that has grown around the issue will not be easily forgotten.

DEMAND FOR PUBLIC RELATIONS

Public relations practitioners serve as a pipeline to move information from organizations to their publics. Demand for public relations activity can be viewed from both ends of the pipe. At one end, organizations demand PR services to get their information out; at the other end, various publics demand PR information from the organizations. Newspapers use PR releases as the basis of news stories; government agencies use PR information in policy decisions; and consumers use PR information as a basis for voting and buying products.

Demand for PR Services

The demand for PR services depends on the types of publics that interact with the organization. In some cases, organizations depend on publics for revenue. Customers of JCPenney form a public for that company. In other cases, the organizations depend on a public for resources. General Motors communicates with its employees, who form a public that supplies labor. Consumers demand certain actions of JCPenney, and laborers demand fair treatment by General Motors. Communication is part of the process that ensures that consumers and laborers get what they need.

Most daily newspapers in the United States belong to the Newspaper Association of America (NAA). Through this membership, publishers constitute a public and express a demand for intelligent lobbying, that is, representing their interests to state and federal governments. The NAA tries to influence legislation that affects daily newspapers, such as laws that limit access to public meetings.

Public relations people deal with two types of publics: those inside their organization and those outside the organization. *Internal publics* include employees, managers, trustees, and stockholders. The inside publics have a much stronger commitment to the organization than do those outside. *External publics* include consumers and voters, government organizations, interest groups, business organizations, and media.

Demand for PR Information

Just as organizations eagerly send out information about themselves, individuals and other groups seek information about those organizations. Press releases, electronic and print, and press conferences are prime ways in which journalists find out about the activities of organizations. Research indicates that small newspapers use press releases more often, sometimes without editing, than large newspapers. Up to 30 percent of the content in some small newspapers comes from press releases.

News media organizations' demand for information from organizations is much like automobile makers' demand for steel and plastic. PR information serves as a raw material for creating news content. Just as steel and plastic vary in quality, so does information. Inaccurate and misleading information, whether purposeful or accidental, does not adequately meet the general public's need for useful information.

SUPPLYING THE DEMAND FOR PUBLIC RELATIONS

Almost every organization has public relations needs. The manager of a small retail store can usually conduct all the public relations the store requires. However, large organizations require public relations specialists. At least four types of groups require public relations to fulfill their goals: political and government groups, interest groups, profit-seeking companies, and nonprofit organizations. All these organizations share the common needs to inform publics about an event, product, or political position and to persuade individual members of the publics to attend the event, use the product, or adopt the position.

Political and government groups inform citizens and advocate political candidates and positions. These groups include political parties, elected and appointed government officials, and candidates for public office. Information is supplied through videotapes, media interviews with politicians, press releases, newsletters, and advertisements. The Michigan Department of Natural Resources distributes information to residents about a variety of outdoor activities such as hunting, fishing, and gardening. Most of the newsletters sent by members of Congress during an election year try to influence the voters to reelect them. Table 3.1 describes different public relations functions used by a variety of organizations.

Interest groups attempt to influence politicians to achieve public policy decisions that favor the groups' interests. The National Rifle Association (NRA) is a powerful interest group that represents the interests of gun owners and manufacturers. For years the NRA has been able to limit legislation to control guns even though a majority of U.S. citizens support control of certain types of weapons.

Almost every cause and profession imaginable has an organized interest group to advocate its political position. Offices for most interest groups are located in Washington, D.C., and state capitals, where they are close to the legislative processes.

Profit-seeking organizations use public relations to create and maintain favorable attitudes toward their goods and services. Consumers who do not trust a company or a particular product will be less likely to purchase it. PR practitioners in profit-seeking organizations use advocacy and information to maintain a positive image in the public's minds.

Nonprofit organizations depend heavily on public relations because much of their support comes from public donations. Organizations such as the Red Cross, the United Way, and the Salvation Army receive a large portion of their funds from individual donations. It is important for those fund-raising efforts that the public recognize the community work they do. In addition, people who use nonprofit organizations' services must be aware of the services they offer if they are going to use them.

The Public Relations Process

Often, public relations practitioners seem to do their jobs effortlessly. But PR works best when it is based on solid planning. Several models of the public relations

table 3.1

PR Functions (by Type of Organization)	
TYPE OF ORGANIZATION	**PR FUNCTION**
Government and political organizations	Political PR
	Fund-raising
	Crisis management
	Event coordination
Interest groups	Political PR
	Fund-raising
	Lobbying
	Event coordination
For-profit organizations	Lobbying
	Crisis management
	Financial PR
	Event coordination
Nonprofit organizations	Fund-raising
	Event coordination
	Lobbying
	Crisis management

Ongoing public relations efforts ensure that the Red Cross is recognized for its disaster work, such as its efforts in the 1999 earthquake in Turkey. Constant public recognition of Red Cross services helps the organization raise money for its efforts.

process are available. In 1955, Edward L. Bernays listed the eight *components of public relations:*[19]

1. Define your objective.
2. Research your publics.
3. Modify your objectives to reach goals that research shows are attainable.
4. Decide on your strategy.
5. Set up your themes, symbols, and appeals.
6. Blueprint an effective organization to carry out the activity.
7. Chart your plan for both timing and tactics.
8. Carry out your tactics.

The public relations process starts with an objective or goal. An automobile company might want to publicize its latest car. Its PR objective would be getting as much mass media publicity as possible. Researching the publics would involve checking the media outlets that are most likely to carry information about a new auto model. These would include automotive magazines, the business and automotive sections of newspapers, and business-oriented television shows. Part of the research might include the probability that the media outlets would write stories about the new model.

key concept

Components of Public Relations The public relations process starts with a goal, requires a plan, progresses through implementation, and then evaluates the plan for effectiveness. Successful public relations campaigns require careful planning and reliance on research.

A political party that seeks support for a candidate is in a similar situation. The party must identify the types of people who are likely to vote for that candidate and the particular issues that will convince them to vote for the person. Part of the research includes surveying the public about issues and reactions to a candidate's position. Without specific knowledge about these two topics, time and money will be wasted on people who will not be swayed or on issues that voters consider unimportant.

On the basis of the research, the automobile public relations practitioners would specify particular goals for publicity. For example, the PR department would aim for long articles in the *Wall Street Journal,* the *New York Times* business section, *Business Week,* and each of a dozen regional daily newspapers. With these goals set, the particular ways of approaching the various media outlets would be designed. These might include personal contact, press releases, videocassette messages, electronic press releases, and press conferences.

In the political example, public relations personnel and political consultants would examine the research, advise the candidate to modify his or her position on

The T-shirts on these children not only identify them as Head Start youngsters, but they also serve an identifying role for the importance of the program itself. Part of the public relations process requires maintaining a message presence before the various publics that an organization or program serves.

certain issues, and select appropriate media outlets and schedule public appearances so that the candidate could advance the message.

The fifth step involves creating the types of messages that will be used. For the automobile company, these messages would include special attributes of the car such as safety features, a sporty image, or mileage performance. A political candidate usually attempts to provide a cohesive and consistent message, which is often referred to as a campaign theme.

The sixth step requires specifying how people and financial resources will be used to carry out the campaign. Who will write what? Where and when will press conferences be held? Who will test drive the new car? Who will promote the candidate, raise funds, and plan public appearances? What is the budget for each type of activity?

As a seventh step, the PR practitioner plans the detailed tactics or processes that will be performed. This includes the timing of the various activities. For example, the car might be announced at a press conference, which would be followed by interviews with company officials and test drives by journalists. Tactics include national announcements and efforts to provide public relations at regional levels. The political candidate might tour a factory, meet with spouses, and give a speech on the factory steps.

Finally, the tactics are fulfilled. After the process begins, the results must be evaluated for the short term and the long term. An effective plan includes monitoring how the tactics are working as the plan is being executed. The practitioners monitor stories run in magazines, newspapers, and on television. Evaluation allows the PR practitioner to adjust the tactics as the plan unfolds. Finally, after the plan has been completed, the practitioner evaluates the overall success of the plan.

The unifying activity of all steps in the planning process is decision making. At each step, decisions must be made. Effective decisions are based on two important aspects of the process: specifying goals and conducting research. All PR activities should take place with a goal in mind; otherwise, the effort may be wasted. The goal may be to improve a car manufacturer's image or to increase the donations at a university, but without goals, efforts cannot be focused and cannot be evaluated. Research is the second critical activity because all planning must be based on knowledge.

Conducting External PR

External communication deals with publics outside the organization. Common PR activities in this area include lobbying, political PR, financial PR, fund-raising, crisis management, and event coordination. This list is far from exhaustive, and even these activities vary with the publics addressed, the goals pursued, and the communication methods employed.

Public Relations Agency Businesses and political organizations often rely on agencies rather than in-house public relations personnel to plan and conduct external campaigns. The emphasis is on strategy and technique, and goals and knowledge of the company are supplied by organizational leaders.

External public relations activities can be handled in-house by organizational employees, or they can be handled by consultants who are usually affiliated with a *public relations agency.* Each method has advantages and disadvantages. In some situations, a combination of in-house practitioners and consultants might work best. For example, media training might best be handled by a combination of internal media relations practitioners advising corporate officials on how to stick to a corporate theme, and consultants might provide on-camera training.

In-house practitioners are usually more familiar with the company's managers and operations than consultants. This gives them more credibility with media and allows for informal interaction with the press. This familiarity can make the PR practitioner a valuable member of the management team. In addition, an in-house public relations staff usually costs less than outside consultants unless PR activities are only periodic.

Despite the in-house advantages, it is not always the best approach in all situations. Some organizations do not need ongoing external PR activities. For example, a small firm that sells manufacturing equipment to furniture companies deals with a small identifiable public and does not require extensive public relations. In such a case, an in-house PR staff would be an unnecessary expense.

PR consultants also may be used in specialized situations even if a company has an in-house public relations staff. If a cereal company plans to sell a new offering of public stock, a financial public relations firm might be hired. Most companies do not have in-house financial public relations personnel.

Public relations firms vary greatly in size. A few collect more than $100 million in fees annually; others have only a few employees. Small PR firms survive in a world of big companies because the heart of PR is mediated and interpersonal communication. From writing press releases to persuading a legislator to support a new bill, PR involves people with communication talent. Many of these people prefer to work for themselves rather than for larger companies.

Several of the larger PR firms work as subsidiaries of advertising agencies. Because PR and advertising are both in the business of promotion, it often makes sense to have both types of services available in the same organization. A client can have both the public relations and ad campaigns planned and executed by the same organization. Table 3.2 shows the PR fee income for the top ten independent PR firms. Of these firms, seven are associated with an advertising agency.

table 3.2

2001 PR Fee Income for Top Ten Independent Firms

FIRM	2001 NET FEES (MILLIONS OF DOLLARS)	EMPLOYEES	% FEE CHANGE FROM 2000
1. Edelman PR Worldwide	$220.7	1,941	−5.0
2. Ruder Finn	80.3	543	−4.5
3. Waggener Edstrom	58.6	431	+1.3
4. Schwaetz Communications	30.4	156	−8.5
5. PR21	15.7	107	+7.2
6. Dan Klotes Communications	14.8	85	+7.6
7. Hoffman Agency	13.5	71	+15.4
8. Gibbs & Soell	12.0	90	−5.6
9. Rogers & Associates	11.4	94	+3.2
10. Sterling Hager	11.3	62	−17.3

Source: O'Dwyer's Directory of Public Relations Firms (New York: J. R. O'Dywer, 2002), www.odwyerpr.com/pr_firm_rankings/independents.htm.

This Dave Matthews Band concert at Madison Square Garden required extensive public relations activity, from organizing the tour to informing music media organizations about the logistics.

Lobbying ✦ **Lobbying** is an effort to influence the legislative and administrative activities of government. Legislators need information when they are writing a law or considering whether to vote for it. They need to know who will be affected by the law, what will be the cost of administering it, and what effects, positive and negative, it is likely to have. A lobbyist provides the information that supports his or her organization's position.

For example, lumber and paper companies might ask the Department of the Interior to open up sections of national forest for more logging. Their lobbyists would argue that doing so will provide much-needed wood-based material and keep down the price of these products. Lobbyists for the Sierra Club would argue that the logging will have a negative impact on wildlife in these areas by removing their habitat. They also would argue that the logging could reduce tourism income to the areas. Lobbyists on both sides of the issue would produce research to support their position. Lobbying often is accomplished through one-on-one encounters, although the use of mass media to sway public opinion can sometimes help lobbying efforts.

Political PR ✦ Political PR activities resemble lobbying efforts, but the voters form the public of interest. Political public relations tries to get a certain person elected or to influence public opinion about a political issue such as abortion or tax reform. During an election campaign, PR practitioners write news releases; set up print, radio, and television interviews; prepare campaign literature for voters; distribute yard signs and bumper stickers; answer questions from journalists; and plan advertising campaigns.

Events Coordination ✦ Public relations also includes coordinating events. These range from concert tours to political campaigns. A concert tour by the Dave Matthews Band requires public relations activity to help organize the tour, buy advertising, and communicate with various music media organizations. The PR practitioner creates and distributes **media kits** about the tour, coordinates media interviews for the artists, writes press releases, and makes sure reporters cover the tour stops.

Financial Public Relations ✦ Financial public relations, sometimes called **investor relations,** are efforts by corporations to communicate with their investors, potential investors, and other interested parties, with the goal of maintaining the financial value of the company. The financial public relations practitioner communicates with three publics: investment analysts, financial journalists, and institutional investors.[20]

lobbying: Persuading legislators and other government officials to enact or support legislation favorable to one's cause.

media kits: A package of video and print news releases and other information to make it easy for reporters to follow up on a public relations–generated event or issue.

investor relations: Communication with those who invest in the company, that is, those who buy stock.

Web, Satellite, and Downlinks

Public relations is no longer simply a process of sending out press releases to the local media. Telephone calls, faxes, and mailings are being replaced with video news releases (VNRs) and satellite technology. Large PR firms are trying to incorporate all these technology services under one roof to better serve their clients. Today's large PR firms have divisions within the company that can, for example, create and update a client's web site, produce videos, and use satellite communications.

Most companies would agree that a web site is a critical public relations tool. Institutions are increasingly expected to have a web site that can communicate information quickly and easily. Large PR firms have the capability to create and service web sites for their clients. The web site might contain press releases, profiles on company executives, and important news about the company. Often it is not the customer who needs the information, but reporters and news agencies. A web site makes it easy for reporters to get valuable information they might need for their stories.

VNRs and e-mail are replacing older methods of distributing press releases. VNRs can be easily placed on the company web site,

which reduces distribution time and cost. The latest events or press conferences involving a company can be placed on the web site for everyone to see. Live feeds that people can log on to and watch are becoming a PR tool as well.

Because of these developments, video production has become more important. PR companies now have in-house production capabilities, that allow the company to produce VNRs as well as executive videos without hiring an outside production firm. The videos are often used internally for employees or externally to inform customers. And, as mentioned earlier, they are often placed on a company web site so they can be viewed by many more people.

PR firms are also turning to satellite technology to deliver messages. Television stations no longer have to attend news events. Instead, the PR firms can use their own production people to video-record the event. The firms then uplink the video using satellite distributors and simply inform the television stations that they can downlink the information.

In a crisis, it becomes very important to spread a message quickly and accurately. New technologies become crucial, and the PR firm that has immediate access

to all this technology can quickly and appropriately deal with a crisis. Many PR firms now have their web site divisions create "dark" web sites for crisis scenarios. These web sites are constructed in preparation for any crisis and can be activated immediately so reporters as well as customers have access to the latest official statements, reactions, and answers to frequently asked questions about the crisis. As a crisis evolved, the web site would be activated with all relevant information as well as names and numbers of people to contact. An intranet site might be set up that can be accessed (usually with a password) by company employees and crisis team staff members so that they are all using the same talking points and key messages. The PR firm's ability to video-record press conferences and transmit them to news organizations via satellite is crucial to getting out the message quickly. Statements and sound bites can then be taken directly by the news organizations without having a reporter on-site. The message gets delivered by the right person to the correct media outlets quickly and accurately.

—by Keith Kincaid

Investment analysts advise the public about buying stocks and securities, and institutional investors represent investment organizations such as mutual funds that have large amounts of money to invest. Financial journalists from such publications as the *Wall Street Journal* provide information about businesses to a variety of audiences. Financial PR firms such as Financial Brokers Relations of Houston, Texas, usually provide a range of services. This includes finding financial support for projects such as expanding production plants and promoting the company's stock among mutual funds, retirement fund managers, and other institutional investors.

Fund-Raising ◆ Some public relations practitioners participate in fund-raising for nonprofit organizations. Public broadcasting stations exemplify this activity. Twice a year PBS stations interrupt their regular programming to ask viewers to donate money to pay for the station's operations. Many stations also hold auctions, soliciting donated goods and services from the community and then selling them to raise money. Philanthropic organizations, such as United Way, and universities and colleges also participate in fund-raising activities. Immediately on graduation, if not sooner, college students receive solicitations for donations from their college's public relations department, which is usually called the development office.

Crisis Management ◆ Public relations personnel develop long-range plans for managing issues so they can help companies avoid crises. Nevertheless, sometimes an unexpected catastrophe hits, and the public relations staff is called on for *crisis management.* Typical crises include product tampering, product recalls, serious accidents, and even some labor disputes. In addition to the potential financial damage done to a company by the crisis, the organization's image can be damaged if the crisis is not handled well.

key concept

Crisis Management This increasingly important dimension of public relations requires that organizations develop plans for dealing with crises such as oil spills, media attacks, or other events that could create antagonism between an organization and any of its publics. The emphasis is on determining what crises could occur and planning in advance of the event so that reactions help to alleviate the crisis rather than promote it.

The American Red Cross had a dire need for crisis management as a result of the $564 million it raised following the terrorist attacks of September 11, 2001. The Red Cross decided to use half of the Liberty Funds for future needs, including potential terrorist attacks. However, this decision resulted in criticism and congressional hearings in November 2002. Critics of the decision said people gave money to the fund expecting it to go to the 9/11 victims and their families. In January 2002, the Red Cross announced a plan that would use 90 percent of the fund to help people affected by 9/11.[21] As a result of the criticism, the American Red Cross drastically changed their fund-raising policy in June 2002. The aim of the changes is to make sure donations are used as the donor intended.[22]

Crisis management requires **contingency plans** that anticipate possible crises. These plans include who will communicate with and what should be communicated to news media and what actions should be taken with products if they are involved. The plans play a crucial role in management actions. An unexpected crisis can cost an organization millions of dollars and even destroy a business.

External PR Tools ◆ Public relations uses a variety of tools; most either generate information or communicate information. Information-generating tools include research methods such as surveys, focus groups, and databases. PR specialists conduct *surveys* using telephone, mail, and personal interviews. In each situation, the respondent answers questions about topics of interest to the PR practitioner. The questions may concern a company's image, use of a product, or opinion about an issue. The answers to the questions are analyzed using computers, and the information facilitates planning and executing PR plans.

The second set of tools includes communication methods, both mediated and interpersonal, to inform and persuade people. A record company faxes news releases about a new album to music critics at newspapers and magazines. The releases provide information about the group, the album title, and the release date in order to get the critic to listen to the album and review it. A day or two after the release arrives, a PR practitioner will call to remind the music critic about the album. Both of these efforts are part of a larger plan to create publicity for the album. Interpersonal communication tools for PR range from giving speeches to one-on-one discussions.

contingency plans: Plans designed well in advance to accommodate situations in which the turn of events was unpredictable; such plans help organizations cope with possible undesirable outcomes.

spin doctors: Public relations personnel, usually associated with political communication, who try to get journalists and other publics to believe a particular interpretation of an event or information.

Spin Doctors and New Tools ◆ Although spin doctors operate in the business world, the term is more often associated with those who work on political campaigns to "spin" a candidate's message. **Spin doctors** lobby journalists to influence coverage.

The practice first gained attention during the 1988 presidential contest between George Bush and Michael Dukakis when the campaign managers contacted the press corps daily to put their candidate's spin on the coverage. Eventually, the spin doctors themselves became subjects of news stories.

Spin doctors provide information, but their real goal is to persuade journalists to at least look at an issue from their client's perspective. Spin doctors first master an understanding of the reporting and editing process and then use that understanding to appeal to journalistic routines and values to get reporters to pay attention to a particular candidate's point of view.[23]

Political spinning seemed to reach its peak after the disputed 2000 presidential election when both parties tried to influence the courts' and the public's perceptions of the election outcome. Democratic candidate Al Gore even appeared on television in an effort to influence the recount in Florida.

Problems Facing the Practitioner ✦ Public relations practitioners deal with two primary problems: budget vulnerability and the need for respect. When the economy takes a downturn, many companies cut budgets to preserve profit levels. Because PR does not contribute directly to the production of goods and services and PR people do not run machines or wait on customers, communication departments often face the sharpest edge of the downsizing ax. PR budgets are cut, and resources for outside consultants are reduced.

In addition, company managers do not always understand—or respect—the fact that PR practitioners have particular expertise in understanding the impact of communication. Managers assume that people in their organization who can write and speak well know as much about communication as the PR experts do. However, exercising the mechanical process of communicating is not the same as understanding how that communication will affect people.

PR practitioners also encounter respect problems because their contributions are difficult to measure. Managers can determine how many people hours it takes to produce a car, but they cannot tell how many practitioner hours it took to get the public to think well of those cars. As a result of these managerial assumptions, PR people sometimes can be treated like comedian Rodney Dangerfield: They get no respect.

In spite of problems, external PR remains important to a company's success. In fall 2002, for instance, Microsoft ran an ad on its web site about a woman who said she had switched from a Mac to a PC computer. The ad was a response to a series of Apple Computer television ads that represented people who had switched from PCs to Macs. Unlike the Apple ads, the Microsoft ad did not include the woman's name. Microsoft took down the ad after Internet users pointed out that the photograph of the woman was a stock photo that could be bought. An employee of a public relations firm that worked for Microsoft admitted to being the person in the ad after the Associated Press tracked her from personal information in the advertisement.[24]An experienced external PR practitioner might have predicted the response of Internet users to the anonymous ad and saved Microsoft some embarrassment.

Conducting Internal PR

Internal public relations activities include all of the formal communications activities within an organization except for interpersonal communication in the organization's daily activities. Broadcasting a company news program to Ford plants around the United States is internal PR; an assembly line foreperson telling a welder to speed up is not.

As with external PR activities, internal activities are planned and sustained. They include company publications about social activities, communication about policies and goals, and training activities. Such communication becomes crucial if a company

Good "internal communication" has been a buzzword and selling point of Saturn automobiles. Public relations constituencies vary, but they sometimes overlap. Good internal communication is a selling point for customers as well as employees.

wants its employees to cooperate effectively and efficiently in achieving the organization's goals.

Both managers and employees of a company continually make decisions. The decisions affect the company's production and services and the lives of the people who work for the company. Employees deserve to know the truth about the company in which they work, and managers must know about their employees if they are to motivate them. Internal PR is a classic case of two-way communication, and much of PR success is determined by how much employees are "listened to" rather than "told to."

Who Communicates with Whom? ◆ Internal communication involves four *directions of information exchange:* downward, upward, horizontal, and diagonal.[25] Figure 3.1 illustrates these four directions.

Downward communication (managers communicating with employees) is best exemplified by a president presenting a policy to employees. There are five main reasons for downward communication: (1) to explain the duties of a job and how to do them; (2) to provide a reason for doing a job and to explain how the job fits with

key concept

Directions of Information Exchange Good public relations and good business require more than one-way communication. Communication horizontally, or among publics, as well as from the top down and bottom up, is essential for harmonious production of products or services.

figure 3.1

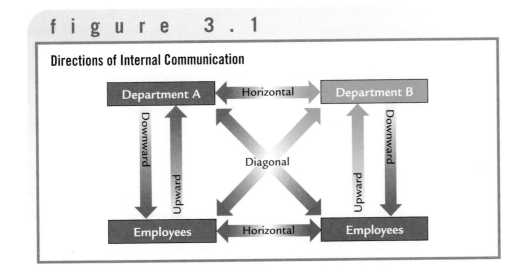

Directions of Internal Communication

other jobs; (3) to communicate an organization's policies, procedures, and practices; (4) to give employees feedback about their performance; and (5) to provide employees with a sense of the organization's missions and goals.[26] All of these are essential for employees to perform well. Upward communication (employees communicating with their supervisors) provides seven types of information: (1) feedback for managers about employees' attitudes; (2) suggestions for improving job procedures; (3) feedback about the effectiveness of downward communication; (4) the ability of employees to achieve company goals; (5) requests for assistance and supplies; (6) timely expressions of employee grievances; and (7) stimulation of employee involvement.[27] All effective communication requires feedback. Upward and downward communication feed each other; it is a mutual and symbiotic relationship. Without both, organizations cannot achieve their greatest potential.

Horizontal and diagonal communication, which involve communication between departments at different levels or between employees at similar levels, are just as crucial to an organization's performance as upward and downward communication. A reporter may need to talk to the circulation director (diagonal communication), or directors of two different departments, such as editorial and circulation, may need to communicate (horizontal communication). These conversations usually involve direct communication among managers and employees without the intervention of a PR practitioner. Diagonal and horizontal communication typically involve small numbers of people, so interpersonal communication works best without someone intervening.

Methods of Internal Communication ✦ Company officials communicate with their employees through media and interpersonally. Many of the tools used are the same as those used in communicating to external publics. The more important the information is to the receiver, the more effective interpersonal communication will be. Information about layoffs and drastic changes in working conditions should be delivered face-to-face by the employees' supervisors. Under such conditions, the employees will have questions that need to be answered. E-mail notices or newsletters can be effective in explaining changes in policies and procedures.

The type of communication also depends on the number of people involved. Interpersonal communication with 10,000 people is not feasible, but a television broadcast would work. Many large companies with multiple plants have daily TV broadcasts with satellite distribution to keep employees up-to-date on corporate events and concerns.

The employees' media habits must be considered if communication is to work. Companies with large numbers of unskilled laborers will communicate more effectively through television and radio than through a newspaper. White-collar companies with highly educated staffs tend to use e-mail, newsletters, and memos to communicate.

Finally, the nature of the company itself is a factor. Some companies are scattered across the globe; others locate their branches close together or have a single location. Because of current technology, distance should not hamper good communication, but it will affect the method chosen.

Converging technologies have increased companies' abilities to function worldwide. The U.S. Postal Service's two electronic newsletters, *Postal Link* for managers and *Straight Talk* for line supervisors, are examples of internal advances.[28]

The term *intranet* did not exist until 1994. By the year 2000, the number of intranet web servers reached about 4.7 million. 3M boasts 180 intranet sites worldwide hosted on forty servers with a three-tiered web site. Tier 3 is a personal web site where managers and employees communicate; tier 2 is for work groups; and tier 1 consists of enterprise web sites, or those combining private and public information.[29] At Hewlett Packard, the intranet connects more than 100,000 computers and 145,000 employees in 160 countries.

Problems Facing Internal PR Practitioners ✦ Internal PR is usually conducted by practitioners who are hired by the organization and work for a supervisor or executive who controls information. The practitioner cannot release more information than is authorized. For public relations practitioners, trust between management and employees is essential in carrying out information tasks. Internal practitioners need support and honesty from management in order to communicate effectively. In addition, good internal public relations relies on credibility. One former PR person told of a manufacturing plant in which the internal communication department conducted a survey of employees to ascertain their attitudes toward management. The employees were told that they would remain anonymous, but managers used the returned questionnaires to identify trouble-makers. The troublemakers were eventually fired. Additional efforts to measure employee attitudes at the plant had no success.

key concept

Code of Ethics Ethical practice is most likely to exist within a society that values truth in communication and holds the people who have the most access to media to high ethical standards. Ethical practices are endorsed by professional public relations organizations, but practicing good ethics is ultimately the responsibility of the individual.

The Public Relations Society of America plays the most important role in promoting PR professionalism. PRSA has a *code of ethics,* a publication called *Public Relations Journal,* and an accrediting program. To become accredited, a PR practitioner must take an exam that tests knowledge of PR practices and ethics and communication law. Practitioners who pass the exam become accredited in public relations and can use the acronym APR after their names. Research indicates that accredited practitioners make about $20,000 more a year than do nonaccredited personnel. Accreditation is enforced through the code of ethics. Complaints can be filed against APR practitioners, and if they are found to have violated the PRSA Code of Ethics (see Figure 3.2), they can be stripped of their accreditation.

figure 3.2

Public Relations Society of America Code of Ethics

CODE OF PROFESSIONAL STANDARDS FOR THE PRACTICE OF PUBLIC RELATIONS

Declaration of Principles

Members of the Public Relations Society of America base their professional principles on the fundamental value and dignity of the individual, holding that the free exercise of human rights, especially freedom of speech, freedom of assembly and freedom of the press, is essential to the practice of public relations.

In serving the interests of clients and employers, we dedicate ourselves to the goals of better communication, understanding and cooperation among the diverse individuals, groups and institutions in society.

We pledge:

- To conduct ourselves professionally, with truth, accuracy, fairness and responsibility;
- To improve our individual competence and advance the knowledge and proficiency of the profession through continuing research and education;
- And to adhere to the articles of the Code of Professional Standards for the Practice of Public Relations as adopted by the governing Assembly of the Society.

Source: David A. Haberman and Harry A. Dolphin, *Public Relations: The Necessary Art* (Ames: Iowa State University Press, 1988), pp. 413–414. Reprinted by permission of the Public Relations Society of America.

The field continues to be redefined, with an emphasis on integrity of practice. In response to a *Public Relations Journal* article asking practitioners to comment about their role, eighty-four practitioners responded. Of these, 21 percent said that practitioners are advocates on behalf of clients, 7 percent said that practitioners are consensus builders who try to bring competing sides together to find solutions, and 57 percent said that practitioners must be both advocates and consensus builders. The remaining 15 percent said that practitioners should perform other functions, such as those of information broker, strategist, and educator.

However, the dichotomy between advocate and consensus builder misses the key issue that has always defined PR professionalism. The issue is not whether to advocate on behalf of clients but rather to determine the role of truth in PR practice. The question is: Should PR practitioners purposely mislead any of their publics?

The professional practitioner, as defined by PRSA, would answer no to this question. The third article of the PRSA Code of Ethics says, "A member shall adhere to truth and accuracy and to generally accepted standards of good taste." However, most PR specialists are not members of the PRSA. The tobacco industry's efforts to persuade the public that smoking is not harmful is a classic case of questionable public relations.

TRENDS

As with all type of businesses, changes in technology and international economics continually reshape the PR industry. In a 2001 book, the executives of the GCI Group listed the Internet, the explosion of media outlets, globalization, and the shifting power to the grassroots level as forces at work on public relations.[30] The first two such trends represent technology changes and the last two concern globalization of economies and culture. A third and more recent trend affecting public relations concerns a crisis in business because of growing scandals related to greedy managers.

Technological Changes

Technology has transformed the PR industry by allowing easier direct contact between PR professionals and their publics and by increasing the number of media outlets that carry information. The integration of the computer at home and work has contributed to the skyrocketing expansion of the Internet and the World Wide Web. The Internet had about 50 million U.S. users in 1997, and by April 2002, Nielsen Ratings estimated that 166 million people in the United States (59 percent) used the Internet.[31] Even more significant, almost all journalists access news by means of the Internet. A decade ago technology was not an issue in PR. Now it is central to every PR firm.

With the Internet, opportunities seem infinite. A study by the Information Data Group estimated that the number of e-mail mailboxes worldwide would grow to 1.2 billion by 2005, with an average of 36 billion person-to-person messages sent each day.[32] The Internet allows public relations professionals to target specific journalists and individuals for press releases. George Simpson, president of Simpson Public Relations, says that "Ninety-nine percent of reporters I work with like and use e-mail." Reporters appreciate accessibility of information twenty-four hours a day as well as the opportunity to obtain information quickly. More than 9,000 journalists already have signed up for PRN's Press Room e-mail notification system. Journalists say they would like more sites with background information, archives, and new press releases.[33]

As a result of the new technology, the business of sending online press releases is booming. PR Newswire had sales of $178 million and made $50 million profit during 2001. Internet Wire, which was founded in 1999, had eighty-four employees three years later.[34] The technology explosion of the past two decades has not only changed the tools of PR for reaching people directly, but it has also increased the media outlets that can be used to reach people around the world. The Web has allowed thousands of existing magazines, TV stations, radio stations, and newspapers to provide news and information over the Internet, increasing the ways and speed of reaching publics. By 2002 about 500 million people worldwide could access these web sites from home.

The role of technology is reflected in PR education. A survey of 264 universities concluded that most public relations programs emphasize the use of new technology in order to prepare future professionals who are adept at developing advancements. According to one of the respondents, "As far as I'm concerned, an undergraduate PR student who gets a sheepskin without becoming computer literate is useless in the working world. I would not want to graduate, nor would I hire, a PR graduate who doesn't know several types of operating systems and software, can design and layout using a computer, knows Internet publishing, and can research and crunch some basic stats with a PC."[35] Technology is no longer a luxury in PR; it is a staple.

Globalization

The expansion of PR firms across the globe points up several issues and trends. Although a main component of this trend is the acquisition of smaller PR firms by larger firms, an equally important element is the combination of PR, advertising firms, and marketing firms. According to Mark Shadle, executive vice president and managing director of the business-to-marketing practice at Edelman Public Relations Worldwide, "There's more of an expansion of the role of what PR can do for a company. . . . PR isn't just a function of marketing, as it was traditionally viewed. It cuts across the various functions of a business." PR professionals can help businesses communicate such complex and unpredictable messages as international economic developments and the effects of mergers and acquisitions on shareholders and customers. Lee Duffey, president and founder of Duffey Communications in Atlanta, believes that PR will become more involved in expanding business strategies. For instance, his public relations firm assists businesses in the recruitment and retention of employees, researches customer perspectives, and also prices products and services. "Now public relations professionals feel the heat to keep up with rapid changes and use it to work more creatively than before."[36] That's not to say that trade–media relations will become passé. Burke Stinson, senior public relations manager at AT&T, believes that PR professionals should "get back to basics" by maintaining contact with news desks; assuming rapport with reporters, columnists, freelancers, producers, and the like; and protecting clients' credibility.

Furthermore, successful PR strategies need to build credibility at the same time they are building a "buzz." Peter Himler, managing director of Burson–Marsteller in New York, says, "PR practitioners will continue to fulfill the traditional role . . . but they'll be doing it differently by cultivating a more targeted approach."[37]

An equally important component of globalization is the need to be global but also local and specialized at the same time. This emphasizes the role of communication *technology and globalization.* Technology allows companies to connect around the world and create cost savings. However, the need for cultural sesitivity, as discussed in the Global Impact box, also concerns good business practices.

Public Relations Goes Global

The Disney song "It's a Small World After All" could easily describe conditions in the public relations industry. The growing threat of international terrorism, the continuing expansion of a global economy, and the increasing importance of international events such as the World Cup and the Olympics demand PR firms that span the globe. PR, which started as an American phenomenon, has become global.

For example, as China prepares to host the 2008 Olympics, it must spend $20 billion to build a national infrastructure that will improve air and water quality, housing, and transportation. It also must change its political image as an authoritarian country with a poor record of supporting human rights. To help it accomplish this change, the Chinese government hired Weber Shandwick Worldwide in 2001 to create the Chinese government's first Western-style PR campaign. Weber Shandwick is headquartered in New York, but it has sixty-eight offices and 3,000 employees around the world.

The globalization of PR is not new, and it has had its critics. One of the earlier concerns was that these Western companies would not be sensitive to variations in cultures around the world. This has not been as big a problem as thought. Formerly solely Western PR companies often win awards in other parts of the world. For instance, Ogilvy won three top Asian PR awards in 1999, and Burson–Marsteller won the top French PR award in 2002. These awards represent sensitivity to national needs within a global company.

The solution to the sensitivity problem has been to hire PR professionals from other countries and to train those who relocate to another country. The future holds more of the same.

Sources: "Ogilvy Tops Asian PR Awards for the Second Consecutive Year," *Business World* (December 29, 1999): 20; "WSW Seeks Long-Term China Ties," *O'Dwyer's PR Daily,* (July 16, 2001), www.odwyerpr.com; "Burson–Marsteller Wins Top French Award," Press Release (May 27, 2002), www.bm.com/newsroom.

A specialty can be a type of business, such as health care, or it can be a type of public relations, such as lobbying. Rossman, Martin & Associates of Lansing, Michigan, specialize in political public relations. They help interest groups influence legislation and work with candidates who are running for office. Often, specialization exists within larger PR agencies. The need for specialization reflects the growing role of PR practitioners as advisers and not just communicators. Carole Howard and Wilma Mathews advise future practitioners:

> We must demonstrate that we have a solid grasp of both our organization's objectives and the world in which we are operating, so that we can provide concrete assistance in articulating and dealing with the complex problems top management faces in relating to this ever-changing environment.[38]

Growing Business Crisis

A final trend affecting the PR industry concerns the growing scandals in the business world. Although scandal has always existed in business, the excesses of the late 1990s' rapid economic expansion yielded a bumper crop of these scandals. Beginning with Enron and Arthur Andersen and running through WorldCom, 2002 yielded a long list of businesses engaging in illegal activities. Even good-living icon Martha Stewart became involved in an insider stock trading controversy. Stewart sold $228,000 worth of ImClone shares the day before the Food and Drug Administration announced it would not review ImClone's cancer drug. Following an appearance on *The Early Show* and a *Newsweek* cover story, Stewart hired Brunswick Group to help her deal with the media.

The business scandals certainly have increased interest in crisis management PR, but there are hidden dangers for the PR industry, dangers that go to the heart of the PR function and stir memories of Ivy Ledbetter Lee and John D. Rockefeller. Can PR professionals represent clients who committed dishonest and even illegal acts and not lie to their publics? The PR ethics code contends that professionals should not lie or mislead, but the pressure to do so can be tremendous. The reactions to the pressures reflect individual as well as professional ethics.

Scandals, such as the investigation into Enron, pose a core question for PR professionals: How long do they support clients when the clients abuse the public trust? The documents in this picture were shredded after the federal government began its investigation of the company.

summary

- Public relations concerns planned and sustained unpaid communication from organizations to publics.

- PR practitioners communicate with internal and external publics.

- Any of an organization's many publics can influence whether that organization achieves its goals.

- The goals of public relations are to inform, persuade, and seek information from the organization's publics.

- Public relations did not become recognized by the general population until after World War II, although some corporations had used PR for almost one hundred years.

- External PR activities include lobbying, political PR, financial PR, fund-raising, crisis management, and events coordination.

- Public relations specialists can work in-house for an organization or as a consultant for an organization.

- The public relations process includes setting goals, conducting research, creating a PR plan, and evaluating the success of the plan.

- The problems facing practitioners include low budgets and lack of respect from managers.

- Internal communication includes downward, upward, horizontal, and vertical communication.

- Ethnic, racial, and gender bias continues to plague the public relations field.

- A variety of technologies are available for PR communication, and the type that is used must be appropriate for the information needs and habits of the publics.

- PR practitioners debate whether public relations is a profession and what the PR practitioner's role is. The key question concerns whether PR practitioners should purposefully mislead members of their publics.

- The growth of the international economic system has created global public relations, which in turn has created additional problems for practitioners.

navigating the web | Public Relations on the Web

The World Wide Web is an ideal public relations tool. In fact, many web sites are promotional sites for organizations or corporations. In addition, various public relations firms maintain sites. Also included are trade publications that provide information about public relations.

PR Newswire
www.prnewswire.com
PR Newswire presents press releases and articles about industries in the United States and around the world. It organizes companies by industry and provides an overview of business and industry.

Public Relations Society of America
www.prsa.org
PRSA is a professional society that accredits PR practitioners. The site contains information about PRSA and its membership requirements, publications, and professional activities. This site also links to the PRSSA (Public Relations Student Society of America) site. The

PRSSA promotes professional public relations on college campuses.

Burson–Marsteller Public Relations
www.bm.com
Burson–Marsteller is the largest public relations firm in the world. This site provides information about the services it offers.

PR Watch
www.prwatch.org
The site is run by the Center for Media & Democracy, a nonprofit organization that criticizes the PR industry for trying to manipulate the public. The site sells books and provides PR Watch online.

O'Dwyer's PR
www.odwyerpr.com
This is an excellent site for news and data about the PR industry. It offers O'Dwyer's PR Daily with news and pages aimed at PR students.

questions for review

1. Define public relations in your own words.
2. Describe public relations as an interactive process between an organization and its publics.
3. What contributions did Edward L. Bernays make to public relations?
4. What four groups require public relations in order to reach their goals?
5. What are the eight steps in the public relations process? Describe each briefly.
6. Why is respect an issue for public relations personnel?

issues to think about

1. What is meant by the concept that public relations evolved to serve social needs?
2. What is the relationship between public relations and propaganda?
3. What is the significance of spin doctors in the world of politics and democracy?
4. Analyze the importance of directional communication in internal public relations.
5. What is the significance of global public relations?

suggested readings

Beder, Sharon. *Global Spin: The Corporate Assault on Environmentalism* (White River Junction, VT: Chelsea Green Publishing, 1998).

Cutlip, Scott M. *Public Relations History: From the Seventeenth to the Twentieth Century: The Antecedents* (Hillsdale, NJ: Lawrence Erlbaum Associates, 1995).

Ries, Al, and Laura Ries. *The Fall of Advertising and the Rise of PR* (New York: HarperBusiness, 2002).

Shelburne, Merry. *Walking the Highwire: Effective Public Relations* (Madison, WI: CourseWise Publishing, 1998).

Simmons, P. J., and Chantal de Jonge Ondraat, eds. *Managing Global Issues: Lesson Learned* (Washington, DC: Carnegie Endowment for International Peace, 2001).

Advertising

The Korean team became Cinderella. Fans saw the Germans as big and dull. The Brazilians performed with beauty and grace, led by a magician and hero named Ronaldo.

Hundreds of millions of fans around the world thought the 2002 World Cup was about soccer, athletes, and national pride. It was, but even more, it was about money.

Big international sporting events such as the World Cup and the Olympics have become one of the few ways international and even national corporations can attract large numbers of viewers to watch their advertisements. As a result, the outcomes affect far more than the teams and fans. France's exit from the World Cup during the first round caused a 1.2 percent decline in stock price for TF1, France's largest commercial broadcaster. TF1 had planned to charge higher advertising prices if team France had made the quarterfinal round.[1] In Italy, RAI, the Italian-owned broadcaster, threatened to take action against soccer's governing body FIFA because it claimed the Italian team lost to South Korea due to errors by the referees. The Italian broadcasters had paid $140 million to broadcast the 2002 and 2006 World Cup matches domestically.[2]

Despite the growing fragmentation of television audiences, companies continue to seek the large audiences that once characterized television. This is especially true for international television because large corporations sell their goods throughout the world. For better or worse, advertising increasingly permeates the social and cultural fabric not only of the United States but also of the world. It clearly influences how we dress, eat, and even think, but advertising comes from biased sources. Some consumers see advertising as an effort to trick them into buying what they do not need. Some journalists see advertising as an unwanted influence on news coverage. Parents resist the brand-name appeals made to children and teenagers. Yet many consumers rely on advertising for information about products and to get a good deal. Each of these perspectives contains some truth.

Advertising is defined as a paid mediated presentation of information about services, products, or ideas with the specific goal of persuading consumers to act or think in a particular way. Advertising differs from news coverage and public relations activities because the advertising message is created, produced, and paid for by the advertiser, and the source of the information is clearly identified. Public relations practitioners must hope that a reporter will relay a message accurately; advertisers simply buy the message they want.

Advertising usually tries to sell products,

Advertising has been a controversial fact of American life. Because advertising has an economic and a social effect, the issues that it raises are complex:

◆ Advertising is most prominent in a free-market economy. As you read this chapter, try to analyze how and why advertising and the free market are related.

◆ Advertising uses social images and appeals to people's psychological and physical needs. Its content may sell a product or persuade people to adopt a specific lifestyle. Given this impact, think about how advertising is related to the marketplace of ideas.

◆ Some individuals think that certain types of advertising should be banned because well-produced messages have an enormous impact. After you read about the various types of influence advertising has on society, try to decide whether advertising significantly changes our society.

◆ Politics has changed with advertising, particularly as political managers have learned to master television. After you learn about how political advertising has changed, think about its effects on a democratic society.

◆ Internet advertising is still in its infancy compared to more traditional forms of advertising. A major issue is how advertising will make use of the new electronic technologies in the long run. What are the implications here for the Internet, online services, and older media?

Advertising *in Your Life*

Advertising as a Political and Social Message

Advertising is a controversial subject in the United States. Think about your own reactions to the ads you see, read, and hear. As you read this chapter, look for clues about the positive and negative aspects of advertising. Think about which forms of media you rely on for advertising and which forms of advertising you think are credible or effective.

WHICH MEDIA DO YOU MOST RELY ON FOR ADVERTISING? (Rank in Order of Importance to You)		WHICH MEDIA DO YOU MOST TRUST? (Rank in Order of Trustworthiness)		DO YOU THINK ADVERTISING FOR SOME PRODUCTS IS MORE CREDIBLE THAN FOR OTHERS? (Rank in Order of Credibility)		WHICH TYPES OF POLITICAL ADS ARE MOST EFFECTIVE? (Rank in Order of Effectiveness)		WHICH TYPES OF POLITICAL ADS CONTRIBUTE MOST TO DEMOCRACY? (Rank in Order of Contribution)	
Magazines	___	Magazines	___	Cosmetics	___	Issue-oriented	___	Issue-oriented	___
Newspapers	___	Newspapers	___	Household goods	___	Attack	___	Attack	___
Television	___	Television	___	Clothing	___	Personal	___	Personal	___
Radio	___	Radio	___	Cars	___	Informative	___	Informative	___
Direct mail	___	Direct mail	___	Appliances	___	Mood creating	___	Mood creating	___
Internet/online	___	Internet/online	___	Services	___	Other	___	Other	___

such as soda, and services, such as health care. However, some ads try to promote ideas. All ads share the goal of trying to influence people in some way.

The effort to persuade is not a serious problem for consumers as long as they understand the purpose of advertisements. Many ads serve the basic media social function of coordinating economic activities. Advertising allows sellers to tell buyers what products and services are available at what prices and in what places. Without this exchange of information, consumers would waste time and money.

However, advertising has real and social costs. Some people argue that it raises the price of goods. Others fear that it alters social norms; affects the attitudes of children and adults; and undermines the influence of family, religious institutions, and schools. Commercialization through advertising, they argue, directs society away from serious issues and raises the art of acquisition to a new level.

For the service of connecting buyer and seller, U.S. media organizations receive large amounts of money. In 2000, media companies took in $243.3 billion in advertising. The bulk of the money went to newspapers, television, direct mail and radio; newspapers received 20 percent, broadcast and cable television received 24.3 percent, direct mail received 18.3 percent, and radio about 7.9 percent.[3]

1477. First handbill advertisement in England
1622. First English newspaper advertisement
1704. First newspaper advertisement in America
Late 1700s. Commercial notices grow as proportion of newspapers.
1830s. Penny press gets heavy advertising support.
1869. Rowell & Ayers publish newspaper directories for advertising.
Late 1800s. Printing technology allows visually appealing ads.
Late 1800s. Magazines provide a vehicle for mass national advertising.
Late 1800s. Advertising agencies grow in importance.
1906. First Pure Food and Drug Act is passed.
1914. Federal Trade Commission is created.
1922. First radio advertisement
1930s. Radio advertising booms as the audience grows.

1400–1700	1800	1860	1880	1900	1920	1930

1620. Pilgrims land at Plymouth Rock.
1690. *Publick Occurrences* is published in Boston.
1741. First magazine is published in America.
1776–1783. American Revolution
1830s. The penny press becomes the first truly mass medium in the United States.
1861–1865. American Civil War
1892. Thomas Edison's lab develops the kinetoscope.
1914–1918. World War I
1915. *The Birth of a Nation* marks the start of the modern movie industry.
1920. KDKA in Pittsburgh gets the first commercial radio license.
1930s. The Great Depression
1939. TV is demonstrated at the New York World's Fair.
1939–1945. World War II

ADVERTISING IN AMERICAN LIFE

Advertising dates to the ancient Greek and Roman civilizations. In the cities, **criers** walked the street announcing commercial ventures, as well as providing information about religion, politics, and other public matters.[4] In a sense, these criers were verbal newspapers, with a mixture of news and advertising similar to that found today.

A more traditional definition of a medium would connect early advertising to printing. The earliest known printed advertisement was the **broadside,** or handbill, which was first produced in England in 1477, and the first known broadside was an advertisement for religious books. Although some disagreement exists, the first English newspaper advertisement has been dated from August 1622. A weekly publication of "Newes" carried an advertisement for two earlier copies of the newspaper.[5] Almost eighty years later, the first advertisement appeared in a U.S. newspaper, the *Boston News-Gazette.* The ad offered to sell advertising in the *News-Gazette.*

crier: In ancient Greece and Rome, a person who walked through the streets crying out news to the people. Preceded printed news.

broadside: Handbill, also called broadsheet, that was printed only on one side of the paper.

1950s. TV replaces radio as a national ad medium.

1971. Cigarette advertising is banned from TV.

1980s. Cable grows as a segmented ad medium.

1980s. Advertising agencies become global.

1985. Consumer spending on media exceeds advertising expenditures.

1990s. Advertising moves to the Internet.

1996. Broadcast and cable advertising exceeds newspaper advertising.

1999. Expansion of e-commerce

2000s. Pop-up ads increase on the Web.

2000s. Concerns grow over privacy of data collected online for marketing.

2001. Advertising reviews for media decline.

| 1940 | 1950 | 1960 | 1970 | 1980 | 1990 | 2000 |

1949. First commercial electronic computer is produced.

Early 1950s. Rock 'n' roll begins.

1969. First person lands on the moon.

1970s. VCR is developed.

Late 1980s. National Science Foundation creates the basis of the Internet.

1989–1991. Cold War ends and the USSR is dissolved.

1996. Telecommunications Act

2000. Presidential election nearly tied.

2001. Terrorist attacks on New York and Washington, D.C.

The Mercantile Press and Advertising

As commerce grew in the American colonies, so did advertising in the **mercantile press.** The mercantile press was aimed at shopkeepers and other small business owners rather than at participants in political discussion. The first issue of the first U.S. daily newspaper, the *Pennsylvania Packet and Daily,* which began in 1784, contained 63 percent advertising. The next year a daily was started in New York with similar success in advertising. These cases suggest a *connection between demand for news and for advertising.* Demand for both promoted the creation of daily newspapers in the United States.[6]

Although most of today's newspaper ads are aimed at consumers, many of the mercantile press ads tried to sell goods to other businesspeople, often for use in their businesses. A shipping company would advertise a shipment of clothing so that retailers would buy it for resale. Early advertisements also promoted real estate, services,

key concept

Connection between Demand for News and Advertising Demand for news and for advertising created a demand for newspapers. Early newspaper ads were simple paragraphs of type promoting real estate, services, and goods for sale to retailers and consumers.

mercantile press: Early American newspapers that served businesses, shopkeepers, and tradespeople. These newspapers also contained political news.

Advertising in the mercantile press often targeted other businesspeople. Today the tradition is carried forward at trade shows where businesses or companies try to attract product users through promotional favors.

and goods for sale, just as newspapers do today. However, advertisements often read like announcements. For example, a small ad in the November 18, 1771, *Pennsylvania Packet and General Advertiser* read: "A few barrels of Carolina Pork to be sold by John Murgatroyd, in Water-street, near Tun-Alley."[7] By the 1820s, the mercantile newspapers had become important commercial bulletin boards with advertising and announcements for the business community.

Despite similarities in purpose, early advertisements looked nothing like the ads that are found in today's newspapers. Only a few crude illustrations were used, and printing technology limited the diversity of type. Ads were typically one column wide and rarely contained graphics.

The Development of Mass Advertising

Because of their focus on business and trade, the mercantile newspapers were poor advertising vehicles for consumer goods. Their small targeted audience kept their circulations low. In 1816 seven New York dailies sold only about 9,400 copies in a city of 125,000.[8] Average people could not afford these papers, nor did they like the content.

The penny press vitalized the consumer market and revolutionized **mass advertising.** By 1842, New York circulation had grown to 92,700 daily; two-thirds of these issues cost two cents or less.[9] Now merchants could reach large numbers of customers with one newspaper.

In addition to expanding the advertising market, the penny press changed the nature of advertising. Penny newspapers ran want ads similar to those found in English newspapers. They charged advertisers by a unit of space rather than the flat price charged by the mercantile press, and they separated advertising and news content.

Not everyone praised the penny press for its changes. The mercantile papers, which charged six cents for a copy, attacked various penny newspapers for printing patent medicine ads. These advertisements sold liquids and salves that at their best did no harm but at their worst could kill. These ads reflected the *let the buyer beware philosophy* of the newspapers. The criticism of penny newspapers was justified, but the mercantile press ignored the fact that some of its newspapers had been carrying patent medicine ads for decades.

After the Civil War, advertising increased rapidly. The Industrial Revolution contributed to an expanding middle class and encouraged an influx of immigrants, both of which increased the demand for goods and services. Businesses met the increasing demand for goods by advertising in the thousands of newspapers that were spring-

mass advertising: Advertisements that aim to reach the largest number of people possible.

ing up around the country. Between the Civil War and 1900, printing and graphic technology facilitated visually appealing advertising. Ads with graphic illustrations became more common.

The post–Civil War period also saw the maturation of magazine advertising. An expanding national economy and a consumer thirst for the information and entertainment that were found in magazines created a national advertising market. A few magazines had reached large circulations before this period, but printing technology and localized economies had limited their advertising. Advertising became the mainstay of the big, high-quality monthlies. The November 1899 edition of Harper's magazine, for example, had 135 pages of advertising and 163 pages of editorial material, which reflected 45 percent advertising, only slightly lower than the percentage of advertising carried by many magazines today.[10]

Because of changes in the economy and mass media, *advertising agents* became more important in the late 1800s. They bought space in publications and resold it to advertisers. An agent could place an ad in a number of newspapers and magazines around the country for one price. This made advertising more efficient and simplified the process for the advertiser, who no longer had to buy ads separately for each newspaper and magazine.

Although several agents were in business before the Civil War, agents had no accurate listings of publications, circulation levels, and advertising rates. These problems were reduced by the George P. Rowell and N. W. Ayers & Sons agencies when they began publishing newspaper directories in 1869. The directories provided some information about where an ad might be placed to achieve a desired effect.

Even though the mercantile press had attacked the penny papers in the early part of the century for their reliance on patent medicine advertising, newspapers and magazines continued to carry ads for the popular medicines. Patent medicines did not cure people, but the high alcohol content in many of them often made people feel better, at least temporarily. Unfortunately, some patent medicines contained addictive drugs and deadly poisons.

The selling and advertising of patent medicines contributed to passage of the Pure Food and Drug Act in 1906, the establishment of the Federal Trade Commission (FTC) in 1914, and the establishment of the Food and Drug Administration (FDA) in 1931. These government initiatives represented efforts to connect *product responsibility and advertising.* Such regulations are based on the assumption that companies should be responsible for the impact of their products by truthfully labeling those products. The FTC and FDA had the power to limit false advertising of patent medicines, but the agencies continued to fight some of these companies into the 1940s.[11]

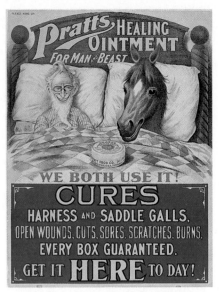

The graphics used in this patent medicine poster, circa 1880, were much more elaborate than the counterpart ads appearing in newspapers. In 1931, the Food and Drug Administration was created to address the patent medicine industry, requiring labeling of products.

The Arrival of Broadcast Advertising

The creators of radio did not envision it as a mass medium, much less an advertising mass medium. It was supposed to be a form of wireless telephone. However, that idea did not last long.

Radio programming developed to sell radio sets, but as the cost of programming increased, more money was needed. In 1922, WEAF in New York sold five ten-minute advertising spots to Long Island real estate promoters. Radio advertising was born. Twenty years later, radio advertising was a $100 million business.[12]

Radio advertising prospered for several reasons. Radio was the first instantaneous national medium. Magazines circulated nationally, but they arrived in the mail and on newsstands days and weeks after they were printed. Radio was heard all across the country simultaneously. That's why General Motors spent $500,000 on radio advertising in 1928.[13] GM could announce the arrival of new car models to thousands of listeners at the same time.

Radio advertising also grew because the U.S. economy boomed through most of the 1920s. After World War I, industrial production and consumer buying expanded, and the middle class continued to grow. People had more discretionary income to spend on goods and services other than food and housing. Advertising helped them decide how to spend that money.

Broadcasting gave modern advertising agencies more choices to offer their clients. As agencies became full-service organizations, they bought advertising space, wrote copy, developed illustrations for ads, placed ads in newspapers and magazines, researched the wants and needs of the audience, and coordinated advertising in more than one publication. Now they could advise clients on where best to place their ads.

Until the early 1950s and the advent of television, radio was the prime broadcast advertising medium. But soon television eclipsed radio; consumers went wild for it, and advertisers capitalized on the fact that viewers could both see the product and hear the national message. In 1950, only 9 percent of U.S. homes had television sets; by 1960, 87 percent had television.[14] Advertisers could reach increasing numbers of people, and the ability to create positive images of a product on the new visual medium seemed limitless. The growth of television advertising contributed to the growth of a *consumer culture* in the United States, in which advertisements influenced not only economic decisions but popular culture as well.

key concept

Consumer Culture Advertising—paid information about services, products, and ideas—is designed to entice an audience to buy a product or an idea. Critics argue that for U.S. consumers advertising has become the dominant form of popular culture and that values have become commercial, rather than emanating from traditional institutions such as the family, school, and religious institutions.

By the 1970s, most of the current mass advertising options had developed, advertising expenditures were growing rapidly, and various forms of mass media were competing for advertising dollars. The amount of money spent on advertising grew from $2.1 billion in 1940 to $19.6 billion in 1970, a 933 percent increase. When adjusted for inflation, advertising increased by 337 percent during this thirty-year period.

A changing distribution of ad dollars among media also marked this period. Television enjoyed the great growth, moving from 3 percent of all advertising expenditures in 1940 to 18 percent thirty years later. The increasing proportion of ad dollars for television came at the expense of newspapers and radio. Magazines and direct mail also experienced a small decline as television boomed.

The growth of cable attracted advertisers during the 1980s. Cable, with its dozens of channels, provided segmented audiences for advertisers. Rather than advertising to mass audiences, advertisers could identify groups that watched specialized channels who might be more interested than the public at large in their products. Although cable offered more effective advertising than broadcast television could, it did not eliminate mass advertising. In 1999, the popular TV show *ER* sold thirty-second commercial spots for $565,000 each.

Interest in online and Internet advertising grew during the mid-1990s. However, advertising expenditures were relatively modest because of concerns about how many people were viewing the ads, how viewers might use these ads, and how to reach particular groups of viewers. Total advertising revenue on the Internet reached about $3 billion in 1999; in 2001 revenues declined 14.7 percent from 2000, from $2.83 billion to $2.50 billion. During the first half of 2002, revenues had increased by 1.90 percent.[15] This will still be a smaller percentage of all advertising expenditures than traditional media.

key concept

Advertising Affects Prices Critics debate whether advertising raises or lowers the prices of goods. In some instances, economies of scale allow producers, in response to demand created by advertising, to manufacture larger quantities at a lower price. However, many critics argue that advertising, particularly on television, is expensive and that the cost of such advertising is often added to the product price.

Advertising and the Price of Products

Economists disagree about how *advertising affects the prices* consumers pay for goods and services. Some argue that advertising increases prices because the money companies spend on advertisements is tacked onto the price of the goods. Campbell's tomato soup costs more than the store brand, they argue, to pay for Campbell's national advertising budget. Typically, nationally advertised products cost more than generic and regional brands.

Other economists argue that advertising reduces the cost of goods because it results in increased production. The more cans of Campbell's tomato soup produced, the less each can costs to make. The average cost of almost all goods will decrease as the number of units increases, up to the capacity of a production plant. Economists call the savings that result from producing large quantities **economies of scale.** The economies occur because a company has to invest a certain amount of money in a plant no matter how many units of the product are made. Producing the first 10,000 cans of tomato soup requires equipment to cook and can the soup. If a plant is already making 10,000 cans of tomato soup, producing another 1,000 will add only the cost of the ingredients, the cans, and some extra labor time.

Because advertising can increase the number of units people will buy, it decreases the average cost of making the product. The average cost per can of 11,000 cans of soup is less than the average cost per can of 10,000 cans. However, research is not conclusive on the impact of advertising on price. In some situations, the lower cost of increased production will be passed on to the consumers as price breaks. In other cases, the price of the product will be kept high, and the company will keep the difference as profit. Similarly, the advertising costs that companies pay may be added to the price of the product in some cases but not in others. The impact of advertising on price varies based on a variety of factors, but a key element is competition. If consumers can buy the same quality of goods at a lower price, companies will probably not pass on the cost of advertising to consumers.

Advertisements appealing to families to vacation together within the United States proliferated after September 11, 2001. Here, the recreational vehicle industry appeals to family themes.

Interestingly enough, whether a similar good is perceived to be of equal quality to another sometimes depends on advertising. For example, advertising convinces some people that Campbell's tomato soup is better than the store brand. Much of television advertising aims to convince consumers that a product is better than other similar products. Nike spends millions of dollars to get people to believe that their athletic shoes are worth paying three times more than some other athletic shoes cost. Burger King has long advertised its hamburgers as flame broiled rather than fried, implying that its burgers are better. This is called **differentiating the product,** that is, getting the consumer to believe one product is different in quality from other products.

Just how advertising affects price is a complicated process that varies from product to product. It depends on the level of demand, consumers' perceptions of quality, the scale of production, and a variety of other business factors. Consumers can make better choices if they understand how these factors work.

CULTURAL AND POLITICAL IMPACT OF ADVERTISING

Advertising serves society in positive and negative ways. It brings buyers and sellers together in economic markets that supply the goods and services that people need and want. It also distributes economic resources for society. Advertising contributes to these processes by providing consumers with information.

On an individual level, advertising makes life easier. Without advertising, just getting the basics for living would be far more difficult and expensive. Imagine hunting for an apartment with no advertising except signs on apartment buildings. You would have to drive to each apartment to find out how much it cost. Without ads, you would not know which grocery store was offering the best specials each week. Price comparison would take enormous amounts of time.

economies of scale: As the number of units produced at a plant increases, the average cost per unit decreases. This comes about because the company has to invest large amounts of money just to produce the first unit.

differentiating the product: The process of trying to get the consumer to perceive one product as being different in nature and quality than other products.

Social Costs of Advertising Advertising can be manipulative and can influence news and entertainment content. Television critics argue that the primary criterion for media programming is to cater to advertisers' needs, not to perform social, cultural, or political functions.

However, the social contributions of advertising also have a *social cost.* The cost comes from negative effects that advertising can have on society. Some of these effects are direct, such as the manipulation of people's spending behavior; others are more indirect, such as the influence of advertising on news media and politics. Critics question the impact of advertising, especially in connection with television and radio, media on which children and young adults rely heavily. The concern is not only about short-term effects, but also about whether advertising actually changes expectations of normative behavior. For example, a short-term effect might be that teenage girls buy more lipstick. But a long-term effect of campaigns such as Benetton's and Calvin Klein's advertisements showing emaciated young people might be to persuade young people that they have to stay ultrathin, no matter what the cost to their health.

Political Advertising

Joe McGinnis published a book in 1969 called *The Selling of the President, 1968.* McGinnis claimed that Richard Nixon used television advertising techniques to win the presidency and that the 1968 election forever changed the nature of political advertising.[16] Since the 1968 election, advertising aimed at persuading, especially on television, has come to dominate elections at the state and national levels.

According to estimates, candidates for federal office spent more than $2.5 billion on advertising during the 2000 election campaign. This was a $500 million increase over the 1996 election.[17] Harold Ickes, an advisor to Hillary Rodham Clinton during her Senate race, said of the sum: "It even staggers me, and I'm pretty hard-core."

Critics of this trend are concerned about the content of ads and the influence that the candidates' need of advertising funds gives political donors. Political TV advertising often appeals to voters' emotions in an effort to persuade rather than inform. Images of crime and violence contribute little to the marketplace of ideas, but they do arouse concern among voters. Such ads attempt to identify a candidate's opponent with negative images and do not provide information for a rational political decision. Scholars and critics are concerned that such advertising emphasizes trivial problems and plays down the issues that are most urgent.[18] Even the heads of large advertising agencies question the usefulness of advertising in the political process.[19]

Political web sites are an integral part of candidates' or public officials' communication with their constituents or potential contributors. Here, presidential hopeful John Kerry reassures the public that, despite his recent surgery for cancer, he will be back on the campaign trail soon.

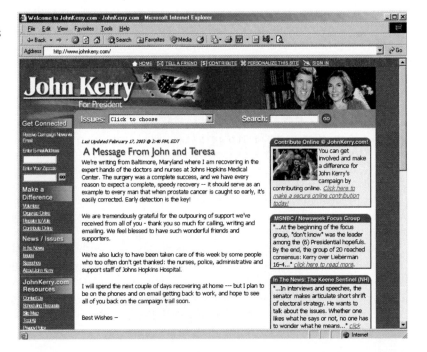

Critics also express concern about the influence that donors of advertising funds can have on political candidates. The spending in 2000 resulted in the reintroduction of national financial reform legislation. Republican Senator John McCain, a cosponsor of the reform bill, said: "Campaign contributions up to the hundreds of thousands of dollars from a single source are not healthy for democracy. Is that not self-evident?"[20] The common supposition is that companies that fund political campaigns will demand a return on their investment when the candidate is elected. Some political managers note, however, that campaign contributions are directed toward parties—parties that in general support the position favored by the contributor.

Manipulation by Advertising

Even though advertising serves the legitimate function of bringing buyers and sellers together, not all advertising is designed simply to provide information. Many ads aim to persuade consumers to buy unneeded goods and services or to pay higher prices for particular brands.

Of particular concern in this area is advertising aimed at children. Children develop **rational thinking abilities** at about the age of twelve. Before that, children have trouble understanding the nature and purpose of advertising. Research indicates that children under the age of four cannot tell programs from the commercials. Often the commercials, with quick camera cuts and lots of action, appeal even more to children than do the programs. The result is that parents hear their children say, "I want that" every time the children see a toy or cereal ad on television. Luckily for parents, advertisements have less influence over children as they grow older.

Advertising's Influence on Journalism

Because advertising provides all of the revenue for television news and 70 to 80 percent of the revenue for newspapers, media critics often raise the question of advertisers' influence on news content. The concern is justified. Advertisers do sometimes succeed in altering news coverage.

Advertisers often have an impact on what is covered as well as on what is not covered. For example, the Bellevue, Washington, *Journal American* ran stories for four days about the reopening of an enlarged Nordstrom's department store. The stories included front-page coverage and full-page "shoppers' guides" of the store. It seems unlikely that it was just coincidence that Nordstrom's is an advertiser in the *Journal American*.[21]

News departments sometimes respond to complaints by advertisers, but they also avoid pursuing stories that would create problems for big advertisers. A newspaper might downplay stories about union concerns at a local department store chain because of the advertising the department store buys. Class action suits against a company might not make the front page in a community with a plant owned by that company.

Even though television stations make high profits, they can still experience pressures. In 1999 two investigative reporters filed suit against a television station in Tampa, Florida, alleging that the station fired them because of pressure from Monsanto, the company that produces a genetically engineered chemical used to increase milk production in cows. The reporters prepared a story raising the issue of how people who drank the milk might be affected. They said that after Monsanto threatened to sue, the station managers decided not to run the story. The news director at the TV station said the reporters' contracts were not renewed because they were "difficult people to work with."[22]

The basic conflict is that information that serves the advertiser may not serve the reader. A story telling readers how to get the best deal for a car can lead to lower profits for auto dealers. This conflict comes from serving the consumer and advertising markets with the same media product. Just who wins depends on the size of the media organization and the beliefs of the managers. Big media companies, which have a large number of advertisers, can withstand advertising boycotts better than smaller ones can. And managers who accept the social responsibility of news organizations will be more likely to side with readers, listeners, and viewers than with advertisers.

rational thinking abilities: The cognitive processing of information by considering options based on conscious comparison of influencing factors.

STRUCTURE OF ADVERTISING AND DEMAND

Advertising is a form of promotion. **Promotion** involves all the ways of gaining attention for a company, product, or service. In addition to advertising, these include public relations, packaging, personal selling, and gifts. Marketing experts divide the marketing process into four elements: product, price, place, and promotion. To market a product successfully, companies must start with a good product, price it correctly, place it well, and promote it. Advertising is interrelated with other aspects of marketing. Advertising cannot sell an inferior product for long, and advertising cannot convince most adults to buy overpriced, low-quality services and products.

The economics of advertising concerns the interaction of supply and demand in the advertising market and the connection between the advertising market and the consumer market. Advertisers buy ads in media because they want to reach the audience that is attracted by the information in the media. Some of the audience seeks the information in advertisements. Economists call serving two markets with the same production process a **joint product.**

To promote goods and services, a company enters the advertising market. Producers and sellers of goods and services pay media companies, which provide space and time in their media products. When a company spends more than $400,000 for thirty seconds on *Monday Night Football,* this exchange takes place in the advertising market.

There is also a connection between the advertising market and the consumer market. In the consumer market, people exchange their time and money for information. A person who watches *Monday Night Football* is part of the consumer market. This person is exchanging his or her attention for the entertainment of the game. The viewer would have no game to watch if advertising did not pay for it, and the advertiser would have no one to see the ads if the game was not provided.

The difference between the two markets is more clear-cut with media that consumers buy. Readers buy newspapers for the information they contain, which comes in the form of news and advertising. Advertisers buy space and reader attention from the newspaper company. As a result, the newspaper simultaneously serves two different but interconnected markets with the same production process.

The Influence of Advertising on Consumer Behavior

The study of how advertising affects people is called *consumer behavior.* There are *two perspectives of consumer behavior:* cognitive and behavioral. The *cognitive* view concerns the effects of mental processes such as perception and knowledge on people's behavior. The *behavioral* approach concentrates on how people's actions are reinforced by other people and media. Both of these concepts involve several theories about how people process information and act. Neither can fully explain the way advertising influences people. People's thoughts do affect their actions, but we also base our behavior on patterns of reinforcement.[23]

The cognitive approach assumes that individuals are active decision makers who use information to make rational and effective decisions. Advertising provides information that helps people select a product or service that meets their needs. Applying the cognitive approach to buying a house, people look for information about the quality and price of various houses and the desirability of living in a particular neighborhood. Some of this information comes from advertisements. After collecting this information about several houses, the buyers select the one that best suits their budget and lifestyle. They have acted rationally by collecting information and evaluating the information systematically.

Cognitive advertising provides people with information about price and quality. Behavioral advertising appeals directly to emotions and the images people have of themselves. It assumes that the environment plays a primary role in people's actions. Print ads work best for cognitive advertising, and television provides the best outlet for behavioral ads.

key concept

Two Perspectives of Consumer Behavior The cognitive perspective assumes advertising changes attitudes and knowledge. The behavioral perspective assumes advertising reinforces people's actions.

promotion: Promotion involves the ways a company gains attention for its product or service, including advertising, public relations, packaging, and personal selling.

joint product: Term economists use when one production process serves two markets. For instance, the process of printing magazines serves readers in the consumer market and companies in the advertising market.

Some television ads affect behavior by connecting a product with a good time and by getting people to identify with appealing characters. These are called *identity advertisements*. Soon after John Elway retired from the Denver Broncos in 1999, Coors beer began running a series of advertisements featuring his career. In these commercials, a sports announcer would describe one of Elway's many heroics on the football field. Then the ads showed a close up of Elway endorsing Coors. The goal was to have the viewers identify with a celebrity of almost mythic proportions. The unspoken message was that viewers might not be able to play football like Elway, but they could share his taste in beer.

By identifying a product with good times, the enjoyment of using the product is reinforced. Over time the ads and the use of a product create a habit for some consumers that the producer wants to reinforce. Identity advertisements are behaviorally based and assume that consumers will be more likely to buy products that have pleasant activities associated with them. Companies that produce goods that are similar to other products often use identity ads. Most best-selling beers and colas have similar recipes, which gives them similar tastes. As a result, the advertisements cannot feature the different tastes of the drinks. Instead, the companies use emotional appeals to create positive but different images of their products.

Although the "Got Milk?" campaign has been successful in gaining attention, it is not clear whether it has been successful in increasing milk consumption.

Identifying Consumers as Types

By using sophisticated social science methods, advertising agencies can identify the types of people who will likely buy a product. People are most often classified for advertising by demographics, geographics, and pyschographics. *Demographics* concerns characteristics of people and households such as age, gender, income, marital status, and family size. *Geographics* concerns physical locations (state, region, or country) of potential buyers. *Pyschographics* concerns the lifestyles and activities of people such as movie attendance, hobbies, and types of physical exercise.

Effectiveness of Advertising

Some critics describe advertising as manipulating people's behavior and getting them to buy things they do not need. Others think advertising is a useful sort of information that allows people to make better consumer decisions. The truth of advertising lies somewhere in between.[24]

People find some advertising valuable. One study reported that 46 percent of readers regularly look at the Sunday newspaper advertising inserts. Another 26 percent occasionally look at them.[25] A person may throw away one clothing catalog that came through the mail and order a shirt from another.

The same people who find supermarket advertising useful may use their remote control to avoid looking at television advertisements for a medical product. Yet television can be very effective at telling people that something is available. McDonald's has not sold billions of burgers because it produces the best food in the world. The company produces fast food that has an acceptable taste for most people and effectively advertises its products, especially to children.

From society's perspective, the best consumer of advertising is the one who understands the purpose of ads and how ads are made. Understanding allows people to use advertising information for their purposes, not the purposes of the advertiser.

Advertising's Effects on Consumers

Advertising influences consumers in four ways: (1) It makes people aware of a product or service; (2) it provides price information about a product or service; (3) it provides information about the quality of a product or service; and (4) it tries to persuade consumers to identify a product or service with a particular person or activity.[26]

Rap and Advertising: Where Culture Goes, Advertising Follows

Rap music began in the 1970s in the South Bronx as African American alternative music. The use of turntables to create music led to break dancing and a hip-hop culture. More than twenty years later, rap has become mainstream. Rap recordings had become more than 10 percent of music sales by the beginning of 2000, and rap had become a promotional tool for such mainstream movies as *Men in Black II.*

The advertising industry has never been reluctant to incorporate popular culture trends into its efforts, and rap is no exception. Calvin Klein followed this trend when it hired Foxy Brown to sell jeans. L. L. Cool J. promoted Fubu clothing. As Dennis Lazar, president of Harbor Footwear Group, said, "Hip hop hits the youth market, we sell to the youth market, and that has been the case for some time. I have a nineteen-year-old and a sixteen-year-old, and they live in a middle-class suburb and they listen to hip hop. It cuts across a huge spectrum of young people."

Using popular culture and music for advertising is an old practice. Companies appeal to young people by getting them to identify their products with good times, and young people depend heavily on music to entertain themselves. The relationship between advertising and popular culture is symbiotic. Just as music promotes products through advertisements, advertisements promote the music it incorporates. Performers know that appearing in advertisements can help their careers.

The mainstreaming of alternative music such as rap raises the issue of how advertising can alter the nature of music, homogenizing it so that it loses its edge. Rap evolved as protest music that examined the problems of urban life in the United States. But protest lyrics do not necessarily evoke the images of good times that advertisers want.

Will the commercialization of rap turn it into simply another form of popular music, which means losing the edge and vitality that marked its development? Are the monetary rewards from advertising worth the impact it has on any form of music? Many of the rock 'n' roll greats, Eric Clapton and Ray Charles, for instance, have appeared in advertisements. Should the complex interaction of popular culture and advertising that influences young people be a matter of concern?

Sources: Monica L. Haynes, "The Hipness of Hip-Hop: Rap Inspired Movement Influences Every Aspect of Popular Culture," *Pittsburgh Post-Gazette* (September 9, 1999): E-1; "Rap Pushes Products from Soda Pop to Shoes," *USA Today* (June 25, 1999): 2E.

The simplest effect is *awareness*. Consumers must know that a product or service exists before they can decide to buy it. In the 1980s, when General Motors planned to create a new car, the Saturn, it spent hundreds of millions of dollars to make the public aware of the car's existence. The advertisements began running before a single Saturn had been produced.

Price information plays an important part in advertising. From a business perspective, advertising that features special prices can attract customers to a store. Supermarkets run grocery prices in the local newspaper to bring customers into the store. The supermarket won't make much, if any, money on the advertised specials, but the customer will buy other products that are not on sale. From the customer's perspective, price advertisements save them time. A person who wants to buy a car will not waste time looking at models that are out of his or her price range.

Quality advertising strives to influence the buyer's impression of how good a product or service is. Quality claims can be vague and unsupported, such as "the best burger in town." But quality claims can also have some authority behind them, such as the *Motor Trend* Car of the Year Award. Quality claims can influence the decision to buy, but they will not get consumers to buy a second time if the product turns out not to have the quality that was claimed.

Identity advertising attempts to get a customer to associate a product with a particular person or enjoyable activity. People in beer commercials always enjoy themselves. Only young, healthy people smoke cigarettes in magazine ads. If consumers associate products with pleasant activities and people, they will be more likely to buy them.

How effectively an advertisement achieves its purpose depends on several factors. Media type is among the most important. Price advertising seems to be most effective in print. Print is more permanent, and the listed prices can be cut out and kept. Prices that are broadcast over television and radio have to be remembered or written down, and both of these are inconvenient. Television works well with identity ads because of its visual nature. Influencing young people to mentally connect beer with fun at parties is much easier when the party is shown on television than when it is described in print.

A second important factor in advertising effectiveness concerns the consumer. Not all people can be reached effectively by the same medium. As a result, most advertising campaigns, especially for large companies, use several media. McDonald's, for example, advertises on television, billboards, and public transportation vehicles. Advertising agencies help design plans that incorporate more than one medium to reach a variety of people with a variety of ads.

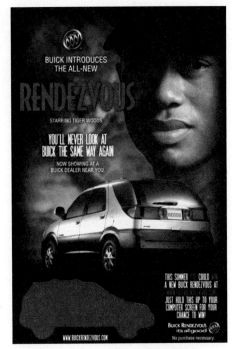

Companies often use advertising to identify a celebrity with their product. In 2001, General Motors connected Tiger Woods with Buick Rendezvous in a cross-media advertising campaign that used 3-D optics online to decode game pieces. The advertising agency distributed game pieces such as this in movie theaters, and players went to a web site to see if they had won anything in the sweepstakes.

SUPPLYING THE DEMAND FOR ADVERTISING

A business that wants to advertise its product or service faces an almost staggering number of advertising forms and advertising outlets. Businesses no longer can depend on just one form of advertising. Companies need to use a mix of media to reach all of their potential customers. This multimedia advertising approach explains why old advertising forms continue to survive as new forms develop.

Table 4.1 shows advertising revenue and proportion of revenues by medium for 2001. In 1988 about $118.4 billion was spent on advertising in the United States. In 2001 the figure was $231 billion.

t a b l e   4 . 1

Advertising Revenues and Proportions, 2001					
Print	REVENUE (BILLIONS OF DOLLARS)	PERCENTAGE OF REVENUE	**Electronic**	REVENUE (BILLIONS OF DOLLARS)	PERCENTAGE OF REVENUE
Daily Newspaper	$44.3	19.2%	Broadcast TV	38.8	16.8
Direct Mail	44.7	19.3	Radio	17.9	7.7
Miscellaneous	39.6	17.1	Cable	15.5	6.7
Yellow Pages	13.6	5.9	Internet	5.8	2.5
Magazines	11.1	4.8	Total Electronic	78.0	33.7
Total Print	153.3	66.3			

Sources: Newspaper Association of America (newspapers), McCann–Erikson, Inc. (all other media). Parts of this table came from the booklet *Facts About Newspapers 2002.* Reprinted with permission of the Newspaper Association of America.

This photo of a billboard illustrates two advertising media. First is Real California Cheese's billboard itself, seen by passersby. Second is their web site, which they hope interested consumers will visit to find out more about their product.

Advertising Support for Media

The growth of mass media during most of the twentieth century was interwoven with a simultaneous growth in advertising. As U.S. economic growth became more dependent on consumer spending, companies sought to reach increasingly larger audiences through their advertising. Media companies rightfully saw advertising as their biggest source of revenue. This gave advertisers more influence over media content than consumers had.

Times have changed, however. In 1984 slightly more than 50.0 percent of all communication industry revenue came from advertising.[27] By 2002 advertising was expected to account for 39.3 percent of all communication revenue. Predictions were that consumers would pay for 31.4 percent, and the remainder of revenue would come from institutions such as business and government. The main reason for the change in the relative contribution of consumers and advertisers is the growth in cable, home video, recorded music, pay-per-view, and online communication. The increasing importance of information in business activities also plays an important role in explaining the changes in media support.

Types of Advertisements
◆ Advertisements can be classified in a number of ways, but the two most common ways of classifying **types of advertisements** are geographic coverage and purpose. *Geographic coverage* is defined as the market in which the advertisements are placed and the advertised product is sold. The *purpose of the ad* reflects the type of influence the advertiser seeks to have over the customer.

k e y   c o n c e p t

Types of Advertisements Advertisements can be classified in several ways. Two common ones include geographic coverage and purpose of ads. Geographic coverage involves national, regional, and local advertising. The purpose of ads includes business ads, public service ads, and political ads.

Geographic Coverage. Traditionally, geographic coverage was divided into national and local. *National advertisements* are ads for products and services that are available throughout the country. *Local advertisements* are ads for companies that serve a much smaller market such as a city or metropolitan area. Typically, national agencies or companies in New York, Chicago, or Los Angeles place national ads in media. Ads for Nintendo, McDonald's, and Coca-Cola are national. Local ads are placed by a company such as a supermarket that has only a local market.

The two types of advertisements are sometimes combined. Burger King, for example, has national TV ads, but the local outlet might run ads in the student newspaper about special prices. Most nationally advertised companies do not own retail outlets; therefore, both local and national ads sometimes promote the same item. The local department store benefits from national Nike ads but also runs its own ads to tell customers when Nike shoes are on sale.

A hybrid form of geographic coverage grew during the 1980s. *Regional advertisements* are local and regional ads that are placed in national media. The USA cable network, for example, might carry ads for a local bookstore. These ads are inserted into predetermined time slots by the local cable company. Regional ads allow local companies the prestige of advertising in national media without the high prices for ads that reach the entire country. *Newsweek* magazine has carried advertisements for Detroit television stations, but only in magazine copies that are distributed in the Detroit area. When the magazine goes to press, space is left for ads that are inserted at the regional printing plants.

Geographic coverage is important because some media serve local businesses better and some serve national businesses better. Newspapers excel as vehicles for local businesses, and television has traditionally been strong for national advertising because of its national audience. But as cable has fragmented the TV audience, many network programs have become less attractive for mass national advertising. As a result, businesses are increasingly using national advertisements targeted to narrower, demographically defined groups of consumers. For example, Lifetime had the highest average ratings for a cable channel during the 2000–2001 season, but its programs and ads were aimed mostly at women.

Geographic coverage also affects the price of advertising. The price that a business pays for an advertisement depends on the number of people who will be exposed to the ad. *Time* magazine charges more for an ad than *Crain's Chicago Business* does. The first is a national publication; the other is a regional publication. A business that sells computers only in Chicago would be foolish to buy a national ad in *Time*. A regional ad in *Time* or an ad in *Crain's* would be more effective and efficient.

Advertisement's Purpose. Although most advertisements promote a product or service, not all do. Advertisements fall into three categories: business ads, public service ads, and political ads.

Business ads try to influence people's attitudes and behaviors toward the products and services a business sells, toward the business itself, or toward an idea that the business supports. Most of these ads try to persuade consumers to buy something, but sometimes a business tries to improve its image through advertising. This often occurs when a company has been involved in a highly publicized incident that might negatively affect its image. Exxon had to rebuild its image after the *Valdez* accident in 1989, in which an Exxon tank spilled millions of gallons of oil in Prince William Sound and damaged the Alaskan coast. Many people saw Exxon as having a callous attitude toward the environment, so the company used advertising to try to change this public perception.

Public service ads promote behaviors and attitudes that are beneficial to society and its members. These ads may be either national or local and usually are the product of donated labor and media time or space. The **Advertising Council** produces the best-known public service ads. The council, which is supported by advertising agencies and the media, was formed during World War II to promote the war effort. It now runs about twenty-five campaigns a year. These campaigns must be in the public interest, timely, noncommercial, nonpartisan, nonsectarian, and nonpolitical.[28] The Ad Council has consistently run campaigns against illegal drug use and in support of such organizations as the United Negro College Fund.

Political ads aim to persuade voters to elect a candidate to political office or to influence the public on legislative issues. These advertisements run at the local, state, and national levels. They incorporate most forms of media but use newspapers, radio, television, and direct mail most heavily. During a presidential election year, more than $1 billion is spent on political ads.

Political advertising receives a lot of attention because it provides a way of increasing voter identification of a candidate. It also gives candidates a way to define the issues during an election. During the 1988 presidential campaign, George Bush's organization ran an advertisement featuring a convicted murderer named Willie Horton. The ad claimed that an early-release program sponsored by his opponent, Massachusetts Governor Michael Dukakis, had allowed Horton to get out of prison and kill again. Many people questioned the truth of the ad, but it was effective in helping to frame the issue of crime during the election campaign.

Mass versus Targeted Ads ✦ As part of advertising planning, companies must decide how large an audience they want to reach. Not every product or service is designed for mass consumption, nor is it available in every geographic location. Advertising the performances of the Dallas Symphony Orchestra during an episode of Comedy Central's *South Park* would be inefficient and ineffective. Most viewers

The Ad Council, funded by advertising agencies and media, creates campaigns that serve the public, such as making people aware of the coalition of environmental organizations called Earth Share.

Advertising Council: Formed to promote the civilian efforts in World War II, the Advertising Council is supported by advertising agencies and media companies. It conducts advertising campaigns in the public interest.

would be too far from Dallas to attend the symphony even if they wanted to, and the audience that watches *South Park* is probably not interested in attending symphony concerts.

key concept

Targeted Advertising Increasingly, advertisements are designed to appeal to a limited group of consumers who can be defined by demographics, geographic location, and psychographics.

Advertisements that target the largest audience possible constitute *mass advertising*. Advertisements that seek to reach a selected audience are classified as **targeted advertising.** Yellow pages serve as mass advertising because every household that has a telephone gets them. Direct mail catalogs from retailers such as Lands' End are targeted advertising because they are mailed to people who are likely to buy clothing through the mail. The most appropriate type of advertising depends on the nature and price of the product or service.

Classifying groups is not enough to produce effective target advertising. Media products have to be available to reach those targeted groups. Magazines, direct mail, and radio are traditional forms of delivering targeted advertising, but the 1980s and 1990s have seen a growth in other possible advertising vehicles. Cable now includes audiences based on geography, demographics, and psychographics.

Who Produces Advertisements?

The nature of jobs in advertising is diverse. Some involve creative writing and art; others consist of selling and buying advertising space and time. Most advertising personnel work either in an advertising agency or in the advertising department of a company. Others work within media advertising departments. Ad agencies try to connect advertising buyers with media organizations. Table 4.2 shows the amount of money billed by the top ten advertising agencies in the United States. The advertising departments within companies may handle most of the same activities as an agency, or they may be small departments that rely heavily on agency services.

The most common services advertising agencies provide include creative production, media buying, research services, merchandising, and advertising planning.[29] *Creative production* includes all the steps in creating advertisements for various media. *Media buyers* place the advertisements in media outlets. *Research* involves determining

table 4.2

2001 Top Ten Advertising Agencies (in millions of dollars)

AGENCY	U.S. GROSS	NON-U.S. GROSS	WORLDWIDE GROSS
McCann–Erickson Worldwide	$1,431.4	$1,600.8	$3,032.2
DDB Needham Worldwide	1,342.1	1,142.0	2,484.1
BBDO Worldwide	974.8	1,358.1	2,332.9
Lowe (The Partnership)	1,212.5	701.0	1,913.5
Euro RSCG Worldwide	755.4	1,050.3	1,805.7
Grey Worldwide	815.5	899.8	1,715.3
J. Walter Thompson Co.	674.3	970.6	1,644.9
Ogilvy & Mather Worldwide	556.3	1,014.0	1,570.3
Young & Rubicam	655.7	863.7	1,519.4
Leo Burnett Co.	529.2	600.2	1,129.4

Source: www.adage.com. Reprinted with permission from www.adage.com and the April 22, 2002, issue of *Advertising Age.* Copyright Crain Communications Inc., 2002.

the effectiveness of advertising. *Merchandise experts* oversee other forms of promotion besides advertising. *Advertising planning* incorporates all of these services.

There are two types of advertising agencies. *Full-service* advertising agencies offer a client all five services just mentioned. A *boutique* agency often specializes in creative services and restricts its activities to a few specialties. A large company, such as a soup manufacturer, would probably use a full-service agency to plan and produce multimedia advertising campaigns. The company's advertising manager would work closely with the agency. A small mail-order company might do most of its work in-house and then contract the creation and production of a catalog to a boutique agency.

Full-service agencies have account teams that serve clients. The account teams provide the basic services previously mentioned. Typically, the account teams are headed by an account executive, who is the agency's contact with the client. The team also includes a media planner, who buys ad space and time; a research director; and creative people, who produce the ads. The creative process involves writing copy and creating illustrations. The copy director oversees the copywriters, and the art director supervises the artists and layout people.

The positions found in an agency team also can be found within the advertising departments of large companies. Larger companies such as department stores often have an in-house ad department because it cuts their expenses and gives them greater control over their advertising. These departments have media buyers and planners as well as creative staff.

TRENDS

Advertising in the twenty-first century faces changes generated by the same trends confronting all media. Technological change, globalization, and the relationship between economic concentration and issues of quality will alter the advertising industry during the next decade. Technological change has created new advertising forms on the Internet, but consumers and businesses have yet to embrace these to the degree they accept more traditional advertising. The trend started in the 1980s and 1990s toward large, concentrated global advertising agencies continued during 2002 but at a slower pace.

Concerns about the impact of advertising on society persist in the new century as well. Advertising has grown even more important in the political process, a fact not welcomed by many politicians and political observers. In addition, ethical issues have been raised by purposeful confusion over whether advertisements are trying to inform or persuade and by the promotion of harmful products.

Infomercials

Concern about ads aimed at children caused Congress to pass the 1990 Children's Television Act, limiting the amount of advertising time in children's television programs. An hour of children's programming may not have more than ten and a half minutes of commercials on weekends and twelve minutes during weekdays. The law did not outlaw programs based on toys and candy. However, if these programs run commercials for the same products that are featured in the show, the shows become program-length commercials and violate the Children's Television Act.

The trend toward global advertising is seen in this Pepsi sponsorship of a marathon in Vietnam.

Efforts to manipulate through advertising are not limited to child audiences. During the 1980s, program-length commercials for a wide range of products from car waxes to exercise machines began to pop up on television stations. These long advertisements are often labeled "infomercials." A company buys time from a station or cable network and controls the content. As cable channels have proliferated, so have infomercials, especially after midnight when it is difficult to sell regular advertising.

These programs most often involve demonstrations of a product and testimonials from people who use, or supposedly use, the product. The Federal Trade Commission oversees the truth of claims made in these programs, but often the claims stop just short of deceptive practices. Even if claims are false, limited resources prevent the FTC from checking all of these commercials.

The format of program-length commercials can affect the credibility viewers give them. During the 1980s, some of the long ads started using a format that made them look like local television news programs. An older man and a younger woman sitting behind a newsroom-style desk might announce a remarkable discovery about how to reduce weight. The program that followed would have **stand-up shots** of people who looked like reporters and a continuation of the news anchor format. The format of these ads was problematic because it confused some people as to whether they were commercials or news programs. This *commercial and information blending* did not become widespread because stations became concerned that selling products with the news format would reduce the credibility of their local news shows. However, these advertisements continue to appear periodically on television. The convergence of media online also raises concern about commercial and information blending. Consumers may not realize that a web site with information about a company's product is designed to persuade and not to provide an objective evaluation of that product.

Online Advertising

Always eager to reach customers, businesses began moving cautiously online during the early 1990s. The caution came from not knowing much about this new medium for reaching customers. In 2000 the amount of such advertising grew to $4.33 billion. Despite this growth, *online advertising* is less than 2 percent of the $443 billion spent annually on advertising in the United States.[30] Although advertising online has grown, the earlier predictions of huge increases in advertising dollars have not held up. Many media managers remain unsure of what role advertising will play online, and some have even questioned the advertising-supported model of the Web. News articles predicting the end of the free Web began to appear during 2002. That year, twenty of Norway's biggest media companies joined to charge visitors to their sites. "We cannot produce content without someone paying for it. It's hard to sell banners and get sponsorship, so the content has to be paid for," said Christian Lind, head of sales and Internet at TV-2.[31] Another article pointed out that some newspapers are beginning to experiment with online subscriptions, but many newspapers remain free. CNN and ABC are charging monthly fees for access to video.[32] Yahoo!'s return to profitability in the second quarter of 2002 was credited to new revenues from fees and other nonadvertising activities. The company reported that 40 percent of its revenues now come from nonadvertising sources.[33] Part of the problem with the free, advertising-supported model of the Web results from consumers' reactions to the advertising. Banner ads, which allow a Web user to click on the ad

stand-up shot: Photographs of active people who appear to be news sources or reporters.

profile

Leo Burnett

As the founder of one of the top advertising firms in the world, Leo Burnett influenced what Americans and others around the world buy.

Burnett was born in a small town in Michigan in 1891 and lived to be seventy-nine. He claimed that his name was supposed to be George, but because of his father's tendency to abbreviate, coupled with bad handwriting, the "Geo" turned out to be "Leo"—and the name stuck.

Burnett's parents owned a small store in Michigan, and his first memory of advertising was seeing the store's name and slogan on the umbrella of its delivery cart. While he was growing up in Michigan, he claimed, "you could hear the corn growing on hot nights." By the time he reached Chicago and opened his advertising agency in 1935, he was forty-four years old.

In contrast to the stereotype of the gregarious advertising man, Burnett was shy. He was also short, slope-shouldered, and had a paunch. The front of his head was bald and freckled, and his lapels were often sprinkled with Marlboro cigarette ashes. His most prominent feature, however, was his lower lip, which became the focal point of his writers' and art directors' attention. The more displeased Burnett was with an idea, the farther out his lip would jut.

To Burnett, the most powerful ideas were nonverbal. Their true meanings were too deep for words, such as the large, playful Tony the Tiger and the strong Marlboro man atop his horse. A successful ad, he said, was one that made an audience respond not with "That is a great ad!" but with "That is a great product!"

For Burnett it was important to find the inherent drama of the product and present it. If no inherent drama could be found, it had to be created. Usually, the creation would be through *borrowed interest*, a concept that allows the drama to come from someone, such as the Lonely Maytag Repairman, or something, such as Morris the cat. Other successes for Burnett included animations such as the Keebler Elves, Charlie the Tuna, and the Jolly Green Giant.

In his sixties, Burnett had an enviable vitality that would not quit. David Ogilvy once said that he turned down Burnett's proposal to merge because Burnett was the only person he knew who worked harder than he did, and "[t]he thought of Leo ringing me in New York at 2 A.M. and asking me to meet him in Chicago for breakfast with some fresh campaign ideas was more than I could bear."

Burnett continued working hard into his seventies, and his loyalty to his clients was unwavering. When he grew faint from low blood sugar, someone ran for a candy bar. "Make sure it's a Nestlé," he cried hoarsely.

Sources: Michael L. Rothschild, *Advertising* (Lexington, MA: D.C. Heath, 1987), p. 217; Simon Broadbent, ed., *The Leo Burnett Book of Advertising* (London: Business Books, 1984), pp. ii and 1–8.

---

to go to the advertiser's web site, had become the dominant form of online advertising by 1999, but few people were using them. Research indicates that only about 0.55 percent of visitors were clicking on them.[34] As a result of disappointment with banners, companies have begun to experiment with a variety of other online ads, especially pop-up ads, which jump on computer screens seemingly from nowhere from a range of sources.

In 2002, some of the largest online news publishers, including the *New York Times* and the *Wall Street Journal*, filed suit against Gator Corporation, an online marketing firm, because of pop-up ads. The complaint centered around the publishers' claim that Gator sells ads that pop up on online delivery sites, obscuring content and even competing with the ads the site owners sell. Gator counters that their software enters a consumer's computer only after the consumer has agreed to view ads in echange for the ability to download a variety of other products such as games and file-sharing programs.[35] The problems confronting the development of online advertising can be overcome. The medium provides for efficient targeting, but the consumer can easily leave the site and delete unwanted ads. The Web is likely to be financed by a variety of revenues, and advertising will contribute to those revenue streams. The key will be finding the types of advertising that are most appropriate for the medium. It may not be advertising in the traditional sense. Perhaps it will encompass **e-commerce,** which takes advantage of the interactivity of the Web.

e-commerce: The selling of goods and services online.

Tracing You to Sell Ads

Many advertisers will not mourn the passing of mass media. The ability to target advertising to people who will likely buy a product makes their advertising more efficient and effective. But how do they know who the targets should be? Before computers and the Internet, collecting information could be expensive and full of error. Now, every time you visit the Internet you are leaving electronic footprints. Opening the door to the Internet to let information in also lets information out.

Companies online have a variety of ways of tracking information about you. Your IP address, which is used to connect with the Internet, can be easily identified as you visit sites or send e-mail. When you download software, the computer that is sending the program can gain access to your hard drive. It can download programs you don't even know about that will allow someone else to run your computer over the Internet. Cookies, text files placed on your computer

while you are visiting a web site, will allow other computers to collect information, and forms you fill out to gain access to sites collect in databases.

The aim of much of this data collection is to target you with advertising for products and services you will probably want to buy. At issue is the loss of your privacy. The data can be sold to anyone once it is collected.

One of the best-known companies to collect Internet information is DoubleClick. Begun in 1996, DoubleClick sells advertising space for web companies. The company collected ad profiles for several years and connected names to web activities. This practice ended in 2002 after a privacy suit was filed in 2000 and after public criticism of the practice.

However, the decision of one company doesn't mean the actions have stopped. KaZaA, a company for sharing files over the Internet, joined with Altnet in 2002 to download a program, without the users'

knowledge, that could distribute advertising and collect information about the user. After the story hit the news, KaZaA changed its policy so that no personally identifiable information would be collected by its partners, such as Altnet.

In many ways, collecting information to target ads toward specific people can serve the consumer as well as the advertiser. It prevents people online from being bothered by ads for products they don't buy. But as always, there is no guarantee that this will happen, and furthermore, consumers are allowing information about their behavior to be controlled by people unknown to them.

Sources: Tom Spring, "KaZaA Sneakware Stirs Inside PCs," IDG News, May 7, 2002, accessed through CNN.com, www.cnn.com; Stefanie Olsen, "DoubleClick Turns Away from Ad Profiles," CNET News, January 8, 2002, news.com.com; Patrick Thibodeau, "DoubleClick Paying $1.8 Million to Settle Privacy Suit," Computerworld, April 1, 2002, computerworld.com.

Worldwide Advertising

During the late 1980s, advertising agencies accelerated the trend to become worldwide organizations through a series of mergers and joint agreements. Advertising agencies that served clients throughout the world had existed previously, but this period saw a boom that reflected the changing world economy. Two important trends pushed agencies toward worldwide status. First, companies have increasingly become transnational corporations. Such a corporation "runs its business and makes its decisions based on all the possible choices in the world, not simply favoring domestic options because they are convenient."[36] U.S. companies such as Coca-Cola, IBM, and Xerox are transnationals, as are companies that are headquartered in other countries, such as Shell Oil, which is a Dutch company. These transnational companies need advertising agencies that can prepare and deliver ad campaigns throughout the world. Using such an agency is more efficient than dealing with a different agency in every country. Ford Motor Company, which also owns Mazda, Volvo, and Jaguar, demonstrated the worldwide reach of advertising in October 1999. It ran a two-minute advertisement about its entire family of cars throughout the world on the same day at 9 P.M. in each time zone. The ad ran on five broadcast networks and thirty-four cable channels in the United States.

A second trend promoting worldwide agencies is the opening of new consumer markets around the world. As Communist governments in Europe and Asia accepted more international trade during the 1980s, Western companies gained access to billions of potential customers. Many markets, such as China, have continued to expand beyond 2000. These new markets, combined with growing television markets around the world, presented transnational corporations with great opportunities to sell more products. But to sell those products, consumers must know that they exist. This is the role that worldwide advertising agencies have come to fill. Today, people on every continent know the round red and white Coca-Cola symbol.

The international approach of advertising is reflected in the research conducted by the agencies. Roper Starch Worldwide, a research company in New York, interviewed 35,000 people in thirty-six countries in the late 1990s and came up with six psychographic groups based on belief systems and behavior that represent consumers around the world.[37] In 2002, McCann–Erickson WorldGroup researched soccer fans in forty countries to discover why they followed the World Cup. The information will prove useful when companies want to advertise during the next World Cup in 2006.

Advertisers and marketers of products such as cigarettes think globally in promoting their lines throughout the world. Even if the demand for cigarettes shrinks in the United States, the worldwide market undoubtedly will remain competitive, and cigarette makers look to expand their markets.

Ethics and Responsibility in Advertising

Dating back to early patent medicine ads more than 150 years ago, advertising has raised issues about the ethics of advertising and whether advertisers were being responsible in their messages. These concerns involve issues of misleading advertising, advertising harmful products, and not telling people that what they are receiving is advertising.

Most television viewers between 1999 and 2001 had heard of Miss Cleo, the psychic. Ads for the card-reading fortune-teller seemed to run almost constantly until seven states and the FTC filed suit against Access Resource Services, the Florida company behind Miss Cleo. The phone service often substituted scripts instead of card readings, but it had more than six million callers and generated as much as $400 million a year.[38]

Although not as blatant as false advertising, the practice of search engines taking money for favorable placement in search results raises ethical issues. Mark Nutritional Inc., makers of Body Solutions weight-loss system, sued AltaVista, Kandoole.com, FindWhat.com, and Overture Services in 2002. Mark Nutritional stated that competing sites would use the term *body solutions* and then pay search engines to place these competing sites higher in the results list than the real Body Solutions site. Part of the problem is that all of these companies except AltaVista are more like advertising sites than search engines, according to Danny Sullivan, a consultant who maintains the Search Engine Watch web site.[39] But the public doesn't know this.

Another area of concern among critics of advertising is the effort to promote dangerous products. Many people thought the 1998 $206 billion settlement between cigarette manufacturers and forty-six states would help reduce cigarette advertising. After all, the cigarette companies banned advertising on billboards and public transportation and curtailed free merchandise with cigarette company logos. However, the cigarette industry spent $9.5 billion on advertising and promotion during 2001, an increase of 16 percent from the year before. Instead of traditional advertising, most of their money is now spent paying store owners for prime shelf space and on buy-one-get-one-free types of promotions.[40] Despite best efforts to regulate unethical and irresponsible advertising, companies who want to take advantage of consumers often find a way around the regulations or find new ways to trick consumers. Even today buyers need to continue to be aware of potential manipulation by advertising.

summary

- Advertising serves a basic economic function in the United States. It allows sellers and buyers of goods and services to find one another in the marketplace.
- Advertising sometimes aims at mass audiences and other times concentrates on segmented audiences.
- Segmented audiences can be classified by demographics, psychographics, and geography.
- Advertisements can be classified by the geographic area they cover, the purpose of the ads, and the effect the ads have on consumers of media.
- Most advertising plans incorporate more than one type of medium.
- Cable, home video, and other new technologies compete for advertising that was supported in the past by traditional mass media.
- Not all of advertising's effects on society are positive. Some advertisers attempt to manipulate audiences to buy certain products and services.

This is especially problematic with very young television viewers.

- Advertisers sometimes influence the news coverage of media organizations with advertising boycotts and informal pressure that affects the contents of stories that are run.
- Most advertising jobs are found in advertising agencies or in the advertising departments of large companies including media organizations.
- Political advertising can become problematic when it emphasizes emotion or allows contributors to gain influence by donating money.
- Online advertising will likely include more marketing elements than traditional mass media.
- Online advertising will increase, but there is some doubt that it will be sufficient to keep web content free to users.
- Advertising agencies have become both concentrated and global in nature.

navigating the web | Advertising on the Web

More and more, advertising is seen on the World Wide Web. Many sites have advertising, but information about advertising is not plentiful. The following list presents a range of sites related to advertising.

American Association of Advertising Agencies
www.aaaa.org
The AAAA site is maintained by a national trade organization for ad agencies. The association promotes integrity and ethics in advertising. The site

contains information about the organization and its goals.

Scarborough Research
www.scarborough.com
This market research organization conducts research for media and advertisers. The site contains information about the services it offers.

Advertising Age
www.adage.com
Advertising Age is the dominant trade magazine for advertising. It contains a wide range of information about

media that carry advertising. Its web site is the online version of the print magazine.

Yahoo!
www.yahoo.com
Yahoo! carries the most advertising of any site on the Web. It also provides information.

Advertising Online
www.advertising-online.org
This site carries some news about the advertising industry and has an extensive collection of links to advertising, research, and marketing organizations.

questions for review

1. What is the difference between advertising and news?
2. What is the difference between online advertising and e-commerce?
3. What factors contributed to the development of mass advertising?
4. Why did some publications begin to refuse patent medicine advertising?
5. Why are advertisers concerned about geographic coverage?
6. What are the primary tasks of an advertising agency?

issues to think about

1. What is the economic role of advertising in a free-market society?
2. How does cultural change affect advertising?
3. What impact did the arrival of broadcasting have on advertising?
4. How does advertising have both a negative and a positive effect on journalism?
5. Does advertising coerce people into buying things they do not need?
6. What are the implications of heavy political advertising on television?
7. How will advertising find its place on the Internet?

suggested readings

Aronson, Brad, et al. *Advertising on the Internet,* 2nd ed. (New York: John Wiley & Son, 1999).

Ewen, Stuart. *Captains of Consciousness: Advertising and the Social Roots of Consumer Culture* (New York: McGraw-Hill, 1976).

Heath, Robert. *The Hidden Power of Advertising* (Oxfordshire, England: World Advertising Research Center, 2001).

Marchand, Roland. *Advertising the American Dream* (Berkeley: University of California Press, 1989).

O'Guinn, Thomas, et al. *Advertising and Integrated Brand Promotion* (Mason, OH: South-Western Publishing, 2002).

Schudson, Michael. *Advertising: The Uneasy Persuasion* (New York: Basic Books, 1984).

Twitchell, James B. *Adcult USA: The Triumph of Advertising in American Culture* (New York: Columbia University Press, 1997).

Books

Maxwell Perkins, in 1919, put his career on the line to persuade his superiors to sign F. Scott Fitzgerald to a contract for his first novel, *This Side of Paradise.* In 1926, Perkins had to do a repeat performance to get Ernest Hemingway (shown here) published. Charles Scribner, head of the publishing house, was afraid that *The Sun Also Rises* was just another dirty book and that publishing it would destroy the reputation of his quite respectable publishing house.[1] Both Fitzgerald and Hemingway, of course, became classic writers of the 1920s generation and are still read by high school and college students as a part of their literary education.

Since merchants first began to sell books to the general public, critics have wondered whether the desire for profit would overcome good judgment. But definitions of quality and a publisher's ability to discern quality have always been elusive. Publishing *The Sun Also Rises* may have seemed like pandering to the popular taste at the time, but it resulted in the preservation of an enduring classic. It was an economic success for the publisher, and despite its enduring quality, some might still argue that it's nothing but a dirty book. On those grounds, people have even urged that the book be banned, that political control be exerted.

Charles Scribner's concern reflected more than the caution of a respectable man. It reflected a continuing publishing dilemma. That dilemma includes the following issues:

◆ In a market system driven by popular acclaim, is there a relationship between quality and profit?

◆ Who defines quality? Are literary elites in a better position than the general public to define quality? Is there a relationship between quality and popular acclaim?

◆ How do books help transmit the heritage of a society?

◆ What are the social and economic impacts of publishing decisions?

◆ What is the role of books in creating stories? How do books function as the basis for electronic media content?

GROWTH OF LITERARY CULTURE

In nearly all cultures, books have been viewed both as the transmitters of knowledge and as the tools of radicals. During medieval times, the reproduction of books was restricted by the Catholic Church for the most part to monasteries, where scribes hand-copied treasured manuscript books that then made up the important libraries of Europe. In that *scribal culture*, copying books was an art, which we can appreciate when we look at rare books on exhibit in museums. Scholars often traveled across Europe to the famous libraries to have access to knowledge. Such scarce books rarely, if ever, were owned by individuals, and students relied on teachers to read books to them, producing the "lecture" system of education that is still prevalent in U.S. and European colleges and universities. When your professor lectures to the class, he or she is reenacting an ancient tradition born of necessity.

key concept

Scribal Culture In the Middle Ages, before the invention of the printing press, written material was reproduced almost exclusively by monks who served as scribes, or copyists. As the sole repository of books, the medieval church was able to control what information reached the population.

With the advent of the printing revolution in the mid-1400s as a result of Gutenberg's cast-metal movable type, books became objects to be printed and sold. They were no longer confined to libraries but become the domain of public culture. Soon books, printed in lots of 200 to 1,000 copies, circulated among the wealthy classes. The production of books opened the way for printer–merchants, who published books and searched for new markets for their products. The Bible, soon printed in English as well as in Latin, circulated freely. No longer did the educated classes depend on the authorities to interpret the word of God; they now could develop their own interpretations. The circulation of books threatened the power of church and state because knowledge, a powerful tool and weapon, was accessible to anyone who could read. In European towns, the printer's shop became a meeting place and educational center. As the British settled the North American colonies, bookshops there also became important cultural centers.

Because of the perceived power of books, nearly all governments and societies at one time or another have sought to restrict the printing or distribution of books. From the early 1500s until the end of the 1600s, printing in England was strictly controlled

Books *in Your Life*

Judging Their Quality

You be the judge. If you're familiar with any of these books, give them a couple of letter grades: A, B, C, D, F. Judge their quality and their popularity according to how you think most of your friends would rate them. Think about whether quality and popularity can be combined in the same package.

As you read this chapter, you will find these books mentioned in connection with important issues for the book industry, including the apparent dilemma of quality versus popularity. Do you think quality and popularity are mutually exclusive?

BOOK TITLE	QUALITY RATING	POPULARITY RATING
Harry Potter and the Sorcerer's Stone (J. K. Rowling)		
A Clear and Present Danger (Tom Clancy)		
Little Women (Louisa May Alcott)		
Lord of the Rings (Tolkien)		
Paradise (Toni Morrison)		
For Whom the Bell Tolls (Ernest Hemingway)		
A Day Late and a Dollar Short (Terry McMillan)		

by the monarchy. In 1529, Henry VIII issued a list of prohibited books and imposed a system of **prior restraint** that required printers to have a license before printing. However, in spite of the severe punishments that were handed down to those who printed outside the system, by the mid-sixteenth century in England, nearly one-third of all books were printed outside the official channels. In 1695 the British Parliament allowed the licensing system to expire, and newspapers and books flourished throughout London and the provincial towns.[2]

BOOKS IN AMERICAN LIFE

As the printing business expanded into the provinces in Britain, it also expanded in the British colonies in America. Information was a highly prized commodity in British America, and colonists bought books to read for pleasure as well as to maintain their connections to the British homeland. Because books were expensive, the industry at first appealed to elite sensibilities and to those who had extra money and leisure time. However, throughout the nineteenth and twentieth centuries, the book industry was democratized. Today, books are produced cheaply and quickly and appeal to all classes of people.

Throughout the seventeenth century, almost all books in the colonies were imported from Europe, although a few religious books and histories were published in Cambridge, Massachusetts. Later, as colonists sought more books, printers such as Benjamin Franklin imported books for sale and helped to establish public libraries. Franklin and a group of his Philadelphia friends contributed forty pounds in British sterling to start the Library Company in Philadelphia in 1731 to import books for reading and discussion. The colonists imported mostly religious books, but they also asked for professional books to expand their knowledge of law, medicine, and navigation. Popular literature also was imported and then published in the colonies. Such material included cheap

prior restraint: Restricting publication before the fact rather than banning material or punishing an individual after the material is already printed.

The first national best-seller, *Uncle Tom's Cabin,* was a sentimental depiction of the evils of slavery and intensified the national discussion about slavery.

forerunners to paperbacks, sixteen- to thirty-two-page pamphlets known as **chapbooks,** which included tales of pirates and highway robbers. Cookbooks, household manuals, fortune-telling books, and even primitive weather forecasts also were published separately or were included in popular almanacs.

Books posed a problem when it came to circulation. They were bulky and expensive to distribute, and postage rates did not favor distribution through the mail. Before the Civil War, many books were circulated by book peddlers, who traveled from town to town with a horse and cart, selling books or exchanging stock with other dealers. Romantic novels, as well as the traditional religious, professional, and historical books, were sold throughout the rapidly expanding United States. The industry was well enough developed by the mid-1850s to play an important role in social movements and in creating a popular culture.

Books and Social Change

Harriet Beecher Stowe propelled the issue of slavery into the popular culture of the 1850s and in the process created the first mass-market best-seller in the American book business. She wrote *Uncle Tom's Cabin,* a novel that depicts the horrors of slavery, which was published in book form about two weeks before the last installment appeared in **serialized** form in the magazine *National Era.* Within three weeks, 20,000 copies of the book had been sold, and by January 1853 that number had grown to 200,000. Stowe received more than $10,000 in royalties on three months' worth of sales of *Uncle Tom's Cabin.* No American or European author had made so much money from a single book. Students at the University of Virginia publicly burned the book, and peddlers were sometimes driven from southern towns as they attempted to distribute it.[3]

The expansion of the book publishing industry provided outlets for other antislavery voices as well. Frederick Douglass, a slave born of a white father and a black mother, escaped from slavery and became one of the principal lecturers for the Massachusetts Antislavery Society. He first wrote for newspapers, but in 1845, when he was only twenty-seven years old, he wrote an autobiography, *Narrative of the Life of Frederick Douglass.* Between stints as a newspaper editor, he wrote *My Bondage and My Freedom* (1855) and then took his message abroad. Douglass's voice was one of only a few black voices that found its way to the pages of the published book; his work represented a nineteenth-century practice of authors writing and updating their life stories while they were still alive. After the Civil War, Douglass continued to fight for black voting rights, urban development, social justice, and women's rights.[4]

key concept

Democratization of Knowledge As books became more accessible in the 1800s, knowledge spread widely among the middle and lower classes, creating an increasingly democratic reading public. Wide distribution of books depended on cheap postal rates, inexpensive book production, and the portrayal of various classes of people in fictional works.

chapbooks: Cheaply printed paperback books produced during the 1700s.

serialized book: A book printed in parts in a magazine or newspaper over a certain period of time.

Paperbacks and Popular Culture ✦ The development of the paperback book industry signaled to society that books were no longer for elites only and that the middle and lower classes would read popular fiction. For many years, books had belonged to the elites, and access to "refined" and "socially respectable" forms of reading reinforced elite values. The development of inexpensive paperbacks created the perception of pandering to popular taste and appealing to those who could be entertained by formulaic fiction. Accessibility to reading material helped to expand the middle class, but it also challenged elite social control. The result was a *democratization of knowledge,* or expansion of information to a wide group of individuals.

cultural impact

Bits about Banned Books

Books—even those we consider to be classics—have been banned at various times, in various places, and for a variety of reasons. Consider these historical vignettes:

- In Mark Twain's lifetime, his books *Tom Sawyer* and *Huckleberry Finn* were banned from the library in Concord, Massachusetts, home of Henry Thoreau. In more recent times, some high schools have banned *Huckleberry Finn*—or parents have demanded that it be dropped from reading lists—because it is considered to be racist. Some of the debate surrounds the use of the word *nigger*, which also got *Uncle Tom's Cabin* challenged in Illinois.

- In 1701, John Locke's philosophical *Essay Concerning Human Understanding* was expressly forbidden to be taught at Oxford University.

- Thomas Paine, eloquent writer who supported the American Revolution, fell on hard times in England when he was indicted for treason in 1702 for his work *The Rights of Man,* which defended the French Revolution. Several English publishers were also prosecuted for printing Paine's *Age of Reason,* in which he argued for Deism against Christianity and Atheism.

- Shakespeare's works have been banned in various places. In Michigan one high school

excluded *The Merchant of Venice* because of its treatment of the Jewish character Shylock. Savannah, Georgia, high school students in 1999 had to obtain permission slips before they could read *Hamlet, Macbeth, or King Lear.* The school board had eliminated the books from class reading lists because they contained "adult language" and references to sex and violence. Many parents and students protested the policy.

Source: The Online Books Page, http://onlinebooks.library.upenn.edu/banned-books.html, accessed on October 18, 2002.

Economic and political conditions fueled the development of paperbacks. First distributed before the Civil War, paperbacks benefited from the less expensive printing technology associated with newspapers and from a lack of government regulation. Because the U.S. government refused to recognize foreign **copyrights,** books from other countries could be cheaply reproduced as paperbacks.

Further, newspapers printed cheap editions of French and English novels that masqueraded as newspapers so they could be distributed by newsboys and sold in the mail using inexpensive newspaper rates. Later in the nineteenth century, publishers printed books that resembled pamphlets and tried to distribute them as magazines. The practice ended in 1901 when the postmaster general declared that book publishers could not use second-class mailing rates under any conditions. Publishers took their case to court but ultimately lost. By 1914, *book distribution* finally gained a favorable mailing status. The move laid the groundwork for the development of book clubs in the 1920s, which promoted popular consumption of best-sellers as well as histories and biographies. Publishers sold hardback books through the clubs, successfully competing with the paperback industry.

Popular Paperback Formats ◆
The growth of the paperback industry stirred the debate over *quality versus quantity,* and in 1884 *Publishers Weekly* reported, "In the rage for cheapness, we have sacrificed everything for slop, and a dainty bit of bookmaking is like a jewel in the swine's snout."[5]

key concepts

Book Distribution The ability to produce and distribute more books to more people depended on publishers' ability to make books known and physically available to potential readers. Wealthy social elites tended to favor limiting wide distribution and opposed low postal rates for books. However, cheap postage and improved marketing techniques eventually made books accessible to large numbers of readers.

Quality versus Quantity Book publishers traditionally have faced an apparent dilemma: Must they choose between publishing high-quality material or publishing to maximize their profitability? Different publishers have responded to this dilemma in different ways. Some have found that they can make a profit by producing work of high literary quality; others choose to produce work that appeals to more stereotyped and fleeting tastes.

copyright: A law that protects authors, playwrights, composers, and others who construct original works and keeps others from reproducing their work without permission.

The availability of dime novels expanded reading for middle- and working-class people. Heroic tales appealed to men and women.

During the Civil War, publishers encouraged inexpensive, relatively short fiction that became known as the **dime novel;** it was a form well suited to popular taste. Soldiers in the field wanted to fill their time, and reading provided portable entertainment. Between 1860 and 1861 alone The Beadle Brothers sold four million copies of formulaic pocket-size novels written with specific plots focusing on romance and violence similar to the plots of television entertainment or the romance novels of today.

Paperback stories reflected men and women in factories and fictionalized situations they might encounter in that new world of work. The stories were produced through what writers often called the **fiction factory,** in which publishers dictated the story lines, characters, plots, and sometimes specific scenes. The stories were aimed at the working class: mechanics, farmers, traveling salesmen, shop and factory workers, secretaries, and domestic servants. The story lines included traditional, heroic war and frontier stories, as well as tales of outlaws, detectives, male factory operatives, and young women who worked in the mills. Religious themes declined, but the virtue of women remained a hot topic. "Fiction that heroized women outside the domestic sphere," wrote Christine Bold, "offered working-class women some kind of accommodation and justification, some means of negotiating the transition from private to public."[6]

New York publishing houses promoted the popular **Horatio Alger** rags-to-riches novels of individual achievement, which soon gave way to adventures of athletes and western heroes. Science fiction also gained readership, attesting to the development of technology.

Book Publishing Enters the Modern Era

Establishing the book industry in the modern era was tied directly to the solution of the distribution issues that had stymied the industry since its beginning. Once books gained favorable postal rates, the industry boomed. The founding of book clubs—the Book-of-the-Month Club in 1926 and the Literary Guild in 1927—allowed publishers to reach a national but targeted group of readers through direct-mail promotion techniques. Such distribution opened the markets for an astounding array of new titles. Publishing dollars rose steadily and declined only during the early 1930s as a result of the worldwide financial depression.

After World War II, book publishing was characterized by specialization. Publishers significantly increased the number of scientific and technical books they published and shifted emphasis to subjects that emerged from war-time trends. Themes reflected the struggle to maintain individualistic, small-town American values while taking advantage of new technology. Americans were ready to move forward technologically. Popular subjects included science fiction, aeronautics and aircraft manufacture, automotive construction and maintenance, radio, television, navigation, and radar. Books that probed the human personality, including those in the areas of psychology, psychiatry, and psychoanalysis, flourished. "How-to" books in home construction, furniture design, and interior decoration catered to those faced with housing shortages or lack of skilled labor, as well as to people interested in manual craftsmanship.

Expansion of secondary schools and the creation of the GI Bill, which financed higher-education programs for returning GIs, created a demand for educational texts. College enrollment increased from 1 million in 1940 to 12 million in 1960. A variety of federal legislation packages created programs that expanded libraries, both in and out of schools, thereby creating an even larger demand for books. Most of the major book publishers developed extensive educational divisions.

TODAY'S MARKET STRUCTURE

The major issues in book publishing—quantity, profits, and quality—are debated today, even as the market structure changes. Although critics lament that nobody in the United States reads anymore, the book publishing industry thrives. Book sales in-

dime novel: Cheap, paperback fiction produced in the mid-nineteenth century.

fiction factory: Late nineteenth-century publishing of formulaic books, in which publishers dictated story lines.

Horatio Alger story: This story began as a real account of how Horatio Alger worked his way up the social and economic ladder, but soon developed into a term to represent the glorification of individualism in American life.

creased in 2002 to $26 billion, a 5.5 percent increase over 2001. Overall, trade sales rose 8.8 percent, with sales of $6.93 billion. Adult trade hardbound sales rose 11.8 percent ($2.94 billion), whereas paperbound sales rose 12.1 percent ($2.16 billion). Juvenile hardbound sales were up 3.1 percent ($957.2 million); however, paperbound sales were down a slight 1.3 percent with sales of $876.3 million.[7]

For the third year in a row, spending on juvenile books outpaced other categories, growing 14.5 percent in 2000. Juvenile books are expected to account for 19.1 percent of all consumer book spending in 2001. The publication of the Harry Potter books, written by J. K. Rowling and published by Scholastic, gave the children's category a huge boost. The three Potter titles published in 1999 sold more than 10 million copies in hardcover and another 3.2 million in paperback. The titles also attracted more boys to reading, which delighted publishers, who have difficulty selecting titles for boys.[8] Book publishers are fully aware that their market is narrow. The biggest audience of literature includes people under age twenty-five, who are probably spurred by the requirements of college professors, and people over sixty-five, who buy the most popular fiction. Moreover, a vast majority of book buyers are white. In a nation in which the minority population is growing faster than the majority, subsequent generations of booksellers will need to target new audiences if they are to continue to experience market growth.

Media Conglomerates in the Book Business

Book publishing has undergone radical economic and structural changes since World War II. During the 1940s and 1950s, publishing was almost a cottage industry; as John Baker wrote, it was "a comparatively small business producing a comparatively limited number of books for a cozily elite readership whose access to bookstores was limited by geography."[9] Like many other companies, small, independent book publishers were swallowed up by conglomerates, although a variety of small, new firms still are being created today. The large inventories needed after World War II to supply increasing demand required large capital investments. Capital came from a variety of sources, including **public investment**; books, like newspapers, went public. Magazine publishers and motion picture magnates plowed some of their profits into the book industry; electronic companies, in anticipation of the computer revolution, also invested. Ownership went international. By 1992, five of America's largest book publishers were foreign owned.[10] Even more significant, a few publishing houses dominated the industry. In 2001, five conglomerates—Random House, Simon & Schuster, Penguin-Putnam, HarperCollins, and Time Warner—accounted for about 86 percent of the hardcover books produced. Table 5.1 indicates the power of the big houses.

public investment: The buying of stock in a company by the general public.

table 5.1

Ranking the Big Publishing Houses, 2002		
PUBLISHER	**NUMBER OF HARDCOVER TITLES**	**WEEKS ON BEST-SELLER LIST IN 2002**
Random House	64	385
Penguin Putnam Inc.	41	228
Simon & Schuster	29	199
Time Warner	30	195
HarperCollins	22	177

Source: *Publishers Weekly*, January 15, 2003, http://publishersweekly.reviewsnews.com.

Mid-1400s. Gutenberg invents movable metal type.

1529. Henry VIII issues list of banned books.

Early 1700s. English Crown reduces control of presses.

1770–1780s. Books and pamphlets promote revolution.

1845. Frederick Douglass writes autobiography.

1850s. *Uncle Tom's Cabin* becomes world best-seller.

1860s. Dime novels and paperbacks flourish.

1890s. Rise of popular formula fiction

1914. Cheaper mail rates for books

1920s. Influential book editors, such as Max Perkins, emerge.

1926. Book clubs are founded.

1930s. *Gone with the Wind* becomes worldwide best-seller.

1400–1700	1800	1860	1880	1900	1920	1930

1620. Pilgrims land at Plymouth Rock.

1690. *Publick Occurrences* is published in Boston.

1741. First magazine is published in America.

1776–1783. American Revolution

1830s. The penny press becomes the first truly mass medium in the United States.

1861–1865. American Civil War

1892. Thomas Edison's lab develops the kinetoscope.

1914–1918. World War I

1915. *The Birth of a Nation* marks the start of the modern movie industry.

1920. KDKA in Pittsburgh gets the first commercial radio license.

1930s. The Great Depression

1939. TV is demonstrated at the New York World's Fair.

1939–1945. World War II

key concept

Media Consolidation From the 1960s onward, books, movies, and other media products have increasingly become linked as part of the process of consolidation—the merging and combining of diverse companies under the same ownership. A few large corporations now control many publishers, film studios, and other media outlets. Although the consolidated companies may produce more books and movies, limited ownership of media may restrict the types of information transmitted to the public.

The Simon & Schuster story reveals what *media consolidation* has meant to the industry. Begun in the 1920s, Simon & Schuster developed a solid reputation as a publisher of scholarly, scientific, and artistic books that appealed to popular taste. In 1944, the Chicago department store magnate Marshall Field III bought a substantial interest in the company and simultaneously invested in Pocket Books, a paperback publisher. In 1966, Simon & Schuster acquired Pocket Books, and in 1976, both companies were brought under the Gulf + Western umbrella, which later became Paramount Communications. In 1983, Simon & Schuster acquired Allyn and Bacon; in 1984, it acquired the venerable publishing firm of Prentice-Hall; and in 1991, it acquired Macmillan Computer Publishing. Then in 1993, Simon & Schuster, under the umbrella of Paramount, acquired Macmillan, a publishing firm with English origins dating to 1843.

In February and March of 1994, Viacom, Inc., and QVC Network, Inc., battled for control of Paramount. Viacom won by bidding more than $10 billion. The pur-

1941–1945. World War II boosts book sales in the United States.

1950s. Publishing houses specialize.

1970s. Book company mergers increase.

1970s. Movie tie-ins and paperback rights begin to drive the book industry.

1980s. Books become part of multimedia packages.

1980s. Foreign ownership of book companies grows.

1990s. Book superstores dominate distribution, and Big Five conglomerates dominate publishing.

2000s. Selling books through web sites grows.

2001. Expansion of e-books.

1940	1950	1960	1970	1980	1990	2000

1949. First commercial electronic computer is produced.

Early 1950s. Rock 'n' roll begins.

1969. First person lands on the moon.

1970s. VCR is developed.

1989–1991. Cold War ends and the USSR is dissolved.

Late 1980s. National Science Foundation creates the basis of the Internet.

1996. Telecommunications Act

2000. Presidential election nearly tied.

2001. Terrorist attacks on New York and Washington, D.C.

chase affected all media industries, not just publishing. In addition to its massive publishing holdings, Paramount also owned Paramount Pictures and a vast movie library, television studios, a theme park division, the New York Knicks National Basketball Association team, and the New York Rangers of the National Hockey League. Viacom also has many other holdings, including MTV, VH-1, and the Nickelodeon networks. In 1994, as a unit, Viacom and Paramount owned twelve television stations, fourteen radio stations, Showtime, the Movie Channel, syndicated reruns such as *Cheers*, and 3,790 films. They controlled 1,927 movie screens, 3,500 home video stores, and 507 music stores.[11] But the story doesn't end here. In November 1998, Viacom sold Simon & Schuster's Education, Reference, Business, and Professional divisions to Pearson Education, a British firm, for $4.6 billion.

Conglomeration and Media Convergence

Concentration has advantages and disadvantages. Book publishing is a risky business; only 20 to 40 percent of books published make a profit. Therefore, concentration allows for greater profit by producing fewer books in large quantities. However,

Toni Morrison

Toni Morrison has brought into the best-seller mainstream a number of novels about African American life in the United States. When she was named the Nobel Laureate in Literature in 1993, it was said that through her novels she had "characterized by visionary force and poetic import . . . an essential aspect of American reality."

Morrison was born Chloe Anthony Wofford in 1931 in Lorain, Ohio, where she graduated with honors from high school; she received a B. A. degree from Howard University in English, then her master's from Cornell. In the late 1950s Morrison taught at Texas Southern University in Houston before returning to teach at Howard. At Howard she became friends with a number of individuals active in civil rights. One of her students was Stokely Carmichael, who became a leader of the Student Nonviolent Coordinating Committee.

Morrison began writing after she moved to Syracuse, New York, as an associate editor in a textbook subsidiary of Random House. She moved in 1967 to New York and became a senior editor at Random House. In 1970 she published her first novel, *The Bluest Eye,* to great critical acclaim but with little financial success. In 1973 her second novel, *Sula,* became an alternate selection of the Book-of-the-Month Club. Excerpts were published in *Redbook* magazine, and *Sula* was nominated for the 1975 National Book Award for fiction. While a visiting lecturer at Yale University, she published a third novel, *Song of Solomon,* in 1977. It won the National Book Critic's Circle Award and the American Academy and Institute of Arts and Letters Award. In 1988 *Beloved*

won the Pulitzer Prize for fiction. And in 1993, she received the Nobel Prize in Literature.

Toni Morrison recently has won praise for *Paradise,* her seventh novel, which is a story about an Oklahoma convent that is assaulted by a group of men from a nearby Oklahoma town. She now teaches fiction writing at Princeton University.

In an interview in *Salon,* Morrison said that critics have become more intelligent in their approaches over the years. "There was a time when my books, as well as everybody else's books, were viewed as sociological revelations. Is this the best view of the black family, or not? I remember once, in the *New Yorker,* being reviewed, I think it was *Beloved,* and the reviewer began the review and spent a lot of time talking about Bill Cosby's television show—the kind of black family to be compared with the family in *Beloved.* It was so revolting. And that notion—once I was reviewed in the *New York Review of Books,* with two other black writers. The three of us, who don't write anything alike, were lumped together by color, and then the reviewer ended by deciding which of the three books was the best. And she chose one, which could have been [the best], but the reason it was the best was because it was more like "real" black people. That's really discouraging. So if you have that kind of reduction to the absurd, you just have to keep on trying."

Sources: "Distinguished Women of Past and Present," www.netsrq.com/~dbois/morrison.html; Zia Jaffrey, Interview with Morrison, *Salon,* www.salonmagazine.com/books/int/1998/02/cov_si_02int.html, January 27, 2000.

---

it also tends to contribute toward homogenization. If one type of book is successful, publishers look for a similar book to appeal to the same broad audience. This in turn can negatively affect the marketplace of ideas because fewer ideas will be available for discussion. The building of **conglomerates** has resulted in the production of packages in which books, movies, television programs, and other products are viewed as parts of the same media package.

conglomerates: Large companies formed by consolidating two or more small companies.

trade book: Most mass marketed books sold at bookstores or through book clubs. Excludes textbooks.

textbooks: Books used for elementary school, middle school, high school, and college classroom work.

AUDIENCE DEMAND IN BOOK PUBLISHING MARKETS

The market can be divided by types of publishing houses as well as by types of books. Publishing houses can be further divided by size. Large publishers often have several divisions and publish different types of books within each division. A large house such as Pearson Education, for example, may have a **trade book** division as well as a **textbook** division. Trade publications, or books published for general distribution, include (1) hardcover books, (2) quality paperbacks, and (3) mass market paperbacks. Textbook divisions include (1) college textbooks, (2) high school textbooks, and (3) elementary school textbooks. In addition, some **specialized publishers** may produce a particular type of book, such as children's books, religious books, and professional books. Scholarly books occasionally are published by large houses, but they are more commonly the province of university presses. **Niche publishers** target tiny specialized audiences such as antique collectors. Publishers strive to supply the demand within a well-defined market.

Financing and Convergence

Books traditionally have relied little on advertising for financial support; rather, they have been financed by individuals, such as by those of us who buy books. Increasingly, as the audience demands varied products in addition to a book, the industry is supplying the content for packages that include several media. Movie rights, television specials, and other related products often boost the proceeds for a publisher and an author while supplying audience demand.

When *Titanic* won eleven Oscars in 1998, at least thirty new and backlist titles related to the disaster hit the best-seller lists. Children's books such as *Voyage on the Great Titanic,* as well as older accounts of the disaster, suddenly became popular.[12] Such packaging represents one type of media convergence adding to the blurring of definitions between media—in this case, between books and films. During 1996, Oprah Winfrey became a new force in the book industry. Oprah began a reading club for her television program, and the selection of a book for Oprah's show pushed it to the top of the best-seller lists. The first book selected for the reading club was *The Deep End of the Ocean* by Jacquelyn Mitchard. It went from 100,000 copies in print to 640,000 within weeks. This example shows the power of celebrity, but it also illustrates a potential new source of demand for books. In 1998, Oprah's show helped Toni Morrison's *Paradise* and Wally Lamb's *I Know This Much Is True* climb to the top of the sales charts. In an industry in which 30,000 copies represents a big sell, Oprah's choices often sold one million copies. Oprah often chose books that spoke about how individuals overcame adversity, and most of her books were written by women.

In April 2002, Oprah announced the end of the club, saying that she was finding it harder to find a new book every week that she could be passionate about. However, Oprah's magic was waning, ratings for the book club shows were down, and some speculated that the loss of popularity was a bigger factor than Oprah's lack of passion for books. Some protested. "For her to say that she can't find enough books to be passionate about is insulting, because there are so many wonderful books out there yet to be discovered," said Nora Rawlinson of *Publishers Weekly.*[13]

Electronic Publishing

Because the book industry deals with nonstandard formats and sometimes small print runs, it was difficult for publishers to justify early investments in page-making software. Today, however, the use of computerized artwork, cover designs, and promotional pieces is standard. Skill, or at least familiarity, with computerized technology is rapidly becoming a requirement for entry-level professionals who must use technology-related tools such as specialized graphics and database software. One result of the new technology has been more streamlined production, which results in the publication of "instant books" such as the *Starr Report,* a publication of Kenneth Starr's investigation into the relationship between former President Bill Clinton and Monica Lewinsky.

Books on Disk ◆ Books on disk take various forms, including reproduction of books in print as well as enhancements for print volumes. CD-ROM also is used for the production of customized textbooks, in which professors might choose particular passages and articles to be reproduced for their students in one newly created text.

specialized publishers: Publishing houses that produce a particular type of book, such as religious or children's books.

niche publishers: Small publishing houses that serve very narrowly defined markets.

The Chicago Public Library is trying to capture the video game generation by experimenting with hand-held computers capable of storing one hundred books in memory.

One of the reasons that CD-ROMs and electronic books (e-books) are better marketed as enhancements is because print remains a relatively cheap, popular, portable, and accessible medium. It is hard to envision leisurely reading a popular novel on a computer screen while sitting in a lounge chair at the beach. However, some small e-book readers have made portability a positive factor for many people who travel, and increasingly books are available for downloading on small computer devices similar to palm pilots or other personal organizers.

Audiobooks ✦ Audiobooks, which began as cassette tapes, now take more sophisticated forms. At least two publishers are selling books in MP3-CD format, in addition to cassette and CD. An MP3-CD has the advantage of holding up to twelve hours of audio, enabling publishers to fit an unabridged title on a single disk. The disks can be played on an MP3-CD player, as well as on most computers and laptops. "Because we can fit up to twelve hours on one CD, audiobooks in this format cost much less to duplicate and package than cassette editions," said Delia White, owner of The Reader's Chair, a publisher of audiobooks. "Consequently, we are able to offer them at very reasonable prices. In this format, listeners can now own these stellar performances for about the same price as the hardcover."

MP3-CDs offer other advantages as well. "MP3 audio has a wider frequency range than cassettes do," said White. "Bookmarking is easy, as each audiobook is divided into scenes—the way the author intended. Users can navigate through their audiobooks with just a click of a mouse or press of a button." The publisher takes advantage of convergence as well, selling MP3 players on its web site, www.readerschair.com.[14]

Market Dimensions of a Best-Seller

By the end of May 2002, the Harry Potter books had sold over 164 million copies worldwide. In the United Kingdom alone, where Bloomsbury published the Scottish author's work, the books won numerous prizes, including three Smarties Gold Awards, two Children's Book Awards, two British Book Awards for Children's Book of the Year in 1997 and 1998, the Young Telegraph Paperback of the Year Award in 1998, and the Whitbread Children's Book of the Year in 1999. Scholastic, Rowling's U.S.-based publisher, reports that over 70 million copies have sold in the United States alone.

The Harry Potter stories chronicle the life of a young wizard and his band of cohorts at the Hogwarts School of Witchcraft and Wizardry. They were written by J. K. (Joanne Kathleen) Rowling. Rowling graduated from Exeter University and moved

to Portugal in 1990 to teach English. She married a Portuguese journalist. When their daughter was born in 1993, she had already begun the book, but after her marriage ended in divorce, she moved to Edinburgh to be near her sister. She was struggling to support herself and her daughter Jessica on welfare while she completed the first of the Harry Potter books, which she finally sold—after several rejections—for about $4,000.

Rowling's second Potter book, *Harry Potter and the Chamber of Secrets*, was published in 1998 and hit the adult hardback best-seller lists within a month of publication. It also won numerous prizes, and Rowling was voted BA (Bookseller Association) Author of the Year in 1999. In 1999, just as *Harry Potter and the Prisoner of Azkaban* was published with much press attention, the *Philosopher's Stone* was topping the paperback charts. (The book was titled the *Sorcerer's Stone* in the United States.) The fourth book in the series, *Harry Potter and the Goblet of Fire,* was published during the summer of 2000 with a record first printing of 5.3 million copies; it quickly broke all records for the greatest number of books sold on the first day of publication, as well as shooting to the top of the best-seller charts.

Warner Brothers bought the rights to the first two books in the Harry Potter series, releasing the first film during November 2001; the second was released in November 2002. In its opening weekend in the United States, *The Sorcerer's Stone* debuted on a record 8,200 screens and smashed the previous box office record, earning an estimated $93.5 million ($20 million more than the previous recordholder, 1999's *The Lost World: Jurassic Park*). It ended the year as the top-grossing movie of 2001. By the summer of 2002, it has grossed $966 million worldwide.

Harry is all over the Web. Much of this information is readily available on the U.K. publisher's web site, www.bloomsburymagazine.com/childrens/authors.asp. Information about Rowling is also available at A&E's www.biography.com. The U.K. publisher has a link to the Harry Potter web site, www.bloomsburymagazine.com/harrypotter/, and Harry has a U.S. web site tied to Scholastic. Harry also has a Warner Brothers web site, http://harrypotter.warnerbros.com/home.html, where fans can access magic games, get Harry Potter instant messaging tools and talk to other fans, or download Harry Potter and various characters to your desktop.

During the summer of 2002, Rowling was said to be working hard on a fifth book—*Harry Potter and the Order of the Phoenix*—in a projected series of seven books. Meanwhile, *Harry Potter and the Sorcerer's Stone* was released by Warner Home Video on video and DVD. During the first five days after its May 28, 2002, release, it became the best-grossing first-week rental title ever in U.S. video stores, with rental revenues topping $19 million. It also broke records in Japan and the United Kingdom.

During the summer of 2002, just as *Harry Potter and the Goblet of Fire* went on sale, Book Sense (www.booksense.com) and Scholastic cosponsored a Birthday Celebration Sweepstakes. On Warner's Harry Potter site, you can order toys or school supplies with Harry Potter characters emblazoned on them. A religion-oriented web site, www.facingthechallenge.org/potter.htm, gave Christian parents clues about how to deal with Potter: "The aim of this article is to examine the Harry Potter phenomenon itself, to explore the different Christian responses, and to encourage careful thought and discussion, whatever conclusions you and your family reach." Television's A&E profiled Rowling, web sites appear in multiple languages, and ABC has secured the television movie rights to *The Sorcerer's Stone*. You can also order a boxed set of four Potter books from www.amazon.com.

SUPPLYING THE AUDIENCE'S DEMAND

Markets and processes in the book industry differ depending on the publisher; trade books and textbooks are published using different processes. Trade books gain greater publicity than do textbooks, but they constitute only 25 percent of the market. The bulk of the market is composed of textbooks, scientific books, reference and scholarly publications, Bibles, and other specialized books.[15]

Textbooks

Producing books for elementary and secondary schools is a process that is exceedingly **capital intensive** and politically and culturally sensitive. In school publishing, authors play the role of consultant–contributor more than that of writer. They contribute to the production of a book or educational package that is constantly shaped and reshaped in response to what market leaders want as analyzed by marketing professionals. The process is predominantly driven by the big state bureaucracies in California and Texas, which are large enough to have the power to determine content. Sample modules are tested on groups of students and teachers who record what works and what doesn't, providing feedback that might send a project back to the drawing board before a final huge investment is made. Sometimes special editions are printed to cater to local demands if printing cost can be justified. Often, videotapes or CD-ROMs are given away or sold at cost to encourage schools to adopt specific books. Because at the public elementary and secondary level taxpayers usually pay for the books, culturally sensitive issues often hit the media and become political footballs for citizens' pressure groups of all kinds. The danger, of course, is that catering to the educational demands of large states such as California and Texas also requires catering to the cultural needs and demands of powerful groups in those states.

Although the college book industry also is market driven, there are significant differences between it and the public school market. In the college market, authors are the writers; students, rather than taxpayers, usually pay for the books; the economic stakes are much lower; and books that grate on culturally sensitive nerves sometimes are used for a purpose. Although professors often generate ideas for college textbooks, sales representatives and editors evaluate whether those ideas will produce books that are competitive with other books in the field. The author's primary responsibility in the college textbook field is producing the manuscript. The contract between the publisher and the author determines who will locate photographs, provide rough sketches for charts and graphs, write photograph captions, and provide an index.

key concept

Markets and Processes in the Book Industry The book industry serves the distinct market needs of general consumers, educators, and professionals. The processes of book production and distribution vary to fit these distinct markets.

capital intensive: A production process that requires a large investment of money.

The textbooks used in this middle-school Spanish class have undergone a rigorous production process resulting in a product that is politically and culturally acceptable to a wide range of school systems.

Once the book is finished, it is marketed by the publisher's marketing department. For public school adoptions, the marketing professionals contact curriculum committees in states and municipalities; for college adoptions, they contact professors at various colleges and universities who might adopt the book for their classrooms or departments.

Thus the publisher assumes almost all the financial responsibility for the book, as well as for production and promotion. The publisher selects what will be published, produces the book, advances the financing for production, promotes and distributes the book, and, if the book is successful, makes a profit. The authors risk time. They produce the copy, examine the changes made by copyeditors, sometimes locate photographs, read page proofs, and sometimes provide an index.

The Trade Market: Fiction and Nonfiction

Trade books can be broadly classified as fiction and nonfiction. Nonfiction books usually start with a proposal. For both fiction and nonfiction, an author usually hires an agent to market a proposal. However, in an exceedingly small number of cases, authors send completed manuscripts to a publisher. A manuscript is read by a reader hired specifically to scan incoming manuscripts. The manuscript is then forwarded to an editor and accepted for publication (or rejected). Sometimes an author is successful first with a small publisher, and then a larger publishing house will entice the author away, as happened to best-selling author Tom Clancy, who struck it rich on the publication of his first novel, *The Hunt for Red October.* Clancy's book was first published by the obscure Naval Institute Press, but he soon joined with the Putnam-Berkley Group, Inc., and increased sales with each successive book he wrote. Altogether, Putnam-Berkley has shipped more than 31 million copies of his books.

Once a book is accepted, an editor is assigned to work with an author. In trade divisions, the editor has a great deal of power and often helps the author shape the book. Through the 1960s, editors helped develop great writers. Probably the best-known editor was Maxwell Perkins, who in the 1920s and 1930s worked with F. Scott Fitzgerald, Marjorie Kinnan Rawlings, Ernest Hemingway, and Thomas Wolfe. Editors such as Perkins regarded themselves as part of the literary class and were aware of their roles as developers of culture and literature and as contributors to the marketplace of ideas. During the past twenty

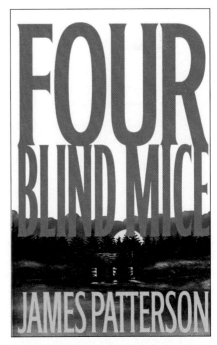

The best-seller lists are heavily influenced by book sales at superstores.

table 5.2

Publishers Weekly 2002 Longest-Running Best-Sellers

HARDCOVER	NUMBER OF WEEKS ON 2002 LIST
Fiction	
The Nanny Diaries by Emma McLaughlin and Nicola Kraus (St. Martin's)	32
The Lovely Bones by Alice Sebold (Little, Brown)	25
The Summons by John Grisham (Doubleday)	21
Skipping Christmas by John Grisham (Doubleday) (6)	17
The Beach House by James Patterson and Peter de Jonge (Little, Brown)	16
Nonfiction	
Who Moved My Cheese? by Spencer Johnson (Putnam) (103)	51
Self Matters by Phillip C. McGraw (Simon & Schuster) (4)	44
Body for Life by Bill Phillips and Michael D'Orso (HarperCollins) (122)	36
Stupid White Men . . . and Other Sorry Excuses for the State of the Nation by Michael Moore (ReganBooks)	31
A Mind at a Time by Mel Levine (Simon & Schuster)	22
Good to Great: Why Some Companies Make the Leap . . . and Others Don't by Jim Collins (HarperBusiness)	22

Source: Publishers Weekly web site, http://publishersweekly.reviewsnews.com, January 13, 2003. Reprinted by permission.

years, power has shifted to some degree from those editors to people in subsidiary rights and marketing. Although editors are still influential in shaping a work, they tend to have less power in the organization and often remain anonymous to the general public. Nevertheless, many editors helped shape the best-sellers listed in Table 5.2.

Production ✦ Book publishing has long made use of the process of contracting out work. The typical production process involves a book being formatted into one of several standard designs produced by in-house artists and designers or being designed by an independent firm under contract to the publisher. If a design contract is commissioned especially for a project, the author may work with the designers in all phases of the production process. Freelancers and other suppliers usually copyedit, typeset, and print a book. The freelancers may be individuals, or they may be production or printing firms outside the geographical confines of publishing centers. With the evolution of word-processing programs and desktop publishing, documents can be formatted directly on the computer, and the outsourcing trend will probably continue. The publisher has access to people with specialized skills without hiring full-time employees for what may be seasonal work. The publisher does not have to pay for benefits associated with full-time employees and does not have to provide office space or other amenities such as child-care facilities. Specialized employees are able to work from their homes, which can be advantageous for parents and other groups but which often means lack of benefits such as health insurance.

Distribution ✦ Chain bookstores are now the primary distribution network and account for almost half of bookstore sales. The top three chains are Barnes & Noble, with 521 stores; Borders, with about 180; and Books-a-Million, which has 175.[16] Crown ranks fourth but filed for bankruptcy in late 1998 and reorganized. The marketing of books through suburban bookstores affiliated with these chains actually has historical roots: Nineteenth-century novels were published in great numbers as the middle class, especially women, began to read for leisure. Waldenbooks specifically targets suburban, middle-class readers, many of them women. Furthermore, the chain stores provide statistics on sales that often are used by publishers to determine in advance the number of books to be printed. Surveys show that the average per-book press run is 10,000 copies. To appear on a best-seller fiction list, a book must sell about 100,000 copies. Unless the suburban book chains carry the book, it is unlikely to reach best-seller status.[17] However, there are major exceptions to this rule: *Snow Falling on Cedars*, *The Joy Luck Club*, *Cold Mountain*, and *Midnight in the Garden of Good and Evil* were all sold by devoted independent sellers before they became best-sellers.[18]

TRENDS

The book industry has remained relatively flat for the past few years. Book industry analysts suggest the industry will see (1) continued growth in electronic and online sales, (2) increasing multimedia packages and multimedia promotion, and (3) continued impact by superstores. These trends will continue to pose questions about quality versus popularity. As books increasingly become the content base for other media, potential profits in the movie or television sector may directly influence book content.

Electronic and Online

The phrase "books online" carries several meanings. E-shopping, or online sales of books, continues to be a major factor in the publishing industry, although they are still fledgling entities. In what was considered dramatic improvement, Amazon.com lost only $94 million dollars in the second quarter of 2002, compared to $168 million in the same quarter the previous year. Why is a company that loses this much money considered a success? Amazon's sales stagnated during 2001, despite predictions by

media convergence

Multimedia Packages

The impact of converging technologies on the creation of multimedia packages can be seen by viewing web sites devoted to books and their spin-offs. For example, if you access www.lordoftherings.net, you will get to the homepage of the film; the page is produced by New Line Productions, Inc. The site shows the integrative possibilities of the Web, but the information found at the site reveals the increasing multimedia impact of a basic print.

If you click on "New Teaser Poster," you will get a film poster of the *Two Towers*, released in December 2002. You also can see movie trailers or order DVD packages. If you go to www.sideshowtoy.com/lotr_home.html, you find a site produced by weta, a production facility in New Zealand that calls itself a site for fans of Tolkien. You can order figures of characters and read comments by other readers. Or you can go to www.tolkienonline.com, a site that focuses on the author and includes letters written by Tolkien, as well as other memorabilia. The combination of books, toys, and films creates a multimedia approach to commercialization of media.

entities such as *Publishers Weekly* that online sales would skyrocket. Increases in sales of the four online book sales companies had increased 322 percent in 1998. But increases, although they seem to be much smaller, are steady, and when this book went to press, Amazon expected to post a profit for the year. Companies such as Amazon benefit not only from book sales but also from their sales of electronics, music, videos, and housewares. They also cut deals with other firms. For example, Amazon is the online outlet for Borders, the massive chain bookstore.[19]

A second type of book online is the author-to-consumer direct sales. Some authors, such as Stephen King have offered chapters or entire books for sale online. Customers send King the money in order to be able to download the book.

A third type of electronic delivery is the e-book. The e-book is itself electronic and can take the form of a CD-ROM or a smaller disk or cassette that is viewed on a computer screen or a small e-book device. Some e-book devices use disks, but more often they rely on the ability to download the book from a particular consumer outlet.

Promotion: Celebrities and Multimedia Products

Multimedia packaging and promotion is increasingly successful in boosting a book to the best-seller charts, especially when the book is promoted by someone of celebrity status. When Oprah Winfrey's cook produced *In the Kitchen with Rosie: Oprah's Favorite Recipes*, the book set a record for the fastest-selling book of all time. It was published in April 1994 with a 400,000-copy first printing. Ten months later, after thirty trips back to the press, the number of copies in print totaled 5.6 million. The book was successful largely because of Oprah Winfrey's television presence, which was a big marketing advantage for those promoting the book.[20]

Multimedia efforts to sell products are standard fare. Just visit www.lordoftherings.net, a *Lord of the Rings* site, and you can play games, order books, and select posters. Such activities on the Internet extend the life of the books and the movies.

Superstores

A significant trend during the past decade has been the book superstore: Borders, Crown Books, Books-a-Million, and Barnes & Noble. The superstores feature a wide selection of books, comfortable browsing surroundings, and coffee shops. Membership in the American Booksellers Association, composed primarily of independent booksellers, dropped significantly during 2000 and 2002 but may be stabilizing at about 16 to 20 percent of the market share. However, superstore and independents represent just less than half of all book sales. Alternatives ranging from book clubs to supermarkets to online sales are claiming a growing market share.

Barnes & Noble, the largest of the superstore chains, enjoyed increased sales in the 1990s, while independent booksellers' share of the market was cut almost in half. But both the superstores and independent stores are losing market share to online sales and other outlets.

discussing trends

In discussing trends, the most elusive factor is content. During the last two years, children's books have become favorites and big sellers. But one never knows if this is a trend or a blip on the screen. Publishers and editors, in an interview with *Publishers Weekly,* indicated they all speculate about what the next "hot topics" will be. After September 11, 2001, editors thought that inspirational and patriotic books might surge, as they did. Despite the focus on technology and distribution, companies recognize that books are an important source of information and inspiration. "Content is king" is a concept that book publishers have not abandoned. Heads of publishing companies anxious to do multimedia deals and provide electronic products insist that "the book is the beginning in the content chain that leads to other products," "books are the seeds in the soil from which other projects spring," and "the core assets for many of these new delivery systems come from print." Time Warner's Trade Group Chair Larry Kirshbaum notes that "everything starts with a story and our role is to be the originator of those stories."[21] So the questions become related to content. For example,

■ Are online sales directly affected by new content trends, or will backlists be a staple of the online sales industry?

■ In devising multimedia approaches, what approaches are best for varied age groups?

■ How many people benefit from Internet links to product and chatroom links?

In an effort to promote sales, Borders inaugurated a new training program for store managers called "category management." Their goal is not only to increase sales by targeting "categories" and standardizing information across its many stores, but also to create a relationship with publishers that goes beyond buying and selling and includes sharing information about customers, markets, sales, merchandising, and other pertinent material.

summary

◆ Books are the oldest commercial form of mass media. They have evolved from serving a highly elite audience to serving the masses of ordinary people. Books have become a form of popular culture that has spread throughout most literate societies.

◆ Publishing as an economic enterprise progressed from the control of the church, to small printers in European cities, to the provinces, including the American colonies.

◆ Throughout history, publishers have been confronted with a quality-versus-quantity dilemma. However, publishers have been willing to risk profits to publish controversial or idea-provoking works both in the history of ideas and in popular fiction.

◆ The advent of the paperback in the nineteenth century, the development of book clubs in the 1920s, and the current widespread publication of all types of books in paperback form helped to democratize the book industry.

◆ Book publishing has moved from business conducted in the atmosphere of a "gentlemen's club" to conglomerate ownership.

◆ The high costs of books are still borne primarily by individuals. Therefore, books continue to appeal to a predominantly middle-class audience.

◆ Online sales represent a significant trend in book sales, but online companies are having to invest significantly in marketing and infrastructure, and therefore are experiencing losses rather than profits.

◆ With the development of conglomerates, the book industry has become more multimedia oriented. Book success is often related to technological convergence. Successful films and audio or video products can hike book sales.

◆ Books often provide the stories, or content, for other media.

navigating the web | Books on the Web

Book-oriented World Wide Web sites take three forms: those that promote books and bookstores, those that provide information about books and the industry, and those that are order sites. You can find information about the art and commerce of publishing on the following sites:

Bookwire
www.bookwire.com
Bookwire deals with a wide range of book issues and also has links to several good sites about books and the industry. It is a server for reviews, and it has a database of books, best-sellers, and publishing companies.

Book Industry Study Groups, Inc.
www.bisg.org
This industry association is concerned with a variety of publishing issues. The site carries news releases about the industry, including yearly data.

***Publishers Weekly* Interactive**
www.publishersweekly.com
The online version of the leading trade publication for the industry, this site gives access to a wide range of

articles about authors, publishing companies, and the industry itself, although it does not provide the full content of the magazine.

The following site publishes reviews of books.

Hungry Mind Review
www.bookwire.com/hmr

Order sites include:

Amazon.com
www.amazon.com
Amazon.com is one of the original high-volume book order sites on the Internet.

Barnes & Noble
www.barnesandnoble.com
Barnes & Noble is providing competition for Amazon.com.

questions for review

1. What developments signified the emergence of mass market best-sellers in the United States?
2. What trends in book production were represented in the fiction factory?
3. What were the first two book clubs, and when were they founded? Why were book clubs a significant development?

4. What is a media conglomerate?
5. What is the difference between a trade book and a textbook?
6. How does selling books online affect the industry as a whole?

issues to think about

1. During the American colonial period, information was a highly prized commodity. Do you think it is still so highly valued? How do converging technologies affect this concept?
2. Discuss the evolution of postal policy that affected the distribution of books in the United States. Why is postal policy an important factor in the development of print media?
3. Discuss the importance of the paperback industry to widening access to fiction and other printed works.
4. What does the trend toward multimedia packaging mean for the book industry?

5. What are the implications of producing schoolbooks for children and young adults that are targeted to the most populous states of the nation? Who makes the decisions about those books? Why are the decisions sometimes political?
6. How does consolidation of the book industry affect the circulation of ideas in an intellectual marketplace?
7. Why do critics lament that the public does not read when, in fact, book sales either remain the same or increase each year?

suggested readings

Ativeh, George, ed. *The Book in the Islamic World: The Written Word and Communication in the Middle East* (Albany: State University of New York, 1995).

Coser, Lewis A., Charles Kadushin, and Walter W. Powell. *Books: The Culture and Commerce of Publishing* (New York: Basic Books, 1982).

Davis, Kenneth. *Two-Bit Culture: The Paperbacking of America* (Boston: Houghton Mifflin, 1984).

Dessauer, John. *Book Publishing: What It Is, What It Does* (New York: R. R. Bowker, 1981).

Johns, Adrian. *The Nature of the Book: Print and Knowledge in the Making* (Chicago: University of Chicago Press, 2000).

Stern, Madeleine B. *Publishing for Mass Entertainment in Nineteenth-Century America* (Boston: G. K. Hall, 1980).

Newspapers

Katie orders a coffee-to-go and sits down at the keyboard. She is interning this summer with the U.S. Park Service in the Mount Rogers Wilderness area near Damascus, Virginia. When she gets a day off, she goes into town, stops at the Side Track Cyber Café, orders coffee, and reads newspapers. Although it's tough to get a print version of the *New York Times* in Damascus, she can easily access it online and her hometown newspaper as well. She also accesses her college newspaper to see if the back-to-school edition has appeared.

As she reads, Katie realizes that the only print newspaper she's read in two months is the *Bristol Herald Courier,* a small daily that serves not only Bristol and Mountain City, Tennessee, but also Abingdon and other southwest Virginia towns.

Damascus is a small town only a few miles from where North Carolina and Tennessee touch the southern border of Virginia. No daily serves the region very well. The Bristol newspaper focuses on Tennessee, and the closest Virginia daily focuses more on the New River Valley, fifty miles to the north. Yet Damascus is an interesting and historic town, where the Appalachian Trail runs down the main street and a fifty-seven-mile bicycle trail, The Virginia Creeper, attracts many visitors who shuttle up the mountain and ride down the trail, observing spectacular mountain views in the process.

The café is not the only public Internet site in town—the public library also has four computer terminals. The library's print newspaper collection includes most of the small newspapers throughout the region, but its terminals give citizens access to news of the world.

Katie's situation—not having access to print newspapers from her hometown, her nation, and her current locale—illustrates how newspapers can reach out to populations that are physically scattered. On-line news attracts young and old alike with its ability to provide large amounts of information on request. Some observers have predicted that the Internet, along with other societal changes, will eliminate newspapers as a print medium. But to paraphrase a comment by Mark Twain, rumors of the newspaper industry's death are greatly exaggerated.

Most newspapers continue to be two to three times more prof-

Despite indications of prosperity, newspapers' role in society continues to change, bringing several challenges for the industry. Newspapers face the following issues:

◆ Changing reading patterns. Readers increasingly say they do not have the time to read a newspaper every day. As the percentage of households subscribing to a daily newspaper declined during the past fifty years, the percentage of households getting weekly and Sunday newspapers grew.

◆ Changing community demographics. Most daily newspapers during the mid-twentieth century appealed to white male readers. This segment has been shrinking as a proportion of the total population. The percentage of Americans who are African American, Hispanic, Asian American, and Native American is growing.

◆ Aging readers. The baby boom generation, which grew up during television's infancy, is aging. These individuals form the bulk of the daily newspapers' readership. Younger readers do not read daily papers as often as their parents and grandparents.

◆ Changing content needs. The news and information that people want and need today differs from what newspapers provided even thirty years ago. Most parents work outside the home, which increases the demands on people's time. They need information to help them deal with these demands. Also,the growing diversity of the population requires a growing diversity of content.

◆ Changing technology. As the World Wide Web evolves and the delivery of video content becomes digital, newspapers must find their place in people's lives. Newspaper managers must decide how and when to use developing technology to deliver the news, information, and advertising their organizations produce. They also must react to the growing competition for time and advertising that technology brings.

Newspapers *in Your Life*

What Are Your Newspaper Reading Habits?

Some of the things you look for in a newspaper depend on who you are, how old you are, and what things are important in your life. Newspapers are divided into sections such as national news, international news, sports, travel, business, local news, and comics.

Think about what you do when you read newspapers. Which sections of the newspaper do you read most? Why? What parts of the newspaper do you like best? Why? What parts of the newspaper do you like least? Why? What could the managers of your campus or local newspaper do to make it more interesting to you?

	NATIONAL AFFAIRS	INTERNATIONAL AFFAIRS	TRAVEL	SPORTS	BUSINESS TRENDS	COMICS	LOCAL NEWS
Which sections of the newspaper do you read most?							
What parts of the newspaper do you like best?							
What parts of the newspaper do you like least?							

itable than the average business and remain the primary source of news about social events, city and county government, and school events.[1] The amount of money spent on newspaper advertising grows each year, and newspapers serve as the principal source of daily news for people with high levels of education and income.

People tend to read only sections or individual stories in newspapers rather than browse the entire paper. The feature Newspapers in Your Life asks you to think about ways you use the newspaper. As you read the rest of the chapter, you will encounter many issues that confront this changing but profitable medium. How it fits among other media will be determined by how it fits in your life and the lives of people throughout the world.

NEWSPAPERS IN AMERICAN LIFE

Throughout the history of the United States, newspapers fulfilled two important roles: They served as a guard against governmental abuses of power, and they defined their communities by providing information about the daily and weekly activities of their

1690. *Publick Occurrences* is published in Boston.

1704. John Campbell publishes the Boston *News-Letter*.

1734–1735. John Peter Zenger is tried in New York for seditious libel.

Mid-1700s. Newspapers promote dissatisfaction with English rule.

1827. First African American newspaper is started.

1830s. Penny press becomes the first truly mass medium in the United States.

1846. Newspapers begin to use telegraph to send news.

1847. Frederick Douglass starts the *North Star*.

1849. First newsgathering association is founded.

1861–1865. Press is censored during the Civil War.

1890s. Period of yellow journalism

1917–1918. Government imposes censorship during World War I.

1920s. Tabloid journalism flourishes in large cities.

1400–1700	1800	1860	1880	1900	1920	1930

1620. Pilgrims land at Plymouth Rock.

1690. *Publick Occurrences* is published in Boston.

1741. First magazine is published in America.

1776–1783. American Revolution

1830s. The penny press becomes the first truly mass medium in the United States.

1861–1865. American Civil War

1892. Thomas Edison's lab develops the kinetoscope.

1914–1918. World War I

1915. *The Birth of a Nation* marks the start of the modern movie industry.

1920. KDKA in Pittsburgh gets the first commercial radio license.

1930s. The Great Depression

1939. TV is demonstrated at the New York World's Fair.

1939–1945. World War II

town, city, and county. Both roles were established from the beginning of the newspaper industry and continued to evolve as early editors fought for political independence and as politicians battled over postal laws that would determine where newspapers could circulate and at what price.

Local Newspapers and Challenges to Elite Authority

During the early colonial period, newspapers focused primarily on foreign events and covered local events to a lesser degree. Newspapers both challenged and cooperated with the British government. Benjamin Harris in 1690 published the newspaper *Publick Occurrences Both Forreign and Domestick*, but the royal government was not ready to tolerate critical comment on local affairs. It prohibited Harris from publishing a second issue. By 1701 postmaster John Campbell circulated a handwritten *News-Letter*,

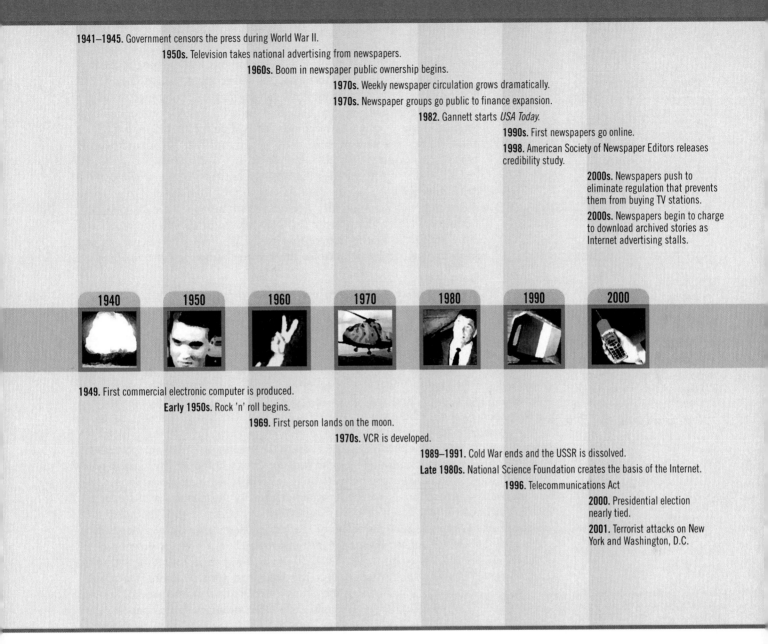

1941–1945. Government censors the press during World War II.

1950s. Television takes national advertising from newspapers.

1960s. Boom in newspaper public ownership begins.

1970s. Weekly newspaper circulation grows dramatically.

1970s. Newspaper groups go public to finance expansion.

1982. Gannett starts *USA Today*.

1990s. First newspapers go online.

1998. American Society of Newspaper Editors releases credibility study.

2000s. Newspapers push to eliminate regulation that prevents them from buying TV stations.

2000s. Newspapers begin to charge to download archived stories as Internet advertising stalls.

| 1940 | 1950 | 1960 | 1970 | 1980 | 1990 | 2000 |

1949. First commercial electronic computer is produced.

Early 1950s. Rock 'n' roll begins.

1969. First person lands on the moon.

1970s. VCR is developed.

1989–1991. Cold War ends and the USSR is dissolved.

Late 1980s. National Science Foundation creates the basis of the Internet.

1996. Telecommunications Act

2000. Presidential election nearly tied.

2001. Terrorist attacks on New York and Washington, D.C.

published "with authority," or approval, of the British governor. In 1704 the newspaper was circulated in printed form from Boston. Campbell's newspaper, operating under prior restraint, summarized news dispatches from abroad, from the government, and from private businesses. His goal was not to present timely accounts of local events as newspapers do today but to present historical summaries of news from abroad.

Being a postmaster gave a publisher several advantages, including free distribution and government allotments. In 1719, William Brooker succeeded Campbell as postmaster. Because Campbell refused to relinquish his editorship of the *News-Letter*, Brooker started a competing newspaper, the *Boston Gazette*. In 1721, James Franklin began the *New England Courant*.

Franklin is often credited with starting the first local newspaper and the first newspaper crusade because he confronted the local Puritan establishment and introduced items of wit and humor. The *New England Courant* covered local public controversies,

PUBLICK
OCCURRENCES

Both FORREIGN and DOMESTICK.

Boston, Thursday Sept. 25th. 1690.

IT is designed, that the Countrey shall be furnished once a moneth (or if any Glut of Occurrences happen, oftener,) with an Account of such considerable things as have arrived unto our Notice.

In order hereunto, the Publisher will take what pains he can to obtain a Faithful Relation of all such things; and will particularly make himself beholden to such Persons in Boston whom he knows to have been for their own use the diligent Observers of such matters.

That which is herein proposed, is, First, That Memorable Occurrents of Divine Providence may not be neglected or forgotten, as they too often are. Secondly, That people every where may better understand the Circumstances of Publique Affairs, both abroad and at home; which may not only direct their Thoughts at all times, but at some times also to assist their Businesses and Negotiations.

Thirdly, That some thing may be done towards the Curing, or at least the Charming of that Spirit of Lying, which prevails amongst us, wherefore nothing shall be entered, but what we have reason to believe is true, repairing to the best fountains for our Information. And when there appears any material mistake in any thing that is collected, it shall be corrected in the next.

Moreover, the Publisher of these Occurrences is willing to engage, that whereas, there are many False Reports, maliciously made, and spread among us, if any well-minded person will be at the pains to trace any such false Report so far as to find out and Convict the First Raiser of it, he will in this Paper (unless just Advice be given to the contrary) expose the Name of such person, as A malicious Raiser of a false Report. It is suppos'd that none will dislike this Proposal, but such as intend to be guilty of so villanous a Crime.

THE Christianized Indians in some parts of Plimouth, have newly appointed a day of Thanksgiving to God for his Mercy in supplying their extream [illegible] from them, as what is in the Forces lately gone for Canada; made them think it [illegible] impossible for them to get well through the Affairs of their Husbandry at this time of the year, yet the season has been so unusually favourable that they [illegible] find any want of the many hundreds of hands, that are gone from them; which is looked upon as a Merciful Providence

While the barbarous Indians were lurking about Chelmsford, there were missing about the beginning of this month a couple of Children belonging to a man of that Town, one of them aged about eleven, the other aged about nine years, both of them supposed to be fallen into the hands of the Indians.

A very Tragical Accident happened at Water-Town, the beginning of this Month, an Old man, that was of somewhat a Silent and Morose Temper, but one that had long Enjoyed the reputation of a Sober and a [illegible] Man, having newly buried his Wife, The Devil took advantage of the Melancholy which he thereupon fell into, his Wives discretion and industry had long been the support of his Family, and he seemed hurried with an impertinent fear that he should now come to want before he dyed, though he had very careful friends to look after him who kept a strict eye upon him, least he should do himself any harm. But one evening escaping from them into the Cow-house, they there quickly followed him found him hanging by a Rope, which they had used to tye their Calves withal, he was dead with his feet near touching the Ground.

Epidemical Fevers and Agues grow very common, in some parts of the Country, whereof, tho' many dye not, yet they are sorely unfitted for their imployments; but in some parts a more malignant Fever seems to prevail in such sort that it usually goes thro' a Family where it comes, and proves Mortal unto many.

The Small-pox which has been ragi

Publick Occurrences, one of the earliest newspapers in America, was shut down by authorities because of its controversial content.

which was a clear challenge to the elite authority. Thomas Leonard wrote, "Defiance was the soul of the *Courant*, the spirited cry of newcomers bumping against an old elite, of artisans mocking the more respectable classes, of provincials picking up the language of London coffee houses, and of eighteenth-century men recovering the nerve to mock and amuse in the face of the grave."[2] When Franklin turned his satirical pen toward the government, however, he landed in jail. While he was in jail, he continued to run the newspaper through his brother, Benjamin Franklin, a noted printer, philosopher, and inventor. James Franklin was released on the condition that he not publish his newspaper, and in 1726 he moved to Rhode Island and became a government printer.

Governors in the colonies did not like criticism of themselves or the British government. As you read in Chapter 2, John Peter Zenger, who printed the *New York Weekly Journal*, was imprisoned for his criticism. The colonial editor had to walk the line between independence and political loyalty. As the country moved toward the War for Independence, patriot editors showed little tolerance for those who championed Britain.

Postal Rates and Serving the Community

From the time that the founders began to shape the laws of the United States, Congress and publishers have debated whether newspapers should be local entities or the fabric that binds the nation together. Should newspapers be the vehicles of communication that enable communities to identify themselves as part of a nation and a federal government? The establishment of postal rates for newspapers, books, and magazines was pivotal in the debate because out-of-town newspapers were distributed by mail.

Although magazines did not gain favorable postal rates until the mid-nineteenth century, Congress considered newspapers from the beginning to be important vehicles of public communication. The fight was not over whether to give newspapers favored status. It was over whether economic favoritism should be used to preserve local voices and traditional values or whether big-city newspapers and forces for modernization should be given the advantage. In an effort to give the advantage to urban newspapers, some members of Congress attempted several times during the early 1800s to abolish newspaper postage altogether. If postage did not exist, the urban newspapers could freely distribute their newspapers to wide geographic areas. But the U.S. Post Office Committee argued that such a move would allow city papers to displace local papers. The decline of the rural papers, they said, would mean that "freedom, that manliness of spirit, which has always characterized the great body of the common people of our country, and which constitutes the safeguard of our liberties, will gradually decline."[3]

Benjamin Franklin—colonial printer, inventor, and diplomat—financed the beginning of several early American newspapers, extending his printing dynasty from Pennsylvania to South Carolina along the major trade routes of the colonies.

Congress resolved the postal rate issue with a compromise that ensured the survival of the local paper. A new postal law in 1852 greatly simplified newspaper rates. In-county newspapers could be distributed free, but any newspaper could cross the continent for a penny.[4]

The early postal battle over newspapers established an important principle: Newspapers were significant factors in the building of a society across wide geographical territory and across the social boundaries of varying value systems. Congress recognized the value newspapers had for the new nation and for serving local communities with news and information.

Serving a Diversified Society

U.S. newspapers always have reflected the diverse interest of our society despite historians' failure to adequately chronicle the history of *nonmainstream media.* When people moved west and trade routes developed across the Alleghenies, ethnic newspapers developed alongside English-language publications. Immigration patterns produced ethnic enclaves that naturally created concentrated market segments for ethnic newspapers. These nonmainstream publications were essential to ethnic and racial minorities. The mainstream publications either failed to serve the needs of these groups or worked to deny them equal rights.

From as early as 1739, foreign-language newspapers provided immigrants with news from home. German-language newspapers were among the first to appear. They dominated the ethnic-press field until World War I, but newspapers written in French, Welsh, Italian, Norwegian, Swedish, Spanish, Danish, Dutch, Bohemian, Polish, Portuguese, and Chinese all appeared during the nineteenth century.

As the descendants of Europeans pushed Native Americans westward and onto reservations, the Native Americans developed newspapers to protest this treatment and to preserve their cultures. For instance, the *Cherokee Phoenix*, printed in English and Cherokee during the 1830s and 1840s, informed Native Americans of actions by whites as well as about tribal concerns. As with all frontier newspapers, Native American newspapers had primitive formats and usually did not remain in circulation for long.

African Americans, who faced slavery in the South and segregation in the North, developed a press about the same time as Native Americans. Samuel Cornish and John Russwurm printed the first known black newspaper, *Freedom's Journal*, in 1827. The newspaper included poetry and reprinted articles as well as original articles about slavery in the United States and other countries. Several other black newspapers were developed in the 1830s, and in the 1840s and 1850s, some of the best-known newspapers, such as Frederick Douglass's *Ram's Horn* and the *North Star*, were issued.

Competition in a New Century

Diversity was also reflected in how newspapers viewed local communities. During the 1840s, Washington, D.C., supported a variety of competing newspapers. The *National Intelligencer* focused on politics; one hardly knew from reading the *Intelligencer* that the city itself existed. Washington was, according to the *Intelligencer,* Capitol Hill. However, the *Georgetown Advocate,* though it followed politics, was more interested in city development and constantly covered the expanding city services and street pavings that were of major concern in the business community. Because the harbors at Georgetown and nearby Alexandria, Virginia, were busy trading ports in the 1840s, the *Alexandria Packet* and the *Advocate* also covered shipping news. In addition, Washington, D.C., supported a temperance newspaper, which viewed all action in light of the evils of alcohol and gambling, and a penny newspaper called the *Saturday Evening News and General Advertiser.* This penny paper printed business cards on at least one full page of the four-page newspaper and published comments about prison reform, public education, and almshouses for the poor, as well as news about city improvements and debates over where to locate public buildings. The *Saturday Evening News* described the social city of Washington beyond the boundaries of politics and business. Each newspaper had a distinct role as a local arbiter of cultural values. The *Intelligencer* catered to the political elite; the Georgetown and Alexandria newspapers promoted local business; and the *Saturday Evening News* recognized a society in the city that was not necessarily intellectual, business oriented, or wealthy.

Frederick Douglass, a freed slave, became an eloquent spokesman for the Antislavery Society, traveling in England and the United States. He published a newspaper to argue for the emancipation of slaves.

Rise of the Penny Press

By the 1830s, New York City was the undisputed center of newspaper activity. It had replaced the important colonial city of Boston in economic and political importance, becoming the nation's largest commercial city. New York City spawned a variety of competing newspapers edited by men who championed different social classes in the city and by men who intended to make a profit. Before 1830 most newspapers had **circulations** between 2,000 and 3,000 and appealed to the commercial interests of the city. But Benjamin Day, who started the *New York Sun* in 1833, and James Gordon Bennett, who established the *New York Herald* in 1835, increased their circulations by selling their newspapers cheaply—for one cent a copy. These *penny press* publishers no longer relied on letters from abroad, political documents, or letters written by members of the elite for news. They hired reporters and managing editors and began to seek news. They recognized the power of timely news and cultivated reporters to get the scoop, or to beat the competing newspaper to a good story. The era of the penny press intensified the focus on local communities.

key concept

Penny Press In the early 1830s, a new class of newspapers targeted to lower- and middle-class audiences earned the name *penny press* because they were sold for a penny a copy. In addition to traditional news about commerce and politics, they included lively stories about social life in the city.

The penny press newspapers targeted middle-class audiences involved in trade, transportation, and manufacturing. However, they were no longer bound to commerce and politics; they reflected the increasing social activity in their urban surroundings. Benjamin Day announced his *New York Sun* with this comment:

> The object of this paper is to lay before the public, at a price within the means of every one, ALL THE NEWS OF THE DAY, and at the same time afford an advantageous medium for advertising. The sheet will be enlarged as soon as the increase of advertisements requires it—the price remaining the same.[5]

The National Stage

By the 1890s, newspapers in towns as small as Emporia, Kansas, where William Allen White edited the *Gazette,* accepted national advertising and carried national and international news provided by the Associated Press or other wire services, thus becoming national in scope. Nevertheless, White and like-minded editors still regarded the local community as the audience for their newspapers. In large cities such as New York, Boston, Philadelphia, and Chicago, newspapers played on a larger stage, but their audience remained primarily local. During the 1850s, Horace Greeley marketed his New York *Tribune* to westerners as well as New Yorkers, and later in the century, William Randolph Hearst with the *New York Journal* and Joseph Pulitzer with his *New York World* commanded large national circulations and claimed influence with major political figures. Newspapers published in large eastern cities had an audience in Washington, D.C. Nevertheless, New Yorkers were their main subscribers, and New York advertisers paid most of their bills.

Advertising took on a national scope during the mid-1800s. Editors carried advertisements for nationally distributed brands as well as local products. For editors such as William Allen White, this posed a dilemma. To accept national advertising was to encourage readers to buy from the large surrounding cities and from mail-order houses rather than from merchants in their hometowns. White carried national advertising but constantly exhorted his readers to "buy at home."

Meanwhile, technology was changing, which facilitated large print runs and large circulations. The rotary press, which printed from rolls of paper rather than from sheets, new folding machines, and new techniques for making plates into paper mats that could be bent around a cylinder to accommodate rolls of paper all contributed to the expansion of the newspaper business.

In the expanding market, newspaper editors competed for circulation, using information, entertainment, and the sensational presentation of news as their tools. Henry Raymond, who started the *New York Times* before the Civil War, appealed to

circulation: The number of copies sold by a newspaper during its production cycle (week or day).

the business classes of New York and Washington, D.C., and established a reputation for solid information without entertainment. Charles Dana, who bought the *New York Sun* in 1868, advocated artisan republicanism, a philosophy maintaining that all people, including the working class, should have equal rights and full participation in the political system. Ultimately, however, Dana could not compete with Joseph Pulitzer's *New York World*. Pulitzer and William Randolph Hearst, with his *New York Journal,* played to the crowds. Catering to the working and middle classes, their newspapers hummed with the vitality of New York City life. They covered stories that had not been covered before, reporting New York gossip among the social set as well as political debates over the organization of labor and the rights of property owners.

The newspapers pursued what has become known as *yellow journalism,* which is the printing of stories that emphasize crime and personal tragedies presented with big headlines and illustrations. These newspapers were highly sensationalistic, although Pulitzer, except during the most highly competitive years, operated from a sense of journalistic integrity. Pulitzer introduced an editorial platform that called for taxing luxuries, inheritances, large incomes, monopolies, and privileged corporations, which he viewed as tools of the rich. He also called for reforming the civil service and punishing corruption in political office. The *New York Times* countered the sensationalists with a sober writing style and point of view.

The New York City papers were not the only ones to capitalize on new developments. E. W. Scripps offered a different kind of competition. Avoiding the urban cities of the Northeast, he established dailies in medium-size cities in the Midwest, supporting organized labor and advocating independence from powerful advertisers. After acquiring a number of newspapers in Ohio, Scripps expanded to the West Coast. With his Midwest papers and significant holdings in Oregon, Washington, and California, he shaped one of the first effective newspaper chains. Scripps required his editors to operate on a very small budget. His formula included heavy reliance on subscriptions and on revenues from multiple advertisers because he feared the power large advertisers might gain if a newspaper relied too heavily on them. Scripps, who disliked the sensationalism of Hearst and Pulitzer, sought to provide local information as the mainstay of his smaller newspapers.[6]

Maturation

Shortly after the beginning of the twentieth century, the number of daily newspapers began to decline as the industry grew more concentrated and profitable. Advertisers were looking for efficient advertising, and they placed their ads in the largest newspapers. Those newspapers that increased circulation experienced a growth in advertising and thus in profit. Those that did not eventually went out of business.

As daily newspapers began to consolidate and close, radio confronted the industry with a new form of competition. During World War II, both newspapers and radio faced some government censorship, but on the whole they cooperated with the government in reporting the war effort. Radio's role in news became increasingly important, particularly in reporting international events. President Franklin Delano Roosevelt's "fireside chats" and Edward R. Murrow's reports from London challenged newspaper superiority in reporting on the war. Nevertheless, it was not until the 1960s, when news of civil rights and subsequently of the Vietnam War exploded on television screens in American homes, that newspapers faced their ultimate challenge from television news.

With some exceptions, the strength of newspapers is still the local audience. National newspapers have difficulty achieving financial stability, let alone high profit margins. During the 1960s, the *National Observer* acquired a national, politically sophisticated audience with its well-written interpretive pieces, but it never obtained the advertising that would have enabled it to succeed in its appeal to a relatively elite national readership. The *Wall Street Journal* succeeds as a specialized national newspaper, appealing to the business community across geographical boundaries. *USA Today* targets a middle-class national audience. After two decades, it reached a 2.3 million daily circulation with a stable advertising market.

The *New York Times*, while definitely targeted toward New Yorkers, also maintains a loyal audience among intellectuals across the nation and at times has exerted major influence nationwide. For example, *New York Times v. Sullivan*, a landmark libel case, resulted when an Alabama police commissioner sued the newspaper because he resented the influence the *New York Times* had in the civil rights movement. The *Times* has begun a campaign to expand its national edition, including a readership program on many large college campuses.

TODAY'S MARKET STRUCTURE

Newspaper **markets** have been defined in a variety of ways. Newspapers are considered vehicles of mass communication that target generalized audiences within a local geographic area. However, exceptions are common. The *Wall Street Journal*, for example, targets a national market when defined by geography, but a specialized market when defined by editorial or advertising content. Furthermore, communities are being identified differently than they were in the past; suburban dailies not only compete with metropolitan newspapers but also supplement them with even more local news and information. In the Washington, D.C., metropolitan area, residents of the northern Virginia suburbs often subscribe not only to the nationally renowned *Washington Post* but also to one of the suburban *Journal* newspapers. For example, the *Fairfax Journal* prints swim team scores, stories on the actions of the Fairfax County board of supervisors, and notices of road repairs and construction. The *Post*, despite its weekly sections for northern Virginia and nearby Montgomery County, Maryland, cannot compete with the level of detail that the *Journal* newspapers provide.

The ***market structure for news*** determines the degree of competition in a media market and, therefore, how responsive newspapers must be to readers. The market structure for newspapers has three components.

The first component is how many choices are available within the market. Residents of Lawrence, Kansas, a town centered between Kansas City, thirty miles to the east, and Topeka, thirty miles to the west, have several choices. They can buy the *Kansas City Star*, the *Lawrence Journal-World*, or the *Topeka Capital-Journal*. Because Kansas City straddles the Missouri–Kansas state line and is a large city, the *Star* offers more cultural news for the area, Missouri state government news, national and international news, and advertisements for shopping in a larger city. The Topeka newspaper offers more Kansas state news. The Lawrence newspaper offers the best local news. Now the question becomes "How will residents deal with this choice?" Will they buy one newspaper? Several newspapers?

The second component is the probability that buyers will substitute products. For example, what is the probability that a person living in Lawrence will buy the *Kansas City Star* instead of the *Lawrence Journal-World*? The component of substitution becomes increasingly important when different types of media are available. Then people have the ability to substitute television, for example, for newspapers.

The third component is the number of barriers new firms face when trying to enter the market. In any major market area, new publishers find it exceedingly difficult to crack an already established newspaper market with a newspaper that competes for the same audience and the same advertisers as an existing newspaper. To challenge the *Washington Post*, for example, requires enormous resources. Although the *Washington Times* has spent huge sums of money, it has been unable to compete successfully with the *Post*'s broad advertising and subscription base. The *Post* serves its advertisers better than the *Times* does because the *Post* can reach more potential buyers at less cost. The overwhelming advantage held by most established newspapers in major markets remains the most important barrier to new competition.

AUDIENCE DEMAND IN NEWSPAPER MARKETS

Editors and owners are having increasing difficulty determining what content readers want, in part because they do not understand the three components of market structures discussed in the previous paragraphs. In the 1950s, white male editors of the mainstream newspapers concentrated on the city beat and basic suburban themes such as road development, schools, and protection from crime and focused on a middle-class white audience. Newspapers included a women's section that focused on fashion, food, and children. Ethnic and minority newspapers targeted specific audiences. However, the composition of the United States has changed dramatically in ethnic diversity, the distribution of power, the number of women working, and the makeup of the typical family. The proportion of young people reading newspapers has declined since the 1950s as the use of other media has grown. Editors must serve a more diverse audience, and they face great difficulty in selecting the specific content that divergent segments of their market want to read. For example, professional women may want newspaper content that is more similar to the content that professional men read rather than to what women who work at home read. Although market research increasingly is used to explore readers' needs and preferences, this "fuzziness," or blurring of the boundaries of desired content, increases the difficulty of identifying the factors that would make an individual or family buy a particular newspaper rather than turn to another source of news.[7]

Newspaper editors no longer can assume that most middle-class households will subscribe to a newspaper. Even though the number of daily newspaper copies

t a b l e   6 . 1

Change in Weekday Circulation at Ten Large Metropolitan Newspapers

NEWSPAPER	MARCH 31, 2002	MARCH 31, 1998	PERCENTAGE CHANGE
New York Times	1,194,491	1,110,143	+7.6
Los Angeles Times	1,001,610	1,095,006	−8.5
Washington Post	811,925	808,884	+0.4
New York Daily News	733,099	727,089	+0.8
Newsday [Long Island]	577,796	571,283	+1.0
Houston Chronicle	545,727	553,387	−1.6
Chicago Tribune	536,469	654,408	−18.0
Dallas Morning News	526,430	509,775	+3.3
Arizona Republic	496,373	484,630	+2.4
San Francisco Chronicle	525,369	475,324	+10.5

Source: Audit Bureau of Circulation, www.access.abc.com.

sold is greater now than it was in 1950, the **household penetration** (the percentage of households in a market subscribing to a newspaper) has steadily declined. Between 1977 and 2001, the percentage of the adult population reading a daily newspaper regularly fell from 65.0 percent to 54.3 percent. More recently, the number of copies of daily newspapers sold declined to 55.6 million in 2001 from a peak of 62.8 million in 1987. However, as Table 6.1 shows, the decline in circulation does not occur evenly at all daily newspapers. As a result of declining circulation, the number of daily newspapers has decreased from 1,772 in 1950 to 1,468 in 2001, a drop of more than 16 percent.[8] Nevertheless, daily newspapers still reach more than half of all American households, and weeklies reach about 70 percent of households.[9]

The advent of radio and television, with their ability to inform and entertain even while the consumer is eating, working, or performing some other task, has presented new choices for newspaper readers. Television and radio have the advantage of providing dramatic visual or auditory stimuli. More recently the Web began to offer an increasing number of electronic specialized information sources as well as general sites run by print and broadcast news organizations.

With increasingly diverse market structures, newspapers can no longer count on the generalized mass markets that supported their development throughout the nineteenth and early twentieth centuries. Faced with the difficulty of identifying content demanded by diverse readership and the expense of producing this content, newspaper managers have begun to think of newspapers as media aimed at the market's educated and high-income citizens. Some reporters for the *New York Times*, for example, say they write not for the general public, but for the political and intellectual elite as well as for other newspaper reporters and editors.[10] Newspaper publishers have to decide whether to continue as mass media or to turn toward segmented audiences. If newspaper managers adhere to the basic concept of a newspaper as news for everyone, they need to identify themselves as suppliers of information, not just of news, because the demand for content will be wide ranging. If they turn instead to specialized audiences, their markets may be easier to define. They can choose, for example, to aim at the political elite; at business entrepreneurs; or at the under-thirty, entertainment-oriented upper middle class.

Newspapers have some advantages over other media. Their role in the community has a historical tradition as well as solid First Amendment protection. To maintain that traditional role, however, newspapers need to be seen by community

household penetration: The number of households subscribing to a newspaper compared to the number of potential households in an area.

members as essential reading. Newspapers may need modernized forms of delivery, such as fiber optics, telephones, satellite transmission, and computers. Diversifying newsrooms in terms of the lifestyles, economic backgrounds, gender, education, and ethnic origins of reporters and editors can help newspaper managers respond to audience demand.

SUPPLYING THE AUDIENCE'S DEMAND

During the last four decades of the twentieth century, the newspaper industry experienced rapid change. Most newspapers came under group ownership, other forms of media expanded and developed, and competition among newspapers declined. During this same period, newspapers experienced a significant decline in their credibility among the general public. Many people no longer trust journalists and the content they create.

Ownership

Newspaper ownership may be *public,* meaning the public can buy shares of ownership in the form of stock traded through a public stock exchange, or it may be *private,* meaning the public cannot buy stock. In addition, newspapers may have *independent ownership* if a company owns only one newspaper, or it may have *group ownership* if the company owns more than one newspaper. Most corporations that own newspaper groups, such as Gannett and Knight Ridder, also own several types of media. In the twenty-first century, there is an increased probability that these media corporations will be bought by conglomerates, which own both media and nonmedia companies. For instance, General Electric now owns NBC television. The percentage of newspapers owned by groups has increased, as Table 6.2 shows.

Corporations buy newspapers because, despite declining penetration, they generate profit rates two or three times greater than the rates of most businesses. This continuing profitability results from strict cost control and newspapers' domination of classified advertising. Factors contributing to increased corporate ownership include the fact that families who own newspapers sometimes have difficulty resolving tensions among their members about how the business should be run, and the tax structure encourages families to sell inherited property rather than keep it. Furthermore, it is much easier for a group to acquire a newspaper and manage it successfully than to start a new one. Starting a daily newspaper requires millions of dollars to buy printing presses and to run the newspaper for years while it builds name recognition. In Washington, D.C., the *Washington Times* was started to compete with the *Post,* but the *Times* has yet to earn a profit. It continues to exist because it is subsidized by a religious organization.

During the 1990s, the concentration of newspaper ownership continued in a new form. Companies began to "cluster" their newspapers by buying several newspapers in the same geographic region. In late 1998, for instance, the Liberty Group bought thirty-eight weekly and twice-weekly newspapers near Chicago. Clustering

table 6.2

The Growth of Newspaper Group Ownership

YEAR	NUMBER OF GROUPS	NUMBER OF PAPERS OWNED BY GROUPS	PERCENTAGE OF NEWSPAPERS OWNED BY GROUPS
1920	31	153	8
1940	60	319	17
1960	109	560	32
1980	158	1002	57
1986	127	1158	70
1996	126	1124	74
2001	120	1106	75

Sources: John C. Busterna, "Trends in Daily Newspaper Ownership," *Journalism Quarterly* 65 (1988): 833; Raymond B. Nixon and Jean Ward, "Trends in Newspaper Ownership and Inter-Media Competition," *Journalism Quarterly* 38 (1961): 5; *Editor & Publisher International Yearbook, 1997* (New York: Editor & Publisher, 1997); *Editor & Publisher International Yearbook, 2002* (New York: Editor & Publisher, 2002).

profile

Nelson Poynter

Nelson Poynter, who owned the *St. Petersburg Times* until he died in 1978, expressed concern about the impact of public newspaper ownership long before it became fashionable among news media critics. He was concerned about the interference of stockholders in newsroom operations and the negative impact that having to pay short-term dividends might have on the finances of the newspaper. However, unlike most critics, Poynter did something about his concerns: He turned the *St. Petersburg Times* into an excellent newspaper and guaranteed that no public corporation could own it.

Poynter was born into an Indiana newspaper family in 1903. He worked as a reporter, editor, advertising salesman, and director at various newspapers before buying a controlling interest in the *Times* in 1947. He believed a newspaper owner held a "sacred trust and a great privilege" that carried with it a responsibility to the community.

The responsibility he felt toward St. Petersburg became a commitment to a quality newspaper that encouraged racial integration in the South and fought government mismanagement. The *Times* won its first Pulitzer Prize in 1964 for public service. Poynter's legacy continued after his death. The *Times* won five more Pulitzer Prizes during the 1980s and 1990s.

Poynter prevented a corporation from taking over his beloved newspaper by willing his stock to The Poynter Institute for Media Studies in St. Petersburg. The Institute has become one of the most respected private journalism educational facilities in the world. Its board of trustees is composed of executives from the *Times*.

Poynter's resistance to corporate ownership and commitment to journalistic excellence have made him a legendary figure in newspaper history. As journalism professor David Coulson wrote, "He was a rare publisher who, in a day of chain ownership, elected to sacrifice any ambitions of amassing great wealth—choosing instead to devote virtually all his time and energy to providing one city with the best newspaper possible."

Sources: David C. Coulson, "Nelson Poynter of the *St. Petersburg Times:* An Independent Publisher with Unique Ownership Standards," *Mass Comm Review* 12 (1985): 11–17; "Nelson Poynter, The 50 Most Important Floridians of the Twentieth Century," November 15, 1999, www.theledger.com/top50/pages/Poynter.html.

---

allows companies to provide better advertising coverage in an area by placing the same ad in all their newspapers. It also allows them to cut circulation expenses because their newspapers no longer compete with one another. This decline in competition has been criticized as leading to reduced newsroom budgets and lower quality.

Ownership concentration also continued in the 1990s as groups started to buy the alternative weekly papers found in most large cities. The weeklies were first published during the cultural movements of the 1960s and totaled more than 250 in 1999 with more than $400 million in yearly revenue. These newspapers typically emphasize politics and entertainment. Some of these alternative newspapers joined together to avoid being bought by daily chains.

In 2002, New Times, Inc., of Phoenix owned twelve alternative weeklies and the Ruxton Group, which sells advertising for twenty-eight newsweeklies in major metropolitan markets. Some observers express concern that group ownership will change the independent, irreverent nature of alternative weeklies, whereas others argue that the increased financial support will help them improve their journalism.[11] To date, it appears that the latter is true, because the newspapers continue to put resources into extensive local political and business coverage.

Group ownership has been criticized since the first chains were formed during the nineteenth century. Some community leaders and journalists fear that group ownership will standardize newspapers at the expense of their local distinctiveness, that absentee owners are less likely to invest in the newsroom, and that ownership groups will impose their editorial will on a local newspaper. Supporters of group ownership argue that financial strength makes groups less vulnerable to manipulation by advertisers or political groups; that groups have more money to invest in staff and equipment; and that when managers are moved from one location to another, they are less likely to become part of the local power establishment with policies and interests to protect. Researchers have found that many of these problems have little to do with whether a newspaper is owned by a group or by an individual or family. The impact of ownership comes from local commitment and management goals—two elements that vary among newspapers regardless of whether owners are groups or individuals. For instance, research indicates that publicly held ownership can negatively affect local newspapers. The more stock is owned by the public, the higher the profit rate a newspaper company will pursue.[12] This reflects management goals. The high profit keeps stock prices up, but the result is reduced newsroom budgets that can lower the quality of the local coverage.

Competition

Direct competition among daily newspapers has all but disappeared. In 1920, 552 of 1,295 U.S. cities with daily newspapers had two or more dailies owned and operated by different companies. By 1960, only 61 of 1,461 cities had separately owned and operated dailies. Currently, about twenty cities have two or more daily newspapers that are separately owned and operated.

Why this downward trend? Newspapers serve more than one market. The diverse reading audience chooses from a variety of media outlets in the consumer market as discussed in Chapter 1. Potential advertisers compose another market. These advertisers want to reach the most people possible for the least amount of money per individual. Accordingly, advertisers buy newspaper space according to the number of readers. This factor is referred to as cost-per-thousand, or the price an advertiser pays to reach 1,000 subscribers. In a two-newspaper town, the newspaper losing readers has a higher cost-per-thousand because newspapers rarely reduce their advertising prices. As a result, advertisers take advantage of the better buy at the other paper. Because readers buy newspapers for ads as well as for news, readers of the trailing newspaper switch to the competing one. Once a newspaper begins to lose readers, it also loses advertisers, and as it loses advertisements, subsequently it loses readers. A downward spiral begins. One newspaper gains a disproportionate amount of advertising, and before long, a two-newspaper town becomes a one-newspaper town.

Competition is an important factor in newsroom quality. Research shows that competition gives the reader choice and, therefore, power. Usually, as the intensity of competition increases, publishers spend more money on the newsroom, resulting in better-quality reporting. With more news and advertising space available in each market, advertisers get lower advertising rates, and reporters and editorial writers strive for new ideas for stories. The existence of two editorial sections also increases the possibility that the marketplace of ideas will become more lively and that readers will have access to varied points of view.

With these competition factors in mind, Congress in 1970 created the Newspaper Preservation Act, which allows two newspapers in the same town to combine all of their operations, such as business and circulation, with one exception: the newsroom. This legislation exempts newspapers from the antitrust laws that regulate

Although newspaper competition has declined in local markets, journalists still compete for stories at the national level. Photojournalists from dozens of news organizations take photographs during testimony by Enron CEO Key Lay to a Senate Committee.

competition. Congress felt that the political role played by newspapers in a democracy warranted efforts to maintain two daily newspapers in the same city. In 2002, twelve of the twenty-seven joint operating agreements (JOA) approved by the Justice Department since 1970 remained in operation. Research indicates that the quality of JOA newspapers is not as good as that in competitive markets but that it is much better than the quality in cities with one daily newspaper.[13] However, JOAs do not end the downward circulation spiral that forces newspapers out of business, and eventually at least one newspaper in all the JOAs will close.

Even though daily newspapers lost most of their daily newspaper competition, other forms of competition have taken its place. Televisions national cost-per-thousand for common items such as household soaps and soft drinks is much lower than that of newspapers. As a result, newspapers carry little national advertising, but they retain local advertising. Also, as the number of big mass market newspapers declined, other portions of the industry restructured. The number of weeklies has grown dramatically, and regional competition has become a factor. Metro dailies have responded to competition from regional and suburban newspapers by zoning their coverage.[14] For example, the *Washington Post* includes Fairfax County and Montgomery County sections once each week to compete with the *Journal* papers. Such sections also allow local advertisers to reach smaller, geographically zoned areas at reduced costs. Zoning has earned profits for newspapers only when the zones are designed narrowly and the sections carry information that readers want and believe they can use.

Declining Credibility

Newspapers cannot prosper as suppliers of news and information unless their readers trust what they read. The decline in newspaper *credibility* has become a primary issue facing newspapers at the beginning of the new century. A study conducted by *Time* magazine in 1998 found that newspaper credibility had sunk to a level at which only 21 percent of Americans believed all or most of the content in the local newspaper, representing a decline from 28 percent in 1985.[15]

In response to the continuing decline, the American Society of Newspaper Editors (ASNE) began a $1 million project to improve credibility. In another 1998 survey, ASNE discovered that the public finds too many factual and spelling/grammar errors in newspapers, too little respect for and knowledge about their communities, too much influence of reporters' biases on what is covered and how it is reported, too much sensationalism to increase sales, and too much concern with profit. A 1999 follow-up study showed little change.[16]

The fact that all news media have seen a decline in credibility does not make newspaper publishers and editors feel any better about their slipping public image. As a follow-up to the survey, eight daily newspapers in 1999 undertook multiyear projects to reverse the trend and improve readers' trust in them. These efforts have expanded. The National Credibility Roundtables Project worked with sixty-three newspapers in forty-nine states in 2001 to "host local reader discussions and to take additional steps to build trust." The project was funded by the Ford Foundation and administered by Associated Press Managing Editors, a national organization of editors at AP-member newspapers in the United States and Canada.[17]

Minority and Ethnic Press

Social groups often have information needs that are not met by large commercial newspapers. Historically, immigrants and other minority groups used their newspapers to protest their treatment by the mainstream society or to fight for changes in laws. These newspapers not only serve as political tools, but they also reaffirm membership in communities and reinforce ties to native cultures. For example, African American newspapers that developed after the Civil War challenged segregation laws established in the 1870s, and they printed news of social events, marriage engagements, and weddings. During the 1960s Chicano movement, Spanish-language newspapers fought discrimination against Hispanics. The ethnic and minority press is an important part of society today as well as historically, and immigrants who speak no English start newspapers in their native tongue just as they did one hundred years ago.

Despite their cultural importance, the minority press has constantly struggled with adequate financing. African American newspaper publishers still report that their main threat to survival is lack of advertisements.[18] Publishers of minority newspapers believe that a single-billing, multiple-placement approach to advertising will enable advertisers to improve financial support for minority newspapers. To address the problem, Hispanic newspapers formed the Latino Print Network, which bills an advertiser only once for placement in more than 120 Hispanic newspapers. A similar organization, Amalgamated Publishers, serves about 200 African American newspapers. In 1999, these two organizations joined with the Newspaper National Network, a marketing organization run by the Newspaper Association of America, to make single-billing advertising in 320 minority newspapers available to advertisers. In 2002, Latino Print Network reported that its database includes over 1,500 publications.

African American Press ✦ The number of African American newspapers has varied throughout U.S. history. The variation is because of the financial factors mentioned previously, as well as cultural trends. One scholar estimates that the United States has had more than 5,539 African American newspapers since 1827.[19] In 1998 about 400 newspapers served African Americans nationwide.[20] During the segregation years prior to World War II, newspapers such as the *Chicago Defender* and the *Pittsburgh Courier* circulated nationally among African Americans. As African Americans migrated north, they sent copies of the paper south to family and friends. Newspaper conductors dropped batches of newspapers from trains at designated southern crossroads.[21] African American newspapers expanded during the 1960s as the civil rights movement grew. These newspapers helped promote the movement and provided an outlet for discussion that was not provided by mainstream newspapers.

Although the influence of the African American press seemed to decline during the waning years of the civil rights movement, as the 1990s came to a close, the African American press seemed to become more vigorous. The growth of the African American population and its wealth attracted new investors. The *New Amsterdam News*, a newspaper founded in 1909 in New York, saw its competition for African American readers increase as four African American newspapers started between 1993 and 1997. This vigor will be tested as general circulation dailies increase their efforts to attract the growing minority population.

In 2002 more than 200 newspapers belonged to the National Newspaper Publishers Association, also known as the Black Press of America. This sixty-two-year-old federation of black community newspapers has also served as the industry's news service since World War II. It initially competed with the Associated Negro Press, but that organization dissolved in 1970.

Native American Press ✦ Like the African American newspapers, many early Native American papers were established because of mistreatment by European Americans. As with most weeklies during the 1800s, preservation of Native American newspapers was erratic, and an exact count of the number of titles is impossible. One scholar estimates that 250 papers were published in the Indian Territory before 1900.[22] A 1984 bibliography of Native American and native Alaskan periodicals identified 1,164 titles between 1828 and 1982.[23] Today, about 280 reservation newspapers and 320 other publications serve Native Americans.[24] Many of the reservation newspapers are owned and run by the tribal government. As such, the leaders can censor them. For example, the *Cherokee Nation* staff was fired in 1997 by the tribal government as the paper investigated the tribal chief.

Most Native American publications take the form of newsletters, a format that reflects the small Native American audience served by these publications. The audience size reflects a historically important difference between African Americans and

Latino presses have become tools of political and social activism as well as mechanisms for social control. They strive to reflect ethnic culture and values.

Native Americans: The African American population grew during the 1800s and 1900s, whereas the Native American population declined.

The Native American Journalists Association has been active in working with Native American media as well as with journalists in the mainstream press. In 2002 the organization conducted, in coordination with *NewsWatch*, an examination of coverage of Native Americans in the nation's largest circulation newspapers. They found that although Native Americans are being covered more than they used to be, coverage falls into three basic categories: reservation stories that for the most part reinforce stereotypes of barren living conditions, stories about casinos and gambling, and stories about mascot team names.[25]

Hispanic Press ◆ In 2002, Hispanics and Latinos made up the fastest growing segment of the U.S. population. However, Hispanics constitute diverse groups, having come from a variety of Spanish-speaking countries at different times in U.S. history. Because the United States seized large amounts of land from Mexico, the largest group of Hispanics are of Mexican descent. Newspapers serving these descendants are called the Chicano press and are printed in Spanish, English, or sometimes both languages.

The Chicano press can trace its roots to the area that is now Texas. Newspapers such as *La Gaceta* and *El Mexicano* were printed in the 1810s as Mexico sought independence from Spain.[26] The number of Latino papers is difficult to determine, but some have estimated that 372 Mexican American newspapers, mostly weeklies, were established before 1940.[27] The 1960s saw growth in the Chicano press as Hispanics battled for political power and civil rights. From 1990 to 2002, Hispanic dailies and weeklies grew from 355 to 550, with circulation well over twelve million.[28]

Latino newspapers play a variety of roles in their communities. Felix Gutiérrez lists three such roles: (1) an instrument of social control, (2) an instrument of social activism, and (3) a reflection of Latino life.[29] In addition to the same monetary problems that the African American newspapers face, the Latino press must deal with language barriers. Publishing in only English or Spanish limits readership, but publishing in both languages doubles the cost.

NEWSPAPERS AS ORGANIZATIONS

By the mid-nineteenth century, newspapers had begun to expand their staffs. The small papers of the colonial and early republic years generally were four pages long and were published by a printer–editor or by a printer who compiled writings by anonymous behind-the-scenes editors. As newspapers expanded in size and circulation, editors began to hire reporters. Throughout the nineteenth century, the reporter was a hired hand, paid space rates by the column inch, and not given job security or benefits. The few women who were hired as reporters had the same lack of security. During the late nineteenth and early twentieth centuries, reporters joined together in press clubs to establish themselves as professionals. Their desire for professional status reflected a growing movement in many of the occupations of the day.

Newspaper Departments

To most people, the term *newspaper staff* brings images of reporters and photographers chasing a story. Although these jobs are crucial to a newspaper, getting the news and advertising to readers also requires other activities. Newspaper organizations typically divide their staffs into newsroom, production, advertising, and circulation departments. The content starts in the newsroom and the advertising department. The newsroom staff produces the stories and photographs and graphics (drawings, cartoons, tables, and charts) that make up the news and information in the newspaper. The newsroom staff organizes the elements of each page on a computer screen in a page layout. At the same time, the advertising department sells ad space and creates the advertisements for the space not given to news and information. The production department runs the newspaper copies on the presses after receiving the laid-out pages from the newsroom and ad department by means of computers. As the newspaper copies come off the press, the circulation department puts them in trucks to be delivered to carriers, news racks, and newsstands.

These four departments have been a part of newspapers for more than 150 years. More recently, newspapers and newspaper groups have added marketing departments. The marketing department conducts research, develops promotional activities, and creates advertising to sell the newspapers to readers and advertising space to businesses and individuals. Newspapers that emphasize the role of the marketing department in creating news and information are called *market-oriented newspapers*. These newspaper organizations typically require communication among the various departments in order to increase sales to readers and advertisers.

Critics of market-oriented newspapers fear that the advertising department will influence content to the detriment of readers and that newspapers will produce only

cultural impact

Commitment Ceremonies in the News

The *New York Times* announced in August 2002 that it would begin publishing announcements of same-sex commitment ceremonies along with its wedding announcements. These are appearing in the Sunday styles section.

Times editors said, "In making this change, we acknowledge the newsworthiness of a growing and visible trend in society toward pub-lic celebrations of commitment by gay and lesbian couples—celebrations important to many of our readers, their families and their friends.

"We recognize that the society remains divided about the legal and religious definition of marriage, and our news columns will remain impartial in that debate, reporting fully on all points of view," he said.

Wedding announcements are printed by decision of the editors, using newsworthiness, accomplishments, and family background as criteria. Editors said the same criteria would be applied to announcements of same-sex couple commitments.

Source: "*Times* Will Begin Reporting Gay Couples' Ceremonies," *New York Times* (August 18, 2002): I-30.

Reporters are often assigned topical beats, such as the environmental beat. This photograph shows volunteers carrying oil up the rocky shore in northwestern Spain. The oil spilled from the sunken tanker *Prestige.*

news that entertains readers. As a result, independent public affairs reporting will be reduced. Advertisers can influence coverage at some newspapers, and examples of newspapers pandering to potential advertisers are not difficult to find. For example, the *Waco Herald-Tribune,* hoping to attract advertising from a new supermarket, ran a front-page story and two pages inside the paper about the opening of a new store.[30] A 1998 study conducted by Randal Beam, a professor at Indiana University, found that seeking reader input and serving readers' needs and wants through marketing does not necessarily mean pandering by producing only entertainment-oriented news.[31] However, the study also found that at market-oriented newspapers, editors interacted more with managers from other departments, creating the potential for influence across departments.

Newsroom Staffing

Newsrooms typically include reporters, photographers, designers, copyeditors, desk editors, a managing editor, and an editor. Reporters interview sources, conduct research, and write articles. Photographers provide the photographs that illustrate articles. Sometimes several photographs printed together create a picture story that emphasizes images more than words. Copyeditors edit stories written by reporters and write headlines for them. Designers produce graphics for the newspaper and organize the graphics, text, and photographs into the layout that becomes the printed pages. Desk editors supervise other staff members who are assigned to specific areas of news coverage. The city editor supervises the staff that covers the city in which the newspaper is located, and the sports editor supervises reporters and editors who put the sports section together. The managing editor supervises the daily operations of the newsroom, which includes coordinating the activities of the various desk editors. The editor is the top manager in the newsroom with responsibility for all activities and staff in the newsroom.

As the size of the paper increases, so do the degree of editorial specialization and the staff. For example, the advertising departments of large newspapers employ several people who specialize in classified advertising, including salespeople and designers as well as people who specialize in demographics and client relations. On the editorial side, the number of editors increases. Large metropolitan dailies tend to be organized by **desks,** or departments, which may be classified as national, business, news, city, education, health and science, and real estate. Reporters are assigned to each desk, and the editor in charge of that department ensures that reporters cover regular **beats,** such as the police department, county courthouse, city hall, or statehouse. General assignment reporters pick up developing stories, **spot news,** and **features.**

The traditional bureaucratic structure of newspapers has been highly criticized in recent years; some critics believe that the traditional structure creates barriers to innovative stories and coverage. In reaction to the criticism, some newspapers have created different ways of structuring the newsroom. In addition to the traditional beats organized around government organizations such as the police and city hall, newspapers have created topical beats such as science, the environment, and minority issues. These beats allow reporters to consider a broad range of topics and issues in depth.

Topic beats are only one of the developments identified with the modern newsroom. Some newsrooms now pursue a team approach. The teams include reporters, photographers, and designers who have a team leader, not an editor. The team leaders help team members develop stories rather than telling them how to cover the stories, as traditional editors might. As part of a marketing approach, newspapers such as the *Orange County Register* and the *Minneapolis Star-Tribune* created teams to cover certain topics in order to better serve readers. Debate continues over the impact of teams on the quality of news coverage, but a study of the health and science team at the *Portland Oregonian* concluded that it produced better coverage than the traditional approach.[32]

desk: A newspaper department with an editor in charge. Most newspapers, for example, have a city desk and a sports desk.

beats: Beats are regularly covered topics of news such as police and science. Reporters contact sources on a beat regularly to check for events that might be newsworthy. Desks have one or more beats connected with them.

spot news: News based on one-time events such as accidents or crimes.

features: Stories that emphasize activities of people instead of "hard news events" such as crime and disasters.

An important member of the news teams is the designer. At some newspapers, the way the news and information is packaged is as important as the news and information itself. A newspaper's **design** must attract and retain readers; it has become a key part of the marketing approach practiced by some newspapers.

Newspaper Design

The trend toward more readable news and graphic displays began with the introduction of Gannett's *USA Today* in 1982. The newspaper distributes 1.8 million copies a day. It provided a wake-up call to the nation's newspaper editors, serving notice that readers would respond to "news you can use" and to graphic displays that made information more accessible. *USA Today* also has pioneered technological developments by using new digital photographic techniques and satellite distribution to regional printing plants. The *New York Times* and the *Wall Street Journal* use similar techniques to produce and distribute those newspapers nationally.

Much of the attractive design that now appears in newspapers came from research conducted during the late 1980s by several newspaper chains. Publishers wanted to find out, in a scientific fashion, what readers would read and what attracted them to newspapers. Thus began the new period of market-oriented newspapers, which emphasized design.

Knight Ridder launched a project at the *Boca Raton News* in southern Florida that led to major changes in newspaper design, although Knight Ridder papers enjoy local autonomy in applying the design lessons learned through market research. Another major effort by a group to get its newspapers in touch with their readers and look to the future was Gannett's News 2000 project. In June 1991, Gannett introduced the program to 230 Gannett executives, instructing each publisher to address the issues that were in the minds of the community. Using surveys, **focus groups,** and readership studies, Gannett staff developed comprehensive designs for each paper. Many of the changes involve presentation, including dramatic designs, **breakout boxes,** and fewer stories that jump from page to page.

Reflecting the importance of design in the industry is the formation of the Society for News Design, an international professional organization with more than 2,500 members in the United States, Canada, and fifty other countries. Members include editors, designers, graphic artists, publishers, illustrators, art directors, photographers, advertising artists, web site designers, students, and faculty.

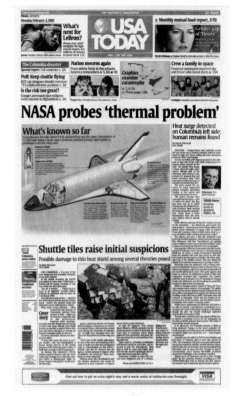

During its first year, *USA Today* was criticized for being "fluffy." However, its coverage has evolved to include excellent graphic representations of news stories, along with writing that is designed to inform consumers how major events affect them.

Newspaper Content

Newspapers contain a variety of information, most of which is not news. The information falls into five broad categories: advertising, opinion material, news, graphics, and photojournalism. Each category has several subcategories.

Advertising ✦ Advertising includes three major types: classified ads, display ads, and inserts. Classified advertisements are the lists of ads set in small type that advertise jobs, items for sale, and garage sales. Display advertisements, found throughout the paper, incorporate photographs, drawings, and large type. For example, when the Al Pacino movie *Simone* opened in theaters during the summer of 2002, many newspapers carried large display ads for the film. Inserts, which are similar to small catalogs, most often advertise merchandise for sale at department stores and supermarkets.

Opinion ✦ Opinion appears on the editorial and op-ed (short for "opposite the editorial") pages. On these pages, editorial writers, political **pundits,** and local citizens express their opinions about current political and social issues. These pages make up the heart of the marketplace of ideas. For example, the opinion pages of the *Lansing*

design: Visual elements, including headlines, photographs, and graphics, organized to make the newspaper interesting and easy to read.

focus groups: Groups of individuals representing different interests who are assembled to discuss a topic. A form of research used to get in-depth information, but not information that is representative of an entire audience.

breakout boxes: Shorter pieces of information, often direct quotes, that are connected to the larger story being covered. They are used to emphasize specific points and for design relief.

pundit: An expert on a particular topic; a person consulted because of his or her knowledge.

State Journal carry letters, columns, and editorials about conflicts between Michigan State University students and permanent residents in East Lansing. Permanent residents want limits on late-night parties, whereas students want lower-priced housing. Ideas exchanged through editorial material allow the community to explore better ways for these two groups to live together.

News ✦ The bulk of nonadvertising information is news. As you read in Chapter 2, news can be hard, soft, or deep. News includes features, current events, and investigative series. Because newspapers tend to emphasize local news, proximity is important for most staff-prepared stories.

Graphics ✦ The term *graphics* covers a range of newspaper content, from the information graphics that present data in tables and graphs to comics and political cartoons. Newspapers have included graphics for more than two centuries, starting with political cartoons before the American Revolution. Currently, newspapers use graphics extensively to create visual interest and to communicate complex ideas and data.

The comics and political cartoons remain the mainstay of newspaper graphics. According to the Newspaper Association of America, more than 70 million people in the United States read newspaper comics and look at political cartoons every day. Comics provide entertainment and a lighter look at some of people's problems. Political cartoons comment on political, social, and cultural events and the people who influence those events. Comics appeal to the consumer market; political cartoons contribute to the marketplace of ideas. The difference between the two is not always obvious because some comics aimed at entertaining, such as "Dilbert," also provide commentary on social and cultural issues.

Any newspaper editor can explain the importance of a comics section to readers. About 95 percent of all daily newspapers carry a separate and identifiable comics section on Sunday,[33] and more people read comics regularly than read sports, editorials, letters to the editor, food pages, and in-depth investigative reports.[34]

The use of information graphics boomed in the late 1980s and became a newspaper mainstay because of offset printing, the use of computers, and the development of *USA Today*. Information graphics such as tables, maps, and graphs have become so important that the number of newspaper graphic artists and designers has grown significantly. Most important news stories have a designer who packages the story, and the nature and extent of graphics and photographs available to tell the story can affect the location of the story. At many papers, a story without good art (graphics and photography) will not make the front page.

Photojournalism ✦ Photojournalism, which integrates words and photographs, attempts to explain people's behavior and the nature of the world. Effective photojournalism involves skilled editing and assumes that informing the public is essential.

Photojournalism is capable of powerfully affecting an audience's interpretation of an event and often defines public memory. People's memories of September 11, 2001, will forever be defined by the photograph of firefighters raising the flag at the site of the World Trade Center.

Photojournalism may be more critical to society than other forms of photography because its goal is to alter our vision of the world and it is mass distributed. Photojournalism opens up arenas of action and images that people would otherwise never see.

TRENDS

In 2002, newspapers, although highly profitable, are struggling to attract a younger audience and to determine how to use the Internet to advance the interests of newspapers and of the media companies that own them. Newspapers have changed enormously since the 1980s, first with livelier news and graphics formats and second with efforts to enhance credibility and expand coverage of diverse populations. Cable and the Internet were two attractive technologies that reduced newspapers' ability to attract readers. However, the American Society of Newspaper Editors has found that communities feel strong and affectionate ties to their local newspapers, despite public skepticism about accuracy and accountability.[35]

As a result, newspapers are aggressively experimenting with new technologies as one way to build bridges to the communities they serve. Although electronic delivery systems are showing a profit for newspapers only in rare instances, publishers recognize the importance of being involved at the experimentation stage. Questions about how to integrate print news into web sites, what types of advertising will sell on the Web, and how much reader participation to allow on newspaper web sites continue to confront newspaper managers.

Another crucial issue for newspapers is diversification. Newspaper staffs are more diverse than they once were, but they still include few minorities. Studies show that diversification in content and staffing can attract new audiences.

Pursuing Young Readers

Publishers realize that they must be attuned to the needs of children and young adults because they will form the readership group for the twenty-first century. Before television gained popularity, young people learned the newspaper-reading habit from their parents. With television's arrival, families began to move away from newspapers as their source of entertainment. A 1999 study found that only 3 percent of the 1,200 teenage participants thought newspapers were "enjoyable" or "entertaining."[36] To counteract this trend, newspapers pursue young readers in a variety of ways, including Newspapers-in-Education (NIE) programs that encourage reading newspapers in public schools, special sections in newspapers aimed at children and young adults, and youth-oriented web sites run by newspapers. For example, in 2002 the Journal Newspapers organization that publishes dailies for Fairfax County, Virginia, Alexandria, Virginia, and Montgomery County, Maryland, among others, began to recognize student achievement in areas other than sports, with awards for high school drama and music stars.

Young readers have not deserted newspapers entirely. Almost 70 percent of teenagers look at a newspaper at least once during the week, and more than 60 percent believe newspapers carry information useful to them in their daily lives. However, newspapers ranked behind television and radio, but above the Internet, in amount of use.[37]

Content is the key to attracting young readers, or any readers for that matter, and newspapers use market research to help them identify the content that readers want. A focus group of sixteen-year-olds conducted by the Survey Research Lab at Northwestern University suggested the following topics as ideal newspaper subjects:

- Crime but not a lot of violence
- World events and how they affect me
- Money (how to make it, how to save it, how to spend it)
- Earth issues and the environment
- Social issues and how I can help
- Analysis, perspective, and explanations of events and controversial issues
- New products and technology
- Fashion ins and outs
- Sports and in-depth interviews with sports stars
- News of upcoming concerts
- Music reviews by people my age
- Things to do
- Getting along with people who are different from me
- Careers and life after high school
- Shopping[38]

Identifying topic areas, however, is only the first step. The news and information must be prepared and delivered in a format appealing to younger readers.

Convergence and Newspapers

A second trend is delivering news online. Despite the staid image of newspapers, the companies that own newspapers fight for readers and advertisers every day on an electronic battlefield. The almost limitless ability of the Internet and World Wide Web to deliver information, news, entertainment, and advertising into people's homes has led newspapers, television, radio, magazines, and even nonmedia companies into a war for the attention and money of people around the world. More than 1,300 daily newspapers in North America have launched online services; worldwide, there are more than 5,000 daily, weekly, and other newspapers online.

Even though the number of news sites grows rapidly, the long-term nature of newspapers' presence on the Web continues to evolve. Few newspaper web sites are making a profit even as the number of hits and visits grows. However, in 2001 more than 2,200 daily and weekly newspapers in the United States have sites on the World Wide Web.

The first few years of online newspaper publishing revealed three important observations about the future of electronic newspapers. First, most newspapers must provide their news and information for free. One study found that only a small percentage of current readers will pay to access newspapers online.[39] The exception seems to be the *Wall Street Journal*, which in 2002 charged $79 annually (or $39 annually for those who also subscribed to the print version).

Second, the advertising battle on the Web will center first on classified advertising. Even though the Web holds promise for selling banner ads for retailers, the battle for the important classified advertising market is underway. Classified advertising fits the Web well. Creating classified ads requires little work, and the ad can be removed quickly after the item is sold or the job is filled.

The third observation concerns content. A lot of the news and information produced for the print version can be put on the Web, but newspapers have to do more than simply reproduce the text from the print version on the Web. Some newspapers, such as the *Tampa Tribune*, have a staff exclusively devoted to generating news for their Web version. Other newspapers add features that the print version cannot supply, such as the *Minneapolis Star-Tribune*'s up-to-the-minute traffic and commuter conditions, whereas still other newspapers experiment with opening their web sites to the community. For instance, the *Philadelphia Inquirer* allows community organizations to put information on the *Inquirer*'s web site. The web sites allow for very local zoning of information. The first week of the *Inquirer*'s southern New Jersey site featured the community's oldest residents and announced the winners of a children's coloring contest.[40] The *Inquirer* sometimes publishes the Web information in its zoned edition. The experimental nature of newspapers on the Web will continue. Newspapers remain local in nature whether on the Web or on paper. The features and types of information that generate advertising revenue and reader interest will likely vary from community to community.

There is some evidence that newspaper organizations have not utilized the Web efficiently. A study of newspaper web sites on September 11, 2001, revealed that many regional daily newspapers simply did not provide information on their web sites. In fact, 65 percent of the sample studied had nothing about the attacks on their web sites in the morning. In the afternoon, 38 percent still had no information online. If newspapers are to compete on the Web, they will have to understand their online competition and the need for speed.[41]

The Attempt to Diversify

Newspaper newsrooms differ from the average workplace in the United States. About 85 percent of the daily newspaper journalists and 77 percent of the weekly newspaper journalists have college degrees, compared to about 20 percent of the general population. About 54 percent of the college graduates at daily newspapers and about 41 percent of the graduates at weekly newspapers majored in journalism. Women make up only one-third of newsroom employees at daily newspapers, which is below the percentage of women in all newspaper jobs (43 percent) and below the percentage for the total U.S. labor force (48 percent). The disparity is curious because more than 60 percent of the graduates from journalism schools during the past fifteen years have been women.[42]

In the early twentieth century, newsrooms were all-male bastions. Although efforts to integrate them have been slow and less successful than desired, today's newsrooms include minority and female journalists as well as white males.

In 1978 the ASNE realized that journalists who make decisions about what and how to cover news should be representative of groups who might read the newspaper. However, racial minorities made up only 3.95 percent of newsroom employees. As a result, the ASNE announced its goal of having the percentage of journalists who are minorities equal the percentage of minorities in the general population by 2000. By 2001, 12.07 percent of daily newspaper journalists were minorities, but minorities represent more than a quarter of the general population. The ASNE revised its goal and set the year of reaching equivalence at 2025. Many journalists expressed disappointment that the goal had been moved so far into the future. Not only have changes been slow, but also newsroom managers and minorities often have different perceptions of newsroom reality. A survey conducted by the National Association of Black Journalists (NABJ) indicates that African American journalists feel that they work in an unfriendly, unsupportive environment. Although 94 percent of newsroom managers said that their organization showed a serious commitment to retaining and promoting black journalists, 67 percent of the black journalists disagreed. NABJ's investigation of the coverage of the 1992 Los Angeles riots found that the lack of African American decision makers in determining story coverage was a critical problem according to black reporters who were assigned to cover the riots. Many black reporters indicate that they are afraid to bring up racial issues because they believe it will hurt their careers. Although many newsroom executives seemed surprised at this claim, Geneva Overholser, former editor of the *Des Moines Register,* said that it is not just blacks who are afraid to speak up in newsrooms, but "[w]omen are afraid to speak out, young people are afraid to speak out. I certainly know that people of color are afraid to speak out."[43]

discussing trends

Communities have ties to their newspapers. Newspaper associations have repeatedly discovered this when trying to analyze credibility and other factors. As you read in the chapter on journalism, rebuilding that tie was the core goal of civic journalism. Newspapers are profitable and hope to stay that way. But the challenge for newspaper owners is how to capture a younger audience, how to use technology in productive ways, and how to diversify to attract wider populations. Otherwise, as the now over-fifty age group becomes the over-seventy group, newspaper audiences could dwindle dramatically. Some of the questions that need to be answered include:

■ If you were a newspaper publisher, how would you attract young readers?

■ What would cause you to read a newspaper?

■ Do you think newspaper publishers could use the Internet more effectively to build audience loyalty?

■ If so, how would you do that?

■ Are newspapers worth preserving, or are they a dying medium?

■ If you were analyzing these trends as a newspaper editor, how would you address the issues?

summary

- Newspapers historically focused on their local communities and provided information about local events. However, they also carried national and international news, and Congress debated early the relative merits of local versus national circulation of newspapers.
- During the revolutionary period, newspapers helped to develop political rhetoric that supported independence. In doing so, they were seldom tolerant of competing voices.
- With developments in manufacturing during the nineteenth century, newspapers began to carry national advertising and expand their markets.
- Newspaper markets today are determined by several components, including the number of choices available within a geographic area, the probability of product substitution, and barriers to entering the market.
- Changing demographics make it difficult for newspaper editors to understand the components of the market. Publishers can no longer assume that middle-class readers will subscribe to the newspaper.
- Newspaper readers now have many choices. They can choose to read a newspaper, subscribe to cable television, listen to the radio, watch network television, or subscribe to a computer online database service.

- Newspaper content includes advertising, opinion material, and news. It comes from newspaper staff reports, wire and news services, and feature syndicates.
- To combat changes in the markets, newspaper executives are trying new approaches. Some newspapers use survey research and focus groups to determine the needs of their particular communities and then target their reporting and writing to those needs. Others have reorganized their newsgathering operations, relying less on institutional news and more on topically defined news.
- Newspapers will remain an important component of the media mix, as long as their staffs take advantage of new technologies and ensure that their content serves their audiences.
- Newspaper publishers recognize the opportunities of online delivery of information, but they have not yet determined how to be profitable using this new technology.
- Newspaper owners must learn to attract younger and more diverse audiences if they are to maintain a steady audience base.

navigating the web | Newspapers on the Web

Web sites about newspapers contain information about the industry and online versions of newspapers. With the Internet, a person can access newspapers from all over the world and find articles and data about the industry.

Newspaper Association of America
www.naa.org

The NAA represents more than 1,500 newspapers in the United States and Canada. Its site provides a variety of information about marketing, public policy, diversity, and operations in the newspaper industry. The NAA "Facts about Newspapers" page carries detailed data about the industry in the United States and Canada.

E & P Interactive
www.mediainfo.com

The leading newspaper trade publication, *Editor & Publisher*, runs this site about electronic news-

papers. The site contains regular columns and articles about newspapers on the Web as well as links to an extensive list of online newspapers around the world.

Associated Press Managing Editors
http://apme.com

The APME is maintained by newspaper managing editors who are members of the Associated Press, which is a news service that serves news media around the world. The site carries information about a variety of news media on the "Industry News" page, and it has links to several other newspaper industry pages, including the Associated Press web site.

questions for review

1. Discuss the significance of colonial newspaper editors in the debate over independence and revolution.
2. List the characteristics of the penny press.
3. What is a newspaper market?
4. If most newspapers are making a substantial profit, why are publishers worried?

issues to think about

1. If newspapers have traditionally appealed to local readers, what should they do to attract young readers who will make up the buying public during the next ten to twenty years?
2. Why should newspaper newsrooms reflect the demographic makeup of society? How can newspapers reach the goal of having newsroom demographics reflect those in society?
3. If you, as an editor, were to redefine how your newspaper was organized, what ideas might you have for change?
4. Suggest some innovative ways to integrate newspapers with the Internet.

suggested readings

Bagdikian, Ben. *The Media Monopoly,* 4th ed. (Boston: Beacon Press, 1997).

Bogart, Leo. *The Press and the Public: Who Reads What, When, Where and Why in American Newspapers,* 2nd ed. (Hillsdale, NJ: Lawrence Erlbaum Associates, 1989).

Underwood, Doug. *When MBAs Rule the Newsroom: How Marketers and Managers Are Reshaping Today's Media* (New York: Columbia University Press, 1993).

Woods, Keith, ed. *2001 Best Newspaper Writing Winners* (St. Petersburg, FL: Poynter Institute, 2001).

Magazines

A licia's professor had given her magazine design class an assignment: Find five recent start-up magazines and analyze their content and target market. Alicia checked several newsstands, but it was hard to determine how new each magazine was. Then she went to the library and looked at *Folio: The Magazine for Magazine Management.* It was here that Alicia found her start-ups.

The August 2002 issue listed *ePregnancy Magazine,* described as a magazine focusing on "everything pregnancy." By studying *Folio,* Alicia discovered that the magazine's initial distribution in July 2002, was 466,000, and that a full-page ad sells for $23,000. Looking through several other 2002 issues of *Folio,* Alicia discovered start-ups such as *Get Up & Go,* a magazine for involved grandparents; *Grace Magazine,* a magazine for the "full-fashioned, full-figured woman"; and *Global Gaming Business,* designed for people in the casino gaming industry.

After completing her assignment, Alicia went to see her adviser to discuss her interest in journalism. She left with an issue of *Quill,* the magazine published by the Society of Professional Journalists, to help her decide whether she was interested in becoming a journalism major. When she arrived home, Alicia fired up her computer, logged onto her web browser through the university network, and read a critical commentary about the college ranking system of *U.S. News & World Report.*

The kinds of magazines Alicia encountered highlight some of the trends in the industry today. Women's magazines such as *Good Housekeeping,* fashion magazines such as *Vogue,* and general-interest magazines such as *Reader's Digest* have been popular for decades. Today, however, the industry increasingly depends on specialized magazines devoted to particular interests such as sports or travel, specific professions, or computers. Specialized magazines are also aimed at specific age groups. *Jane,* a magazine started by the founding editor of *Sassy,* is aimed at women ages eighteen to thirty-four and just celebrated its fifth year anniversary. At the same time, *Modern Maturity* thrives on articles with titles such as "Elder Cool" because it targets baby boomers turning fifty. Fifty-one-year-old former model Cheryl Tiegs, who appeared on the cover of *Time* in 1975 clad in a white see-through bathing suit, graced the cover of *Modern Maturity* in 1999. Publishing director Shirley Ramsey said the way in which Tiegs was dealing with aging was important to her readers. "People are not looking at aging the same way they did in the past," said Ramsey. "They are living longer and their lives are healthier and more meaningful. The magazine needs to reflect that. They're more interested in seeing if they can prolong health and fitness and vitality."[1] So we see that even traditional magazines are adapting to new demographics (characteristics, such as age and income, of the population). Furthermore, magazine content is increasingly appearing on the Internet and on other online services. Small magazines, called *zines,* are appearing online and bypassing paper publication altogether.

In a world in which individuals have unprecedented choice regarding which media to buy and use, magazine industry personnel have to consider the following issues:

◆ How are converging technologies affecting magazine content, audience, and distribution?

◆ As the U.S. population continues to age, how are magazines adapting to changing demographics?

◆ How do magazines succeed in periods of economic downturn and reduced advertising revenues?

◆ Will specialized magazines—which are so successful today—be able to function as conveyors of social knowledge? Will they continue to connect people?

Magazines *in Your Life*

Do Magazines Bring People Together?

As you read this chapter, consider whether magazines connect people. Think about the types of magazines you, your friends, and your family read. Are your family's magazines so specialized that you don't enjoy them? What about your magazines? Would your parents or your children read them? Or do you think that magazines are so specifically targeted to special interests and to age groups that they have lost their ability to bring people together? What kinds of magazines bring people together?

TYPES OF MAGAZINES	TITLES YOU READ	TITLES YOUR FAMILY READS	OTHER PEOPLE WHO READ YOUR MAGAZINES
News			
General Interest			
Specialized			
Men's			
Women's			

Throughout our nation's history, magazines have been the collectors, producers, and distributors of contemporary social knowledge. ***Magazines have helped connect, or correlate, different aspects of society,*** explaining to millions of readers how small bits of information fit into a larger context. With today's trend toward specialized magazines, however, that traditional function may be in jeopardy.

key concept

Magazines and Correlating the Parts of Society People from various social groups have used magazines to discover and make sense of the behavior of other groups. Information about others in magazines may help a group bring into perspective, or correlate, the actions of one part of the society with the actions of another.

Magazine publishing is a risky business that generates billions of dollars. There are more than 31,000 magazines published in the United States, and total magazine revenues in 2001 exceeded $16 billion. About 350 new launches occurred in 2002. People in the United States are buying more magazines than ever. From 1965 to 1999, total magazine circulation in the United States increased more than 74 percent.[2] Since 1998, magazine readership increased 5.3 percent, outpacing the 4.4 percent growth in the adult population during the same period, despite an economic downturn and the continued growth of media alternatives such as the Internet. Total circulation exceeds 358 billion. Many magazines are launched each year, and many magazines fail. In a random survey of 8,000 consumers, 48 percent said they trusted magazines, compared to 32 percent who trusted network television.

1741. First magazine is published in America.

1800s. Increasing literacy and technology enhance magazine growth.

1850. Number of magazines published in the United States reaches 685.

1863. Price to ship magazines by mail declines.

1890. 4,400 magazines reach eighteen million circulation.

1893. *McClure's* starts mass circulation of muckraking magazines.

1904. *Ladies' Home Journal* passes 1 million circulation.

1915. Magazine muckraking dies out.

1922. *Time* becomes first news-weekly.

1936. *Life* becomes first U.S. picture magazine.

1400–1700	1800	1860	1880	1900	1920	1930

1620. Pilgrims land at Plymouth Rock.

1690. *Publick Occurrences* is published in Boston.

1741. First magazine is published in America.

1776–1783. American Revolution

1830s. The penny press becomes the first truly mass medium in the United States.

1861–1865. American Civil War

1892. Thomas Edison's lab develops the kinetoscope.

1914–1918. World War I

1915. *The Birth of a Nation* marks the start of the modern movie industry.

1920. KDKA in Pittsburgh gets the first commercial radio license.

1930s. The Great Depression

1939. TV is demonstrated at the New York World's Fair.

1939–1945. World War II

MAGAZINES IN AMERICAN LIFE

The magazine business, like all business ventures, has been dependent on supply and demand. Once magazines became established in the British colonies in America, they successfully occupied a niche within the world of print and publishing as the nation's conscience, the conveyors of social knowledge. Although newspapers supplied quick information and books offered professional materials and fiction, magazines provided the long, thoughtful essays that encouraged people to think about politics, to plan their travels, and to engage in debates about social policies. At first magazines catered to the elite, but they soon began to reach a broader class and became a *unifying force in American life.*

key concept

Magazines as a Unifying Force in American Life Magazines have allowed people across class, social, and racial divisions to read common material, thus providing the basis for mutual understanding.

Magazines Experience Slow Growth

The colonists were eager for information from their home countries and from adjacent colonies where they had family and friends. They imported books from England and read the fledgling newspapers in the colonies. Magazines developed more slowly be-

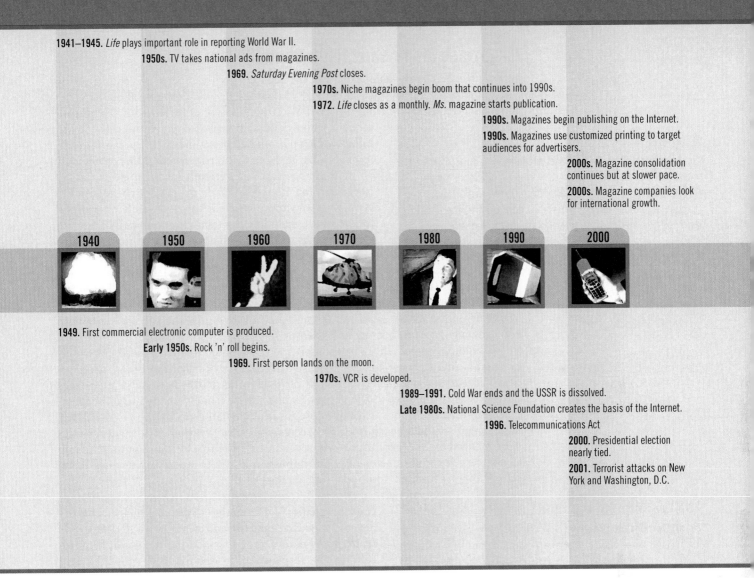

1941–1945. *Life* plays important role in reporting World War II.

1950s. TV takes national ads from magazines.

1969. *Saturday Evening Post* closes.

1970s. Niche magazines begin boom that continues into 1990s.

1972. *Life* closes as a monthly. *Ms.* magazine starts publication.

1990s. Magazines begin publishing on the Internet.

1990s. Magazines use customized printing to target audiences for advertisers.

2000s. Magazine consolidation continues but at slower pace.

2000s. Magazine companies look for international growth.

| 1940 | 1950 | 1960 | 1970 | 1980 | 1990 | 2000 |

1949. First commercial electronic computer is produced.

Early 1950s. Rock 'n' roll begins.

1969. First person lands on the moon.

1970s. VCR is developed.

1989–1991. Cold War ends and the USSR is dissolved.

Late 1980s. National Science Foundation creates the basis of the Internet.

1996. Telecommunications Act

2000. Presidential election nearly tied.

2001. Terrorist attacks on New York and Washington, D.C.

cause they were expensive, postal regulations did not favor their distribution until the mid-1800s, and early America lacked a professional class of writers to supply articles.

In fact, it was a full fifty years after the first newspaper was published in the colonies that Andrew Bradford sold the first magazine: *American Magazine, or A Monthly View of the Political State of the British Colonies* first appeared on February 13, 1741. Although Benjamin Franklin had intended for his *General Magazine, and Historical Chronicle, for All the British Plantations in America* to be the first magazine in the colonies, Bradford's was published three days earlier. Bradford's magazine lasted three issues; Franklin's survived six. The first American magazines boldly published articles that appeared in British magazines and rarely used local material.

Reading magazines was a pastime of the colonial elite, who not only had the education to read but also the time. Because most colonists were engaged either in subsistence agriculture or the trades, they had little leisure time for reading. Inadequate distribution and printing methods contributed to the slow growth of magazines. Magazines never enjoyed the favored postal rates to which newspapers quickly grew accustomed. To reach audiences outside the growing towns of Boston, Philadelphia, and New York, magazines traveled by stagecoach, which had to contend with rough and sometimes washed-out roads. Most publishing operations were family owned, sometimes with husband and wife sharing equal responsibilities, and profits could be earned more easily from printing, stationery sales, or newspaper publishing than by publishing magazines.

Magazines in the Nineteenth Century

Although only 12 magazines existed at the beginning of the nineteenth century, nearly 100 were in existence by 1825, and by 1850 that number had grown to about 685. Despite a severe setback during the Civil War, the industry experienced a sharp turnaround, with 3,300 magazines in circulation by 1885. The *Industrial Revolution* that began in England in the late eighteenth century had a major impact on *magazine technology.*

The change from an agricultural to an industrial society after the Civil War made magazines cheaper, more attractive, and more efficient to produce. New printing technologies, including the steam press, **stereotyping,** and **electrotyping,** sped up production. These innovations also reduced the amount of heavy labor needed, often allowing young women, who could be paid less, to handle many aspects of publishing, thus reducing labor costs. Papermaking machines allowed paper to be produced in continuous rolls. Photographic and engraving developments also were important to magazines because they allowed publishers to use engravings and drawings more frequently at less cost.

Technology improved transportation and contributed to an advanced postal system that facilitated faster and less expensive distribution of magazines across wider geographical areas. Newspapers could rely on local forms of distribution, but magazines were expensive and needed a wider geographical base from which to attract readers.

In 1845, a five-ounce magazine cost six and one-half cents to mail; by 1852, the same magazine could be mailed for five cents. If postage was paid in advance, charges were reduced by half. Postal laws were even more favorable by 1863, setting the rate at one cent for four-ounce magazines published less than weekly, with rates rising proportionally for each additional four ounces.[3]

A rapidly growing population, a steady migration to cities, and national distribution of products helped consolidate the magazine audience and create an *era of democratic reading.* As manufacturing made the transition from locally produced products to nationally distributed brand names, magazines became the perfect national advertising vehicle. They circulated to all regions and appealed to national businesses and national audiences. Magazines gave meaning to situations and helped readers understand significant social, economic, geographic, industrial, and educational events. Children were expected to read in order to become good citizens, and young adults strived to expand their knowledge in order to advance their careers. The search for social knowledge was important to those seeking upward mobility.

With this historical context in mind, think about the magazines you listed in Magazines in Your Life at the beginning of this chapter. Can you think of magazines you read today that help you understand significant social and political events?

Quality Monthlies ◆ The showcase magazines of the mid-nineteenth century were the quality monthlies, known for their travelogues, light fiction, and political commentary, as well as for their elegant covers and finely drawn illustrations. Among these were *Century Magazine, Scribner's, Atlantic Monthly,* and *Harper's.* Those magazines helped to develop a class of American writers and created a forum for criticism of American art and literature. By 1870, *Harper's,* which relied heavily on British authors, had a circulation of 150,000. This magazine, owned by The Harper Brothers, Inc., provided an excellent advertising vehicle for books produced by the company. The *Atlantic Monthly* was one of its chief competitors, building its reputation on American authors such as Ralph Waldo Emerson.

key concept

The Industrial Revolution and Magazine Technology In the mid- to late nineteenth century, developed societies were completing a transition from an economy based on handwork and agriculture to one based on mechanized industry. The shift from handwork to mechanized production increased efficiency and radically lowered the cost of printing, which made magazines and newspapers affordable for a large population.

key concept

Era of Democratic Reading By the mid-nineteenth century, thanks to the availability of cheap publications, all classes of society were encouraged to become readers. The new democracy of readers eagerly devoured newly created magazines and newspapers.

stereotyping: The use of a paper mat to make cylindrical molds for printing.

electrotyping: A metal plate used in letterpress printing by coating a lead or plastic mold of the page to be printed.

Mathew Brady and his photographers chronicled the Civil War. Magazines such as *Frank Leslie's Illustrated Weekly* carried engravings of the photographs to inform the nation of the carnage of the war.

Financing a New Industry

Advertising not only provided the funds for magazine growth but also provoked social and cultural controversy. Some magazine publishers shunned advertising, believing that ads for such items as **patent medicines** cheapened their product. However, some publications sold space publicizing contraceptives and abortion-inducing drugs, forcing readers to confront the issue of unwanted pregnancies. Magazines such as *Ladies' Home Journal* eventually abandoned patent medicine advertising and published articles to educate middle-class women about the alcohol content of drugs they routinely took.

Although the growing magazine industry provided an outlet for the work of American authors, they were poorly paid. Elite publishers, who believed writing should be an avocation rather than a trade, were reluctant to pay the young, middle-class authors who wanted and needed money for their work. The *Atlantic Monthly* paid $5 a page to new writers, $6 a page to published writers, and $50 for a poem. Louisa May Alcott was paid $50 for her first story; Ralph Waldo Emerson, $50 per essay; and Harriet Beecher Stowe, $400 for her serialized version of *Uncle Tom's Cabin*. During the nine months that *Uncle Tom's Cabin* ran in the *National Era*, the antislavery journal sold a magazine record of one million copies. As the number of professional writers or "magazinists" grew, so did the practice of paying writers.

General-interest and women's magazines dominated the nineteenth-century market; however, publishers began to recognize the value of **market segments,** or specific categories of readers. By midcentury, publishers began to develop specialized magazines, targeting particular social and economic interests. Early *specialization in publishing* focused on subjects such as southern living, public affairs, agriculture, antislavery, medicine, law, education, banking, and the insurance industry. By the end of the nineteenth century, specialized audiences included druggists, hardware dealers, railroad enthusiasts, telegraphers, coach makers, children, and literary types. In the twentieth century, targeting specific market segments enabled magazines to survive economic hard times and competition with new media such as radio and television.

The best example of large-scale specialization and technological innovation appeared in the specialized market of philosophy and religion. The American Bible Society and antislavery societies circulated publications as an integral part of a widespread religious revival that preceded the Civil War. These societies were the first to use technological innovations. They used newly developed, inexpensive methods of printing and expanded the distribution of their messages to create the illusion that their movements were larger than they really were.

key concept

Specialization in Publishing As early as the mid-nineteenth century, magazines adopted the practice of targeting specific segments of an audience rather than appealing to the general public. Magazines continue this trend in the twenty-first century.

patent medicines: Packaged drugs that can be obtained without a prescription. Before the Food and Drug Administration was created, these drugs often contained large amounts of alcohol and sometimes opium.

market segments: The target audience. The group of individuals a magazine selects to target for its readership.

Mass Production and Assembly-Line Magazines

The magazine industry mushroomed, fueled by technological change and a rising middle class. The technological improvements allowed magazines to increase their circulations. By 1890, 4,400 magazines were being published and circulated to eighteen million readers. Circulation reached sixty-four million fifteen years later. In 1915, advertising revenues for general-interest and farm publications combined topped $28 million. The elite magazines of the nineteenth century, such as *Harper's* and *Godey's Lady's Book*, gave way to mass-produced, assembly-line products.

Magazines exploited the social trends and changing values that emerged with the rising middle class. Public education, opportunities for college education, and business expanded. More significant, business had become a national phenomenon. The number of trademarks registered with the U.S. Patent Office, for example, jumped from 1,721 in 1910 to 10,282 in 1920. In this new world of rapidly developing products and new technology, national advertisers bought magazine space to appeal to the middle-class potential consumers of new products.

Publishers strove to achieve large circulations, realizing that advertisers would tolerate higher advertising rates if they could gain wide exposure for their products. Increased advertising rates enabled publishers to reduce subscription prices, which made magazines available to a larger audience.

Magazines began to define their audiences broadly, but they remained an expensive medium. The quality monthlies sold for a quarter, whereas a newspaper sold for two or three cents. However, in the late 1890s, the muckraking magazines dropped their prices to ten cents in order to broaden their targeted audience. The *Ladies' Home Journal* had more than a million circulation in 1904, but until World War I few magazines fared as well.[4] Among those that did were *Collier's, Cosmopolitan, McCall's,* and the *Saturday Evening Post*. Most of the successful magazines of the first two decades of the twentieth century were general-interest magazines such as *McClure's, American Magazine, Independent, Literary Digest, Leslie's Weekly, Scribner's Magazine, Century Magazine,* and the *Saturday Evening Post*.

Before television became a nationwide visual medium for mass audiences, general-interest family magazines, such as the *Saturday Evening Post* or *Collier's,* were dominant and accessible forms of visual information.

The Muckrakers

The dramatic social force on the magazine front was the inexpensive muckraking magazines. Despite massive economic growth and an improved standard of living during the late nineteenth and early twentieth centuries, a growing recognition of corporate greed and political corruption provided the raw material for a literature of exposure. The magazine industry began to attack corporate giants and their struggle for political power. Theodore Roosevelt, despite his own inclinations toward reform, called these writers **muckrakers.** Roosevelt likened the writers to the man with the muckrake in John Bunyan's seventeenth-century *Pilgrim's Progress:* "A man who could look no way but downward with the muckrake in his hands; who was offered the celestial crown for his muckrake, but would neither look up nor regard the crown he was offered, but continued to rake the filth of the floor." Through the **dime magazine,** crusading journalists reached almost three million readers. They used the magazines as responsible tools for public education, describing the close relationship of politics and government and pointing out the advantages of the wealthy and privileged classes. *McClure's,* for example, published articles on the consolidation of the oil industry, corruption in state government, and right-to-work laws. Such magazines, including *McClure's,* the *Munsey,* and the *American Magazine,* thrived until the start of World War I.[5] Although exceedingly popular, the muckraking magazines were relatively short lived. Muckraking as a social phenom-

key concept

Muckrakers The label *muckrakers* was introduced by Theodore Roosevelt and has long been applied to investigative reporters who dig into backgrounds of people and organizations, often exposing corrupt political or business practices. The label sometimes connotes sensationalized or even irresponsible and unethical reporting.

dime magazines: Magazines that cost ten cents and appealed to a broad class of readers. These magazines were less expensive than the quality monthlies that preceded them.

enon has been the focus of critical dispute about the role of magazines and how they reflect, respond to, or influence social and economic forces. Muckraking magazines came of age during the early 1900s, when Congress passed the Pure Food and Drug Act, the Clayton Antitrust Act, the Federal Trade Commission Act, and other pieces of legislation to curb business excess—or at least to create the appearance of doing so. That period saw social reform issues arise in all media, from the reform press to the photography of social reformers such as Lewis Hine. It is possible that by 1915 when the magazines lost popularity the public was tired of reform or believed that corruption had subsided. Perhaps the public had shifted its attention to the looming war in Europe. Nevertheless, the muckraking magazines were a social force that informed readers about corporate and political behavior inappropriate for a democratic society.

News and Pictures Revolutionize Magazines

Issues of social reform did not belong to the muckrakers alone. As the Kodak box camera began to revolutionize public photography after 1900, the development of the **35-millimeter** camera and **fast film** created new opportunities for photojournalism, which was an extension of the type of photography social reformers had used between 1880 and 1915 to document the negative social effects of the Industrial Revolution.

Some journalists tried to expose these problems through articles and illustrations. Muckrakers, who often were magazine journalists, and their newspaper counterparts attacked corporations and fought for changes in labor, agricultural, and business laws. Jacob A. Riis and Lewis W. Hine photographed the plight of the poor and homeless to show what can happen to unskilled workers in an unregulated capitalist economic system.

In the 1920s, social documentary photography was greatly enhanced with the introduction of the small Leica camera, made by E. Leitz of Germany. With the Leica, a photographer could work unnoticed while recording a scene. In addition, film became "faster," needing less light and less time to record an image. These technological changes led to flourishing picture magazines, first in Germany, then England, and then the United States. Magazines that used high-quality paper and printing processes benefited more than newspapers from the new technology.

Henry Luce, who later developed the Time, Inc., publishing empire, capitalized on the need for news, the development of the 35-millimeter camera, and the public's desire for interpretation of social and political events. He and Briton Hadden started *Time* magazine in 1923, at first clipping and rewriting items from daily newspapers

35 millimeter: Photographic film that has a frame for exposure 35 millimeters in length. It is used for both still and moving pictures.

fast film: Generic term for the film that photographers use to stop fast action. Does not need long exposure to light to capture the photographic image.

The photojournalism magazines captured emotion as no medium had before. Here on the pages of *Life,* C. P. O. Graham Jackson plays "Goin' Home," expressing his own and the nation's sorrow at the death in 1945 of Franklin Delano Roosevelt.

Roy Stryker of the Farm Security Administration employed talented photographers in this New Deal program, designed to put artists to work and to photograph the Great Depression. Many of the photographers later became famous.

and later adding their own staff and building the weekly into one of the most renowned news vehicles in the nation. In 1930, when the Great Depression was already under way, Luce successfully founded the business magazine *Fortune*. Although some thought he was foolhardy to initiate such a venture at that time, he recognized that businesspeople and the public needed to understand the consequences of business decisions.

Then, in 1936, he created *Life*. *Life* and Gardner Cowles's *Look* became showcases for photojournalists who chronicled the later years of the Depression and set the standard for war photography during World War II. Unlike photographers in previous wars, *Life* and *Look* photographers, with their small cameras and fast film, could photograph action. They conveyed the horrors and glory of war, including the blood, effort, and grief, transporting readers to the battlefields.

Perhaps the most notable group of photographers during the depression years worked for Roy Stryker and a government agency, the Farm Security Administration (FSA). Some continued to photograph conditions for the Office of War Information during the early 1940s. Photographers such as Arthur Rothstein, Walker Evans, Dorothea Lange, and Gordon Parks photographed migrant farmers in California, African American sharecroppers in the South, drought-stricken farmers in Oklahoma and Texas, and federal work projects throughout the country. The FSA photographers' records of that period demonstrate how effectively a camera can function as a sociological commentator and historical recorder.

Maturation and Competition

Despite improved printing technology and the audience appeal of photojournalism, magazines struggled through the 1930s. A massive economic depression, in which one-third of U.S. workers were unemployed, resulted in lower advertising and subscription revenues. Although the end of the war in 1945 generated prosperity and record amounts of buying, it also resulted in rising costs, including an 89 percent increase in postal rates.

Advertising—the golden financier of magazines—became a commodity for which to fight. It had fueled the magazine industry, but as radio and television entered the media picture, magazines began to lose their competitive edge. Now they had to share advertising resources not only with newspapers but also with new and dynamic media that captured people's ears as well as eyes. Ads with sound and motion made stronger impressions on consumers than print ads. And the cost for television ads was cheaper: In 1971 the expense per thousand persons reached through *Life* was $7.71; by means of television, it was about $3.60.

Three historic general-interest magazines ceased publication with the growing popularity of television. The magazines failed not because of loss of circulation but because of loss of advertising. Although the *Saturday Evening Post* had a paid circulation of 6 million and a **pass-along rate** of 14 million readers, it ceased publication in 1969. *Look*'s paid circulation was 8 million with an estimated 18 million readers when it folded in 1971. *Life,* which boasted a circulation of 7 million and was read by 21 million people, folded in 1972. (*Life* was later revived as a feature magazine published monthly.) These giants had retained huge circulation lists, but they lacked the advertising money needed to keep them afloat financially. Whereas television's share of national advertising more than doubled in the 1960s from $1.5 billion to $3.5 billion, magazines' share went from less than $1.0 billion to only $1.2 billion.

pass-along rate: The total number of readers who read a magazine regularly, including those who read copies that were given, or passed along, to them.

Specialization, however, kept the magazine industry in business by targeting specific audiences and addressing changing **demographics.** Specialized magazines thrived because, rather than competing for the same audiences as broadcast television, they delivered to advertisers audiences with particular interests and consumer habits. For example, advertisers can count on subscribers to *Skiing* to buy advertised skiing products. Particularly successful niche magazines have addressed changing demographics, trends, and technologies. For example, they have targeted increasing numbers of working and single women, emphasized fitness and health, and exploited the popularity of computers.

TODAY'S MARKET STRUCTURE

The magazine industry, like other media industries, is big business. Ownership also is highly concentrated. According to data compiled by the Audit Bureau of Circulations, the number of single titles of U.S. *consumer and business magazines* has grown from 13,541 in 1988 to 17,815 in 2000. More than 347 new titles were introduced in 2001, only a few of which will last for more than five years. Only 15 percent of all magazines have a circulation of 1 million or more, but these magazines represent 64 percent of all circulation. Slightly more than 51 percent have a circulation of 250,000 or less.[6]

Magazines on the Web

Magazines exist on the Web either as independent entities or as a supplement to print magazines. Although originally small magazines making their debut on the Web were called **zines,** the stabilization of the genre has led us further away from this entrepreneurial term, although it is still used occasionally.

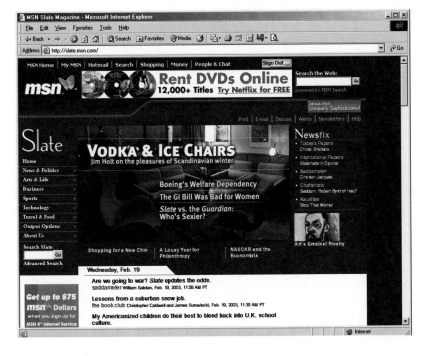

The most successful Web magazines creatively use the interactivity of the Web—like Slate's "The Fray" reader forum or "build your own Slate" feature—to make their products different from the traditional printed magazine.

Magazine publishers have had a difficult time deciding how to profitably create an online presence. Early in their efforts, editors tended to "shovel" print copy onto web sites. Now editors have discovered that magazine web sites are good marketing tools for their print products and for products they advertise.

Magazines may have an important niche in online shopping. The Magazine Publishers Association conducts an ongoing online survey to determine how readers use magazine web sites. They find that web site visitors say they usually find web addresses of sites they visit from magazine ads. Sixty-eight percent of magazine web site visitors have used their credit cards to purchase a product or service online, and they say they enjoy online shopping because they don't have to talk to a salesperson.

Sixty-three percent of respondents say they prefer to read both the printed and online versions of a magazine, and 75 percent of magazine web site visitors also subscribe to or buy at a newsstand the printed version.

Magazines do exist as stand-alone titles on the Web as well. *Slate*, a magazine of news and opinion, succeeds. Other on-the-Web-only magazines tend to address highly specialized audiences.

Economic Hard Times

Changes in the magazine industry are related to broad economic trends as well as to the publishing industry's specific environment.[7] For instance, during the 1990s magazine publishing followed U.S. corporate trends of decentralizing and downsizing, and during the early 2000s, advertising revenues declined. Cost-saving measures included cuts in full-time staff and an increased use of freelancers. Throughout the 1990s, magazines continued to lay off employees, and tight economic times forced editors to edit less and spend increasing time in business meetings, struggling with budgets, creating ideas for advertorial sections, and spinning off satellite projects.

Consumer Magazines

Consumer magazines are those directed to the consumer. They may be of general interest or specialized and they often follow trends. The number of consumer magazines increased slightly each year from 1989, when there were 12,797 published, to 1998, when 18,606 were published. They then declined slightly, with 17,815 published in 2000.[8] Specialization is still the key to success. The top ten areas of growth include comics, regional interest, lifestyle, management, environment and ecology, computers and automation, travel, women's, music, and family magazines. Although the trend toward an increased number of shelter magazines began before September 11, 2001, the attacks on New York City and Washington, D.C., seemed to inspire more interest in home magazines. Three new launches during the fall of 2002 included *LivingRoom*, *Chic Simple*, and *Budget Living*. Other new magazine launches have been directed toward teens and toward young men. Listed in Table 7.1 are the top paid-circulation consumer magazines.

Business Magazines

Business magazines occupy a large segment of the magazine business. They address specific business needs, and many are distributed through controlled circulation. Traditionally, the top ten categories of business magazines have been computers, health care, engineering and construction, media, automotive, banking and finance, business, building, advertising and marketing, and industrial manufacturing.[9] Health care, business, and computers held the top circulation categories in 2001.[10]

Many of the top-circulation consumer magazines, such as *TV Guide* or *Reader's Digest*, appeal to the general population. Others, such as *Essence*, focus on a narrower segment of the reading public for their audience.

Top Paid-Circulation U.S. Consumer Magazines, January–July 2002	
1. NRTA/AARP Bulletin	21,712,410
2. AARP Modern Maturity	17,538,189
3. Reader's Digest	12,212,040
4. TV Guide	9,072,609
5. Better Homes and Gardens	7,602,575
6. National Geographic	6,890,852
7. Good Housekeeping	4,708,964
8. Family Circle	4,671,052
9. Woman's Day	4,167,933
10. Time—The Weekly News Magazine	4,114,137

Source: Magazine Publishers of America, www.magazine.org. Reprinted by permission.

In **controlled circulation,** magazines are sent free to individuals within an industry. This method was developed as a distribution technique in the specialized business-press arena and, unlike consumer magazines, more than half of the specialized business publications use this method of circulation. For example, *Offshore Engineer* is mailed only to named individuals who prove they are involved in specifying and buying equipment and services for the offshore industry.

However, controlled-circulation magazines are recognizing that they need to try different approaches to support growth. **Association magazines** in particular can no longer afford to exist on dues alone. "They have to generate revenues from selling ads and doing all the things that consumer publications do," says Elissa Myers, vice president and publisher of *Association Management,* the 21,400-circulation magazine published by the American Society of Association Executives based in Washington, D.C. Myers points out that the average association now draws only 40 percent of its revenues from dues, compared to the 95 percent drawn in the 1960s. As a result, more and more association magazines are beginning to consider nonmembers as subscribers.[11] Association magazines are a traditional and solid approach to conveying information. Nearly every organization, from county medical societies to the Home Builders' Association, publishes a magazine for its members.

Magazine Ownership

Despite the growth in small-circulation magazines, magazine publishing is big business, and a handful of **conglomerates** dominate as they do in other industries. Some owners publish in a variety of subject categories, and others specialize. Market analysts predict that the pace of consolidation will slow, but magazine publishers will continue to realize benefits by being big. Size brings decided advantages in marketing and distribution. However, companies are more concerned about whether a particular magazine fits the company's business profile. Those that don't fit into an apparent long-term strategy may be sold off.

Conglomerates also have the advantage of staff pools. When one of the conglomerate's magazines is successful, its editor may be moved to another of the conglomerate's magazines. Nevertheless, critics continue to worry about the standardization that comes with conglomerate ownership. If conglomerates prevail, how will the independent magazines—the *Rolling Stones*—survive? Industry analysts and some critics answer that there will always be room for a good editorial product.

controlled circulation: Technique of sending magazines free to individuals within an industry to increase identification with an organization.

association magazines: Magazines published by various associations to publicize their activities and communicate with their members.

conglomerate: A corporation formed by merging separate and diverse businesses.

AUDIENCE DEMAND IN MAGAZINE MARKETS

A magazine has to be in demand to succeed. People can be looking for news on a general topic, advertising about companies or products, or information about new ideas. In response to demand, magazine publishers produce certain kinds of content. The two major markets are consumer, with magazines selling editorial content to readers, and advertising, with magazines selling readers to advertisers.

Consumer Market

All publications need to find a **market niche**. Magazine publishers have done so by providing information in greater depth than newspapers and by being more disposable than books. In addition, they carefully target their audiences. Audiences may be defined through various categories. Some are listed below.

- Geography—worldwide (*National Geographic*); regional (*Southern Living*); state (*Texas Monthly*); city (*Atlanta*)
- Gender—female (*More, Sassy*); male (*Esquire*)
- Ethnic background—African American (*Ebony*); Hispanic (*Hispanic Times*)
- Age—children (*Sesame Street Magazine*); teenagers (*YM*); seniors (*Modern Maturity*)
- Lifestyle—raising children (*Parents Magazine*); owning a home (*Coastal Living*)
- Occupation—*Farm Journal, Nursing, Chemical Engineering News, Editor & Publisher*
- Hobby or sport—*Art & Antiques, Game & Fish Magazine*
- Socioeconomic background—wealth (*Fortune*); education (*Harper's*)
- Application—entertainment (*TV Guide*); decision making (*Consumer Reports*)
- Ideology—liberal (*Mother Jones*); conservative (*National Review*)

Almost every literate person in the country is a potential magazine consumer. Many *market segments for magazine advertisers* overlap, but rarely do two magazines target the identical audience. For example, audiences for *Working Woman* and *Working Mother* overlap, but some readers of *Working Woman* are not interested in motherhood. Similarly, some readers of *Redbook*, a magazine targeted at young mothers, also read *Working Mother*. Furthermore, *Modern Health Care* might also compete for the audience of any of these three women's magazines.

Changes in audiences force magazines to change their content. Therefore, as social change enabled more African Americans to earn higher incomes, advertisers began to recognize that African Americans had increased purchasing power. Publishers then began to target magazine content to specific African American interests, convinced that they could attract advertisers for the new market. Thus economic and cultural forces intertwine—as do consumer and advertising markets.

> **key concept**
>
> **Market Segments for Magazine Advertisers** Each magazine strives to sell content and advertising to a specific segment of the total population that the publisher has selected as its target readership. The tastes of the target audience determine the nature of the magazine's offerings.

Advertising Market

Initially, magazine publishers relied primarily on subscriptions for revenues. However, they soon recognized that they could broaden their audience by allowing advertisers to pay part of the costs. Today, advertisers search for media that are most appropriate for their product and message. Magazines compete with all media for consumers and for advertising. However, a few magazines, such as *Ms.* and *Consumer Reports,* publish without advertising because their publishers wish to avoid advertiser control and also have found that some subscribers support content that does not appeal to advertisers.

Magazines allow companies to match their messages with specific audiences. For example, suppose that a national software company that publishes an interactive

> **market niche:** Portion of the audience a particular magazine gains as subscribers or buyers.

Teen Magazines

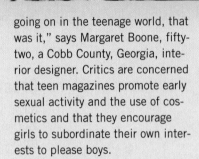

Probably more than any other type of magazine, the teen magazine reflects and shapes change in society. *Seventeen,* twenty-eighth on the list of largest-circulation magazines, was fifty-eight years old in 2002, with a circulation of 2.4 million. Gruner + Jahr's *YM* was closing in on *Seventeen,* with a circulation of almost 2.3 million. *Teen,* which has been a close third, declined from a high of more than 2 million in 1999 to 1.6 million in 2002.

Much of the effort has been directed at teenage girls, with boys earning little attention. In 2000, Transworld publishers attempted to change that with their launch of *Stance.* At the time of the launch, Fran Richards, editorial director for the magazine, said, "We're trying to create a broader interest magazine for teen boys. There's been a huge focus on Generation X, with a lot of publishers vying for that readership. We felt that there's a whole culture below the adult mainstream radar—a culture of brands, sports activities, music and fashion—which is very much geared toward and generated by kids between 12 and 24." The magazine was chugging along in early 2003.

YM, which has been struggling to pass *Seventeen,* benefited from Gruner + Jahr's 2001 purchase of *Jump,* a teen fitness magazine. *Jump* launched in 1997 and was published eight times a year. Gruner + Jahr folded the magazine into *YM.*

Other challenges in the teen market have emerged in recent years. In 1999, *CosmoGirl,* published by the owners of its sister magazine *Cosmopolitan,* was launched and was still on course in late 2002. Other teen magazines target specialized audiences such as Latin American girls *(Latin Girl)* and girls who cannot fit into the "skinny model" clothes pushed by many teen mags (for example, *Girl,* launched in 1998 by *Mode Magazine).* *YM* claims to be a fashion and beauty magazine, but *Seventeen*'s editor says that *YM* has a sensationalist approach, with cover lines such as "I Slept with My Best Friend's Boyfriend," which *Seventeen* avoids.

The teen market is growing. According to the U.S. Census Bureau, the teen population, now estimated at 25 million, will grow at nearly twice the rate of the rest of the population. *Dallas Morning News* writer Tom Maurstad notes, "These teens are coming of age in the Age of AIDS, the Age of Media, the Age of Marketing, the Age of Multiculturalism and Political Correctness." Teen magazines include articles on body piercing, tattoos, and sex (including AIDS and sexual abuse) as well as on the fame, power, and money of celebrities.

Seventeen brought a new self-awareness to girls. "I read it in the mid-'50s and it was like the Bible. If you were wondering what was going on in the teenage world, that was it," says Margaret Boone, fifty-two, a Cobb County, Georgia, interior designer. Critics are concerned that teen magazines promote early sexual activity and the use of cosmetics and that they encourage girls to subordinate their own interests to please boys.

Sources: Janet Ozzard, "Teens: Survival of the Fittest: These Days, Everyone's Making a Run at Seventeen," *Women's Wear Daily* (October 28, 1994); Tom Maurstad, "Fashion! Dallas: Something Different," *The Dallas Morning News* (August 24, 1994): 3E; Jean Marbella, "Attacking the Teen Market—by Design," *Baltimore Sun,* (March 26, 1994): 1D; Valerie Seckler, "Who's Making Money?" *Women's Wear Daily* (October 28, 1994): S18; Angela D. King, "Seventeen Editor Gets Top Spot in New York," *New York Daily News* (October 10, 1996): 73; Catherine Fitzpatrick, "Magazines Your Daughter Is Reading Encourage Sex, Promote the Pursuit of Cosmetic Perfection, and Tell Her to Subordinate Her Interests to Please Boys, a Study Says," *Milwaukee Journal Sentinel* (May 30, 1999), Lifestyle sec., p. 1; "Gruner + Jahr Acquires Weider's Teen Magazine *Jump,*" online exclusive, March 12, 2001, www.foliomag.com; and Susan Thea Posnock, "Lead Launch: Taking a Stance," March 1, 2000, www.foliomag.com, accessed in October 2002.

database for evaluating entry-level jobs wants to reach people in their late teens and early twenties. Radio and newspapers tend to be too local, and national television advertising costs too much. That leaves national magazines that appeal to young people. *Jane* would allow the software company to reach young women, and *Details* would allow it to reach young men.

SUPPLYING THE AUDIENCE'S DEMAND

To continue making money and survive as a business, magazine organizations have to stay in touch with their readers. As society changes, so do readers' wants. For example, *Seventeen* magazine caters to teenage females. Every few years, the magazine's audience "ages out," and *Seventeen* has to recruit new readers. The magazine targets not a set of particular women, but a particular age group whose demographics, backgrounds, wants, and needs are always changing.

The readers change, and so do the topics that interest them. Today's *Seventeen* includes stories and information that were not considered necessary or even proper ten or twenty years ago. *Seventeen*'s October 2002 web article, "Are You Ready to Go All the Way?" would probably never have appeared in the 1970s. Whereas the 2002 article cautions that having sex "won't make you a mature woman," a 1970 version probably would have focused on the dreaded fear of pregnancy. Chances are that in 1970 gun violence in the schools and beepers for staying in touch would not have occurred to an editor of a teen magazine as possible topics. If your mother or aunt read *Seventeen* or *Teen* when she was a high school student, she probably read a far different magazine than the one teenagers read today.

Creating and Financing Magazines

Ideas for new magazines start with a concept that gets refined through the reactions and suggestions of others.[12] This process is referred to as *magazine start-up and financing*. Only one in every ten ideas presented to publishers makes it to the start-up stage, and even then, market success is not guaranteed. An idea must be original, but not so far outside the mainstream that it will not attract an audience. Furthermore, a magazine must have staying power: If it addresses a trend, the trend must be here to stay. For example, computer magazines have proliferated, addressing a permanent new development in our society. In 1988, as the computer trend gained strength, about 180 ideas for computer magazines were presented to major magazine publishers. Eighteen were seriously pursued, but only three were still in existence three years later. Of course, many specialized computer magazines now are available on newsstands.

More important than a great idea is its execution; an idea must be packaged as a marketable product. Table 7.2 shows some start-ups and what happened after their first five years. An entrepreneur must be both an editor and a marketer.[13] As marketer, the entrepreneur must secure financial backing.

Initial financial support for starting commercial magazines comes from three sources. First, entrepreneurs can seek support from companies already established in the industry—for example, major publishers—to launch a new idea. Second, they can look for **venture funding** from small investors who are willing to endure higher risk for bigger payoffs than traditional capital investors. For that, a strong business plan is crucial. Third, start-ups can be funded by private investors who know the publisher and believe in that person's ability to make the magazine work.

Not all magazines are commercial ventures. However, they usually are financed by governments, special interest groups, or commercial companies.

Government ◆ Although some government agencies publish magazines, they tend to be geared to government employees. Usually government publications are newsletters or pamphlets.

Special Interest Groups ◆ Some organizations, such as a city chamber of commerce or a nonprofit organization, publish magazines. Some associations, such as the National Association of Home Builders, publish magazines that rival commercial publications in quality and cost. Others publish smaller, less professional magazines.

key concept

Magazine Start-Up and Financing New magazines may get financial support from government or special interests, but most often the support comes from business financiers who have experience in the industry or are willing to take risks in hope of high returns. Some magazines seek funds from subscribers and patrons only (avoiding ads) or from advertisers only (offering the magazine free to readers), but most magazines are supported by a combination of advertising and subscriptions.

venture funding: Funding of an enterprise with cash from several investors who are interested in innovative enterprises that carry both risk and the potential for large profits.

table 7.2

The Fate of Magazine Start-Ups

TITLE/PUBLISHER	TARGETS	FATE
Chance: The Best of Gaming, ARC Publishing, June 1997	Quarterly magazine devoted to gambling; initial distribution of 100,000 to newsstands, gaming outlets, and select consumers	Folded in early 2002
Working at Home, Success Multimedia Enterprises, September 1997	Quarterly publication aimed at telecommuters; initial advertising rate base of 300,000 circulation	Folded during the summer of 2001
Coastal Living, Southern Progress, subsidiary of Time, Inc., April 1997	Shelter/travel magazine launched as a bimonthly with a rate base of 300,000	Still bimonthly, rate base currently 450,000
Jump, Weider Publications, August 1997	Targeted girls age 15 to 18; initial distribution was 300,000; bimonthly	Acquired by Gruner + Jahr USA in March 2001 and folded into *YM*

Source: Material adapted from several issues of *Folio*, 2001–2002.

Commercial Companies ✦ The vast majority of magazines are commercial, and their financial support comes from readers, advertisers, or a combination of the two.

Advertising

Advertising is the primary source of revenue for most magazines. However, as previously discussed, some are financed through other means. Nevertheless, magazine publishers always must make a decision about advertising. The decision often reflects the philosophy of the magazine's owners.

Advertising-Free Magazines ✦ Some magazines survive without advertising; they are supported solely by readers who pay for subscriptions or for issues on the newsstand. These magazines are published by individuals who believe that advertising would compromise the integrity and principles of the magazine. For instance, *Ms.* magazine, after initial disputes with advertisers, reinvented itself as a nonadvertising publication. Because the magazine's editorial stance is that a woman looks and feels best without excessive use of cosmetic products, *Ms.* wanted to avoid the hypocrisy of printing advertising that contradicted the editorial position. The editors also wanted to avoid advertising cigarettes and alcohol, products that the editors had denounced as dangerous. *Ms.* magazine has had a difficult time sustaining its readership, however. In December 1998, it was purchased by Liberty Media for Women, a newly formed consortium of feminists including the original founders. In October 2002, *Ms.* was searching for a new editor-in-chief and planning a move of its editorial offices to the West Coast.

Free Magazines with Advertising-Only Financing ✦ Although some magazines are supported by readers only, others are financed by advertising only. Consumers read or receive the magazines at no charge. Membership in the American Association of Retired Persons, for example, guarantees a subscription to its flagship publication, *Modern Maturity*.

Combination Financing ✦ A third type of financing is a combination of advertising and circulation. Most commercial magazines fall into this group, and advertising rather than circulation provides most of the revenue stream. Magazines that rely on a combination of advertising and reader support traditionally competed for readers, but now they more often compete for advertising dollars. Advertising rates are closely tied to circulation figures, so publishers must be careful not to price their magazines out of the market. If they do, the decrease in circulation will result in a subsequent decrease in advertising revenue. Therefore increased costs often must be absorbed by increased advertising revenue.[14]

Advertising Tie-Ins ✦ Although prestigious newspapers have established their independence from advertising pressures, magazines have allowed, and sometimes even courted, editorial/advertising **tie-ins. Package deals** are commonplace for many magazine editors who guarantee preferential editorial treatment to advertisers. Take, for example, one issue of *Where to Retire*, a magazine aimed at baby boomers considering retirement in the next ten years. An article featuring Georgetown, Texas, as an award-winning hill country town, is surrounded by advertisements for Georgetown Village, a retirement community, and Texas travel guides from the Texas Department of Economic Development.

Advertisers and Editorial Content ✦ Advertisers also specify placement of some ads and react negatively when editorial content does not support their products. Many advertisers even hire resident censors who sit in the ad departments of major magazines. Dow specified that ads for its Spray 'n Wash products had to be adjacent to pictures of children or editorials about fashion, and ads for its bathroom cleaner next to home-furnishing and family features. Revlon refused to advertise in a magazine because the Soviet women on the cover were not wearing makeup. (The story later won a prestigious Front Page Award.) And during the Gulf War, Procter & Gamble successfully stopped *Sassy* from running a page covered with the word *peace*.

However, if a magazine too often crosses the fine line that separates credibility and promotion, the industry and the magazine's readers may lose faith in it. If circulation drops as a result, advertisers lose interest as well, and the magazine is left to wither from lack of reader or advertiser support.

Publishing a Successful Magazine

The masthead, or list of owner, publisher, and staff of a magazine, usually appears near the table of contents in the first few pages of a magazine. The list emphasizes that *publishing is a process.* The number and size of departments and types of positions vary with each publication; large consumer magazine staffs may employ several hundred people, whereas small specialized business publications might have fewer than ten people. The positions and departments in the following sections are common for all sizes of magazine staffs.

Publisher ✦ The publisher, to whom all staff members are ultimately responsible, may also be the magazine owner or editor. The publisher defines the personality of the publication and works to ensure its financial success. Some publishers with particularly forceful personalities and deep pocketbooks can breathe life into a publication or kill it with an easy blow. When *Lear's* ceased publication in March 1994, the *New York Times* reported that the magazine had died as it had lived. "It was created by Frances Lear, who, after a bitter divorce from television producer Norman Lear, was at a crossroads. She invented the magazine for a particular reader: herself. She gave the magazine her vision, her energy, her money and her name. She sustained it with her enthusiasm, and when she lost interest, she pulled the plug."[15]

Editorial ✦ Once the publisher has defined the magazine's personality, the editor develops and shapes its identity. To successfully complete an editor's mission, the managing editor, the articles editor, and department editors work together to give readers the information they want. Editors edit and proofread stories, approve design and graphics, accept freelance submissions, and contract with designers.

Large-circulation magazines pay from seventy-five cents to $1.50 a word. For example, if you write a 5,000-word article, you could expect to earn about $5,000.

tie-ins: The connection made when a magazine runs a story about a product advertised in the magazine.

package deals: A series of media tie-ins.

However, this is true only if you have already established a reputation and have created a relationship with an editor. Now, to have a gross income of $50,000 (before taxes and expenses), you would have to write ten such articles each year—and be successful at placing all of them. *Salon Magazine* reports that many freelancers are willing to accept $1.00 a word for the visibility they get at a publication such as the *New York Times Magazine*, which a *Times* editor says now pays star writers $80,000 for four pieces. Only a few writers, such as Norman Mailer, achieve real fame and real money. Mailer reportedly was paid $140,000 for two pieces for the now defunct *George.*

Advertising ✦ Advertising is often a magazine's lifeblood. According to Magazine Publishers Association figures, advertising revenue has increased steadily but slowly from $6.7 billion in 1990 to $17.7 billion in 2000.[16]

Advertising staffs may include only an advertising director and several salespeople. At larger magazines, divisional managers contribute specialized knowledge about readers and advertisers in specific geographic areas or about specific types of products.

Design and Production ✦ Convergence of technology is readily apparent in the design and production departments of large and small magazines. The design department designs the actual paper product that readers hold. The production staff includes artistic experts, technological wizards, and people who buy supplies for production, such as ink and paper. **Desktop publishing**—the integration of design and production—has saved magazines millions of dollars and cut production time. For example, when the National Geographic Society converted to desktop publishing for *National Geographic Traveler and World,* it saved $200,000 annually.[17] Technology also has allowed publishers to print split runs and use selective binding, in which pages are changed according to geographic locale. Advertising copy may be based on zip codes. Geographically divided runs allow publishers to better target their markets.

Circulation ✦ The circulation staff gets the magazine to the reader through either subscriptions or newsstand sales. Each method has different costs. A new subscription costs publishers about $15 in promotion expenses; each renewal costs about $3. For single-copy sales, every stage of transport between publisher and newsstand takes a percentage of the copy price.

Soliciting subscriptions is one facet of circulation, and experts have become adept at using demographic background information about individuals in personalized, target-market selling. Publishers also design web sites aimed at attracting subscribers.

Newsstand, or single-copy, sales go through a variety of stages before hitting the display racks. Each publisher works with one of about ten national **distributors.** The distributor supplies the printer with the mailing labels of some of the four hundred regional **wholesalers.** The printer mails bundles of issues to the wholesalers, which deliver the copies to dealers. Popular newsstand dealers include owners of grocery stores, convenience stores, pharmacies, and bookstores. At the same time that magazines are delivered, the wholesaler picks up and discards the previous week's or month's unsold ones.

Magazine Employees ✦ Salaries for editorial assistants and fact checkers—beginning jobs on magazines—pay between $22,000 and $28,000. Some companies, such as Time Warner, pay overtime, which can double your income. But to do so means working sixty hours a week. At the *New Yorker,* fact checkers make $30,000 to $35,000. Beginning staff writers and reporters at Time Warner make between $35,000 and $50,000. At Condé Nast, writers and editors at the lowest levels make $30,000 to $40,000. Senior writers and editors at *Sports Illustrated* may make as much as $150,000. Top editors at Time Warner make about $250,000, with the editors-in-chief making $500,000 to $1 million. In addition, "some of the top people are getting bonuses equal to good salaries," says a Time Warner writer. Executive editors at Condé Nast make $200,000 to $300,000. Photo editors can make from $125,000 to $200,000. Art directors make $180,000 to $225,000. Pay is better on the advertising side. A junior ad salesperson, the typical starting job, makes between $45,000 and $70,000, and senior salespersons can make around $150,000. Publishers' pay packets depend on the profile of the magazine, ranging from $200,000 to

desktop publishing: Writing, illustrating, and designing publications with a personal computer.

distributors: Companies that help get magazines from the printer to the wholesalers.

wholesalers: Companies that deliver magazines from a warehouse to dealers, such as bookstores.

profile

Gloria Steinem

In September of 2002, *Mother Jones* magazine published this intro to an article about Gloria Steinem:

> More than two decades after founding *Ms.* magazine, Gloria Steinem remains America's most influential, eloquent, and revered feminist. Her 1992 book, *Revolution from Within: A Book of Self-Esteem,* was a number one bestseller and has been translated into 11 languages. Last winter, shortly after publishing a book of six essays titled *Moving Beyond Words,* she canceled a national speaking tour because of a rare nerve disorder that left her bedridden. Now rejuvenated, the 61-year-old Steinem spoke with us about politics, aging, and why her best activist days are still to come.

Since the founding of *Ms.* magazine in 1971, Gloria Steinem has been a feminist ideal for young women and men. She has devoted her life to persuading all kinds of women to believe in themselves, has lent an influential voice to the cause of immigrant farmworkers in California, and has helped to persuade Democratic political leaders to include women's issues in their platforms.

As a feminist, Steinem has had a major impact on the magazine industry. She developed a solid reputation as a reporter and magazine writer, founded *Ms.* in 1972, and later helped convert it to a no-advertising publication to avoid the impact of sexist advertising on its content.

Steinem grew up in a tenement in Toledo, Ohio. Her emotionally ill mother, Ruth, had been a newspaper journalist who wrote under a male pseudonym. Steinem's parents were divorced when she was ten.

When Steinem was old enough, she worked evenings and weekends as a waitress and shop assistant. She also tap danced in chorus lines. She graduated from Smith College and then spent a year in India with the followers of the spiritual leader Mahatma Gandhi before starting her professional career. She advises women to use their backgrounds to learn and to grow.

When she returned to the United States from India, she wrote for *New York Magazine* and *Esquire,* building a reputation as a reporter and establishing a network. Her political involvement in women's causes began in 1969 at an abortion-law reform rally, where she heard women talk about being offended by sexist jokes and about having abortions and other experiences, some of them similar to hers. Inspired, Steinem cofounded the national feminist publication *Ms.* Although the magazine went through several changes of ownership, in December 1998, Gloria Steinem and a group of investors bought the publication from MacDonald Communications Corp. The investors, a group of women who call themselves Liberty Media for Women, paid between $3 million and $4 million for the magazine.

Today, Steinem remains active in women's issues as president of the Voters for Choice Education Fund and through other volunteer work.

Sources: Sarah Lyons, "Daughter of the Revolution," *South China Morning Post* (July 6, 1996), Books sec., p. 8; Joan Smith, "The Unexplained Feminist," *Financial Times* (May 4, 1996), Books sec., p. 11; Rosie Boycott, "Sex and Feminism," *Daily Mail* (April 20, 1996), p. 36; Maureen Freely, "Gloria and Me," *The Guardian* (April 18, 1996), Features sec., p. 6; Katie Donovan, "Feminist Enigma," *The Irish Times* (April 9, 1996), News Features sec., p. 9; and "New Group Buys *Ms.* Magazine," Associated Press via abcnews.com, http://abcnews.go.com/sections/business/dailynews/ms magazine981201; Cynthia Gorney, "Gloria," September 2002, www.motherjones.com/mother_jones/ND95/gorney.html.

$800,000, with bonuses that can double these figures. In fact, bonuses are a plus at almost all levels of magazine publishing.[18]

TRENDS

Today's magazines are operating in a climate of massive change. The business climate and advanced technological developments indicate that magazines will continue to be geographically decentralized and to operate with smaller staffs and increasing contractual arrangements. The word for the twenty-first century is *demographics. Social and economic change* intertwined with the growth of the aging population challenges magazine editors to provide new types of content for **fragmenting markets.** *Technological change* is affecting how magazines address demographic change, as well as increasing the choices for distribution. Magazines can be delivered as paper products or online.

In the midst of these changing times, Bruce Sheiman, managing director of the Jordan, Edmiston Group, Inc., in New York City, exhorts editors to remember that magazines provide subtle benefits. He argues that magazines continue to hold a unique place in American society because they "crystallize, articulate and reinforce a person's identity."[19] They offer intimacy and depth not offered by electronic media. Sheiman argues that people relate to magazines as friends, experts, and role models.

Demographics

Magazine publishers are targeting new audiences for the twenty-first century. In the United States, slower population growth, an aging society, changing lifestyles, and an increasingly diversified population are making new demands on magazines. And these changes are not strictly American characteristics, but are occurring throughout the world. If magazines are to survive, magazine publishers must learn how to satisfy the new demands.

One glance at *American Demographics* in late 2002 introduces these demographic issues: (1) the degree to which the American mind-set changed after September 11, 2001; (2) the baby boom in the Middle East and its impact on Arab populations and values; (3) the lack of nurses and the major career opportunities in the field; (4) the steady trend of social segregation when it comes to marriage—interfaith and interracial marriages still constitute a tiny proportion of all marriages; (5) an increasing number and the increasing wealth of the Asian American population; and (6) shifts of spending priorities for different age groups.[20] Population growth is slowing and the population is growing older. Despite the teen boom that magazines have addressed, the two fastest growing age groups today are people age forty-five to fifty-four and eighty-five or older. Publishers targeting today's baby boomers (ages forty to fifty-five) with active lifestyles will have to redirect their publications to attract tomorrow's aging baby boomers.

Economic and Social Change

The adaptation of magazines to social and economic change has enabled them to continue to connect people and events. In 1969, *Life* magazine published pictures, letters, and interviews with family and friends of 220 of the 245 men killed in Vietnam during the week of May 28 to June 3, 1969. The magazine received 1,300 letters from readers praising and criticizing it for this personal look into the reality of war. The massive pictorial essay represented a distinct change in attitude toward the war by Time, Inc., and generated a national conversation about the gains and losses of the war in Vietnam.[21]

However, some magazine editors argue that economic and social change has driven magazines toward new goals rather than preserving a journalistic tradition. For example, Simon Dumenco writes in "The Glossies: The Un-Magazines" that

> We magazine people think we're part of some great narrative, journalistic tradition. But, in fact, the most interesting and successful stuff that's going on in magazineland these days involves the pouring of a different sort of media ethos into magazine-like vessels.
>
> Sometimes this is obvious: *In Style* is a catalog. So is *Lucky.* Of course, the big fall issues of the fashion glossies sell so well every year not because they're magazines, but because they're catalogs that out-catalog real catalogs.
>
> Other magazines are actually catalogs of another sort: They're repositories of a fixed body of knowledge that is reiterated ad infinitum in magazine form. *Men's Health,* for instance, is basically the coolest, sexiest health-and-nutrition book ever, serialized over and over again and updated incrementally. (The "Hard-Body Instruction Manual" that appeared in a recent issue is not a whole helluva lot different from the "Hard Muscle: Your Start-Up Plan" article that appeared in an issue two years ago. With apologies to Gertrude Stein, a biceps curl is a biceps curl is a biceps curl.)[22]

Magazines are increasingly addressing the personal needs of an aging population. As people get older, they look for different content in their magazines. For example, seniors and those caring for them need to know more about health care and financial planning. Take the case of eighty-five-year-old Sarah K. Goldstein, who threw her back out while shoveling snow. Her daughter, Carol Abaya, who ran an advertising and public relations business, found it almost impossible to get information about health-care systems and to cope with the needs of her mother as well as those of her own demanding life. In 1992 she started a magazine, the *Sandwich Generation,* designed to provide information to the nation's 76 million baby boomers who were caring for more than 32 million people age sixty-five or older. The magazine originally circulated only in Monmouth and Ocean Counties of central New Jersey, but it now circulates in forty-two states. Abaya claims that her circulation has increased 500 percent since the first year, and her distributor says that her growth is 15 percent ahead of the national average for newsstand magazines. Abaya was invited to testify before the U.S. House Ways and Means Committee in January 1995 to discuss elder care and tax credits. In 1997 the magazine won awards for its design, and the publication continues as a strong force. Abaya has been written about in the *New York Times,* as well as by other major media outlets. By 2002 she was employed as a syndicated columnist and circulates her magazine online.

Social issues affect not only the content of magazines but their production as well. Recycling, for example, has become an important issue. Many publishers are aware that the magazine industry must initiate a voluntary recycling program to keep Congress from enacting mandatory recycling requirements for the industry. Some major publishers are still reluctant to use recycled paper because of its high cost, low quality, and limited availability. However, as publishers demand high-quality recycled stocks, paper producers will attempt to produce what is in demand.

Magazine development is tied to economic change. The 1990s and early 2000s witnessed a significant increase in paper costs, which led to price increases and a decline in circulation. Coupled with slow growth of advertising revenues, increased costs indicate a difficult time for magazines.

In 2002 a "hot" competitive market emerged in the world of city magazines. City start-ups are using a tried and successful strategy—they are specializing, carving out a single niche within a metropolis to compete against the big city slickers.

During economic downturns such as that being experienced in 2001–2002, national advertising shrinks, but city and regional magazines and their advertising markets tend to be more resilient because they rely on local advertising. For example, in 2001 advertising pages in city and regional titles were down just 0.3 percent from 2000, but national magazines were down 11.7 percent.

Although many city magazine editors dismiss the challengers as only temporary, some magazines can create real competition. In the Miami market, *South Florida* went unchallenged for years, but when *Ocean Drive* went after the upscale South Beach party scene, it gained circulation and advertisers, edging out *South Florida,* which ceased publication in 2001 after nine years of competition. Some new competitors in the fall of 2002 included *At Home in Memphis, Bliss* (Birmingham, Alabama), and *Surprise!,* a business magazine competing against *Seattle.*[23]

Converging Technology

Technology is driven, at least in part, by economic need. As publishers see the need for innovation in order to maintain profits, they finance the development of technology. At other times, technological developments in fields other than publishing can be adapted for innovation.

Computer publishing has greatly decreased the cost of producing magazines. But an even more costly area had been distribution. The newsweeklies pioneered satellite transmission of electronic pages to tighten editorial deadlines but still meet distribution schedules. Now *Vanity Fair* can close some pages just hours before press time because it uses totally electronic page composition and transmission to its printer. Publishers also take advantage of the Internet and online systems.

Magazines Online ◆ Consumers have accessed magazines and newspapers using commercial online services, such as CompuServe Information Services Inc., since the mid-1980s. However, readership online has shown slow growth. In 1995, 3.7 million Americans read online magazines. In 1997, that number grew to 4.6 million. Online magazine readers tend to be highly educated and to read print magazines as well as those online. The Magazine Publishers Association reported in 1999 that 1,170 print magazines had established web sites. Readers use online versions to browse, search, and seek information on subscribing.

However, in 2002, magazine publishers were talking about ways to *enhance* magazine content with online features, rather than merely shoveling information onto the site. "Imagine," says Jillian S. Ambroz, "what might have happened if *Travel & Leisure* had established online ancillary operations that might have negated the impact of Expedia and Travelocity."[24] Ambroz says that many publishers rushed to the Web, only to later slash their Internet budgets and close down sites. She also comments that online activities take two directions: one represents the publishers who have prepared editorial for multiple delivery systems, including handheld wireless devices, and the other represents the publishers who create "digital duplicates" for onscreen delivery.

The challenge, Ambroz notes, is to make use of the magazine format. Daniel Okrent, former Time Inc. editorial executive and writer, says "If you believe the magazine form has validity, then to do it digitally means that you don't disaggregate it." Foreward-thinking companies explore the possibilities for wireless handheld devices and greater functionality on magazine web sites.

International Markets

Mailing costs and lack of access to lists of potential foreign consumers have slowed the growth of international circulations, but those difficulties may be overcome as international readers begin to show more of an interest in U.S. consumer magazines. In some countries, censorship prevents distribution of U.S. magazines. Nevertheless, some publications already have successful foreign markets. *Reader's Digest* is read in about 163 countries; *Time* produces about thirty-four foreign editions; and in April 1994, *Cosmopolitan*, on sale in about 84 countries, became the first major women's magazine published in the former Soviet Union. Hearst Corporation has joined with Televisa S.A. of Mexico to translate more of its titles into Spanish-language editions for the Latin American market. Currently, Spanish-language editions of Hearst's *Cosmopolitan, Harper's Bazaar, Popular Mechanics,* and *Good Housekeeping* are distributed in Latin America. A Canadian edition of *Sports Illustrated*, launched in 1993, encountered protests from Canadian magazine publishers. Under new Canadian government regulations, U.S. companies will have to obtain government approval for future Canadian editions of their magazines. The Canadian government restricts Canadian editions because it fears the impact those magazines could have on Canada's economy and on Canadian culture. As a further indicator of the international emphasis, the Magazine Publishers Association, founded in 1919, in 2002 had 240 U.S. members and 80 international members. The international members represent 800 titles in 31 countries.[25]

Car and Driver, published by the French publishing giant Hachette Filipacchi New Media, is read all over the world in editions specially tailored for each market.

global impact

International Distribution of Magazine Content

Lagardere, a French company, is the eighth largest media company in the world. Lagardere is an example of an international company that distributes magazines all over the world. In February 2001, it created a new division to be able to distribute content across the cable, interactive television, wireless, broadband, and Internet platforms. It has separate operating units in North America, Europe, and Asia.

Lagardere owns Hachette Filipacchi Media, the world's largest publisher of consumer magazines. Recognizable titles include *Car and Driver, Elle,* and *Woman's Day.* In addition to its magazine holdings, it owns a production company that supplies original television programming for TNN. It also has relationships with AOL, Vivendi Universal, Canal Plus, and Liberty Media.

Largardere has targeted *Car and Driver* and *Elle* for new media development and for expansion into television—creating new delivery options internationally for magazine content.

Source: Robin Berger, "Lagardere Positions for Interactive Push," Crain Communications Inc. (February 19, 2001), accessed via Lexis-Nexis on November 10, 2002.

summary

- Magazines helped develop the nation's social conscience.
- Limited technology and lack of an economic base, together with a primitive postal system, hampered the development of the U.S. magazine industry.
- Rapidly advancing technology and mass marketing of goods reduced production costs and created an advertising base that fostered magazine development.
- A rising middle class, increased public education, and the opportunity for social advancement encouraged a reading audience. By 1900 that educated middle class used magazines as the medium for social protest.
- Magazines survived competition from radio and television by targeting groups of readers. This specialization was attractive to both the audience and the advertiser.
- In today's market, specialization is key. Consumer magazines and literary journals make up the bulk of magazine publishing.
- Huge business conglomerates are the primary owners of magazines. However, in response to the recession of the early 1990s, magazine publishers downsized and decentralized.
- During the economic downturn of the early 2000s, magazine advertising revenue declined.
- Many new magazines do not survive. Those that do have solid financial backing, a specific advertiser base, and a staff of highly trained professionals.
- Demographic changes force magazines to attract new audiences. Magazines must meet the needs of changing audiences and of advertisers.
- Combined—or converging—technologies foster new methods of production and distribution. Magazine publishers increasingly are enhancing their products with web sites and online magazines.
- Editors argue about whether magazines will continue to function as important generators of a national conversation about political and social issues, or whether they will emerge as "super catalogs" and other forms of media.

navigating the web | Magazines on the Web

Magazine web sites include sites for the magazines, sites for companies that publish magazines, and sites for information about the industry. Although industry information and company sites are usually free, some magazine sites require users to purchase a subscription.

American Business Press
www.americanbusinesspress.com/resources/facts.htm
The goal of the association is to enhance knowledge and practices of leading publishers and to provide information for business, professional, and specialized consumer markets worldwide.

Magazine Publishers Association (MPA)
www.magazine.org
The MPA site provides research material about magazines and news about the industry.

The Write News
http://writenews.com
Writers who are targeting magazines use the Write News site, which contains writing tips, job information, and other helpful ideas.

Ziff-Davis Magazines
www.zdnet.com
Ziff-Davis is one of the largest publishers of computer and electronic media magazines. This site connects to the texts of magazines published by Ziff-Davis, including *PC Magazine* and *Family PC.*

Miller Freeman, Inc.
www.mfi.com
The homepage for the Miller Freeman Corporation, which publishes seventy business and trade publications, contains information about the magazines and the company.

Media Central
www.mediacentral.com
The Media Central site is home to several publications, including the material from *Folio* that is available online.

Some magazines online include the following:

People
http://people.aol.com/people

Business Week
www.businessweek.com

PC Magazine
www.pcmag.com

questions for review

1. Why were magazines slow to develop in the early United States?
2. How did mass production affect magazines?
3. How are magazines financed?
4. How is technology used for distribution?
5. How are magazines adapting to online possibilities?

issues to think about

1. What social roles have magazines occupied?
2. How are economics and cultural issues intertwined in magazine development?
3. Should magazine editors and consumers be concerned about influence on content by advertisers? If so, why?
4. What are the advantages and disadvantages of conglomerate ownership?
5. Will magazines use online technologies to enhance the print product or to replace it?

suggested readings

John, Arthur. *The Best Years of the Century* (Urbana: University of Illinois Press, 1981).

Vincent, Theodore G., ed. *Voices of a Black Nation: Political Journalism in the Harlem Renaissance* (San Francisco: Ramparts Press, 1973).

Wilson, Christopher. "The Rhetoric of Consumption: Mass-Market Magazines and the Demise of the Gentle Reader, 1880–1920," in *The Culture of Consumption,* Richard Wightman Fox, and T. J. Jackson Lears, eds. (New York: Pantheon, 1983), pp. 39–64.

Wilson, Harold S. McClure's *Magazine and the Muckrakers* (Princeton, NJ: Princeton University Press, 1970).

Yagoda, Ben. *About Town: The* New Yorker *and the World It Made* (New York: Scribner's, 2002).

The Movies

Moviegoers probably did not notice the battle in the theaters during 2002. It was easy to miss, but it raged nonetheless. Young ticket buyers voted with their money on the next generation of Hollywood heroes. The film business knew that the old tried-and-true action heroes—Arnold Schwarzenegger, Clint Eastwood, Bruce Willis, and Harrison Ford—had passed their prime. Young people needed new types of heroes, and Hollywood responded with several options. The movies offered an extension of the older hero type with Ewan McGregor as Obi-Wan Kenobi in *Star Wars: Attack of the Clones;* new multicultural, testosterone hulks such as the Rock and Vin Diesel; and unusual heroes such as Frodo Baggins in *Lord of the Rings: The Fellowship of the Rings.*

Most of these new heroes performed well at the box office, although not all achieved equal success with critics. But the hands-down winner among the viewing public was Tobey Maguire in *Spider-Man.* As the nerd turned superhero, Maguire helped take the surprise hit of the year to fifth on the list of all-time top domestic grossing films, with $404 million in ticket sales. To everyone's surprise, *Spider-Man* passed *Harry Potter and the Sorcerer's Stone* and *Lord of the Rings* to take the top spot during the summer season.[1]

Spider-Man contained something for everyone. The sensitive hero played by acclaimed actor Maguire appealed to teenage girls, and the state-of-the-art special effects and Kirsten Dunst as Spider-Man's girlfriend attracted teenage boys. Add a well-written script, and the United States has the new action hero—a flawed character who possesses a strong-enough will to rise above those failings.

The action film remains a foundation of the film industry that allows viewers to escape to worlds that exist only in their imaginations. "Above all, Hollywood captures the popular imagination," wrote Douglas Gomery "because it is still the nation's (and the world's) 'dream machine,' projecting private hopes and fantasies and fears onto a big screen for all to see and share."[2]

Child psychologist Dr. Bruno Bettelheim wrote that as an adolescent he went to the movies as often as he could and that they "provided unique opportunities for letting down one's defenses and experimenting with being in love. . . . I do not recall having ever laughed as heartily and unrestrainedly as I did when watching funny scenes in these pleasure palaces. In fact, watching the movies thus carried me away so that I was no longer quite myself. Instead, we were part of the world of the moving picture."[3]

Fascination with the moving picture has focused on the way in which entertainment appeals to certain psychological needs: to have a fantasy life, to be loved, to be beautiful, to take one's place in the world. Films have helped to create culture as well as perceptions of society and culture. However, because films have been

As you read this chapter, consider the following issues facing filmmakers and those who are interested in the impact of moviemaking and moviegoing:

◆ What are the economic and cultural impacts of film viewing? Are films significant in shaping the culture of our future?

◆ Economic interests are an important component of filmmaking. How do you think corporate interests and the studio system have contributed to (or limited) the subject matter and impact of film?

◆ Increasingly, film production houses are internationally owned. How will this increased international economic concentration affect film as a "culture machine"?

◆ How do you think new technologies will affect the production and delivery of film and its convergence with other media?

◆ Film viewers can choose different settings in which to see films in a variety of technological formats. "Movies in Your Life" outlines some of the choices available and points out that different types of viewing may serve different functions.

The Movies *in Your Life*

How Do You Watch Movies?

College students are major consumers of movies. How important are they in your life? As you read this chapter, think about the different ways in which you view movies. Do you think your viewing habits and those of your friends influence the movie industry? What do your friends think?

Take a moment to think about how the form, type, and function of movies you view are intertwined. Do you view movies on videocassette for relaxation and in a theater for social reasons? Do your goals differ when you view movies in different places? Are the results different? For example, do large-screen films viewed in a theater have a greater impact on you than a film viewed on a television does? Is form—or the convergence of technology—affecting the impact, the content, or the use of film? As you read this chapter, you will see that the movie industry is concerned about some of the very same considerations that influenced you in responding to these issues.

FORM OF VIEWING	TYPE OF FILM	TIME/DAY	PURPOSE OF VIEWING
Movie theater			
Broadcast TV			
Cable TV or direct broadcast satellite			
VHS/DVD (rental)			
VHS/DVD (own film)			
Computer			
Other (please specify)			

financed by commercial, often large corporate interests, the cultural perspectives are related to the industry's desire for profit. From the beginning, critics were interested in the impact of film, although they usually worried more about declining standards of morality than about commercialization. Parents, community censorship boards, voluntary associations, and religious interests all believed that film would have a major impact on the nation's youth. Today, critics are still concerned about the cultural influence of film.

FILM IN AMERICAN LIFE

Louis Giannetti and Scott Eyman wrote that moving pictures were, for some, "art, science and schooling all in one."[4] They also are—and have been since 1920—big business. The emergence of moving pictures was part of the experimentation with entertainment in the United States during the 1880s and 1890s that included concert saloons, peep shows, and vaudeville variety acts.

Technological and Economic Development

The fascination with pictures in motion goes back to ancient Greek and Arab civilizations, but not until the mid-1800s did technology make such pictures available to broad audiences. Motion pictures evolved from two sets of developing technologies: experimentation with photographic processes and the development of moving picture devices. Photographic processes that evolved in the mid-nineteenth century paved the way for moving pictures. By the late nineteenth century, a French scientist had developed a camera that produced twelve pictures on a single plate. The development of gelatin emulsions and the production of celluloid during the 1880s furthered photographic technology. In 1878, Eadweard Muybridge achieved a sense of motion by positioning cameras at different intervals along a race track and arranging for the shutters to click in sequence. In the early 1890s, several scientists were experimenting with viewing devices in the United States, Thomas Edison's labs produced the **kinetoscope**, a device that allowed for viewing a film by moving loops of film over a series of spools.

A contemporary observer wrote,

> The ends of the film are joined, forming an endless band passing over two guide drums near the top of the case. One of these drums is driven by a motor and feeds the film along by means of sprocket teeth which engage with perforations along the edges of the film. Just above the film is a shutter wheel having five spokes and a very small rectangular opening in the rim directly over the film. An incandescent lamp . . . is placed below the film between the two guide drums, and the light passes up through the film, shutter opening, and magnifying lens . . . to the eye of the observer placed at the opening in the top of the case.[5]

The new motion picture technology set the stage for the peep show, which featured short films that could be viewed by looking through a viewfinder on a machine about the size of an upright piano. Kinetoscopes became popular in hotel lobbies and other public places, but they never produced the great profits Edison had anticipated.

Vaudeville provided the entertainment milieu in which technical projection developed as a form of theater. Vaudeville acts were popular from the beginning of the nineteenth century, though their form and acceptance varied with specific historical periods. Until the 1880s, vaudeville was considered legitimate theater and appealed to all classes. During industrialization in the late 1800s, audiences developed a greater sense of class consciousness, and upper-class theatergoers began to object to the "lower class" that cheered and booed from the galleries. The upper class then excluded the working class from theater, and variety acts became more important as entertainment in working-class neighborhoods, often in saloons. However, entertainment entrepreneurs, not content to appeal only to a drinking crowd, sought to establish the *vaudeville show in a theater* environment that would attract working-class and middle-class audiences. Once variety moved back to the stage—this time as its own genre rather than as an extension of theater—it was established as vaudeville with high appeal to the middle class. In this environment, entrepreneurs marketing new technologies made inroads.

In the late nineteenth century, agents who booked acts for vaudeville, looking for new acts for their demanding audiences, often sought visual presentations to enhance their shows. "Magic lantern" slide shows had been popular during the 1880s, but the invention of projection machines posed interesting possibilities for new types of entertainment. Several competing machines entered the market at about the same time. Auguste and Louis Lumière introduced the Cinématographe, Francis Jenkins and Thomas Armat the Vitascope, and Edison the kinetoscope.

Initially, films were short exhibitions of moving images. They were popular in the Far East, Europe, and the United States. Between 1896 and 1903, travelogues, local features, comedy, and news often were the subjects of short films. Depictions of movement also were used to create a physiological thrill. In 1902 and 1903, Edwin Porter produced several American films, including *Life of an American Fireman* and *The Great Train Robbery*. These twelve-minute productions pioneered storytelling techniques in film and led the way to the development of feature films.

key concept

Vaudeville Show as Early Movie Theater In the early 1900s, popular comedy, dramatic skits, or song-and-dance entertainment was presented in local vaudeville theaters. Early silent films, usually with piano accompaniment, were also shown in these theaters.

kinetoscope: A boxlike mechanism used to view short films during the late 1800s. The viewer looked into an opening and watched film move past a lightbulb.

media convergence

DVD Delivers

If it were a 1950s sci-fi movie, it would be called *The Incredible Shrinking VHS.* A trip to the local movie rental store will demonstrate dramatically the transition in movie technology occurring in U.S. households. The shelf space with VHS videotapes gets smaller and smaller by the week, as the space given DVDs grows. Just as cassettes replaced records and CDs replaced cassettes, a similar transition is occurring in film technology.

DVD players were introduced in 1997, and by August 2002 they had reached more than 30 percent of U.S. households. Millions more can play DVDs on personal computers and games such as Sony PlayStation 2. Estimates are that 47 percent of U.S. households will be able to play DVDs by the end of 2003. It appears that the technology to play DVDs is spreading faster than any entertainment technology since black-and-white TV sets during the 1950s.

The boom in DVDs has occurred for at least three reasons. The quality of DVDs is twice that of VHS tapes, and DVDs contain a variety of material in addition to the movie because they hold more digital information. This additional material includes interviews with stars and directors, alternate endings, and even additional versions of the movie in languages other than English. Equally important is the drop in DVD player prices from about $700 in 1997 to $150 in 2002.

In response to the growth of DVD players, consumers can rent DVDs online and have them delivered by mail. These companies charge a fixed fee, and consumers can order a certain number of titles each month.

Some experts have marveled that this spread has occurred despite the inability of most existing DVD players to record programs from the television, as VCRs can. This one drawback will soon vanish as the prices of recordable DVD players drops from about $500 to $200.

The manufacturers of DVD players should not feel overly confident, however, as broadband cable and computer distribution raise the specter of video-on-demand. This will allow consumers to order the movie they want when they want.

DVD delivers today, but some day it might join the 8-track tape and audiocassette as technologies of historical interest.

Sources: Theoden K. Janes, "DVDs Reach 1 Billion Mark," *Lansing State Journal* (August 11, 2002): 3D; Peter M. Nichols, "Home Video: Choosing Bells or Wishes," *The New York Times* (October 26, 2001): E1, 27; Susan Stock, "DVD: Digital Video Demand," *Lansing State Journal* (April 15, 2002): Business Extra 1–2; and Susan Stock, "DVDs Zoom into Local Mailboxes," *Lansing State Journal* (July 11, 2002): 7C.

Films were shown in the vaudeville theaters and by traveling showmen, who projected them at tent shows or fairs. By 1906, storefronts known as **nickelodeons** exhibited films that attracted working-class audiences. To broaden their audience, nickelodeon operators began moving their operations into theaters and adding one or two vaudeville acts to the attraction. This small-time vaudeville relied more heavily on motion picture entertainment and less on live acts than did the traditional variety show. By 1910, nickelodeons attracted an audience of 26 million each week, a little less than 20 percent of the national population. By 1914, the weekly audience had increased to 49 million.[6] The moving picture was now considered respectable middle-class entertainment, and theaters began popping up in middle-class neighborhoods and small towns.

In 1908 a variety of companies were competing in the movie industry. Industry leaders were spending so much energy defending their patents and jockeying for position that, in an effort to increase profits and to standardize the industry, they decided to form a monopoly. Led by the Edison Manufacturing Company and the American Mutoscope and Biograph Company, they formed a trust called the Motion Picture Patents Company (MPPC). Creating trusts was a common business strategy in the late nineteenth century to acquire and pool patents. For a short time, the MPPC controlled production of raw film, manufacture of motion picture and projection equipment, distribution, and exhibition. All members were required to

nickelodeon: Small storefront functioning as a theater; popular about 1910. These preceded the grand movie palaces.

Short action films were among the first popular films to appear in theaters of the early 1900s. One of these, Edwin Porter's *The Great Train Robbery,* helped launch the popularity of the cowboy movie.

purchase film from the Eastman Kodak Company, and the company refused to sell to outsiders.

The trust was dissolved in 1915 because of the government's success in *United States v. Motion Picture Patents Co.,* an antitrust case against the MPPC. The MPPC certainly had increased its own profits and was known for its strong-arm tactics, which included raiding independent studios and smashing equipment. However, it also had ended squabbles among different segments of the U.S. film industry and had improved film quality. Through competition and standardized distribution and exhibition practices, the MPPC helped create an internationally competitive motion picture industry.[7]

Although members of the MPPC had tried to eliminate independent movie production, its standardization of production and distribution became too rigid. The MPPC clung to the concept of short films and at first rejected the multiple-reel feature films that became successful during the teens. Independents saw big feature films as a way to gain a market niche and sought financing on Wall Street. By 1915 the MPPC was gone and independents were producing feature films. Film exhibition moved from the storefront nickelodeon and the small vaudeville houses to theaters that were designed exclusively for the showing of movies. The movies had become big business.

The Audience and New Expectations

When D. W. Griffith's long, controversial, and popular feature film *The Birth of a Nation* opened in New York's Liberty Theater on March 3, 1915, it established the importance of feature films. The three-hour film was based on a popular novel published in 1905 that had become a successful play. This story of the aftermath of the Civil War roused enormous controversy because of its underlying racist message. The film depicted a northern family and a southern family adapting to the postwar period, but the point of view was decidedly southern. African Americans who were not loyal to their southern masters were depicted as subhuman. The last half of the film was dominated by Ku Klux Klan activity that would never be condoned today. Nevertheless, the film opened to a packed audience. Each audience member paid two dollars for a reserved seat, an orchestra accompanied the performance, and costumed ushers handed out souvenir programs. The exhibition format resembled that of an upper-class theater. The film played for forty-four consecutive weeks at the Liberty and showed in leading theaters across the United States, breaking records and generating controversy because of its racist tones. The three-hour production yielded $5 million on an investment of less than $100,000.

Pioneer filmmaker D. W. Griffith perfected the art of cinematic continuity and storytelling necessary for the modern feature film. His film *The Birth of a Nation,* a controversial story dependent on racial stereotypes, was a box-office hit, but his subsequent film *Intolerance,* loaded with pacifist scenes, failed to gain an audience on the eve of World War I.

Griffith's follow-up picture, *Intolerance*, ran three-and-one-half hours, and although the film is regarded as an artistic classic, it failed miserably to reward its financial backers. Griffith, who personally stood behind the losses, never recovered financially.

Why did *Intolerance* fail? Critics debate the issue. Griffith's message of love, tolerance, and the uselessness of war might have been popular before 1916, when Americans were resisting involvement in what many considered a European war. However, by 1916, when the film was released, the message alienated many viewers as the United States prepared to go to war.

Griffith made other successful films, but he was a poor businessman and always struggled with finances. By 1920, his films were no longer regarded as groundbreaking. Nevertheless, Griffith's innovative film techniques redefined the expectations of film audiences. He created grand epics with spectacular scenery and introduced lighting and **editing** techniques that established film as a medium for exploring social and cultural themes.

Sound and Money

Companies that experimented early with adding sound to motion pictures were the first to realize vast profits from introducing the technology, but this introduction changed the industry economically. Once big money was needed for big technology, few companies could make the switch without help from bankers. The adoption of sound also signaled a solidifying of big business interests.

As audience reaction to feature films and the appearance of stars ensured that movies would indeed continue to be an important entertainment medium, companies such as Western Electric, Warner Bros., and Fox experimented to develop technology for sound, hoping that it would accelerate profits. Although some critics thought such investments were a waste of money, sound soon became accepted through an economic process of invention, innovation, and diffusion.[8] In 1926, Warner formed the Vitaphone Corporation in association with Western Electric, a subsidiary of American Telephone & Telegraph Co., to make sound pictures and to market sound production equipment. Although Warner lost $1 million in 1926, the loss was anticipated and was necessary to finance the expansion. Vitaphone initiated a sales campaign to encourage exhibitors to introduce sound equipment. Such planning paved the way for the success of *The Jazz Singer,* which premiered in October 1927. Because Warner was first to market sound, it earned extraordinary profits. During the last half of the 1920s, Warner was able to solidify its position by acquiring other companies with production and exhibition facilities.

After the success of *The Jazz Singer,* most of the major companies rushed to switch to sound. RCA developed a competing sound system called Photophone. The company became a massive firm by merging with a motion picture giant, the Radio-Keith-Orpheum Corporation, and with the Keith-Albee-Orpheum circuit of vaudeville houses. Major companies had signed long-term, exclusive contracts with AT&T, but RCA challenged the giant with unlawful restraint of trade and reached an out-of-court settlement in 1935. By 1943, RCA supplied about 60 percent of all sound equipment. Production costs rose as a result of the new technology. The major companies and studios were able to make the capital investment needed to switch to sound, but smaller independent companies did not have enough financial backing or capital to make the transition. Many of the independents simply closed their doors or sold out to the bigger companies. By 1930 the industry was an **oligopoly.**

The Studio System

By the 1920s, the movie industry had moved to California, where the studios could use nearby locations to depict desert, mountain, or ocean scenes and the weather permitted year-round filming. However, many decisions affecting the industry were made in New York offices by film company executives. The corporate chief executives (such

editing: The technique of joining pieces of film or of digitally manipulating images in a creative process.

oligopoly: A business situation in which a few dominant companies control enough of the business that each one's actions will have a significant impact on the actions of the others.

The star system could punish or reward actors. It made a superstar of Clark Gable, shown here with David O. Selznick and Louis B. Mayer of MGM signing for the part of Rhett Butler in the 1939 film *Gone with the Wind*.

as Harry Warner, Nicholas Schenck of Loew's/MGM, and Joseph M. Schenck of Fox) made the most important decisions, such as the titles and number of films to be produced in any given season, total production budgets, and the number of **A and B pictures**. Once the New York executives had prepared a release schedule, the head of the studio took control. But the chief executives who controlled the business aspects of the industry made the most important creative and business decisions. Because they valued stability, they used popular stars in familiar roles. In this way, economic structures affected film style and content.

Unlike the chief executive officers (CEOs), the heads of the studios were familiar to the public: Louis B. Mayer at MGM, Darryl Zanuck at Twentieth Century Fox, and Jack Warner at Warner Bros. The heads promoted and negotiated contracts with the stars, ensured that production schedules were met, and assigned material to producers.

The glamourous stars were encased in a *star system* created by studio heads and had little control over their own lives; the studios controlled many of their personal and private actions. Their contracts usually ran for seven years, and the studios could drop or renew the contracts yearly. A star who rebelled could be loaned out to work for other studios on pictures that had little chance of succeeding. Furthermore, stars were cast repetitively in similar roles. Once the studio discovered someone with star potential and groomed the actor, it tried to stay with the winning formula. Such formulaic casting made it difficult for stars to get more demanding roles. Publicity departments at the big studios promoted the stars and worked hard to ensure the public would view each star in a particular wholesome but glamorous light. Moviegoers contributed to the development of the star system as they began to select movies on the basis of particular stars who were cast in them. Thus the studio heads, combined with audience responses, contributed to the star system.

Domination by the Big Five

By 1930, five companies dominated United States movie screens: Warner Bros.; Loew's, Inc., the theater chain that owned Metro-Goldwyn-Mayer; Paramount; RKO; and Twentieth Century Fox. Each company was vertically integrated; each produced motion pictures, operated worldwide distribution outlets, and had a theater chain. Three other companies—Universal, Columbia, and United Artists—had significant holdings but no chain of theaters. Universal and Columbia supplied pictures to the majors, and United Artists was a distribution company for a small group of independents. Theaters owned by the big five companies formed an oligopoly and took in more than 75 percent of the nation's box-office receipts. Through the 1930s and 1940s, these eight companies defined Hollywood.

The depression of the 1930s caused movie revenues to plummet. The major studio companies had difficulty meeting their financial obligations. They had overextended themselves in a market that was declining rather than expanding.

When President Franklin D. Roosevelt introduced the National Recovery Act (NRA), with provisions for cutting competition among industries, the federal government allowed the big five to continue practices they had already established to limit competition. These included **block booking** (requiring all theaters to buy a season's package of films rather than individual productions) and **blind booking** (forcing a theater owner to buy a season's package of films sight unseen). The NRA also allowed the companies to continue the **vertical integration** they had established, which brought them great profits. In return, the studios were supposed to make certain concessions. Although the studios had vociferously opposed unionization, now they readily recognized trade unions of production personnel, which formed some of the least expensive parts of the business, as a way of complying with the act. However, they continued to fight to keep stars outside the collective bargaining system.

Growth in the Domestic Market

When World War II began, the film industry lost most of its worldwide business that had been established during the late 1930s. But the *domestic market, dominated by five major studios,* improved dramatically because U.S. citizens were earning relatively high wages and had few commodities on which to spend them. Movies were affordable and available. Domestic **studio film rentals** for the top eight studios increased from $193 million in 1939 to $332 million in 1946. In this peak year, an average of 90 million Americans, or 75 percent of the U.S. population, went to the movies each week.

Post–World War II Decline

The movie business declined at the end of the war—even before the rise of television. Returning soldiers bought houses in the suburbs, went back to college on the GI bill, and started families. The decline in movie attendance paralleled a restructuring of the industry after the Supreme Court in 1948, in *United States v. Paramount Pictures, Inc., et al.,* forced the companies to divest themselves of their theater chains and thus limited the vertical integration that had been the norm for thirty years. The Supreme Court's *Paramount* decision ended block booking, fixing of admission prices, and other discriminatory practices, which were declared to be in restraint of trade.

With the *Paramount* decision came increased freedom for producers and stars. Although the major companies continued to dominate the industry, the number of independent producers more than doubled from 1946 to 1956. In response, the major studios competed to provide space and facilities for such producers. Foreign films had more access to the U.S. market, and small **art theaters** sprang up, particularly in university towns and large urban areas. Stars were more reluctant to sign long-term, exclusive contracts, so their talent became more widely available.

Nevertheless, the big companies continued to dominate the production business, both at home and abroad. Because access to movies made in the United States had been limited during the war and many European production facilities were shut

studio film rentals: Movies produced by studios to rent to distributors and/or theaters.

art theater: Outlet for films designed for their artistic quality rather than for their blockbuster audience appeal that usually are produced by independent companies rather than by the big studios.

The post–World War II decline in major movies opened the market for independent producers such as Ingmar Bergman, who experimented with new film techniques. Bergman's *The Seventh Seal* is still shown regularly at university film series.

down, studios made huge profits from European rentals. Foreign operations, both rentals and production, continued to gain importance; by the 1960s, more than half the revenue of the major studios came from operations overseas.

Response to Television

By the early 1950s, the movies had a major contender for audiences' time: television. For young families with children, television was simpler and less expensive than going to the movies. For older people, television did not require as much effort. The motion picture industry formulated its *response to television,* using the natural advantages of the theater format. Studios began to produce more films in color, to experiment with screen size, and to introduce **Cinerama** and **3-D.** The most lasting innovation was **Panavision,** which was introduced by Fox in 1962 and gave the illusion of depth without seeming contrived.

Before long the film industry began to collaborate with television. In 1949, Columbia converted a subsidiary into a television department that produced programs for *Ford Theater* and the comedy series *Father Knows Best.* In 1953, when television made the transition from live to filmed production, Hollywood became the center for television production.

By 1955, Hollywood was also releasing many of its older pictures for television broadcasting. For example, RKO sold its film library to a television programming syndicate for $15 million. During the 1960s, however, the studios realized that they had undervalued their old films. ABC paid Columbia $2 million for the 1957 film *The Bridge on the River Kwai,* and when the film was shown on television on September 12, 1966, sixty million people watched it. Television became a regular market for films, and competitive bidding continued to rise.

In the late 1960s, studios began producing made-for-television movies. In television movies, production costs were kept low, and these movies soon glutted the market, diminishing the demand for older movies. Between television movies and acquired film libraries, the networks discovered that they had enough films stocked for several years and stopped bidding for studio productions. The studios retrenched, but by 1972 they were again selling to the networks. ABC, the youngest network, increased its ratings and forced CBS and NBC to be more competitive. The three networks bid the prices of movies such as *Alien* as high as $15 million in the early '80s. When cable became widespread in the 1980s, movies became an even hotter commodity. Film ultimately benefited from *converging technologies.* The coming of television and cable increased film viewing.

The development of cable television and direct satellite broadcasting has altered the use of movies on television. Home Box Office (HBO), a cable television channel that began operation in 1972, allowed its subscribers to see movies after their theatrical release but before the major broadcast networks could acquire them. HBO's success led to the establishment of other premium channels such as Showtime and Cinemax.

In the 1990s, the expansion of channels made possible by fiber-optic cable allowed cable companies to offer pay-per-view movies. These differ from premium channels in that the viewer pays for each viewing rather than a flat monthly fee. Pay-per-view makes films available to the cable and broadcast satellite subscriber at the same time that the movie appears in video stores, before it appears on a channel such as HBO. Some hotels even offer pay-per-view showings of movies that are currently in first-run movie theaters.

Increasingly, movies, whether made for theaters or directly for television, have become a basic building block of television content. The strong film libraries held by Disney, Turner Broadcasting System, and Time Warner were important factors in the mergers between Disney and Capitol Cities/ABC and between Turner Broadcasting System and Time Warner. Television and theaters are no longer competitors. Instead, they are different distribution systems for reaching viewers.

key concept

Response to Television In the 1950s, the movie industry, desperate to recapture audiences lost to television, competed by offering technical novelties, including 3-D Panavision. Soon Hollywood also collaborated with television, providing studio facilities for making innovative TV series.

Cinerama: Trade name for process that produces wide-screen images.

3-D: Film technique designed to create a sense of depth. Viewers wore special glasses for viewing.

Panavision: System of lenses used in filming that enabled a film shot in one wide-screen version (Cinemascope, for example) to be shown in theaters without the lenses for that type of projection.

Some movies, such as *Road to Perdition* released in 2002, deal with abstract themes like sacrifice and redemption. This movie tells the story of gangster Michael Sullivan's, played by Tom Hanks, efforts to save his son from a mob execution. Hanks is shown here with Tyler Hoechlin, who played Michael Sullivan, Jr.

CULTURAL AND POLITICAL DEVELOPMENTS

Before 1952, when the Supreme Court handed down a decision that granted First Amendment protection to film, movies were considered a simple amusement, like a circus. The courts had previously ruled that movies were not a "significant medium for the communication of ideas." However, from the early days of movies until recent times, civic and religious groups have tried to institute censorship because they feared the power of the movies. Early research labeled movies as emotionally powerful. These contradictory views persist today. But through the generations, the movies—America's dream factories—have given generations of children, adolescents, and adults the opportunity to escape from routine work, from inhibition, and from the doldrums of everyday life.

Movies as Art and Social Commentary

The studio, the star system, and a system of repeating popular **genres** enabled the Hollywood studios to maximize profits. They also guaranteed that a certain type of movie would emanate from Hollywood. U.S. filmmakers left intellectual movies to foreign producers. During the silent era, slapstick comedies, Westerns, and melodramas were the most popular genres. However, D. W. Griffith and his contemporaries in the teens and early twenties introduced more sophisticated narratives dominated by characters who were not only goal oriented but also in a hurry to succeed. These narrative structures were linear and came almost directly from the stage. Griffith's *The Birth of a Nation*, for example, was a stage play before he adapted it to film.

Popular culture films such as gangster pictures, musicals, and screwball comedies became popular during the talkie era, and the studio and star systems propelled Hollywood to produce big-budget spectaculars. Yet despite the emphasis on popular culture films and the box office, Hollywood managed to produce, sometimes by accident, lasting classics. Certain artistic directors earned international recognition. For example, Orson Welles wrote, directed, and starred in *Citizen Kane* in 1941, when he was twenty-six years old, and became known throughout the world for his contribution to cinematic technique. *Citizen Kane* was based loosely on the life of newspaper tycoon William Randolph Hearst. Welles included unusual camera angles, backlighting,

genre: A kind or style of movie.

and condensed time sequences and introduced other film techniques that continue to influence moviemakers today. Many film critics consider *Citizen Kane* to be the greatest American film ever made. However, it was a box-office failure when it was released because Hearst used his immense power in the newspaper and entertainment industries to encourage negative reviews and to force theater owners to boycott the film.

From the 1940s to the early 1960s, films used a narrative structure that featured wholesome heroes and heroines. Although there were attempts at *social realism,* such as Tennessee Williams's *A Streetcar Named Desire,* positive tones and outcomes dominated the big screens. In *Streetcar,* Marlon Brando played Stanley Kowalski, a brooding, unkempt antihero who brutalizes both his wife and her sister. In the 1960s, film content and character changed in dramatic ways. Some critics date the shift to the 1967 production of *Bonnie and Clyde,* a movie about two 1930s gangsters, which critic Pauline Kael described as a film of violence that "puts the sting back into death."[9] The strident films of the 1960s reflected the nation's conflicts over the Vietnam War, youthful rebellion, the civil rights movement, and militant black power efforts. Social conflict and social statement films dominated the decade and the early 1970s. After 1977 and the production of *Star Wars,* a science fiction epic, many films turned to escapism. Filmmakers also moved away from the structured narrative that had dominated through the 1960s to more episodic narratives with less foreshadowed endings. Heroes were sometimes amoral, and sex, often fused with violence rather than with romance, moved onto the screen in unprecedented fashion. *M*A*S*H* (1970) depicted interrelationships among characters thrown together in a medical unit during the Korean War. The exploits of the medical team were presented in episodic fashion.

Many traditional film themes are repeated in filmmaking today. The classic Western with a loner, good-guy cowboy is repeated in films about loner heroes in a postnuclear anarchical society. An Australian film, *The Road Warrior,* exemplifies this category. But characterization varies over time, and moviegoers today see much more complex characters than usually appeared in the films of the past. During the 1940s "Golden Age of Hollywood," Jimmy Stewart took on corrupt Washington in Frank Capra's *Mr. Smith Goes to Washington,* and Henry Fonda cleaned up Tombstone as Wyatt Earp in John Ford's *My Darling Clementine.*

Movies during the last two decades show how the industry follows changing trends. In the mid-1990s, *Pulp Fiction* and *Natural Born Killers* sparked discussions about the role of violence in films. Steven Spielberg's tribute to World War II veterans of the Normandy invasion, *Saving Private Ryan,* brought the sounds, blood, and emotion of that conflict to the movie screen. At the same time, Disney continued the string of hits started by *The Little Mermaid* in 1989 with *Aladdin, The Lion King, Toy Story 2,* and *Monsters, Inc.,* all of which sold more than $200 million in tickets within the United States. The early 2000s saw the rise of fantasy and sci-fi as *Spider-Man, The Lord of the Rings: The Fellowship of the Ring, Harry Potter and the Sorcerer's Stone,* and *Star Wars: Attack of the Clones* all earned more than $300 million in domestic box-office revenues. Of the ten highest grossing films domestically, only two were released before the 1990s. Table 8.1 details these successful films.

key concept

Social Realism A genre of films critical of society's structure that has maintained its thread throughout the years of movie production, although it rarely dominates the big screens. Such films have played an important part in the marketplace of ideas.

t a b l e   8 . 1

Top Grossing Films in the Domestic Market

MOVIE	TOTAL GROSS	YEAR RELEASED
1. *Titanic*	$601	1997
2. *Star Wars*	$461	1977
3. *E.T.*	$435	1982
4. *Star Wars: The Phantom Menace*	$431	1999
5. *Spider-Man*	$404	2002
6. *Jurassic Park*	$357	1993
7. *Forrest Gump*	$330	1994
8. *Harry Potter and the Sorcerer's Stone*	$318	2001
9. *The Lord of the Rings: The Fellowship of the Ring*	$313	2001
10. *The Lion King*	$313	1994

Reprinted with permission of MovieWeb; www.movieweb.com. Updated in 2002.

Movies and the Marketplace of Ideas

Hollywood has rarely produced explicitly political films. Despite the cultural and social impact of movies, the motion picture was not considered "speech" until 1952 and therefore was not protected by the First Amendment to the U.S. Constitution. In 1915 in *Mutual Film Corp. v. Industrial Commission of Ohio,* the U.S. Supreme Court declared that exhibiting films was a business pure and simple, a decision that allowed for the control of film content. To avoid including film under the protection of the First Amendment, for nearly forty years courts adhered to the "simple business" standard and did not recognize movies as "a significant medium for the communication of ideas." However, in 1952 in *Burstyn v. Wilson,* the Supreme Court declared that film content entertained and informed and therefore was subject to First Amendment protection.

In 1922, the motion picture industry voluntarily organized the Motion Picture Producers and Distributors of America (MPPDA) and named Will H. Hays as its president. The move was designed to avoid government regulation and to combat negative publicity about stars, divorce, and the prevalence of drugs in the industry. Twelve years later, a group of Catholic bishops organized the National Legion of Decency to develop lists of films that were acceptable and not acceptable for Catholic viewers. Hollywood responded by establishing a production *code of film content* that forbade sex, excessive violence, and vulgar language. Violators of the code were to pay a $25,000 fine to the MPPDA, although the fine was never publicly invoked. The code, although often skirted or challenged, remained on the books until 1968, when the industry adopted a ratings system. The ratings system shifted responsibility to the movie viewer by specifying the type of audience the movie had been designed to attract. In 1984 and again in 1992, the industry revised specific ratings, but the principle of alerting the audience rather than controlling content remained as the guide.

> ### key concept
>
> **Code of Film Content** Various regulations have been in place, particularly at the local level, to control the content of films shown in communities. The film industry, constantly facing pressure to produce exciting films yet avoid moral injury to young audiences, developed a production code to comply with various local government restrictions. In 1968 the industry altered its position from controlling content to developing a system of ratings to identify levels of sexual and violent content and adult language.

Government opinions of the motion picture industry's activity during World War II were mixed. Major producers cooperated to produce war films on what they termed a nonprofit basis. Nevertheless, during 1941 and 1942, the Army Pictorial Division alone spent more than $1 million in Hollywood. Critics claimed the producers filmed for the government during slack times, or when the studios otherwise would have stood idle, and that by cooperating, the industry managed to remain relatively untouched by the war. Therefore, despite Walt Disney's portrayal of Donald Duck's willingness to pay taxes with patriotic enthusiasm and Frank Capra's direction of the Why We Fight series designed to train new soldiers, the motion picture industry still had a variety of enemies in Congress.

The Motion Picture Bureau, a division of the Office of War Information (OWI), attempted to influence Hollywood producers to support the war effort. One of its tasks was to try to motivate producers to incorporate more realistic pictures of African American life into films. A 1942 survey conducted by the Office of Facts and Figures revealed that 49 percent of the African Americans in Harlem thought they would be no worse off if Japan won the war. In response to this evidence, OWI wanted Hollywood to tone down its racist images of African Americans to foster a sense of unity in the country.[10]

Although the industry had catered to the Legion of Decency and various economic groups, when OWI attempted to promote more positive images of African Americans, the industry cried censorship. For example, MGM in 1938 had hand carried its script of Robert Sherwood's antifascist play, *Idiot's Delight,* to Italy for approval after drastically altering it to avoid offending Benito Mussolini. Warner Bros.'s coal mining saga, *Black Fury,* was altered to blame labor unrest on union radicals rather than on mine operators after the National Coal Association protested.

OWI efforts to promote positive African American images had little effect. A 1945 Columbia University study found that of one hundred African American appearances

1878. Eadweard Muybridge uses stop-action photography.

1892. Thomas Edison's lab develops the kinetoscope.

1895. Vaudeville theaters begin to show magic-lantern shows.

1903. *The Great Train Robbery,* the forerunner of feature films, is shown.

1900s. Nickelodeons become popular.

1915. *The Birth of a Nation* marks the start of the modern movie industry.

1927. *The Jazz Singer* popularizes sound in feature-length films.

1930. Five large movie companies dominate the industry.

1934. Studios establish decency code for films.

1939–1945. Movie industry helps government promote war effort.

1400–1700	1800	1860	1880	1900	1920	1930

1620. Pilgrims land at Plymouth Rock.

1690. *Publick Occurrences* is published in Boston.

1741. First magazine is published in America.

1776–1783. American Revolution

1830s. The penny press becomes the first truly mass medium in the United States.

1861–1865. American Civil War

1892. Thomas Edison's lab develops the kinetoscope.

1914–1918. World War I

1915. *The Birth of a Nation* marks the start of the modern movie industry.

1920. KDKA in Pittsburgh gets the first commercial radio license.

1930s. The Great Depression

1939. TV is demonstrated at the New York World's Fair.

1939–1945. World War II

in wartime films, seventy-five perpetuated stereotypes, thirteen were neutral, and only twelve were positive. OWI hesitated to push very far, claiming the war came first.[11]

Congressional frustration with the film industry was not limited to its concern about treatment of minorities in wartime. In the late 1940s and 1950s, conservative members of Congress attacked the industry in hearings before the House Committee on Un-American Activities. This committee and Senator Joseph McCarthy's parallel committee in the Senate pummeled the media industries, taking special delight in attacking the motion picture and broadcast industries. Congressman and committee chairman Thomas Parnell intended to prove that the film industry had been infiltrated by Communists who introduced subversive propaganda into the movies.

At the 1947 hearings, ten screenwriters, later dubbed the Hollywood Ten, refused to say whether they had been members of the Communist Party, invoking the First Amendment guarantee of freedom of the press and freedom of association. The

1948. Supreme Court breaks up the industry's vertical integration.

1950s. Television begins to affect movie attendance.

1952. Supreme Court extends First Amendment rights to film.

1960s. Networks begin showing movies during prime time.

1968. Film industry begins using a ratings system.

Late 1960s. Graphic violence and sex become prominent in independent films.

1972. HBO starts satellite distribution to cable systems.

1980s. Video recorder technology is sold to consumers.

Late 1980s. Cable channels increase their financing of feature films.

1990s. Movies are promoted on the World Wide Web.

1990s. Cable systems experiment with movies on demand.

2000s. Movies become increasingly international.

2000s. DVD replaces VHS for viewing movies at home.

2002. Movies, dominated by sequels, break box-office records.

1940	1950	1960	1970	1980	1990	2000

1949. First commercial electronic computer is produced.

Early 1950s. Rock 'n' roll begins.

1969. First person lands on the moon.

1970s. VCR is developed.

1989–1991. Cold War ends and the USSR is dissolved.

Late 1980s. National Science Foundation creates the basis of the Internet.

1996. Telecommunications Act

2000. Presidential election nearly tied.

2001. Terrorist attacks on New York and Washington, D.C.

Hollywood Ten all went to jail for contempt of Congress. Although recent research shows that these writers had in no way tried to formally propagandize or commit any type of subversion, Hollywood did not stand behind them. Rather, it panicked. Many Hollywood liberals such as Humphrey Bogart and John Huston supported the writers initially, but most support disappeared when the heads of the large studios threatened the supporters' careers. The Hollywood Ten were suspended from work, and executives invited Hollywood's talent guilds to help them eliminate any subversives from their ranks.

From 1951 to 1954, a second round of hearings investigated Hollywood further. Director Elia Kazan, who would later win an Academy Award for *On the Waterfront,* eagerly testified and lost many friends. The result of the hearings was an informal blacklist of actors, directors, writers, and producers whom the major studios would not hire. A few found work with independent production companies, often using

An anticommunist witch-hunt fueled attacks on Hollywood stars during the late 1940s and early 1950s. Ten film writers were jailed for refusal to answer trumped-up charges of communist affiliation. A chill effect followed, with panicky Hollywood executives refusing to employ many actors and producers.

false names. The actor Kirk Douglas hired Dalton Trumbo, who had been one of the Hollywood Ten, to write the script for his 1960 blockbuster *Spartacus*, but more than 320 people were blacklisted by the studios.

Once the national scare ended and Senator McCarthy was exposed as an irrational manipulator of fear, the film industry enjoyed relative freedom from government interference and regulation. Even during the 1990s, with renewed emphasis by some special interest groups on family values, congressional rhetoric and action focused more intensely on the television industry than on film. While campaigning for the Republican presidential nomination in 1996, Senator Bob Dole attacked Time Warner for its production of violent films, but within the context of the entertainment industry as a whole.

Despite varying degrees of freedom, the U.S. movie industry usually avoids explicit depictions of *politics in the movies*. Exceptions, such as *Meet John Doe* (1941), *Bob Roberts* (1992), *Wag the Dog* (1998), and *Primary Colors* (1998) do exist, but they seldom draw large audiences. Over time the main contribution of movies to the marketplace of ideas has been in the area of social and cultural issues and trends.

key concept

Politics in the Movies Even before McCarthyism and the Red Scare of the 1950s, some politicians saw films and television as sources of corruption of society's political or moral values. The U.S. film industry, seeking to avoid such criticism, has typically discouraged controversial political content in movies.

The Role of Women in Movie History ✦ Since the beginning of feature films, most women in the movie business played second billing to men, just as minorities played minor roles. *Stereotypes of women and minorities* abounded. A female actor could not open a movie, which means "attract a large audience," by herself. Even acclaimed actresses such as Katharine Hepburn and Bette Davis were defined in most films as much by their leading men as by their own star power. Few women were movie executives, and even fewer directed films.

Today, women have a greater impact in the movie business. Actors such as Sandra Bullock and Julia Roberts open films and attract large audiences. Women sit on executive boards of major studios, and female directors produce quality, money-making movies. Penny Marshall directed *Big* and was executive producer of *A League of Their Own*. Nancy Meyers directed *The Parent Trap* and *What Women Want*, both of which were hits. Oprah Winfrey also won kudos for her production of Toni Morrison's best-selling novel-turned-screenplay, *Beloved*.

Despite their advances, women still face problems in Hollywood. Young actors often feel typecast in roles that depend on looks more than talent, and these roles often stereotype women. In 2002, Halle Berry won the Oscar for best actress in *Monster's Ball* after Angela Bassett, who was nominated for best actress in the 1993 movie *What's Love Got to Do with It*, turned down the role because she said the role was

key concept

Stereotypes of Women and Minorities Despite a steady evolution toward more positive roles and the elimination of the most insulting stereotypes of gender or ethnic behavior on screen, most movies continue to show only relatively narrow ranges of behavior and few substantial roles for minority and female actors. Rarely are African Americans, Hispanic Americans, Asian Americans, or Native Americans portrayed in films outside a small set of social settings, and seldom are women shown in strong or dominant roles.

a stereotype of black women's sexuality.[12] Interestingly, the controversy involving this stereotypical treatment of women received far less media attention than the treatment of women in the 1991 movie *Thelma and Louise*. This film was labeled as male bashing, mostly by male columnists, because it showed two strong women refusing to be intimidated by men.

profile

Jodie Foster

Jodie Foster, one of the few actors in Hollywood who ensures worldwide box-office attention, had her first role as the little Coppertone girl in pigtails whose swimsuit bottom was being pulled down by a mischievous dog. Then came television shows such as *The Courtship of Eddie's Father* and Disney movies including *Freaky Friday* and *Candleshoe*.

While other children were watching her in Disney movies, Foster and her siblings were watching French and Italian movies. Her mother chose similarly off-beat movies in which Foster could act. The most memorable, garnering Foster an Oscar nomination when she was only fourteen, was *Taxi Driver* (1976). It also made her the obsession of John W. Hinckley Jr., who attempted to assassinate then-President Reagan in 1981. *Taxi Driver*, rereleased in 1996, starred Robert De Niro as a Vietnam veteran turned late-night taxi driver in New York City. He becomes obsessed with rescuing a twelve-year-old prostitute played by Foster and goes on a bloody killing spree in an attempt to cleanse the city of moral degeneracy.

After Foster graduated from the Lycée Français in Los Angeles, she became an honors student in comparative literature at Yale. On her return to Hollywood, she had to stand in line to try out for movie roles. She had been away from the industry too long for her name to be an automatic box-office draw.

Foster's star power was still there, however. In 1988, she won an Oscar for best actress for her role as a rape victim in *The Accused*. Her second Oscar came three years later in *Silence of the Lambs* for her portrayal of an FBI agent trying to get information from one vicious killer in order to find another. In addition to acting, Foster has focused her talents on directing. She acted in her first feature film as director, *Little Man Tate* (1991), the story of a brilliant child. The movie is more about character than plot. Her second directing success was *Home for the Holidays* (1995), the story of a young woman who goes home to have Thanksgiving with her dysfunctional family. In 1995, she received her fourth Academy Award nomination for her portrayal of an autistic woman in *Nell*.

Foster continues to interweave her acting, producing, and directing talents. In 1999, she appeared as Anna in a remake of *Anna and the King* (of Siam) at the same time she was casting for *Flora Plum*.

Foster has been pragmatic in managing her career and is known for her sense of perspective about life. Reviewers repeatedly comment that success does not corrupt her. CEO of her own production company, she is an accomplished producer, director, and actor.

Sources: Stephen Rebello, "Jodie Foster: Nice Girls Do Finish First," *Cosmopolitan* (April 1996): 176; The Internet Movie Database, December 1999, http://us.imdb.com/AName? Foster,+Jodie.

People of Color in Film

An analysis of movies and race begins with the history of stereotypical treatment of people of color by white filmmakers. From the early presentation of people of color in film during the 1890s, the images have been inaccurate and limited. During the 1930s, 1940s, and 1950s, movies presented African Americans as lazy and slow thinking. This stereotype has been called the "Step 'n Fetchit" role—a term that came from the stage name of Lincoln Perry, who made a career of playing this type of character. Native Americans have been presented either as the "noble savage" or the "bloodthirsty savage."[13]

The stereotypes associated with Hispanics and Latino movie characters have varied from the Latin lovers of the 1920s to the bandidos of the 1930s and 1940s to the gang members and drug dealers of the 1960s. Early portrayals of Asian Americans often showed them as scheming and untrustworthy. However, more often than not, Asian Americans were just missing from films or had minor roles.[14]

Often ignored in history are the films made by filmmakers of color. The first black film company, for example, was the Lincoln Motion Picture Company, formed in 1915 in Los Angeles to showcase black talent. In 1916 the Frederick Douglass Film Company formed on the East Coast to counteract antiblack images in the movie *The Birth of a Nation*.[15] Hampered by financing and distribution problems, both companies closed during the early 1920s. They were replaced by other African American film companies. Oscar Micheaux became the best-known black filmmaker of this period, producing dozens of silent and talking films. Many of these films dealt with racial issues and presented African American life in greater variety than was found in major studio films.

From the late 1930s to the 1950s, a variety of companies produced movies with all–African American casts for the segregated theaters of the black community. These films tended to imitate films produced by whites and were made cheaply. As film historian Daniel J. Leab said, "The leads remained very Caucasian-looking and spoke good English; the villains and comic figures, who were more Negroid in features and darker skinned, tended to speak in dialect."[16] The failure to present African Americans in a more realistic fashion in these films can be largely attributed to the financial and distribution control that whites continued to hold over the black film industry. In order to be seen, films about African Americans had to fit white stereotypes.

Movies by Chicano and Hispanic filmmakers in the United States came much later than those by African Americans. Although a few films were produced by Chicano filmmakers during the early and mid-1960s, the early 1970s saw the blossoming of Chicano-made movies. Mostly documentaries, such as *Requiem-29: Racism and Police Repression against Chicanos* by David García, these films dealt with the problems confronting Chicanos and were part of the overall social unrest of the late 1960s and early 1970s.[17] However, fictional films by Chicanos and Hispanics developed even later.

In the 1960s, major studios discovered that African American actors could make money at the box office. Sidney Poitier became an acclaimed actor and bankable star. The change in Hollywood reflected the changing mood of a nation whose consciousness was being raised by the civil rights movement. The late 1960s and early 1970s saw the arrival of the black action film. *Shaft*, directed by famous black photographer Gordon Parks, came out in 1971. It was a violent film, not unlike similar white-oriented detective movies. It cost $1.1 million to make and made $6.1 million.[18] Hollywood liked these profits, and similar films followed, including two *Shaft* sequels. Although these films starred African Americans, they were produced by major film studios, and some critics said they exploited the anger that black audiences felt about the lack of changes in society. In fact, they are now referred to as "blaxploitation" movies. These films were no closer to the average African American's life than the James Bond films are to the average white British person's life. But white people saw a larger variety of self-images in film than did people of color.

In the 1980s and 1990s, young African American filmmakers Spike Lee and John Singleton gained financial support from major studios. Lee's *She's Gotta Have It,* an independent production, attracted the interest of Columbia Pictures, which financed half his second film, *School Daze* (1988). However, black filmmakers' projects typically receive less financial support than do projects by white directors. Lee's later films such as *Do the Right Thing* (1989) and John Singleton's *Boyz N the Hood* (1991) received critical acclaim and made a profit. Lee continued in the late 1990s with *4 Little Girls* (1997) and *He Got Game* (1998). Despite the high quality of acting, writing, and production, some critics see in many of these films new stereotypes that continue to reflect the financial control of white-run studios. Film scholar Jacquie Jones concluded:

> Unfortunately, even a cursory examination of the recent wave of black films financed with studio capital reveals that age-old ghettoization of black products remains unchanged. The industry's wholesale investment in films that explore only ghettoes and male youth ignores the existence of a black community beyond these narrow confines—inclusive of women as valuable participants—as well as films that refuse to cater to these prescriptions.[19]

Some would argue that this is an oversimplification of the movies by these African American filmmakers. Spike Lee's 2000 *Bamboozled,* a satirical look at the way white media portray African Americans, was not consistent with this criticism.

Although the number of titles remains small, Latino and Native American filmmakers began to produce movies during the 1980s. *Zoot Suit* (1981) and *La Bamba* (1987) by Luis Valdez, *Born in East L.A.* (1987) by Cheech Marin, and *American Me* (1992) by Edward James Olmos were early Latino films. More recently, Robert Rodríguez, whose first film *El Mariachi* in 1992 was made with $7,000 and earned more than $1.8 million, has moved into the movie mainstream with the critical and box-office successes *Spy Kids* and *Spy Kids 2.*

Films made by Native American filmmakers are even more of a rarity. In 1998, *Smoke Signals,* a film advertised as the first feature film written, acted, directed, and produced by Native Americans, was shown to rave reviews at the Sundance Film Festival in Utah. The movie was directed by Chris Eyre from a book by Sherman Alexie titled *The Lone Ranger and Tonto Fistfight in Heaven.* Despite this film's critical success, it continues to stand alone as an example of how Native Americans can find their own voice to speak about themselves.

Acclaimed African American director Spike Lee's early work explored some of the dynamics of white–black interaction in such movies as *She's Gotta Have It.* Some critics fear that if Lee and others concentrate too much on exploring violent roles for African American males or on ghetto settings, they may promote still another Hollywood stereotype for African Americans in film.

Nominated for the 2001 Best Picture Academy Award, *Crouching Tiger, Hidden Dragon* succeeded at the box office and with the critics despite using English subtitles. Here, Ang Lee directs Chow Yun Fat.

Asian American filmmakers have yet to emerge as a force in Hollywood. This may reflect the strength of the Asian film industries in Japan, China, and Taiwan. For example, *Crouching Tiger, Hidden Dragon,* directed by Ang Lee, was nominated for the Academy Award as best picture in 2001, and Jackie Chan, who was born in Hong Kong, has had several American hits, such as *Rush Hour* and *Rush Hour 2.*

Although people of color continue to be stereotyped in films and struggle for roles in Hollywood, events in 2002 raised hopes that improvement is underway. For the first time ever, a woman of color, Halle Berry, won the Oscar for best actress, and Denzel Washington won the Oscar for best actor. This occurred on the night Sidney Poitier was recognized for his lifetime achievements as an actor and director by the Academy of Motion Picture Arts and Sciences. In August of 2002, *Newsweek* ran a cover story naming M. Night Shyamalan, whose parents are Indian, the "next Spielberg." His 1999 film *The Sixth Sense,* with Bruce Willis, grossed almost $300 million in the United States, and his 2002 film *Signs,* with Mel Gibson, grossed $118 million in two weeks.

TODAY'S MARKET STRUCTURE

The film industry is still dominated by a group of major studios. It has survived repeated challenges, including the breakup of theater networks; the rise of television, cable, and pay-per-view; and the popularity of the videocassette recorder (VCR). The studios have not only survived, but they have also adapted, prospered, and grown. For example, Rupert Murdoch, the Australian press lord, merged Twentieth Century Fox with his chain of metropolitan television stations acquired from Metromedia Television. The Fox television stations give the corporate family instant access to wide distribution of a film after it appears in the nation's theaters.[20] In 1985, Ted Turner bought MGM and acquired its film library for his superstation before reselling the movie company. The major studios still control about 80 percent of the business in the United States and about half the market in Sweden, West Germany, several other western European nations, and Asia. Although the number of independent producers has increased during the past twenty years, all of them contract with the studios to distribute their films.

The key to the studios' success continues to be their domination of movie **distribution.** The studios see all the forms of distribution—theaters, DVD/VHS, pay-per-view, television networks, cable channels, satellites, and premium networks—as windows of opportunity for distributing their films. In each of the windows, consumers pay a different price for the same material. Watching a movie in a theater costs more than buying it through pay-per-view on cable or renting a DVD. Renting a DVD costs more than getting a movie as part of HBO, and HBO costs more than

distributors: The people of the movie industry who arrange to engage movies in theaters, then on television.

Special effects are a critical part of today's action movies. Here, Yoda looks at a projection of Obi-wan Kenobi, played by Ewan McGregor, in *Star Wars Episode II: Attack of the Clones.*

Sequels Dominate the Summers

In Hollywood, if something works once, try it again. Each summer the theaters fill with sequels from previous hit films. In 2002, it was *Austin Powers III, Spy Kids 2, Stuart Little 2, Men in Black II, Star Wars Episode II—Attack of the Clones* (it was really the fifth Stars Wars film), and *Halloween: Resurrection,* to name a few. In summer 2001, it was *The Mummy Returns, Rush Hour 2, Jurassic Park III,* and *American Pie 2.*

Films that continue the same characters are called "franchise" films. The characters become a brand that people know and like enough to see again and again. The idea of the franchise is not new. For example, the Thin Man character from the Dashiell Hammett book appeared in six films during the 1930s and 1940s. However, more recently they have come to dominate the summer season.

Franchises have the advantage of reducing risk for a film, which is worthwhile if a studio is going to spend $60 to $100 million to make a film. If the previous movies were successful at the box office, then the sequels are more likely to be successful. In addition, the amount of advertising necessary to make people familiar with a character declines with a sequel. The advertising must only convince the potential audience that this installment is as good as the previous ones.

Sequels also offer fading actors a chance to revive their careers. Arnold Schwarzenegger, for instance, hasn't had a hit since *True Lies* in 1994. In an effort to correct this, the fifty-five-year old will release *True Lies 2* and *Terminator 3: The Rise of the Machines.*

Critics and studio representatives disagree about the impact of franchise films. Critics argue that by concentrating on sequels, more serious films do not get made or receive little distribution and promotion. In response, defenders of the system argue that the franchise films make money that allow studios to experiment with smaller, more artistic films. They also point out that independent filmmakers, supported by such organizations as the Sundance Institute, produce far more films today than thirty years ago.

Whatever the impact on the film industry, franchise films will not leave anytime soon. The Spider-Man and Harry Potter franchises promise to run for a long time. Each summer Hollywood will become "déjà vu all over again."

Sources: Mark Caro, "Summer of the Franchise II," *Chicago Tribune* (May 12, 2002); 7:1, 7:13; and Malcolm Johnson, "When Action Stars Age: Sequel Cash Is Alluring Despite Fading Credibility," *Hartford Courant* (February 7, 2002): CAL, 16.

watching a movie on the TNT cable network. In each window, consumers pay less, but they have to wait longer after the initial distribution to see the film.[21] Movies hit the video stores and pay-per-view about six months after they leave theaters. After another six months or so, the film will be on HBO. This "windows" process allows studios to reach people who will not pay $7 to $10 to see a film in the theater. It also explains why studios have become part of multimedia corporations. By controlling the windows, the corporations squeeze more profit out of each viewing opportunity. This is why Viacom, for example, owns the CBS Network, Paramount Pictures, Showtime, and Blockbuster video stores.

AUDIENCE DEMAND IN MOVIE MARKETS

Despite, or maybe because of, the economic downturn of 2001 and 2002, movie demand experienced growth in both years. U.S. movie ticket sales reached $8.35 billion in 2001, an increase over the $7.7 billion in 2000.[22] By August of 2002, the year's ticket sales had hit $5.6 billion, which was 15 percent ahead of the 2001 ticket sales at that time.[23] Six of the top twenty box-office hits of all time were released during 2001 and 2002. These 2001–2002 films appealed to a wide range of ages. *Gosford*

Park was aimed at an older audience, whereas *Spider-Man* drew teenagers and *Monsters, Inc.* attracted younger viewers.

In the early days, movies catered to the family audience. From the era of the nickelodeon to the age of Panavision, mothers, fathers, and children flocked to neighborhood movie houses and to the theater palaces in the cities. After the advent of television, as couples settled down to raise children in the suburbs, the movies became less attractive. For parents, going to a movie meant paying for a babysitter, tickets, and transportation, so many chose to stay home and watch television. Slowly, the audience changed, and from the late 1960s until the late 1980s, the seventeen-year-old was the most reliable moviegoer. Demographics have changed, however, and aging baby boomers now far outnumber teenagers in the United States and present a viable group for studios to target.

The movie viewing audience became older during the 1980s and early 1990s, according to data published by the Motion Picture Association of America. In 1981, 24 percent of moviegoers were between the ages of sixteen and twenty, but by 1992, that percentage dropped to 15 percent. Admissions for people between forty and forty-nine rose from 6 percent to 16 percent during that period. However, since 1992 the age distribution of moviegoers has remained relatively stable.

Younger viewers retain great influence over which films are made. People between ages twelve and twenty-four made up 23 percent of the U.S. population but 38 percent of total theater admissions in 2001. Nearly half of all teenagers go to the movies at least once a month, compared to just one in four adults. Young people rarely wait for recommendations and reviews; they go to movies as soon as they open. They attend movies as part of their social activity with friends, choose movies on impulse, and are heavily influenced by television advertising. By contrast, older adults attend movies selectively, preferring films that represent more sophisticated fare than they can find on television. They choose movies after reading reviews and listening to their friends' recommendations.

Adults accompany young children to family movies and appreciate the music, acting, story lines, and animation. Adults, as well as the children they accompany, are partly responsible for the success of films such as the Harry Potter movies, along with classics such as *Beauty and the Beast, Aladdin,* and *Home Alone.* The movie industry's ratings system has emerged as a *labeling system targeted to specific demographics.* In general, films rated G and PG earn more money than films rated R or NC-17. According to *Variety* magazine, from 1972 to 1991, movies with G or PG ratings earned the most at the box office. None of the top ten all-time grossing films has an R rating. Nevertheless, the number of R-rated movies produced has increased from 39 percent in 1972 to 74 percent of all movies in 2001. R-rated movies appeal to youth, particularly urban youth, who report in focus groups that they want to see movies dealing with the reality of their lives, which often are surrounded by violence and drug use.[24]

As a reaction to the violence in films, the Federal Trade Commission and U.S. Congress held hearings during 2000. Theaters started checking IDs and making it more difficult for people under seventeen to buy tickets. Teenagers reacted by buying tickets to a non-R film and then going into the R-film auditorium at the multiplex. Hollywood reacted by increasing the sex and violence in PG-13 movies. Parental watchdog groups call this "ratings creep."[25] The movie industry's defense against the criticism is that they are merely showing what teenagers can see on television. The percentage of U.S. films that carried a PG-13 rating grew from 16 percent in 1999 to 22 percent in 2001.

Increasingly, the U.S. audience in all its various segments is only a portion of the audience to which U.S. movies are directed. Profits can be doubled by showings in the international market. Furthermore, studios are measuring the popularity of particular stars and genres in the international markets before film scripts are even developed.

key concept

Labeling for Audience Demographics Movie ratings systems have been developed to target the various demographics that constitute the filmgoing public. As family audiences gave way first to the teenage audience, then to the baby boomers, the ratings system adapted. The current ratings system is as follows: G: general audiences; PG: parental guidance suggested; PG-13: special guidance for children under thirteen; R: people under seventeen must be accompanied by an adult; NC-17: no one under seventeen admitted.

SUPPLYING THE AUDIENCE'S DEMAND

Movies meet the demands of the audience and make profits not only through traditional showings at theaters but also through release to the international market, pay-per-view television channels, home videos, premium channels, and television networks. Movie theaters usually split box-office receipts with distributors, who also charge booking fees to moviemakers. Exhibitors make a good deal of their money, however, on refreshments, which often are marked up by 60 percent over their wholesale cost.

The average gross of the top fifteen films has increased every year since 1990, and the movie industry expected to sell more than $8.5 billion worth of tickets in 2002. Industry observers credit the growth in ticket sales to increased numbers of screens in multiplex theaters and to the action films, such as *Spider-Man* and *Lord of the Rings: The Fellowship of the Ring,* that look much better on big screens. Now a blockbuster movie can open on five thousand to six thousand screens across the United States and make its cost back in two weeks.

The rush to build screens, however, backfired during 2000 and 2001. Six of the nation's largest theater chains filed for Chapter 11 bankruptcy court protection to help them get out of debt. Theater chains had overbuilt new multiplex screens while being locked into leases that kept them from closing older theaters. As a result, the Motion Picture Association of America reported that there was a net loss of 401 screens from 1999 to 2001. But industry observers said that the 36,764 screens still operating in 2001 was too many and that thousands more screens would disappear as older multiplexes close.[26] With the growth of DVD, pay-per-view, and the potential of Internet-delivered films, the number of screens will likely decline even more in the coming decades. Distributing movies will take on a new meaning.

Product Placement: Supplying the Advertising Market

For the first one hundred years of the U.S. movie industry, advertising played a small part in the financing of movies. However, that is changing. Movie companies face blockbuster budgets in excess of $100 million, and companies concerned about people's increasingly cynical response to television commercials constantly search for ways to sell their products more effectively. These two needs have seen an increase in an advertising strategy called *product placement.* This involves displaying a clearly identifiable product in a film, such as having a popular star in a film drinking not just any soft drink, but specifically a can of Pepsi. Critics argue that product placement is deceptive because the viewer does not recognize the ad for what it is. Industry spokespeople have another point of view: Director John Badham notes that film budgets have become so large that producers need to look for new types of revenue. "From a producer's or a director's view, product placement is a great way to reduce the budget and keep the studio quiet."[27]

> **key concept**
>
> **Product Placement** Movie production has been financed primarily by admission revenues rather than sponsored ads. However, since the 1980s, significant indirect advertising income has come from the product placement system, whereby a product, such as a Coca-Cola can, is clearly discernible in the movie.

The technique is not new. In 1945, film star Joan Crawford downed Jack Daniels bourbon whiskey in the Warner Bros. production *Mildred Pierce.* However, in 1982 product placement hit the big time when sales of Reese's Pieces soared 66 percent in three months after the candy was showcased in Steven Spielberg's *E. T. the Extra-Terrestrial.* Hollywood-featured releases became an important element of every consumer marketing program.[28] Spielberg struck again in 2002 with the release of *Minority Report.* Product placement of brands such as Burger King, Century 21, and Guinness brought in $25 million to cover almost a quarter of the film's $102 million budget.[29]

Minority Report was not alone in the increasing use of product placement. The Austin Powers franchise has been aggressive in product placement. Who doesn't know that Dr. Evil stocks Starbucks coffee in his lair? In 2002, Coors Brewing Co. signed a deal with Miramax Films to be the official sponsor of theatrical premieres of Miramax films in the United States. In addition to being served at opening night parties, Coors will appear in fifteen films from 2003 to 2005. With the need to reduce risk for blockbuster movies, studios will continue to aggressively sell placement in their movies. At issue is the influence this may have over viewers.

The Home-Viewing Revolution

Television brought movies into the home, but viewers had no choice but to watch what was available or to turn off the TV set. When Sony introduced the Betamax home videocassette recorder in 1976, people could select what they wanted to watch at home and when they wanted to watch it. With the advent of video rental stores, people no longer had to go to theaters to see the films they wanted to see. However, the high cost kept many people from purchasing VCRs. JVC introduced VHS technology a few months later and provided the competition that drove down the cost and led to the eventual demise of the Beta format.

When the VCR first appeared, it was not a popular piece of equipment among movie moguls. Jack Valenti, president of the Motion Picture Association of America, called the VCR a "parasitical instrument."[30] Valenti was about to witness a *home-viewing revolution.* At first the studios attempted to sell movies on videocassettes directly to the public, but high costs made that impractical. Sensing a business opportunity, some entrepreneurs bought the expensive videocassettes and rented them out at affordable rates. As rental stores began to spring up in neighborhoods, film studios capitalized on the new market by releasing more and more films on video. As more videos became available, more people bought VCRs, and the purchase price of popular videos decreased. Today, popular family movies such as *Harry Potter and the Sorcerer's Stone* first make money at the box office. Then the theater popularity prompts buyers to pay $15 to $20 for a videocassette they can watch again and again.

The home-viewing revolution took a new twist with the introduction of digital videocassette players in 1997. DVDs have sharper images and carry far more material than do tapes and have moved quickly to supplant the VCR as the technology of choice for home viewing. Movie studios continue to increase the number of their older titles available on DVD, which allows them to sell more copies of older titles.

Although households buy a wide range of films, both old and new, the Walt Disney Company was one of the true entrepreneurs in the home-viewing revolution. The company has excelled both at marketing popular theater movies and at using those movies to sell less expensive videos to the home market. For example, after amazing success with the film and video versions of *Aladdin,* Disney began selling *The Return of Jafar,* a home video sequel, in May 1994 and sold 1.5 million cassettes in the first two days. Although *Jafar* never showed in movie theaters and was panned by critics, it was successful because of *Aladdin*'s popularity. Disney continued this tradition in 2002 with the release of *Tarzan and Jane* directly to DVD and VHS. The *Tarzan and Jane* DVD allows children to sing along and to build their own tree house. Because it is a follow-up to the 1999 theatrical film *Tarzan,* it already has built-in promotion among children.

The production of direct home video has obvious advantages. The budget for *Jafar* was about $5 million, which was considerably more than the $500,000 Disney spends on a half-hour of animated television programming but considerably less than the estimated $30 million spent on *Aladdin.* Although critics argue that there is a creative loss, producers claim that the product can get to the market quickly and inexpensively without the cumbersome creative and financial restrictions of filmmaking.[31]

Although the home-viewing revolution is more than a quarter-century old, it remains far from over. The delivery of movies over the Internet and video-on-demand over cable broadband will give viewers even more control and choice, which is something viewers enjoy and will pay for.

SUPPLYING THE INTERNATIONAL MARKET

The potential for international revenues increasingly plays a role when studios decide which films to fund and which stars to hire. Of the top twenty-five all-time box-office leaders, 57 percent of the $17.8 billion in ticket sales was international. Although Europe is an established market, providing about 60 percent of the international revenue, Asia provides another 30 percent.

Genre and star identity often determine a film's success overseas. For example, *Gladiator,* released in 2000 and starring New Zealand actor Russell Crowe, cost $103 million to make and earned $188 million in U.S. revenues. This would have been an acceptable but not outstanding profit, except that it earned another $267 million in other parts of the world to make it both a critical and financial blockbuster. Action is the most foolproof genre for overseas sales, and films such as the *Star Wars* series and *Lord of the Rings: The Fellowship of the Ring* will gross more overseas than in the United States.

Some films encounter international political barriers. *Schindler's List,* which grossed $100 million in Europe, Asia, and Latin America, was barred from many Arab and Islamic nations. Director Steven Spielberg told the *New York Times* that the banning was disgraceful. "It shocks me because I thought the Islamic countries would feel this film could be an instrument of their own issues in what was happening in Bosnia."[32]

International Film

Film has always been an international medium. In 1895 the first public screening of short films occurred in France, the United States, Germany, and Belgium.[33] Today, despite the dominance of U.S.-made films in most markets, movies remain essentially international. Three trends demonstrate the global nature of films: strong domestic film industries in many countries, growing exportation of films from many countries, and increasing coproduction of films across national boundaries. *Competition in the international market,* therefore, takes a variety of forms.

Strong Domestic Film Industries

European countries have had strong film industries for more than one hundred years. British, French, and Swedish films have had a small market in the United States, although Hollywood would often remake the European films with American actors. In addition, many Asian countries with growing populations have developed their own film industries to meet the increased demand for entertainment. The Indian film industry out-produces all other countries with 800 or more films a year, about 100 more films than produced by Hollywood. The Indian industry peaked in 1990 with 945 films in twenty-one native languages.

The Indian film industry has been known as the producer of cheap, low-quality films. However, recently Indian filmmakers decided to compete with Hollywood in production quality. *Devdas* cost $11 million to make in 2002—the most expensive in the history of Indian films. It was released on 900 screens all over the world.[34] Despite this and similar efforts, most of the Indian studios continue to produce films at a low cost. These films may not make inroads into the United States, but they do well throughout Asia.

global impact

Where Is Hollywood?

During the 1990s, the international market for movies became larger than the domestic U.S. market. By 2000, 60 percent of all movie sales by U.S. companies were outside the United States. For example, the all-time box-office leader, *Titanic*, sold $600 million tickets domestically but $1.23 billion worldwide. This change in market masked another change in the movie industry, which mirrored the shift in ticket sales. Hollywood, as a synonym for the movie industry, has become truly international. No longer do Americans make films just in Hollywood; artists from all over the world create them throughout the world.

Perhaps the 2001 and 2002 Academy Awards best represent the growing international nature of the film industry. Of the five films nominated for best picture in 2002, *Gosford Park* was filmed in Eng-

land and *The Lord of the Rings: The Fellowship of the Ring* was filmed in New Zealand. Two of the five best director nominees, Ridley Scott and Peter Jackson, were born outside the United States. Three of the best supporting actress nominees were from England, as were three of the five best supporting actor nominees.

The 2001 Oscars showed a similar pattern. Of the five nominees for best picture, *Chocolat* was filmed in France by a Swedish director; *Crouching Tiger, Hidden Dragon* was filmed in China by a Chinese director; and *Gladiator* was filmed in London, Morocco, and Malta by a British director. Of the four directors nominated as best director (Steven Soderbergh was nominated for two films), three were not U.S. citizens, and of the five best actor nominees,

Javier Bardem is Spanish, Russell Crowe is from New Zealand, and Geoffrey Rush is from Australia.

Because many of the studios that finance and produce films remain headquartered in Hollywood, financial figures show that with the exception of India and China, 70 percent of all ticket sales are for films made by these companies. However, the films are shot all over the world by people from throughout the world. As a result, Hollywood continues to be both a town in California and a symbol of the international film industry.

Sources: Jason Korsner, "Academy Celebrates Foreign Film," *BBC News,* March 25, 2001, http://news.bbc.co.uk/1/low/entertainment/film/1242254.stm; Malcolm Johnson, "The Academy's New Orientation," *The Hartford Courant* (March 25, 2001): G1.

China, Hong Kong, and Taiwan experienced similar growth in films during the 1980s and 1990s. China reopened the Beijing Film Academy in 1978, with a resulting growth in the film industry. In the 1990s, about 120 domestic films a year were produced in China. Throughout the 1960s and 1970s, Hong Kong produced more than 120 films annually, mostly martial arts movies, for domestic and international markets. During the 1980s, some filmmakers moved toward more complex plots. Taiwanese films, which were similar to those released from Hong Kong, also moved toward more socially meaningful themes during the 1990s and 2000s. These film industries will continue to grow and develop as the Chinese economy becomes more commercial and as films become a significant part of Chinese culture.

Growing Exportation of Films

In addition to growing domestic markets, several countries have seen growth in the exportation of their films. Australian and New Zealand movie companies have found both financial success and critical acclaim in the United States. The string of successes include Australia's *My Brilliant Career* (1979), the Mad Max movies, and *Crocodile Dundee* (1986). Following the success of these films, several members of the Australian movie industry, including actor Mel Gibson and director Peter Weir, moved to Hollywood. The Australian film industry continues to enjoy its renaissance, however, with successes in the United States in the late 1990s with films such as *Muriel's*

Wedding and *Me, Myself, I*. Foreign films have succeeded not only in the marketplace but in U.S. award competitions as well. In 1993, *The Piano*, a New Zealand film starring a New Zealander and two Americans, was nominated for an Academy Award for best picture. In 2001, the Australian film *Moulin Rouge* achieved both financial and critical success in the United States.

An important element of the growing exportation of films from a variety of countries is the number of serious filmmakers throughout the world. Beginning in the 1980s, Satyajit Ray of India, Aki Kaurismaki of Finland, Luis Puenzo of Argentina, and Pedro Almodovar of Spain have represented a new wave of serious directors. These filmmakers and others use film to explore personal problems and social relations in a way that transcends geographic boundaries.[35]

International Coproduction

Increasingly, movie companies from different countries are joining together to make truly international films. French financiers, for example, funded *The Oak*, a 1992 Romanian film written and directed by Lucian Pintilie. During the 1980s and 1990s, Akira Kurosawa, one of Japan's greatest filmmakers, directed films that were financed by companies in the Soviet Union, the United States, and France. In 1999, India and Australia began a joint coproduction company. In 2002, Rupert Murdoch's Twentieth Century Fox signed to produce three films as coproductions with two Indian movie companies.

Today, it is common for a film crew from a variety of countries to work on a movie that is financed by multinational companies. A film's financial and artistic prospects are more relevant issues in the quest for financing than are the countries in which the director, producer, and actors live.

TRENDS

As it has in the past, the movie industry will continue to take advantage of new technologies and respond not only to changes in demographics of the U.S. population but also to the demands of the international markets.

Digital Distribution of Movies

The move to digital distribution of content affects the movie industry as it does every other medium. The conglomerates that own numerous media companies are experimenting with new digital distribution of movies to homes and to movie theaters. Digital home delivery already includes DVDs and pay-per-view, but the next step will be movies-on-demand. Such a service differs from pay-per-view movies on cable channels because it allows the selection from a movie library to be ordered and watched at the viewer's preferred times.

Movies-on-demand (MOD) is a subset of video-on-demand (VOD), which currently exists in larger U.S. cities and in many locations around the world. In 2002, worldwide revenues from VOD were estimated at $400 million, but 98 percent was for adult content.[36] Observers expect the worldwide expenditures to reach almost $2 billion by 2006.

Although little doubt exists that VOD will grow, what remains unclear is just which distribution system will dominate the industry. Distribution of films takes a large bandwidth, which requires broadband cable, satellite, or Internet access. Distribution over the Internet has the advantage of more interactivity, which makes ordering easier. However, movie-viewing sets provide a more enjoyable movie-viewing experience than do computer screens. Eventually, the integration of computer and television technology will resolve this problem.

Movie studios continue to discuss the possibility of providing digital delivery of movies to theaters by means of satellite. A few theaters experimented with digital movies in 1999. In 2002 about sixty theaters showed digital versions of *Star Wars: Episode II—Attack of the Clones*. Supporters of digital movies argue that the quality is better and that digital movies don't degrade as film does. However, theater owners say that the $170,000 per-screen cost to convert is too expensive, and they are concerned that they will have to pay specially trained technicians to run digital films.[37] Other observers argue that transmitting digital versions of movies by satellite will make it easier to pirate them and that technical improvements in film technology may make films cheaper and of equal or higher quality than digital versions.

Demographics

Demographics have always been an integral part of the movie business. Film producers and distributors aimed primarily at the family audience during the first sixty years of the industry. This changed when the baby boomers became teenagers and dominated the moviegoing market. The aging of the baby boomer generation has seen a growth in moviegoing among those older than fifty. However, the younger market still has an edge on influencing filmmakers.

Women emerged in the mid-1990s as an important demographic group. In 1996, for example, *The First Wives Club* earned $105 million because its tale of women gaining revenge on their former husbands appealed to women. Conversely, the critically acclaimed *The People vs. Larry Flynt* failed at the box office after criticism from feminists that it degraded women. Industry sources explain that teenage males choose movies to attend for dates more than do teenage women. And teenage men like action. But in the thirty to fifty age range, women play the dominant role in selecting movies. This rule may be changing, however, as Hollywood moves toward action films such as *Spider-Man* and *Lord of the Rings: Fellowship of the Ring* that offer more depth of character than traditional action movies. In addition, the growing strength of women as movie consumers may pressure Hollywood to offer more managerial opportunities for women in the movie industry.

Influences of the International Market

Movies can no longer achieve success by merely performing well in U.S. theaters. To achieve blockbuster status, a movie must attract audiences outside of the United States. Of the top ten grossing Hollywood movies, seven made more money in international markets than in domestic ones. Number one *Titanic* made $600 million in the United States. and $1.23 billion internationally. *Harry Potter and the Sorcerer's Stone* grossed twice as much internationally than in the United States ($648 million to $318 million). The three films that did not make more money overseas were *Star Wars, E.T. the Extra-Terrestrial,* and *Spider-Man*. Hollywood released the first two of these before the international market had developed extensively; *Spider-Man* is expected eventually to gross more internationally than domestically.

Because the market is lucrative, international audience demands affect the types of films that are produced in the United States. All of the top ten grossing movies have action elements. Comedies and romantic films traditionally have done less well. However, occasionally even nonaction films, such as *Forrest Gump* and *Rain Man,* will perform well overseas.

International markets will continue to influence Hollywood films for at least two reasons. First, Hollywood makes more movies now than three decades ago, and as a result, the cost of promoting the movies continues to grow. Higher promotion costs cause lower profits. The studios need the international markets in order to generate more profit. Second, the populations of some other countries are not only much larger than that of the United States, but also they are growing faster. These markets will continue to expand at a faster rate than the U.S. market.

discussing trends

The movie industry has always been a fluid industry. As demand for certain types of movies came and went, the studios reacted to that demand. This reflects the commercial nature of movies and the desire of studios to make a healthy profit. Because the cost of production is directly reflected in profit, the desire for profit affects how films are made and distributed. New technology, audience demographics, and the international market also will affect how movies are made. Some of the questions that need to be answered include:

■ How will increasing digital distribution affect the types of movies you see and the form in which you see them?

■ Does the quality of movies differ between digital and film versions?

■ In order to appeal to a wide audience, is it possible to make films that cross age and gender barriers?

■ Will the baby boomer generation become more influential in Hollywood than teenagers?

■ Do common concerns exist across cultures that would lead to similar films based on age or gender rather than on nationality?

■ Why do action films attract so well across national boundaries?

Some observers fear that the need to generate higher profits abroad, where action plays well, will limit studios' willingness to invest in quality smaller films, such as those by directors Woody Allen and John Sayles. However, so far, this fear remains unconfirmed.

summary

◆ U.S. filmmaking has been dominated by large studios since the early years of the industry.

◆ Films first targeted family audiences, then, with the advent of television, switched to the teenage audiences that spent their money indiscriminately on movies.

◆ Film represented two lines of development: the perfection of the photographic process and the fascination with moving pictures.

◆ Vaudeville influenced the content and style of the first projected shorts.

◆ Edwin Porter's 1903 short films *Life of an American Fireman* and *The Great Train Robbery* pioneered storytelling techniques that led toward feature-length films.

◆ The Motion Picture Patents Company controlled early film production. Although it edged out independents, it also stabilized a fledgling industry.

◆ During the teens and early twenties, film became middle-class entertainment, and studios introduced the star system to attract large audiences.

◆ By 1930 five movie companies dominated the U.S. film industry.

◆ The peak year of movie attendance in the United States was 1946.

◆ After World War II, the domestic audience dwindled because of the population shift to the suburbs, the baby boom, and ultimately more attention to television.

◆ However, the foreign audience grew and by 1960 provided nearly half of the U.S. film industry's revenues.

◆ Movies constitute art, social commentary, and entertainment.

◆ Movies were not given free-speech protection until 1952.

◆ Movies usually target a young audience, although aging baby boomers constitute a dynamic secondary market.

◆ Product placement is a form of advertising in which identifiable brand-name products are consumed or used by characters in movies.

◆ The advent of the VCR created a new challenge for the film industry. The industry responded by supplying videos through rental stores and directly to the consumer, increasing revenues by $15 billion.

◆ Merchandising products is a successful profit-making venture of movie studios.

navigating the web | The Movies on the Web

Movies and films are at the top of the popular culture list of web sites. Sites cover the history, business, and criticism of film. Many are created by interested individuals; others are produced by the large movie corporations. Some experimentation inevitably will be done with showing movies directly on web sites, but as yet movies are still more suited to the television set or the big screen for general viewing.

The following sites contain research material about movies and their history.

Cinemedia
www.cinemedia.org/welcomes/you.html
Cinemedia claims to be the largest index and directory of film-related sites on the Web and provides a rich array of resources.

MovieWeb
www.movieweb.com
MovieWeb has information about current movies and those screening within the past five years. It also contains useful statistical information about movies.

Classic Films
wwwgeocities.com/classicflicks2000/classicfilms.html
This site has text, photographs, and posters about classic movies, stars, and directors from the 1930s through the 1970s.

The Academy Awards
www.oscar.com
The Academy Awards site, maintained by the Academy of Motion Picture Arts and Sciences, lists all Academy Awards and includes a summary of the films that have screened over the years.

The following two sites contain information about the entertainment industry. They have current information about the film industry, including upcoming films and box-office receipts.

The Hollywood Reporter
www.hollywoodreporter.com

Premiere
www.premieremag.com

questions for review

1. What type of technology did magic-lantern shows use?
2. Which studios have retained dominance over time?
3. Why was the First Amendment not applied to film until 1952?
4. What is the star system and why is it important?
5. Why is *Bonnie and Clyde* sometimes considered a turning point in the development of modern film?
6. What is the home-viewing revolution?

issues to think about

1. Some people argue that movies have been the U.S. dream machine. As more films are made with an international audience in mind and more international films are imported into the United States, how will the dream machine transmit social and cultural heritage?
2. How does the technological form of film watching affect the content and reaction? Do you react differently if you watch a film on a VCR at home or in a dark theater? With friends or parents?
3. How has the Hollywood system affected the development of U.S. film?
4. What do you think the technology of the future will be? How will it affect the production, distribution, and marketing of movies?
5. What are the implications of product placement?

suggested readings

Adair, Gilbert. *Flickers: An Illustrated Celebration of 100 Years of Cinema* (Boston: Faber & Faber, 1995).

Corrigan, Timothy. *A Cinema without Walls: Movies and Culture after Vietnam* (New Brunswick, NJ: Rutgers University Press, 1991).

Ellis, Jack C. *A History of Film,* 2nd ed. (Englewood Cliffs, NJ: Prentice Hall, 1985).

Giannetti, Louis D. *Flashback: A Brief History of Film,* 3rd ed. (Englewood Cliffs, NJ: Prentice Hall, 1996).

Gomery, Douglas. *Movie History: A Survey* (Belmont, CA: Wadsworth, 1991).

Radio

"**I** wrote 'Your Revolution' as a response to the music on mainstream radio, which often treats women as sex objects and playthings," singer Sarah Jones explained in early 2002 after filing suit against the Federal Communications Commission. The suit resulted from a $7,000 indecency fine against KBOO-FM of Portland, Oregon, which had played Jones's song as part of a public affairs program. The song has explicit sexual lyrics that the FCC said were intended to "pander and shock."[1]

The FCC did not include Jones in the fine, but she sued because by calling it indecent, the FCC has effectively eliminated play time for her song. Interestingly, the FCC reversed a $7,000 judgment against KKMG-FM for playing "The Real Slim Shady" by Eminem, who has been criticized for being misogynistic. The station said it was playing an edited version of the song.

This particular incident is one of a growing controversy surrounding radio and television content. Broadcasters are prohibited from playing indecent material between 6 A.M. and 10 P.M., but both music and talk programming increasingly include material that some listeners find offensive. In 2002, FCC Commissioner Michael Copps said, "It's become a rare morning when I don't walk into my office and find 30 [complaints] in one day."[2]

The conflict over the nature of radio content represents two of radio's many faces. Radio influences individuals and groups within society through ideas and information. Government regulators often see their goal as making sure the impact is not negative. At the same time, radio is a commercial medium that attracts listeners through entertainment. Listeners' attention is sold to businesses in the advertising market. Some stations care little how they attract that attention and purposely play controversial material. Radio has had other faces as well. The powerful medium once was an innovative journalistic tool that brought a war home to listeners around the world. In countries where television is not widely available, radio is still a primary source of news and entertainment. It remains one of the most portable mediums available, as well as one of the most influential information and propaganda tools. Perhaps the most notable characteristic of radio is its availability. According to UNESCO, households in developing countries are ten times more likely to have radio sets than TV sets.

The most consistent characteristic of radio has been its ability to survive in emerging competitive markets. Radio began as a medium for live entertainment and short news broadcasts. It developed situation comedy programs and dramatic fare that eventually transferred to television. After television sapped the best performers and programs from radio, radio altered its format, turning primarily to music, news, and talk. In the 2000s, especially in developed countries, radio faces increased competition from computer-based interactive technologies. Listeners can play music on CD-ROMs that are integrated into computer video. Software allows online listeners to hear live music broadcasts from rock and blues clubs. Users of the Internet and online services can access the latest news on demand. Even radio's grip on talk could be loosened as individuals communicate with one another over the Internet. As radio continues to compete with other media and enters the world of converging technologies, the major issues will be the following:

◆ Will interactive programming delivered by satellite and Internet force broadcast radio to shift content, or will radio's music, talk, and news formats still appeal to tomorrow's population?

◆ How will radio reflect or contribute to cultural life?

◆ What role will radio have in political campaigns and decision making in the United States? Will "talk radio" make radio content informative and persuasive as well as entertaining?

◆ Will the growing use of sexually explicit material lead to increased government content regulation?

◆ Will radio continue to be significant as a carrier of international news and information, crossing boundaries of countries that try to block external influence?

Radio *in Your Life*

How Many Roles Does Radio Play?

Think about your own use of radio: What purposes does it serve for you, your family, and your friends? Do you use it for news? For entertainment? For background study music? Do you listen to the talk shows? Do you find yourself using the computer to listen to radio?

As you read the chapter, think about how you use radio and how many minutes a day you spend listening to rock, alternative rock, Top 40, country, rap, classical music, jazz, talk, and news.

TYPE OF STATION	USE	HOURS PER DAY	OTHER MEDIA USED FOR SAME PURPOSE
Rock			
Alternative rock			
Top 40			
Country			
Rap			
Classical			
Jazz			
Talk			
News			
Public radio			
Other			

RADIO IN AMERICAN LIFE

Radio was the first national electronic mass medium, and politicians, corporate managers, and advertisers were quick to recognize its potential power. Radio allowed millions of people throughout the country to listen simultaneously to the same carefully tailored message. Despite the introduction of newer technologies, people throughout the world still use radio more than any other mass medium for information and entertainment. Even in the United States, where television seems to dominate the mass media, radio retains a significant audience—and significant political and social influence. By the beginning of 2001, the United States had more than 12,700 licensed radio stations.

Delivery of news is a critical radio function; more than 1,900 stations listed themselves as either news/talk or news stations in 2001.[3] These news and talk stations provide information and often try to persuade though opinion. Radio's ability to entertain with music is also important; in fact, music, especially music heard on the radio, has defined several generations of youth. This music often shapes norms and beliefs while entertaining.

The Magic Starting Point

As with most technology, finding an exact starting point in *broadcast radio* history is not easy. Radio was not invented by one person. Rather, a variety of inventors contributed

David Sarnoff, airwave pioneer and radio czar, began his career in radio's infancy. His role in forming RCA and the NBC network dramatically shaped the broadcast industry as a commercial medium.

to specific aspects of radio development. The scientific understanding gained by James Clerk Maxwell and Heinrich Hertz during the 1870s and 1880s furthered radio's development. Nathan Stubblefield experimented with transmitting voice and foresaw radio not merely as a point-to-point communication form, but as a method of transmitting news.[4] In 1895, Italian inventor Guglielmo Marconi produced a device that sent a message without wires. The message, however, was in code, like that of the telegraph. For radio to be a significant force, voice and wireless transmission had to merge.

Others contributed as well. John Ambrose Fleming developed a type of vacuum tube, Lee de Forest made amplification possible, and Reginald A. Fessenden experimented with the technology and began broadcasting. Edwin Howard Armstrong and de Forest fought bitterly in court over the patents to the regenerative circuit—a circuit that used the **audion** as a transmitter, amplifier, and detector in a radio receiver. Although engineers familiar with the technology believed that Armstrong understood the process far better than de Forest did, the court awarded de Forest the patent. Armstrong later invented frequency modulation (FM), but its development was hampered by Radio Corporation of America (RCA). Armstrong committed suicide after losing his legal battles and watching FM languish in the shadow of television development.

By 1915, the technology to send and receive music and voice was well established. On September 30, 1915, David Sarnoff, then a lowly employee of American Marconi Company but later president of RCA, wrote a memo to his boss. He predicted that the "Radio Music Box" would become as common in households as the piano or phonograph. But it took more than five years for radio to become a commercial enterprise because the demand had not yet developed and because of patent infringement disputes.[5]

The development of the radio station ensured that radio would be a mass medium that sent content to a large number of radio receivers, rather than remaining a wireless telephone. Several stations claimed to be "first." The first experimental license after the federal government began regulating radio was given to St. Joseph's College in Pennsylvania. The University of Wisconsin was granted an experimental license in 1919, two years after it first broadcast music; this license became a regular license in 1922.[6] KDKA in Pittsburgh was the first radio station to schedule programming and to offer continuous voice service. It received a commercial license on October 27, 1920, to experiment with voice transmission for a year. KDKA's first broadcast was election returns from the Harding–Cox presidential race. The station also broadcast church services, sports, and market reports. Less than a year after KDKA started broadcasting regularly and shortly before its experimental license was converted to regular status, WBZ in Springfield, Massachusetts, received the first regular broadcasting license.

audion: A three-electrode vacuum tube amplifier, which was the basis of the electronic revolution that permitted the development of radio.

Radio as a Mass Medium

Radio became a mass medium during the 1920s. This decade saw rapid growth and change in the number of stations, the percentage of U.S. households with radio receivers, the forms of financing radio, and the nature of programming.

The United States went from 30 licensed commercial AM stations in 1922 to 618 by 1930. Despite radio's development as a broadcast medium, the influence of the telephone company persisted. American Telephone and Telegraph (AT&T) invented the broadcast network, simultaneously broadcasting on January 4, 1923, over its stations in New York and Boston. Two years later, AT&T had regular *network broadcasting* over 26 stations from New York to Kansas City.[7]

In 1926, AT&T withdrew from the radio industry and sold its radio subsidiary to RCA. RCA soon acquired all stock in the National Broadcasting Corporation

(NBC) and began to build a dominant network. Starting with 19 stations in 1926, NBC had 56 stations two years later. The network grew to 154 stations in 1938 and 214 by 1940. There were actually two NBC networks: the Red and Blue networks. The Blue network's flagship station was WJZ, NBC's first station in New York. The Red flagship station was WEAF in New York, which NBC acquired from AT&T. Each network offered its own programming.

NBC soon had competition when Columbia Broadcasting System (CBS) emerged as the second network. CBS had 16 stations in 1929 and had expanded to 113 by 1938. In 1934, Mutual Broadcasting Network entered the field with 4 stations; by 1940, it had 160 outlets. Mutual differed from the other networks in that it did not own any stations but shared programs among independent member stations. In 1943, when the Federal Communications Commission (FCC), in an effort to reduce the power of the networks, forced NBC to sell one of its networks, the American Broadcasting Company joined the competitive field. FM stations continue to proliferate, although growth has slowed.

Cecil Brown reported on World War II on the radio for CBS. By the beginning of the war, the network had established itself as a highly credible news source.

Networks provided programs at lower cost than it would have cost individual stations to produce them, which meant higher profits. From an advertiser's perspective, networks simultaneously connected homes throughout the United States. A company could reach millions of people with the same message at the same time. A modern mass medium had arrived.

Although networks could connect the people in the United States, people had to want to be connected—and they did. Demand for radio receivers expanded as fast as radio stations did in the 1920s. With radios selling for as low as $9, the percentage of households with radios rose from about 7 percent in 1923 to 20 percent in 1926 and 35 percent in 1930.[8]

These broadcasts often used wire service material that was available from newspaper sources. During the 1920s, the news services—the Associated Press (AP), United Press (UP), and International News Service (INS)—waffled in their stance toward this potential competitor. They were unsure whether allowing wire service reporters to supply news to radio should be part of their service or whether radio would threaten their newspaper clients.

However, when radio networks used wire service material to beat newspapers in delivering election results of the 1932 Roosevelt–Hoover presidential race, the radio–newspaper war was officially declared. Journalists became embroiled in an industry battle. After the 1932 election, the AP, a newspaper-based and -funded service, refused to sell news to radio networks, ordered newspapers with radio stations to limit broadcasting of AP news to brief bulletins of thirty words, and charged additional fees for the use of its material on radio. UP and INS created similar constraints on radio.

The news service actions led to the growth of separate radio newsgathering organizations. CBS started the fledgling Columbia News service soon after the AP decision, though it was discontinued when NBC and CBS signed an agreement to end the radio–newspaper war. This agreement, which limited the networks' ability to gather their own news, lasted less than a year. The wire services provided only limited copy to the networks and maintained a structure that favored newspapers. The radio industry was not strong enough to consider staffing its own worldwide bureaus.

Competition emerged from a news service that was not tied to the newspaper industry. Transradio Press Service, begun in 1934, acquired 150 clients during its first year and provided news from other wire services such as Havas in France and Reuters in England as well as domestic news. The service sent an average of 10,000 words a day. Fearful of the competition, the wire services declared independence from newspaper dominance and began to sell news to radio stations. The networks also returned to gathering their own news.

Order Now! for delivery Christmas Morning
Let Majestic's
COLORFUL TONE
flood your home with
year 'round enjoyment

Majestic
RADIO

Radio was initially conceived as a technological device to be experimented with in garages and workshops, but as programming developed, the device was encased and moved into the living room as a piece of furniture. Radio was advertised as a cultural device that could bring the best symphonies into every middle-class home.

As you read in Chapter 1, Edward R. Murrow made radio news a household term during World War II with his remarkable coverage of the European front. Murrow's broadcasts were expanded as CBS expanded its activities abroad.

The Advent of Advertising

As late as 1922, the primary purpose of radio programming was to sell radio sets. Without programs, no one would buy radio receivers. That year, AT&T started *toll broadcasting,* or the selling of time, at WEAF in New York. Secretary of Commerce Herbert Hoover feared that a speech by the president would "be used as the meat in a sandwich of two patent medicine advertisements." Nevertheless, station owners quickly envisioned a future of broadcasting financed by advertising. By 1929, advertising had been included in the first National Association of Broadcasters code of standards. NBC made more than $15 million in advertising that year.[9]

Because radio was new, the audience responded even to relatively simple and inexpensive programs. On 1920s radio, dance music reigned supreme. Many stations broadcast bands and orchestras live. Religious programming was also popular. University stations and, to some degree, networks broadcast educational material. Educational programming declined during the 1920s as university stations closed from lack of funding, and commercial stations, whose owners actively opposed licenses for educational institutions, got control of more radio frequencies.

Early Regulation

Technological chaos ruled in the early days of radio. Stations attempted to broadcast over the same **radio frequencies,** resulting in noise rather than useful programming. The problem of allocating stations to the limited number of airwaves led to several regulation efforts. The Radio Act of 1912 gave the Secretary of Commerce and Labor the right to license radio stations and assign frequencies. However, failing to anticipate that demand would far exceed availability, the act created no criteria for licensing.

Finally, Congress passed the Radio Act of 1927 and established the Federal Radio Commission (FRC) to regulate broadcasting. Such legislation represented a major departure from the government's stance toward the press. Regulation of radio was justified on the basis of *airwave scarcity,* and the commission was instructed to act in the "public interest, convenience and necessity." However, this departure was acceptable to industry representatives. The Radio Act ensured that commercial interests would dominate the medium, networks would retain power, and government would not interfere too directly. The number of educational licenses fell from 129 in 1925 to 52 in 1931.[10]

Even though the FRC reduced the chaos in the radio industry, several agencies still shared regulation of radio, telephone, telegraph, and cable; this overlap created confusion as to which regulations applied. Congress passed the *Federal Communications Act of 1934,* establishing the Federal Communications Commission (FCC) as the regulator of wired and wireless communication. Congress also charged the FCC with recommending action on the long-standing debate between *commercial and noncommercial broadcasting,* but the pattern set by the 1927 act persisted. The

radio frequency: An electromagnetic wave frequency used in radio transmission.

commercial forces, well financed and well organized, dominated the debate. Non-commercial interests were unable to create a unified front that would present a cohesive message to Congress. It would be decades before frequencies would be set aside specifically for educational purposes.

Radio's Golden Age

During the 1930s, radio matured as a mass medium. Through the 1940s, radio was the electronic bridge to world affairs, quality entertainment, national sports events, and urban progress. The 1930s and 1940s were the Golden Age for radio. The number of homes with receivers, the interest of advertisers, and the types of programming expanded rapidly. News, comedy, drama, mysteries, and "entertainment news" emerged in radio programming. As the medium matured, audiences began to regard radio as a reliable source of news and information. The World Series was carried by some stations as early as 1922, and sports became a mainstay by the end of the decade.

Drama was a favorite, and in 1934 the *Lux Radio Theater* began presenting radio adaptations of films, using movie stars to provide the voices. Soon, more than 30 million people listened weekly. Because of radio's credibility, influence, and popularity, when Orson Welles and his *Mercury Theater* players broadcast an updated version of H. G. Wells's *War of the Worlds* on Halloween night in 1938, some listeners did not realize that it was meant to be entertainment. The program started with dance music, which was interrupted by a realistic-sounding news flash announcing that Martians had landed in New Jersey. Although the program contained periodic statements identifying it as a dramatization, tens of thousands of listeners reacted as if it were real.

The mix of drama and news entertained and informed, and some early radio programming foreshadowed the television docudrama. *The March of Time*, which began in 1931, dramatized news, using actors to recreate (sometimes in altered form) actual news events. *The March of Time* was broadcast on and off for the next fourteen years, reaching as many as 9 million homes at one point, and it spawned several imitators.

During the day, soap operas such as *Guiding Light* and *Backstage Wife* attracted a primarily female audience. At night, game shows such as *Twenty Questions* and *Truth or Consequences* were family listening fare. Mysteries, crime shows, Westerns, and comedy series added diversity. Comedy shows ranged from *Amos 'n' Andy*, which used racist stereotypes of African Americans, to *Blondie*, which featured a bumbling, unlucky husband named Dagwood Bumstead. The king of the radio comedians was Jack Benny. By 1938, Benny had an audience of 7 million families and was making $25,000 a week.

The growth of radio listening during the 1930s reflected an increase in radio ownership and a hunger for news and entertainment spawned by the Great Depression. Between 1930 and 1940, the number of radio sets in the United States increased from 13 million to 51 million.[11] During the depression, people bought the relatively cheap radio receivers and sought escape from their everyday difficulties.

As radio matured as an advertising medium, companies bought time to sponsor particular shows rather than simply airing commercials. For example, General Foods' Jell-O sponsored Jack Benny. Networks rented time to companies, which were responsible for the content of the entire program. This enabled advertisers to dictate the type of programming that aired. A similar pattern dominated the early years of television.

Competition from TV

At the end of World War II, radio was at the height of its dominance as a mass medium. By this time, 14.6 percent of advertising expenditures went to radio, up from 6.5 percent only ten years before. But ten years later, the percentage had dropped to 6.1 as television moved into households across the nation.[12]

1895. Guglielmo Marconi sends a message without wires.

1912. Radio Act of 1912

1920. KDKA in Pittsburgh gets the first commercial radio license.

1922. First advertising is sold for radio.

1926. NBC becomes the first radio network.

1927. Radio Act of 1927

1932. Radio networks begin their own newsgathering.

1934. Federal Communications Act of 1934; the FCC is established.

1938. Orson Welles's *Mercury Theater* broadcasts "War of the Worlds."

1938. Edward R. Murrow begins broadcasting reports of war in Europe.

1942. Voice of America begins broadcasting in several languages.

1400–1700	1800	1860	1880	1900	1920	1930

1620. Pilgrims land at Plymouth Rock.

1690. *Publick Occurrences* is published in Boston.

1741. First magazine is published in America.

1776–1783. American Revolution

1830s. The penny press becomes the first truly mass medium in the United States.

1861–1865. American Civil War

1892. Thomas Edison's lab develops the kinetoscope.

1914–1918. World War I

1915. *The Birth of a Nation* marks the start of the modern movie industry.

1920. KDKA in Pittsburgh gets the first commercial radio license.

1930s. The Great Depression

1939. TV is demonstrated at the New York World's Fair.

1939–1945. World War II

The advent of television caused a rapid decline in the comedy and drama shows on radio. As radio stars such as Jack Benny, George Burns, and Gracie Allen moved to television, many critics predicted an end to radio as a mass medium. But radio reshaped itself and survived, becoming the music box of a new generation. Radio created a forum for ethnic music. And furthermore, millions of young baby boomers found rock 'n' roll, which distinguished them from their parents' generation.

New Technology and the "Music Box"

The development of **FM** radio and the creation of the transistor, which made portability possible, combined to recast radio as the music box it had once been. FM had three major advantages: (1) it had better sound quality than **AM;** (2) smaller communities that were bypassed by other media forms would have access to

FM: Frequency modulation attaches sound to a carrier wave varying the frequency of the carrier wave.

AM: Amplitude modulation attaches sound to a carrier wave by varying the intensity, or amplitude, of the carrier wave.

1948. Transistor radio is invented.

1950s. TV's development forces radio to use music format.

1971. National Public Radio begins operation.

1990s–2000s. Radio industry concentrates as a result of the Telecommunications Act.

1995. Radio begins transmitting over the Internet.

1996. Telecommunications Act

2000. Radio changes to digital broadcasting.

2002. FCC expresses concern over indecency on radio.

1940	1950	1960	1970	1980	1990	2000

1949. First commercial electronic computer is produced.

Early 1950s. Rock 'n' roll begins.

1969. First person lands on the moon.

1970s. VCR is developed.

1989–1991. Cold War ends and the USSR is dissolved.

Late 1980s. National Science Foundation creates the basis of the Internet.

1996. Telecommunications Act

2000. Presidential election nearly tied.

2001. Terrorist attacks on New York and Washington, D.C.

frequencies; and (3) with its wider **wave band,** FM could carry the new **high-fidelity** and stereo recordings that were enhancing the quality of recorded music. The **transistor,** invented in 1948, made possible portability and better car radios. By the late 1950s, teenagers could listen to rock 'n' roll anywhere and just about any time they wanted.

AM radio stations send long wavelength, low-frequency radio signals, and FM stations send short wavelength, high-frequency signals. The longer the wavelength, the greater the distance the signal will travel because it is not easily absorbed by the ground and other solid objects. This explains why a person in Montana can pick up an AM station in Forth Worth, Texas, late at night when atmospheric interference is low. High-frequency signals, however, produce higher-quality sound.

FM stations dominate radio ratings today because of the higher sound quality. Music is the primary format on radio, and FM provides higher fidelity for stereo radio.

wave band: An electromagnetic wave within the range of radio frequencies.

high fidelity: Reproduction of sound with minimal distortion.

transistor: A small electronic device containing a semiconductor. A key component of an integrated circuit that paved the way for portability.

Stations Wave Hello to Digital Radio

For well over a century, radio stations have broadcast their programs by creating an electronic signal and attaching it to radio waves. The use of radio waves will continue, but the electronic signal of the future will be digital. The signals will be coded into series of zeros and ones before being attached to the radio waves.

The change to digital radio, which reflects a similar change in television, will have significant ramifications for radio. Engineers say digital radio will improve audio quality, making AM stations sound like FM stations and allowing FM stations to send CD-quality music. But digital radio also will affect convergence and competition.

Creating digitized audio will make sending the music and news over the Internet and by satellite much easier. Digital audio can be easily combined with other digitized formats (video, photographs, and text) for multimedia content. By

making digital transmission easier, more forms of competition will develop for traditional broadcast radio. The delivery of music and news over the Internet, by satellite, and through broadband cable systems will become easier, and these systems allow for more interactivity and selection by consumers.

Despite the advantages for consumers, the transition will face some difficulties. First, consumers will have to buy new receivers or adapt older ones. Digital receivers should be available in early 2003, but they will cost about $300 initially, and even when prices decline due to mass production, they will cost about $100 more than the analog sets we now have. Second, there are still some technical problems in delivery. AM-only stations are concerned about the interference their digital signals encounter at night. The interference comes from the 50,000-kilowatt, clear-

channel stations that have more power because they broadcast during national emergencies. The AM stations fear they will go out of business if they cannot broadcast clearly at night.

The process of moving entirely to digital radio may take up to a decade, and most experts say the speed will be determined by how quickly car manufacturers put digital receivers in their cars. However, the outcome has been determined, and analog radio is destined to go the way of 8-track tapes and the 78-RPM record.

Sources: Paige Albiniak, "Too Little Night Music On-air," *Broadcasting & Cable,* June 10, 2002, www.broadcastingcable.com; David Lieberman, "Radio Close to Increased Digital Transmission; Ibiquity CEO Says Hiss, Static to Go Away," *USA Today,* April 11, 2002, www.USAToday.com; "Digital Radio Service to Finally Take Hold in Consumer Markets," TVinsite, May 13, 2002, www.tvinsite.com.

Nevertheless, AM radio staged a comeback in the 1990s, as talk radio boomed. Talk and information do not require high-quality transmission, and the long reach of AM opens up a big market for the talk shows.

TODAY'S MARKET STRUCTURE

By the end of the 1960s, as television became the favorite mass medium for national advertising, radio lost its mass appeal. Local stations began to tailor their formats to attract specialized audiences. The shift has been a lucrative one. In 2001, radio received just under $18.0 billion in advertising revenues, compared to $15.5 billion for cable and $11.0 billion for magazines.[13] Most communities have the choice of a number of stations in several formats. Rural areas, of course, have access to fewer stations and formats.

These formats, which are described in Table 9.1, deliver a particular type of audience to advertisers, who buy time to present their goods and services. The audience for each format is carefully defined by music or content taste, age, lifestyle, and buying habits. Stations use a variety of strategies to build a loyal audience, often creating programming around distinctive **on-air personalities.** Stations with similar formats compete

table 9.1

Commercial Radio Formats—by Frequency of Use

Country: Country music in a variety of forms: traditional, contemporary, and country-rock. Appeals to ages 25 to 64 with a variety of socioeconomic backgrounds.

News-Talk: Twenty- to thirty-minute cycles of local, state, national, and international news and a variety of talk and call-in shows. Targets listeners between 25 and 65 and can narrow the group according to content.

Religion: Music, information, and talk designed to appeal to people who support the religious beliefs of the organization that runs the station. Aimed mostly at adults.

Adult Contemporary: Current and former popular music. Attracts wide range of adults between 18 and 35.

Oldies: Mostly rock 'n' roll hits from the 1950s and 1960s. Targets people over 35.

Top 40: Current top-selling 40 rock and pop songs. Targets ages 18 to 24 but has many younger listeners.

Middle of the Road: Variety of music and information. Music list includes contemporary popular music. News, sports, weather, traffic, and talk are included in the mix. Attracts 25- to 45-year-olds.

Album-Oriented Rock: Emphasizes current and old hits of particular artists. Album cuts and entire sides are played. Particularly attractive to people 18 to 35, especially men.

Alternative Rock: Plays rock music from lesser-known groups and singers who would not appeal to Top 40 listeners. Aimed at people in the 18 to 30 age group.

Spanish: Variety of music, news, and talk in Spanish. Aimed at Spanish-speaking people in a particular market.

Urban/African American: African American–oriented music, ranging from soul, gospel, and rhythm and blues to jazz and rap. Aimed at African Americans between 18 and 49. Also attracts many white listeners.

Classic Rock: Music mostly from the 1960s, 1970s, and 1980s, with an emphasis on particular artists. Aimed at those over 35, especially men.

Easy Listening: Slow, instrumental versions of current and older hits. Aimed at older listeners.

Jazz: Jazz music, from big band to fusion. Appeals to a limited number of upper-income listeners.

Classical: Recorded and live opera, symphony, and chamber music. Aimed at educated groups.

---

for advertisers, particularly during the *highly lucrative drive times*—6:00 to 10:00 A.M. and 3:00 to 7:00 P.M.

In 2001, 81 percent of people over age twelve listened to the radio during morning drive time at least once a week. The percentage was 79 percent during afternoon drive time, but 76 percent between 10 A.M. and 3 P.M. The lowest rate was between 7 P.M. and midnight, when 54 percent listened to radio at least once during the week.[14]

Syndicated programming increasingly dominates radio, especially in non-drive-time periods. A disc jockey (DJ) at a central location plays songs and supplies chatter to stations around the country through telephone lines and by satellites. Standardized programming, which sometimes eliminates the DJ, is often less expensive than local programming. Syndication has become particularly prevalent in the talk format, in which hosts such as Rush Limbaugh, Dr. Laura, Don Imus, Tom Joyner, and Howard Stern draw millions of listeners from across the United States. However, this type of programming lacks local flavor and reduces diversity. Even though syndicated radio does not have local flavor, some supporters argue that there simply is not enough talent to provide high-quality DJs, news, and talk for the more than 12,000 radio stations throughout the United States.

Radio Station Organization

Organizational patterns are similar for AM and FM stations. A general manager supervises the entire operation; makes business decisions with the assistance of other department heads; and runs the business department, which handles payroll, hiring, billing of advertisers, and buying of supplies.

key concept

Drive-Time Broadcast Significant audiences are available to broadcasters during the morning and afternoon periods when people are driving to and from school and work. These drive times represent prime markets for radio—and for radio advertisers.

on-air personalities: One of the attractions of radio has been listeners identifying with a personality they tune in to regularly on the radio. Whether the radio host reads the news or announces music, the on-air personality gives a station a singular identity.

syndicated programming: Nationally produced programming that is supplied to stations through telephone lines and by satellite.

At least three departments—programming, sales, and engineering—report to the general manager. The programming department and its manager select and produce all of the station's programming. If a station has a news format or substantial news programming, it may have a separate news department and news director.

The sales department sells radio time—and, implicitly, the attention of its listeners—to advertisers. A sales manager runs the department, and account executives sell time and serve the advertisers. This service includes helping advertisers pick the best time for their ads to air and helping them develop the advertisements.

The engineering department, headed by the chief engineer, is responsible for the technology at the station. This includes a variety of equipment, from CD players to **modulators** and antennas. Members of this department make sure the station's broadcasting meets the requirements of the FCC.

The **traffic** manager works with the sales and programming departments. She or he prepares a log of what is supposed to play every day and keeps a record of what actually goes on the air. The traffic manager supplies the information that is used to bill advertisers for time on the radio.

Large stations may have additional departments, such as a promotions department, which is in charge of advertising and public relations for the station. At small stations, the general manager usually handles these responsibilities.

Radio Ownership

Congress drastically changed ownership rules for radio stations with the 1996 Telecommunications Act. Before the act, companies could own no more than thirty stations, and those stations could have no more than 25 percent of the national audience. The 1996 law removed all national limits on audience and stations. It also expanded the number of stations a company could own within a market, which varies by market size.

As a result of the changes in ownership limits, large radio corporations grew rapidly, buying independent stations and other groups. By 2001, at least seventeen radio companies owned more than 30 stations. The largest was Clear Channel, with more than 1,200 stations in 190 markets. The company received about 27 percent of all radio revenue during 2001.

The expansion of these large companies has generated a range of concerns from many quarters. Some critics say this concentration has reduced minority and women ownership. Others say it has reduced the number of independent voices in local markets, which limits those who have access to the airwaves. The American Federation of Television and Radio Artists claims that the large corporations use cookie-cutter playlists that keep independent artists off the radio. The companies have denied they require such playlists.[15]

Whether the critics or the companies are right, the federal government has reacted. In July 2002, the FCC stopped three station acquisitions by Clear Channel because the acquisitions might not be in the public interest. Each will be investigated, but the process will take until spring 2003.[16] About the same time, Senator Russ Feingold of Wisconsin introduced a bill that would control the alleged abuses resulting from ownership concentration.

AUDIENCE DEMAND IN RADIO MARKETS

Radio does not aim for the mass. It aims for targeted audiences. Station managers strive to identify content that will appeal to dedicated listeners with particular demographic characteristics. Gaining a loyal and identifiable segment of the audience, rather than trying to attract a large percentage of the total available audience within a given geographic area, has enabled radio to survive in a competitive media environment. The attention of the targeted audience is sold to advertisers, which connects the *markets for consumers and advertising*.

modulator: Device that processes the carrier wave so that its amplitude or frequency varies. Amplitude modulation (AM) is constant in frequency and varies the intensity, or amplitude, of the carrier wave. Frequency modulation (FM) is constant in amplitude and varies the frequency of the carrier wave.

traffic: Department that controls movement of programming through the day, logs what goes on the air, and supplies information for billing advertisers.

Consumer Market

Radio listeners demand music, news, and talk. A few nostalgia stations continue to carry radio drama and comedy, and some stations broadcast sports, but music makes up the bulk of programming.

Demand for Music ✦ Music programming provides background for people's daily lives. Students study, mechanics repair cars, and commuters drive, all to the sound of radio music. Music helps us to endure exercise and to transcend boring tasks, and it bonds us with people who share common interests. It is the shared interest that makes the format approach work. In general, people who want to listen to country music tend to have some common characteristics—characteristics that can be associated with certain buying habits that attract advertisers. Without correlations between demographics and music and demographics and buying habits, radio advertising would lose its effectiveness.

Radio stations often sponsor concert series that appeal to specific age groups.

Demographics that lead to demand for a particular type of music might involve educational level, race, or gender, but they most often reflect age. Music has been the language of adolescence, and the various demographic groups have been given names that reflect their music tastes in adolescence. The members of the so-called Generation X tend to share musical tastes, as did the bobby-soxers and baby boomers before them. The Xers have rap and grunge, the boomers had folk rock and acid rock, and the soxers had Frank Sinatra and swing. The radio and recording industries have addressed the music of each generation, capitalizing on the ability of radio to create and spread popular music to those who want to listen.

The connection between age and radio format can be seen in the numbers of stations within format types. These formats reflect consumer demand. For example, in 2001, 616 stations carried the top-40 format aimed at younger listeners, while 1,195 carried the Oldies format, which aims mostly at baby boomers. Another 1,918 carried the adult contemporary format, which fits in between the oldies and top-40.[17]

Demand for radio is fairly strong across age groups. A 2002 study by Arbitron found that 95 percent of everyone above the age of twelve listens to radio during the course of the week. The lowest percentage is among people over sixty-five, with 87 percent, and the highest is among those twelve to seventeen, with 98 percent.[18]

Format is not just a function of age, however. More than 2,390 stations carried country music in 2002, which was about 22 percent of all commercial stations. Country music formats can appeal to the entire range of audience, depending on the types of country music they carry.

Demand for News and Talk ✦ Radio news ranges from the in-depth reporting of national and international news found on National Public Radio to a quick survey of the city's most important stories. In between falls extensive coverage of local news. Large markets have enough demand for these types of news to support either an all-news or a news-talk station. Smaller markets must often rely on public radio stations to meet the demand for news.

A 2002 study by Scarborough found that about 22 percent of all Americans over age eighteen listen to news-talk radio. The percentage varies with the market, with about 40 percent of the adults in St. Louis listening and only 9 percent in Houston listening. Listeners tend to be older with a higher level of education. The median age is fifty-two, and only 3 percent of talk listeners are between the ages of eighteen and twenty-four. People with postgraduate degrees are 82 percent more likely to listen to news-talk radio than those without.[19]

Advertising Market

Advertising demand is expressed by the potential advertiser, not by the audience. Because each radio station targets a demographically defined group of people who listen to a specific format, no station can deliver an audience that would include all

Ratings and Shares for the Pit Viper

	TOTAL MARKET (BASIS FOR RATING)	TOTAL LISTENERS WITH RADIO ON DURING SEGMENT
May 15 Segment: 8:15 A.M. to 8:30 P.M.	1,000,000	100,000
Pit Viper's hard rock listeners	10,000	10,000

Rating:

$$\frac{10{,}000}{1{,}000{,}000} = 0.01\ (1\%)$$

Share:

$$\frac{10{,}000}{100{,}000} = 0.10\ (10\%)$$

the people a business might want to reach. Therefore, businesses often buy radio advertisements as a part of a total media package. A pizza parlor might run a coupon in the local newspaper and buy radio ads on one, two, or several stations to tell people about the special price. One study of two medium-size cities found that the average company bought ads from about five different types of media outlets.[20]

Advertising rates reflect an independent assessment of audience size. Advertisers learned early not to rely on media companies to estimate audience size and supported the rise of ratings companies, whose sole job is to measure audiences. Arbitron, the primary radio ratings service, assigns counties to 250 geographic regions, labeled **areas of dominant influence (ADI)**, and reports listener data for these areas and smaller geographic components on either an annual or a quarterly basis.

The numbers of listeners are reported in two forms: rating and share. A *rating* is the percentage of *all people in a market* who are listening to a particular station during a fifteen-minute segment. A *share* is the percentage of *people with their radios on* who are listening to a particular station during a fifteen-minute segment. The data come from surveys in which randomly selected listeners fill out a week's worth of daily logs detailing their radio listening.

To understand ratings and shares, look at the Pit Viper's hard rock drive-time program on station JIMI. The ratings service estimated that 10,000 people listened to the Viper's show from 8:15 to 8:30 A.M. on May 15. Of the 1 million listeners in the ADI, 100,000 were listening to the radio at that time. Table 9.2 shows how the rating and share for the show are computed.

SUPPLYING THE AUDIENCE'S DEMAND

The type of content broadcast by a radio station depends on its purpose and who owns it. As shown in Table 9.3, there are eight *radio station types,* which can be classified on the basis of ownership and type of financing: commercial, state-run, public, shortwave, educational institution, community, special-interest, and pirate stations. The types of stations available vary by country, depending on the nature of government and regulation. In the United States, about 85 percent of all stations are commercial, although all eight types can be found. In Asia and Africa, state-run and commercial stations are the most common.[21] U.S. commercial stations program primarily music, and public radio remains the prime source of news and information. Talk radio has emerged as a cultural force, and it has emerged on commercial and public radio, special-interest stations, and shortwave.

The Public Radio System

In 1967, after a period of concern that television was becoming a "vast wasteland," Congress responded to the recommendations of a prestigious study group, the Carnegie Commission, and created the Corporation for Public Broadcasting (CPB). In 1969–1970, CPB joined with public television and radio stations to form the Public Broadcasting Service (PBS), which serves television and National Public Radio (NPR). These organizations provide programming for noncommercial stations.

areas of dominant influence (ADI): Areas defined by the ratings company Arbitron for purposes of reporting listener data.

table 9.3

Types of Radio Stations

Commercial: These stations seek to make a profit. Programming is mostly music, interview and call-in shows, and news.

State-run: Owned and operated by governments with direct control of content on a day-to-day basis.

Public: Noncommercial stations that receive money from the general public, private foundations, and governments. Receive government grants but are shielded from day-to-day government intervention.

Shortwave: Shortwave radio is used to beam international programming. During 1995 it gained new attention in the United States because of its use by the militia movement.

Educational: Educational radio stations are owned and operated by universities, colleges, and even high schools. More than 800 U.S. educational institutions have broadcast licenses.

Community: Low-power stations that promote community participation in solving local problems. In the United States, many serve ethnic communities.

Special Interest: Financed by noncommercial groups that advocate particular political or religious beliefs.

Pirate: Unlicensed stations. For example, WTRA/Zoom Black Magic Liberation Radio in Springfield, Illinois, battled the FCC over the right to broadcast without FCC approval. The low-power station promoted communication among people who lived in a low-income housing project.

Sources: Carolyn Weaver, "When the Voice of America Ignores Its Charter," *Columbia Journalism Review* (November–December 1988), 36–43; Michael C. Keith, *Radio Production: Art and Sciences* (Boston: Focal Press, 1990), p. 228; Robert Chapman, *Selling the Sixties: The Pirates and Pop Music Radio* (London: Routledge, 1992); and Ron Sakolsky, "Zoom Black Magic Liberation Radio: The Birth of Micro-Radio Movement in the U.S.," in *A Passion for Radio,* Bruce Girard, ed. (Montreal: Black Rose Books, 1992), pp. 106–113.

NPR started in 1971 in one room with part-time journalists. Early programming was offbeat, and the small budget encouraged an emphasis on feature stories. One reporter writing in a closet commented on whether Wint-o-Green Life Savers spark in the dark when someone bites them.[22] By 2001, NPR had almost 20 million listeners weekly, and member stations draw almost 29 million listeners each week. Its combination of features and in-depth news programming such as *All Things Considered* and *Morning Edition* has brought it millions of regular listeners. As NPR has become successful, its product has been criticized for becoming too much like commercial radio news. However, NPR programs are often the only radio news available in small towns and cities. As such, they are serving the purpose envisioned by noncommercial radio proponents as early as 1920.

NPR makes up an important part of public radio, but the 680 public radio stations produce the bulk of programming, including news and talk shows. Classical music and jazz also make up a significant proportion of program time on many stations. Public radio stations tend to reflect the needs and wants of those in the community who supply the money that allows the station to operate, a practice that has opened the system to charges of elitism.

Each public station operates independently as a public corporation. Each station originates its own programming but also carries NPR programs about national and international issues. About 49 percent of public radio programming is produced locally, 19 percent comes from Public Radio International, which distributes programs such as *A Prairie Home Companion,* and 9 percent comes from other sources.[23]

Some public radio stations face increasing pressures to attract listeners. In 1980 only 15 percent of public radio funding came from membership contributions, but twenty years later, that percentage had more than doubled.[24] This trend reflects declining support of public radio and television by the federal government, and it places pressure on public radio stations to broadcast programs that attract listeners. As a result, many public radio stations' programming increasingly resembles that found on commercial stations. Such a trend raises concerns because public radio was created as an alternative to commercial radio.

profile

Garrison Keillor

When Mark Twain said that rumors of his death were greatly exaggerated, he may have been predicting his reincarnation as Garrison Keillor, the gentle and observant writer, humorist, and host of public radio's *A Prairie Home Companion*. No radio comedian since Will Rogers has been better at sharing the joy of a well-crafted story or at pointing out the humor in our everyday lives.

Born in 1942 in Anoka, Minnesota, Keillor yearned as a teenager to be a writer. He graduated from the University of Minnesota in 1966 and went to New York to find a job writing for a magazine. After a month and no job, he returned to his home state. Three years later he became a professional writer when he began working for Minnesota Public Radio and writing for *The New Yorker*.

It was a magazine story about the Grand Old Opry that led to the creation of *A Prairie Home Companion* in 1974. The show is a combination of storytelling, comedy, and folk music. Keillor ended the program in 1987 and moved to New York, where he started *The American Radio Company* in 1989. Keillor said of his New York program, "Despite attempts to strike out in new directions, it was still the same show, so we brought it back to St. Paul and in 1993 resumed the name 'A Prairie Home Companion.'"

Keillor has become the writer he wanted to become, having written eleven books and dozens of magazine articles. However, he remains most noted for his radio program, which is carried over National Public Radio on Saturday nights. No one in radio is better known or more respected.

When asked about public radio in 1997, Keillor said:

Public radio is absolutely necessary in this country, given that commercial radio over the past decade has abandoned any sense of public service. Commercial stations are chasing after particular segments of the market—the eighteen to twenty-five-year-old male who is into hearing loss, the fifty-plus male who is into conspiracy theories—and it's left to public radio to fulfill the great dream of radio as a medium that brings people together and disseminates information accurately and swiftly and creates national bonds of understanding and brings great music and poetry and drama to the far corners of the land.

Sources: "It's Just Work: Garrison Keillor on Radio, Writing, and His Personal Revolt against Piety," *Atlantic Monthly*, October 8, 1997, www.theatlantic.com; "Garrison Keillor," Minnesota Public Radio, www.phc.mpr.org/cast/garrison_keillor.shtml; Christina Gomez, "Garrison Keillor Biography," Mindspring.com, www.mindspring.com/~celestia/keillor/bio.htm.

Producers of entertainment for public radio fear that commercial pressures resulting from government budget cuts will hurt the independent artists and experimental music from which commercial stations shy away. One person who is already speaking out is folksinger Iris DeMent, who is defending what she believes is public radio's true service: providing an oasis from the barrage of commercial messages and commercially motivated programming that create a false impression of U.S. society. "That's not an accurate picture of who we are as a people," says DeMent. "Public radio maintains that balance."[25]

Commercial Radio News

The growth and development of NPR coincided with a decline in the amount of commercial radio news, especially in smaller markets. The growth of television, the development of FM radio, and deregulation all combined to restructure radio news after 1960. However, commercial radio news continues to survive and even shows signs of resurgence.

Commercial radio stations that carry news generally list themselves as news or news-talk. Both types of format have content other than straight news. All-news formats have interview programming and even call-in shows. The difference between the two is primarily one of degree and emphasis. All-news stations emphasize the information elements, whereas talk programming includes a greater element of persuasion as guests and listeners express their opinions. At the beginning of 2002, about 1,200 stations listed their format as news-talk and another 758 as news.

All-news stations typically have ongoing news packages, similar to *CNN Headline News* on television, that summarize important happenings around the world, nation, state, and local community. A second form of commercial news can be found on music format stations. However, this news is usually limited to short news summaries that run for a minute or two on the half-hour. The thirty-one radio networks often syndicate these reports, with stations adding local news from the newspaper.

Deregulation and increasing competition for radio advertising have hurt smaller news operations. Before the deregulation of the 1980s, most radio stations provided news every thirty minutes as part of their public service requirement for a license. When the public service requirement was dropped, about 8 percent of the stations dropped news. The increasing number of stations chasing dwindling advertising funds in the early 1990s contributed as well. Many stations simply cannot afford news. The number of stations with newsrooms dropped from 5,500 in 1994 to 4,500 in 2001.[26]

Talk Radio

Between 1990 and 1995, the number of stations that devote the bulk of their programming to talk almost tripled, from 405 to 1,130. Since 1995 the number increased slightly to about 1,200 at the beginning of 2001. With talk, radio stations have discovered a way to boost their ratings among higher-income older audiences and to attract advertisers who want to reach this group. By 2002, about 22 percent of the adult U.S. audience listened to talk radio during a given week.[27]

Talk radio as a format was developed in the 1960s by conservatives Joe Pyne and William Buckley. Murray Levin, a Harvard professor who wrote *Talk Radio and the American Dream* in 1980, told a *Los Angeles Times* reporter in 1995 that talk shows today capitalize on emotional subjects in much the same way they did in the 1960s. "When I studied talk radio," Levin said, "there was no issue that aroused as much anger and emotion as homosexuality. The talk-show hosts, they knew this. They would talk more about it than the subject warranted. They'd get heated debates and would push people to further extremes. That boosted ratings."[28]

The popularity of talk radio has created a wide diversity of hosts. They range from conservative Rush Limbaugh to outrageous Howard Stern and include a range of political figures including perennial presidential candidate Pat Buchanan, who was among the first to realize the potential of talk radio as political communication.

In 1993, political scientist Richard Hofstetter surveyed San Diego County and found that about one-third of adults had listened to political talk shows at one time or another. Those who were more interested in political issues and well informed about candidates were more likely to listen. Most were mainstream in their views, Hofstetter said. Eighty percent said that they disagreed with the talk show host at least occasionally, but 30 to 40 percent said that they disagreed often. "That was surprising,"

Syndicated programming is a mainstay of radio content. Tom Joyner and Travis Smiley host ABC Radio's syndicated *Tom Joyner Morning Show.*

Commerce and Culture: Who Decides What We Hear?

The U.S. Congress and the Federal Communications Commission have long wrestled with the issue of how big a broadcast company can become before it has too much power to influence what people see and hear. The issue resurfaced with a vengeance in 2002 as a result of Clear Channel's aggressive acquisition of radio stations, with more than 1,200 stations and efforts underway to acquire another 186. The federal government reacted by postponing and investigating these acquisition plans and by introducing legislation that would control potential abuses from economic concentration.

At the forefront of the complaints is a wide range of organizations that represent artists, including the Recording Association of America, American Federation of Musicians, American Federation of Television and Radio Artists, and the Recording Academy. Their complaints center on the practices of using a national playlist that limits the variety of music heard locally, of

artists and recording companies financing station promotions and receiving airtime for particular artists, of stations not playing artists who do not use Clear Channel's concert-promotion service, and of using other companies to buy radio stations and hold them for Clear Channel in anticipation of policy changes at the FCC.

Critics argue that all of these practices, if true, limit consumer access to a wider range of content and stop smaller companies from buying stations. Hillary Rosen, president of the Recording Industry Association of America, says, "There is no question that radio consolidation and radio promotion have raised questions about access to the airwaves."

Executives at Clear Channel have denied the charges. Randy Michaels, chief executive officer for Clear Channel Radio, says no national playlist exists. He says the company has computer software to help build databases if they want, and that program directors in

smaller markets can ask for help from those in larger markets.

Clear Channel is not the only large radio company. A coalition of ten opposition groups issued a statement in May 2002 that said four companies control 63 percent of all stations with contemporary-hit and top-40 formats and 56 percent of all country-format stations.

All radio companies affect what listeners can hear and the culture that grows from that listening. At issue is whether those decisions should be placed in the hand of fewer people through economic concentration. Congress, the FCC, and federal courts will make the decision.

Sources: Paige Albiniak, "Clear Channel Challenged," *Broadcasting & Cable,* January 28, 2002, www.broadcasting cable.com; Bill McConnell, "Clear Channel Fights Back," *Broadcasting & Cable,* May 13, 2002, www.broadcastingcable. com; Paige Albiniak, "Music Biz Asks for Radio Probe," *Broadcasting & Cable,* May 27, 2002, www.broad castingcable.com.

Hofstetter told the *Los Angeles Times.* "That suggests this is a sort of titillating, cheap thrill for these listeners. I think what's happened is people stuck in automobiles want to listen to something besides music."[29]

The popularity of talk radio has caused critics and scholars to speculate about why it has been so successful. One argument holds that talk radio is the new town meeting of a fragmented society whose members never meet in person but use electronic media such as radio and the Internet to connect. In this town meeting, the populace speaks rather than relying on official voices. In fact, in *Talk Radio,* Levin attributes the public fascination with talk radio to an increasing distrust of official institutions.

Critics often attack talk radio as a negative force. Peter Laufer, in *Inside Talk Radio,* concludes that many hosts put forth "fallacy" as "fact," "uninformed opinion" as "thoughtful commentary," and "groundless innuendo" as "investigative journalism."[30] Critics suggest that talk radio exploits and fans groundless fears and feeds paranoia.

INTERNATIONAL RADIO

Radio is a powerful medium in many countries. Even with new technologies, radio continues to be significant because programming is inexpensive to produce, can be transmitted across borders, and does not rely on expensive receiving equipment. These features, combined with portability, make radio a tool both for governments and for those who seek to challenge governments. In countries where print media are not widely distributed or where governments deny access to news, portable radios often are the only connection to factual information.

BROADCASTING ACROSS BORDERS

Broadcasting across borders dates to 1926, when the Soviet Union ran a brief radio propaganda effort against the government of Romania. The first ongoing broadcast for people outside a country occurred in 1927, when Holland directed domestic programming to Dutch citizens living abroad. During the next seven years, Germany, France, Great Britain, the Soviet Union, and Japan created their own "colonial" broadcasts.[31]

During World War II, several combatant countries broadcast programs aimed at the enemy's population in an effort to undermine opposition, lower morale, and create confusion. Germany, for example, broadcast anti-British messages into India in eight Indian languages.

Known personalities tended to attract listening audiences. One of the most famous of the radio personalities, "Tokyo Rose," broadcast to the Allied troops in the Pacific in an effort to lower their morale. After the war, an American typist, Iva Togura, was convicted of treason and spent ten years in prison for being the infamous Tokyo Rose. Togura, who was trapped in Japan during the war, admitted to working for Japanese radio. In reality, Tokyo Rose did not exist. The name had been applied to every woman announcer on Japanese radio.

From the end of World War II until the late 1980s, the Cold War, a war of ideology, relied heavily on the dissemination of information and propaganda. The Western and Eastern bloc countries fought for domination through propaganda extolling the virtues of one political system over the other.

The two dominant broadcast units for the West were the British Broadcasting Corporation (BBC) and the Voice of America (VOA). The BBC began broadcasting to the Soviet Union in 1946, and the VOA followed a year later. The VOA reached its zenith under then-President John Kennedy in the early 1960s, when it also received its greatest support from Congress.

It is difficult to say how much international broadcasting contributed to the changes that swept the world during the past decade. However, Western radio broadcasts to other countries claimed audiences in the tens of millions throughout the Cold War period. Chinese immigrants talk about listening to the broadcasts while they were banished to the villages during the Cultural Revolution, and others profess to have learned English by listening to the broadcasts.

Europe

Most European countries have mixed systems with both public and commercial stations. Public stations are financed by license fees, which theoretically represent licenses to obtain radio content but in practice are fees for using a radio receiver. Commercial stations raise revenue from advertisers, and during the 1980s they increasingly took advertising revenues from other media. In Austria, Ireland, Portugal,

France, and Greece, a higher percentage of advertising dollars is spent on commercial radio than in the United States.[32]

Programming on European public networks includes classical and popular music, sports, news and current affairs, and educational material. As in the United States, commercial stations in Europe target segmented audiences, and during the 1980s European radio became less national and more local.

Africa

African radio systems continue to use the same approach as the BBC and French radio systems, which were established when the African countries were European colonies. The BBC-derived systems are run as public operations with boards of governors appointed by the national government, and they operate nationally and regionally. Typically, 70 to 80 percent of revenue in these systems comes from advertising; the rest comes from government through the boards.

The French-derived systems have less autonomy than the British-derived systems because they advertise less and receive more direct government subsidies. They are usually run by the country's Ministry of Culture or Ministry of Information. The number of stations has remained relatively small in most African nations because it is in the interest of the elite class to limit the number of stations and thus limit access to information and power. A few African nations, such as Nigeria and Madagascar, experimented with privately owned radio stations during the mid-1990s. The effort, however, has remained limited in scope.

Latin America

Despite Latin America's colonial background, its radio system differs greatly from Africa's. Most Latin American countries have diverse systems, including stateowned, special interest, educational, community, and commercial stations. The difference between radio in Africa and radio in Latin America probably reflects the dominance of the BBC in Africa and the generally stronger economies of Latin America. Latin

Radio is still the medium of choice in many countries. It's inexpensive, it's portable, it plays music, and it brings information to young and old.

NPR Heard around the World

In July 2002, National Public Radio began broadcasting twenty-four hours a day throughout the world by means of WorldSpace, a satellite broadcast system. This publicized something that listeners may have already recognized—NPR is truly "international public radio." Although much of the content deals with U.S. domestic issues, much of it also involves either international news or topics that have universal relevance.

This is not NPR's first effort to reach the world. In addition to WorldSpace, the NPR web site (www.npr.org) explains that NPR can be accessed internationally through the Internet, by shortwave radio, and over cable in Japan, Sweden, and Switzerland.

The international nature of NPR has been building for years. In April 2002, the Overseas Press Club, composed of international correspondents, awarded National Public Radio the Lowell Thomas Award for its coverage of September 11, 2001. It was NPR's fourteenth Overseas Press Club award in the organization's thirty-two years. When the Mideast conflict grew during 2002, NPR created a Mideast web site with audio and transcripts of its coverage. As NPR Online Vice President Maria Thomas said, "This online area enables users to access at any time throughout the day content produced for NPR's radio news programs that they otherwise may not have the opportunity to hear."

NPR's international influence as a news organization will likely grow as it expands the number of technologies that can be used for listening. Radio remains the most often used form of communication in areas other than North America and Europe.

Sources: "Overseas Press Club Honors NPR," NPR press release, April 26, 2002, www.npr.org; "Mideast Web Portal at NPR.org Extends Access to Mideast Coverage," NPR press release, June 6, 2002, www.npr.org; "NPR Now Portable in Europe, Africa and the Mideast on Worldspace," NPR press release, July 25, 2002, www.npr.org.

American countries average twice as many radio receivers per one thousand inhabitants than those in Asia or Africa. Commercial stations are strong in Latin America because the greater number of receivers and higher standard of living, compared to Africa, help to sustain a system funded by advertising revenue.

Commercial programming in Latin America is similar to that found in North America, with an emphasis on music and entertainment. Some countries experienced a growth in community and pirate radio stations during the 1980s. During this period, hundreds of illegal FM stations sprang up in Argentina, which had no federal licensing agency. They served people in small communities by running local information and educational programs and by offering advertising to small businesses. When politicians discovered in 1991 that these stations provided an effective way to reach voters, the central government tried to close them down. However, many pirate stations continue to operate today.

Asia

Radio in Asia has similarities with radio in both Latin America and Africa. Because of European colonial influence, countries such as India have adopted systems modeled after the BBC. However, Asian radio stations, like those in Latin America, provide more diverse programming than do African stations. Some Asian nations such as Singapore have highly developed commercial systems. Some, such as South Korea, have radio systems with extensive religious programming.

In China the government has traditionally maintained tight control of radio at both national and local levels. Lately, the control has loosened, but control remains stronger than in most other populous countries.

The variety of systems reflects variations in economic and political development. People in some countries, such as Bhutan and Bangladesh, have limited access to radio sets, whereas people in countries such as Japan and Korea have nearly as many radios per inhabitant as in Australia or the United States. The importance of radio as a mass medium varies as well. In some isolated parts of China, radio is the primary source of national news. In Japan a highly developed television system has replaced radio as the primary source of information.

Australia

Australia, with its vast geography and scattered population, has a natural demand for radio. The distances between population centers far exceed the broadcast capabilities of nonsatellite television. Australia has almost 1,300 radio sets per 1,000 inhabitants, second in the world only to the United States.

The Australian radio system is overseen by the Australian Broadcasting Commission (ABC), which also provides programming through a network of stations. The programming is similar to that of public stations in the United States, with music and news making up most of the content. During the 1980s, ownership rules were changed to allow more stations per company, and commercial radio grew in popularity.[33]

TRENDS

Radio may change during the early 2000s as a result of four important trends: consolidation of radio ownership, the growth of *Internet and satellite radio,* and regulation of content. These trends will determine both how we receive radio and the nature of radio content.

Consolidation of Radio Ownership

The consolidation of radio ownership into large corporations will continue unless the FCC and Congress reverse themselves, which is unlikely. Just how this consolidation affects radio content remains uncertain, but early results of corporate ownership suggest a variety of changes. Consolidation reduces expenses for the company, but this typically means a reduction in the number of radio jobs. There is concern that music will be standardized across stations because of centralized control of programming. In addition, the need to pay off large loans used to buy stations could cause companies to increase the number and duration of commercials.[34]

Not everyone sees consolidation as a negative trend. One company owning more stations reduces duplication of formats in medium-size markets. So, instead of having two oldies stations, a market might have an oldies station and a sports talk station. Others argue that without consolidations, radio stations would find it difficult to survive financially with the increasing options offered by new computer technology.

The reaction to the rapid growth of radio companies after the 1996 Telecommunications Act led to the introduction of legislation in 2002 to control potential abuses of this concentration. However, the radio companies remained aggressive. In 2002, they were pushing the FCC to eliminate the rules limiting the number of stations a company can own in a single local market.[35]

Another economic element entered the debate about consolidation during the middle of 2002. The removal of the head of Clear Channel's radio division in July led to rumors of accounting irregularities of the type that plagued many corporations. Despite denials by the company, stock prices for Clear Channel dropped as a result of the rumors.[36]

Internet Radio

Between 1996 and 2001, radio programming delivered over the Internet boomed. The number of stations programming over the Internet increased from 56 stations to 5,000.[37] Estimates were that by the end of the 1990s, 31 million people worldwide listened to Internet radio daily, despite erratic quality.

The potential for reaching national and international audiences through the Internet seemed unlimited once technology improved, but technology was not the only issue. In 2001 the Internet radio industry began to backtrack because of concerns over unauthorized use of advertising online. In 2002 the industry took an even stronger blow when a three-judge arbitration panel announced the royalty fees that must be paid to recording companies for broadcasting their music online. As a result, some stations have stopped streaming audio, and some observers claim that the use of Internet for radio music is dead.

Advertisers began to pull their radio ads off Internet broadcast in 2001 because they would be liable to pay the actors additional fees under a contract with the American Federation of Television and Radio Artists. Some stations simply quit webcasting, and others, such as those owned by Clear Channel, began to sell separate ads for the Internet versions. This problem didn't affect Internet-only broadcasters.[38]

A much greater impact has been felt following the decision about what Internet broadcasters must pay recording companies to webcast their music. Commercial radio stations must pay 0.07 cents per performance per listener to simulcast a song, whereas noncommercial broadcasters pay 0.02 cents. Songs that are webcast only must pay 0.14 cents per performance per listener. In addition, everyone must pay another 9 percent and a $500 license fee.

The fee was about ten times more than broadcasters asked for and less than the 0.4 cents asked for by the recording companies. As a result, a radio station that simulcasts twenty songs an hour for twenty-four hours to 10,000 listeners would pay $3,360 a day, plus $302, which is 9 percent.[39] Webcast-only stations will have to pay $6,720, plus $605.

Many Internet-only radio executives don't believe they can make a profit with these rates. Eddie Fritts, president of the National Association of Broadcasters, says, "If the powerful record-company interests' goal was to strangle a fledgling new service to radio listeners, it may have succeeded beyond its own expectation."[40] Because the rates are higher for stations that webcast only, critics of the rates say it will hurt smaller operations more than the larger companies that webcast simultaneously. They claim that one more possible source of diverse entertainment will be lost. The rate was set under the direction of the Library of Congress, but some radio companies have said they will challenge the rates in court.[41]

Satellite Radio

Even newer than Internet radio is satellite radio. XM began broadcasting in late 2000, and Sirius came onboard the next year. XM charges about $10 and Sirius about $13 per month for one hundred channels. Satellite service accommodates radio listening on long trips because signals are not lost as a car moves from one signal area to another. The development of digital radio and the installation of satellite receivers in cars will give satellite a big boost. A California consulting group predicts that satellite radio will have nearly 5 million subscribers by 2004. Receivers cost between $150 and $200.[42]

Satellite radio gives new meaning to the concept of portability. Included in many luxury automobiles, the radio picks up the satellite feed regardless of location, allowing occupants to listen to their favorite station at any time.

Traditional broadcasters are concerned that the satellite radio will begin to compete with them at the local level, just as cable competes with broadcast television. XM has denied they have such plans. However, if listeners substitute satellite radio for local broadcast, broadcast ratings will decline and advertising support will follow. It is difficult to believe that satellite will not have a long-run impact on broadcast radio.

Content Regulation

Because the airwaves belong to the people, radio and television have never been given complete First Amendment rights. As a result, the FCC has a right to regulate material that it considers indecent. This is "programming that describes or depicts sexual or excretory organs in a patently offensive way."[43] The degree of regulation has varied over the years, but recent events suggest that we may be in for a period of growing regulation.

In early 2002, FCC Enforcement Bureau Chief David Solomon announced, "If the station can't refute information in the complaint, we'll assume the complaint got it right."[44] Many observers say this is a reversal of a policy that has dismissed decency complaints when evidence was not available.

The growing concern about radio content, which receives the bulk of decency fines, reflects what many see as an increasing raunchiness of talk shows and the explicit lyrics found in many rap songs. Three decency cases during 2001 and 2002 illustrate this. WKQX-FM in Chicago was fined $14,000 in early 2002 for two shows that included explicit discussions of sex acts. KKMG-FM in Pueblo, Colorado, was fined $7,000 for playing Eminem's song "The Real Slim Shady" in 2001. The fine was dropped when the station claimed they had run an edited version of the big hit. As mentioned at the beginning of the chapter, KBOO-FM, a noncommercial station in Portland, Oregon, was fined $7,000 for playing Sarah Jones's "Your Revolution" during a public affairs program. The song uses explicit lyrics to attack popular rap songs that demean women. Jones has sued the FCC over the fine.

The heart of this conflict is the issue of just how much regulation government should exercise over broadcast content. A more conservative FCC, which reflects appointments by President George W. Bush, suggests that regulation may grow. Yet the popularity of mainstream rap with explicit lyrics indicates that commercial music interests and many listeners may not want increased regulation.

discussing trends

Changes in trends occur for a variety of reasons, and these often are related to technology and regulation. A new president, for example, appoints new members to regulatory boards such as the FCC, and these new members bring new interests. Currently, the FCC is concerned about the sexual content on radio. This concern is far from new. However, with each generation the material seems to become more explicit. The reemergence of this issue raises the following questions:

■ Why do sexually explicit lyrics offend some people?

■ What sort of negative impact can these lyrics have?

■ Should FCC fines for such lyrics be removed?

■ Should the context of playing these lyrics—information versus entertainment—be considered when the FCC investigates a complaint?

Regulatory boards are not the only groups in Washington, D.C., that react to trends. Congress has become concerned about the concentration of ownership and has introduced legislation to control potential abuses. At the heart of this issue is whether abuses have occurred or whether there is the potential for such abuses. Think about these questions concerning the negative impact of ownership concentration:

■ Has the concentration of ownership limited the number of different formats available in your radio market?

■ Does concentration make it more difficult for independent artists to have their music played on the radio?

■ Is it wrong for recording companies to pay for radio promotional events and then to receive play time for their music in return?

The final two trends are connected by the move to digital radio. By digitizing the content signal sent by radio stations, it has become very easy to distribute the material in ways other than broadcast waves. Today, digital radio can be sent by satellite and Internet, but both of these distribution systems face difficulties. The Internet has a new fee structure for using recordings that many think will cripple the Internet as a stand-alone distribution system. Questions to be answered include:

■ Does the difference in fees paid by simulcast stations and Internet-only stations seem fair? Why or why not?

■ What impact will the burden of higher fees have on the availability of independent music?

■ On the other hand, satellite radio will require new receivers that will cost more than analog sets. Do you think many people will purchase satellite radio?

■ Will satellite and Internet radio run local broadcast radio stations out of business?

summary

◆ Radio began as a point-to-point communication form before becoming a mass medium during the 1920s.

◆ Radio became the center of home entertainment during the 1930s, much as television is today.

◆ During World War II, radio news gave war coverage a speed and intimacy that never existed before.

◆ A central debate throughout the history of radio is whether it should be a commercial medium serving owners or a noncommercial medium serving society.

◆ In the United States, radio has become a medium that attracts demographically defined audiences and sells the attention of those audiences to advertisers.

- Music for entertainment makes up most of radio's programming, but news and talk radio remain important sources of information, especially in larger markets.
- More than two dozen music formats are available to radio stations.
- There are eight types of radio stations: commercial, state-run, public, educational institution, community, special interest, shortwave, and pirate.
- Radio remains the most used medium throughout the world.
- International broadcasts grew during the 1980s as more countries used improved technology to communicate their ideologies.
- Radio stations face increased competition during the twenty-first century from Internet and satellite distribution of radio.
- Radio ownership concentration has increased greatly as a result of the 1996 Telecommunications Act, and some critics fear this will reduce the diversity of news and information.
- Driven by talk radio and the explicit lyrics of rap music, the debate over regulation of radio content has reemerged during the past few years.

navigating the web | Radio on the Web

Radio on the Web is growing as stations set up web sites. The availability of RealOne Player software will increase the broadcasting of radio on the Web. RealOne Player can be downloaded at www.real.com.

Inside Radio
www.mstreet.net
Inside Radio provides insider radio news on the Web or by means of fax.

Sites also include information about the history and current state of the radio business. The following sites contain historical and industry information.

Old-Time Radio
www.old-time.com
Programming logs, pictures, and catalogs of tapes from the Golden Age of radio are available at this site. It contains historical material about the 1930s and 1940s.

The Museum of Television and Radio
www.mtr.org
The MTR site is an introduction to the two museums about radio and television. One is located in New York and the other in southern California. The site contains

information on the museums, which have scholarly material about the history of radio and TV.

Television and Radio News Research
www.missouri.edu/~jourvs/index.html
Professor Emeritus Vernon Stone of the University of Missouri maintains this page. It contains a large amount of research conducted by Professor Stone and others for various electronic news organizations. It has information about radio and television salaries, internships, and pros and cons of broadcast journalism careers.

The following sites have information about radio news and radio companies.

Westwood One Radio Networks
www.westwoodone.com
The Westwood site is maintained by the Westwood radio networks. It contains information about the company, its programming, and its affiliate stations.

National Public Radio
www.npr.org
The home site for the National Public Radio network contains audio and text versions of news events and information about NPR, its programs, and its affiliates.

questions for review

1. Was radio first conceived of as a broadcasting system?
2. What is a network?
3. When did radio journalism become significant?
4. What is significant about radio formats?
5. How might the development of Internet and satellite distribution of radio affect local radio stations?
6. Describe the types of radio stations.
7. How did the Telecommunications Act of 1996 affect ownership?
8. Why is the FCC considering increased regulation of radio content?

issues to think about

1. Describe radio's flexibility across the years. How has this contributed to its staying power as a mass medium?
2. Does specialization strengthen or trivialize radio as a news and information medium?
3. Does public radio make a unique contribution to society? How might the reduction of federal support for public radio affect content?
4. Why is radio a significant international medium? How does it differ from other media in this respect?

suggested readings

Chantler, Paul. *Local Radio Journalism* (Oxford, England: Focal Press, 1992).

Land, Jeff. *Active Radio: Pacifica's Brash Experiment* (Minneapolis: University of Minnesota Press, 1999).

Murray, Michael D. *The Political Performers: CBS Broadcasts in the Public Interest* (Westport, CT: Praeger, 1994).

Seib, Philip M. *Going Live: Getting the News Right in a Real-Time, Online World* (Lanham, MD: Rowman & Littlefield, 2000).

Sklar, Rick. *Rocking America: An Insider's Story: How the All-Hit Radio Station Took Over* (New York: St. Martin's Press, 1984).

Television

Cliff Huxtable never bit the head off a live bat. But he was head of the number-one TV family of the 1990s, found on *The Cosby Show*. Welcome to the 2000s and a new kind of Father Knows Best— Ozzy Osbourne. Rock 'n' roller Ozzy shares the Osbourne household with his wife, Sharon, daughter, Kelly, and son, Jack. Together they constitute the most popular series in MTV history.

The family of the former lead singer for Black Sabbath burst onto MTV in spring 2002 and quickly gained as many as six million viewers per episode. The series won the 2002 Emmy for best nonfiction program on television. Episodes showed Ozzy and his family wrestling over issues such as Kelly's tattoo and struggling to make the TV set work. The characteristic that made the show different from other so-called reality shows was the almost continuous use of foul language by all members of the family. MTV blipped the words, but Canadian television ran the uncensored version when it picked up the series from MTV.

Not everyone fell in love with Ozzy and his family. The Parents Television Council, a nonpartisan organization that monitors television content, studied reality programs during 2001–2002 and called *The Osbournes* the most offensive reality program on cable.[1]

Arguments about television programs do not surprise media historians. Television has always been a controversial factor in U.S. life. Newton Minow, chair of the Federal Communications Commission (FCC) in the early 1960s, called television "a vast wasteland."[2] Critics have argued that television provides not only sound but also pictures in our heads, and that those images destroy our ability to use our imaginations, which is the essence of creativity. Others have long worried that television presents violent behavior as acceptable within society. Some believe that television advertising creates a desire for products and services that people may not need and cannot afford. Some believe that television is replacing the vitality and diversity of folk and ethnic cultures with a bland, homogeneous consumer culture.

Television has a positive side as well. It expands the world of people who have limited opportunities to experience faraway places and events. At times, programming pushes cultural boundaries; at other times, it reinforces the status quo. For many, television is the great entertainer and informer. Television also brings the world to our homes and can create common experiences among Americans. These range from entertaining spectacles such as the Super Bowl to tragedies such as the shooting at Columbine High School.

As you read this chapter, you will see that changing technologies affect how people watch television as well as what they watch. Television content and the amount of television being watched remain concerns for people who are interested in individual development, social change, political life, and the evolution of a democratic society. Consider the following issues:

◆ Television in the United States has been, for the most part, a commercial venture. How has the commercial nature of television shaped its content? Is content shaped by advertisers? By public need and desire? By the overwhelmingly commercial structure of the medium?

◆ Until recently, the broadcast television industry was dominated by three networks. Now many viewers have access to more than one hundred channels. Has this change benefited the public?

◆ Television is a force for political and social change. How do you think the content of television has shaped or changed U.S. culture and society? Has television fostered democracy? Has it turned politics into entertainment? Has it made people more accepting of violence? Has it encouraged tolerance of diversity?

Television *in Your Life*

How Do You Watch Television?

People watch television for a variety of reasons. What motivates you to look at television? Do you watch to see people with whom you can identify? Do you watch to learn about people who are different? Do you use TV to escape and relax? Do you learn ways to solve your daily problems from TV?

People also watch television in a variety of situations. It can be a solitary or social activity. How do you most often look at TV? Do you watch by yourself, or with your family? Do you watch television as part of a sorority or fraternity? Do you watch TV when you're on a date? How and why you watch television changes how it affects you. As you read this chapter, think about the ways television affects you and how content is shaped to have that influence.

MOTIVATIONS	WATCHING ALONE	WITH FAMILY	WITH FRIENDS	ON A DATE
To see people I can identify with and enjoy				
To see people who are different from me				
To escape and relax				
To watch action, adventure				
To find good role models				
To learn ways to solve daily problems				
To learn about different cultures and lifestyles				

TELEVISION IN AMERICAN LIFE

The history of television is a history of technology and policy, economics and sociology, and entertainment and news. Television has never been a static medium. Rather, it evolved through changing technologies, including changes in presentation (such as color programming) and distribution (by cable, satellite, and fiber optics). These changes have been affected by government regulation. But television was not merely a technical invention. It changed people's lives, even down to the arrangement of their homes. As Lynn Spigel has demonstrated, for example, women's magazines of the 1950s discussed how to rearrange household furniture to accommodate the television as a replacement for the fireplace and the once traditional piano. The magazines also noted that television could provide a unifying influence in family life.[3] In later decades, televisions were often placed where they could be watched during meals. Today, many households have more than one television, and family members may watch individually rather than together. Television revolutionized not only the home, but also news, politics, and information. Some say that it revolutionized an entire society.

Development of Television

Television resulted from a long line of early experiments by many inventors, including Vladimir Zworykin, Philo T. Farnsworth, Edwin Armstrong, and Lee de Forest. The finished product represents the efforts of combined technologies and vicious patent disputes. Although experimentation began a century ago, the first test broadcasts did not begin until the mid-1920s. Development of television was

Television arrived in the home and changed not only people's vision of the world but also the spatial arrangements of their homes. Household furniture was shifted to accommodate the television as a replacement for the fireplace and the once traditional piano.

not an exclusive American phenomenon; television was on the air in England in the mid-1930s.

Battles between the radio networks such as Columbia Broadcasting System (CBS) and electrical giants such as Radio Corporation of America (RCA) determined the course of television in the United States. David Sarnoff of RCA became the dominating force in both radio and **television network** development. In 1933, Sarnoff opened the RCA Building in midtown Manhattan, which included a studio designed to provide live TV programs. RCA first demonstrated its all-electronic television system to the **trade press** in 1935, and television sets went on sale in a Bronx furniture store in 1938. In 1939 many people in the United States saw their first television on five- and seven-inch screens at the New York World's Fair.

During 1939, several radio networks and radio manufacturing companies, including General Electric, RCA, CBS, and DuMont, began transmitting from experimental television stations in New York. RCA and DuMont, which manufactured early receivers, slowly increased the size of the viewing screen to twelve inches. After several years of debating technical standards, the FCC authorized a standardized system for resolution quality and transmission.[4] By the end of 1941, which was television's initial year of commercial operation in the United States, CBS and NBC had converted their New York stations from experimental to commercial status, and about ten-thousand sets were sold.

Television's progress came to a halt in 1942 as manufacturers devoted themselves to war production. New television sets could not be made, and old ones could not be repaired. Only six experimental stations stayed on the air, and these for only an hour or so a week.

Although the technology was in place and regulation allowed for expansion, commercial television faced major challenges at the end of the war. First, TV station start-ups were expensive, requiring $1.5 million (about $7 million in today's dollars) or more. Second, the nation still suffered a shortage of critical materials. Third, advertisers were wary of television's high costs. Owners correctly expected their stations to operate at a loss for several years before a large enough viewing audience began to attract advertisers.

Each segment of the industry was reluctant to commit resources because of uncertainty in other segments. Station owners were concerned about whether consumers

television network: The radio network system became the model for developing television, and network-affiliated TV stations shared programs. The individual stations, which also produced local programs and sold local advertising, rebroadcast the programs to viewers in a geographic area.

trade press: Periodicals that target a specific industry. *Broadcasting & Cable* magazine, for example, targets the broadcast and cable industry and is an example of a trade magazine.

could afford sets to receive their broadcasts; set manufacturers needed on-air programming to entice set buyers; programmers needed advertisers' financial support; and advertisers needed viewers. One entity had to create the impetus for the other players to take the plunge, so development was slow. Nevertheless, the potential market encouraged risk-taking, and each segment stumbled its way to success.

Postwar Challenges

After World War II, television began to emerge as a mass medium, and networks rapidly became the dominant force in shaping station ownership and programming. In 1948, because of signal interference and because the number of channels assigned for television proved inadequate to meet the demand, the FCC froze the granting of television station licenses. Until it ended in 1952, the freeze limited stations to the 108 that were already in operation. During the freeze, a few big cities had several stations, and many had none. In areas that had no television, people used ingenious methods to get signals. In some communities, companies built tall antennas on hilltops to receive station signals and then transmitted those signals through **coaxial cable** to subscribing homes, thus initiating *community antenna television (CATV)*. By 1952, about 15 million homes (10 percent of the U.S. population) had TV sets, and advertising revenues were about $324 million. Total advertising revenues for radio in the same year were about $445 million.

By late 1948, four television networks broadcast from New York with limited links west to Chicago. Three of the networks—ABC, CBS, and NBC—were based on radio networks; the fourth, which was television only, was run by DuMont with help from its partner, United Paramount Theaters of Hollywood.

Good programming and solid *network affiliate* stations developed because they allowed the local broadcast stations to share the expense of producing quality programming. Local stations could not afford individually to pay national radio stars such as Jack Benny, but by forming networks, better programs could be produced and broadcast locally. CBS and NBC offered the strongest programming and so gained the most affiliates. ABC and DuMont competed for the rest. DuMont was the only network that had no radio connections; its financial support came from a successful television manufacturing business. DuMont hoped to pick up stations along the Atlantic seaboard and then move inland as the number of receivers increased and as the AT&T coaxial cables necessary for carrying television signals moved west. But the new stations tended to affiliate with one of the major networks. Unable to compete financially, DuMont closed its doors in 1955.[5] ABC, CBS, and NBC continued to dominate television until the coming of the Fox network in the late 1980s.

During the 1950s, CBS and NBC competed for the top spot. One of their early battles involved the development of color television. CBS, RCA (which owned NBC), and other companies had experimented with color systems beginning in 1940. As often happens with innovative technologies, technical standards clashed. In 1948, CBS claimed it could implement its system, but RCA argued that further experimentation was necessary before standards could be set. In 1950, after considerable political pressure from Congress and from CBS, the FCC first chose CBS's partly mechanical color system. However, in 1953 the FCC reversed its decision and authorized the all-electronic RCA system, which was compatible with black-and-white sets. David Sarnoff, chairperson of the board of RCA, announced on television that color had arrived. "This day will be remembered in the annals of communications," he said, "along with the historic date of April 30, 1939, when RCA-NBC introduced all-electronic black-and-white television as a new broadcast service to the public at the

key concept

Community Antenna Television (CATV) The first form of cable system, CATV was created in 1948. It used signals that were beamed to widespread communities via hilltop antennas; coaxial cable then carried the signals to households. The CATV system brought television signals to many rural areas that previously were unable to get them or received only poor-quality signals.

key concept

Network Affiliate A television station typically contracts to carry one network's programming and commercials; the station thus becomes an affiliate of that network. In return, the network pays the station for use of its time. The three major networks—CBS, ABC, and NBC—historically gained much of their strength through powerful affiliation agreements.

coaxial cable: Cable that contains two conductors: a solid central core surrounded by a tubelike hollow one. Air or solid insulation separates the two. Electromagnetic energy, such as television transmission signals, travels between the two conductors.

opening of the World's Fair in New York. At that time we added sight to sound. Today, we add color to sight."[6] However, Sarnoff's claim was mostly public relations hype, and it was not until the mid-1960s that color receivers became widely available.

Policy and Politics

Industry players cooperated with the government to ensure a profitable commercial broadcast system. By 1934, regulation of broadcasting had been assigned to the FCC, which was created by the Communications Act. Broadcast regulation is treated thoroughly in Chapter 11, but it is important to note here that the basic outlines of radio regulation were applied to television, guaranteeing that it too would be primarily a commercial medium. The act extended principles of the 1927 Radio Act that assigned licenses to *broadcasters as "trustees" of the airwaves* and charged broadcasters with operating in the public interest.

The FCC had difficulty addressing the issue of radio and television political content, particularly when it involved opinion, from the early days forward. The FCC argued that broadcasters' editorializing might not serve the public interest because broadcasters might propagate their own opinions without providing airtime for opposing points of view. Therefore, in a 1941 broadcast licensing hearing, the FCC ruled in the *Mayflower* decision that a broadcaster could not advocate a specific point of view. In 1946 the FCC codified much of its previous thinking into a document titled "Public Service Responsibility of Broadcast Licensees," generally referred to as the "Blue Book." This document outlined the rationale for FCC programming regulation and set standards for public service. It also argued that some profits should be reserved for public service programming. The TV industry attacked the Blue Book, arguing that the FCC was moving too close to censorship, which is prohibited by the U.S. Constitution. In 1948–1949 the FCC reconsidered its position on editorializing and encouraged reasonably balanced presentation of responsible viewpoints.[7]

This FCC policy statement became the basis of the *fairness doctrine*. Under the fairness doctrine, a station broadcasting one side of a controversy had to offer time to someone representing the other side of the controversy. The doctrine was eliminated in 1987, when the FCC concluded that the growing number of media outlets provided for enough diversity of opinion about public controversies.

The Communist Scare ◆ In the aftermath of World War II, fear of Communism infected U.S. society. Legislators, business groups, and others attacked the film and television industries, labeling performers, producers, actors, and writers **fellow travelers,** or sympathizers with those who advocated bringing Communism to the United States. In the atmosphere of anti-Communist hysteria fostered by Wisconsin Senator Joseph McCarthy, the entertainment industry faced sharp challenges from the House Un-American Activities Committee.

In 1950, Counterattack, a right-wing political group, published *Red Channels: The Report of Communist Infiltration in Radio and Television,* which named many writers, performers, and other broadcast employees as Communist Party members or sympathizers. This and other **blacklists,** many of which went unpublished, destroyed the careers of many aspiring broadcasters because those named on the blacklist were denied employment in the industry.

Entertainment Programming

Television programming successfully adapted radio's best offerings by the early 1950s. This movement from radio to TV served the networks because their programs had recognized stars, and it served the stars because it gave them access to a new, growing audience. **Anthologies** quickly became standard fare. *Kraft Television Theater, Studio One,* and *Fireside Arena Theatre,* produced live from New York, mimicked live stage performances. With live television, "every night was opening night," recalled costume designer Bill Jobe, "with fluffed lines, ties askew, flies open, and overstuffed merry widows."[8] Critics acclaimed the tasteful performances, and sponsors seeking sophisticated audiences raced to finance independently produced high-quality programming.

Comedy–variety shows hosted by successful radio comedians, quiz shows, dramas, and Westerns were standard prime-time television fare. Local programming also increased as stations began to broadcast during the day. "Every station had its cooking expert; a late afternoon children's program host, usually a cowboy or a clown; a general interview host for daytime shows; and a small local news staff."[9]

By the late 1940s, the networks had added situation comedies (sitcoms), which were mostly borrowed from radio. One of radio's most popular comedies was *Amos 'n Andy,* which debuted under the name of *Sam 'n Henry* in 1926. In 1931, the two white radio actors who spoke as *Amos 'n Andy* on radio starred at the *Chicago Defender*'s second annual picnic. The *Defender* was Chicago's nationally known black weekly newspaper. But even as actors Charles Correll and Freeman Gosden appeared at the *Defender*'s picnic, another prominent black newspaper, the *Pittsburgh Courier,* attacked *Amos 'n Andy* for being demeaning to African Americans.

Amos 'n Andy became a television hit in 1951, with black actors replacing the white radio voices. It was the first television show to have an all-black cast. The black community was split in its response. The NAACP denounced *Amos 'n Andy* for depicting "the Negro and other minority groups in a stereotyped and derogatory manner" that strengthened "the conclusion among uninformed or prejudiced people that Negroes and other minorities are inferior, lazy, dumb, and dishonest." But the *Pittsburgh Courier,* which had panned the radio show, found the television version to be "well-paced, funny more often than not, directed and produced with taste." *Amos 'n Andy,* the television show, won an Emmy nomination in 1952, but CBS did not renew the program for a third season. CBS syndicated the show, however, selling it to local stations and foreign countries until 1966. Correll and Gosden continued to act a radio version of the program until 1960.[10]

Other popular sitcoms soon became part of television fare. *I Love Lucy, Father Knows Best, Our Miss Brooks,* and *Burns and Allen* enjoyed long runs. However, many programs lasted only a few months.

Live performances continued to dominate television programming through the mid-1950s, but broadcasters soon realized that television lent itself to recorded programs. Filming programs for later broadcast was efficient and economical. By the late 1950s, the national programming from New York and much of the creative local programming that had originated in Chicago had moved to Hollywood. There, television producers had access to the technology and talents of the film studios, and the climate allowed outdoor filming all year. Film was the primary recording method; videotape was not in widespread use until the early 1960s.

Television comedy borrowed from its predecessor, radio. *The Red Skelton Show* specialized in slapstick that contained vestiges of vaudeville.

The Influence of Advertising on Programming

From the beginning of television, advertising and programming were intertwined through network personnel and through sponsorship. For example, Harry Ackerman, appointed vice president to head network programs for CBS in Hollywood in 1951, had worked at CBS radio and then for the prestigious Young & Rubicam Advertising Agency. At first, television programs were owned by advertisers, which based the content of the shows on the interests of the audiences they wished to reach. The names of the anthology dramas reflected their sponsors: *Kraft Television*

anthology: A favorite television format of the 1950s that consisted of stage plays produced for TV.

dateline: Television in our lives

1927. First experimental broadcast

1934. Federal Communications Commission is established.

1939. TV is demonstrated at the New York World's Fair.

1948. FCC freezes television station licenses to examine allocation policies.

1948. Cable television systems begin.

1400–1700	1800	1860	1900	1920	1930	1940

1620. Pilgrims land at Plymouth Rock.

1690. *Publick Occurrences* is published in Boston.

1741. First magazine is published in America.

1776–1783. American Revolution

1830s. The penny press becomes the first truly mass medium in the United States.

1861–1865. American Civil War

1892. Thomas Edison's lab develops the kinetoscope.

1914–1918. World War I

1915. *The Birth of a Nation* marks the start of the modern movie industry.

1920. KDKA in Pittsburgh gets the first commercial radio license.

1930s. The Great Depression

1939. TV is demonstrated at the New York World's Fair.

1939–1945. World War II

1949. First commercial electronic computer is produced.

Theater and *Goodyear TV Playhouse,* for example. The sponsor's advertising agency bought time from a network, and the agency produced and controlled the program and supporting ads. Sometimes the line between advertising and entertainment blurred. "A girl breaks into song," the *New Yorker* reported, "and for a moment you can't quite pin down the source of her lyrical passion. It could be love, it could be something that comes in a jar."[11]

Through the 1950s, networks and advertisers struggled over who would control content. NBC introduced the concept of *magazine programming,* which meant selling time to several advertisers to share the support of a single show. The networks improved their production facilities and brought more production in house. As the expense of programming and advertising rates increased, TV networks and stations increasingly sold time, not shows. At first only one product or service appeared in each commercial break, but later each break contained multiple ads.

The downfall of the *single-sponsor system* came with the 1950s **quiz show** scandals. These popular shows were cheap to produce because they required little in the

key concept

Single-Sponsor System In the early days of television, a single advertiser often sponsored an entire show. This system declined as television time became more expensive and the reputation of sponsors suffered from the quiz show scandals of the late 1950s.

quiz show: Show on which contestants answer questions that show their knowledge of selected material.

Early 1950s. 15-minute network news broadcasts

1952. FCC unfreezes station licensing.

1952. Networks cover presidential campaign.

1955. DuMont network closes, leaving three broadcast networks.

1960. First televised presidential debates between Kennedy and Nixon

1963. NBC starts 30-minute network newscasts.

1960s. Color television becomes popular.

1972. HBO becomes first premium cable channel.

1979–1980. *60 Minutes* becomes first news program to top the ratings.

1980. CNN begins operation.

1980s. Large-market local television expands newscasts from 30 minutes.

1987. Fox network begins broadcasting.

Early 1990s. Direct satellite broadcast starts using 18-inch dishes.

1996. Telecommunications Act

2000. Direct satellite broadcast increases its share of pay television.

2006. All broadcast TV stations must change to digital broadcasting.

1950	1960	1970	1980	1990	2000

Early 1950s. Rock 'n' roll begins.

1969. First person lands on the moon.

1970s. VCR is developed.

1989–1991. Cold War ends and the USSR is dissolved.

Late 1980s. National Science Foundation creates the basis of the Internet.

1996. Telecommunications Act

2000. Presidential election nearly tied.

2001. Terrorist attacks on New York and Washington, D.C.

---

way of sets or staging. Individuals appeared onstage and answered questions, much like *Jeopardy* contestants do today. The shows appealed to large audiences. The famous *$64,000 Question,* developed by an advertising agency and sold to Revlon, achieved one of the highest ratings of the decade. But the *$64,000 Question* and other highly rated quiz shows, including *Twenty-One,* were rigged to make them more exciting. The scandal broke during the summer of 1957. In the fall of 1958, Charles Van Doren, star contestant on *Twenty-One,* confessed that the producers (and by implication the sponsors) had given him advance answers to the questions he would be asked.[12] (Van Doren's story was the basis for the 1994 film *Quiz Show.*) Although the networks were in some cases reluctant to take over the management of advertising and programming, they used the scandal to claim that because sponsors were too greedy for high ratings, the networks themselves should control programming.[13]

Charles Van Doren was first a celebrity, then an outcast, on the TV quiz show *Twenty-One.* Quiz shows, many of which were proved to be fraudulent, attracted wide audiences.

Polls and Television

Each presidential election year, the television networks race to see who can predict the election outcome first. The predictions are based on exit polls, which involves asking people about their votes as they leave the polls. In 2000 the networks created confusion because early in the evening their exit polls predicted Democratic candidate Al Gore would win the popular vote in Florida. They later reversed this prediction and said Bush would win Florida. The voting was so close that the final winner of Florida and the presidential election were not declared for six weeks.

The networks used the polling of the Voter News Service. An article in the *Washington Post* cited three problems with the exit polls: the sample contained too many Democrats, a miscount of votes in the Jacksonville area, and some false assumptions about the election.[14] The problems encountered during the 2000 election will not stop the use of exit polls for predictions, but the networks will be more careful in the process of collecting and analyzing data, as well as timing the release of exit poll information.

TODAY'S MARKET STRUCTURE

Until the mid-1980s, television was dominated by three major networks: CBS, NBC, and ABC. Cable was targeted at a small, largely rural audience. However, in the 1980s cable companies took advantage of satellite technology to expand their distribution. They found that even urban viewers, with a range of network affiliates and small local stations to choose from, would pay to receive the additional channels that cable offers. In addition, some new networks arose to challenge the dominance of the big three. Today, seven commercial networks offer programming through broadcast television stations.

Four New Networks

Although networks had long dominated television, by the early 1990s forecasters were predicting their death. The share of prime-time audience held by ABC, CBS, and NBC eroded from a high of 91 percent in 1978–1979 to 41 percent during the first week of the 2002 fall season.

The lost audience moved to the four new networks—Fox, UPN, PAX and WB—and to cable. However, predictions of the networks' deaths were premature. The companies that own the networks remain financially strong as a result of deregulation in the 1990s. These companies provide original content and continue to attract viewers to their stations and networks.

Fox ✦ Rupert Murdoch, who started his career managing a family-owned newspaper in Adelaide, Australia, managed to do in ten years what no one in the United States had been able to do in the past—pose a serious competitive challenge to CBS, NBC, and ABC. Targeting a young audience, Murdoch took advantage of the FCC's desire to foster competition against the networks and used his own resources and nerve to battle the dominant business structure of U.S. television.

Murdoch built a single paper into a chain of tabloid newspapers, then moved to London in 1969 to buy a tabloid weekly, *News of the World*. By 1985, Murdoch and his News Corporation had collected a group of powerful media companies in Britain, including the *Sun*, the nation's largest-circulation daily, and the prestigious *Times*, and had begun laying the groundwork for a satellite television service called Sky Channel, which beams programs to cable systems throughout Europe. In 1985, Murdoch's News Corporation moved into electronic media with the purchase of Twentieth Century Fox Film Corp., with its rich film library. In the same year, Murdoch bought six big-city television stations from Metromedia in New York, Los Angeles, Chicago, Dallas, Houston, and Washington, D.C.[15]

Fox competes with more established networks with innovative programming such as *American Idol,* designed to attract performers who compete for the opportunity to win a recording contract to produce a CD.

Murdoch's deal needed approval by the FCC, but he was not a U.S. citizen, and the Communications Act prohibits ownership of broadcast stations in the United States by foreigners. Murdoch changed his citizenship as soon as legally possible, and the FCC seemed to ignore the fact that his News Corporation was made up primarily of foreign investors.

Ten years after Murdoch started the network, which he named the Fox Network, the foreign ownership issue resurfaced. After an eighteen-month investigation, the FCC reversed its 1985 decision, declaring that Murdoch's company, despite his U.S. citizenship, was indeed a foreign company. However, the FCC simultaneously granted Murdoch a waiver from the foreign-ownership rule, allowing him to continue business.[16]

Murdoch and Fox again pushed for changes in FCC regulation in 2003. They owned thirty-five TV stations that reached more than 40 percent of the households in the United States. This exceeded the FCC cap of 35 percent of national households for network-owned and -operated stations. The FCC was considering abandoning the cap in 2002, but if it does not, Fox will have to sell some of its stations.

UPN and WB ✦ As Fox illustrated that a new network could achieve success, two others joined the competition. United Paramount Network (UPN) and Warner Bros. Network (WB) joined the field during 1994 and 1995 respectively. In their first season, UPN reached an average of about 4 percent of households, and the WB reached about 2 percent. By 1999 the new networks reversed these positions, as the WB became the fifth-ranked network.

By fall 2002, both networks were averaging about 4 percent of households. UPN's highest-rated program during the first week of the fall season in 2002 was *WWE Smackdown,* and the WB's highest-rated program was *7th Heaven.*

PAX TV ✦ The number of networks grew to seven in August 1998 when Lowell "Bud" Paxson, founder of the Home Shopping Network, started a broadcast station network, PAX TV, built on reruns of family shows such as *Touched by an Angel.* By fall 2002, the network covered 86 percent of U.S. households. During its first year, PAX TV came close to averaging 1 percent of U.S. households watching the network programs. However, the ratings remained about the same four years after the network started.

Some analysts wonder whether family-oriented shows that appeal generally to older audiences will command enough of an advertising market to support the network. One of PAX TV's advantages is that it owns 65 of the more than 120 stations that carry the network and therefore will benefit from selling both local and national advertising. It also operates at low cost because of a decision not to originate or carry local news and to handle all promotions, marketing, and scheduling from corporate headquarters.

The future of these three newest networks—WB, UPN, and PAX—is uncertain. Each lost millions of dollars in its first year, and financial analysts predict that one or more will fail because there is a limited amount of advertising money available to support all television programming.

Television Delivery Systems

About 100 million households in the United States have one or more television sets. In 2002, 71.8 million households subscribed to a cable system, and 11.9 million of these had broadband cable. Another 18.4 million subscribed to a direct broadcast satellite (DBS) system, which was more than an 80 percent increase since 2000. Together, cable and DBS reached more than 90 percent of all households in the United States.

Broadcast Stations ✦ The United States has about 1,700 **full-power television stations.** More than 1,300 are *commercial,* in business primarily to make a profit. They are licensed by the FCC, transmit programs over the air, and carry commercial messages to pay costs and make a profit. *Noncommercial* stations, often referred to as educational or public television, are not operated for profit. These 380 stations are financed primarily by grants from foundations, viewers' donations, and government funds and carry no traditional advertising. *Low-power broadcast* stations serve limited areas because the stations' signals cannot reach long distances. There are about 2,100 low-power broadcast stations. Broadcast operations can be further classified according to their spectrum location in the very high frequency (VHF) or ultrahigh frequency (UHF) band. The 720 VHF broadcasting stations use larger radio waves to carry their television signals than do the 1,000 UHF broadcasting stations. The VHF signals travel farther and provide a clearer picture than UHF TV signals.

Cable Industry ✦ The $50 billion cable industry profits mostly by selling cable service to subscribers, although many systems and networks also sell advertising. Cable systems originally functioned as boosters for broadcast signals, but in the 1950s they began to augment programming by producing limited local programs. Later, cable companies offered additional features, such as movies without ads, for an extra charge to their subscribers.

By the mid-1960s, broadcasters began to fear the power of cable competition and asked the FCC to design protective regulation that would keep cable operators from competing with traditional broadcast stations. From 1966 until the late 1970s, the FCC imposed heavy restrictions on cable development. However, such regulations did not hold up under Supreme Court scrutiny, and during the late 1970s the FCC reversed its position on cable regulation. In 1984, Congress passed a strongly deregulatory Cable Communications Policy Act, which limited interference in cable operations by local communities, state governments, and the FCC. Recent disputes over cable have centered primarily on subscriber rates, with a fair amount of government and private concern directed toward the rapidly increasing costs of cable television to the consumer.

Deregulation paved the way for cable **superstations.** In 1976, Ted Turner turned the lowest rated Atlanta TV station, UHF Channel 17, into superstation WTBS. He contracted with a satellite company to **uplink** his signal to RCA's SATCOM I for distribution to cable systems. At first, only twenty systems **downlinked** WTBS, but within two years more than 200 systems downlinked programs from the station, and by 1979 more than 2,000 systems were participating.[17] Using WTBS, Turner made the Atlanta Braves, which he also owns, one of the most popular baseball teams in the United States.

full-power station: A station that reaches a large percentage of households in its market and that must broadcast a schedule of programs.

superstation: A station that reaches hundreds of markets throughout the country by means of satellite distribution of a signal to cable systems.

uplink: Transmitting an electronic signal to a satellite for storage or further distribution.

downlink: Transmitting an electronic signal from a satellite to a ground facility.

During the past two decades, cable advertising revenues have grown considerably. In 1981, cable television had less than 1 percent of the total television advertising pie. By 2001, its share had risen to almost 7 percent. It was one of the few advertising categories that did not see advertising revenue drop from 2000 to 2001, as the economy slumped.[18] The average cable system offers more than sixty-five channels, but this average will grow with increasing use of fiber optics and digital signals by cable systems. One industry observer predicts that the percentage of cable subscribers using digital will exceed 50 percent of the total by 2004.[19]

Even though the United States has more than 11,000 cable systems, a few companies own most of them. These companies are called multiple system operators (MSO). AT&T, which owned no cable companies in early 1998, joined with Comcast Corp. in November 2002 to create the Comcast MSO, which served more than 27 million subscribers, or 29 percent of the pay-television audience. Comcast Corp. and AT&T share ownership, but AT&T has the majority share of stock. In 2002, Time Warner was the second largest MSO in the United States with 13 million subscribers.

Satellite Distribution ✦ Direct broadcast satellite (DBS) distribution has become the fastest growing segment for delivering TV content. The number of DBS subscribers increased from 10.0 million in 1999 to about 18.4 million in 2002. DBS's rapid growth resulted in part from the approval in 1999 of federal legislation that allows satellite systems to distribute local station broadcasts into those stations' home markets. This had been illegal and had been the largest stumbling block for DBS in its growing competition with cable systems.

Mergers in the industry during the late 1990s reduced the number of major DBS providers to two, EchoStar and DirecTV, in 2002. When these two attempted to merge, the FCC declined to approve the merger in October 2002. The FCC said the merger would have eliminated competition.

Television Station Ownership Patterns

When buyers consider purchasing a television station, they must first examine the other media they own within that market. FCC regulations limit multiple ownership of the same medium and cross-ownership of other media (radio and newspaper) within the same market. The intent is to prevent a controlling media monopoly and to encourage a variety of voices within the marketplace.

Of all ownership types, *network-owned and -operated ("O and O") groups* receive the most attention. The stations in these groups tend to be in larger markets such as Chicago, New York, and Los Angeles because they attract larger audiences and profits than they would in smaller markets. The seven networks generate or acquire programming that runs on their own stations and on affiliated stations. The networks make money not only by carrying network advertising, but also by selling advertising time on single stations. Because of declining network ratings and increasing production costs, networks make more profit from their stations than from network advertising.

Other companies besides the networks own groups of stations. Some of these companies are major players in the media industry. For example, Gannett, which is known more for its newspapers than for television stations, owned twenty-two stations in 2002, and Media General owned twenty-six stations. Stations that are owned by groups may or may not be affiliated with networks. Affiliates make money from networks, which pay them to run programming, and by selling advertising at their stations. Affiliated stations use network shows and also buy syndicated programs.

Independently Owned Stations ✦ Independently owned stations are owned by individuals or families. They are not part of groups and may or may not be affiliated with networks. Programming can be expensive for independently owned stations that do not have a network on which to rely. However, independent stations have total freedom in deciding content, and much creative programming has originated at these stations.

Public Television Stations

◆ Public broadcast stations do not carry direct advertising; they are supported mostly by private donations, tax revenues, grants, and corporate underwriting. Corporate underwriting, in which a large company or corporation provides funding for a series, a program, or a particular time slot, is reflected in statements such as "This program is made possible in part by . . . " Public television is known for its long-running popular educational programs such as *Sesame Street* and *Masterpiece Theatre* and explorations of nature and science. In addition, its multipart social and cultural programs such as Ken Burns's *The Civil War* often attract large audiences of people who do not regularly watch public television. Public television is also known for carrying important congressional proceedings such as the Senate Judiciary Committee's confirmation hearings when Clarence Thomas was nominated to the Supreme Court. However, C-SPAN and CNN now generally provide more thorough coverage in this area.[20]

C-SPAN is a private, nonprofit company created in 1979 by the cable television industry as a public service. Their mission is to provide public access to the political process. C-SPAN receives no government funding; operations are funded by fees paid by cable and satellite affiliates who carry C-SPAN programming.

The federal government supports public television by giving money to the Corporation for Public Broadcasting (CPB), a private, nonprofit corporation created by Congress in 1967, which in turn partially funds one thousand public radio and television stations. With some of this money, public stations produce or buy programming. Television stations buy shows such as *The News Hour with Jim Lehrer* from the Public Broadcasting Service (PBS), a network created by CPB. The federal government's portion of the $2.3 billion spent on public television continues to decline; it was only 13.6 percent in 2000. Congressional critics of CPB argue that its programming has a liberal bias. PBS supporters reply that if federal funding were eliminated, many small stations might go out of business. Figure 10.1 illustrates where public television gets its money.

As a result of declining federal funds, PBS stations increasingly carry underwriter spots that look like commercials. For example, one spot showed a clip of the Mitsubishi Galant with a voice saying, "This program was brought to you by Mitsubishi. The all-new Galant, proof that sedans and pulses can harmoniously exist."[21]

Generation Xers who grew up watching *Sesame Street* are now watching it with their own children.

figure 10.1

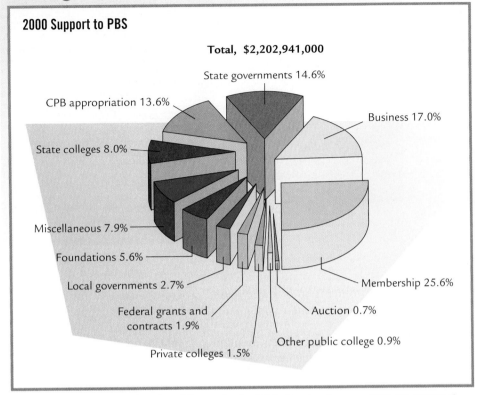

2000 Support to PBS

Total, $2,202,941,000

- State governments 14.6%
- CPB appropriation 13.6%
- Business 17.0%
- State colleges 8.0%
- Miscellaneous 7.9%
- Foundations 5.6%
- Local governments 2.7%
- Membership 25.6%
- Federal grants and contracts 1.9%
- Auction 0.7%
- Private colleges 1.5%
- Other public college 0.9%

Source: "Frequently Asked Questions," Corporation for Public Broadcasting, www.CPB.org. Reprinted with permission.

In fall 2001, the FCC voted to let PBS stations carry advertising on the six extra digital channels they will have when the conversion to digital transmission is complete. PBS station managers say they will need to find additional revenues to replace what they are losing from the federal government.

AUDIENCE DEMAND IN TELEVISION MARKETS

Television caters to the advertising market and the consumer market with news and entertainment. Networks, cable systems, direct broadcasters, and syndicates provide programming that supplies the demand. The chief goal, except in public television, is to make profits, which is usually done by achieving high ratings. However, high profits are increasingly associated with targeted audiences rather than mass audiences. In such cases, lower ratings can still attract advertisers. For example, golf events on television earn low ratings but are still attractive to advertisers because people who watch golf on television are high earners with disposable income to spend.

Consumer Market

TV shows can be divided broadly into two types: entertainment and news. Most television stations and networks have separate departments for providing these types of programs. The distinction does not mean that information cannot and should not be entertaining. Traditionally, the distinction has been that entertainment is mostly fictional and information concerns real events. This difference seems less identifiable,

Syndicated reruns, such as *X-Files,* remain popular fare for television viewers.

however, with the proliferation of reality-based programs such as *Cops,* magazine programs such as *Entertainment Tonight,* and fictional dramas (docudramas) based on recent news events.

People's demand for news reflects an interest in international, national, and local affairs. In nightly newscasts, networks provide national and international news, but stations traditionally broadcast local news as well. In the early days of TV news, the lack of portable cameras and the use of ordinary, fixed news sets led to low production quality. Often the local newscast represented no more than a station's effort to satisfy the FCC's policy of serving the public interest. However, in the 1980s the realization that local news programs could make enormous profits prompted stations to adopt new portable technologies and to hire consultants to redesign and expand their news formats. Now local news ratings of stations in big markets often exceed those of network news. Large-market stations regularly include national and international news using satellite technology.

Demand for entertainment is as diverse as the population. Most entertainment programming falls into standard categories such as comedy, drama, sports, talk, game shows, children's programs, documentaries, and reality-based shows. Within these categories there is a great variety. Drama includes weekly series, such as *CSI: Miami* and *ER,* and made-for-TV movies, such as *Prince William.* Comedy programs can be equally disparate, ranging from *Everybody Loves Raymond* to *South Park.* These programs air in prime time (between 8 P.M. and 11 P.M. EST), when most people watch television.

In addition to prime-time programming, most of the networks or their stations provide morning shows such as *Today* and *Good Morning America,* daytime soap operas, and late-night shows such as *Nightline* and the *Late Show with David Letterman.* Local stations usually fill the remaining time with local news, **syndicated material** (such as *The Oprah Winfrey Show* and *Soul Train*), movies, cartoons, and reruns of prime-time programs.

Cable networks run movies, sports, music videos, and syndicated programming, but they may also produce original material. By 2002, critics praised HBO as the best-quality network on television, and its program *The Sopranos* was considered the best drama.[22] As the number of cable channels proliferates, cable networks will invest the premiums they receive from subscribers in greater amounts of original programming to draw viewers from broadcast networks.

Theoretical structures for predicting success on television do not exist. Neither are there measuring systems that truly rate what audiences would watch if they had

syndicated material: Programs made available for sale directly to stations or cable channels rather than distributed by networks to affiliates. Examples are *Xena: Warrior Princess* and *The Oprah Winfrey Show.* Discontinued network shows that have had long successful runs, such as *Cheers,* are also candidates for syndication.

a wide range of choice. Although ratings reflect how audiences choose between available programs that are already on television, they do not reflect what *could be* on television. Audience research has been designed primarily to determine how viewers react to what is available, not what viewers might like to watch if they had the chance.

Advertising Market

Advertisers use media to persuade potential buyers. Television advertisers have traditionally addressed a mass market, and products that are advertised on television reflect such an audience. A popular actress, Betty Furness, opened refrigerator doors on television repeatedly during the 1950s to advertise Westinghouse refrigerators to homemakers; Procter & Gamble advertised its cleaning products on Ed Sullivan's Sunday night variety program in the 1950s and 1960s; and a new line of automobiles rolled across the screen each year on Dinah Shore's variety show sponsored by Chevrolet.

With the development of multiple cable channels, advertisers increasingly use television to target audiences through use of *demographics* and *psychographics*. Although traditional demographics give advertisers some guidance in targeting audiences, some larger audiences are bound together more by attitude than by demographics. The Discovery Channel, for example, has "different demographic groups but they share a psychographic tie that binds them together," says Chris Moseley, senior vice president of marketing and communications for Discovery. "They want information and they want to be entertained." Through research, Discovery divided its audience not merely into people over and under fifty years of age, but into categories that included "scholars," "practicals," and "boy's toys."[23]

Advertising and Television Content ✦ Company sponsorship of individual television shows declined in the 1960s after the quiz show scandals. Today it is rare for an entire program to be sponsored by one advertiser. Rather, networks or stations sell time for ads, known as *spots*, during a show. Does this mean that advertising has little impact on programming? No. The influence remains, but it is more subtle. Individual advertisers occasionally affect content, but advertising as a form of financing has a more pervasive impact.

Because cable television fragmented audiences during the 1980s, advertisers increasingly appeal to precise demographic groups. To provide efficient advertising within these groups, programs need to attract as large a proportion of the targeted group as they can. A company selling jeans to eighteen- to twenty-four-year-olds wants to reach as much of that audience as it can with one program because buying the ads on several programs cuts into the company's profit margin. Therefore, the company may prefer a program that concentrates on sex, action, and violence, which have a visceral impact that attracts many viewers in the target age group. But some programs, such as the hospital drama *ER*, are high-quality shows that may include sex and violence but do not rely heavily on them. The muscular chests and jiggling breasts of the lifeguards on *Baywatch*, for example, attract viewers, whereas the occasional shot of Detective Sipowicz's buttocks probably does not significantly increase the audience of *NYPD Blue*. High-quality dramatic shows attract viewers with complicated plots, character development, and sophisticated writing.

NYPD Blue provides an example of the declining influence of advertisers on adult programming. The program first aired in the fall of 1993 amidst controversy over its language, violence, and occasional nudity. During its premiere season, automotive, food, and beer advertisers stayed away because they were frightened by protests from some organizations. As it turned out, the violence did not exceed that found in the earlier *Hill Street Blues,* and the language could be heard daily on talk shows. The sex, although racy by traditional network standards, proved to be mild by cable standards. Nine years after it began, *NYPD Blue* continued to rank among the top twenty-five programs on television. Advertisers flocked to reach its audience.

Audience Measurement and Station Survival: The Ratings Game ✦ Measuring audience demand for particular programs is important because prices charged for advertising are based on the number of households and people watching. The measurement also helps programmers evaluate the demand for various types of shows. If dramas about police departments get high ratings one season, more such programs will surely appear the next season.

A. C. Nielsen Media Research dominates the audience measurement business. Nielsen measures viewing of programs and breaks down the number of viewers into a variety of demographic and psychographic categories. Using statistical techniques, the Nielsen reports can tell an advertiser how many people between the ages of eighteen and thirty-four who make more than $40,000 a year watched *Friends* on Channel 10 in Lansing, Michigan, on October 28, 2002.

Nielsen uses a variety of techniques to measure audiences. These include diaries, people meters, and set-tuning meters.

✦ *Diaries.* Viewers keep journals detailing what they are watching. Although the results might seem precise, a diary measures only what a viewer is willing to write. It reflects the viewer's perceptions, not an actual response.
✦ *People Meter.* People meters measure what is being watched and who is watching. A box is placed in five-thousand randomly selected households in the United States. Each person presses a button to record when he or she is watching.
✦ *Set-Tuning Meters.* Nielsen places these meters on the back of TV sets in randomly selected households in the forty-nine largest TV markets. They record what is watched on a daily basis.[24]

Ratings are a key factor in how long a television series stays on prime time and will help determine the longevity of CBS's top-rated 2002 series *Crime Scene Investigation.*

The proliferation of cable channels, videocassette recorders, and digital video disk has complicated the ratings process. Many people do not watch programs at scheduled times but record them for viewing later. People also watch one program while recording another. It's difficult to conclude that audiences rated one program higher than another if viewers plan to watch both, but at different times.

Nielsen Media Research measures audiences for television much the way Auditron measures audiences for radio except that the unit measured for television is sometimes the household as well as individual people. In addition to the number of viewers watching a program, Nielsen reports findings in the form of ratings (the percentage of TV households in a market watching a program). Nielsen found out, for example, that during the week of October 14 to 20, 2002, *CSI* was watched by more households nationally than any other program, and it achieved a rating of 18.6. One rating point equals 1,055,000 television households, so almost 20 million households were watching *CSI.*

Nielsen also reports its findings in the form of shares (the percentage of households watching television that are tuned to a particular channel). Shares are significant figures because they show how watching is distributed among channels, and they can be compared across markets. *CSI,* with its 18.4 rating, had a share of 29. The next closest program during the same time period was *ER,* with a share of 27 and a rating of 16.2.[25]

The accuracy of audience measurements can be a controversial issue. Different methods can produce different ratings and shares. Advertisers re-

It appears one career is not enough for Bill Cosby. In his forty years as an entertainer, he has been a standup comedian; broken racial barriers as a costar of the 1960s television series *I Spy;* changed the face of television situations comedies with *The Cosby Show;* sold four million copies of his first book, *Fatherhood,* and two million of his second book, *Time Flies;* had two comedy albums in *Billboard*'s Top 10; and been awarded eight gold records and five Grammy Awards as well as Emmy Awards for *I Spy* and *The Cosby Show.*

Much of Cosby's work is based on his family life and his experience as a father—areas he says he knows best. Cosby believes in keeping comedy and situation comedies clean, and he has been successful doing so.

Cosby was born in Philadelphia on July 11, 1937, and was the first of three boys. The family lived in a housing project, where, he says, their needs were met and there was no place for prejudice. His mother, Anna Pearl Cosby, was his role model; she raised the boys while working sixteen hours a day as a domestic. His father served in the navy.

Cosby was the captain of his high school track and football teams, but he dropped out of school in his sophomore year. He joined the navy, finished high school through a correspondence course, and received his GED. He went to Temple University on a track scholarship but quit three years later to concentrate on his comedy career. He later obtained his degree from Temple and went on to obtain master's and doctorate degrees in education from the University of Massachusetts. His wife, the former Camille Hanks, also has a doctorate in education. The Cosbys have four daughters; their son Ennis was murdered in 1997.

Cosby played the first minority lead role in television when he starred with Robert Culp in *I Spy* from 1965 to 1968. Before the series was over, he had won three Emmy Awards. Cosby went on to perform in other TV shows, several specials, and many successful concert performances. He also has recorded more than twenty comedy albums and has written four books during his career.

His most famous accomplishment was *The Cosby Show,* a family show in which the parents were strict but loving and children and parents learned from each other. Cosby took his idea to all three networks, but only NBC accepted it. By its second season, *The Cosby Show* was the highest-rated weekly television series, attracting 60 million viewers. The show ran for eight years, from 1984 to 1992.

However, Cosby's success as a creative entertainer and his wealth have not protected him from tragedy. On January 16, 1997, his son, Ennis William Cosby, a doctoral student at Columbia University, was found shot to death near his car on the side of a road in California.

In the 1996–1997 season, NBC introduced *Cosby,* a new situation-comedy series that was soon dropped from the schedule. Today, Cosby is one of the richest people in the entertainment business, and he has been number one on *Forbes*'s list of top-earning entertainers several times.

Sources: Don Heckman, "Common Cos," *The Los Angeles Times* (June 11, 1995), Calendar sec., p. 8; Bob Thomas, "Cosby Talks," *Good Housekeeping* (February 1991): 167; and Todd Klein, "Bill Cosby," *Saturday Evening Post* (April 1986): 42.

quire that the ratings be measured by an independent company because stations might inflate their own audience measures to increase ad rates.

SUPPLYING THE AUDIENCE'S DEMAND

Supplying the demands of the consumer market and supplying the demands of the advertising market are intertwined. Sometimes, while trying to target (attract) a certain segment of the audience, television executives manage to deter other segments, causing lower ratings and decreased advertising support. This happens when networks provide programs to attract specific age groups, but it also can occur with other types of demographic groups. During the summer of 1999, the National Association for the Advancement of Colored People (NAACP) threatened to boycott the four largest networks because not one of the twenty-six new shows set for the fall lineup featured an African American in a starring role. Why? African Americans are not being targeted by the networks.[26] In a reaction to the criticism, NBC revised some of their programming to include minority characters.

Because content reflects the interests of targeted advertising groups, the issue of which groups of people will be represented on television and which will not promises to be a continuing controversy in the future. Traditionally, broadcast stations are supposed to serve the public in general, but this becomes increasingly difficult in times of targeted advertising.

Efforts by network television to attract African American viewers did not last long. By spring 2002, only seven network programs were aimed primarily at African American households. This was down from eighteen in 1997.[27]

Station Organization

Most television stations contain six core departments. The size of each department depends on how big the station is. The engineering department manages the technical equipment used by all departments, especially the news and programming ones; the news department produces newscasts and public affairs reporting; the programming department buys and produces content to attract viewers for advertisers; the advertising or sales department solicits advertisers; the business office maintains financial records; and the promotions department uses advertising, special events, and public service to attract viewers and develop a positive image of the station.

Television Transmission Technologies

Television, just like newspapers and magazines, has to be distributed to the audience. Television transmission technologies can be either wireless, such as broadcast, microwave, and satellite, or wire based, such as coaxial or fiber-optic cable. Many of these technologies are used in combination with each other.

Broadcast television is similar to broadcast radio in that the information is transmitted from a station antenna on a specific spectrum frequency or channel to a receiver, usually a TV set's antenna. Each TV station has a designated channel on which it transmits. The spectrum space needed for television is six megahertz, larger than radio, because more information is transmitted.

Before 1998, all broadcast television stations used **analog technology** to transmit their signals. However, FCC regulations now require that the television industry convert its programming to **digital technology** by 2006. Since television began, a variety of transmission technologies besides broadcast have developed.

Wire Transmission ✦ Cable television transmits its programming through coaxial or fiber-optic cables instead of broadcasting it over the air. Cable transmission has several advantages: Cables, strung on utility poles or laid underground, are not subject to line-of-sight obstruction or most other electronic interference; two-way interaction back and forth along the same cable is possible; and a subscriber can receive many channels, typically sixty-five but sometimes as many as two-hundred, from one cable system instead of one channel from one broadcast station.

The disadvantages for cable operators are often financial. Because the initial cost is so high, a number of households must subscribe for it to be financially viable to bring cable into a neighborhood. In rural areas, the distances between houses greatly increase the cost of laying cable, so many rural areas do not have access to cable. Furthermore, cable operators must employ salespeople and pay for promotions to encourage people to buy the service. Broadcast operators, by contrast, worry only about transmission costs because households buy their own antennas to catch signals, and broadcast television is directly supported by advertisers, not consumers.

The hair-thin strands of glass known as fiber-optic cable carry audio, video, and digital information on lights produced by laser. More information is carried more quickly and in a narrower space by fiber optics than by coaxial wires. For example, one pound of fiber-optic cable can carry eighty times more information than one pound of coaxial cable.[28]

Fiber-optic cable's potential for delivery of information will grow with the increased use of digital transmission. **Broadband** transmission refers to digital trans-

analog and digital technologies: Analog technologies transform one form of energy into another to transport content. For example, analog broadcast TV changes the actions of actors into electronic impulses that can be carried by the energy waves of the electromagnetic spectrum. Broadcast digital technology transforms the actors' actions into a binary code of zeros and ones, the same code used for computers, that can be carried by energy waves. Digital technologies are more efficient and carry more content for the same amount of energy than analog technologies.

broadband: Fiber-optic cable with the capacity to carry large amounts of information.

mission over fiber-optic cable. Broadband transmission will promote the convergence of television and computers in the future.

Direct Broadcast Satellite (DBS) ✦ Satellites provide a relatively inexpensive way of transmitting information nationally or globally and have made instantaneous global communication possible. Most communications satellites orbit 22,300 miles above the equator. At this distance, they seem to remain stationary over one point on Earth. As a result, these satellites can continuously receive uplink signals from Earth dishes and send downlink signals to Earth dishes within their footprint. The *footprint* is the geographic area that can be covered by a satellite. For almost two decades, travelers noticed the eight-foot satellite receiving dishes in rural areas that cable and broadcast stations could not reach. However, since spring 1995, eighteen-inch receiver dishes, about the size of a large pizza, can receive more than 150 channels with high-quality digital reproduction. As a result, the large dishes are no longer being installed and cable television now faces competition in urban areas.

DBS systems offer a variety of viewing packages at prices comparable to those of expanded cable packages. However, some systems require subscribers to buy a satellite dish to receive the signals. The future of DBS brightened in 1999 when Congress passed legislation allowing these systems to rebroadcast local station signals into their local markets. The inability to do this had placed DBS at a disadvantage when competing with cable.

The number of DBS subscribers grew from 5.3 million in 1997 to 18.4 million in 2002. Predictions are that this total will reach 26.0 million by 2006, which would be close to 24 percent of all U.S. households.[29] The accuracy of this prediction will depend on the reaction of cable to the DBS competitive challenge and on whether additional DBS providers enter the U.S. market. In 2002, for instance, SES Americom, a company owned by European SES Global, asked the FCC if it could launch a satellite that would allow content providers such as Fox and AOL Time Warner to send signals into U.S. households. The service, called Americom2Home, would start in 2004 at the earliest if it is approved.[30]

Multichannel Distribution Service ✦ Multichannel distribution service (MDS), also called wireless cable, uses higher broadcast frequencies than traditional broadcast television frequencies and a converter box to send multiple channels of cablelike programming. Initially designed for cities that did not receive cable, MDS had less expensive installation and start-up costs. MDS faces an uncertain future because most cities now are wired for cable and DBS also provides competition.

Low-Power Television ✦ Low-power television (LPTV) is comparatively inexpensive to both producer and viewer because it operates on conventional television broadcast frequencies at very low power, covering distances less than fifteen miles. LPTV's local nature, more defined target audience, and cost are advantageous; however, competition makes financial stability difficult. Because large numbers of consumers watch network broadcast and cable television, advertisers are less inclined to spend money reaching the small audiences of the low-power stations. To overcome the competition obstacle, groups of LPTV stations are forming to offer larger audiences that will attract advertisers. In addition, nonprofit groups such as religious organizations have been applying for low-power frequencies.

Supplying News and Information: The World in Our Living Rooms

Local stations, national networks, CNN, and news syndicates generate programming in a variety of *TV news and information formats.* Local stations usually produce their own community news, and satellite technology allows them also to carry national and international news. CNN, Fox News Network, and MSNBC use cable and satellite technology that provides twenty-four-hour access to news. TV news syndicates take the form of either a video exchange by local stations joined in a cooperative or a pay service.

Evening Newscast ✦ The evening news format, as exemplified by the network shows featuring Peter Jennings, Dan Rather, and Tom Brokaw, is the most basic news presentation model. Chet Huntley and David Brinkley popularized the anchor format, in which one or two anchors present the news, usually with video or other visual accompaniment.

Local stations have their own news teams. Teams include the anchors and supporting team members who report on local weather, sports, and other topics, such as health and consumer information. Station reporters videotape reports or report live from story sites. There also may be remote feeds, usually from stations affiliated with the same network, for stories of special interest. For example, during the trial of Zacarias Moussaoui, who fought with the Taliban in Afghanistan, many local news broadcasts around the country featured live reports from Virginia.

Newsmagazines ✦ Magazine programs contain several stories in each segment. Newsmagazines reached the level of prominence they enjoy today in the late 1990s. Magazine programs such as *Dateline NBC* air more than once a week, and they often receive high ratings, especially during summer when most entertainment programs are reruns.

The shows vary in the degree of hard and soft news they carry and in the degree of sensational treatment. However, they are profitable because they cost less money to produce than a prime-time drama, and they allow the networks to share the high salaries of news personalities among several programs.

Interview Shows ✦ *Meet the Press* and *Face the Nation*, in which journalists interview one or more prominent people in the news, are some of the longest running programs. They provide the public with the opinions of prominent politicians, military leaders, and other important public figures. In doing so, these programs serve the marketplace of ideas.

Morning News Shows ✦ Morning news shows have completed a circle, arriving where they were when the *Today Show* started on NBC in 1952. The early *Today Show*, hosted by Dave Garroway, provided news, but in a very broad sense of the term. Celebrity interviews, a large picture window through which people on the street could hold up signs of greetings, and even chimpanzees named Mr. Kokomo and J. Fred Muggs greeted viewers in the morning. Eventually, the *Today Show* spawned a variety of imitations. The morning shows took on a harder edge during the late 1960s and early 1970s. But *Good Morning America* started a return toward softer news in the mid-1970s. This sometimes sensational news approach became the norm for morning shows after 1979, when *Good Morning America* replaced the *Today Show* as the ratings leader for morning news shows.

The morning time slot can generate a large amount of advertising for the networks. As a result, the morning shows became a battleground in 1999. In order to boost sagging ratings, ABC moved Diane Sawyer to *Good Morning America*. CBS retaliated by bringing Bryant Gumbel back to the early morning competition. Gumbel had drawn a large audience at *Today* before leaving NBC. Both Gumbel and Sawyer were gone from the morning shows less than three years later, but the investment of star power showed how eager NBC, CBS, and ABC are to attract the morning audience.

Tabloid Television ✦ Tabloid television includes confrontational talk shows such as *Jerry Springer*, gossip shows such as *A Current Affair*, and so-called reality-based shows such as *Cops* and *America's Most Wanted*. These are inexpensive to make, easy to syndicate, and wildly profitable. Tabloid shows continue to receive criticism because of their emphasis on sex, reenactments, and the practice of paying sources. During the 1990s, some programs toned down their excesses in these areas, but the emphasis on sex and violence is part of what defines tabloid shows.

Supplying Entertainment

Because it is difficult for programming directors to predict the success of shows, they rely on *entertainment formulas* that have worked in the past. Costs are high and risks are great. When a network's new show pulls good ratings, other networks quickly produce shows with similar plots or casts of characters. This *copycat programming* increases the chance of success. Thus programming often goes through three stages: *invention*, in which new genres or types of shows are developed; *imitation*, or copycat programming; and ultimately *decline*.

cultural impact

We Are Family: From Ozzie and Harriet to Homer and Marge

Programs about families have always been part of television, but just how much a part has varied from season to season. Although crime dramas seemed to dominate the 2002–2003 season schedule, family programs made a charge to regain the throne as the top TV formula. However, of the dozen new family programs that premiered during fall 2002, some fit the Simpson and Osbourne dysfunctional model more than the Huxtable and Nelson traditional family mode. In addition, not all TV families were made up of mother, father, and children.

The new TV family fare saw a range of plots, including a remake of the 1960s program *Family Affair*, in which three children move in with their uncle; *8 Simple Rules,* with a father and mother dealing with raising their two daughters; *Greetings from Tucson,* a story of an Irish mother and Mexican father

who help their teenagers cope with U.S. culture; and *Half & Half,* showcasing daughters from a father's first and second marriages who live in the same building.

Television observers have speculated that the growth of family shows represents a desire of the post–9/11 U.S. audience to return to simpler times with stronger family connections. However, a second factor appears to be the push of advertisers for more family-friendly programs. The Family Friendly Programming Forum, which is composed of forty-eight companies such as Coca-Cola, Ford Motor Company, and Proctor & Gamble, organized in 2000 to promote family-oriented programming through which they could advertise their products. The forum subsidizes the development of new scripts and pilots. They backed the *Gilmore Girls* on the WB in 2000–2001, a show that gained audience and critical praise. In 2002–2003,

five forum-subsidized programs were on television.

Whatever the reasons, programs about families have come a long way since the 1950s. They now represent a wide range of families. Critics argue about whether television reflects reality or helps create it. It does both. But there is little debate that TV shows must attract audience to continue, and programming formulas rise and fall with ratings.

Sources: Robert Blanco, "Gather Round: Fall TV Is for Family," *USA Today* (September 20, 2002): 1E; Stuart Elliott, "The Media Business: Advertising; Family-Friendly TV, with Crucial Support of Advertisers, Wins More Time in Prime Time," *The New York Times* (June 3, 2002): C9; Diane Holloway, "Some 'Family' Shows Not for All in the Family," *Chattanooga Times/Chatanooga Free Press* (October 6, 2002): E1; Paul Fahl and Lisa de Moraes, "For TV Networks, It's a Family Affair," *The Washington Post* (May 25,2002): C01.

The Sopranos, initially designed to end in 2002, was scheduled for an additional year. The show, an HBO original, has evolved through time. In 2002, viewers watched the Soprano family relationships deteriorate; viewers had to wait until the 2003 season to see whether the family would come together in the end.

With the large number of broadcast and cable channels available, viewers see several different types of formulas generating copycat programming during the same season. For instance, in 2002 the television lineup seemed riddled with crime programming. In the spring, three shows using the title *Law & Order* were available. With syndication, the *Law & Order* franchise could be seen twenty-seven times a week.[31] Not to be outdone, *CSI* (crime scene investigation) added *CSI:Miami* in fall 2002, and both were in the top ten programs by the third week of the season. Crime was not the only formula alive and well in 2002. The headline of an October 15, 2002, article in the *New York Times* stated: "Mom, Dad and the Kids Reclaim TV Perch."[32] The number of situation comedies in the top thirty increased from three in 2001 to nine during the first month of the fall 2002 season. Most of these were family sitcoms. Even though it was fading, the reality formula continued as well in 2002 prime time with *Survivor Thailand* and *American Idol in Vegas.*

Entertainment programming includes prime-time network shows, which run between 8:00 and 11:00 P.M. EST. Syndicates' prime-time shows are first-run shows that are sold through syndicates and not by networks. Other programming is composed of syndicated reruns, which are former or current successful prime-time shows that produced enough episodes to run five days a week. Still other programming includes movies, sports programming, and public broadcasting.

Who produces entertainment programming? Overwhelmingly, television shows have been produced by Hollywood studios. However, freed from regulation during the early 1990s, networks began producing more of their own television programs. This allowed them greater control of the program content, but it also raised concerns among independent producers. With network-produced shows taking up more time slots, networks will buy fewer independent programs. As media companies have merged, corporations increasingly look to own a production company and a television company to distribute the film and video. For instance, Disney owns ABC, and Murdoch owns both the Fox Network and Twentieth Century Fox.

Issues about Entertainment Content ✦ Although First Amendment considerations prevent government action in most content areas, Congress and public interest critics have repeatedly raised concerns about the impact of sexual and violent content on television, particularly its effects on children.

Sex and violence remain standard components of successful movies and television programming. Kiefer Sutherland stars as a police officer in *24*, a critically acclaimed but violent series on Fox. Television's emphasis on violence and sex worries critics, who complain that television has a negative impact on today's children.

Programs aimed at young people typically emphasize relationships between boys and girls, which translates on television into sex. MTV has been successful in attracting young viewers with relational programming such as *Real World*. This age group is attractive to advertisers because teenagers spend much of their money on consumer goods and services. These programs also attract teenagers who see themselves as young adults. Proponents argue that these programs introduce social issues and teach teenagers how to deal with them. Critics are quick to point out that choices made by the characters seldom have lasting consequences and are unrealistic.

The public and Congress express even greater concern about the impact of programming on young children, particularly in regard to violence. Some people argue that parents should monitor what their children watch, others support installing V-chips that can block specified programming, and still others advocate outright control of content production.

Increased concern about the influence of television content on children and the impact of violent programming on society led to a television program ratings system in 1997. The television industry developed the system not out of altruism but because the 1996 Telecommunications Act mandates a system that can be used with a computer chip. The industry hopes the ratings system will help to blunt any further efforts to control content.

The Motion Picture Academy of America helped to develop the ratings system, which is similar to the one used for movies. The system has been adopted by the networks and most basic cable channels. The system has six levels that are indicated by icons in the upper left corner of the TV screen during the first fifteen seconds of the program. The levels are based on age and run from TV-Y, which means that the program is suitable for all children, to TV-M, which means that it is not suitable for children under age seventeen. Table 10.1 lists all of the new ratings.

The ratings system has not received unanimous support. Critics argue that the ratings should address content more specifically and that separate ratings should be available for sex and violence. Others argue that determining the suitability of TV content should be left to parents, not a ratings system.

table 10.1

Television Ratings

TV-Y—All Children: The program is suitable for all children. It should not frighten young children.

TV-Y7—Older Children: Designed for children age 7 and older; may contain mild physical or comedic violence that may frighten children under 7.

TV-G—General Audiences: Program is appropriate for all ages. It contains little or no violence, no strong language, and little or no sexual dialogue or situations.

TV-PG—Parental Guidance Suggested: Program may contain limited sexual or violent material that may be unsuitable for young children.

TV-14—Parents Strongly Cautioned: Program may contain some material that many parents would find unsuitable for children under 14 years old.

TV-M—Mature Audiences Only: Program is specifically designed to be viewed by adults and therefore, may be unsuitable for children under 17.

A survey published in 2001 found that only 28 percent of parents said they often used the age-based ratings system.[33] Bradley Greenberg, a professor at Michigan State University, explained in his book *The Alphabet Soup of Television Ratings* that the lack of use was due to confusion over the meaning of the rating symbols and inadequate information about the ratings of programs before the programs are shown.[34]

Supplying the Advertising Market

Several different entities—networks, groups, individual stations, and cable systems—sell advertising time. The price of the time varies with the geographic location and type of audience, which also varies in kind and number with the time of day. For example, advertising time within a network show is much more expensive than time within a local show because of the larger, national audience that the network can reach. The price for an ad within a Chicago local program would depend on the size and demographics of the audience.

The number of viewers a particular program attracts determines the fee that the network or station charges advertisers. The formula for determining the *cost per consumer* is called the cost per thousand (CPM), which is the dollar amount it costs to reach a thousand viewers with an ad. Take, for example, a thirty-second advertisement on *ER*. The charge for such a spot in 2002 was about $440,000.[35] On a good night, the program might have 30 million viewers. The cost per thousand viewers would be $14.66. Here is the formula broken into two parts:

$$\frac{\text{Total number of viewers}}{1{,}000} \qquad \text{Example: } \frac{30{,}000{,}000}{1{,}000} = 30{,}000$$

$$\frac{\text{Cost of ad}}{\text{Result of first equation}} \qquad \text{Example: } \frac{440{,}000}{30{,}000} = \$14.66 \text{ per thousand}$$

The same formula can be used for radio, magazines, and newspapers. Thus the cost of reaching a thousand people with a TV program can be compared to the cost of reaching the same number of people in other media. The higher a show's rating, the more a station can charge for a minute of advertising, as long as the CPM does not become too much higher than that of other media.

Television regulation also affects how stations and networks supply the advertising market. For example, cigarette advertising is prohibited. Cigarette manufacturers got around the ban on television advertising by putting cigarette ads in football stadiums, baseball parks, and basketball arenas, which appeared on TV. The Justice Department said that Philip Morris had ads placed near the field or scoreboards in fourteen football stadiums, fourteen baseball parks, and five basketball arenas. In 1995, Philip Morris agreed to remove such advertisements.[36]

The latest move toward regulating advertising concerns liquor advertisements. From 1948 until 1996, the companies that produce distilled spirits voluntarily refrained from advertising on television. But in fall 1996, Seagrams ran advertisements for Chivas Regal Scotch in Texas and Massachusetts, sparking discussion among FCC commissioners and members of Congress about regulating liquor advertising.

In December 2001, NBC announced they would accept distilled spirit ads, but they backed away from that decision in early 2002 after national protest from a variety of parent groups. Some critics point out that this position can be considered hypocritical because wine and beer companies already spend about $1 billion on advertising, much of it on television.[37]

TELEVISION AND THE INTERNATIONAL MARKET

Technology and corporate activities continue to make television an international medium. During the 1990s, satellite transmissions of video material and changing government systems opened up areas of the globe that once had limited access to television. MTV can now be seen in Asia, Europe, and Latin America as well as in North America. International television involves importing material into the United States and exporting U.S. products to international markets. Further, the United States must compete with imports and exports among other countries, such as from the United Kingdom to India and vice versa. Four *market factors in international television* will determine the nature and

Although *Baywatch* is one of the best-selling internationally syndicated television programs, many critics object to Western values creeping into other cultures.

extent of this trend: the availability of distribution systems, the availability of programming, cultural resistance, and international corporate cooperation.

Availability of Distribution Systems

At the center of global television proliferation are companies such as News Corp., which provides service on seven continents. News Corp. and other satellite companies use eighteen-inch satellite dishes to provide packages of channels to viewers in a variety of countries and are able to reach audiences without the expensive task of laying cable. Such corporations wield enormous power. Although NBC challenged News Corp.'s right to own U.S. TV stations, arguing that it violated FCC regulations because it was foreign owned, NBC dropped its complaint after News Corp. agreed that NBC could use Star Television's satellite to reach Asian markets.

Availability of Programming

Offering 150 channels will not attract viewers unless the programs have appeal. With the proliferation of channels, content becomes increasingly important in determining who watches what, and some of the communications mergers of the 1990s sought to broaden access to content. CNN joined news organizations in Turkey in 1999 to create a cable news network called *CNN Turk*. Run by Turkish journalists, the network has access to CNN international news coverage. In 2002, Disney launched channels or strategic partnerships in Indonesia, South Korea, and Poland.

Many countries' governments help supply the demand for content. The European Union spends about $60 million a year to develop television programming. Canada invests in film and video and has emerged as the biggest foreign supplier of television programming in the United States.

Cultural Resistance

Not all countries embrace expanding access to television. Many countries in developing areas fear that Western programming will corrupt the morals of their people and forever alter indigenous cultures. They see the expansion of television as a form of *cultural imperialism*, which involves the forcing of one country's culture on another through media content dominance. For example, Iran bans satellite dishes because of concerns about the clash of values found in U.S. programming, such as those on MTV, with Muslim beliefs.

Fears about cultural imperialism are both economic and cultural. Both stem from the popularity of U.S. programming. With their high production values, focus on action, emphasis on sex, and simple plots, many U.S. television shows and movies attract audiences across cultures. Economically, imported programs undermine indigenous television production. Such programming also often contradicts cultural values. For example, in a country that holds older people in high esteem, a U.S. program that caters to a young audience by portraying older people as inconsequential could be offensive. Europe reacted against the power of the United States in the video industry in 1999. Companies in France, Germany, Italy, and other countries increased their investments in television programming to improve production quality and provide the types of programs that Hollywood produces. As one journalist said, "After years of worrying that *Dynasty* and *Baywatch* would corrupt their kids, Europeans have discovered that they can do the corrupting themselves."[38] The investment paid off in France in 2002, when admissions to U.S. films dropped 16 percent, and admissions to French films rose 63 percent. However, 30 of the 204 films produced in France in 2001 made half of the total revenue. Many films are never distributed.[39]

International Cooperation

Because resistance to external video programming is widespread and shows no sign of subsiding, global conglomerates have turned to cooperative ventures for developing international television content. For example, Hearst Entertainment and PRAMER SCA of Argentina partnered in 2002 to start a twenty-four-hour channel called Cosmopolitan Television Latinamerica.

As the world moves toward 200-channel satellite and cable systems, programming demand increases. If 200 channels averaged eighteen hours of programming apiece each day, the system would require more than 10,000 hours of programs per month. In an entire season, the four major U.S. television networks provide only about 500 hours of new programs.

TRENDS AND INNOVATIONS

Trends and innovations in television can be categorized according to technology, ownership, and content. Just as they have been in the past, the three will continue to be interdependent.

Technology: Digital Television

Technology and economics will drive many of the expected changes. **Interactive television** is on the horizon, but marketers have not determined yet exactly how much interactivity audiences want, what types of interactive programs they will watch, how willing they will be to use complex technologies, and how much they will pay for it. Interactive trial runs have been inconsistent. Although some experiments have been welcomed in households, few consumers seem willing to pay for the service after the free trial period ends. The most popular services seem to be movies-on-demand, games, children's services, and content created specifically for interactive television.

Thanks to an FCC decision in April 1997, the next generation of TV sets will have a higher-quality picture and will connect easily to the Internet. After years of debate and experimentation, the FCC began allocating additional spectrum space for *digital television (DTV)*. DTV uses digital technology to improve the quality of the TV picture by increasing the number of lines on the screen. Until 2006 each television station will send two signals. One signal will be the current analog signal, and the other will be the same programs in digital form. In August 2002, 461 stations were broadcasting a digital signal in 136 of 210 TV markets. This was about a third of all stations. By the end of 2003, the percentage should be about 70 percent. After 2006, people either will have to buy a digital TV set or use a converter for their old TV sets.

Although all stations must broadcast digitally by 2006, debate continued in 2002 as to whether the broadcasts would be standard digital TV (SDTV) or *high-definition TV (HDTV)*. HDTV has even more lines on the screen and produces the sharpest picture possible. The FCC requires some form of digital but not necessarily HDTV. Some station owners would rather see lower-quality digital transmission because that would allow stations to broadcast multiple signals. The multiple signals could be used for more television signals, data, or even voice communication. Multiple signals instead of one HDTV signal would bring in more money for the stations. Unless regulations change, in 2006 prime-time network programming will be

---

key concept

Digital Television (DTV) Digital television converts TV programming into a digital format rather than the analog format used since television was invented. By sending the programs as a series of ones and zeros, the picture is sharper than it would be with analog distribution. All TV programming must be digital by 2006.

key concept

High-Definition Television (HDTV) By presenting the picture with a greater number of lines projected on a TV monitor than that found with standard digital television (SDTV), HDTV produces the highest level of TV reproduction quality. However, HDTV takes a larger bandwidth than SDTV. Some TV companies would rather send SDTV and use the excess bandwidth for other purposes, such as data transmittal and wireless telephones.

interactive television: The ability of computers and TV sets to jointly send messages to and receive messages from the company that provides the television signals. Typically, viewers can access video-on-demand and interact with program hosts and audiences in studios.

We're Digital. Now What?

The debate over whether and when television programming will be digital has come to an end. With the increased use of satellite and digital cable, the percentage of households already receiving digital programming grew during the 1990s and into the new century. In 2002 the Federal Communications Commission decreed that by 2007 all television sets larger than thirteen inches must be produced with a digital tuner so they can receive digital broadcast signals.

Although the distribution technology debate has been decided, many issues remain about digital television. First, whether most people will receive TV programming through cable or from satellite remains unclear. Cable has for years dominated the nonbroadcast distribution of TV programming. However, signs of weakness have emerged. In 2002, 76 percent (71.8 million households) of the cable–satellite market subscribed to cable. However, only ten years earlier, cable had 95 percent of the market. At issue during the next decade will be whether satel-

lite delivery continues to make inroads into cable's share and whether competition will develop within the cable industry from telephone companies.

Questions of what services to provide in an all-digital television environment have emerged even within corporations. Time Warner cable started offering some digital cable subscribers technology that allows consumers to fast-forward through commercials. Time Warner also offers video-on-demand for movies and some network programs. Although this made viewers happy, it has had the opposite effect on executives within the Turner Broadcasting and Warner Brothers divisions within AOL Time Warner. These divisions sell advertising and fear that giving viewers more choice will have a negative impact on advertising rates as fewer viewers pay attention to commercials.

The movement of programming choice from sellers to consumers results from efforts to get cable subscribers to pay for digital cable and from competition with direct broadcast satellite companies

that already provide some of these services. It remains unclear what prices people will pay to have more choice.

To make the future even more complicated, the combination of improving streaming technology and increasing broadband access will move the Internet closer to being a viable video distributor. The Internet already exceeds any other medium in allowing consumer control over content. Corporations such as AOL Time Warner also have online divisions, as well as broadcasting and cable. It appears that decision making within multimedia corporations will become more difficult and interesting.

Sources: John M. Higgins, "The Demand of Demand," *Broadcasting & Cable,* July 22, 2002, www.tvinsite.com; Ken Kerschbaumer, "Getting It All Together," *Broadcasting & Cable,* December 10, 2001, www.tvsite.com; David D. Kirkpatrick, "A TV House Divided," *The New York Times* (October 28, 2002): C1–C4; Heather Newman, "Federal Ruling Makes Digital TV a Certainty," *Detroit Free Press* (August 9, 2002): A1–A2.

HDTV, but stations will be able to broadcast lower levels of digital during other time periods.

Initially, HDTV was developed to improve picture quality, but the growth of the Internet also pushed the television industry toward digital transmission. The move to digital may have been the most important element in the adoption of HDTV because it will lead to the convergence of television and computers. *PCTV* is a combination of the acronyms for television (TV) and personal computers (PC), and it represents the convergence of television and computers. PCTV will connect homes to electronic distribution systems such as the Internet even when customers don't have both a television and a computer. The future of interactive television also got a boost from the creation of digital video discs (DVD). The introduction of DVD in 1997 increased the likelihood of consumers buying sets with digital monitors so the picture would be digital quality. Eventually, PCTVs will become the basis for sophisticated interactive home entertainment systems.

Even though the FCC continues to push toward a 2006 conversion of broadcast television to all-digital transmission, consumers have not moved as readily toward buying digital TV sets. First, confusion reigns over what is needed. Should it be HDTV or just SDTV? Many salespeople don't know that sets must have both a digital monitor and a digital tuner to receive digital broadcast signals. In addition, a thirty-four-inch set with a digital monitor and decoder still costs about $3,000. Not surprisingly, a 2002 survey found that 32 percent of people over age eighteen had never heard of HDTV, and 56 percent had no idea about how to receive HDTV signals.[40] Despite consumers' lack of information, the move to adopt HDTV got a boost in 2002 with several programming changes. CBS announced it would broadcast twenty-seven hours of high-definition television a week, and ABC committed to thirteen hours a week.[41]

Ownership and Delivery of Services

The passage of the Telecommunications Act of 1996 guaranteed massive changes in television station ownership and the mix of delivery services. The act changed regulations governing broadcast television and cable ownership, programming, and cable rates. The far-reaching law affects all areas of the television industry and will alter the nature of the industry well into the twenty-first century.

Old rules limited companies to ownership of twelve TV stations reaching up to 25 percent of the national audience. The 1996 act eliminated the limit on the number of stations one entity could own and increased to 35 percent the national audience a company's stations could reach. Companies quickly grew in size, and the broadcast lobby continues to push for a higher national audience percentage, which will make the media corporations even bigger.

As a result of the act, networks and TV stations now can own cable systems, and cable systems can own TV stations. A network can own a second network, provided it starts the second one rather than buying an existing network. The new law also requires the FCC to consider whether it should relax the rule against a broadcaster owning only one TV station in a market. The FCC has taken a liberal stance toward ownership of a TV and radio station in the same market.

The conglomeration of media described in earlier chapters also affects television as a result of the Telecommunications Act. In 2000, Viacom, which owns Paramount and cable networks, acquired CBS. As with Fox and ABC, critics fear that the integration of movie studios with television cable and broadcast outlets will reduce the chances that networks will buy independently produced programs.

Perhaps the most drastic changes are in the cable industry. With the ending of rate regulation in 1996, cable rates outpaced the inflation rate by 200 to 300 percent. The success of cable-rate deregulation hinges on telephone companies' ability to provide programming. Regional operating companies can deliver programs as a cable system, which will require a franchise agreement from local government, or as an **open video system.** Open video systems do not have to get local franchise agreements and are subject to limited federal cable regulations. In return for more freedom, the open systems make cable channels available to unaffiliated programmers without discrimination in one of two ways: The system operators can rent entire channels to programmers without control of the content, or the systems can make a channel available that will vary in its content. A person or group could buy an hour of time on a given day to broadcast any message that falls within the limits of the law.

Open video systems allow greater access to people and organizations that are not affiliated with an existing network or television station. Economists would say that this lowers barriers to entry for nonestablished businesses and will make content more diversified.

open video system: A system that rents entire channels or time on channels to unaffiliated programmers without discrimination.

Just as telephone companies can enter the cable business, cable companies can begin to provide telephone service. Existing telephone companies must negotiate with new service providers about interconnections and a variety of other issues required to keep telephone use simple.

Almost as soon as the 1996 act was signed, corporations began to lobby the FCC to deregulate even further. As 2003 began, the FCC was considering several changes in regulation, including removing the 35 percent cap on households a company could reach with "O and O" TV stations, removing the radio–television cross-ownership limit, allowing a company to own more than one network, removing the limits on the number of radio stations a company could own in a market, and removing the ban on local newspapers owning broadcast stations. The FCC commissioned a series of studies in 2002 that generally, but not entirely, supported these positions. However, critics of deregulation were not convinced that the studies were entirely unbiased.[42]

Television Content and a Diverse Society

Because of immigration patterns and birthrates, each year the population of the United States becomes more racially diverse. With this diversification, one would expect television content to reflect the changes in society. However, this has not been the case. A study of the racial composition of TV characters in 1993 found that Native Americans, African Americans, Asian Americans, and Hispanic/Latino characters composed 16.4 percent of all TV characters, although they made up about 24 percent of the U.S. population.

Almost a decade later, some signs of improvement have been seen, but representation in television equivalent to the population demographics remains a distant goal. About 16 percent of TV characters are African Americans, but most are minor characters. The number of TV programs with African Americans in lead roles actually declined from eighteen in 1997 to seven in 2001.[43] Hispanics/Latinos are being served not by network television, but by Spanish-language television, which has grown with NBC's alliance with Telemundo. Few prime-time network characters are Hispanic/Latino, and even fewer are Asian American or Native American.

The absence of characters who are people of color downplays the importance of people who are not white. Children learn a great deal about how they should behave from watching television. If they are denied role models who look like themselves, their development of self-esteem can be damaged. The desire to watch characters of color can be seen in a study of African American viewers by Nielsen in 2000. Nielson compared the top-ten rated prime-time programs for African Americans with the top ten programs for white Americans. The only common program was *Monday Night Football*. Eight of the other nine programs in the African Americans' top ten were from UPN and the WB and had African American lead characters.

It is possible that no racial group will constitute a majority in the U.S. population by 2050. Television companies will need to do a better job of representing society if it hopes to attract an ever-fragmenting audience.

summary

- Television, as a medium and as content, has always been controversial in U.S. society.
- Television station licensees are charged with operating in the public interest.
- Getting the television industry on its feet after World War II was difficult because each important element (station owners, set manufacturers, programmers, consumers, and advertisers) was waiting for someone else to begin the process.
- Although blacklisting did not alter the structure of the television industry, it reminded television executives of their vulnerability and underscored the necessity for free expression.
- Three networks, CBS, NBC, and ABC, dominated television during the first forty years. This dominance declined during the 1980s and 1990s because of cable television and the advent of additional broadcast television networks: Fox, UPN, WB, and PAX-TV.
- Early television programming borrowed from radio and was broadcast live.
- Early advertising took the form of sponsorship, and advertisers controlled the content of specific programs.

- Television combined with changes in the political landscape to shift power from political parties to television. The emphasis is on the candidates' images rather than on substantive discussions of the issues or investigations of the candidates' past positions.
- Broadcast stations profit by selling an audience to advertisers, whereas cable stations profit by selling programming to subscribers and, to a lesser degree, audience to advertisers.
- Television involves a variety of distribution technologies such as broadcast, cable, satellite, fiber optics, and combinations of these and other transmission processes.
- Ownership categories include group ownership, independents, public stations, and multiple-system cable operators. Some stations are owned and operated by networks; others are affiliated with networks; and some are independent, broadcasting local and syndicated programming.
- For some people in the United States, cable is not available because the nearest cable company determined that laying cable to those potential subscribers is not profitable.

- Although a program may have many viewers, a broadcast station might choose not to broadcast it the next season because it does not attract the consumers that certain advertisers wish to reach.
- Audience measurement, such as ratings and shares, affects programming because it affects an advertiser's willingness to buy time in connection with specific programs.
- Changes in the regulation of satellite distribution during the late 1990s has increased competition between direct broadcast satellite and cable companies.
- Digital television, in the form of high-definition television (HDTV), will improve the quality of reception, and households will move toward convergence with PCTV.

navigating the web | Television on the Web

You can find sites related to your favorite television programs, or you can use television web sites to find information about the industry. There also are sites that lead you to current news and information and station promotion.

Broadcasting & Cable
www.broadcastingcable.com

Broadcasting & Cable is the television trade magazine. The online version contains information about the print version as well as some content from the print edition.

TV Acres
www.tvacres.com

TV Acres provides easy access to information about prime-time and Saturday morning television programs

from 1940 until the present. It has a variety of databases for searches.

TV Guide Online
http://tvguide.com/tv

This site provides information about current and historical television content. It is the online version of *TV Guide* magazine, which has a circulation of nine million.

TV Radio World
www.tvradioworld.com

This site is a directory for television and radio stations and networks around the world. It also provides information about technical information and regulations applicable to particular countries throughout the world.

questions for review

1. What is the difference between cable systems and broadcast stations?
2. What was the *Mayflower* decision and why was it important?
3. How do public and commercial television differ?
4. What is the significance of the Fox network?
5. How does television measure its audiences?
6. What are the implications of the federally mandated move to digital television?

issues to think about

1. How has the primarily commercial ownership of television in the United States affected its development?
2. What changes do you see in politics since the advent of television? Do these changes foster democracy?
3. Has television content deteriorated, or is it merely the reflection of changes in society?
4. How do varying distribution technologies affect the development of television content?
5. As cable and new networks compete with ABC, CBS, and NBC, what changes do you foresee?
6. What will be the impact of interactive television?
7. What has been and will be the impact of the Telecommunications Act of 1996?

suggested readings

Barnouw, Erik. *The Golden Web: A History of Broadcasting in the United States, 1933–1953* (New York: Oxford University Press, 1968).

Blumenthal, Harold J., and Oliver R. Goodenough. *The Business of Television* (New York: Watson-Guptill Publications, 1998).

Douglas, Susan. *Inventing American Broadcasting, 1899–1922* (Baltimore: Johns Hopkins University Press, 1987).

Garner, Joe. *Stay Tuned: Television's Unforgettable Moments* (Kansas City, MO: Andrews McMeel Publishing, 2002).

Gitlin, Todd. *Inside Prime Time* (New York: Pantheon, 1985).

Lasswell, Mark, ed. *TV Guide: 50 Years of Television* (New York: Crown Publishing, 2002).

Walker, James R., and Douglas A. Ferguson. *The Broadcast Television Industry* (Boston, MA: Allyn & Bacon, 1998).

11

Music and the Recording Industry

E minem's third album, *The Eminem Show,* zoomed to the top of the charts in May 2002. Wrapped in controversy, the album symbolized both the history and the future of popular music.

Eminem's success as a white rapper of African American music brought memories of white singers making hits of rhythm and blues music in the 1950s. Eminem even mentions the impact of race on music in the song "White America," when he sings: "Let's do the math—if I was black, I would've sold half."

Some critics trace Eminem's popularity to the controversy that surrounds his music. Just as teenagers found rebellion in early rock 'n' roll, young people today find expressions of their discontent in his lyrics that attack a variety of people, from Vice President Dick Cheney's wife to his own mother. But Eminem seemed to be making a move toward the pop mainstream with the fall 2002 release of his movie *8 Mile,* which was embraced by some mainstream movie critics.

Music journalists continue to debate whether the singer purposefully creates controversy to sell his music or simply is expressing his view of the world. But the most prophetic part of *The Eminem Show* release may be what happened on the Web. The album was released nine days before the scheduled date because pirated copies were being downloaded. More than 280,000 copies were sold over the Memorial Day weekend despite little prerelease publicity, but the future of any big album release remains uncertain.

This ongoing relationship between young people, music, and technology reflects the important cultural force music has become in the twenty-first century. Music has played a cultural role throughout history, but the recording and distribution technology for music that developed during the past century amplified that impact. This cultural impact affects individuals through the very personal experiences and images music creates, but it also affects society through the ideas expressed in the music and adopted by the groups that identify with that music. Because the lyrics and rhythms of songs that are popular among the young tend to push the boundaries of contemporary culture, they often are controversial. In the 1960s, "Beatlemania" offended at least some of the older generation; now sexually suggestive music videos on MTV draw the wrath of critics.

Controversy over music increased once music could easily be disseminated through mass media. Recording technology took music out of the carefully controlled parlor with its piano or phonograph into the automobile with its portable radio. Adolescents were able to listen to music far from the ears of their parents. Today, parents often do not know what their children are listening to.

In this world of mediated music, economics and technology pose significant issues such as the following:

◆ Music is a cultural force. Critics wonder whether music can continue to push the cultural boundaries of society without encountering crippling political and social resistance. Are the bounds of good taste and artistic innovation at odds? Do cultural clashes represent the differences between generations and social classes?

◆ The recording industry is for the most part a corporate world. Will the industry's focus on profits mean more promotion of mainstream music and the exclusion of aspiring artists who experiment with varied musical forms and lyrics? Will independent musicians and small companies be strong enough to continue innovation?

◆ Will converging technologies alter the form of music itself? Will video images and self-promotion made possible by technology destroy music in its purest forms? Or will it make a wider variety of musical forms accessible?

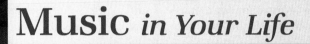

Music *in Your Life*

Music as Rhythms and Ideas

Music can be listened to merely for entertainment, but it also may educate. Think about how music has affected your life. Why do you listen to it? What does it do for you?

As you read this chapter, think about the many ways in which music pervades life in the United States. Think about how you use music—to tell stories, to relax; to worship. Also try to relate some issues to the commercialization of music and the impact of corporate music makers on popular content.

WHAT YOU LEARN	TECHNOLOGIES YOU USE	PEOPLE YOU LISTEN WITH	PURPOSES OF MUSIC
New ideas	Radio	Friends	Religion
About people who are different from you	Television	Date	Excitement
About people who are like you	Compact discs	Family	Making friends
About the world around you	Tapes/records	People in restaurants/bars/stores	Relaxing
About emotions	Internet/computer	Colleagues at work	Other

Unwilling to listen to the "noise," they leave it to their children to choose their own artists, songs, and lyrics. The ability to listen outside parental influence and issues of taste have caused dilemmas for the recording industry; for radio broadcasters, who balance specific audience needs and tastes with broader cultural boundaries; and for advertisers, who seek to attract adolescents who have money to spend on recorded products.

The economics of the music industry also have changed. The recording industry has become concentrated. Music promoters and broadcasters, seeking to please audiences and advertisers, tend to favor established artists. Concentration of the industry means fewer independent recording companies and may signal a more difficult time for entrepreneurs and new artists to break into the business.

PRINTED AND RECORDED MUSIC IN AMERICAN LIFE

Europeans brought their own music with them to America. Clinging to familiar traditional forms, they disregarded the music that existed on this continent long before they arrived. Native American music, like that of Europeans, was central to religion, but it also served as oral history. Most tribes had no written language, so music helped them remember and teach the stories that make up their histories.

Native American music is still not a key ingredient of U.S. popular music.[1] Most of the music that has become popular through sheet music, phonograph, radio, television, and compact discs has two major cultural strains: African American music forms, which evolved into blues and jazz; and European religious and popular music, which evolved into bluegrass and country music. Ultimately, strains of all the popular forms made their way into a blend called rock 'n' roll.

African American Music

African music arrived in Virginia with the slave ships even before the *Mayflower* landed in New England, and it appeared in printed form during the Civil War. It evolved into black spirituals, work songs, blues, and jazz. Although the Africans sang tribal songs with a **syncopated beat** that was foreign to most European songs, during the 1700s and 1800s the early African Americans blended these songs with European religious music to create spirituals. The first black spiritual appeared in print in 1862, and the first collection of black spiritual sheet music was published five years later.[2] African Americans sang work songs on the docks and in the cotton fields of the South. These songs had no instrumental accompaniment, and workers used them both to help them bear harsh working conditions and as clandestine protest songs, which created the base of the blues tradition.

Blues songs were personal music about an individual's troubles. After the Civil War, wandering musicians helped to spread the spontaneous music with impromptu lyrics, and at the turn of the twentieth century, W. C. Handy immortalized the genre with his song "The St. Louis Blues." The song was so popular that it earned Handy $25,000 a year in royalties forty years after it was written.[3]

African Americans also composed music for entertainment and dancing. These fast-paced banjo songs were adopted by white performers in the traveling **minstrel** shows that were popular among white audiences from the 1840s to the early twentieth century. In these shows, white men blackened their faces with burnt cork and sang black songs. Successful songwriters such as Stephen Foster gained fame by imitating the songs of black Americans, who were not allowed to perform their own music. Such music eventually made a successful transition from performance to motion picture. Al Jolson, famous for his blackface movie roles, carried the minstrel tradition into the twentieth century. Despite its appeal to some white audiences, African Americans felt minstrel shows mocked their tradition.

In the late 1800s, the minstrel shows also gave rise to ragtime, which originated in the African American dance music called the cakewalk. Ragtime emphasized in-

syncopated beat: The regular metrical accent shifts temporarily to stress a beat that is normally weak. Syncopation is important in African and African American musical traditions and is considered the root of most modern popular music.

minstrel: An entertainer, with blackened face, performing songs and music of African American origin.

Early jazz music developed from the ragtime and blues played in New Orleans and was spread northward by musicians such as Louis Armstrong, whose career paralleled the growing popularity of jazz. Elements of jazz and blues ultimately became a critical element in rock 'n' roll.

tricate syncopated rhythms in march tempos. Ragtime composer Scott Joplin, who first studied classical European music, stunned his audiences with songs such as the "Maple Leaf Rag." Ragtime developed as commercial music, particularly in urban areas with large concentrations of African Americans.

At the turn of the twentieth century, African American musicians performed in the bars and brothels of the Storyville section of New Orleans. They combined ragtime and blues forms, creating jazz in the relatively tolerant environment of the southern port city.[4] City authorities closed down Storyville in 1917 under pressure from the U.S. Navy, which had a large military base in New Orleans. New Orleans' loss was the United States' gain as jazz spread through the nightclubs of Chicago, St. Louis, New York, Kansas City, Memphis, and San Francisco. In the 1920s, the economy boomed, young people looked for excitement, and jazz thrived.

A decade later jazz became the basis for the big band, or swing, sounds of the 1930s and 1940s played by black, white, and mixed bands. Many jazz musicians criticized swing because it sanitized jazz to make it more commercial. Nevertheless, jazz flourished and grew in complexity. It underwent a revitalization in the 1950s and is found in a variety of forms today.

European American Music

Europeans brought both religious and *folk ballad traditions* with them to America. The religious songs came with the settlers, many of whom were escaping religious persecution in Europe. The folk songs came with the sailors and adventurers who saw the New World as a way to make money and with the peasants and farmers who settled on the expanding frontiers. Serious music did not gain a foothold until the first half of the nineteenth century, when an elite class began to look toward European forms of entertainment.

Because of the efforts to break away from Europe, patriotic songs were popular in this early period. British soldiers used "Yankee Doodle" to taunt colonists, but during the American Revolution it became a standard on the battlefield. Patriotic songs remained popular throughout the 1800s and reached their peak with the marches of John Philip Sousa in the latter part of the nineteenth century.

Origins of Western, Bluegrass, and Country Music ✦ European folk music blended with other traditions. In some urban areas, folk ballads were integrated into African American minstrel music, and in the West they formed the basis of western songs, expressing the tales of the lonesome cowboy. Hill music—bluegrass, hillbilly, and country—had its roots in European folk music. In the mountains of Tennessee, Kentucky, Virginia, and North Carolina, people used folk tunes and religious songs, played on traditional instruments such as the fiddle and banjo, to ease the burdens of life.

Urban Popular and Tin Pan Alley ✦ The popularity of music culminated in the late 1800s in *Tin Pan Alley,* which was both a place and an approach to commercial music. The popular music industry was centered in New York City around Union Square. Here, the music houses employed people to write songs for sheet music, vaudeville, and theater. Writers incorporated classical and folk melodies and wrote their own tunes to please the taste of the average person. In 1893 the music producers moved to West 28th Street. Monroe H. Rosenfeld, a press agent and journalist,

1600s. African and European folk and religious music arrive in America.

1800s. Blues develops from African roots, and country music develops from European roots.

Late 1800s. Sheet music sales boom.

1887. Edison invents the recording machine.

Early 1900s. Records are mass produced.

1930s. Swing grows from jazz.

1940s. Les Paul invents the electric guitar.

1940s. Tape recording develops.

1947. Columbia develops 33⅓ rpm long-play records.

1948. RCA develops 45 rpm records.

1400–1700	1800	1880	1900	1920	1930	1940

1620. Pilgrims land at Plymouth Rock.

1690. *Publick Occurrences* is published in Boston.

1741. First magazine is published in America.

1776–1783. American Revolution

1830s. The penny press becomes the first truly mass medium in the United States.

1861–1865. American Civil War

1892. Thomas Edison's lab develops the kinetoscope.

1914–1918. World War I

1915. *The Birth of a Nation* marks the start of the modern movie industry.

1920. KDKA in Pittsburgh gets the first commercial radio license.

1930s. The Great Depression

1939. TV is demonstrated at the New York World's Fair.

1939–1945. World War II

1949. First commercial electronic computer is produced.

named the street Tin Pan Alley after the sound made by a piano that had been modified with newspaper strips woven through its strings to muffle the noise.

Tin Pan Alley dominated popular music for almost twenty-five years, producing thousands of mostly forgettable songs for sheet music sales. It ended in the 1920s as radio, phonographs, and movies began to distribute not only notes and lyrics, but sounds as well. Today the term describes formula commercial music aimed at pleasing large numbers of people.

Elite Music ✦ Although music aimed at the educated and wealthy elite did not develop as quickly as popular and religious music in the United States, it made giant strides from 1865 to 1920 and even today is significant as a form of music available on radio, tape, compact disc, and even television.[5] The increased availability of higher education, the expansion of the middle class during the Industrial Revolution, and the invention of the phonograph created large audiences for serious music. Private cit-

Early 1950s. Rock 'n' roll begins.

1950s. High-fidelity and stereo technology is introduced.

Early 1960s. Beatles become the most popular rock group ever.

Late 1960s. Rock 'n' roll fragments into various strains of rock.

Mid-1970s. Punk and new wave music develop.

Late 1970s. Hip-hop develops in South Bronx.

1979. Sony Walkman is invented.

1980s. Compact disc is invented.

1981. MTV begins broadcasting.

1985. Digital audiotape is introduced.

1990s. Music begins broadcasting over the Internet.

1990s. MP3 technology is developed for the Web.

2000s. Rap becomes international and more mainstream.

2001. Sales of recordings decline and some blame web downloading.

1950	1960	1970	1980	1990	2000

Early 1950s. Rock 'n' roll begins.

1969. First person lands on the moon.

1970s. VCR is developed.

1989–1991. Cold War ends and the USSR is dissolved.

Late 1980s. National Science Foundation creates the basis of the Internet.

1996. Telecommunications Act

2000s. Presidential election nearly tied.

2001. Terrorist attacks on New York and Washington, D.C.

izens funded conservatories and concert halls, and by 1920 symphony orchestras had been established in New York, Philadelphia, Chicago, Cincinnati, Minneapolis, Pittsburgh, San Francisco, Cleveland, Detroit, and Los Angeles. Opera did not fare as well, with only two permanent opera companies performing in 1920.[6]

From the 1930s to Rock 'n' Roll

By the middle of the 1920s, African and European music had become interwoven to form specific strains of popular music, and radio facilitated the wide distribution of popular forms of music. The United States had jazz, blues, country, western, theatrical and movie songs, Tin Pan Alley tunes, and dance music. Jazz entered the mainstream musical arena and paved the way for *rock 'n' roll.*

Elvis Presley incorporated rhythm and blues with rockabilly roots to establish himself as a rock 'n' roll star.

The hot jazz of the 1920s, born in the brothels of New Orleans, gave way to **swing** during the late 1920s. Gone were the small improvisational groups, replaced by bands of more than a dozen musicians. Some African American swing musicians, such as Duke Ellington, garnered an audience and a reputation during this period, but swing was dominated by predominantly white bands headed by Benny Goodman, Glenn Miller, and Artie Shaw.

Even as mainstream singers such as Frank Sinatra, Bing Crosby, and the Lennon Sisters sold millions of records during and after World War II, some areas of music were changing. In jazz, African American artists such as Charlie Parker and Dizzy Gillespie reacted against swing and the white commercial exploitation it represented. They developed **bop,** which returned jazz to its improvisation roots and boosted its ability to compete in the recording industry.

The bop movement represented only one genre of African American music that flourished. Count Basie gained white fans with his **jump music,** and blues singers such as Blind Lemon Jefferson and Big Mama Thornton recorded hits. The term *rhythm and blues (R&B)* was applied to all kinds of black music, replacing the term *race music.*[7]

Country music flourished along with rhythm and blues. The lonesome songs of Hank Williams, the western songs of Gene Autry, and the foot-tapping bluegrass of Bill Monroe made country music commercially attractive for the recording industry. The Grand Ole Opry in Nashville broadcast weekly over radio, and performing there became the goal of every country-and-western singer.

Blending Music to Make Rock 'n' Roll

People disagree about who invented rock 'n' roll, but everyone agrees that it vitalized the recording industry. Many say that Louis Jordan's rhythm and blues music of the 1940s was rock 'n' roll. Others argue that Bob Wills and his Texas Playboys' western swing of the 1930s was the root of rock 'n' roll. Other influences include urban blues singers such as T-Bone Walker, who adopted Les Paul's solid-body electric guitar during the late 1940s.[8] Elements of gospel music can also be heard in early rock 'n' roll.

Without question, however, rock 'n' roll was born in the deep South, and it emerged from rhythm and blues. By living in the South, young musicians were able to hear the black R&B and white hillbilly music that formed the core of rock 'n' roll. Two streams emerged. One involved identifiable rock 'n' roll music from rhythm and blues, by musicians such as Little Richard, Bo Diddley, and Chuck Berry. The other stream was the rockabilly music, which dated to Bob Wills but incorporated more rhythm and blues. Early rockabilly musicians, such as Johnny Cash, Carl Perkins, Buddy Holly, and Elvis Presley, folded gospel and rhythm and blues into their music. Often they covered R&B artists' music, as Elvis did with Big Mama Thornton's "Hound Dog." At the same time, some African American artists, such as Chuck Berry, found influence in the country music they heard growing up in the South.

Alan Freed, a Cleveland disc jockey, helped to popularize the music in the North. His show boomed in popularity after June 1951, when he began playing the R&B records he had heard on African American radio stations. Freed called the music "rock 'n' roll."

Though early rock 'n' roll made African American rhythms more acceptable to white audiences, the major recording companies resisted. Company executives saw no future in music that adults considered too loud, and the sexual energy demonstrated in rock 'n' roll dancing alarmed adults. This was "trash" music to most white people older than age eighteen. Early production and distribution of rock 'n' roll were left to small record companies such as Sun Records of Memphis and Chess Records of Chicago. Figure 11.1 illustrates the evolution of rock 'n' roll and other strains of music in the United States.

swing: Big band music played with a jazz rhythm that was popular during the 1930s and early 1940s. Swing enjoyed a revival during the 1990s.

bop: Jazz that developed during the 1940s as a reaction to big band swing music. Usually performed by small groups with fast tempos and conflicting rhythms. Also called be-bop.

jump music: Small band music that merged swing and electric blues during the late 1940s. Jump developed into rhythm and blues music.

The Evolution of Rock 'n' Roll

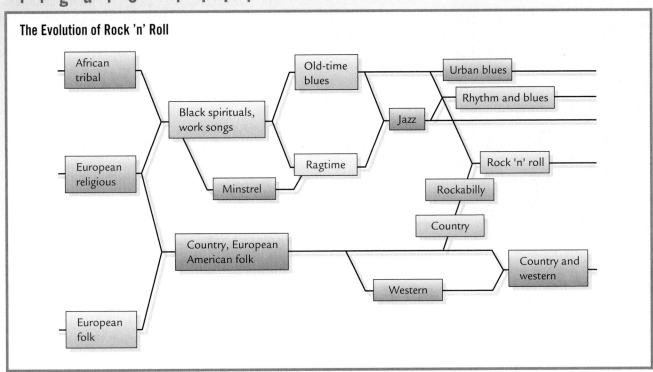

SOCIAL AND CULTURAL IMPACT

Three elements have guided the evolution of popular music in the United States: rebellion, the blending of different types of music, and commercialization. These elements signify the controversial nature of music distributed by mass media and its impact on social change. Rarely was a musical form adopted by the mass media without enormous controversy. Even elites who wanted classical music to dominate argued that trying to broadcast classical music would diminish its quality; they believed that only in a concert hall or parlor could an audience truly appreciate the nuances of classical music. Political figures and social reformers balked at putting jazz on the radio. They feared that such forms of music would corrupt society's youth, encouraging them to dance cheek-to-cheek, and more. The same arguments were made when rock 'n' roll began to climb the charts. Recently, gangsta' rap has come under attack by parents, Congress, and public figures.

Music and Rebellion

Music—particularly music as a form for mass media—has served each generation as a *forum for rebellion* against the status quo. As rock spread into a variety of subgroups defined by varying ethnic backgrounds, cultures, and classes, its breakthroughs and barriers in the recording industry represented cultural tension, not merely a change in musical form.

As each generation matures, its members see the world with a new perspective and with new values. The lyrics and music written by artists who are members of the new generation often express these values, which inevitably conflict with values held by their parents. When Bob Dylan wrote "The Times They Are A-Changin" in 1963, he told parents to either help change society or get out of the way of young people

key concept

Music as a Forum for Rebellion Popular music has often served younger generations as a way to express and encourage rebellion against existing social rules and norms. Music helps express the emotions people feel about their lives.

The Supremes attracted black and white audiences who rebelled against the previous generation by listening to "crossover" Motown soul music.

who wanted to make the changes. Dylan's words were adopted by many baby boomers as an expression of their discontent with what they saw as an unjust and valueless society. Three decades later feelings of alienation among the children of baby boomers found expression in the rebellious lyrics of grunge and rap.

Sometimes the rebellion in music expresses itself through lyrics; other times the music itself is rebellious, as in the syncopated beat that made early rock 'n' roll different. Often the music represents the results of social change. The same generation that embraced the rebellion in folk music associated with Dylan accepted the blues of Ray Charles, which led to soul music and to the Motown sound from Detroit. The Supremes, Aretha Franklin, Four Tops, Temptations, Stevie Wonder, and Smokey Robinson and the Miracles sold millions of records to young white people whose parents would have condemned the music as "race music" just a generation before. The times did change.

The rock 'n' roll musical rebellion of the 1950s affected Europe as well as the United States. Young British rock 'n' rollers listened to American music on Radio Luxembourg and cheered when Buddy Holly and the Everly Brothers toured Britain during the late 1950s. The Beatles brought British rock to the United States and became the best-selling musical group in history. Hard rock, pop, and psychedelic rock boomed during the 1960s. Bands such as the Grateful Dead and Jefferson Airplane carried the rebellious hippie culture of the San Francisco Bay area to the rest of the United States.

Rock splintered during the 1970s and 1980s as major recording companies increasingly commercialized popular music and artists reacted to that commercialization. Taking its name from the discotheque (dance club), disco music had a relatively short life but made a big splash on television and in the movies. Disco, sung by groups such as the Bee Gees, was based on a heavy beat that was easy to dance to. It lacked the soul of other types of rock and, like Tin Pan Alley music, became crassly commercial.

As a reaction to this commercialization, rock returned to its rhythm and blues and country roots during the mid-1970s led by Bruce Springsteen and the E Street Band. Springsteen initially set his socially critical lyrics to a hard-driving beat that was reinforced by the saxophone of Clarence Clemons. A VH-1 television documentary about him proclaimed that Springsteen killed disco. By the 1990s, Springsteen was singing personal songs that resembled the sounds found in the Great Depression music of Woody Guthrie.

During the late 1970s, punk rock also emerged as a reaction to the commercial success of rock. Groups such as the Sex Pistols and the Ramones played angry, nihilistic music that projected little hope for the future. A somewhat milder form of rebellion against traditional rock came in the form of new wave groups such as the Talking Heads.

A second form, heavy metal, evolved from the acid and hard rock of the late 1960s. Led Zeppelin and Queen began the movement, and other groups such as Van Halen, Judas Priest, and Def Leppard carried it through the 1980s. Heavy metal underwent a resurgence in 1994 with Megadeth, Pantera, and several other groups, but it never regained the popularity of the earlier period.

Grunge and hip-hop carried the punk tradition into the 1990s. Grunge, led by groups such as Nirvana, originated in the northwest United States and projects images of a painful, materialistic, and uncaring world created by the earlier rock generations. The success of grunge is a contradiction because of grunge musicians' disdain for materialism. One of grunge's leaders, Kurt Cobain of Nirvana, killed himself in April 1994, becoming, at least for some, a cult figure and martyr.

Although grunge appealed primarily to white, young people, hip-hop music emerged from the African American tradition. Hip-hop developed in the South Bronx in New York City during the late 1970s and formed the backdrop for 1980s rap music. DJs such as South Bronx's Lovebug Starski and Grandmaster Flash experimented with turntables as musical instruments, deftly stitching together pieces of different songs, which tended to have a heavy beat. Some DJs would rap while the music played. The first rap single, "Rapper's Delight," was released in 1979 by Sugarhill Gang. Rap and hip-hop have their roots in African call-and-response music and, more recently, the Watts poets in 1960s Los Angeles, Bo Diddley, and Cab Calloway.[9]

As rap moved into the 1990s, it diversified and attracted political attention. Some rappers, such as M.C. Hammer, had a softer sound, whereas gangsta' rap, with its emphasis on harsh ghetto conditions, has a violent edge. Gangsta' rap came under fire from Congress because of its emphasis on violence and its demeaning attitude toward women. Today, the beat and lyrical patterns of rap have become a strong element of the music industry. White, suburban young people listen to gangsta' rap, and some, such as Kid Rock, perform it.

Blending Musical Forms

A second defining feature of music in the United States is the *blending of forms*. Often this happened casually, as musicians adopted features of music they had heard. Sometimes, however, musicians have searched deliberately for exotic styles of music. Singer and songwriter Paul Simon has stayed popular, according to *Newsmakers 1992*, "precisely because he is continually 'rediscovering' musical styles—from folk-influenced rock ballads to rollicking gospel, blues, jazz, and reggae-fueled tunes to an eclectic brand of 'world music.'" However, Simon's blending of styles became controversial when he chose to cross cultural lines.

Introduced by a friend to the *township jive* songs of black South African musicians, Simon was so impressed that he traveled to Johannesburg and recorded several partial tracks with prominent South African musicians. These tracks became the basis for a highly acclaimed album, *Graceland*. Winner of the 1987 Grammy Award for best album, *Graceland* experimentally mixed the distinctive *mbaqanga* beat of the South African musicians with Simon's lyrics. It received little airtime but was a commercial and critical success. *Graceland* and its accompanying tour exposed enormous audiences to South African variations of **world music**. The album gave Western audiences the opportunity to hear such musicians as Ladysmith Black Mambazo, Hugh Masekela, Youssou N'Dour, and Miriam Makeba. Robert Browning, director of the World Music Institute, called *Graceland* a "milestone."

However, Simon's tour created intense political controversy, showing once again that music is not just music, but a form of communication and often a political statement. A number of groups attacked Simon for traveling to South Africa and recording there; these groups considered those activities a refutation of the cultural sanctions that the United Nations had in place against South Africa before **apartheid** was overthrown. In addition, when Simon performed in 1987 in Zimbabwe, two exiled South African musicians, Hugh Masekela and Miriam Makeba, joined Simon before a racially mixed crowd. Simon wrote a letter to the U.N. Special Committee against Apartheid explaining that he had refused to perform in South Africa and that he unequivocally supported the boycott.

By the time Simon performed in Johannesburg in 1992, the U.N. General Assembly had lifted the cultural boycott against South Africa. However, a radical black consciousness group, feeling that genuine political reform had not yet occurred in South Africa, joined with the Pan Africanist Congress and threatened violence, if needed, to stop Simon from performing. Nelson Mandela's African National Congress (ANC) and the predominantly black South African Musicians Alliance supported Simon's efforts to perform, which he did, despite a grenade attack on the office of the concert's promoters. In spite of the controversies caused by this tour, Simon refused to back down under outside pressures, even violent ones. As he once explained to *Esquire*, "By nature I'm a tenacious person."[10]

Jimi Hendrix, Simon's contemporary, created his own blend of music. Starting from his rhythm and blues roots, he combined a unique style of playing electric guitar and a lyric sense he copied from Bob Dylan to create the Jimi Hendrix Experience. He blasted onto the rock music scene at the 1967 Monterey Pop Festival, playing guitar by a new set of rules. More than thirty years after his death, his unique mix of music and words continues to sell a quarter-million CDs and cassettes each year.

Evidence of the blended nature of music can be found in the difficulty of separating music formats. Alternative rock, country, rap, and R&B often dominate play lists at Top 40 radio stations. Musical artists see no boundaries as they refine and develop their music.

Commercialization

The third trend in popular music is *commercialization,* which is a process that tends to move power from the artists to the recording executives and audiences. Popular music has two purposes. It can be an expression of an individual's vision and emotions, such as Bruce Springsteen's songs, or it can be a processed product aimed at a specific demographic group, such as the disco music of the Bee Gees. Although many people regard music that incorporates an individual's vision as more sincere than processed music, for recording companies, the music of individuals is risky. It is difficult to predict just whose music will have immediate popularity and whose will gain stature over the long term. To reduce risk and retain power, recording companies often look for the short-term profits of processed music. This was the approach of Tin Pan Alley, and it has been the approach of many recording companies since then.

crossover artist: A top-selling musical artist in more than one music segment. Country and rhythm and blues often cross over with Top 40 music.

Other Forms of Popular Music

Rock has come to dominate the popular music scene in the United States, but that domination is far from complete. Country in its many forms is next in popularity to rock. Traditional country music, such as that played at the Grand Ole Opry during the 1940s and 1950s, flourished until the mid-1970s, when Willie Nelson, a songwriter who had enjoyed limited success as a singer in Nashville, led a revisionist movement. His simple-sounding lyrics in songs such as "Crazy" evoked powerful emotions and memories of Hank Williams's songs of the 1940s and 1950s. Nelson, Waylon Jennings, Jerry Jeff Walker, and Kris Kristofferson incorporated rock, western swing, and blues in their songs and helped to reshape country music.

Traditional country music experienced a revival during the 1990s with artists such as Garth Brooks, Reba McEntire, and LeAnn Rimes. Brooks ranks second only to the Beatles in career record sales. In 1999, Shania Twain and the Dixie Chicks emerged as successful country artists and **crossover artists.** More recently, artists such as Toby Keith, Faith Hill, Deana Carter, and Lucinda Williams demonstrate the wide range of music that falls under the umbrella of country.

Jazz, too, continues to change. The bop of the 1940s and 1950s gave way to three types of jazz in the 1950s and 1960s: cool, hard bop, and free jazz. Cool jazz had an intellectual quality, with sophisticated arrangements. Hard bop combined bop jazz with old jazz forms from New Orleans. Free jazz dropped the rhythm and tune of jazz and explored personal, impromptu music.[11] Since the 1960s, jazz also has incorporated rock elements. This fusion music continues today as jazz begins to merge with hip-hop and rap music.

In 1997, jazz began to gain recognition as a more serious musical form. The Pulitzer Prize board awarded Wynton Marsalis a Pulitzer Prize for *Blood on the Field*. Marsalis uses music from classical traditions, but his music dif-

In the 1990s, the jazz musical form continues to evolve as Wynton Marsalis combines elements of classical music with jazz improvisation.

fers from classical forms because of his use of improvisation, which is traditional with jazz. Marsalis is the first jazz musician to win the award, and music writers have speculated that this recognition will encourage further recognition for jazz.

As the population of Latino Americans and Hispanic Americans grew, Latin-based music became a fast-growing segment of music during the late 1990s, reaching almost 5 percent of all recording sales by 1999.[12] In May 1999, Ricky Martin had the number one album and single in the United States.

In 2002, newspapers declared a new Latino music, *nuevo latino*, which drew inspiration from a wide range of music. As journalist Brendan Kelly wrote, "it's the product of a new generation of Latin musicians who grew up listening to the Ramones alongside calypso king Mighty Sparrow, and took their Bob Marley with a little Celia Cruz on the side."[13] Notable artists in the movement include Manu Chao, P18, Sergent Garcia, and Los De Abajo.

Manu Chao, one of the stars of nuevo latino music, performs at the Roskilde music festival in Denmark.

Elite Music

Music for elite audiences, often referred to as classical music, has always had difficulty acquiring popular support and financing in the United States. This held true in the 1990s, but classical music still survives as a segment of the music and recording industry. In the 1990s, the sales of classical music recordings and the number of classical music radio stations continued to decline. The percentage of all recording sales that were classical totaled 2.7 percent in 2000 and 3.2 percent in 2001.[14]

Declining support from the National Endowment for the Arts, labor disputes among orchestras, an aging of the audiences, and the closing of some prominent civic orchestras in cities such as Sacramento and San Diego indicate difficult times ahead for elite music.[15] However, attendance at recitals by well-known artists increased and opera attendance grew. The *Chicago Tribune* music critic John von Rhein offered a prescription for elite music artists and businesspeople in 1997:

> We must accept the fact that serious music is in a state of change, and change can be unpleasant, even downright brutal, sometimes. The days of classical music preaching to the already-converted elite, and doing so in the same old manner, are fast disappearing. All aspects of the music business will need to reinvent themselves, to a degree, if they want to be useful and enriching to more than a privileged elite of the most educated citizens.
>
> In short, classical musicians and presenters must get out of their ivory towers and learn to adapt better to the social, economic and cultural shifts of the world in which it exists. Their challenge will be to devise ever more creative tactics to attract new consumers while keeping the integrity of the music foremost.[16]

THE RECORDING INDUSTRY

The technological and economic processes for creating and delivering music come together in the recording industry. A small portion of the industry involves producing nonmusic recordings, such as books on tape and motivational recordings. However, for the most part the recording industry and music continue the symbiotic relationship that has existed since the first records were pressed. Developing computer technology will not change the process of recording music, but computers will drastically change the system of delivering music to consumers.

The precursor to recording technology was the printing press. During the 1880s, entrepreneurs cranked out sheet music to sell to budding pianists and singers. Some songs sold more than a million copies, and in 1910 two billion copies of sheet music were sold.

The phonograph hit the sheet music industry hard. By 1877, Edison had developed a machine that could record on a tinfoil cylinder, but it was not until the 1890s that Emile Berliner developed a way to engrave a zinc disk and mass produce copies of records. He joined forces with Columbia Phonograph, a company that developed a method of creating disks with wax in the early 1900s. The modern recording industry was born.

The famous opera singer Enrico Caruso became the first recording star to earn big royalties in the industry. He began recording records in 1901 and accumulated more than $2 million in royalties between 1904 and his death in 1921.

The recording industry boomed between 1910 and 1920. Industry sales reached $158 million in 1919, but the banking depression killed the boom. The Great Depression of the 1930s also caused low record sales. After World War I, radio promised to revive the industry, but the worldwide depression of the 1930s stunted its growth. In 1927, 104 million records were sold; in 1932 the figure dropped to 6 million. The economic recovery and improving technology during the 1930s and 1940s brought the recording industry back to prosperity.

Phonographs and Records

After World War II, the recording industry experienced a period of rapidly improving technology. Within a thirty-year period, companies moved from the 78 rpm record to 33⅓ rpm LPs (long-playing records) and 45s—the inexpensive "singles" that music-loving young people collected. Like many industries, the recording industry encountered *competing technologies*. The first records played at 78 revolutions per minute (rpm), and we get the term *album* from those days, when a long work or collection of songs consisted of several 78 rpm records packaged in a cardboard case that resembled a photo album. In 1947, Columbia developed the long-playing record that, at 33⅓ rpm, could play for longer than an hour. The next year RCA introduced the 45 rpm record, which played for only a few minutes, about as long as the old 78 rpm records. The 45 had one song per side and required an adapter to play on most record players, but RCA wanted to recoup its investment. The company pushed ahead in the battle of the speeds.

> **key concept**
>
> **Competing Technologies** The 1950s saw an interruption in the steady advance (from zinc to wax to shellac to plastic disks) that major recording companies had developed in marketable audio technology. When an explosion of new technology confused buyers with three competing turntable speeds and two record disk sizes, the major recording companies decided on a standard (33⅓ rpm) disk to regain the market. The smaller (45 rpm) record remained as a secondary format until the 1980s.

With so many types of records, the public was confused, and sales dropped dramatically until 1950. Columbia and RCA called a truce, and machines were manufactured that could play both 45s and LPs. The 78s disappeared almost immediately, and the 45s slowly gave way to the LPs, which could hold many more songs, as the most popular record format.

Audiotape and Digital Technology

Early radio popularized listening to performed music, and inventors searched for better ways to preserve musical performances. Initial efforts to record on wire were scratchy and unreliable. During World War II, the Germans developed magnetic tape-recording technology. Some Americans smuggled those machines to the United States, and U.S. engineers improved on them. In 1946, Bing Crosby—who wanted to have more time for his golf game—was the first to tape-record his radio show, proving that a star could be successful without performing live.

During the late 1940s, the Minnesota Mining & Manufacturing Company (3M) perfected plastic recording tape, and Ampex developed reliable reel-to-reel tape recorders. However, the recorders and tape players remained expensive and cumbersome. In the 1970s, reel-to-reel recorders gave way to portable cassette players for personal use, and their popularity skyrocketed after Sony introduced the Walkman in 1979. Portability, as well as quality, was now a characteristic of tape machines.

Despite the increased use of magnetic tape, entrepreneurs continued to improve record quality as well. High fidelity, a side benefit of wartime English sonar technology, could pick up a wider range of tones; it was followed by stereo records, which were introduced in 1958.

Records, cassette tapes, and **8-track tapes** dominated the market during the 1970s, but in the mid-1980s they lost ground quickly to the compact disc with its almost flawless reproduction quality. Sales of CDs soared from $17.2 million in 1983 to $930 million in 1986. As a result, the major companies closed their record plants; most new vinyl records now being produced are novelties. Currently, CDs are absorbing the market for prerecorded cassettes, which are found in shrinking numbers in most stores.

During the 1970s, the recording industry viewed the development of magnetic tape in cassettes skeptically. The industry feared that the simplicity and portability of tape dubbing would increase album pirating—and they did. Estimates of losses from pirating run from $350 million to $1.5 billion a year. The industry's concern led to several hearings before Congress. The Sound Recording Act of 1971 made copying for one's own use legal, and in 1984 the Supreme Court ruled in favor of home recording in the Betamax case. It seemed that the fears had subsided until 1985 when the Japanese introduced digital audio tape (DAT). The fear reemerged because DAT can make perfect copies from CDs and would become a better way of pirating.

Congress resolved the DAT controversy with the Audio Home Recording Act of 1992. DAT recorders sold to consumers are equipped with a microchip that limits the owner to one digital recording of a prerecorded tape. In addition, the law levies a tax on DAT recorders and blank cassettes, which is paid to recording artists for lost royalties. This solution seems excessive; DAT never became popular as a consumer recording technology, and other digital recording technologies have developed.

In 1992, Sony developed the 3½-inch MiniDisc (MD) as an alternative to CDs. It is durable and easy to carry, but MD players will not play larger CDs. Available as players and recorders, the MD format made some progress as a competitor for CDs during 1998 with a growth spurt in Europe. Sony sold its five millionth MD recorder that year, and recording company EMI began producing MD recordings. Until then, Sony was the only major recording company to release MiniDisc recordings.

Despite the progress made by MDs, CDs should remain popular, at least partly because an agreement among electronics firms in 1995 created the enhanced CD, which is a standardized compact disc that works in audio players and in computer CD-ROM drives. Enhanced CDs can contain video and other multimedia content, allowing CD-ROM users to do more than simply listen to the music.

The development of MP3 (MPEG Layer 3) technology during the late 1990s changed music forever for three reasons. First, it combined production and distribution into one step. By downloading music onto a PC, listeners can transfer the digitized file to an MP3 player or burn the music onto a CD. No longer must recorded CDs be shipped by truck and train to music stores and then carried home. Second, without needing to ship CDs and tapes, one of the two main functions of recording companies—distribution and promotion—is becoming increasingly inexpensive. This allows more people to produce and distribute music without having to go through one of the big five corporations.

Finally, music online is easily pirated by sending files from one computer to another. As a result, companies and artists are unable to collect royalties from people copying their music. In 2002 more than 17 percent of all adults who use the Internet had downloaded music, and some experts attribute the 10 percent decline in number of albums sold from 2000 to 2001 to music piracy.[17]

8-track tape: A plastic cartridge that holds a continuous recording tape. Invented primarily for automobile play during the 1960s, its eight tracks allowed high-quality stereo reproduction in an easy-to-handle cartridge.

TODAY'S MARKET STRUCTURE

By media industry standards, the recording industry is small but growing steadily. Between 1984 and 1998, its revenues more than tripled, from $4.4 billion to $13.7 billion, which is about 5 percent of all money spent on media.[18] But it is an important industry, and the figures are misleading because they ignore the need for music and its impact on other media industries such as radio, television, and movies.

Of the three media goals mentioned earlier in the book (entertainment, information, and persuasion), the primary one in the recording industry is entertainment. Although music often can aim to inform and persuade, as occurred with the folk songs of the Great Depression, the protest music of the 1960s, and rap of the 1980s, the recording industry's commercial nature causes most recorded music to aim at entertaining listeners.

The world recording industry is dominated by five *major recording companies,* though independent companies fill an important niche that often is more innovative than the territory dominated by the majors. A proposed merger

media convergence

Who Will Control the Music and Make a Profit?

The recording industry has a long history of technologies battling for dominance. In the past, the players have been the giant recording companies and the consumers. But now the sharing of music through the Internet has brought the musicians into the fray.

Because 97 percent of all recordings fail to make money from the sale of albums after costs are deducted, musicians do not necessarily side with the record companies in the downloading controversy. These musicians make money from merchandise and tours. They can profit from the Internet because it eliminates the business functions—distribution and promotion—that give the major labels power. CDs have to be produced, shipped, and sold in stores. That gives businesses physical control. With the Web, each computer becomes the equivalent of a factory and tractor-trailer. Any musician can produce,

ship, and sell over the Internet. The Artist Formerly Known as Prince, for example, has been selling music online since the mid-1990s.

Downloading music from the Web also changes promotion. Radio and MTV may lose some of their influence in selling records as listeners sample music online to decide whether they want to invest their money in the CD. Increasingly, musicians will create web sites to promote their tours and sell CDs directly.

These changes raise interesting scenarios for the future of music. Observers have suggested the following:

• Listeners will have access to a greater variety of music because artists can make a living without a major label contract.
• Musicians will make a larger percentage of their income from tours as CD sales decrease,

and ticket prices will probably increase.
• The number of major recording companies will shrink as some merge as a result of shrinking CD sales.
• The majors that survive will sell more of their music online and will concentrate even more on highly popular acts and Top 40 recordings.

Of course, which, if any, of these scenarios will happen depends on what happens in the courts and in the marketplace. But convergence has forever changed the music industry.

Sources: Greg Kot, "You Say You Want a Revolution," *Chicago Tribune* (February 24, 2002): 7:1, 6–8; Jube Shiver Jr., "Hollywood Lobbies for Stricter Copyright Rules," *Chicago Tribune* (April 22, 2002): 1, 5; Joshua Klein, "Artists Taking Matters into Their Hands," *Chicago Tribune* (June 2, 2002): 9.

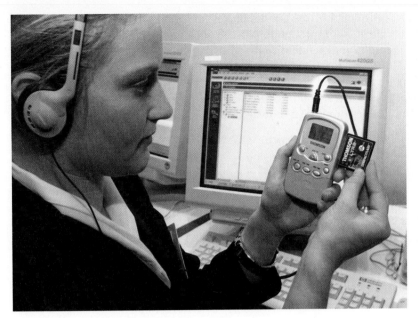

A recordable CD and an MP3 music player are all you need to compile your own collection of music for free. Artists and recording companies are debating how much access will infringe on their copyrights and affect their royalties.

of EMI with Time Warner in 2000 would have reduced the number of major recording companies to four. However, European Union regulators' concerns caused the companies to abandon their plans. The five major companies (Warner Music Group, Sony Music, BMG, EMI, and Universal Music Group) produce and manufacture about 85 percent of the cassettes and CDs in the world.[19] Reports that the recording industry sold about 100 million fewer CDs and cassettes in 2002 than in 2000 has stimulated speculation that mergers could reduce the number of majors in the near future. *Independents,* often termed *indies,* have taken risks when the majors were reluctant to do so. Rock 'n' roll finally hit the charts because indies produced records when the majors thought rock 'n' roll was a dangerous fad. Even today, independents often can offer exposure to regional groups that otherwise would be ignored. For example, grunge might well have remained a local fad if Subpop Records had not offered recording contracts to Soundgarden, Nirvana, and other Seattle bands.

Because of declining production costs, the future is promising for indies. Artists can start their own recording companies through self-recording. In fact, the cost of studio production has been cut in half during the past twenty-five years. A musician can record in a studio with just a guitar for as little as $500. Sophisticated computer software allows musicians to record and burn CDs at a very low cost, and self-recording CDs can be a step in the rise to national prominence. For example, the Dixie Chicks sold their own recordings in Texas long before they became a crossover success throughout the United States.[20]

The recording industry is global, and although worldwide data are elusive, estimates suggest that five recording companies owned by U.S., British, and Japanese corporations control most of the world's recorded music. The industry's concentration in these countries reflects the concentration of buyers. The United States, Japan, Britain, Germany, and France accounted for 68 percent of recorded music sold during the early 1990s.

Market concentration shows no sign of abatement as large corporations continue to acquire other large corporations. Sizable companies have favorable production and distribution economies that allow them to offer lower prices per unit than independents. This ability, along with solid financial backing that allows large companies to open new markets and finance new ventures, gives them a strong edge in the market. Currently, the majors are actively using their financial resources to invest in formerly Communist-dominated countries that promise new and potentially lucrative markets.

The market edge held by the majors makes it more difficult for independents to operate. Nevertheless, lower production costs from less expensive technology resulted in a slight increase in independent shares of the recording market during the mid-1990s. In 2002 in Chicago, for instance, more than thirty independent labels recorded music ranging from jazz and blues to punk rock and country. The long-term success of indies depends on their ability to find creative new musicians and to push the acceptable boundaries of musical innovation.

AUDIENCE DEMAND IN RECORDING MARKETS

People demand music for entertainment and for affirmation of cultural values. Music can distract people from boring or difficult tasks. It also plays important *social roles,* fostering rebellion, blending forms to make new cultural statements, and promoting certain cultural norms through commercialization. It contributes to ceremonies and rituals that define social groups. National anthems praise and affirm the glory of a country. Weddings, funerals, graduations, and other life passages incorporate music as a basic element. Music gives generations of people an identity because the shared values expressed in music create feelings of commitment and membership and help to pass on the social heritage.

Music conveys information while it entertains. In 1993, Bruce Springsteen's theme to the movie *Philadelphia* expressed the isolation from society that people with AIDS often feel. As information, music's strength is its ability to combine the rational and the emotional through lyrics, melody, and beat.

Society demands formal music, such as classical, as well as the many styles of popular and religious music. A current form of demand that we might label *integrated* involves combinations of media. Such integration can be seen in the incorporation of music into movies, television programming, and advertisements.

Changes in musical taste can be sudden and dramatic. The rapid growth in the demand for rock 'n' roll during the 1950s caught many music companies off guard. But a decade later, the music system had adjusted. Between 1988 and 1992, the percentage of money spent on recorded music that was spent on rock music dropped

The demand for music often results in a blending of styles to make new cultural statements. Zydeco music from Louisiana originated as a symbol of cultural survival for the Acadian French but now has a far wider appeal.

from 47.5 percent to 33.2 percent. The growth in country music offset this decline, as the percentage spent on country grew from 6.8 percent to 16.5 percent.

In the nine years following this change, country saw its share decline to 10.5 percent of sales, as rock continued to decline to 24.4 percent. Rap saw a growth between 1992 and 2001 from 8.6 percent to 11.4 percent of sales. Religious recordings' percentage of all recording sales more than doubled, from 2.8 percent in 1992 to 6.7 percent in 2001.

These dramatic changes in demand for music often reflect changes in the music itself. The initial increase in the demand for country music resulted as country adopted a rock beat and new superstars emerged. Music preferences also occur with societal changes. The increase in religious music sales represents changes in the listening habits of older consumers.

SUPPLYING THE AUDIENCE'S DEMAND

The recording industry supplies demand for music in a number of ways. Recordings can be supplied on a variety of disk, tape, and vinyl forms. However, all recording forms start with the recording process, and all forms require financing, distribution, and promotion. Some companies handle all of these processes; other companies may be involved in only one or two. Regardless of ownership structure, the recording process remains the same.

The Recording Process

Musicians create music, but creating music does not guarantee that it will be heard beyond those listening to the music live. It must be recorded. Recording as a technical process can be divided into two types: multitrack and direct recordings. *Multitrack recording* involves recording the various elements of the music (singer, rhythm, and lead instruments) at different times and combining them through an electronic mixing process. Natalie Cole's CD *Unforgettable* is an example of multitrack recording. This popular CD blends the voices of Natalie and her deceased father singing "Mona Lisa" and other songs made famous by Nat King Cole. Multitrack recording also is routinely used to record several layers of instrumental and vocal tracks. In fact, multitrack recording is more common than single-track recording.

In *direct recording*, all the parts are recorded together at the same time. The direct process involves six steps:[21]

1. *Session preplanning:* This includes getting the studio technology ready, preparing music for musicians, and discussing how the session will be run with the musicians in charge.
2. *Creating the sound quality of the recording:* A dress rehearsal is conducted, and factors affecting sound quality are adjusted. A tape of the rehearsal is made.
3. *Consultation with musicians:* The person in charge of recording meets with the musicians, and they review the rehearsal tape to determine whether any changes in sound quality are needed.
4. *Recording session:* The music is recorded in sections. Each section will have more than one **take.** The takes continue until at least two usable takes are recorded. Technicians work on the quality of elements of the recording during this process.
5. *Selection of takes:* The person in charge of recording and the musicians listen to the takes to select the best one for a master recording.
6. *Editing to compile master tape:* Any changes that were decided on during the take selection are made at this time, and a final master tape of the recording is made for reproduction.

take: One effort to record a piece of music.

A new era in the recording process began when the popular group the Beatles produced the breakthrough album *Sgt. Pepper's Lonely Hearts Club Band*. It featured layered sounds using high-tech blending techniques.

Multitrack recording is similar, except that the various tracks are recorded at different times and must be mixed. Mixing can be complicated and involves the input of the recording manager and the creative artist.

The amount of time involved in the *recording process* varies greatly with the type of recording and the artist involved. The Beatles' *Sgt. Pepper's Lonely Hearts Club Band* album required more than seven hundred hours in the recording studio because of the amount of overdubbing and multitrack recording used.[22] The result was an album that changed rock 'n' roll.

Financing

Financing in the recording industry takes many forms. People buy CDs and tapes, which is a direct source of income. Because recording production, distribution, and promotion are expensive, most recording titles that are released do not make a profit. So profit potential of blockbuster recordings is important.

A secondary source of *revenue comes from licensing* existing music. Someone who uses a copyrighted piece of music must pay the copyright holder. Copyright owners receive revenue, known as royalties, under three conditions. Under *performing rights,* the copyright holder is paid every time a song is performed. *Mechanical rights* ensure that the copyright holder is paid when the song is recorded. *Public performance rights* require that the copyright holder be paid when an actual recording is played commercially.[23]

Rights are overseen by music licensing organizations such as the American Society of Composers, Authors, and Publishers (ASCAP) and Broadcast Music Incorporated (BMI) in the United States, the Performing Rights Society (PRS) in England, Gesellschaft für Musikalische Aufführungs (GEMA) in Germany, and the Société des Auteurs, Compositeurs et Éditeurs de Musique (SACEM) in France. The organizations act as agents for the publishers and composers of music whom they represent. The organizations collect fees and distribute money on the basis of formulas that incorporate several factors, such as the number of performances of a particular song and the writer's prestige and seniority.

Distribution

The two keys to a hit recording are *recording promotion and distribution*—getting airplay on radio and television and obtaining adequate distribution of copies. Play time involves promotion, which is the attention-grabbing side of the industry. Distribution tends to be rather mundane in comparison, but it is no less important.

Distribution can take several forms. Recordings are sold in record stores such as CD Warehouse; in department and discount stores such as Kmart; by mail clubs such as Columbia House; and over television, as in the ads for a singer's greatest hits or songs of a certain era. The last two forms often involve direct selling, which means that the production company handles the distribution without another company between it and the buyers. The last two forms involve at least one intermediate company.

Since the early 1970s, the five major recording companies have expanded their distribution branches. The branches sell directly to record stores and to rack jobbers. *Rack jobbers* handle sales of recordings in department and discount stores. They stock the CD and tape racks and split the sales money with the store. Other independent distributors also serve the industry by distributing independently produced recordings and even some recordings from major companies.

In the competition for distribution, the majors have three advantages. They can provide many copies of hit recordings; they can afford expensive national promotions; and they have strong financial backing.

Throughout the twentieth century, music was delivered to people either by radio or through some recording technology that uses a physical object. The move to digital technology at the end of the century is reshaping how people receive music. Satellite radio makes music available on dozens of channels no matter where the radio receiver is located. Fiber-optic cable provides dozens and potentially hundreds of music channels. But the most influential form of distribution has become the personal computer.

The rise of MP3 technology as a system for trading and selling music continues to reshape the industry. Promoted in the beginning primarily through Napster, the exchanging of music files became a threat to the revenue of the music industry. Napster allowed people to exchange copyrighted and noncopyrighted music through the Internet. The five majors responded to Napster with lawsuits for copyright violations. In 2001, a federal judge ruled that Napster had to filter music that was not in the public domain. As a result, Napster shut down in summer 2001 in hopes of returning as a company that sold music online. However, Napster declared bankruptcy when it was unable to find financial backing for the change. Roxio Inc. bought the Napster name, web domain, and technology in November 2002 for $5.3 million.

The big five music corporations have moved slowly into online distribution, but by 2002, Sony and Universal had invested in Playpress.com, and AOL Time Warner, BMG, and EMI had invested in Musicnet.com. The two sites allow listeners to pay a monthly fee and download music that can be played only on a PC with the provided player. All five majors sell their music through both sites, and they also have licensed independent sites, such as Rhapsody and FullAudio, to sell their music.

Promotion

Sales of records or sheet music have always depended on making the largest number of people aware of the music's existence. When sheet music dominated the industry, vaudeville performers increased sales of a particular song by performing it. As radio attracted more listeners, radio airplay became essential to a record's reaching the charts. Today, performance tours supporting a new album and exposure on television, such as on a music video channel, are crucial in promoting recordings. Reaching and staying at the top of the national pop charts requires play time on MTV's *Total Request Live* and dozens of live performances throughout the United States and abroad. Despite the importance of video music promotion, the number of TV video music channels is limited and the time they spend showing music videos declined during the 1990s. So radio remains the most frequently used promotion tool. If a recording can get extensive airplay on radio stations, it has a chance of making the top-selling recordings list. The station format and the location are crucial considerations in promoting recordings on radio. Contemporary hit radio formats that run recordings from the Top 40 chart provide the best exposure. However, recording companies sometimes select stations with other formats for promotions because those stations better fit the recording. Stations in markets with a **cumulative weekly audience** of more than one million are vital for promotion. These markets, such as New York, Los Angeles, and Chicago, generate a high percentage of recording sales. Exposure in these markets can make or break a recording.

Promotion involves sending traditional **press releases** and **media kits** to reviewers and radio stations. However, the key link in recording promotions is the independent promoter, sometimes called a "plugger." Independent promoters are hired by recording companies to help increase record sales. They use a variety of techniques to promote recordings, including providing information to media about the artists and the recording, arranging personal appearances by artists, and helping with tours that promote new recordings. The crucial role of the independent promoter is getting a recording played on the radio. During the late 1980s, promoters became very powerful in either getting or stopping airplay. Without independent promoters, it is difficult for a recording to become a hit.

key concept

Payola in Music Promotion Paying DJs or program producers to play specific songs on a radio station or video channel to enhance the song's popularity. Investigated by Congress since the 1950s, the conspiracy between the recording and broadcasting industries is probably impossible to uproot, especially as combined ownership affects more sectors of the media and recording industries.

cumulative weekly audience: The total number of people who listen to radio during a given week in a given market.

press release: An announcement of some event, such as a recording release, sent to various news media outlets.

media kit: A collection of information about a particular event or person, such as a recording release. The kit can include text, photographs, audiotapes, and even computer discs and CD-ROMs.

Promotion's Influence on Music ◆ Because promotion significantly affects the sales of music, it also is a prime source of corruption. A recurring problem in the record industry has been the phenomenon of *payola,* or paying a programmer or disc jockey to play a specific song. In the 1950s, the situation became so critical that Congress held hearings that revealed an industry in which payola ruled. For example, 335 disc jockeys reportedly received $263,245 in "consultant" fees.[24] Stations offered deals that were thinly disguised payola plans. One station in Los Angeles offered a "test record plan," which cost $225 a week for eight plays a day, and a New York station had a deal of six plays a day for six weeks for $600.[25] As a result of the congressional hearings, the Federal Communications Act of 1934 was amended in 1960 to outlaw payola. Punishment is one year in jail with a maximum $10,000 fine. However, these hearings concentrated only on rock 'n' roll music—a controversial genre in the 1950s—and ignored payola in other areas of popular music. Furthermore, payola is difficult to monitor. Although it has been outlawed, independent promoters are still known to deliver money, gifts, or more tangible services to those in positions to get music on the radio.[26]

A legal variation of payola has developed on the Internet. The digital music site MP3.com started auctioning prime placement of recording links on their main music page or on one of the genre pages. The managers of MP3 call it advertising, but there is concern because other artists receive page placement based on the popularity of their recording.[27] Some critics fear the consumer will be confused about why particular recordings are receiving prominent placement.

Promotion and Controversy ◆ Controversy over rock music is as old as the music itself. In the 1950s, instead of promoting African American artists, the recording

industry used white performers such as Elvis Presley, who either recorded R&B songs or adapted African American sounds to country-and-western music. Presley was controversial to many white parents because he had an African American sound and because he wiggled his hips as he sang. The controversy seemed only to sell more records as young people delighted in the disapproval of their parents.

Although the numerous controversies that have arisen during the years have rarely resulted in successful legal attempts to censor music, society controls its music in the commercial marketplace. The majority of promoters and record companies are reluctant to promote music that offends people and that raises the specter of government intervention into radio content. During the early 1990s, for example, gangsta' rap faced promotion problems because of its emphasis on violence and misogyny. Concerns over the lyrics led to congressional hearings in 1994. Controversial music can gain some attention through independent companies, which foster cutting-edge music. Nevertheless, success usually requires the involvement of the majors, which often means that a group will have to alter its message and its tune.

Influence of promotion was demonstrated in the early 1960s, when an appearance on the *Ed Sullivan Show* could enhance a singer's success. Elvis Presley and the Beatles made their first U.S. television appearances there. However, Bob Dylan refused to appear when CBS wanted to censor his politically oriented songs. The Rolling Stones wanted the exposure and saw no problem in altering lyrics. They changed their lyrics from "let's spend the night together" to "let's spend some time together." Both Dylan and the Rolling Stones continue to have long and prosperous music careers.

Fortunately, the power of promotion to stifle creativity has a limit. Artists who demonstrate star power early in their careers will enjoy more musical freedom. Artists such as the Beatles have survived musical controversies because the recording companies sold records despite or because of the controversies. During the last half of the twentieth century, some musical groups achieved a measure of independence, but no artist ever escaped all the influences of the promotion machine.

Video: A Powerful Promotional Tool ✦ On August 1, 1981, MTV began broadcasting. Within ten years, MTV reached more than 204 million homes in forty-one countries around the world. MTV and other music channels provide another source of income for musicians and recording companies: selling music videos. However, videos are far more important as a promotion tool than as a revenue source. A well-conceived and well-executed video can boost recording sales considerably.

Video promotion is a creative art. Some videos are constructed with story lines that enhance the music; others contain appealing abstract images that may be unrelated to the specific lyrics. Videos have become so important that some top stars can spend more than $1 million on a video. The nature of MTV and other music networks began to change during the 1990s. Ratings declined during the early 1990s, and the networks began to increase nonmusic programming to attract viewers. MTV's *Beavis and Butthead* developed an instant cult following. Currently, MTV shows a variety of nonmusic programs, including *Real World, Cribs,* and the *Osbournes.* VH-1 became the pop music history channel with shows such as *Where Are They Now?* and *Behind the Music.* The resulting increase in viewers has limited the time available for playing music videos but made the remaining video time more important for record sales.

Television video is not the only form of video promotion. Many of today's performers are making movies, and some actors are recording. Eminem's first movie, *8 Mile,* sold more than $71 million in tickets during its first eight days. Jennifer Lopez has established herself as a star in both movies and the music industry. Success in one entertainment field has become a way to promote success in another.

MTV: Making Money and Influencing Culture around the World

Music Television (MTV) changed the face of television in 1981 when it initiated the first twenty-four-hour music channel. The mission was simple: to capture cable viewers between the ages of twelve and thirty-five by adding video to music. The result was a form of television that spread throughout the world and continues to make money and to influence world culture.

The idea of combining video and music existed long before MTV. Rock 'n' roll joined television early with dance programs such as Dick Clark's *American Bandstand.* Later, documentaries about musicians combined video and music. Frank Zappa's 1971 movie *200 Motels* visually represented his surreal music. Short videos were used to promote music. However, MTV changed the music industry by widely distributing promotional videos through satellite and cable transmission.

Within six years, MTV began creating channels to provide music to the world outside the United States. MTV, now owned by Viacom, provides music television to

Australia, Europe, Asia, and Latin America. Dozens of competing music satellite networks are available around the world.

Initially, MTV's ratings rose quickly. In 1986, however, they started to fall, and the network added nonmusic programming. The strategy worked. Even though MTV only averages about a million households at any given time, some programs, such as *Real World,* can double or triple the ratings. As a result, MTV has become the most profitable cable network and ratings were growing in the early 2000s. The greatest growth in profits came from MTV's international business.

The movement toward more nonmusic programming did not reduce MTV's influence over recording sales. *Total Request Live* has become the equivalent of the 1960s *American Bandstand* in its influence. Kid Rock, for example, commented on *TRL* to the *Los Angeles Times:* "It was like boom, overnight. Man, you hit that 'TRL,' that's the biggest thing going in music. Video is more powerful than radio these days, and

who would have thought that we would ever reach that point?"

MTV exerts this type of power around the world. It has increased the flexibility of programming for various countries and cultures. This allows MTV to take advantage of music trends in the United States and other parts of the world.

Some music observers criticize the impact of video promotion, arguing that splashy, high-tech videos emphasize style over substance and that videos have increased the special effects on concert tours. This, they contend, downplays the music in favor of visuals.

Sources: Robert M. Ogles, "Music Television (MTV)," in *The Cable Networks Handbook,* Robert Picard, ed. (Riverside, CA: Carpelan, 1993), pp. 137–142; John Lannert, "Latin Notes: MTV Acts Locally; NYC Fetes Salsa," *Billboard* (September 4, 1999), via Lexis-Nexis; and Geoff Boucher, "The Listeners Are Watching: After a Lull, Music Videos Are Bigger Than Ever to a Generation That Insists on Seeing the Hits Before Buying Them," *The Los Angeles Times* (September 4, 1999): F1.

TRENDS

Threats to the Recording Industry

The late 1990s and early 2000s have not been kind to the music and recording industry. Several trends merged to raise issues about the long-run survival of the industry as currently structured. The headline on a front-page story in the June 5, 2002, edition of *USA Today* read, "Any Way You Spin It, the Music Biz Is in Trouble."[28] The story listed four trends that continue to threaten the industry: piracy, the decline of radio as a promotional tool, the high cost of CDs, and the decline of original and diverse popular music. The article said that these four trends account for the first decline in album sales since 1991. The number of albums sold dropped by 2.8 percent between 2000 and 2001, and the trend continued into the first quarter of 2002.

The impact of downloading music from the Web is well documented, and many of today's young people don't see downloading as wrong. Some observers blame part of this attitude on the rising cost of CDs. The average new CD in 2002 cost $18.98, but that is only a slight increase from a decade earlier when inflation is considered.

Other critics say the problems stem from the tendency of corporations to limit popular music releases to sound-alike groups. They say this limits diversity in an effort to attract young listeners to a few albums that will sell millions of copies. Musicians who develop a following slowly, such as R.E.M., U2, and Bruce Springsteen, will find recording contracts more difficult to acquire in the future.

As the radio industry has become more concentrated, some critics argue that the programming has become more alike and that the morning drive-time programs play little music any more. Play time is reserved for the highly promoted, select few recordings. The result is that many albums do not get the promotion they once received over radio.

The *USA Today* article missed one trend that may be even more threatening to the big five's survival. The recording artists are revolting against the old system. Some artists, such as Gillian Welch and Aimee Mann, have started their own labels and promote them over the Internet. These labels even sell the CDs online.[29]

Other artists have taken a different approach by raising money to support the Recording Artists Coalition. The coalition is lobbying to pass state laws that would limit the length of contracts with musical artists to seven years. A bill has already been introduced into the California legislature. Currently, recording companies often sign artists to long-term contracts that pay the artists little after expenses are deducted. If contracts are limited, a popular artist could switch labels and receive a better deal. This would lower the profit margins of publicly owned record corporations and affect the very nature of the industry. Just how all of these trends will reshape the recording industry remains unclear, but few doubt that changes will occur.

The Commercialization and Globalization of Rap

Rap music developed from its roots in African American and Jamaican music during the 1970s. It started as a protest against the treatment of African Americans and as a reflection of the hip-hop culture that spawned it. Since that time, it has evolved into a variety of forms: from the old school rap recordings of The Sugarhill Gang to the gangsta' rap of Tupac Shakur, Notorious B.I.G., and Snoop Doggy Dog, from the playa' rap of Run D.M.C. and M.C. Hammer to the message rap of KRS-One.[30] What started as a male-dominated music form has evolved into an equal opportunity art form with the success of Queen Latifah, Lauryn Hill, and Foxy Brown.

Although Run D.M.C. and M. C. Hammer popularized rap, it was the success of white rappers that made the music even more commercially acceptable. Vanilla Ice experienced brief notoriety and was followed by the Beastie Boys. These musicians were criticized either for imitating or making fun of African American rappers.[31] The more recent emergence of white rappers such as Kid Rock and Eminem who rap about their own lives has created an even greater demand among white teenagers. In a 1999 article, *Time* magazine reported that whites bought 70 percent of the rap albums.[32] Rap has not remained just an American music form. It can be found throughout the world as it mutates into dozens of forms. Rappers rap in France, Italy, Germany, Japan, Korea, New Zealand, and dozens of other countries. In the book *Global Noise: Rap and Hip Hop outside the USA,* Tony Mitchell states:

> Hip-hop and rap cannot be viewed simply as an expression of African American culture; it has become a vehicle for global youth affiliations and a tool for the reworking of global identity all over the world. Even as a universally recognized popular music idiom, rap continues to provoke attention to local specifics.[33]

Rap began in the South Bronx but has become an international form of music. For example, Israeli Arab rappers Richy Shaby and Mahmoud Shalaby sing about the disillusionment of Israel's Arabs.

The 2001 movie *O Brother, Where Art Thou?* starred Tim Blake Nelson, George Clooney, and John Turturro and become the basis for a multimedia entertainment package. The sound track won the Grammy Award for best album in 2002.

Rap has become a form of music that people all over the world use to protest their conditions and to spread the word about those conditions. Despite its global development, however, the sales of rap recordings continue to be dominated by U.S. rappers.

Multimedia Packaging

Multimedia packaging involves the production and release of recordings with other media products. In the world of commercial music, the recording is often only part of the package, which may also include a video, movie, and concert tour. For example, Michael Jackson recorded a song called "Will You Be There" in 1993 in connection with the small-budget film *Free Willy.* The video of Jackson singing the song played at the beginning of the film and on music television. The video, the soundtrack tape and CD, and the movie all promoted each other. The result was success for both the movie and the recording.

Multimedia packaging can affect all forms of music. Few people expected the release of the Coen brothers movie *O Brother, Where Art Thou?* in 2001 to affect the music industry as it did. Although the movie received mixed reviews, its sound track sold more than five million albums and won the Grammy Award for best album in 2002. Under the supervision of T-Bone Burnett, the sound track combined blues, bluegrass, traditional country, and gospel music. It led to a revived interest in "old-time music" and generated a tour of the sound track musicians in 2002, a television program, and a documentary film of the recording process. It also illustrated the impact of multimedia packaging on all the elements, as well as the difficulty of predicting the success of these packages.

Women in Popular Music

In summer 1997, Lilith Fair disproved the music industry's long-held belief that women performers could not make money on their own. Lilith Fair was organized by Sarah McLachlan and starred such artists as Sheryl Crow, Jewel, the Dixie Chicks, and the Indigo Girls. It helped promote the current expansion of opportunity for women in rock. The concert series made $28.3 million during the summer of 1998, and it continued for a third year in 1999. McLachlan told the Minneapolis *Star Tribune,* "The success [of Lilith] has proven that women are and can be successful in their own right. Because unfortunately, that's the way business is. If you make money, you're taken seriously. We're making money."[34]

Although Lilith Fair gets much of the credit for increased opportunity for women, that credit should be shared with the large number of successful women artists who emerged during the 1990s. Celine Dion, Alanis Morissette, Fiona Apple, Sinead O'Connor, Mariah Carey, and Paula Cole, among others, reached stardom during this period along with Jewel, McLachlan, and Crow. So many women selling so many records was new to the recording business. Throughout much of its history, women were treated as sex objects or as auxiliary artists for the men who dominated the sales charts.

The success of women in the 1990s spread beyond the Top 40 performers. A new generation of women rap artists, as typified by Eve and Sole, emerged in 1999 to take their place alongside Lil' Kim and Foxy Brown.[35] Country music saw a similar trend as Shania Twain established herself as a solid crossover

Avril Lavigne is one of the young women singers who have followed in the footsteps of the 1990s wave of women recording artists who topped the pop and rap charts.

profile

Janis Joplin

During a period of male-dominated rock 'n' roll, Janis Joplin was considered by many to be the most exciting performer of her generation. "She was not just a singer, but a symbol of the liberation and excess of hippy San Francisco in the late '60s," reminisced Harper Barnes, who had reviewed Joplin's performance in front of 11,000 fans at the outdoor Mississippi River Festival in Edwardsville in the summer of 1969. "Joplin simply tore the place up. . . . She flings herself into every song, her voice scooping up notes and slamming them down, her body moving like a bawdy majorette. At one point, she looked out at the audience with the grin of a naughty child and said, 'Now do you know what rock 'n' roll is all about?' "

Janis Joplin was born into a middle-class family on January 19, 1943, in Port Arthur, Texas, an oil town on the Gulf of Mexico. It seemed that the plain, chubby girl and then teenager was often unhappy and had trouble fitting in with others her age. After graduating from high school, she attended the local college briefly, then set out to San Francisco. In North Beach, where the beat writers such as Jack Kerouac had gathered, Joplin sang in bars and coffeehouses, experimenting with folk and blues songs before settling into rock 'n' roll.

For a while, Joplin gave up music. She returned home and started school again in Austin, Texas. But she left after a short stay. Friends in the fading band Big Brother and the Holding Company convinced her to join them in San Francisco in 1966. The band's new sound combined an energetic beat with Joplin's powerful blues- and gospel-influenced voice.

Joplin pursued pleasure with the same energy, and life became an incessant whirl of sex, alcohol, and drugs. When she was not too strung out to sing, she "drove audiences into a frenzy with her harsh yet soaring voice and the highly charged, openly sexual energy of her performances," wrote Barnes.

By 1967, Janis Joplin was a star. She, Jimi Hendrix, and Otis Redding were the hottest American performers in rock 'n' roll. When the album *Cheap Thrills* came out in 1968, she became world famous. Over time, however, the alcohol and $200-a-day drug habit took their toll. In 1970, at the age of twenty-seven, Joplin died of an accidental overdose of heroin. Jimi Hendrix had died from suffocation related to drug use a month earlier.

Some of Janis Joplin's most famous songs included "Summertime," "Ball and Chain," "Piece of My Heart," and "Turtle Blues." Three months after her death, "Me and Bobby McGee" was released and became Janis Joplin's first song to be number one on the pop charts.

Sources: Harper Barnes, "Full-Tilt Boogie Janis Joplin Came and Went Like a Texas Tornado," *St. Louis Post Dispatch* (October 14, 1992), Everyday Magazine sec., p. 1F; Susan Whitall, "Polishing the Tarnished Janis Joplin," Gannett News Service (October 14, 1992).

---

star and the Texas group Dixie Chicks won the best country album Grammy Award for their debut album in 1999.

The new century has seen increased success for women in popular music. Women not only have access, but also the range of the pop music genre for women has grown. From the pop princess music of Britney Spears and Christina Aguilera, to the pop rock of Avril Lavigne, to the hip-hop of Lauryn Hill, women musicians now find success throughout rock music.

discussing trends

As new technologies develop, the music industry will continue to be threatened. However, it has survived and adapted to changes in both content and packaging. Some of the questions to be answered include:

■ How will the trends mentioned in this chapter affect the recording industry during the next ten years?

■ Will rap continue to expand its influence on popular music?

■ Why have men traditionally dominated music? Is this likely to continue?

summary

- Music's primary purpose is to entertain people, but it also serves important social and personal functions.
- Music binds social groups together by creating shared experiences and by serving as part of ceremonies and rituals.
- American popular music evolved by blending music from African and European cultures.
- Popular music depends heavily on the connection between music and young people's rebellion against existing social norms.
- As music has become commercialized, control of the music has moved from the artists to the recording companies.
- The first technology used by the music industry was the printing press to print sheet music during the 1800s.
- During the 1950s, two record formats battled for supremacy. The 33⅓ rpm long-playing format won over the smaller 45 rpm format, only to lose out to tapes and compact discs during the 1970s and 1980s.
- Today's recording industry remains highly concentrated in the United States and the world; only a few companies produce 70 to 80 percent of all recordings.
- The recording process can be direct (all parts are recorded at the same time) or multitrack (different parts are recorded at different times).

- Copyrights allow the holder of the copyright to be paid for reproduction and performances of music.
- Distribution of recordings occurs through record stores, discount and department stores, television, the Internet, and mail-order clubs.
- Because of their size, the major recording companies have economic advantages in distributing and promoting recordings.
- Promotion plays a key role in selling recordings, making people aware of the music, and encouraging demand. It also creates conditions for corruption.
- Music video emerged during the 1980s as an important promotion tool. As a result, TV music channels now influence record sales.
- The recording industry is global in reach, but most of the recording production and sales organizations are located in Britain, France, Germany, Japan, and the United States.
- Trends in the music industry include multimedia packaging, the evolution of rap as a commercial form of music, efforts by artists to reduce the power of the recording companies, and the distribution of music over the Internet.
- In the 1990s, women gained power and influence in the popular music industry.

navigating the web
Music on the Web

Music is a growing presence on the World Wide Web because of improved sound quality. Sites take a variety of forms, from those owned by recording companies to sites on which the music of independent artists can be sampled and their recordings bought. The following sites are information sites for music and the recording industries and sites where music can be downloaded.

Internet Underground Music Archive
www.iuma.com
This site is a place for uploading and downloading music from musicians who do not have recording contracts. In addition, it has information about these artists and links to other sites.

Rock World
www.enn2.com/rock.htm
Rock World provides extensive material about the history of rock 'n' roll and links to other sites related to

artists, bands, record companies, and radio stations, among others.

MP3
www.mp3.com
The MP3 homepage for leading technology for downloading music on the Web also contains music for downloading and news about the music industry.

The following sites contain photographs, text, and music of independent artists.

Virtual Radio
www.vradio.com
Download music in a variety of formats.

Mammoth Artists
www.mammothartists.com

Rock and Roll Hall of Fame
www.rockhall.com
This is the official web site of the Rock and Roll Hall of Fame located in Cleveland, Ohio. It includes information about important musicians in the development of rock 'n' roll, as well as information about events occurring at the Hall of Fame.

VH-1
www.vh1.com
This is the official web site for the VH-1 music channel. It includes music news, tour information, links, the channel schedule, and biographical information about popular musicians.

questions for review

1. How did African American music first appear in the United States?
2. What are the steps in the recording process?
3. How has the blending of different types of music affected the development of rock 'n' roll, and why has it created controversy?
4. What three elements have guided the development of popular music in the United States?
5. List several ways in which the recording industry is financed.
6. How do converging technologies affect the distribution of mediated music?

issues to think about

1. Throughout history, alternative popular music forms such as punk, rap, and grunge have either been adopted by the mainstream or faded as a music form. Why does this happen, and what are the implications for a young musical artist?
2. How does the concentration within the recording industry affect music content?
3. How do promotional needs and efforts shape the music industry?
4. How would you describe MTV as a cultural force?
5. In what way do you foresee the Internet and other online services affecting the delivery of music?

suggested readings

Campbell, Michael. *And the Beat Goes On: An Introduction to Popular Music in America, 1840 to Today* (New York: Schirmer Books, 1996).

Chanan, Michael. *Repeated Takes: A Short History of Recording and Its Effect on Music* (New York: Verso, 1995).

Dannen, Fredic. *Power Brokers and Fast Money Inside the Music Business* (New York: Times Books, 1990).

Farr, Jory. *Moguls and Madmen: The Pursuit of Power in Popular Music* (New York: Simon & Schuster, 1994).

Hamm, Charles. *Putting Popular Music in Its Place* (Cambridge, England: Cambridge University Press, 1995).

Santoro, Gene. *Dancing in Your Head: Jazz, Blues, Rock, and Beyond* (New York: Oxford University Press, 1994).

Unterberger, Richie. *Unknown Legends of Rock 'n' Roll* (San Francisco: Miller Freeman Books, 1998).

Computers and the Internet

Jenny stood looking out of the window of her high-rise apartment on the upper East Side in New York City. She had been cleaning up the kitchen, with the television on in the background. Suddenly a news bulletin announced that a plane had hit one of the buildings in the World Trade Center complex. Her husband's office was next to the World Trade Center. Her children were at school.

Jenny grabbed for the telephone but the circuits were busy. She couldn't get in touch with either her husband's office or her children's school.

Jenny turned on her computer, checked her e-mail repeatedly, and typed in cnn.com. An e-mail appeared shortly. Her husband was fine. He had gotten out of the building and e-mailed her from his handheld Blackberry computer. Soon she had a message from her children's school. The principal had sent a broadcast e-mail to all parents saying the children were safe and would be kept at school until a plan could be developed to send them home safely.

The Internet became an important tool in the lives of many Americans after the attacks on Washington, D.C., and New York City on September 11, 2001. According to a study by the Pew Project on the Internet and American life, people used the Internet to provide assistance to victims, seek assistance, monitor news and information, seek information specifically from the government, and communicate with each other more often. Many used the Internet as a "public commons," a place where expressions of grief and support for others could be delivered.

The Web also became a site for many images. The Pew Project described these as:

- Informative images—to deal with breaking news of the attacks
- Memorial images—to acknowledge the tragedy and show support for victims and rescuers
- Signpost images—to show recognition of the importance of 9/11 events even though the function of those web sites was unrelated to news or memorials (such as e-commerce sites)
- Storytelling images—to show how certain elements of the 9/11 story were unfolding
- Supplemental images—to accompany heartfelt written commentary about the meaning of the attacks or the appropriate way to respond to them
- Logos—to capture some emotional aspect of a web designer's response to the ongoing story.[1]

The events of September 11, 2001, represent—probably more than any single other event—the revolutionary potential of computer-mediated news gathering. It stands alone as a medium and as a technology, but it also

New technology offers not only possibility, but problems as well. The issues here include the following:

◆ How will pricing and information about computers affect access for individuals from all socioeconomic levels of society?

◆ How much of the Internet and the World Wide Web will be devoted to information? To entertainment? To commerce?

◆ How is this new technology related to news content? Does the new technology simply provide an extended delivery service for old content? Or will new forms of mass media and journalism emerge?

◆ As we express ourselves online, will we be able to preserve privacy, maintain security, and preserve the tenets of free speech? How will we protect those who create content as well as those who seek to preserve their privacy and control content for their children?

Computers *in Your Life*

Tools and Toys

Computers are becoming increasingly indispensable for students. Do you use computers? Do you use them for work? For play? As you read through this chapter, think of uses of the computer that we've not yet even dreamed of—or at least those for which we have not yet perfected the technology. Computers and the online world have great potential, but most analysts do not yet know how the technology will be used in the mass media mix.

HOW DO YOU USE COMPUTERS?	HOW MANY HOURS PER WEEK?
Research for school assignments	
Word processing	
Software games	
Games on a network via the Internet, World Wide Web, or commercial service	
Banking service	
At work	
Electronic mail to family and friends	
Electronic mail to teachers	

embodies the convergence of electronic and print media. The merging of audio and video with graphics and text and delivering these electronically creates communication among individuals through e-mail and instant messaging; establishes viable e-commerce; and provides news, entertainment, and information. Flash technology and animation illustrate dramatic news events such as the meltdown at the Chernobyl nuclear plant in the former Soviet Union and the crash of the spaceship *Challenger*. In early 2003, you could access www.nytimes.com/packages/html/magazine/20020908_911_ PLAN/index.html, and get a dynamic illustrated plan designed by the *New York Times* for the redevelopment of Ground Zero.

By providing a unique format for conveying information, computer technology becomes a medium rather than a mere form of distribution. It is through this new technology and the services provided that we come to understand cyberspace. A former editor at Newsweek Interactive noted that at *Newsweek,* "we used to say that code is content, for much the same reason that literary critics say that the form and content are inseparable." Computer-delivered information is a form of mass communication. Interactivity is content.

In 1795, information in the form of books and newspapers was a scarce commodity. Creating and distributing these products were slow and laborious processes. Two hundred years later, people get their information from books, newspapers, magazines, letters, movies, radio, television, telephones, VCRs, audiotapes, electronic mail, interactive CDs, and computer online services.

This information revolution has affected almost every process of *communication*—gathering, organizing, presenting, and disseminating information. Some theorists predict that someday we will have a paperless society in which radio and television combine with a computer for a home information system. However, media industry analysts suggest that this process will take considerably longer than some futurists contend. Print media remain cheap and portable. What remains certain is that text, visuals, and sound are converging as the best elements of television and recording industry technology combine with computers.

key concept

Media Convergence Some scholars argue that media convergence—the blending of television and computers through technology, for example—only creates a new way of distributing information. Others believe that convergence of media technology actually creates new styles and modes of information, which has been transformed based on the way it is delivered.

The term **media convergence** is generally defined as the combination of two or more traditional media into one process. For some industry watchers, media convergence also means the merging of mass media organizations. Traditionally, each medium had one objective. For example, the U.S. Postal Service transported handwritten or typed correspondence from one destination to another. Newspaper organizations presented news and information on newsprint to a reader. Telephone companies made it possible for people in different locations to talk to one another. And television stations provided vivid moving pictures to viewers. Today, innovative companies combine these functions into one process, using a computer and telephone lines or a combination of television sets and telephone lines. When users turn on their computers and go online, they can send and receive e-mail, read information about a bill that was passed recently in Congress, or watch basketball game videos—all from the same source.

However, the possibility of convergence doesn't mean that all media will converge. Readers will still subscribe to newspapers, watch television, and take magazines on vacations. Different media—text for explanation, persuasion, video for emotion—retain specific functions that transcend the ability to converge media into a single process.

Consumers now can talk to each other and buy airline tickets, clothing, books, and even stocks online. Soon such innovations as 3-D technology will grace computer screens. But rich multimedia, such as interactive 3-D "flythroughs" of a news location, will have to wait for higher delivery speeds. Slowing down technology development and adoption is the technical delivery system. As long as consumers stay with dial-up modems, delivery will be too slow to advance some of the new technology. However, as more households go to cable modems, DSL lines, and satellite Internet, which provide far greater bandwith, the power of the computer will expand.

The computer has had a major impact on other media and on consumers. For example, newspapers and broadcast news programs receive syndicated programs quickly and easily; public relations practitioners get information from a database in another country instantly; advertisers approve faxed designs in minutes; broadcasters receive newsfeeds via satellite simultaneously; and freelance writers interview sources electronically.

The computer also presents the possibility of a society interactively linked by a network. In a networked society, people will be able to access mass media services and communicate individually through the computer.

COMPUTERS IN AMERICAN LIFE

Computers have profoundly influenced our society by simplifying complex tasks and by informing and entertaining us in new ways. However, the computer has also complicated simple tasks—have you tried typing a form on a computer? Every day we encounter computing technology, just as we encounter mass media. A computer assists us each time we make a phone call, read a newspaper, watch television, listen to the radio, program our VCRs, get cash from a bank's automated teller, have our purchases scanned at the checkout counter, reserve an airplane seat, or pay with a credit card. In the coming decades, we will use computers even more for information and entertainment. The computer is the heart of interactive television, virtual reality, movies-on-demand, and individualized news delivery. An information or media center in a custom-built home today may well control not only temperature, lights, and appliances, but also the information that household receives and sends. These are representative of our *information society.*

Some historians date the computer to the ancient abacus, a handheld counting device, and mechanical devices that were in use by 1900 for tabulating large amounts of data. However, the military demands of World War II produced the first electronic computers. The breakthrough can be attributed to a variety of people. John Vincent Atanasoff, an Iowa State University professor, and an electrical engineering student, Clifford E. Berry, were in the process of constructing a computer when the war began. A huge computer, the Colossus, helped the British break German military codes, and Harvard mathematician Howard Aiken developed a computer to calculate artillery ballistics. When U.S. leaders saw the possibilities for defense and space applications of computer technology, they channeled government money to finance computer research and development.

In the landmark 1945 article "As We May Think" in the *Atlantic Monthly,* MIT researcher Vannevar Bush suggested that a machine, a "memex," could extend the powers of human memory and association and solve the problem of organizing and accessing information. "A memex," Bush wrote, "is a device in which an individual stores all his books, records, and communications, and which is mechanized so that it may be consulted with exceeding speed and flexibility. It is an enlarged intimate supplement to his memory."[2] Bush envisioned the machine as a desktop device with a keyboard; storage would be on microfilm, and dry photography would be used for input.

> **key concept**
>
> **Information Society** The United States, and to some extent the world, is in the midst of an information revolution that parallels the Industrial Revolution in scope. An information-age society faces the serious question of whether the members who have access to electronic equipment and an understanding of technology will become information-rich while others become information-poor.

The enormous 1955 Remington Rand Univac computer had less processing power than a Pentium desktop computer used today.

Doug Engelbart read Bush's article and recognized the problem he described but realized that the computer, not a microfilm machine, was the answer. The computer could manipulate symbols and allow individuals to compare data.[3] Engelbart went on to direct laboratory research at the Stanford Research Institute and was active through the 1970s in developing computer applications. Engelbart's group at Stanford initiated the field of computer-supported cooperative work and invented **WYSIWYG** word processing, the mouse, multiwindow displays, and electronic meeting rooms.[4]

Although Bush envisioned a mechanical device to sort information, electronic computers were the key to Engelbart's concept of being able to manipulate information. In 1946, the first electronic, general-purpose computer, Electronic Numerical Integrator and Computer (ENIAC), was developed at the University of Pennsylvania. The construction of the computer reflected the earlier work of Atanasoff and others.[5] ENIAC was eighteen feet high and eighty feet long and weighed thirty tons. It used 17,468 vacuum tubes connected by 500 miles of wire to perform 10,000 operations a second. To change its instructions, engineers had to rewire it. The research effort that produced it had been financed by the U.S. government in hopes that a computer would contribute to the war effort, and ENIAC was used to make some of the calculations in the building of the hydrogen bomb in the 1950s.

Engineers recognized at the beginning that computers had many possible applications. Not only could they manipulate numbers and sort information by topic, but they also offered a platform for developing graphics programs that could serve as architectural and design tools. Already in the early 1950s, MIT laboratories were experimenting with **interactive** computing and computer graphics. Ivan Sutherland created Sketchpad, a graphics program in which the user drew directly on the screen using a light pen. Sketchpad introduced software inventions such as the cursor, the window, and clipping. In 1955, IBM released the **computer language** FORTRAN, which was designed to aid scientists in solving engineering problems.

Mildred Koss, one of Univac I's initial programmers, commented, "There were no limitations to what you could accomplish. There was lots of vision and new ideas as to where the computer might be used. We looked at the computer as a universal problem-solving machine. It had some rules and an operating system, but it was up to you to program it to do whatever you wanted it to do."[6]

But computers could be problematic as well. Grace Hopper, a mathematician who worked in computer research at Harvard and developed the first commercial, high-level computer language, gave a name to those problems. While trying to determine what had caused a computer malfunction, Hopper found the culprit—a dead moth on a vacuum tube. From then on, "bug" became a common computer term.[7]

The Move to Micro

With the development of the silicon chip in 1959, the computer industry expanded to become a microelectronics industry. The silicon chip and programming languages enabled the electronics industry to develop **microcomputers** for general use. Software, rather than hardware, determined the application. By the early 1960s, this infant industry was garnering annual revenues of more than $1 billion. As computers were

WYSIWYG: Text on a computer screen that corresponds exactly to the printout: What you see is what you get.

interactive: Interactive systems involve two-way communication. The information receivers act as senders and vice versa.

computer language: An intermediate programming language designed for programmers' convenience that is converted into machine language.

microcomputer: A small computer using a microprocessor as its central processor.

profile

Bill Gates

Until the mid-1970s, computers took up entire rooms. But in 1975, the first microcomputer kit—the Altair 8800—was developed, making computers affordable and usable in the home. Unfortunately, the operating system language for the microcomputer was the same as that for large mainframe computers, filling up most of the Altair's small memory capacity and leaving little room for data.

When Paul Allen read about the Altair 8800, he convinced his friend Bill Gates to work with him on developing a condensed operating system language, which the teenage math geniuses licensed to the makers of the Altair 8800.

One year later Allen and Gates established Microsoft Corporation. The young founders were convinced that they were in the forefront of a computer revolution. Software, said Gates, was where the money would be.

Microsoft's big break came in 1980 when the industry's leader, IBM, asked Gates to develop an operating system for its new personal computer. Gates declined at first, then bought a system from another small company for $50,000, reworked it, and licensed it to IBM for $125,000. He named the operating system MS-DOS, for "Microsoft disk operating system." Gates retained ownership and thus was ready to confront the microcomputer revolution. IBM introduced its PC in 1981, and clones (practically identical machines) using MS-DOS soon followed.

Today, Microsoft's operating systems—MS-DOS and Windows—run more than 90 percent of the world's personal computers.

On July 15, 1996, Microsoft and NBC each invested $220 million to launch MSNBC, the Microsoft–NBC news service that is available on cable and online. The companies claim they are preparing for the time when computers and television merge. Gates is now a billionaire, one of the richest people in the United States.

Gates surprised the computer world in January 2000 by stepping down as Microsoft chief executive officer and allowing his old friend Steve Ballmer to become head of the corporation. Gates became chief software architect in an effort to help Microsoft respond to the changing world of computer communication. Increasingly, the industry is moving away from desktop PC software to software that runs over networks, such as the Internet.

Gates ran Microsoft for twenty-five years. Despite his step away from the day-to-day operations, Gates is likely to continue to shape corporate policy.

In April 2000, after almost two years of legal maneuvers, U.S. District Judge Thomas Penfield Jackson ruled that Microsoft had violated a broad range of antitrust laws. The suit continued for two more years, with court decisions initially indicating that punishment for Microsoft might include breaking up the company. However, in November 2002, a U.S. federal judge signed off on a settlement reached between the U.S. government and Microsoft nearly a year earlier. The settlement imposed no financial penalty but required Gates's software company to disclose some technical information and also barred agreements on Microsoft products that were designed to exclude competitors. The settlement gives computer makers freedom to remove some Microsoft icons from the Windows desktop and instead feature rival software. Microsoft also is prohibited from retaliating against any manufacturers who choose non-Microsoft products.

Many regarded the settlement as a mere slap on the hands to Microsoft. The company continues to market its browser, Explorer, with its Windows systems on many new PCs that are sold.

Sources: Peter H. Lewis, "A Glimpse into the Future as Seen by Chairman Gates," *The New York Times* (December 12, 1993), sec. 3, p. 7; "Bill Gates," *Newsmakers*, Gale Research Inc., August 1993; Joel Achenbach, "The Computer King's Hard Drive; Billionaire Bill Gates, Cult Hero, Cracks Open a Window on the Secret of His Success, *The Washington Post* (April 14, 1993): B1; Cynthia Flash, "Microsoft, NBC Launch News Venture," *News Tribune* (July 14, 1996): 1.

---

used for processing different applications, hardware and software manufacturers rapidly began to develop new products.

In 1974, Intel marketed its first computer chip, the Intel 4004. This chip, which combined memory and logic functions on the microchip to produce a microprocessor, launched the individual computer market. First, workstation terminals that were attached to a large mainframe began to proliferate in the workplace, and then stand-alone desktop computers appeared. However, the personal computer (PC) was designed primarily for ham radio operators and other electronics hobbyists.

In 1975, Paul Allen, the friend of a Harvard student named Bill Gates, was attracted to the cover of the January 1975 issue of *Popular Electronics*. The cover

table 12.1

Number of Years to Reach 50 Percent of U.S. Households for Selected Technologies

TECHNOLOGY/MEDIUM	NUMBER OF YEARS TO REACH 50% PENETRATION
Newspapers	100+
Telephone	70
Phonograph	55
Cable TV	39
Personal Computers	24
Color TV	15
VCR	10
Radio	9
Black-and-white TV	8

Sources: Electronic Industries Alliance, U.S. Department of Commerce, 1996. Courtesy of John Carey.

featured a photo of the very first personal computer, the MITS Altair 8800. After reading that article, Gates and Allen started Microsoft Corporation.

The Altair 8800 was the first practical mass market machine, produced by a hobby company called Micro Instrumentation Telemetry Systems (MITS), and it sold for $397, about the price of the Intel chip that made its production possible. But there was a catch. To be useful, an Altair required a video display terminal, storage disks, and a printer, which brought the price into the $5,000 range. For that price, the buyer had a computer that did real work, such as word processing, file management, and running BASIC, FORTRAN, COBOL, and PL/I programs. Programmers entered data with switches instead of a keyboard. Hobbyists and entrepreneurs loved the Altair. Personal computing had arrived.[8]

In 1977, Steve Wozniak and Steve Jobs, two college dropouts, perfected the Apple II, which sold for about $1,300, contained four **kilobytes** of memory, and came with a jack that converted a television set into a monitor. About the same time, the Tandy/Radio Shack TRS-80s—the first truly portable computer—became available. In 1981, Osborne introduced a machine with a built-in twenty-four-line monitor, and in 1981, IBM entered the market with the first IBM PC. "Totables" or "luggables" included the Kaypro, which sold for about $1,800, and Compaq's suitcase-style machine, which was about the size and weight of a portable sewing machine.

kilobyte: A measure of memory size equal to 1,024 bytes.

user-friendly: Software that is designed for use by individuals who are not familiar with complex computer languages.

operating systems: Programs that tell the computer how to behave. DOS and Windows, produced by Microsoft, dominate the world market for operating systems. The Macintosh operating system is second, used by about one-tenth as many machines as the Microsoft systems.

spreadsheets: Software that allows for organization and tabulation of financial data; commonly used in planning budgets.

databases: Software for recording statistics. Data can be sorted into categories and reports printed in various forms. Used by businesses that need to sort customers by zip code, for example.

graphical user interface (GUI): Arrangement on the screen that imitates a desktop.

Software Revolution

By the mid-1980s, the personal computer had been revolutionized with the advent of **user-friendly operating systems.** The most widely used of these was DOS. DOS-based personal computers and the Apple Macintosh became affordable, revolutionizing not only the workplace, but the home as well. These machines enabled people to use a desktop computer for sophisticated engineering problems and at the same time for other applications such as word processing, graphics, design, **spreadsheets,** and **database** management. Personal computers became even more user-friendly in 1984 with the introduction of the small, light computer named the Apple Macintosh. The Macintosh provided an easy-to-use format characterized by the term **graphical user interface (GUI).** This arrangement used the metaphor of a desktop to display the range of tasks the Mac make possible. In 1990, Bill Gates introduced Microsoft's Windows 3.0, and two years later followed with 3.1. This software replaced DOS's text-based interface with a GUI clearly modeled on the Macintosh. But the lower price of Windows machines, whose manufacturers had to compete with each other, attracted cost-conscious buyers. And as Windows' share of the marker grew, software companies had less and less incentive to write for the Macintosh. This was especially true of the burgeoning video-game sector. The result: Macintosh was relegated to specialized markets such as graphic designers, whereas Windows became the effective industry standard for desktop and laptop machines. Windows had sold 60 million copies by 1995, and Microsoft was supplying 80 percent of the operating systems worldwide. The company launched Windows 95 in August 1995. Subsequent versions of Windows, including Windows 98, Windows 2000, Windows NT, and Windows XP, have since been introduced and dominate the market.

The introduction of user-friendly software, along with the trend toward microcomputers, has made computers a common household item. A study by Arbitron NewMedia shows that home penetration doubled from 29 percent in 1995 to 58 percent in 2001.[9] For comparison, Table 12.1 shows the number of years it took for some other popular technologies to reach 50 percent penetration.

Radio first made possible rudimentary long-distance education, but new media and satellites make it possible for students to participate interactively with instructors and discussion groups.

COMPUTERS AND COMMUNICATION

Once computers became small and inexpensive enough for consumers to buy them as individual PCs, and software opened the door to a variety of uses, the next step was to connect computers in such a way that people could videoconference, send messages, and access information from other computer sources. This was achieved through the Internet, its graphical interface (the World Wide Web), and online services, and has led to the formation of *information-based economies.*

The Internet

The Internet is a **network** of computer networks. These networks include computers found in businesses, universities, libraries, government, media companies, and homes. The Internet is available today because the federal government wanted to link computers in such a way that in times of disaster—either human or natural—defense and communications systems could still operate. In the 1960s, the U.S. Defense Department designed an experimental network called ARPAnet. As the type and number of network systems increased, it became apparent that allowing computers to "talk" to one another regardless of their operating systems would be beneficial to all. In the late 1980s, the National Science Foundation (NSF) created five supercomputer centers. At first the NSF tried to use ARPAnet to connect them, but bureaucracy and staffing problems got in the way. NSF, therefore, created its own network by connecting the centers with telephone lines. Then, through a chain system, the network linked universities and other commercial and noncommercial computer groups. In each area of the country, a group is linked to its neighbor group or institution rather than every one being fed to a central location. This saves primarily in the cost of telephone lines.

The success of the system came close to being its downfall as users multiplied rapidly and the telephone lines could not sustain the use. In 1987, the old network was replaced with higher capacity telephone lines.

The most important feature of the NSF network has been its commitment to universal access, thereby opening up enormous sources of data and conversations for people using computers.[10] What is amazing is that connections occur within seconds, despite being linked from one institution to another across hundreds of miles or around the world.

network: Computers that are connected by communications lines. The computers may be connected within a restricted geographic area, such as a laboratory in a mass communication program. This network is a local area network (LAN). The Internet networks millions of computers worldwide through telephone and fiber-optic lines.

The Internet is the carrier of a variety of services, including newspapers online, original Internet content, electronic shopping, music that can be downloaded and played through stereo and television equipment, and streaming video that offers real-time news feeds. The Internet distributes almost any content that can be imagined.

Commercialization of the Internet

In the early days of the Internet, research and correspondence characterized the content. Commercialization would have been seen as a major gaffe. Now the Internet, particularly the subset called the World Wide Web, is a major site for the advertisement of products, online shopping, promotion of products tied to movies and books, and other commercial ventures. A small indicator of this is that U.S. consumers spent an estimated $32.6 billion online in 2001, compared to $27.3 billion in 2000.[11]

Along with commercialization has been the development of hardware, known today as "Internet appliances." Personal digital assistants, the Web-capable cell phone, and the Blackberry are leading serious people who are familiar with wireless technology to begin to talk about the "Post–PC World." In July 2002, India announced the marketing of a $200 Simputer, a handheld computer designed to be multilingual and inexpensive. The item would sell for about the same price as a cheap color television in India.[12]

In Great Britain, Greek-born entrepreneur Stelios Haji-Ioannou has used the commercialized Internet to foster his easyGroup company. The group encompasses air travel, auto rentals, Internet cafes, free e-mail services, and online financial services. One of his greatest successes was the bare-bones easyJet, which in November 2002 announced annual pretax profits of 71.6 million pounds. Much of his success was due to the fact that the establishment of easyJet coincided with the commercialization of the Internet. Haji-Ioannou bypassed the traditional travel agent business, using the Internet as a business tool. "I was only capable of cutting out the travel agents because I knew nothing about the travel business. I had no allegiances, I had no friends in that industry. I just said . . . we will not do it." He added, "The internet has probably had a bigger effect on people's ability to fly than the jet engine."[13]

Social and Cultural Effects

Economists and social theorists claim that the United States and other developed countries have moved from industrial-based to information-based economies. Creating and distributing information for entertainment, investing, and economic decision making account for a large portion of the U.S. national product. Relying on information creates concern in three basic areas: (1) Who has access to the information? (2) What are the implications for social interaction and political participation in a democratic society? and (3) Is regulation necessary to protect individual privacy while still preserving the tenets of free speech?

Access ◆ Information is a commodity that represents knowledge and the ability to transcend socioeconomic class. A 2001 study shows that 58 percent of all Americans have online access. Major growth during the last year brought 51 percent of U.S. African American households online. In addition, with a growth rate of 28 percent, households earning less than $25,000 a year increased their Internet presence more than any other income segment, bringing total household penetration in this income sector to 36 percent. Internet connections by households earning $25,000 to $50,000 grew 17 percent in 2001 compared to 2000, representing the second largest increase by income segment and bringing total household online penetration in this income range to 56 percent.

For elderly households, Internet connectivity is 27 percent, but in the age category just below that—fifty-five to sixty-four—52 percent of all homes are online. "In 2000, the Internet has continued its growth toward becoming a mainstream medium," said Gian Fulgoni, chairman and cofounder of comScore Networks. "The rapidly growing online penetration into these new demographic segments suggests that Web usage is on its way to becoming pervasive."[14]

Computers tie the elderly to their friends, children, and grandchildren, and to information. Letters and photographs can be distributed easily across many miles. Although there is a significant startup cost, once the equipment is in place, distribution is very inexpensive.

Research reveals that because individuals with higher levels of education generally have more access to mass communication, they gather ideas and new information more quickly than those with less education. One of the concerns about the Internet has been whether the entire population will have access or whether only a select few will. As the Internet developed, scholars referred to this concept as the *"digital divide."* In essence, there was major concern that those who were poor and less educated would be divided from those who had access to information. However, the digital divide seems to be eroding considerably, and if library access, access at places of employment, and the declining cost of computers and related technology continue to erode the digital divide, the Internet could be a major factor in leveling the information playing field.[15]

Social Interaction and Political Participation ◆ Although media reports of incidents such as the 1999 Columbine High School shooting or a story about an Internet-addicted teenage murderer may point to computer use as a factor in a lack of socialization, users report that Internet access enhances their ability to communicate with others. A Wirthlin study reported that only a third of those surveyed "feel that computers and the Internet have made it more difficult to establish relationships with people," while more than two-thirds disagreed with the statement. People cited exchanging e-mails with distant family members, databases for looking up lost acquaintances, and chat groups as ways of staying in touch with others.

Questions about political participation are difficult to answer, and research is primitive in this area. As information becomes more specialized, more technology-based, and more expensive, sociologists and political critics worry that the participation of an informed public, necessary to support the foundations of a democracy, may erode even further than it already has. Sociologists are concerned that we will become a fragmented society in which there is no longer such a thing as "common knowledge." We might have nothing to say to our neighbors anymore because we choose the content and the information sources we want, which might be different from those our neighbors want.

Freedom of Expression ◆ There are many issues having to do with privacy and security and the Internet. As you will read later in this chapter, many individuals are concerned about security of bank accounts and of shopping online. They also are concerned about hackers, and the ability of outsiders to break into their flow of information.

1943. Early electromechanical digital computer is developed by IBM.

1946. First electronic, general-use computer is developed.

1949. First commercial electronic computer is produced.

1954. Computer graphics are introduced by MIT.

1955. IBM invents the computer language FORTRAN.

1959. Silicon chip is developed.

1400–1700	1800	1900	1930	1940	1950

1620. Pilgrims land at Plymouth Rock.

1690. *Publick Occurrences* is published in Boston.

1741. First magazine is published in America.

1776–1783. American Revolution

1830s. The penny press becomes the first truly mass medium in the United States.

1861–1865. American Civil War

1892. Thomas Edison's lab develops the kinetoscope.

1914–1918. World War I

1915. *The Birth of a Nation* marks the start of the modern movie industry.

1920. KDKA in Pittsburgh gets the first commercial radio license.

1930s. The Great Depression

1939. TV is demonstrated at the New York World's Fair.

1939–1945. World War II

1949. First commercial electronic computer is produced.

Early 1950s. Rock 'n' roll begins.

Another aspect of privacy that affects our social and cultural structure is the ability to freely express ourselves without undue interference by the federal government or other entities. With the passing of the 2001 Patriot Act in reaction to the attacks on September 11, 2001, the federal government has increased its ability to "look into" people's correspondence.

Another area that affects freedom of expression has to do with efforts by the government to regulate pornography on the Internet. Here, one must balance the needs of society, the rights of people not to receive information they don't want, and the rights of others to exchange ideas freely.

TODAY'S MARKET STRUCTURE

The computer industry—coupled with information services that make the personal computer valuable—is highly diversified and competitive, although the shakeout of 2001 reduced the overall number of Internet companies. The market consists of access providers such as Earthlink or MCI's WorldCom, hardware manufacturers such as Dell and Intel, software manufacturers such as Microsoft and Broderbund, and online products or services providers such as America Online. Online services and products can be divided into three categories—e-commerce, information, and entertainment. Online services can be accessed through the Internet or through commercial services.

However, the media boom seems to be slowing. Veronis Suhler's *Communications Industry Report* claims that 2000 represented a peak performance level and "clearly

1974. Intel markets its first computer chip.

Mid-1970s. MITS develops the first personal computer, the Altair 8800.

1975. Bill Gates and Paul Allen start Microsoft Corporation.

1976. Steve Jobs and Steve Wozniak perfect the Apple II.

1980. Microsoft introduces MS-DOS.

1981. IBM manufactures its first PC.

1984. Apple introduces the Macintosh.

Late 1980s. National Science Foundation creates the basis of the Internet.

1995. Microsoft introduces Windows 95.

1996. Telecommunications Act

2001. Total advertising revenue online declines.

2002. Microsoft antitrust case is settled.

2000s. Broadband grows as a way to log onto the Internet.

1960	1970	1980	1990	2000

1969. First person lands on the moon.

1970s. VCR is developed.

1989–1991. Cold War ends and the USSR is dissolved.

Late 1980s. National Science Foundation creates the basis of the Internet.

1996. Telecommunications Act

2000. Presidential election nearly tied.

2001. Terrorist attacks on New York and Washington, D.C.

marked the final stages of the remarkable American media industry boom of the last decade." The "dot-com tumble" contributed to a significant shakeout through 2001, made worse by the aftermath of the September 11, 2001, terrorist attacks. "We've seen the media and information business shift rapidly from one of its best years into what is certain to be one of its worst in a decade, but it's important not to lose sight of the larger landscape of an industry that is remarkably diverse and dynamic," said James P. Rutherfurd, executive vice president and head of investment banking for Veronis Suhler.[16]

America Online is the largest publicly reporting consumer Internet company, with $6.9 billion in revenues in 2000. It is followed by Genuity at $1.1 billion, Yahoo! at $1.1 billion, PSINet at $995.5 million, and Earthlink network at $986.6 million.

The Technology of Access

The race is on to be connected to the Internet at high speeds. What this means to the consumer is that in addition to standard telephone modems connecting at speeds of about 56 kilobits per second, there are **cable modems** providing service technically one hundred times as fast, and **DSL** (digital subscriber lines) telephone-based enhanced hookups that are thirty times as fast as a standard 56K modem. Cable modem speeds, however, are somewhat mercurial, given that the speed can vary depending on the number of individuals using the cable service at the same time. DSL speeds also vary because telephone companies want to preserve a distinction between their commercial T-1 service offered at higher prices than regular DSL lines, which they provide more often to consumers. Cost is another critical factor. Consumers need to have a compelling reason to switch from dial-up to broadband.

cable modems: Devices used to connect computers to the Internet and other online services that operate through cable, rather than telephone, lines.

DSL: Telephone lines that foster extremely fast connections to the Internet and other online services.

Media companies are also getting into the business of providing access. In 1999, Cox Communications Inc. traded AT&T shares for AT&T cable systems stock, which gives Cox large cable holdings throughout the South and Southwest and makes it the fifth largest U.S. cable company. The largest cable companies in 2002 were AOL Time Warner and Comcast (which includes AT&T).

The primary contest is between cable services offering high-speed cable modems and telephone companies with loyal subscriber and billing bases. As new communications companies such as IXC Communications built fiber-optic, long-distance networks, **bandwidth** became a more available commodity. Corporate customers and Internet service providers have access to high-speed (T-1 and T-3) Internet lines for 30 percent less than they paid in the mid-1990s. These companies, looking toward the future, are aware that mere possession of the physical networks will not continue to generate large profits. So increasingly they are developing services and connectivity options for individual customers. In late 1999, the Internet service provider Earthlink Network signed an agreement with MCI that allowed Earthlink to have access to DSL lines for fast connections for its customers. Many of the large telephone companies such as AT&T are opting to buy into the cable industry as well, hoping that owning cable lines into customers' homes will enable the company to deliver interactive television, high-speed Internet services, and local phone service. All of these options represent increasing media convergence.

Hardware

Computers, coupled with companies that provide specific parts or peripherals, such as Hewlett-Packard with printers and Intel with computer chips, constitute the hardware industry.[17] The boom in personal computers during the 1990s increased growth and profit among computer manufacturers. According to the Consumer Electronics Manufacturers Association, 6.7 million personal computers were sold in 1994 at a total of $10.08 billion. In 1998, 12.8 million computers were sold worth $16.64 billion. However, analysts in 2002 documented that sales had been overclaimed in the peak years of 2001 and 2002. Conventional wisdom said that hardware sales—at least for personal computers—were down. Companies such as IBM were seeking mergers to expand their base into computer services in order to reduce reliance on hardware.

Nevertheless, in October 2002 DataQuest predicted that computer hardware, including personal computers, printers, servers, and handheld computers, would increase 3.6 percent that year to $38 billion and rise 6.2 percent to $40 billion the following year. Just as hardware sales could not sustain the radio or the cellular phone industry, increasingly standard hardware provides less of the revenue stream for the information industry. Because speed, storage, portability, and capability to manage new applications continue to improve, a demand continues for new computer purchases.

Software

Software is a term for programs, or the instructions that tell the computer's processor what to do. Besides operating systems, software includes communication software, task-oriented software, and entertainment software.

Communication software provides connections from one computer to another. Some programs configure a modem so that a user can fax material, send an electronic message to another person, or access an online service. Other programs, such as Netscape Navigator or Internet Explorer, enable users to browse the World Wide Web.

Task-oriented software includes all the programs that allow people to create text and images and to organize data. Included are word-processing programs such as WordPerfect; page design programs such as QuarkXPress; database organizers such as Filemaker Pro; and spreadsheets such as Excel.

Entertainment software allows consumers access to a variety of media and activities online and from disks and CD-ROMs. Such software delivers thousands of

bandwidth: A measure of capacity for carrying information.

Taboo Surfing

The Internet—a nearly ubiquitous form of chat—allows Iranian youth to bypass cultural norms and Chinese teenagers to escape an authoritarian government. In Iran, cards for prepaid Internet access can be purchased in local markets, nearly every university is wired, and citizens build online communities. The content? Everything from discussing Western styles to downloaded MP3 files to conversations about sex, dating, and marriage.

An estimated 400,000 people in Iran were online in 2001. Why does the Iranian government allow the public to escape the rigid social laws of the country through Internet use? Since 1996, President Mohammad Khatami has sought to expand some individual freedoms in Iran. Further, there is the basic fact that the Internet holds expanded scientific and technical knowledge that promises progress.

In China, where unlike Iran the Internet is subject to controls, individuals can still cruise the Internet with high-speed connections in more than 200,000 cybercafés across the country. The government estimates that more than fifty million people are online.

"Now, young people rush to the Internet cafes rather than rushing to newsstands to buy *People's Daily*," said Liu Junning, a political scientist who favors a less restrictive policy. "The Internet has fundamentally undermined people's dependence on the government-controlled media."

The government still blocks access to what are termed "anti-social" sites and also jams e-mail it deems threatening. Dissident e-mail newsletters have been suppressed. Mr. Liu notes, however, that the Internet still provides a mechanism for free thinking.

Source: Nazila Fathi, "Taboo Surfing: Click Here for Iran . . ." and Erik Eckholm, ". . . And Click Here for China," *New York Times* (August, 2002): 5.

---

stories, poems, photographs, games, and videos to computer users. Simulation games such as Flight Simulator provide a base for spinoffs. They also integrate analytical skill building with entertainment.

Software can be supplied on CD-ROMs, on disks, or through online services, or it can be downloaded into the computer from a web site or electronic bulletin board. Some downloadable programs are free; others can be paid for by credit card, by mail, over the telephone, or directly through the Internet. Downloaded programs are increasingly challenging the "shrink-wrapped" software providers such as Microsoft and Broderbund.

Online Service Providers

Online services are the area of greatest growth. Most of the growth is web based, and services may be provided free or for a fee. The services vary from specialized financial services to web-based banking, from entertainment to shopping online, from news to parodies of news. Audio and video images can be downloaded, and sites can be individually created. The online world is truly interactive; everyone with access to technology and a willingness to endure an often steep learning curve is capable of being online.

Online services took a giant step toward becoming a mass entertainment medium in January 2000 when AOL combined with Time Warner in a $350 billion merger. AOL had the computer and online experience, and Time Warner creates content and has cable systems that provide fiber-optic distribution. If online services expect to become truly multimedia, they need the video, film, and music that content companies create. Among the Time Warner properties are CNN, HBO, *Time* and *People* magazines, Warner Music Group, and Warner Brothers movie company.

This merger represented the first large-scale combination of an "old media" and "new media" company. By 2003, the flood of corporate scandals hovered over the

Steve Case, former chairman and CEO of America Online, and Gerald Levin, former chairman and CEO of Time Warner, celebrate AOL's acquisition of Time Warner in 2000. Two years later, AOL Time Warner had lost $98 billion in one year, and both men had been forced from power. The great experiment of combining "old" and "new" media companies had failed.

conglomerate, and the AOL and Time Warner merger appeared to be unraveling. AOL Time Warner stock value declined precipitously, combined with a government inquiry into the accounting for the company's advertising. After an internal audit of previous years' advertising and sales revenues, the company adjusted downward its previously claimed revenues. By February 2003, the two men who engineered the merger were no longer running the company. Gerald Levin retired as AOL Time Warner's chief executive officer in late 2001, and Steve Case resigned as chairman of AOL Time Warner in 2003.

In an effort to reverse its fortunes, AOL launched AOL 8.0 in late 2002. AOL now claims a worldwide membership of 35.2 million, including 26.5 million in the United States. However, subscriptions declined in the last quarter of 2002 for the first time in company history. The advantages of combining old and new media never materialized, and AOL Time Warner lost $98 billion in 2002, the largest annual loss in history by a corporation.

Many observers began to question the company's survival. AOL based its success on acquiring customers early and often—and on dial-up modems. As broadband continues to be more widely accepted, AOL may lose customers to other services. In 2002, AOL had only a 4 percent share of the 12 million broadband subscribers in the United States.[18]

AUDIENCE DEMAND IN COMPUTER MARKETS

The demand for computers in business is enormous. Nearly every professional office—whether it be a law office, a public relations agency, or a government agency—relies on computers. Educational institutions constantly struggle to fund up-to-date computer facilities in a rapidly changing technological environment. Stockbrokers and financial analysts use computers to keep up with constantly changing market conditions. In doctors' offices, appointments and medical and billing records are kept on computers. Reporters, advertising personnel, and public relations professionals seek information via the computer and then use the computer as a tool for the production of ads, news stories, public relations releases, and illustrations. Convergence is further evident as the advertisements are broadcast electronically for companies sponsoring World Wide Web sites.

Demand for Hardware

Hardware demand—at least for standard computers—is declining. This is driving prices down. In 2003, a fast, well-equipped desktop computer could be obtained for about $1,000, less than half the price of only several years earlier. A family could subscribe to an Internet provider for about $20 a month, with some local services charging even less. Computers now cost about the same as a thirty-inch television set. The computer is still an expensive mass communications tool for some families, but the decline in price makes it more accessible than in previous years.

The demand for computers is slowing both at home and at work, in part because the advances are not viewed as essential by consumers or corporations. In a world in which a variety of computers strive for brand identification, consumers buy less because of price than because of brand.

Demand for Software

Most home computers are sold with a solid complement of software, including the basic operating system. For non-Apple systems, this usually means Windows XP. Consumers take for granted that basic software will be provided. Increasingly specialized applications, however, are available for higher-end users. Digital photography has opened a new consumer, as well as corporate, market. As the price of digital cameras declined, more people took advantage of the ability to e-mail photographs to their family and friends, as well as to print copies. Hewlett-Packard, for example, in 2002 introduced a photo printer that guaranteed prints that would not fade for seventy-five years. As prices dropped, the market expanded for related photo software.

Demand for Privacy and Regulation in Networked Services

Connectivity usually means access to the World Wide Web, the graphical interface of the Internet. With the demand for connectivity and the services it provides, such as online shopping, comes an array of fears about online security. The issues of *privacy and anonymity* exist on many levels, from protecting credit card numbers in online shopping to worrying about access to pornography. Other problematic areas include censorship, copyright and access to information, and developing a system of *regulation in the information age.*

The Pew Project on the Internet and American life suggests that Americans worry first about child pornography on the Internet (92 percent). The other area of major concern has to do with credit card theft (87 percent), fraud (80 percent), and hackers breaking into government and corporate computers (76–78 percent). Nearly 82 percent are also worried about organized terrorists "wreaking havoc" with Internet tools.

Researchers for the project also discovered that a slight majority of the public supports the right of the FBI and other law enforcement agencies to intercept the e-mail of those suspected of crime. Interestingly, this support comes at a time when only 31 percent of Americans say they trust the government to do the right thing. In regard to monitoring e-mail, the public doesn't believe that current legislation affecting monitoring of telephones is adequate; 62 percent of Americans say new laws should be enacted to protect the e-mail privacy of ordinary citizens from government agencies.

During the 1999 Yugoslavian war, messages on the Internet alerted the world to some of the first atrocities committed by Serbs against ethnic Albanians, yet there was a great fear that the messages could be traced, which might have resulted in death for those who sent the messages. Yet traceability is valuable in tracking such criminals

key concepts

Privacy and Anonymity Courts have ruled people have a right to privacy, but sometimes that right conflicts with the need to find those who abuse access to free communication over the Internet.

Regulation in the Information Age In the early days of the Internet, regulation was compared to law in the Wild West—there wasn't much. As more people use the Internet, pressures to make money increase, and issues of security evolve, regulation has grown. However, the extent and nature of Internet regulation continues to be an issue in courts and legislatures and will be for years to come.

as the creators of the Melissa and "I Love You" viruses, which infected thousands of computers in 1999 and 2000.[19] The concern about privacy accelerated after users learned that Intel Corporation embedded unique identification numbers in its Pentium III processors that enabled network operators to identify specific users on the Internet. In addition, Microsoft designed a "globally unique identifier" that appears in Microsoft documents and can be used to trace files to a specific computer. The identifier was helpful in tracing perpetrators of the Melissa virus. In response, companies have developed privacy software such as anonymizer.com, which allows users to remain anonymous online.

Further complicating the picture is the move to wireless. Wireless networks are easily hacked, a situation that should make corporations think twice about going to the uncabled communication system. Also, since September 11, 2001, analysts have become increasingly worried about the vulnerability of the Internet to terrorist attack. Commercialization of the Internet has increased access but at the same time increased vulnerability.

Another form of privacy involves user accessibility. For those hoping to shield their children from certain sites, web filters such as Cybersitter and Clickchoice are available. These software packages block certain sites and words. However, they are not foolproof systems because users have to specify words that are to be blocked. Eliminating specific words may still allow objectionable material through the filter.

Privacy issues are paramount because almost every move a person makes on the computer can be tracked electronically. Databases record when and where you change addresses, subscribe to magazines, and apply for credit cards. The 1994 movie *The Pelican Brief* was realistic in showing that the FBI and others can identify a person's exact location by tracking credit cards used for shopping, hotel accommodations, and ATM machines. Another film, *The Net*, revealed an even darker side of the computer links to a person's identity. Sandra Bullock's character was consistently—and intentionally—identified as someone other than herself. Her own identity seemed nearly lost.

Databases available for finding a person's location or biographical information include Post Office Change of Address, People Finder, Address Search, Phonefile, and Credit Abstracts. Information in these databases includes a person's name, age, date of birth, Social Security number, spouse's name, current and previous addresses, phone number (sometimes even an unlisted one), all residents at that particular address, and neighbors and their phone numbers and addresses.

Some of these databases are put together from information found in standard directories, product response cards, and magazine subscription cards. Herein lies an ethical and perhaps legal issue. Private citizens filling out magazine subscription cards and the like assume they are providing information to one company for the single purpose of receiving a magazine subscription. However, this information is often sold to other companies that use the information to create databases for anyone to buy. The information use goes beyond what the individual originally intended, and at least two companies are profiting from information that a person has provided freely.

Privacy and copyright issues arise in obtaining information from bulletin boards and electronic mail. Many mass media professionals scan electronic networks looking for story ideas, information, and sources to quote. They believe that because these electronic postings are available to the public, they can be repeated in other printed publications or broadcast (and cable) products. However, they might be sued if the source has not granted permission to be quoted or deems that the use of material invaded his or her privacy. Web-based documents are easily downloaded and pasted to other documents. The technological ease of copying material, however, does not ensure that such copying is legal. Furthermore, e-mail messages, such as letters, belong to the originator, not to the recipient. They are not considered part of the public domain. Although media organizations may win specific judgments, they often experience financial and time losses.[20]

SUPPLYING THE AUDIENCE'S DEMAND

Traditional news organizations are taking notice of the growing number of computer users and their willingness to pay for fast, customized information. These organizations are experimenting with the notion that they are in the information business, not just the newspaper or broadcast news business. Many mass media suppliers have created Internet or web sites or are delivering information through commercial on-line services.

Software Products

Software products are designed to meet audience demand for information and entertainment. CD-ROMs are often used as storage devices because of their large capacity. CD-ROM technology first made it possible to store large indices, such as the *Reader's Guide to Periodical Literature* and encyclopedias, on a single disk. Now these services are increasingly provided online, often through web-based products.

Virtual reality products simulate reality, allowing users to "go" places and "do" things they have never done. The ability to simulate real life was once considered nearly impossible, but now has significant applications in military training, health care, education and training, and entertainment. Information highway planners emphasize that equal opportunities for professionals to gain training and upgrade computer skills are essential elements of an information society.

One of the earliest uses of virtual reality was in training pilots. When U.S. pilots went into Bosnia in December 1995, they had trained on virtual reality simulators that turned satellite data into three-dimensional views of Bosnia, which familiarized them with the terrain even though they had never seen the Balkans.[21] Bill Gates, in his book *The Road Ahead*, writes about how convincing being in a simulator is: "When I was using the simulator my friends decided to give me a surprise by having a small plane fly by. While I sat in the pilot's seat, the all-too-real-looking image of a Cessna flashed into view. I wasn't prepared for the 'emergency,' and I crashed into it."[22] Significant use of this technique also can be important in the training of medical students for surgery. With goggles and helmets, they will be able to perform simulated surgery on patients who are computer creations rather than living individuals.

Virtual reality products are not commonly found in the home market yet because they require powerful and sophisticated computer equipment combined with intricate software. However, this is likely to change. Simplified approximations of virtual reality have already reached the home market.

Online Professional and Consumer Services

Commercial online services are designed for either professional or consumer use. Professionals use databases in a variety of ways. For example, a marketing firm might hire a researcher to investigate different types of packaging. That person might connect to Lexis-Nexis and go into its MARKET, an electronic library grouping of databases on advertising, marketing, market research, public relations, sales and

Simulation and virtual reality techniques often are used in training as well as for entertainment. Information superhighway planners emphasize that equal opportunities for professionals to gain training and upgrade computer skills are essential elements of an information society.

selling, promotions, consumer attitudes and behavior, demographics, product announcements and reviews, and industry overviews. Then the user might narrow the search into PACKNG, a database on packaging from January 1989, for the desired information. Professional services are sophisticated but expensive, and most are subscribed to by companies rather than individuals.

News Services

✦ The most popular general **news service** is the Associated Press (AP), which has several hundred news bureaus gathering information in more than one hundred countries and translating it into six different languages. The AP sells its information to more than fifteen thousand different types of media organizations around the globe. About 75 percent of the news (international, national, and state) that U.S. consumers read and see comes from the AP. On the one hand, it is cheaper for media organizations to get information from the AP than to set up bureaus or send their own reporters to all countries where newsworthy events are taking place. On the other hand, it is worrisome to know that most of the information that people receive, whether delivered in print or through broadcast or cable, comes from the same source.

Other news services at home and abroad have played important roles throughout the years. United Press International, initially formed from William Randolph Hearst's International News Service and E. W. Scripps's United Press, has fought desperately to stay alive. International services such as Reuters and Agence-France Press have provided information through the lens of a different national perspective. Specialized news services such as Dow Jones and the Washington Post–L.A. Times News Service provide in-depth features and explanations rather than the spot news on which the AP thrives.

Computers help news sources get information to their subscribers quickly. Most news services have reporters who use computers to write their stories and transmit them through portable satellite dishes, all of which can fit into a big suitcase. The reports can be dispatched immediately to the news service's headquarters, edited, and sent to computers at the subscribing media organizations. Although satellite transmission helps journalists avoid censorship, they still must fear at times for their personal safety. Securing a place from which to bounce a signal off a satellite is not always easy in hostile territory.

Computers have also spurred development of online news services by commercial conglomerates and news chains such as Knight Ridder. Its news organizations transmit every published story to a central database that is available to all Knight Ridder news organizations. Other organizations also may subscribe.

Syndicates

✦ Syndicates provide features, entertainment, opinion columns, and cartoons to media organizations for a fee. Syndicates enable you to keep up with "Dear Abby" or follow the same comic strip in different newspapers in any part of the country. Syndicates also provide news and entertainment videoclips for use by broadcast and cable TV stations.

Syndicates contract with writers, illustrators, and video artists to provide work that can be sold through the syndicate. Media organizations can select specific items to purchase, much like choosing dishes in a cafeteria line. Computers are influencing the way news organizations get their syndicated features.[23] For example, even as recently as 1993, when computers abounded in the media workplace, syndicated comics were sent by postal mail, not electronically. Comic strips had to be completed six months before publication. Syndicate delivery—another example of media convergence—allows comics to be transmitted directly into newsroom computers, and publications now electronically paginate comics pages. Cartoonists now have tighter deadlines, which are especially important to political cartoonists, who need to closely follow political "hot topics."

King Features Syndicate, which handles the largest number of syndicated comic strips, has contracted with the AP to distribute comics electronically using the AP's digital and satellite technology. The AP sends its news photos to subscriber media organizations through a high-speed PhotoStream service. Non-AP material is distributed through PhotoExpress, which uses extra capacity on the PhotoStream service.

news service: Organizations that collect and distribute news and information to media outlets. Some professionals still use the term *wire services.*

Gaming

Games are no longer a video arcade or a simple maze on a PC. Three companies have high-stakes dollars invested in the personal gaming craze, and PC Rooms, first popular in Asia, are spreading rapidly in Los Angeles and San Francisco.

Online gaming is a major sport for teenagers and young adults. In fact, Microsoft, Nintendo, and Sony are battling to gain the largest portion of the online game market. Each of the manufacturers has produced machines for gaming. In the fall of 2002, Sony's PS2 cost about $199, Microsoft's Xbox cost $200, and Nintendo's GameCube

cost $150. Each manufacturer was slashing its prices to win the initial audience. Each device has from fifty to two hundred games.

The easy availability of games and game rooms poses questions for parents interested in their children's computer activities. Half-life Counterstrike, a game rated M—intended for players seventeen years old or older—is readily available in PC Rooms, public gaming rooms that have replaced the old video arcades. Rarely are ages checked. Counterstrike is a bloody, animated battle game in which the goal is to kill

more times than you are killed. Survival is not the issue.

Although games are rated by the Entertainment Software Rating Board, an industry organization, the ratings are rarely enforced. A Federal Trade Commission study published in December 2001 found that 78 percent of teenagers ages thirteen to sixteen who tried to buy an M-rated game were successful.

Sources: New York Times (September 5, 2002): E1, E5; *Detroit Free Press* (May 21, 2002): 1D, 4D; *Chicago Tribune* (April 22, 2002), Business sec., p. 4.

Consumer Services ✦ Commercial services and Internet service providers such as America Online, Earthlink, or other local providers offer some or all of the following services:

✦ Indexed information retrieval for financial and general information such as that found in traditional newsletters, annual reports, newspapers, magazines, radio, and television.
✦ Transactions such as shopping in an electronic mall or participating in a public opinion poll online.
✦ Sending messages to people privately with e-mail or in forums.

TRENDS

Trends on the Internet involve (1) media organizations' use of new technologies such as Flash and 3-D to animate information; (2) creation of increasingly portable hardware; and (3) increased commercialization of the Web, including shopping.

Media Organizations on the Web

As you read in Chapter 2, which explained the history and some of the current issues of journalism in the United States, many media organizations are still following an age-old concept called "shovelware." A Michigan State University study of regional daily newspaper web sites indicates that outside the major national markets, newspapers are not adapting to web use. For example, 65 percent of the regional web sites studied in the late morning of September 11 2001, said nothing about the World Trade Center bombings. Furthermore, 38 percent in the late afternoon still had no news about the New York attack. The Pew Center for the People and the

By using the Web, media organizations are able to present complex information using a combination of text, graphics, and audio clips in an interactive format.

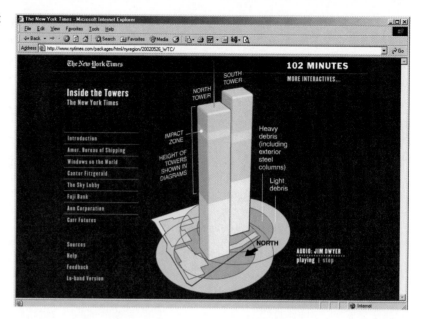

Press also indicates that although 25 percent of Americans go online for news at least three times a week, there's been almost no increase in the percentage during the last few years.[24]

However, some newspapers are striving to exploit unique characteristics of the Web. Reliving September 11, the *New York Times* created a dramatic presentation blending audio, video, text, and commentary. (See www.nytimes.com/packages/html/nyregion/20020526_WTC.) Occasionally, a newspaper does something really ambitious. For example, the *Fort Lauderdale Sun-Sentinel* has a page about Hurricane Andrew in 1992 and even includes a clever gamelike feature. The material is well researched and graphically interesting. One can imagine science teachers using it to explain the origins and impact of hurricanes. (See www.sun-sentinel.com/extras/graphics/news/andrew/index.html.) However, the gamelike feature, called "Hurricane Maker," is hard to find. You have to click on "Andrew's Path," then "Recorded Wind Speeds and Storm Surge," then "Related Items," then "Interactives." This feature is easy to miss—a good example of bad web design.

"Hurricane Maker" is, however, a harbinger of things to come. More and more, news organizations are using technologies such as Flash and Java to create animated information graphics. This approach is useful for animating the ground attack in Iraq or the internal fires that ultimately weakened the metal skeletons of the Twin Towers. In continuing struggles in the Middle East, whether they be ground attacks or invasions of technology, animated graphics could provide excellent comparisons of U.S. weapons technology with the technology in the Gulf War of 1991. The technology is a lot better today. The United States claimed then, for example, that airborne surveillance was able to deliver real-time imagery to aid in target selection. That wasn't true then, but it is now. Unmanned aircraft such as the Predator transmit television images to command-and-control centers far from the battlefield. This technology was tested in Afghanistan in 2001 and in Iraq in 2003 and was found to work reasonably well. An animated infographic would explain it better than a still infographic, and using a voice-over might enhance the emotional immediacy of the action.

Gamelike features also will find their way onto news web sites. In the case of Iraq, for example, somebody will surely think of introducing users to the concept of target selection by turning them into armchair generals, offering them a range of targets—say a Baghdad hospital that Israeli intelligence says is being used as a cover for unconventional weapons development. You as the "general" would have to decide whether you trusted the Israelis enough to accept the certain public outcry that would come from bombing a hospital.

Whoever does this will no doubt be criticized for turning news into entertainment, and under circumstances that raise real questions of taste and propriety. Other innovations include:

+ The weblog, or "blog." Romanesko's *Media News* is a blog, which refers to a rolling, frequently updated set of musings on a given topic, typically supplying users with a message board function so they can join in. The *Arts and Letters Daily,* now published on the site of the *Chronicle of Higher Education,* is another example.
+ Short Message Service, or SMS. This is a cell phone service, wildly popular in Europe, in which it is possible for a company to send 164-character bursts of text to a subscriber. SMS is good for sports scores, stock quotes, and headlines. The service is far faster than web functions on a cell phone.
+ RSS, for Really Simple Syndication. This is a variant of the Web markup language known as XML (for eXtensible Markup Language), which allows a provider of news to publish in a format readable by "news aggregators" like Amphetadesk.

This cellular phone features a camera, personal organizer, and e-mail ability. It represents a new generation of wireless communications and information technology.

Hardware Development

The innovations in hardware development include chips that provide greater stability and speed, but true innovation today comes in the concept of portability. Portability has become the key to new hardware developments. Forget the lightweight laptop. Next in line are multimedia mobile phones and handheld computers that recognize speech and handwritten notes. Mobile phones that take digital photos already are available.

Nokia, for example, released cellular phones in November 2002 that included such features as a flashlight, calorie counter, calendar, foldout keyboard, and the ability to download games and music. But such gadgets are costly: The Nokia sold for $1,300. Camcorders and video players were scheduled to be released in the next generation of mobile phones. Nokia spokesman Antony Wilson said, "What we are seeing is true convergence of things like digital cameras, MP3 players, personal data assistants; all these technologies are starting to converge in mobile devices."

Tablet PCs were also on the horizon in late 2002. Busy executives were expected to be interested in the small computers that would recognize notes written with an electronic stylus.

In the music arena, a handheld Mad Player, at a cost of $750, can be purchased over the Internet. The Mad Player contains 550 sounds that can be mixed in random ways to create a variety of musical styles.[25]

E-Commerce

One of the newest and hottest developments on the Web is *e-commerce.* Although online sales at the beginning of 2000 represented only a small portion of consumer spending, e-commerce has grown tremendously from 1997 to the present. Online sales escalated from a mere $3.01 billion in 1997 to an estimated $32.6 billion in 2001. These figures did not include sales from ticket agencies or online travel services.

Despite these increases, online shopping accounted for only 1 percent of total retail sales in 2001 and did not increase at as fast a rate as regular retail. However, catalog sales accounted for about $72 billion in 2001. Despite the fact that Internet shopping has been available for only a few years, it accounted for nearly half as much as the catalogs.[26]

E-commerce includes advertising as well as sales. Although online advertising declined during 2001–2002, some segments showed increases. One of these is online gambling. Casino ads now appear not only on gaming sites, but on general interest portal sites as well. Middle-aged, lower-income, and childless adults are most likely to hit the gambling sites.[27]

key concept

E-Commerce Shopping online is a growing trend that may change the retail industry worldwide.

discussing trends

The ways in which media organizations address web use, the availability of portable hardware that provides everything from digital video to voice calls, and the expansion of e-commerce mean that computers are ubiquitous. They invade not only the homes of most Americans, but also their very lives. Still, many questions remain to be answered. These include:

- Will media organizations spend more dollars and time creating specific media content for the Web?
- Will individuals respond to flash animation and 3-D technology? Will they take the time to use information delivered in this new form?
- Will portable gadgets be just that—gadgets? Or will individuals use the many applications soon to be provided? How important is cost?
- Will e-commerce continue to expand? How will it affect regular retail? How big a factor will security play?

summary

- Computers are used in every application by traditional mass media organizations. They are also a medium in their own right and are used directly by consumers.
- Convergence—or the combining of more than one communication form into a single distribution process—is increasing rapidly.
- The computer began as an attempt to create calculating machines, then evolved as scientists sought efficient means to organize, retrieve, and process information.
- Although the computer industry is highly diversified and competitive, giants such as IBM and Microsoft have held leading roles and dominated different portions of the industry at different times.
- Computer research and networking have been heavily funded by the U.S. government because of the implications for defense and strategic applications.
- The development of the silicon chip in 1959 made it possible for the computer to shrink in size.

- The modem is the connection to the computerized world, the device that makes possible the concept of an information highway. A major issue is whether the cable industry or telephone companies will win dominance to provide access to computer users.
- The Internet is a series of computers networked to other computers that provide the fundamental basis of an information highway.
- CD-ROMs and DVD technology help meet the demand for text, audio, and video storage that is portable and that can be periodically updated.
- Commercial online services provide information, usually at a cost, to high-end business users as well as to consumers.
- Most news services and syndicates are now computer based.

navigating the web | The Internet on the Web

Obviously, people who use the Web are interested in computers, technology, and the potential of the information highway. On web sites, you can find information on the history of computers, new technologies, and the business of technology.

Internet World Online
www.internetworld.com

Covering a variety of Internet topics in columns and articles, *Internet World* is also available in print.

ZDNet
www.zdnet.com
The ZDNet Webzine comes from Ziff-Davis, the largest publisher of computer magazines. It covers news about computers and the world of online businesses.

Media Central Interactive
www.mediacentral.com
Cowles Media maintains Media Central Interactive, which provides in-depth articles about online media and daily short stories about events in a variety of media.

Privacy Issues
www.epic.org
EPIC is a public interest research center in Washington, D.C. It was established in 1994 to focus public attention on emerging civil liberties issues and to protect privacy, the First Amendment, and constitutional values. EPIC is a project of the Fund for Constitutional Government. It works in association with Privacy International, an international human rights group based in London, and is also a member of the Global Internet Liberty Campaign, the Internet Free Expression Alliance, the Internet Privacy Coalition, and the Trans Atlantic Consumer Dialogue (TACD).

Zero Knowledge Systems
www.zeroknowledge.com
Programs to protect privacy on the Internet are available at Zero Knowledge.

questions for review

1. What was IBM's role in the development of computer technology?
2. Why is Microsoft a significant player in computer delivery of mass media?
3. What is an operating system?
4. Describe several online services that target professional users.
5. How will e-commerce affect retail sales, for example, of clothing?
6. What is the digital divide?

issues to think about

1. What are some obstacles that will have to be overcome in developing the Internet so that it is accessible? So that it protects individual privacy? So that people can use it for functions such as transferring money and know that their funds are secure?
2. Describe ethical issues that emerge from virtual reality technology.
3. Develop your idea for a web site that would meet the needs of a professional today. How would you structure the content of such a site and what links would you include?
4. What is the role of the mass media professional in the development of the World Wide Web?
5. If you were designing a newspaper for the future, how would you incorporate new technology?

suggested readings

Carey, John. "The Interactive Television Puzzle." Freedom Forum Media Studies Center Paper, 1994.

Diamond, Edwin, and Stephen Bates. "The Ancient History of the Internet." *American Heritage* (October 1995): 34–46.

"Internet, Free Speech and Industry Self-Regulation." Report by The Information Technology Association of America Task Force on Internet Use, November 1995. This and other reports can be obtained from the association at 1616 North Fort Myer Drive, Suite 1300, Arlington, VA 22209. The association's web site is www.itaa.org.

Kovach, Bill, and Tom Rosenstiel. *Warp Speed* (New York: The Century Foundation Press, 1999).

Negroponte, Nicholas. *Being Digital* (New York: Alfred A. Knopf, 1995).

Ethics

In May 2002, CBS aired edited portions of a videotape showing Pakistani Islamic fundamentalists murdering Daniel Pearl, a reporter for the *Wall Street Journal*. Showing the tape drew criticism from U.S. government officials and from some ethicists.

On May 31, shortly after the debate had begun, *The Boston Phoenix*, a weekly alternative newspaper, posted a link to an edited version of the tape that includes Pearl's neck being cut with a knife and images of someone holding his severed head.[1] The *Phoenix* also ran a photo in its newspaper of Pearl's severed head. The debate about what should and should not be shown elicited national attention.

CBS used some of the less disturbing images from the video footage to illustrate a story about how terrorists used the video as propaganda in Muslim countries. CBS was criticized because the Pearl family did not want the footage shown. Andie Silvers, a CBS spokeswoman, explained: "We thought it was important as responsible journalists to show the American people what is being put out there and the effect it is having on the Arab world."[2]

Controversy over CBS's story faded as critics responded to the *Phoenix*'s use of the video and still images. Critics said the video had no news value, it was used just to gain attention for the newspaper, and the *Phoenix* showed disrespect for the family.

Not everyone agreed that the *Phoenix* was wrong in running the images. Some said the video had news value and historical importance and that withholding and editing it was "paternalistic."

"There are awful things that happen in the world, and I don't believe people should be prevented from seeing them," Paul Lester, a professor at California State University, Fullerton, told the *American Journalism Review*. "Awful acts need to be shown, and we need to see as humans what other humans are capable of in this world. Visual images show this more powerfully than words can ever do."[3]

The issues surrounding the Pearl video get to the heart of news decisions. Were the images crucial to CBS's story? Did other news organizations buckle under to government pressure not to use the images? Who should decide the nature of images given to viewers and readers? Should news media consider the feelings of family members when using images? Do media organizations use gruesome images to gain audience, which will affect how much money they make?

Welcome to the world of media ethics. In this world, political and economic pressures can affect the media content that consumers receive. *Ethics* is easily defined as standards of conduct and moral judgment. However, defining moral judgment requires judging the goodness or badness of human behavior and character. This is a difficult task both for those who supply news to reporters and for those who process news. When people question whether mass media employees have ethics, they are really asking whether these influential professionals have standards to guide their decisions and

Ethical decision making is not easy to understand or to do. But because mass media permeate our society and are our primary sources of information, we need to address ethical issues. Some of those addressed in this chapter include the following:

◆ Why is adherence to ethical behavior an important consideration for media workers?

◆ How is ethical behavior related to political and social issues?

◆ How do economic issues influence ethical behavior?

◆ What is the relationship of ethical behavior to the marketplace of ideas and to the preservation of U.S. society?

Ethics *in Your Life*

Whom Do You Trust?

Do you trust journalists to behave in ethical ways? What about public relations practitioners? If you had a discussion with your friends, what would they say? Do you think credibility is an important issue for information gatherers? As you read this chapter, think about the various individuals who try to control the flow of information. To what extent does their credibility have an impact on your life?

WHOM DO YOU TRUST?	WHO IS MOST LIKELY TO ADHERE TO ETHICAL BEHAVIOR?
Print journalists?	
Reporters and anchors for network television news?	
Reporters for special news programming, such as newsmagazines?	
Reporters and anchors for local news?	
Public relations practitioners who work for nonprofit companies?	
Public relations practitioners who work for profit-making companies?	
Advertisers?	
Sources for news: Politicians?	
Sources for news: People who hold high positions in the business world?	
Sources for news: Social and political activists?	

conduct and whether they adhere to those standards. News reporters and editors have long claimed that they adhere to standards of truth without obligation to any economic imperative, but research reveals that economics and politics often have dictated news content. Furthermore, although public relations personnel are often thought to be more loyal to the organization that employs them than to the truth, standards of professional conduct also are applied to decision making in public relations. Public relations professionals consider part of their job to be convincing upper management of the ethical position that a company should take regarding public service and information.

ETHICS IN AMERICAN LIFE

Media critics have long been concerned with ethical standards. That concern, reported as early as the eighteenth century, was part of a continuing dialogue about the role of a free press in a democratic society. If the media are to be protected—that is,

Sensational stories, such as those about murders and love triangles, have always been standard fare for newspapers. Critics have argued about whether the editor should decide what the reader needs to read or whether the reader can make intelligent individual choices. After World War II, the idea of a socially responsible press gained credence, and critics viewed it as the obligation of the press to report the news in the full context of political and social events.

if freedom of expression is to be paramount—then the public must be able to trust the media to adhere to well-understood standards. The political importance of ethical behavior is strongly connected to the concept of a free-flowing marketplace of ideas that is the foundation of a democratic society.

History of Journalistic Standards

Ethical standards are intrinsically related to the political and cultural milieu in which the media operate. In colonial days, newspapers were highly partisan, and *ethical decision making* focused on whether editors should print points of view of competing parties rather than just the views of the party they supported. As newspaper editors adopted an **information model** during the middle of the nineteenth century, they remained partisan but also began to include stories about common people. This focus on individuals gave rise to new discussions about ethics. Critics denounced editors for trivializing the news, claiming that giving public notice to ordinary people was harmful to the public and "misled most people . . . into thinking them[selves] important."[4] After 1850, however, critics began to focus on the relationship between press and society, and they increasingly addressed press issues. They attacked editors for publishing trivial gossip and argued that publishing details of people's lives, such as accounts of weddings, invaded individuals' privacy.

With the rise of sensational journalism in the 1890s, critics began to focus on attributes of news. They argued that fact and opinion should be separated, that care "beyond the profit principle must be exercised in news selection," and that material that violated good taste and judgment should be avoided. Critics, of course, differed in their definitions of good taste. Some thought crime stories were not in good taste. Others thought editors should print only certain details about crime stories. Critics also noted that business and editorial operations should be separated. These discussions paved the way for the development of journalism education, ethics codes, and other means of monitoring journalistic conduct.[5]

key concept

Ethical Decision Making Making ethical decisions has been a concern of journalists since at least the early twentieth century, when many reporters wanted to be among the emerging groups of professionals. However, attempts to determine exactly what standards of conduct and moral judgment constitute ethical behavior have resulted in a continuing debate rather than absolute standards.

In a study of journalistic standards, Marion Marzolf noted that by the end of the nineteenth century, commercial concerns were beginning to shape newspaper standards. Even though the newspaper was still seen as educational, with a moral obligation toward the public, profit goals were beginning to tip the press toward a "degrading vulgarity."[6] Marzolf's work reflects a concern that dominates criticism of the media today: the controversy between commercial gain and the traditional democratic values that a free press was thought to foster.

Development of Standards for Public Relations

By the end of World War I, extensive use of propaganda techniques during the war raised ethical issues for practitioners of public relations as well as for journalists. In 1923, Edward L. Bernays, who had developed campaigns for the War Department, published *Crystallizing Public Opinion*, which argued that the modern public demanded information and made up its own mind. However, because society was growing in complexity, Bernays said, someone was needed to bring specialized information to the public in an honest, ethical way. He and his colleague and wife, Doris Fleishman, coined the term "counsel on public relations" to describe the work of the public relations practitioner. In essence, Bernays argued that in the marketplace of ideas the job of the public relations counsel was to get a client the best possible hearing for a legitimate message.[7]

information model: Pattern of behavior for disseminating information as news; incorporates values such as objectivity over partisanship.

CLASSICAL ETHICS IN A MODERN SOCIETY

In their book *Media Ethics*, three prominent ethics scholars, Clifford G. Christians, Kim B. Rotzoll, and Mark Fackler, outline five ***theoretical approaches*** for understanding modern ethical decisions. Remember that these are philosophical principles that underlie discussions; they are not prescriptions for solutions, as you can see in the following examples.

1. *The Golden Mean.* Aristotle advocated the Golden Mean. He believed that moderation in life, as well as in eating habits, best serves the individual. Moderation as applied to ethics means operating somewhere between two extremes. For example, in the case described in the opening segment of this chapter, CBS attempted moderation, whereas the *Phoenix* thought truth lies in the raw power of the unedited picture.

2. *The Categorical Imperative.* Eighteenth-century philosopher Immanuel Kant believed that ethical principles should be determined by analyzing what principles could be applied universally. This imperative is related to what some call **absolute ethics.** What is right for one is right for all, and what is right for one situation is right for all situations with similar circumstances.

People who advocate absolutist positions believe that if lying, for example, is unethical, then all variations from the truth are wrong; it would be out of the question to utter a white lie or to lie to protect someone. If an editor decrees that names of suspects will not be published until they have been found guilty, then that rule covers all cases, with no exceptions.

3. *The Principle of Utility.* Nineteenth-century philosopher John Stuart Mill advocated that ethical decisions be made on the basis of what provides the greatest good for the greatest number of human beings within society. One could argue that public relations professionals who promote tobacco and media companies who reap profits from tobacco advertising are not operating according to the principle of utility. Medical science has found that tobacco is deleterious to a great number of human beings within society.

4. *The Veil of Ignorance.* John Rawls espouses a decidedly twentieth-century philosophical position, arguing that justice emerges when social differentiations are eliminated in the process of negotiation. Therefore, information is treated outside of the social context, and power, wealth, and other social factors do not enhance one position over another. This principle means that ABC reporters, for example, when covering Disney, would be able to disregard the power and wealth of the network's parent company.

5. *Judeo-Christian Ethic.* The Golden Rule, "Do unto others as you would have them do unto you," applies here. Individuals who adhere to this religious ethic are encouraged to "love thy neighbor as thyself" and to treat all individuals with respect.[8] In this case, the decision to show the Daniel Pearl tape would require the reporter to ask himself or herself, "If I were Pearl, would I want it shown?"

POLITICAL AND ECONOMIC DEMAND FOR ETHICAL BEHAVIOR

The evolution of journalistic standards and concern about the ethics of reporting information from both journalistic and public relations standpoints clearly reveal that the public, press, educators, and critics demand ethical behavior. The standards

absolute ethics: A code of ethics that allows no deviation from its rules.

are not always clear, and they change as cultural norms within society change. The nineteenth-century critics who thought that reporting on crime was distasteful would be laughed off the television screen, which thrives on realistic reenactments of police investigations.

However, there are also economic demands for ethical behavior because of the enormous impact of information dissemination in a free-market society. Economic demand involves several factors: (1) the **credibility** of the news organization and its ability to make a profit, (2) the economic concentration of media outlets, and (3) the impact on other industries affected by media coverage.

Credibility and Profit

When the public believes that those who work in the mass media act without thinking ethically, then media credibility is at stake. People listen to the radio, watch television, and read newspapers and magazines to find out what is going on in the world around them. If the local newspaper is known for routinely publishing inaccurate information, then people will stop buying the paper and turn to local television or radio for news.

If people question the credibility of one network news department, then they may turn to a more credible network for national news. For any of the news media to survive, *credibility is an economic incentive for ethics.*

The issue of credibility and the growing competition among twenty-four-hour cable news channels was exemplified by the hiring in April 2001 of actress Andrea Thompson, who formerly starred in TV police drama *NYPD Blue*, to anchor *CNN Headline News*. Critics said Thompson was not qualified for the position because she had not graduated from high school and had worked only about a year in local television news. She was hired at a time CNN was firing far more experienced reporters.[9] Observers said the hire would hurt the credibility of *CNN Headline News*. But Bruce Bartlett defended the hire when he wrote:

> So let's cut the hypocrisy. It's getting a little thick. Television news is a business like any other. It has to produce ratings so that advertisers will buy time and pay the network to run their ads. If no one tunes in, as is increasingly the case with CNN, what are they supposed to do? Run losses and take it out of the hides of shareholders? I think not.
>
> Personally, I think it would be better if we just called anchors what they are called in England, "news readers." That's all they do and that is fine. We shouldn't pretend they are anything more.[10]

Adding to the controversy was the discovery before Thompson started on CNN that she had posed topless for photographs earlier in her career. These appeared on the Internet and caused CNN to discuss whether she should go on air. However, she did appear as a *CNN Headline News* anchor. Her work was erratic and she sometimes seemed uncomfortable on camera.

Whether Thompson hurt CNN's credibility remains unresolved. She left the network nine months after she started. Her explanation was that she wanted to spend more time with her child. CNN said the departure was Thompson's idea. It is not clear whether TV news anchors need to be journalists to have credibility. But it is clear that the need to generate audience to make sufficient profit affects decisions that affect credibility.

Ethics and Media Concentration

With the increasing concentration of the ownership of media organizations, critics and the public have become more attuned to the possibilities and effects of unethical behavior. In 1996, Disney acquired two major media organizations: Cap Cities and ABC. Two years later, serious accusations arose about ABC's ability to cover the par-

"Pass the Courvoisier": The Ethics of Persuasion

For decades, critics have chided the movie industry for product placement—taking money for prominently placing a product in a film. Critics say this subtle, unacknowledged form of advertising manipulates people without their being aware of this fact.

In an expanding world of media often funded by advertising, such issues will only grow. Whether it's Busta Rhymes helping Courvoisier brandy with his hip-hop hit or television news departments selecting sources from their advertisers, such behavior raises issues related to the ethics of persuasion.

Much of the criticism of media organizations concentrates on two issues: persuasion aimed at promoting harmful activities and unidentified persuasion. The former has been an issue for as long as advertising has been sold and can be traced to the patent medicine ads of the 1800s. The belief that it is unethical to use advertising as a way to persuade people to act in harmful ways was the principle behind outlawing cigarette advertising on television in 1971. This concern arose again more recently with the efforts by television and the alcohol industry to adver-

tise hard liquor. Although advertising hard liquor on television is not illegal, manufacturers of distilled spirits did not run TV advertising between 1948 and 1996. However, because of lost revenue to beer and wine, Seagram began running ads on local stations in 1996. In 2002, NBC decided to reverse its decision to run alcohol ads after protest from the U.S. Congress and groups such as Mothers Against Drunk Driving.

Industry sources argue that it is not unethical to advertise alcohol to consenting adults. Critics reply that the unethical behavior occurs when underage teenagers are exposed to this form of persuasion.

Even worse, ethicists argue, is when content presented as entertainment or news really aims to persuade. Hip-hop has a history of using brand-name products in music. From Run-D.M.C.'s 1987 "My Adidas," to Ludacris singing about Cadillacs in "Southern Hospitality," products have benefited from rap music. The hip-hop artists, however, say they do not charge for mentioning products; they simply sing about what they like. As a result, their work differs from movie

product placement. This distinction could easily be lost as recording companies look for revenue to replace the money lost by declining CD sales.

Money also seems to be behind the trend in some TV news departments of using their advertisers as news sources. As one news director reported in an *American Journalism Review* article, "If we're doing a story on imported cars, we'd rather talk to the Honda dealer who advertises as opposed to the Toyota dealer who doesn't."

The simplest, and perhaps best, ethical standard for media should be that a media consumer be able to identify the purpose of the content she or he is using. Of course, ethical standards can only be as effective as the ethics of the person creating the content.

Sources: Paige Albiniak, "NBC Bows to Pressure from the Government, Industry Watchdogs," *TVinsite,* March 25, 2002, www.tvinsite.com; Lynette Holloway, "Hip-Hop Sales Pop: Pass the Courvoisier and Count the Cash, *The New York Times* (September 2, 2002): C1 & C6; Deborah Potter," News for Sale," *American Journalism Review,* September 2001, www.ajr.org.

ent company. The case involved *20/20*, the ABC newsmagazine. After a top investigative reporter, Brian Ross, and his longtime producer, Rhonda Schwartz, spent months exposing unsavory practices at Disney theme parks, executives killed the story. "A draft story was submitted that did not work," ABC news spokeswoman Eileen Murphy said in a prepared statement. "This does not reflect badly on any reporter or producer involved."[11]

Impact on Other Industries

News stories affect not only readers but also the subjects they cover. They can affect an industry's credibility or a company's profits; they can also affect the amount of government attention an industry gets. Such attention can result in a change in regulation, which may ultimately affect profit. Such coverage does have an impact that can improve or detract from a company's profitability.

A classic example is the story about Food Lion, Inc., that ABC ran on *PrimeTime Live* during 1992. ABC accused the food chain based in North Carolina of selling out-of-date meat and substandard deli products. Within days, Food Lion stock dropped $1.5 billion in value and food sales declined. ABC producers had gotten jobs at Food Lion and hidden tiny cameras in wigs to shoot footage. Food Lion sued for fraud, deceptive trade practices, breach of loyalty, and trespassing.

Although ABC was found guilty on two counts, the fine was reduced to only one dollar for each count. The network maintained that its actions were ethical. ABC defended lying on the applications, the use of hidden cameras, and its selection of sources by saying that serving the public good—protecting the public from being exposed to bad food—outweighed other considerations. It may well have been a false argument because it is doubtful that bad food was ever the real issue. Even Diane Sawyer, the anchor, reported that no cases of illness from bad food purchased at a Food Lion store had been documented.

A more recent example shows how unquestioning news coverage can help a company and hurt readers. For several years, hormone replacement therapy (HRT) had been hyped as an important treatment in helping menopausal women remain healthy. The hype was promoted by public relations releases from pharmaceutical manufacturers. But in 2002, the National Institutes of Health prematurely ended a large study of HRT because the risks were too great for the women participating. The scientists found that HRT increased the risk of heart disease, breast cancer, and blood clots and that it did not help prevent osteoporosis to the degree claimed earlier. It was also reported that a pharmaceutical manufacturer financed the initial research about HRT.

Although the National Institutes of Health's action was treated with surprise by news media, these same problems had surfaced over a number of years in other underreported studies. Drug manufacturers had made millions off the women who used HRT, yet the treatment was not as effective as claimed and was even hazardous to the patients. In this case, poor reporting seems to have aided some of the pharmaceutical companies in their rush for profit.[12]

Basic Ethical Standards in U.S. Media

Professional communicators recognize the value of fundamental standards of ethical behavior. In addition, media audiences have come to expect certain *fundamental ethical standards.* Among these are accuracy, fairness, balance, accurate representation, and truth. The Public Relations Society of America, for example, recognizes, in its code of professional standards, values such as truth, accuracy, fairness, responsibility to the public, and generally accepted standards of good taste.

Accuracy ✦ The bedrock of ethics is **accuracy.** For public relations professionals, reporters, and editors, being accused of inaccuracy is one of the worst charges that can be leveled. However, accuracy is not simple truth but the reporting of information in a context that allows people to discern the truth. Some inaccuracies can be damaging, such as the one revealed in this correction printed in the *Fulton County Expositor* in Wauseon, Ohio: "The *Fulton County Expositor* incorrectly reported in Tuesday's edition that recently deceased John T. Cline of Delta was a Nazi veteran of World War II. The obituary should have read he was a Navy war veteran."[13]

Some issues of accuracy are more complex because the news is more complex. The international movement against corporate globalization has created problems for

Television images of protests can significantly distort the overall picture. This image of the International Monetary Fund/World Bank protests in Washington, D.C., shows a crowd of people, but an audio description is required to explain how many people attended.

the U.S. news media. This movement has a variety of elements, reflecting the wide range of antiglobalization organizations that protest together. As a result, coverage of protests at meetings such as the International Monetary Fund meeting in Prague during 2000 and in Washington, D.C., in 2002 often concentrated on violence. John Giuffo looked at more than two hundred stories by newspapers, newsmagazines, and TV networks and concluded: "The problem is not so much the focus on the small percentage of protesters who acted violently, but that the coverage lacks context." He added, "The protests are difficult to cover—chaotic, partially violent, and complex in their list of complaints and demands. Still, the underlying issues that have brought out hundreds of thousands of people are often glossed over or misrepresented."[14] Accuracy can be an issue of what is not said as well as what is said when news organizations cover difficult issues.

Objectivity ✦ To be truly unbiased is an admirable but unattainable goal. From birth on, society and familial upbringing subtly influence a person's view of the world. However, journalists who accept **objectivity** as a goal need to be aware of their biases and then report and produce as objective a story as possible.

Objectivity is more than simply being aware of personal biases. How objective should a journalist be? Perhaps some interpretation is necessary to present a complete story. For example, in the 1950s the media unwittingly helped Wisconsin Senator Joseph McCarthy to instill a fear of communism in U.S. society that caused serious harm to innocent people. Actors and others who had only attended a meeting of the Communist Party decades earlier were blacklisted and could not get jobs in their profession. McCarthy and his aides understood how the media operated, and they carefully timed speeches and press conferences close to deadlines, knowing that reporters would have to choose between checking facts and being scooped by another news organization. Often, reporters followed the dictates of objectivity, quoting McCarthy verbatim. However, some newspaper reporters questioned McCarthy's actions, and in his television program *See It Now*, Edward R. Murrow exposed the McCarthy witch-hunt.

Objectivity is not a fundamental ethical attribute of public relations and advertising personnel, whose goal is to persuade as well as to inform. But it has been a

> **objectivity:** Reporting facts without bias or prejudice, including a deliberate attempt to avoid interpretation.

After the news media realized they had been duped by Senator Joseph McCarthy, they took steps to ensure that it could not happen again.

fundamental aspect of twentieth-century reporting, and it is one of the factors that distinguishes journalism from public relations and advertising communication.

Fairness and Balance
✦ Fairness and balance often go hand in hand with accuracy and objectivity. Reporters attempt to investigate the many sides of a story. For example, abortion is a much-debated issue in many state legislatures. If the mass media quote and run video only of active demonstrators on the prochoice and prolife sides, the complete story remains untold. Stories need to take into account the range of differing opinions. Often, complexity must be preserved for **journalistic balance** to be achieved.

The more complicated the news, the more difficult it is to provide balance. In 2002, U.S. news media came under fire for lack of balance in their treatment of the Palestinian conflict. However, they were attacked by both pro-Israeli and pro-Palestinian critics.[15] Political coverage often brings such charges. In 2002, congressional Democratic leaders claimed that the cable news networks' coverage was favoring the White House.[16] Such claims usually are based on individual perception and have little scientific support. At issue is whether balance should occur in every story or across time in a series of stories.

Absence of Fakery
✦ One of the most blatant cases of fakery occurred in 1992 when NBC *Dateline* faked a truck explosion for a report about the dangers of crashes involving General Motors pickups. GM sued. NBC broadcast a retraction and NBC News President Michael Gartner resigned. The line between entertainment and news was badly blurred in the competition for viewers. Why did the network do it? "Because one side of the line is an Emmy. The other side, the abyss," said Jane Pauley, one of *Dateline*'s anchors.[17]

Misrepresentation and **fakery** can occur without a journalist's knowledge. Freelance photographer Courtney Kealy took a photograph of hooded Palestinian teenage boys dressed as suicide bombers for a parade. They put a pseudo-bomb on a three-year-old boy and then posed with him for Kealy. In December 2001, the photo ran in several news publications and raised the issue of the impact of war on children. About three months later, the photograph ran in an American Jewish Committee advertisement, which appeared in the *New York Times*. The ad read, "No one is born hating. . . . But too many are taught how!" The ad credited the photograph as courtesy of Kealy and Getty Images, Kealy's agency. But Getty Images had sold the photograph without Kealy's knowledge. Kealy was shocked and frightened that she would be seen as supporting the Israeli side of the conflict, which could place her in danger. The American Jewish Committee said they did nothing wrong and that they

journalistic balance: Providing equal or nearly equal coverage of various points of view in a controversy.

fakery: Posing that which is false to be true.

were told how to credit the photo by Getty. The Getty salesman said he didn't know how the photograph would be used.[18]

Truth ✦ Although journalists cannot always ensure that their stories are true, they can make an extra effort to be truthful and to avoid lying. In August 2002, Mike Barnicle resigned from the *Boston Globe* while on a two-month suspension after he was accused of stealing material and lying about his sources. The *Globe* was highly criticized for suspending Barnicle rather than firing him because a few months earlier it had fired an African American woman, Patricia Smith, after similar charges were made.

It is possible to report material accurately and still not present the truth. Trying to attain truth requires accuracy, fairness, balance, and a variety of other aspects of reporting that combine to create a picture of the "whole truth."

Integrity of Sources ✦ A journalist's story is only as good as his or her sources. In 1981, Janet Cooke, a twenty-six-year-old *Washington Post* reporter, won a Pulitzer Prize for a front-page article called "Jimmy's World." Jimmy was an eight-year-old heroin addict. Soon after receiving the award, Cooke confessed that she had concocted the story; Jimmy did not exist. She returned the prize and left the *Post*.[19]

Reporters who become too loyal to sources risk the possibility of being blinded and missing important cues to stories. The *Washington Post*'s revelations about the Watergate scandal initially came not from reporters covering the White House who had access to top-level sources, but from young metropolitan desk staffers Carl Bernstein and Bob Woodward, who connected one of the burglars who broke into the Democratic Party headquarters in the Watergate complex to the Central Intelligence Agency.

Avoiding Conflict of Interest ✦ Outside business, social and personal activities, and contacts can subtly influence the ability of mass media professionals to conduct objective reporting. This is called *conflict of interest*. It might cause, for example, an animal rights activist not to cover comprehensively and fairly a story on animals and scientific experiments; a city council member might not effectively relate all sides of a housing bill; or the spouse of a political contender might not write objectively about a candidate's platform. The lack of objectivity these reporters experience originates in a conflict of interest—the conflict between trying to do one's job effectively and a belief system that adheres to the moral rightness of a cause or a desire to promote one's own interest.

key concept

Conflict of Interest Along with government officials and others in positions of responsibility, journalists are under pressure to avoid allowing personal activities or interests to interfere with their professional responsibilities. Journalists have an obligation to strive for unbiased coverage of an event or situation.

Stories of conflict of interest abound. For example, Suzy Wetlaufer, editor of the *Harvard Business Review,* had an affair with the married former chairman of General Electric Jack Welch after interviewing him for a story. Similarly, Andrea Mitchell, NBC's chief foreign affairs correspondent, and Federal Reserve Chairman Alan Greenspan dated for twelve years before their marriage in 1997. As Lori Robertson wrote in *American Journalism Review* about the topic, "Other ethicists and editors say that reporters romancing their sources is an issue they rarely face. But what many journalists do encounter is the larger grayer issue of personal relationships bumping up against coverage responsibilities. What if a reporter dates a former source, for instance?"[20]

SUPPLYING ETHICAL STANDARDS

Standards can be imposed through agreements among professionals to behave in certain ways and to punish certain behaviors. Ethical standards are upheld by educating professionals in moral reasoning processes that help individuals and organizations make decisions about how to handle specific situations.

Industry's Response

Media industries have tried to establish official positions that indicate their desire to increase credibility and avoid government regulation. Their responses have taken several forms, including establishing codes of ethics and ombudsman positions.

Codes of Ethics ◆ Media organizations have established *codes of ethics* to standardize media behavior. Although critics argue that many of the codes are shallow, the code guidelines still serve as reminders that ethical standards are considered important for credibility, profitability, and the good of society.

The American Society of Newspaper Editors, in 1923, was the first national press association to draft an official code of ethics. Many news organizations did not adopt formal codes until the 1980s, when ethics became a hot topic for journalists. Instead of using ethics codes, some small news organizations have created firmly established verbal policies or guidelines set by precedent. Currently, the Society of Professional Journalists (SPJ), the Radio–Television News Directors Association (RTNDA), and the Public Relations Society of America (PRSA) are among prominent organizations that have formulated policies.[21] Figure 13.1 is the Society of Professional Journalists' Code of Ethics as revised in 1996.

Several years ago the television Code of Good Practice that the National Association of Broadcasters (NAB) had established was ruled unconstitutional by the Supreme Court. The industry code was seen as a violation of antitrust rules because the code required all broadcast bodies to be answerable to the same uniform policies.

National advertisers, public relations practitioners, filmmakers, TV program producers, and even **infomercial** producers have codes of ethics. These national policies serve primarily as voluntary guidelines for local member organizations. Some organizations simply follow the national or state code, or they modify the standard to fit their own news objectives and geographic areas. However, many media chains have lengthy written ethics policies that they expect their local affiliates to follow.

An organization's codes can be enforced in the same way as any other company policy. Adherence to the national codes is voluntary and cannot be enforced. Many professionals fear the adoption of mandatory codes, arguing that they would be used as the basis for lawsuits that would harm the media.

Ombudsmen ◆ Another effort to enforce ethics originated at the *Louisville Courier-Journal and Times* in 1967, with the appointment of the first newspaper **ombudsman.** The primary function of the ombudsman is to represent the readers and to criticize the actions of the newspaper when the ombudsman believes it has done something wrong. An effective ombudsman will serve as the newspaper's conscience and help to ensure that readers and the community are served and that ethical standards are observed. The international News Ombudsman Organization maintains an active web site, with information about the practice.

Critics' Response

By 1947, increased chain ownership of newspapers meant that fewer newspapers were independently owned. In the 1940s, the Hutchins Commission, which had been created by Henry Luce to analyze the impact of the modern press, addressed the issue of chain-owned media. The commission feared that such media would not freely criticize themselves and recommended the establishment of news councils to counter this trend. In subsequent years, journalism reviews developed as another way of monitoring the press and its behaviors. Today, newspapers print news and editorial comment on press behavior.

News Councils ◆ The Hutchins Commission recommended the establishment of **news councils,** which would hear complaints against news media, investigate each complaint, pass judgment on the complaint, and publicize the judgment.

Society of Professional Journalists: Code of Ethics

PREAMBLE

Members of the Society of Professional Journalists believe that public enlightenment is the forerunner of justice and the foundation of democracy. The duty of the journalist is to further those ends by seeking truth and providing a fair and comprehensive account of events and issues. Conscientious journalists from all media and specialties strive to serve the public with thoroughness and honesty. Professional integrity is the cornerstone of a journalist's credibility Members of the Society share a dedication to ethical behavior and adopt this code to declare the Society's principles and standards of practice.

SEEK TRUTH AND REPORT IT
Journalists should be honest, fair and courageous in gathering, reporting and interpreting information.

JOURNALISTS SHOULD:

- Test the accuracy of information from all sources and exercise care to avoid inadvertent error. Deliberate distortion is never permissible.
- Diligently seek out subjects of news stories to give them the opportunity to respond to allegations of wrongdoing.
- Identify sources whenever feasible. The public is entitled to as much information as possible on sources' reliability.
- Always question sources' motives before promising anonymity. Clarify conditions attached to any promise made in exchange for information. Keep promises.
- Make certain that headlines, news teases and promotional material, photos, video, audio, graphics, sound bites and quotations do not misrepresent. They should not oversimplify or highlight incidents out of context.
- Never distort the content of news photos or video. Image enhancement for technical clarity is always permissible. Label montages and photo illustrations.
- Avoid misleading re-enactments or staged news events. If re-enactment is necessary to tell a story, label it.
- Avoid undercover or other surreptitious methods of gathering information except when traditional open methods will not yield information vital to the public. Use of such methods should be explained as part of the story.
- Never plagiarize.
- Tell the story of the diversity and magnitude of the human experience boldly, even when it is unpopular to do so.
- Examine their own cultural values and avoid imposing those values on others.
- Avoid stereotyping by race, gender, age, religion, ethnicity, geography, sexual orientation, disability, physical appearance or social status.
- Support the open exchange of views, even views they find repugnant.
- Give voice to the voiceless; official and unofficial sources of information can be equally valid.
- Distinguish between advocacy and news reporting. Analysis and commentary should be labeled and not misrepresent fact or context.
- Distinguish news from advertising and shun hybrids that blur the lines between the two.
- Recognize a special obligation to ensure that the public's business is conducted in the open and that government records are open to inspection.

MINIMIZE HARM
Ethical journalists treat sources, subjects and colleagues as human beings deserving of respect.

JOURNALISTS SHOULD:

- Show compassion for those who may be affected adversely by news coverage. Use special sensitivity when dealing with children and inexperienced sources or subjects.
- Be sensitive when seeking or using interviews or photographs of those affected by tragedy or grief.
- Recognize that gathering and reporting information may cause harm or discomfort. Pursuit of the news is not a license for arrogance.
- Recognize that private people have a greater right to control information about themselves than do public officials and others who seek power, influence or attention. Only an overriding public need can justify intrusion into anyone's privacy.
- Show good taste. Avoid pandering to lurid curiosity.
- Be cautious about identifying juvenile suspects or victims of sex crimes.
- Be judicious about naming criminal suspects before the formal filing of charges.
- Balance a criminal suspect's fair trial rights with the public's right to be informed.

ACT INDEPENDENTLY
Journalists should be free of obligation to any interest other than the public's right to know.

JOURNALISTS SHOULD:

- Avoid conflicts of interest, real or perceived.
- Remain free of associations and activities that may compromise integrity or damage credibility.
- Refuse gifts, favors, fees, free travel and special treatment, and shun secondary employment, political involvement, public office and service in community organizations if they compromise journalistic integrity.
- Disclose unavoidable conflicts.
- Be vigilant and courageous about holding those with power accountable.
- Deny favored treatment to advertisers and special interests and resist their pressure to influence news coverage.
- Be wary of sources offering information for favors or money, avoid bidding for news.

BE ACCOUNTABLE
Journalists are accountable to their readers, listeners, viewers and each other.

JOURNALISTS SHOULD:

- Clarify and explain news coverage and invite dialogue with the public over journalistic conduct.
- Encourage the public to voice grievances against the news media.
- Admit mistakes and correct them promptly.
- Expose unethical practices of journalists and the news media.
- Abide by the same high standards to which they hold others.

Source: Sigma Delta Chi's first Code of Ethics was borrowed from the American Society of Newspaper Editors in 1926. In 1973, Sigma Delta Chi wrote its own code, which was revised in 1984 and 1987. The present version of the Society of Professional Journalists' Code of Ethics was adopted in September 1996. Reprinted by permission.

During the 1950s and 1960s, several European countries, including Germany, England, and Sweden, established press councils. In 1972, a consortium of foundations started the Council on Press Responsibility and Press Freedom in the United States. It later became the National News Council, and its role was to investigate public complaints about national news organizations. Newspaper owners reacted to the News Council with the same vehemence they had shown the Hutchins Commission. The vast majority of newspapers did not support the News Council and criticized the very idea of an independent watchdog for news organizations. In 1984, the National News Council closed because of lack of money and support from the news media. The most active remaining council is the Minnesota News Council.

Journalism Reviews ◆ Only a small percentage of newspapers have ombudsmen, and news media have failed to support news councils, but another forum for criticizing media behavior exists: the journalism review. These publications report and analyze examples of ethical and unethical journalism. Three national reviews provide extensive criticism of the media: *Quill, American Journalism Review,* and *Columbia Journalism Review. Quill* is published by the Society of Professional Journalists; *American Journalism Review* is published by the University of Maryland College of Journalism, and *Columbia Journalism Review* is published by Columbia University.

Moral Reasoning Processes for Ethical Decisions

Codes of ethics are good for outlining standard practices and procedures, but they cannot take every situation into account. Media practitioners must go through a *moral reasoning process* to help them make decisions. Instead of simply saying that the decision "felt like the thing to do," professionals need to be able to articulate and justify why a decision was made. Journalists must be accountable.

Several ethical decision-making procedures and models have been developed to help professionals make ethical decisions. We will discuss four of them: (1) an ethical framework advanced by philosopher Sissela Bok; (2) a decision-making process designed by Roy Peter Clark of the Poynter Institute; (3) a values-oriented-series-of-questions approach advocated by media ethics expert H. Eugene Goodwin; and (4) the Potter Box. Not every model or every item within each model will be equally pertinent to every situation; however, decision makers should discuss each item.

Bok's ethical framework is based on three questions designed to help all types of professionals make ethical decisions. Each question is discussed in great detail in her book *Lying: Moral Choice in Public and Private Life:*[22]

1. How do you feel about the action? (Look inside yourself and have a talk with your conscience.)
2. Is there any other way to achieve the same goal that will not raise ethical issues? (Talk to others to find out what they would do. Or think about what a trusted friend or ancient philosopher would suggest.)
3. How will my actions affect others? (Think about what readers, viewers, sources, and those affected by the story might feel or say.)

The moral reasoning model advanced by Roy Peter Clark of the Poynter Institute for Media Studies suggests that all journalists carefully examine their consciences before making deadline decisions. He offers five questions that should be answered before a story is published or broadcast:[23]

1. Is the story, photo, or graphic complete and accurate to the best of my knowledge?
2. Am I missing an important point of view?
3. How would I feel if this story or photo were about me?
4. What good will publication do?
5. What does my reader or viewer need to know?

Goodwin discusses his values-oriented approach in his book *Groping for Ethics in Journalism,* which he wrote after "becoming bothered by some of the things jour-

profile

Heywood C. Broun

Decades ago, Heywood Campbell Broun gave journalists a motto to remember as they work in the marketplace of ideas: "For the truth, there is no deadline."

Broun, a prominent newspaper columnist during the 1920s and 1930s, showed perpetual concern for the underdog. Today, the Heywood Broun Award is given to select journalists who have helped right a wrong or correct an injustice.

Broun began writing for newspapers in 1908 and did not stop until his death in 1939. He wrote novels, political tracts, and pieces about sports and drama. He invented the newspaper column in which writers expressed opinions that could differ from those of the owners. His six columns a week rooted out injustices, and they were read by thousands of people who felt that he was their friend.

Broun was educated at Harvard University. From 1912 to 1920, he was a drama critic and then literary editor for the *New York Tribune.* He and his wife, Ruth Hale, whom he married in 1917, also spent time in Europe, he as a war correspondent and she as editor of a Paris-based edition of the *Chicago Tribune.*

In 1921, he began a daily column, "It Seems to Me," for the *New York World,* but in 1928 he was fired from the *World* because of his support for Italian anarchists Nicola Sacco and Bartolomeo Vanzetti, who were convicted of murder on slight evidence but in an atmosphere of fear of anarchists.

Ruth Hale was the United States' first female movie critic, a reporter for the *New York Times,* and a drama critic for *Vogue.* This professionally successful couple led a somewhat tortured private life and after seventeen years of marriage were divorced, although they maintained what their son called a "special intimacy." Ruth Hale battled the State Department for the right to carry a passport bearing her name rather than her husband's, and she founded the Lucy Stone League, a group of women who championed the right to retain their birth names.

Broun ran for Congress as a Socialist in 1930. A few years later he became the founding president of the American Newspaper Guild. When he died in 1939, more than ten thousand people, some of them readers, attended his funeral. In 1941, two years after his death, the guild established the Heywood Broun Award for outstanding journalistic achievement that reflects "the spirit of Heywood Broun."

Sources: William Hunter, "In Bed with Broun, Star of the Liveliest Sheets," *The Herald* [Glasgow] (March 14, 1995): 14; Mary Anne Ramer, "A PR Practitioner's Memo to Journalists," *Editor & Publisher* (October 10, 1992): 64; Joseph McLellan, "His Mother, His Father, Himself; Whose Little Boy Are You? *A Memoir of the Broun Family* by Heywood Hale Broun," *The Washington Post* (August 8, 1983), Style sec. Book World, p. C8.

---

nalists and news media proprietors do. They do not always seem to have a strong sense of morality, of what is right and wrong." He recorded seven useful questions for successful teaching in journalism ethics and for working journalists:[24]

1. What do we usually do in cases like this? (Consider whether a policy for this situation has been established. Is it a good policy or does it need to be modified?)
2. Who will be hurt and who will be helped? (Recognize that most stories will hurt someone or some group. Weigh that hurt against benefits to the community. "Realizing who is apt to be hurt and whether the benefits can justify that hurt can help us make an intelligent decision.")
3. Are there better alternatives? (Think about all alternatives before making a decision. Harmful results often can be softened or eliminated by going a different route.)
4. Can I look at myself in the mirror again? (You must think about how you feel personally. Can you live with yourself afterward? James D. Squires, formerly of the *Chicago Tribune,* advised media people not to "do anything that your momma would be ashamed of.")
5. Can I justify this to other people and the public? (If you know that you will have to explain your decisions, in an editor's column or television newscast, for example, you are often more careful with your decisions.)
6. What principles or values can I apply? (Some established principles, such as truth, justice, or fairness, take priority over others.)
7. Is this decision appropriate for the kind of journalism I believe in; does it coincide with how people should treat one another? (Your judgments should correspond with the way you believe that media ought to act and how "people in a civilized society ought to behave.")

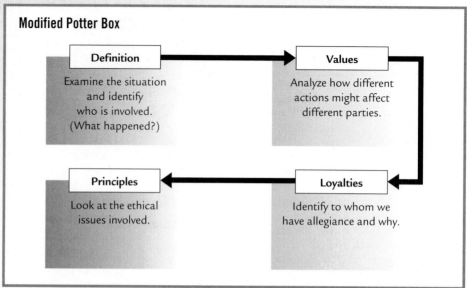

Source: The original version is described in Ralph B. Potter, "The Structure of Certain American Christian Responses to the Nuclear Dilemma, 1958–1963" (Ph.D. dissertation, Harvard University, 1965).

The Potter Box, constructed by Harvard philosopher and theologian Ralph Potter, is a sequence of four steps designed to help people reason their way to an ethical decision:[25]

1. Find out what happened.
2. Analyze the values.
3. Identify loyalties.
4. Look at the principles involved.

Sometimes the initial reaction to a set of circumstances is not the final judgment one reaches after progressing through facts, values, principles, and loyalties. The Potter Box is depicted in Figure 13.2.[26]

ETHICAL SITUATIONS AND DILEMMAS

Some situations are variations on common dilemmas. Because these dilemmas recur often, personnel in many news organizations have developed consistent ways of dealing with them.

Business and Media Content

Most media outlets are businesses, and many depend heavily, if not entirely, on advertising revenue, which often creates ethical dilemmas for people who create media content. Businesses can affect content in a variety of ways, but the most effective impact is created through advertising. Advertisers can withhold advertising in what is called an advertising boycott, or they may seek favorable treatment by buying advertising.

Businesses, religious groups, and civic activists have used advertising boycotts to try to persuade publishers to change their editorial stance. In January 1998, Harry Ashmore died. Ashmore was a civil rights writer who won a Pulitzer Prize for his editorials on desegregating Little Rock's Central High School. Ashmore's fame may have died before he did, but his experience is central to journalism in the United States. Ashmore edited the now-defunct *Arkansas Gazette* in 1957 when Arkansas Governor Orval E. Faubus ordered the National Guard to stop nine black students from entering Little

Rock Central High School. Eisenhower sent in federal troops to counteract Faubus's action. Ashmore urged Little Rock's citizens to accept a desegregation plan, a plea that resulted in death threats, an advertising boycott, and a decline in circulation. In 1959, Ashmore left Little Rock.[27]

Just how advertising and business pressure affects content depends on the ethics of the individual journalists and media managers. Some managers give in to pressure more quickly than others, and some do not give in at all. Allowing advertisers to influence news and information has at least two dangers—one for consumers and one for the media companies. If consumers know that the information they receive represents a business's bias, they can take this into consideration when using that information. If they don't know, as may happen when media are influenced by advertisers, then they can be influenced to act in ways that may not be in their interest.

Harry Ashmore's editorial pleas for a desegregation plan for Little Rock schools resulted in an advertising boycott against the *Arkansas Gazette.* Ashmore won the 1958 Pulitzer Prize for editorial writing, and the *Gazette* survived to become the most influential news organization in Arkansas.

Freebies and Junkets

Until the 1980s, at least some people who worked in mass media took for granted that their low pay would be supplemented by **perks** such as gifts, free meals, and trips—freebies and junkets. These blatant handouts were among the first practices to be attacked as unethical. During the early 1900s, editors began to reject free railroad passes in return for advertising. But freebies persisted well into the 1990s, with sports reporters continuing to accept free rides to accompany teams on trips and movie reviewers accepting free movie passes. Most of these practices have now ceased, not only among journalists, but among public relations practitioners as well. One element of a respectful relationship between journalists and public relations professionals has been an acknowledgment that public relations is most effective when it is based on accurate and convincing information and that journalists can best act with integrity when they are not indebted to specific organizations or people. If journalists are accepting free trips, movie passes, or other perks, they are less likely to report a story with full objectivity.

Anonymous Attribution

The use of anonymous sources has long been problematic with journalists. Richard Blow said of them:

> They [anonymous sources] can say what they want without having to take responsibility if their information isn't accurate. Another problem is that for the subject of anonymous criticism, it's almost impossible to respond; knowing the source of an attack is often crucial to rebutting it.[28]

Research has shown a high dependence on anonymous sources among some national media. In 1984, a study published in *Journalism Quarterly* found that 84 percent of sources used in *Newsweek* were unnamed and that 77 percent of the sources in *Time* were unnamed.[29] More recently, a story published by the *Modesto Bee* reported that of 287 articles about Chandra Levy published in the *Washington Post* during 2001 and 2002, 144 used unnamed sources.[30]

Journalists admit to abuses, but argue that some stories could not be reported without protection of anonymity. Marshall Loeb, a columnist for *CBS Market Watch* and former editor of *Columbia Journalism Review,* said, "In reporting, there is a tension between using named sources and anonymous sources. But I've spent most of my life covering business, and you can't get a story about corporate abuse without granting your source anonymity."

Checkbook Journalism

News organizations, both broadcast and print, sometimes pay sources for story ideas and information. In the past, such **checkbook journalism** occurred mostly in entertainment, but with the lines blurring between news and entertainment, journalistic

perk: Short for *perquisite,* or payment for something in addition to salary.

checkbook journalism: Paying subjects or witnesses for information or interviews.

Tailwind Leaves a Foul Smell

On June 7, 1998, CNN broadcast a report that claimed U.S. forces had used the nerve gas sarin in 1970 while attacking a village in Laos that was believed to be harboring U.S. defectors. The next day, *Time* magazine also reported the story. This report proved to be the inauspicious start to a new venture, a newsmagazine show, "NewsStand: CNN & Time." In early July, CNN and *Time* retracted the reports after CNN commissioned an independent investigation that they believed showed the report's conclusions were not supported by the evidence. Tom Johnson, CNN's chief executive (shown here), apologized for the damage done to CNN's reputation over the issue.

The incident had many implications for journalism and for the media industry. If the story was true, it would mean that U.S. soldiers had committed an international war crime. And if the Pentagon had covered up such a story for twenty-eight years, it would have a disastrous effect on U.S. policies to halt nations such as Iran from stockpiling nerve gas. The primary source for the story was Robert Van Buskirk, who had not mentioned the incident in his 1983 book *Tailwind,* but who claimed he suddenly recalled the incident at the end of a five-hour interview with CNN producer April Oliver.

The most prominent journalist involved was Peter Arnett, although producer April Oliver did most of the reporting. Arnett was reprimanded for his part in the story, and Oliver and her colleague Jack Smith were fired. Peter Arnett's contract was not renewed.

Development of the program represented converging technologies—a blend of television and magazine journalism. Response to the program was an even greater example of convergence in action. Veterans hit the Internet, explaining that they had been involved in the operation, called "Tailwind," and that they had used gas—nonlethal tear gas.

Neither Oliver nor Jack Smith sought to produce an inaccurate story. In fact, they still believe the story to be true. Constitutional lawyer Floyd Abrams, who conducted the independent investigation that caused CNN to retract the story, said,

The CNN journalists involved in this project believed in every word they wrote. If anything, the serious flaws in the broadcast that we identify in this report may stem from the depths of those beliefs and the degree to which the journalists discounted contrary information they received precisely because they were so firmly persuaded that what they were broadcasting was true.

Time editors had questioned the story. Washington Bureau Chief Michael Duffy said that both a veteran Pentagon correspondent and a deputy bureau chief had concerns about "the substance and the sources and the evidence of the story."

---

standards quickly can take a backseat. ABC paid the $25,000 bill for Monica Lewinsky's lawyer so he would persuade special prosecutor Kenneth Starr's office to let Lewinsky be interviewed by Barbara Walters in March 1999.[31] ABC also paid a friend of one of the Columbine killers $16,000 for videotapes and photographs of the killer. The material aired on *Good Morning America* in 1999, a week after the friend, Nathan Dykeman, appeared for an interview. ABC has a policy against paying for interviews but will pay for newsworthy images. An ABC spokesperson said the network did not know the visual material existed when Dykeman was first interviewed.[32]

Most incidents of paying for news content reflect the need to attract audience in order to sell advertisements. This emphasis on profit, wrote Stuart Loory of the *Kansas City Star,* puts "hard news into the same category as major-league sports as

There is no doubt that April Oliver believes her story is true. In fact, she sued CNN and *Time*'s parent company, Time Warner. At the time of the controversy, Oliver turned over her notes to Floyd Abrams, whom CNN asked to conduct an investigation of the Tailwind controversy. Oliver claims that she thought she had an attorney–client relationship and that CNN and the lawyers did not inform her that the information could be used against her. She also claims that the allegations against her constitute defamation. April Oliver's bylined story about the controversy appeared in the July/August 1999 issue of *American Journalism Review*. In that story, she argued that she and Jack Smith were "scapegoated so CNN could preserve its highly valued and all-too-friendly relationship with the military."

What are the issues here? During the 1980s, increasingly concerned about financial survival, television networks cut costs in their news departments and focused on achieving the high ratings that translate into profits. A series of stories during the 1990s issued by TV newsmagazines were challenged as inaccurate. These stories are initiated by producers

who "pitch" stories to network editors; it is difficult for producers to back away from a story once a network has committed resources to it. Unless editors are carefully guiding the development of a story with a jaundiced eye, reporters and producers can get so caught up in their own story that their judgment becomes flawed. Reporters also are cynical about government officials and sometimes simply assume that government officials lie most of the time.

In the CNN story, the Abrams report indicated that producers had ignored contradictory evidence, asked leading hypothetical questions, and turned ambiguous answers into evidence.

Arnett, who anchored the report, shirked his reporter's responsibility, claiming only that he was brought in late, "asked a few questions," and "read the script." *Time* reporters indicated there was concern at the magazine about the truth of the story, but the story ran anyway because magazine editors knew the broadcast was scheduled the day before publication of that week's magazine. The pressure of profit, time, and adherence to the journalistic value of "getting the scoop" may have

taken precedence over a greater value—that of providing truth and accuracy in reporting and interpreting the news of the day.

Such cases do not end easily. Van Buskirk sued CNN for libel because he said CNN indicated he was the source of inaccuracies. Although the case was still working its way through the court system in fall 2002, the court of public opinion had already decided that Tailwind was a foul wind for journalism ethics.

Sources: Susan Paterno, "An Ill Tailwind," *American Journalism Review* (September 1998): 23–33; Christopher Callahan, "An Embarrassing Time," *American Journalism Review* (September 1998): 29; John Elvin, "Battle Continues over CNN's Discredited Report on 'Tailwind' Military Operation," *The Washington Times* (September 20, 1999): 34; April Oliver, "The Wrong Lessons," *American Journalism Review* (August/July 1999): 52–54; Joe Sharkey, "Memories of Wars Never Fought," *The New York Times* (on the Web), June 28, 1998, Week in review sec.; Robin Pogrebin and Felicity Barringer, "CNN Retracts Report That Military Used Lethal Nerve Gas in Laos in 1970," *The New York Times* (on the Web), July 3, 1998, National sec.; and Jane Kirtley, "Tailwind Lessons," *American Journalism Review*, May 2002, www.ajr.org.

a profit center and throws the whole purpose of news presentation—information for consumers versus profit for disseminators—into question."[33]

Privacy versus People's Need to Know

Many media professionals believe that there are times when the public's right to know takes precedence over the **right of privacy** of an individual. When does information change from news to voyeurism? Is it necessary to watch a woman cry on television about the death of her spouse? Is it important to write that the man who rescued a drowning child was also gay? When should journalists report that a political candidate has been unfaithful to a spouse? Although some reporters believe that personal life has nothing to do with business or politics, others think that personal

right of privacy: An ethical and legal area of decision making. The right to be protected from unwarranted intrusion by the government, media, or other institutions or individuals.

actions illuminate character. A candidate who breaks a solemn vow to someone as important as his or her spouse might also break promises to constituents. The question here is whether the account serves a public interest. What constitutes "the public's right to know" is an ethical question that media workers and the public share.

At times, a public event becomes a media circus. The trial of O. J. Simpson for murder is one example. From the summer of 1994 until the fall of 1995, the O. J. Simpson case was a topic or news segment on NBC's *Nightly News,* a regular topic on tabloid television, and the target of farcical skits on Jay Leno's late-night show and *Saturday Night Live.* Almost buried under discussions of prosecutor Marcia Clark's hairstyles and child support problems, defense attorney Robert Shapiro's tailored suits, and Judge Lance Ito's whimsical comments lay the real tragedy of two murdered people.

Public figures are not given as much consideration as private citizens. Public figures such as politicians or movie stars deliberately place themselves in the limelight and know that their lives and movements will be constantly scrutinized by the press. Private citizens, however, usually have indirectly attracted publicity for some other reason. Therefore, ethical journalists look at whether someone is a private citizen or a public figure when considering whether to include some types of information about that person.

Sensationalism, Decency, and Good Taste

Some material, especially visual information, will always be more offensive to some viewers than others. *Sensationalism*—the use of material merely to shock, startle, or violate a person's sense of decency—may attract attention, but it is not newsworthy.

Stanley Forman, a photojournalist for the Boston *Herald-American,* took several photos of a young woman and little girl standing on a fire escape about to be rescued from a burning building. Suddenly, the fire escape collapsed, and Forman took dramatic pictures of the two falling. Although the woman died, newspapers all over the world published the photos, and Forman was awarded a Pulitzer Prize. But, as mass media educator Fred Fedler noted, readers "accused the newspapers of sensationalism: of poor taste, insensitivity, an invasion of the victims' privacy, and a tasteless display of human tragedy to sell newspapers."[34]

The realism of images can create controversy, as it did with video and photographic images from 9/11.[35] Many people, including some of the family members of those who died in the attacks, objected to the use of graphic images on the anniversary of the terrorist attacks. In particular, people did not want to see scenes of people jumping or falling from the World Trade Towers or the towers collapsing. Defenders of using the images argued that people need to know about the horrors of terrorism if the United States is to maintain its resolve to fight it. At the heart of the debate is the fact that different people react to the same images differently.

Images that are distributed electronically can cause as much controversy as printed images. During the 1980s and 1990s, viewers became more concerned about the high number of graphic depictions of violence and sex scenes on television and in movies. How advertisers and public relations firms portray women and minorities in selling products in ads or for product promotions has also concerned different segments of society. Critics are concerned that adults and children may adopt behavior patterns and attitudes that are based at least in part on media portrayals.

The 1999 shooting at Columbine High School in Littleton, Colorado, reinforced the belief of many critics that the constant repetition of graphic violence and sex in all media sends the wrong message, especially to young viewers, about the world around them. The scenes grab viewers' attention but rarely show the consequences associated with violence and indiscriminate sexual acts. Are violent aggressors to be admired? What are the repercussions of casual sex? Although few scholars believe that watching a few indiscriminate sex acts on television will cause a teenager to be sexually active, many are concerned that a multiplicity of such shows helps to shape a child's view of normative behavior. Do excessive violence and sexual behavior become accepted by the viewer as what "probably" goes on in most people's lives?

Concern about sensational media coverage and images remains an international concern. It has been an ongoing concern in Great Britain for decades because their tabloid newspapers continue the types of coverage popularized by Hearst and Pulitzer during the "yellow journalism" period. But as other countries open up their press systems and pursue democracy, many fear that the freedom can be abused. For instance, in January 2002, the Council of Pakistan Newspaper Editors, All Pakistan Newspaper Society, and the Ministry of Information in Pakistan adopted a joint resolution calling for newspapers to avoid sensationalism and obscene material.

Photographers and camera operators, along with editors, must make decisions about the role of good taste in publishing war images, such as this photograph from the Afghanistan war. Is an image sensational? Or does it make a significant point that the public needs to understand?

Direct Quotations

Quote marks signify the exact words of a source. However, research shows that media professionals do not agree on the practice of quoting bad grammar, cursing, ramblings, and accents.[36] Nor do they agree on when a quote should be edited. For example, cursing might be edited out of a quote from a student but left untouched in one from a ball player or politician (or the other way around, depending on the subject). If a quotation has to be changed, it should be paraphrased, using indirect or partial quotations. Journalists almost universally denounce making up quotes, even if they are based on notes and represent a partial reconstruction of what the person might have said.

Correction of Errors

Media sometimes publish or broadcast inaccurate information, yet often the public is never notified of the inaccuracy. When was the last time a network news anchor admitted a mistake was made the previous night? While covering the Gulf War, the networks produced live reports and inevitably broadcast a variety of mistakes while trying to be first with the news. Most of these mistakes were never identified or addressed. Instead, more accurate news was broadcast in a follow-up story.

Newspapers are usually better than magazines, television, and radio about rectifying errors. However, readers rarely know where to look for corrections because notifications are not a standard practice. When a correction is made, it is usually published on an inside page, not in a prominent position. Some newspapers, such as the *Chicago Tribune*, either place corrections at the same location as the original story or put the corrections in the same location every day.

Fiction and Fact

When real-life events provide the basis for entertainment, professionals often are confronted with the issue of mixing fact and fiction. Docudramas mix documentary techniques and dramatic action; they make great viewing. But they often blur the lines between fact and fiction in such a compelling way that viewers remember the visual representation better than the facts. Historians are therefore justifiably concerned about films such as *Mississippi Burning*, the story of the murder of three civil rights workers during the 1960s. *Mississippi Burning* gave Gene Hackman a starring role as a tough and decent FBI warrior and distorted the role of the FBI. In fact, many historical journals have introduced new sections to evaluate historical docudramas and films.

More recently, the 1962 Cuban missile crisis was explored in the 2001 film *Thirteen Days*. The movie reported the story about the confrontation between the United

Kevin Costner plays Kenny O'Donnell in *Thirteen Days*. The issue with docudramas is whether fictionalizing history distorts history. Will the information we pass to the next generation be accurate—or simply dramatic fiction?

States and the Soviet Union through the eyes of presidential assistant Kenny O'Donnell, played by Kevin Costner. Little evidence exists that O'Donnell played as important a role in the crisis as the movie portrays. His character is a device for dramatizing the story.[37]

Oliver Stone is one of the most criticized filmmakers for confusing fact and fiction. His films *JFK* (1991) and *Nixon* (1995) both received critical acclaim, but both were also attacked as revisionist history. *JFK* explored the possibility that a conspiracy lay behind the assassination of President John F. Kennedy in 1963. The film was criticized for its factual errors and questionable assumptions. *Nixon* portrayed the life of Richard M. Nixon, who resigned from the presidency in 1974 after the U.S. Congress began impeachment proceedings in the wake of the Watergate scandal. *Nixon* has fewer inaccuracies than *JFK*, but it did poorly at the box office. Filmmakers such as Stone say they use movie storytelling techniques to get their version of truth to viewers. As one writer put it, "Asked if he believed that art could arrive at the truth even faster than journalism, Stone replied, 'I know it.'"[38]

Altering fact to get one's version of the truth across to people requires ethical decision making. How much alteration is permissible? How much should the viewer or reader be told about the alteration? How can an artist be sure his or her version of the truth is really the truth? How can changing fact reveal truth? These questions pose serious issues about whether the results contribute to society's understanding of its own history.

TRENDS

Ethics are affected by a variety of trends in society and in media industries. Two such trends facing media today include the demands for high profit among media, especially during an economic downturn, and the war on terrorism that may well become a part of world events for years to come.

Economic Demands on Media

Trends in ethics depend on changes in economic structures of media institutions, and increasing competition also has become a factor. As media companies compete for readers, viewers, and listeners, organizations are tempted to emphasize sensational content to get attention, thus accelerating the trend toward infotainment. Whether journalists and media companies choose to resist this trend is problematic. If they do not, some critics predict that U.S. society as a democratic forum in which citizens participate will be endangered.

A second economic force, the segmented audience, also tests the ethics of media managers. As media outlets proliferate, audiences have more choices about what to read or watch. Specialization gives advertisers more power over content because the media company becomes more dependent on a few advertisers. *Glamour* magazine, for example, has a much smaller pool of potential advertisers than *Newsweek* does because *Glamour* has a narrower reader appeal. If an article in *Glamour* upsets the large cosmetic advertisers, an advertiser boycott could reduce the magazine's revenue drastically.

A third economic factor affecting media ethics is the demand for high profits by some publicly owned corporations. Media companies such as Gannett and Knight Ridder must keep their profits high to keep their stock prices from falling. Declining stock prices can result in changes in management and takeovers by corporations that think the media company's stock is undervalued. Companies with high profit margin requirements might be less likely to write or broadcast negative information about their advertisers and more likely to give in to advertiser boycotts.

Although competition often can increase the possibility of unethical behavior, it also can help expose that behavior. Media companies competing for audiences do not hesitate to expose the questionable behavior of their competitors. One network's news department might eagerly expose that another network's news department is paying sources or staging events to create video.

The War on Terrorism

The events of September 11, 2001, the war in Afghanistan, continuing concerns about terrorism, and the 2003 war in Iraq have created ongoing ethical dilemmas for journalists. Real-time television newscasts create tension between ethical standards, the need to present a realistic picture of the horrors of war, and journalists' roles as citizens. Ethical issues such as those surrounding the use of video and photographic images of Daniel Pearl will continue to arise. News organizations trying to gain or keep readers, viewers, and listeners may be tempted to use checkbook journalism and to increase self-censorship. Journalists should be keenly aware of the potential for ethical abuses under conditions of war because their role as information providers becomes even more important.

discussing trends

During times of economic and political crisis, pressures on media organizations and journalists can increase. Media must provide information that is profitable but doesn't compromise the security of the country. As competition for attention increases, ethical standards can become even shakier. This leads to a range of complex questions that can test individual and organizational ethics:

- How can a news organization provide truthful, balanced, and fair coverage of a community with shrinking newsroom budgets?
- Can individual journalists stand up to demands that they cut corners in collecting news?
- Will the need to attract audience in TV news outweigh the desire to maintain ethics in an increasingly fragmented industry?
- Can news organizations use the World Wide Web to provide some of the news eliminated by cost-cutting in hard economic times?
- Will self-criticism within news media help police unethical behavior?

Equally difficult will be covering a war on terrorism and maintaining balanced reporting and ethical behavior.

- What is ethical behavior in war?
- Should news media continue to provide balanced and fair reporting of all sides?
- Should news media fight for individuals' rights as government aims to increase security and curtail the flow of information?
- How can the public and news media differentiate between issues of national security and efforts by government to hide its mistakes?
- How will economic demands and the need to cover war increase the pressure to act unethically?

summary

- Media ethics are important because citizens rely heavily on media to make informed decisions in a democratic framework and because media credibility is necessary to attract and keep an audience.
- Ethical behavior has political and economic implications.
- In the nineteenth century, editors were criticized for trivializing the news when they printed material about the details of people's lives.
- Standards for ethical behavior vary within and across cultures.
- The increasing volume and complexity of information in the early twentieth century led to the development of professional public relations practitioners whose task was to get a client the best possible hearing for a legitimate message.
- If media organizations do not regulate themselves (with standards of good taste and decency), then government is more likely to impose regulations.
- Five classical positions for understanding modern ethical dilemmas include the principles of (1) the Golden Mean, (2) the categorical imperative, (3) utility, (4) the veil of ignorance, and (5) the Judeo-Christian ethic.
- Accuracy, fairness, balance, and accurate representation are fundamental ethical standards accepted by most professional communicators. Objectivity is a basic value of most journalists.
- Some media organizations joined together to support the National News Council, but it lacked support throughout the industry; other organizations have hired ombudsmen to act as internal critics.
- Industry ethics codes are used as guidelines for media professionals. Adherence is voluntary. Many local media operations have devised their own codes, enforcing adherence in the same way that other company policies are enforced.
- Although many media organizations follow a code of ethics, such codes are not enough. Individuals need to develop a process of moral reasoning and understand ethical issues at all levels to articulate and justify the reasons behind their decisions and actions.
- The reliance of media on advertising makes media vulnerable to business demands. However, advertisers also need media.
- Increasing competition, development of a segmented audience, and demands by corporations for high profits are among the trends that foster sensationalism.

navigating the web | Ethics on the Web

Ethics-related web sites provide information about ethics in the United States and in the world. These sites may include journalistic codes of ethics, reports from think tanks, and journalism magazine articles that discuss ethical issues.

EthicNet
www.uta.fi/ethicnet

EthicNet was created by the Department of Journalism and Mass Communication at the University of Tampere in Finland. It includes journalistic codes of ethics from all over the world.

Fairness and Accuracy in Reporting (FAIR)
www.fair.org

FAIR is a liberal media watch group that criticizes media for their biased coverage of minorities, women, and labor. FAIR's site provides reports and a variety of links.

The Media Institute
www.mediainst.org

As a conservative think tank that criticizes media, lobbies Congress about media policy, and supports deregulating media, The Media Institute's site provides articles and reports.

Poynter Online
www.poynter.org

The Poynter Institute for Media Studies is a nonpartisan, nonprofit organization that studies media ethics, management, and graphics. It conducts seminars on a variety of these topics.

AJR NewsLink
www.ajr.org

AJR NewsLink is the online version of the *American Journalism Review*. Maintained by the University of Maryland College of Journalism, this site provides articles and links about journalism performance.

questions for review

1. Why did social responsibility replace the libertarian philosophy as the basis for the U.S. press system?
2. Under what conditions can profit affect news credibility?
3. Why is accuracy a basic element of most communication ethics?
4. What types of impact can advertisers have on media content?

issues to think about

1. How might questionable ethics, such as those in CNN's story about Tailwind, affect the way people think about television news? What could TV news departments do about this?
2. How might media organizations be forced to behave ethically? What drawbacks would this method create?
3. What can companies and industries do if they think the news media are not being fair and balanced in their coverage?
4. How do personal ethics affect professional ethics?
5. Do you use a moral reasoning process in making decisions? How would you describe that process?
6. How would you go about writing a code of ethics for a news organization? Who would you consult about what should be in the code?
7. How are ethical and legal problems similar? How are they different?

suggested readings

Altschull, J. Herbert. *Agents of Power*, 2nd ed. (White Plains, NY: Longman, 1995).

Christians, Clifford G., et al. *Media Ethics: Cases and Moral Reasoning*, 6th ed. (New York: Longman, 2002).

Jaksa, James A., and Michael S. Pritchard. *Communication Ethics: Methods of Analysis* (Belmont, CA: Wadsworth, 1988).

Lynch, Dianne, ed. *Stand! Virtual Ethics: Debating Media Values in a Digital Age* (Boulder, CO: Coursewise Publishing, 1999).

Merrill, John C. *The Dialectic in Journalism: Toward a Responsible Use of Press Freedom* (Baton Rouge: Louisiana State University Press, 1989).

Regulation

The story would have run in any commercial newspaper in the United States. Residents near the school district's bus garage had filed a lawsuit against the district, claiming that diesel fumes from the buses made them sick. But high school journalist Katy Dean, a sixteen-year-old junior at Utica High School in Michigan, discovered she worked under different rules. Her story about the suit would not run in her award-winning high school newspaper. The principal censored the story.

Dean's experience is not unusual. During 2002, Huntley High School administrators in Illinois confiscated issues of the school paper that contained stories about students who suffered from depression. Administrators at East High School in Cheyenne, Wyoming, censored a story about police arresting the debate team for vandalism. When the principal of Leto High School in Florida would not let the student editor run a story about a teacher's police record, the editor put the story on his web site and ran an ad for the site in the high school newspaper. The editor was suspended from the newspaper staff.

These examples are only a few of the hundreds of high school censorship problems that arise each year. The Student Press Law Center, which provides help for student journalists, reported 518 calls for help in 2000.[1] Despite the First Amendment to the Constitution, courts have ruled it is legal for school administrators to censor high school journalism. High school journalists have less freedom than older journalists.

The issue of who loses and who gains freedom is at the heart of regulation. Whenever people interact, conflicts arise. Ethics and social norms provide standards for behavior, but they have no formal power of enforcement. Some entity must balance the rights of individuals against those of society. Ultimately, governments determine which behaviors will be punished as illegal and the form of punishment that will be applied. Therefore, regulation—the process of enforcing rules that mediate societal conflicts—occurs in all societies.

Because of the media's potential for changing society and harming individuals, media content and the behavior of people who work in the media are regulated throughout the world. A person in the United States cannot legally start broadcasting without permission from the federal government. A Chinese journalist can be sentenced to jail for criticizing the government. The degree of speech and press freedoms varies from country to country, but in no country is it absolute.

The issues surrounding regulation are always complex because they involve the rights of society versus the rights of individuals and they must cope with changing technologies and changing economic factors. Some of the issues addressed in this chapter include the following:

◆ As new technologies develop and channels of information proliferate, what justifications will be used to regulate new technologies? Will these be legitimate bases for regulation, or will they merely serve political or economic purposes?

◆ As electronic delivery of information increases throughout the world, how will governments regulate this activity, which freely crosses national boundaries?

◆ How does regulation achieve a balance between the right of free expression and societal concerns about media depictions of violence and sexual activity?

◆ Are journalists' right to access compatible with individuals' rights to privacy and freedom from libel?

◆ Who receives First Amendment protection in the United States and who does not?

◆ How will the need to control information during war affect individual rights of expression?

Regulation *in Your Life*

Freedom and Restraint

As you read this chapter, think about how free speech has been restrained at different times in society. Can you think of some examples that might enrich a discussion of how free speech is important to your life as a student? As you think about your own examples of restrictions on freedom of speech, would you say they fit into the five categories listed below? Or do they fit into other categories?

WHY GOVERNMENTS REGULATE	EXAMPLES OF RESTRICTIONS
Economic reasons	
Product or company has negative impact on society as a whole	
Product or company has negative impact on individuals that outweighs benefits to society	
Preservation of security during war	
Preserve government's power	
Other	

REGULATION IN AMERICAN LIFE

Although few people dispute a government's right to regulate, nearly everyone disagrees about what the regulation should cover. The founders of the United States, fearing that government officials would exercise arbitrary power, created the Bill of Rights to protect citizens from government encroachment on private affairs and to promote the concept that government is by consent of its citizens.

Reasons for Regulation

In the United States, the ***regulatory concept*** is widely accepted. Federal, state, and local governments use regulatory power for five reasons.

1. *Government regulates when people or organizations interfere with the workings of the economic market system.* The United States has a **market economy** based on two assumptions: that competition works best for society and that unfair business practices must not be allowed to reduce competition. Competition has been favored because it is believed to force companies to respond to the demands of the public and keep prices low. Theoretically, the company that produces the best product at the lowest price will continue in business.

Even though competition does not always provide immediate benefits to media consumers, the federal government assumes that in most situations competition is better than monopoly. Such was the assumption when the courts broke the AT&T monopoly in 1984. AT&T, the giant telephone monopoly, was stifling competition for long-distance services and making monopoly profits through high prices. The largest company in the world at the time, AT&T was forced to split its local telephone services among seven independent regional operating systems. It continued to

Deregulation has expanded the long-distance telephone service market and opened up the possibility for telephone companies to provide news and entertainment content as well as the technology to carry messages.

provide long-distance service, competing against providers such as MCI and Sprint, and could enter into unregulated enterprises.

Now long-distance telephone companies compete to set up worldwide communication systems for a variety of businesses. Several of the regional Bell operating systems are exploring mergers with cable TV companies and are generating and distributing information. The competition has led to experimentation and the development of new technology and services in the **telecommunications industry.** As a result of the *1996 Telecommunications Act,* AT&T became the largest cable company before merging with Comcast in 2003.

2. *Government regulates when the use of a product or an industry or company's behavior has a negative impact on society as a whole.* The ongoing struggle between the tobacco industry and the government illustrates this point. By the early 1950s, the U.S. medical community was convinced that cigarettes posed serious health hazards for the public. The tobacco industry responded with a public relations and advertising effort that clouded the issue and sought to minimize health problems related to smoking.[2] In 1964 the U.S. Surgeon General pronounced publicly that cigarettes cause cancer. Seven years later, Congress passed legislation prohibiting radio and television from carrying cigarette advertising. The federal and state governments have taken several regulatory steps to control smoking, including banning and controlling smoking in public places.

The ability of tobacco companies to influence policy declined in 1997 when the cigarette manufacturer Liggett Group released about 175 boxes of internal documents to state prosecutors as part of a lawsuit settlement. Liggett admitted that company executives knew cigarettes were habit forming and caused cancer, something tobacco companies had denied for decades.

Despite the settlement of a class action lawsuit by forty states against the tobacco industry and calls from lawmakers that cigarettes be regulated, smoking continues to threaten the lives of millions of Americans. The fact that cigarettes have not been banned entirely illustrates the influence of powerful and wealthy industries over government regulation.

3. *Government regulates when a product or behavior has a negative impact on individuals that outweighs its contribution to society as a whole.* Laws concerning

privacy, libel, and slander are examples of this form of regulation. In 1942, *Time* published a story about Dorothy Barber, a woman who ate constantly but still lost weight, calling her a "starving glutton." She sued, and the courts ruled for Mrs. Barber, arguing that the hospital was one place you should be able to go for privacy. Her disease, rather unusual at the time, is now more widely known as anorexia nervosa.

A journalist cannot enter a person's house carrying hidden cameras and microphones. When a *Life* magazine journalist and a photographer did this for an article called "Crackdown in Quackery," *Life* was sued for invasion of privacy and lost. The courts ruled that the journalist's entry into A. A. Dietemann's home was an illegal intrusion of privacy even though he was practicing a questionable form of medicine in his home.[3]

4. *Government regulates the flow of information during times of war.* Unrestricted publication and broadcasting could endanger the lives of U.S. troops and could affect the outcome of battles and wars. **Censorship** during war is not mentioned in the Constitution, but courts have supported the government's right to censor ever since the Civil War.

The exact relationship between the press and government during war remains unsettled. Because the Vietnam conflict was never declared a war, formal censorship was never invoked. Since that time, the federal government tried to regulate the media in war by creating **press pools** and by limiting access. In Iraq in 2003, reporters were "embedded" in military units but still faced restrictions.

The relationship between the press and government's control of war coverage became even more complicated with the war on terrorism that followed the attacks of September 11, 2001. This undeclared war has no geographic battle lines and will be fought all over the world. The Patriot Act of 2001 has given the U.S. Justice Department broad powers that affect both individual rights and journalists' access to information.

5. *Government seeks to preserve its own security and power.* Government officials sometimes try to regulate information for illegitimate reasons, to avoid political embarrassment, or to hide illegal activities. Most citizens and journalists would argue that using government laws to avoid embarrassment is an improper use of political power. Two important events came about primarily because citizens, journalists, and the U.S. courts agreed that government officials' use of laws to avoid embarrassment is a misuse of political power: the overturn of the Alien and Sedition Acts and the resignation of President Nixon. The Alien and Sedition Acts, passed in 1798 by a Federalist-controlled Congress, allowed the government to imprison and fine its critics. Representative Matthew Lyon was imprisoned for four months and fined $1,000 for suggesting that President John Adams's administration had "an unbounded thirst for ridiculous pomp, foolish adulation, and selfish avarice."[4] Congress overturned these acts after only two years. Two historic clashes in the early 1970s between the press and President Nixon illustrate cover-up efforts by a U.S. president. The first was the battle between the press and the government over the Pentagon Papers, which are historical documents chronicling the Vietnam conflict. The second was the Watergate affair. Both involved an attempt by government to withhold information because it would be personally (or governmentally) embarrassing.

In the Pentagon Papers case, major newspapers published government documents that they believed had been misclassified, and they were vindicated by the Supreme Court. The government's ability to hide information legally had not been destroyed, but it had been significantly damaged. The term *Watergate* applies to a wide range of illegal and unethical behavior by the Nixon White House during his reelection campaign in 1972. These activities included disruption of Democratic campaign activities, burglary, and taking illegal campaign contributions. Nixon and his advisers got even further into trouble when they tried to cover up their activities as

censorship: Restriction of access to information; deletion of information from a story; or refusal to let a correspondent mail, broadcast, or otherwise transmit a story.

press pool: A small group of reporters selected to gather information and pass it on to the larger group of press people. Used when the number of reporters gathering in one spot is problematic.

the Senate held hearings. Nixon resigned in 1974 when it became obvious that he would have to endure impeachment proceedings if he remained president.

The initial story of a break-in at Democratic headquarters located in the Watergate office complex led to a series of investigations by *Washington Post* reporters Bob Woodward and Carl Bernstein. These reporters won the Pulitzer Prize for their stories, which revealed the corruption and illegal activity within the Nixon administration.

Sometimes reporters have to look beneath the official reason to determine whether government is acting in a legitimate way or is trying to cover up its actions. The Defense Department said that it regulated media access to the Gulf War in 1991 to protect troops and journalists. However, the government seemed just as concerned about criticism from both inside and outside the military as it did about protecting the troops.[5]

Regulation of Media and the First Amendment

Not all media are equal when government attempts to regulate *freedom of expression.* Print media initially gained their freedom through the First Amendment to the Constitution because the founders believed that a self-governing populace needed a free flow of information. The press enjoys a higher level of protection than broadcast and cable media. The limited number of channels available to broadcast and cable technology and public fear of broadcasting's power to influence elections and social values have created an atmosphere in which regulation has been thought necessary and beneficial.

First Amendment press guarantees are not unique. For example, Japan's constitution guarantees freedom of the press and speech. Great Britain also protects its press, although their protection is more limited than in the United States. One difference is that in the United States the balance of power among the executive, legislative, and judicial branches prohibits one branch of government from creating regulation without review. Each branch of government provides a check on the others that limits, but does not prevent, political abuse.

The almost mythical stature the First Amendment has gained over the years hides the controversy that originally surrounded it and the other nine amendments in the Bill of Rights. During the 1787 Constitutional Convention, the Federalists argued against the inclusion of a bill of rights. They said that it was unnecessary because any powers not specifically given the central government would be left to the states. The Anti-Federalists, who were suspicious of a strong central government, said that the absence of specific protections for individuals' rights would allow the federal government to supersede such rights granted at the state level.

Some states were reluctant to ratify the Constitution without a bill of rights. To secure ratification, the Federalists agreed that such a bill would be added as amendments. This compromise allowed ratification of the Constitution by the original thirteen states. The Bill of Rights was drafted by the first U.S. Congress and ratified by the states in 1791.

For almost two hundred years, scholars have debated the exact reason for writing the First Amendment. However, one component is clear. The founders intended to preserve a marketplace of ideas, particularly in the realm of politics. Many who helped write the Constitution believed that distasteful and unpopular content must be protected so that democracy did not become mob rule. Today, as then, the press is an essential contributor to public debate. A valid fear is that censorship of unpopular content can become a precedent for censoring a wide variety of material. The slow erosion of protection could result in a tyranny of majority opinion that would damage the vitality of the entire democratic system.

Teach Your Children Well:
Schools and the First Amendment

A democracy such as the United States exists on the free flow of information and ideas. The First Amendment rests on this foundation, and the preservation of this delicate and crucial relationship depends on citizens understanding it. If the United States must depend on its schools to teach this heritage, its democracy may well be in serious trouble. Since 1988, high school students have had little or no First Amendment protections, and efforts to reduce First Amendment protection for college students continue in U.S. courts.

Until the Supreme Court's *Hazelwood School District v. Kulmeier* decision, high school students could exercise free expression unless it would disrupt school or affect others' rights. The 1988 *Hazelwood* ruling presented school administrators with almost unlimited power to censor high school journalists. Officials use the ruling to control information that might simply be embarrassing.

In 2002, administrators in two Texas high schools refused to let students publish articles about homosexuality. The *Bear Facts* staff at Hastings High School in Houston had planned a two-page spread about the abuse of lesbians and gays, but the articles were censored because administrators considered them too controversial. At Cinco Ranch High School in Katy, Texas, administrators eliminated a yearbook column about "coming out" and said it would have been okay in the newspaper but not in the yearbook. Tara Williams, news-

paper adviser at Baltimore Southern High School, said her contract was not renewed in 2002 because she fought efforts by administrators to censor the student newspaper.

Certainly, many principals and superintendents do not exercise their power to censor, but the fact that they *can* censor content tells their students something about the role of the First Amendment in a democracy. Critics argue that students who are denied free expression in their education are not likely to develop an appreciation for the role of the First Amendment, nor will they be eager to use their rights. There is little evidence for this position, but there is no doubt that support for the First Amendment has been declining. An *American Journalism Review* survey in 2002 found that 49 percent of the one thousand people interviewed said the Constitution goes too far in the rights it guarantees. This was up from 22 percent two years earlier.

Another concern is that the *Hazelwood* ruling will be applied to colleges, which would give college administrators the power to control news and information. An effort by the administrators at Kentucky State to control yearbook content went to the U.S. Court of Appeals for the Sixth Circuit in 2001 before the court ruled that administrators had violated the students' First Amendment rights. In fall 2002, arguments were being made before the U.S. Court of Appeals for the Seventh Circuit after the dean of Governors State University told the printers of the *Innovator,* the

student newspaper, not to print the paper until a school official approved the content. Three student journalists sued. In this case, Illinois Attorney General James Ryan requested that the court apply the *Hazelwood* case to the public college.

Arguments in support of controlling student expression contend that student mistakes could hurt others and that controversy can disrupt school. Critics reply that these are certainly possibilities, but these possibilities can be reduced by teaching students about press responsibility, and that sometimes these mistakes are the price for having freedom.

If U.S. high school and college students are denied protection of expression by the First Amendment, how can they develop an appreciation for the main pillar of democracy in the United States? How can young people support what they cannot experience? Is the danger of harm from exercising First Amendment rights greater than the negative effects of denying those rights to young people? These are the issues that regulation must address.

Sources: Ken Paulson, "Too Free?" *American Journalism Review,* September 2002, www.ajr.org; Jill Rosen, "High School Confidential," *American Journalism Review,* June 2002, www.ajr.org; "First Amendment Groups Will Argue College Censorship Case before Appeals Court," Student Press Law Center, September 25, 2002, www.splc.org; "Two Houston Area Schools Censor Stories about Gay Students," Student Press Law Center, May 24, 2002, www.splc.org.

Regulation in a World without Boundaries

As far back as the 1800s, media companies have been concerned about the pirating of copyrighted material. U.S. magazine, newspaper, and book companies regularly reprinted British articles and books without paying the writers or companies who originally published them. After the development of cassette tapes, CDs, VCRs, and DVD players, U.S. entertainment companies became upset with losses due to domestic and international piracy of the content.

However, in all these previous instances, companies could try to control piracy by controlling the distribution of physical objects. It wasn't always effective, but shipment of books, CDs, and DVDs could be confiscated. The Internet has changed this. Bundles of electrons can speed around the world pirating songs and movies without having to be smuggled physically across a border.

In February 2002, Movie88.com began streaming movies that could be viewed but not downloaded. The cost for viewing the films for a few days was one dollar. The service was located in Taiwan, and authorities closed it quickly. In June the site reemerged as Film88.com, this time located in Iran, a country that does not recognize international copyright law. However, Film88.com used servers in the Netherlands, and the Motion Picture Association of America obtained a court order to close it down.

Later in 2002, the Recording Industry Association of America sued several Internet service providers (ISPs) to shut down a Chinese web site, Listen4ever.com, which was distributing Western music. This was the first lawsuit against an ISP that was aimed at restricting access. The recording industry did not sue the web site, because China has a spotty record in supporting copyright law. The confrontation with ISPs disappeared when the web site went offline.

Companies providing any form of media content must face the threat of piracy from all over the world. It is unlikely that all web sites can be shut down with laws because some will locate in countries that don't recognize copyright law. As a result, pressure on ISPs from the copyright holders will increase. The ISPs do not want to become involved in censoring web sites.

Portions of the Digital Millennium Copyright Act (DMCA), passed in 1998, aimed to clarify this problem. The law provided a way for an ISP to reduce its liability for copyright infringement, but ISPs that knowingly distribute pirated material can still be held liable. Critics argue that corporations are abusing the act and restricting the free flow of information. They have called for Congress to reassess the law.

Sources: David McGuire, "Civil Liberties Group: Copyright Law Unconstitutional," Newsbytes News Network, February 4, 2002, www.newsbytes.com; Pham-Duy Nguyen, "Sony, Labels Withdraw Suit against Internet Service Providers," Detnews.com, August 22, 2002, www.detnews.com; Daniel Sieberg, "Movie-Streaming on Film88.com: Movie-streaming Site Raises Ire of Industry," cnn.com, June 10, 2002, www.cnn.com.

TYPES OF MEDIA REGULATION

Governments in the United States exercise three types of regulation over mass media:

1. Governments regulate the economic behavior of media companies in the consumer and advertising markets. For example, the federal government limits the number of television stations a company can own in a city.
2. Governments regulate certain internal business activities of media companies. For example, a media company must comply with federal laws that prohibit racial and gender discrimination in hiring.
3. Despite the existence of the First Amendment, governments regulate some content and information. For example, a company cannot broadcast a deceptive advertisement that might harm consumers.

These forms of regulation can take place at several levels of government. Local governments pass ordinances about where newspapers can put news racks. States pass libel laws. The federal government has created the Federal Communications Commission (FCC), which regulates telecommunications, and the Federal Trade

table 14.1

Sources of Laws

These are listed in order of power. For example, the U.S. Constitution takes precedence over federal statutory laws. Federal statutory laws can be challenged as being unconstitutional.

- *Federal Constitution:* laws established by articles and amendments to the U.S. Constitution.
- *Federal Statutory:* laws passed by the federal legislative body, the U.S. Senate and House of Representatives.
- *Federal Administrative:* laws established by federal administrative bodies that were set up by statute, such as the FCC and FTC.
- *State Constitution:* laws established by the various state constitutions.
- *State Statutory:* laws passed by various state legislatures.
- *State Administrative:* laws established by various state administrative bodies that were set up by statute.
- *State Common Law:* laws created by judicial interpretation; few apply to communication law.

Source: Todd F. Simon, Professor and Director, A. Q. Miller School of Journalism and Mass Communication, Kansas State University.

Commission (FTC), which regulates advertisements. The higher the level, the more power the government has to affect content.

Media regulation evolved through a series of legislative actions and court interpretations that are sometimes inconsistent and confusing. A valid libel defense in one state may not be a valid defense in another. One court decision may set a precedent that conflicts with another. The inconsistencies reflect the nature of a democratic style of government and the difficulties of interpreting laws on the basis of a constitution written 215 years ago. Table 14.1 outlines the sources of regulatory laws, which range from the federal Constitution to laws created by judicial interpretation. The ability of media organizations to monopolize a market through

more efficient technology did not exist when the Constitution was ratified. Nevertheless, one common thread runs throughout all of the ad hoc public policy: Regulation attempts to balance the information needs of society with the rights of media companies and individual citizens. This is called *balancing theory.*

Economic Regulation

Media economics concerns the way media companies produce and sell products in the information and advertising markets. Two types of regulation affect these markets most often: antitrust laws and direct regulation by government agencies such as the FCC and FTC.

Antitrust Law ✦ Antitrust laws are intended to promote competition in markets and to prevent or break up monopolies. They outlaw several practices aimed at closing down a company's competitors, including selling a product for less than it costs to make and joining with another company to drive others out of business.

The Sherman Act, passed in 1890, and the Clayton Act, passed in 1914, are the core of antitrust law. Congress passed them in part as a reaction to the "robber barons" of the late nineteenth century. Industrialists J. P. Morgan, Cornelius Vanderbilt, and John D. Rockefeller, among others, used unfair business practices to monopolize markets. As monopolists, they were able to increase prices and profit considerably more than they would have if competition had existed.

The underlying assumption of antitrust laws is that *competition benefits consumers*. Experience shows that competition can reduce prices and allow consumers to influence products through their purchasing choices. This holds for news media competition at a local level. Competition among newspapers and among television news departments lowers subscription prices (for newspapers), increases news department budgets, increases amounts of information, and causes journalists to work harder to get news quickly and accurately. These advantages have a cost. Competition also can result in an emphasis on sensationalism and in unethical behavior to get stories.[6]

The impact of competition in the advertising market is more straightforward. Theoretically, competition keeps advertising prices low and improves service from the media companies. However, competition can increase advertisers' influence over editorial content. For example, because of the high degree of competition in the field, magazines are far more likely to allow advertisers to influence content than other media might be. If a company does not like what a magazine has written about its product, the company can ask for a change in that content and threaten to take its advertising elsewhere. Research shows that publications with extensive alcohol advertising also contain favorable editorial content toward drinking.[7] In another study, five large-circulation women's magazines with high amounts of cigarette advertising between 1983 and 1987 carried no feature-length articles about the hazards of smoking.[8]

Newspapers and Antitrust Laws ✦ Despite the early application of antitrust laws to broadcasting and film, some newspapers have enjoyed exemptions from these laws. Initial application of antitrust law to newspapers did not occur until 1945, when the Supreme Court ruled that the Associated Press could not sell its services exclusively to one newspaper in a city. Two decades later the Justice Department once more applied antitrust law and tried to dismantle an illegal agreement called a **joint operating agreement (JOA)** between two daily newspapers in Albuquerque, New Mexico. (Seventeen other cities had similar agreements.) The Supreme Court supported the Justice Department, ruling that the agreement that allowed the two newspapers to set prices and sell advertising together violated antitrust law.

As a reaction to the Supreme Court's ruling, Congress passed the Newspaper Preservation Act (NPA) in 1970. The act made the eighteen JOAs legal by allowing two newspapers in the same city to combine all departments and activities except the newsrooms. Senators and representatives who voted for the NPA said that it would preserve a second editorial voice in cities where two dailies could not survive independently. Some argued that it was the power of newspapers to influence voters that really got the NPA passed.

No matter what the reasons, the NPA preserved editorial voices in only a handful of cities. The same economic forces that have caused direct daily competition to disappear in all but a dozen cities continued to work in JOA cities. Because the NPA doesn't preserve competition in the long run, the daily that has the circulation lead has little incentive to join a JOA. Only thirteen JOA cities existed in 2003. However, as a rule, the quality of JOA newspapers has been higher than that of the average daily newspaper without direct daily competition.[9] The NPA has helped a handful of cities to have better daily newspapers for a slightly longer time than would have happened otherwise.

Direct Telecommunications Regulation ✦ During the early stages of broadcasting, government gave three justifications for *direct telecommunications regulation:* (1) The airwaves are a limited commodity, (2) the airwaves belong to the public, and (3) broadcasters should be responsive to the community and work in its best interest. The first justification reflected the confusion that arose as the number of radio stations grew during the 1920s. Often, two stations would broadcast on the same radio frequency, which meant that one or both could not be heard clearly. Because the

joint operating agreement (JOA): An agreement that allows two newspapers in the same city to operate the business and production sides of a newspaper together in a fashion that normally would violate antitrust law.

stations did not cooperate, Congress decided to regulate signals. The second justification concerns the physics of broadcasting. Radio and television use electromagnetic waves that move through the air. Because the government controls the air, the signal belongs to the public. The third justification reflects the assumption that giving a broadcasting company a license to use the public airwaves means that the company owes the public various kinds of services in return.

A series of congressional acts in 1912, 1927, and 1934 reflected a compromise between the desire to safeguard the public interest and efforts by broadcasters to preserve a commercially oriented broadcasting system.

The Radio Act of 1912 was the first effort to regulate wireless communication. The Radio Act covered regulations for maritime radio behavior and required that the federal government give radio licenses on request. However, the 1912 act did not provide criteria for rejecting licenses, and as the radio industry developed commercially, stations broadcast over the same frequencies, creating chaos in the air.

In 1927, Congress recognized that radio would be more than wireless communication and passed the second radio act, which created a five-member Federal Radio Commission that could assign radio licenses and require records of programming and technical operations. Congress created the FCC with the Federal Communications Act of 1934. The FCC had the power to regulate both wireless and wired communications, which at the time included radio and telephone. Most of the procedures developed under the Radio Act of 1927 continued under the FCC. The act provided for FCC control of broadcast licenses and ownership rules, as well as for regulation of some types of content. The 1934 act was amended and extended in a variety of ways as new technology developed, but federal communication regulations did not receive a major overhaul until 1996.

During the 1960s, citizens began to take an active interest in television content and in access to these channels of information. In this activist period, regulation increased. For example, in the case *Office of Communication, United Church of Christ v. FCC*, citizens gained *standing*, or the ability to take part in a license hearing. In this case, citizens challenged the renewal of a license to a Jackson, Mississippi, television station because of what they believed to be racist policies. During the 1970s, guarantees of equal time to candidates for federal offices had been expanded to include equal access to stations and equality in desirability of air time. For example, a station cannot sell prime time to one candidate and only early Sunday morning time to another.

Deregulation ✦ In the 1980s, technology allowed fifty or more radio stations and a dozen or more television stations in large markets to broadcast without any signal overlap. This improvement in technology, combined with the rapid rise in cable television, caused critics to question whether scarcity of channels was an issue. The political climate also changed. The Republican administrations of Presidents Ronald Reagan and George Bush had a more conservative approach toward federal government policy than previous administrations had had. The FCC reduced its regulation of broadcasting in ways that reflected the Reagan and Bush administrations' aim to limit government activities in economic markets.

The broadcast industry changed drastically as a result of deregulation. Companies no longer have to carry public affairs programs; a station's license does not have to be renewed as often as before; a company can own multiple radio and television stations in the same city; and stations no longer have to observe the *fairness doctrine*, a collection of rules that required stations to air opposing viewpoints concerning controversial issues. However, Congress retained the *equal time rule*, which affects political elections.

> **key concept**
>
> **Fairness Doctrine** The collection of FCC rules that was first passed in the 1940s required broadcast stations to air competing views on controversial issues, although earlier regulations had prohibited such debate. The FCC no longer enforces the rules, and some critics claim that the result has been a watering down of public debate.

Even though regulations requiring public service have declined, the issues are still debated. In December 1998, a twenty-two-member commission headed by Vice President Al Gore recommended that free television time be given to political candidates. In response, Senate Majority Leader Trent Lott introduced legislation that

Cable companies' ability to provide more than 200 channels to a viewer challenges the old notion of broadcasting as a scarce resource, the very principle on which broadcast regulation was founded.

would prevent the FCC from requiring free airtime from broadcasters. The $2.2 billion spending on advertising and the funding scandals in the 1996 elections sparked the call for free airtime. Because Congress and the FCC are split on the issue, the debate continues.

The law that governs direct telecommunication underwent its first complete revision in sixty-two years with the 1996 Telecommunications Act. The package of regulations that govern broadcast, cable, and telephone companies ended several years of congressional debate and altered the relationships among the various types of media.

The act removed barriers that prohibited cable and telephone companies from competing against each other. Now telephone and cable companies can provide entertainment, information, and telephone service. In addition, the Telecommunications Act allows local Bell telephone companies to provide long-distance service if the local companies are competitive for telephone service and the FCC decides that such entry serves the community's interests. Price regulation for cable ended in March 1999.

Ownership regulation changed as well. The number of radio and television stations a company can own nationally is no longer regulated. However, a single company's television stations cannot reach more than 35 percent of all households in the country. Radio stations have no household limit. In radio, a company can own multiple stations in a market, but the number varies with market size. In markets with forty-five commercial stations, a company can own up to eight stations but no more than five of a particular type (AM or FM). In the smallest markets, those with fourteen or fewer stations, a company can own five stations but no more than three of a particular type. Three years after the Telecommunications Act, the FCC ruled that one company could own two television stations and six radio stations in a market with twenty or more unaffiliated newspapers, radio stations, and television stations.

Despite the massive deregulation of the telecommunications industry, large media companies continue to press for more changes in the ownership rules. The three largest radio corporations, Clear Channel, Infinity, and Cox, with more than 1,500 stations in 2002, called for the FCC to repeal the local-ownership rules entirely.[10]

Television companies also joined the demand for fewer regulations. A federal judge ruled in 2002 that the FCC rule about audience and ownership was arbitrary. The rule states that a television network cannot own stations that reach more than 35 percent of all the households in the United States. In 2002, Fox Television and CBS each had stations that reached about 40 percent of all households.

Proponents of the 1996 Telecommunications Act claimed it would promote competition that would lower prices and increase diversity of content. Opponents said it would result in media concentration that would reduce competition and increase prices. It has certainly increased ownership concentration, but the impact on prices and diversity for radio and television remains uncertain. However, deregulation of cable has resulted in price increases above the rate of inflation. Cable rates increased by 7.3 percent between June 1997 and June 1998 and by 3.8 percent between June 1998 and 1999.[11] A more recent FCC study found that the price for basic services and equipment increased by 7.5 percent between July 1, 2000, and July 1, 2001.[12]

The 1996 Telecommunications Act did not entirely deregulate the cable industry. In 1992, Congress passed the Cable Consumer Protection and Competition Act, which required cable systems to carry the signals of local television stations. Cable operators argued that the law violated their free speech rights because they could not open these channels to other cable networks, such as C-SPAN and Comedy Central. If the law did not exist, channels used for smaller local stations would likely be used for cable channels and possibly for pay-per-view programming. In 1997, the Supreme Court upheld the law five to four and required cable systems to continue carrying local station signals.

Business Regulation

Although economic regulations govern the interaction among competitors, the concerns of *business regulation* are less abstract. Business regulations affect the way an organization treats its employees and the impact that it might have on society. Media companies are concerned primarily with labor laws, discrimination laws, and other laws that affect media business practices.

Labor Laws ✦ Treatment of employees makes up a large portion of business regulation. Until the early years of the twentieth century, laborers usually worked six days a week for ten to twelve hours a day. Even children under the age of twelve worked under these conditions. However, in the 1930s the National Labor Relations Act (NLRA) and the Fair Labor Standards Act (FLSA) were passed as part of President Franklin Roosevelt's New Deal package. The NLRA outlawed antilabor activities by employers such as refusing to bargain collectively with employees and firing individuals because they participate in labor unions or publish criticism of an employer. The FLSA established the minimum wage and set limits on the number of hours a person could be required to work.

Many media companies fought against the application of labor laws to their activities. Although they argued that the First Amendment guarantee of freedom of the press should protect them from having to adhere to laws that affected other businesses, media business owners generally were more concerned with the effect on their profits than on their freedom. The NLRA was applied to newspapers in 1937 after the Associated Press attempted to fire Morris Watson for trying to form a union. The AP argued, to no avail, that the NLRA abridged freedom of the press. The NLRA was ruled applicable to broadcast stations the same year. The Watson case was part of the American Newspaper Guild's efforts to unionize reporters; the guild, begun in 1933, continues today with contracts at more than one-hundred newspapers.

key concept

Business Regulation Mass media outlets are usually owned by large corporations. As big businesses, media owners are required to adhere to labor laws, environmental regulations, and such standards as postal law. In many cases, media owners have protested having to abide by these laws, arguing that the laws infringe on their First Amendment rights.

1790. First copyright law is passed.

1791. Bill of Rights (first ten Constitutional Amendments) is ratified.

1798. Alien and Sedition Acts are passed.

1861–1865. Press is censored during Civil War.

1890. Sherman Antitrust Act is passed.

1906. Pure Food and Drug Act is passed.

1914. Federal Trade Commission is established.

1914. Clayton Antitrust Act is passed.

1917. Espionage Act is passed (World War I prior restraint).

1918. Sedition Act is passed (World War I prior restraint).

1927. Radio Act of 1927 is passed.

1931. *Near v. Minnesota* (prior restraint) is decided.

1934. Federal Communications Act is passed (FCC established).

1937. National Labor Relations Act is applied to newspapers.

1400–1700	1800	1860	1880	1900	1920	1930

1620. Pilgrims land at Plymouth Rock.

1690. *Publick Occurrences* is published in Boston.

1741. First magazine is published in America.

1776–1783. American Revolution

1830s. The penny press becomes the first truly mass medium in the United States.

1861–1865. American Civil War

1892. Thomas Edison's lab develops the kinetoscope.

1914–1918. World War I

1915. *The Birth of a Nation* marks the start of the modern movie industry.

1920. KDKA in Pittsburgh gets the first commercial radio license.

1930s. The Great Depression

1939. TV is demonstrated at the New York World's Fair.

1939–1945. World War II

Discrimination Laws ✦ Congress passed a series of laws between 1964 and 1992 that concern discrimination against employees who are members of various groups. The most important law in this area is the Civil Rights Act of 1964. Title VII of this act makes illegal any employment discrimination based on "race, color, religion, sex or national origin." Nevertheless, the percentage of newspaper newsroom employees who are members of racial minorities increased from 4 percent in 1978 to only about 12 percent in 2000. Furthermore, more than 40 percent of daily newsrooms remained all white.[13] There is also resistance to promoting people of color and women to managerial positions within media organizations.[14]

The Americans with Disabilities Act (ADA), passed in 1990, prohibits most employers from discriminating against people on the basis of a disability. As the ADA was phased in during the early 1990s, media companies seemed much more prepared to adjust to the law than they did to the Civil Rights Act. A survey of forty-seven

1941. 1917 Espionage Act is reactivated.

1945. *United States v. AP* is decided (antitrust applied to newspapers).

1964. *Times v. Sullivan* is decided (libel decision).

1970. Newspaper Preservation Act is passed.

1971. Pentagon Papers case is decided.

1972. Watergate scandal begins.

1976. Copyright Act is passed.

1996. Telecommunications Act is passed.

2002. War on terrorism leads to more regulation of government information.

2000s. U.S. government pushes for international enforcement of copyright laws.

2002. FCC further deregulates telecommunications industry.

1940	1950	1960	1970	1980	1990	2000

1949. First commercial electronic computer is produced.

Early 1950s. Rock 'n' roll begins.

1969. First person lands on the moon.

1970s. VCR is developed.

1989–1991. Cold War ends and the USSR is dissolved.

Late 1980s. National Science Foundation creates the basis of the Internet.

2000. Presidential election nearly tied.

2001. Terrorist attacks on New York and Washington, D.C.

media companies in 1991 found that 81 percent would have no compliance problems with the ADA.[15]

Content and Information Regulation

Direct *content regulation* emerged from government efforts to balance the free flow of information and ideas against the negative effects of media products. Part of the news media's role, as H. L. Mencken said, is "to comfort the afflicted and afflict the comfortable." Content regulation tries to reduce *unjustified, unnecessary,* and *unreasonable* harm to people from media content. Such regulation can occur before or after distribution. Some types of speech, such as political speech, are

Levels of Protected Communication

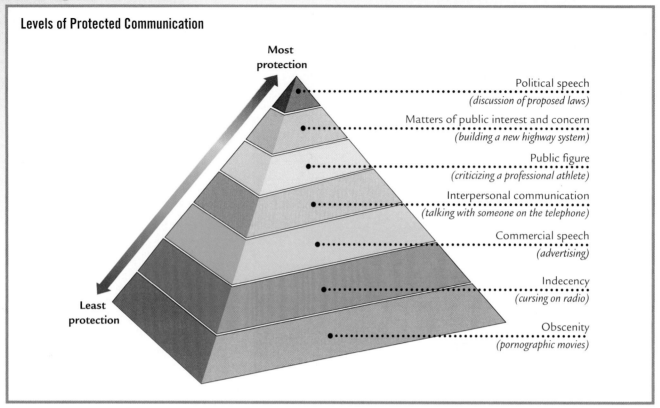

Most protection

Political speech
(discussion of proposed laws)

Matters of public interest and concern
(building a new highway system)

Public figure
(criticizing a professional athlete)

Interpersonal communication
(talking with someone on the telephone)

Commercial speech
(advertising)

Indecency
(cursing on radio)

Obscenity
(pornographic movies)

Least protection

Source: Todd F. Simon, Professor and Director, A. Q. Miller School of Journalism and Mass Communication, Kansas State University.

more protected than others, such as commercial speech. Figure 14.1 outlines the levels of protected speech.

Regulating Content Before Distribution ✦ Regulation of media content before

it is distributed is used to control content in times of war and for economic reasons. Such regulation falls into three areas: prior restraint, controlling government documents, and copyright law. The first two concern access to information about governments and their activities, and the third concerns protection of content created by individuals and organizations.

Prior Restraint. Through prior restraint, a government body prevents the public from getting certain types of information. In some cases, the government body reviews content before publication and censors it. In other cases it mandates that some types of content cannot be distributed.

The classic legal case involving prior restraint on newspapers is *Near v. The State of Minnesota.*[16] In this 1931 case, the State of Minnesota tried to stop the publication of the *Saturday Press*, a smear sheet that viciously attacked Jews and Catholics. In one story, the *Press* charged that gangsters controlled Minneapolis while law enforcement officers turned the other way. The publishers, Howard Guilford and J. M. Near, were charged under a Minnesota statute that prohibited anyone from publishing a "malicious, scandalous and defamatory newspaper, magazine or other periodical." The U.S. Supreme Court overturned the conviction of Guilford and Near and let them continue to publish. Although the Supreme Court allowed the *Saturday Press* to continue publication and, in effect, struck down the Minnesota "press as public nuisance" law, the court also recognized that these press freedoms are not absolute. It said that prior restraint can be exercised under conditions of national security, situations involving obscenity, and when the public order is threatened through violence. Prior restraint was often exercised during the mid-twentieth century when local and state censorship committees ruled on whether a film could be shown or whether it should be banned because of violence, sexual content, or unacceptable moral prescriptions.

Obscenity. Prior restraint often has been exercised when *controlling obscenity* and pornography have been the core issues. Such restraint was employed—sometimes illegally—by postmasters who took it on themselves to censor the mail they handled.
In 1873, Congress adopted the Hicklin Rule, which defined obscenity as anything with a tendency to corrupt people whose minds might be open to immoral influences. Critics later argued that the rule treated all citizens as though they were children. During the 1950s, the Supreme Court adopted a new definition, which eased the standards by which something was deemed obscene. The Roth-Memoirs Rule, named for two Supreme Court cases, declared that material deemed obscene for children was not necessarily obscene for all. The rule also required that the entire work, not just a portion, be considered in judging whether material was obscene. In 1973, with the case of *Miller v. California,* the court devised a three-part rule for determining obscenity:

1. An average person, applying contemporary local community standards, finds that the work, taken as a whole, appeals to prurient interest.
2. The work depicts in a patently offensive way sexual conduct specifically defined by applicable state law.
3. The work in question lacks serious literary, artistic, political, or scientific value.

Because the rules are community based, what is deemed obscene in Shreveport, Louisiana, may be determined by community standards in New York City to be purely artistic. Nevertheless, under any rule it has always been difficult for censorship boards, gossip columnists, and courts to determine whether content is obscene or whether it is artistic or literary. Obscenity laws have been used to ban everything from diving magazines to information about birth control.

Debate over the regulation of obscenity continued to gain attention during 2002 with two important decisions. First, David Solomon, head of the FCC Enforcement Bureau, which oversees obscenity complaints, said radio and TV stations would have to be able to refute complaints in the future. Stations cannot broadcast obscene programs between 6 A.M. and 10 P.M. Some say this will require stations to tape and keep recordings of their content. Most of the 280 formal complaints in 2001 concerned radio, but some observers suggest that television should be concerned about the potential for increased enforcement.[17]

As regulation of broadcast radio and TV content seemed to be increasing, portions of the 2000 Children's Internet Protection Act were overturned during 2002 by three federal judges. The law said public libraries had to block pornography with Internet filters. However, the judges ruled that these filters eliminated content that is protected by the Constitution. School libraries must still use filters.[18]

Censorship during War. Despite concerns about prior restraint, most journalists have accepted some censorship during times of war. The *control of media content during war* dates to the Civil War, when President Lincoln shut down the *New York Journal of Commerce* for publishing a forged presidential proclamation announcing the draft of 400,000 men. But Lincoln was generally tolerant of the press and remanded an order by General A. E. Burnside to close the *Chicago Times,* arguing that such action would be more detrimental than criticism of the war effort.

Congress formalized war censorship of the press during World War I when it passed the Espionage Act in 1917 and the Sedition Act in 1918. These acts prohibited publishing "disloyal" information and bringing the U.S. government into "contempt, scorn or disrepute." The enforcement of these laws was the responsibility of the Postmaster General, who could prevent offending publications from being mailed. At least forty-four publications lost second-class mailing privileges as a result of the Espionage Act.[19]

During World War II, the 1917 Espionage Act was reactivated, and President Franklin Roosevelt declared a limited national emergency, which allowed him to control broadcasting. Hoping to avoid more stringent regulation, the National Association of Broadcasters asked its commentators not to editorialize. Because of widespread fear and public support of the war, the media cooperated in most censorship during that war. The Office of Censorship, created in 1941, administered a voluntary code of censorship and controlled communications coming into and leaving the country.

Because the United States never declared war on North Vietnam, wartime censorship was never imposed during that conflict. The media were free to report the war as they saw it, though military personnel often gave inaccurate information in news briefings. Although research indicates that public protest of the war coincided with official concern about the conduct of the war—and that negative media coverage followed, but did not precede, the official concern—many military officials believed that the media had helped to lose the war in Vietnam. Government efforts to prevent publication of the Pentagon Papers under the guise of national security created further mistrust between journalists and government.

After Vietnam, the military tried to improve its management of the media by controlling access rather than by engaging in official censorship. This strategy was used in 1983 in Grenada and in 1989 in Panama. It also proved fairly successful during the initial stages of the Gulf War in 1991. However, some daring journalists were able to bypass military controls and pursue their own stories. Peter Arnett challenged U.S. control by remaining in Baghdad and reporting from the enemy capital, despite censorship by the Iraqis.

In 2003, Arnett again remained in Baghdad during the early stages of the war in Iraq, but after granting an interview to Iraqi State Television during the first two weeks of the war in which he stated that the U.S. war plan had "failed," he was fired by NBC and *National Geographic*. Many journalists believed that Arnett had "cozied up" to the Iraqi War Ministry to try to get an interview with Saddam Hussein. In doing so, he crossed the line from accurate reporting to airing his personal opinion as fact.

During the 2003 conflict, reporters were embedded with troops and gave real-time coverage to military actions. Government officials hoped such reporting would show how the United States strived to provide humanitarian aid and avoid civilian casualties.

The war on terrorism resulted in the USA Patriot Act, signed in November 2001 by President George W. Bush. The law amended more than fifteen federal statutes, allowing government officials greater power to withhold information and increasing their power to access electronic communication and other information about U.S. citizens. By the middle of 2002, some lawmakers were beginning to question whether the increased powers were too great.[20]

executive privilege: The president's right to withhold information if disclosure might harm the executive branch's functions and decision-making processes.

sunshine laws: Laws requiring that meetings of federal or state administrative agencies be open to the public.

Controlling Government Documents ✦ Prior restraint and censorship are not the only ways in which government controls information. It can also control access to material that affects the decision-making process. Many federal agencies exist just to provide information to Congress and the administrative branch. At the federal level, the president controls information because of the doctrine of **executive privilege,** which dates to the time of George Washington and James Madison. This doctrine states that the president may withhold information when disclosure might injure the public.

During the 1960s, press associations and other citizens' groups lobbied extensively for open meetings and records acts, often called **sunshine laws.** As a result, all fifty states have some form of open records laws. However, just how information is released varies. Some states, such as Florida and New York, allow more access to computerized data than do others. The denial of access to databases reflects a desire to protect individual privacy. However, as more records are stored electronically, states will have to make such databases available as part of open records acts.

In an effort to make government information more available to the public, Congress passed the Freedom of Information Act (FOIA) in 1967. The act specified that a federal agency can withhold information in only nine areas: national security, agency interpersonal activities, statutory exemptions, trade secrets, some intra-agency and interagency memos, issues involving personal privacy, police investigations, protection of government-regulated financial institutions, and information about oil and gas wells.

A difficulty with the FOIA is that agencies have extensive leeway in following the act. Bureaucracies can make information access easier or harder to obtain, depending on what the particular administrator wants to do. For example, the person seeking information is expected to pay reasonable fees for searching and copying. What is reasonable can vary from department to department and across time. The 1986 FOIA Reform Act tried to define the issues of national security and law enforcement exemptions, but it also gave departments more power to make some information less accessible.

Concern over how forthcoming the federal government would be increased in 2002 with the revelation that U.S. Attorney General John Ashcroft wrote a memo to government agencies on October 12, 2001, encouraging them to be more restrictive with FOIA requests for information.[21]

Controlling News Events. At times, reporters need information that cannot be found in documents. During breaking news stories, journalists want access to the people and locations involved in the news. Other important news events include governmental meetings at which ordinances and laws are decided. Because historically many government bodies have sought to close meetings, all states and the federal government have enacted open meetings laws known as *sunshine laws*. These laws require official government meetings to be open to the public, and thus the press, except under specific conditions.

The federal Government-in-Sunshine Act that took effect in 1977 applies to about fifty agencies, departments, and other groups. Their meetings can be closed if circumstances meet one of ten exemptions. State laws vary. Typical exemptions include meetings to discuss personnel matters, lawsuits, and land acquisition. Discussions about personnel could involve private material, considerations of lawsuits might involve confidential client–attorney information, and deliberating over land acquisitions could result in the premature release of information that could affect the price of land.

Public officials often control information. Here, reporters wait for a press conference during the Washington sniper attacks in 2002. Journalists question whether control of information is in the public interest or whether it simply serves to protect the officials.

In breaking news situations, such as the series of sniper killings in the Washington, D.C., area in October 2002, journalists want total access. However, law enforcement officials can legally exclude journalists from crime scenes during and after the crime. Nevertheless, police sometimes restrict journalists when it is not necessary to do so, causing speculation that law enforcement personnel are simply trying to control information.

Copyright Regulation. Copyright law stems from a power granted by the Constitution to Congress. The purpose of copyright law is to promote the publication of information by protecting the property rights of authors. The first U.S. copyright law was passed in 1790. A subsequent law, passed in 1909, stood until Congress revised it in 1976. The 1976 law provided increased protection for the creator of the work. Now the creator of a work has a copyright from the moment of creation until fifty years after his or her death.

Copyright law applies to newspapers, magazines, books, video, film, photographs, computer programs, speeches, web sites, and even professors' lecture notes. By providing the creator with control over the created material, the government hopes to encourage as much participation in the consumer market and marketplace of ideas as possible. People who make their living as writers, journalists, artists, and scholars cannot do so without legal control of the material they create.

Copyright covers the content but not the ideas in a publication. The words of this book are copyrighted, but the ideas are not. Often it is impossible to determine who generated an idea. Individuals build on a set of ideas by adding or altering existing ideas. Allowing ideas to float freely in the marketplace fosters public debate.

Although the law has protected creators of information, it has not been proved perfect in its promotion of an active marketplace of ideas. For example, **fair use** is a problematic issue. Teachers, reporters, book reviewers, and researchers exercise fair use when they excerpt material for scholarly use or comment and criticism. However, it is often difficult to determine just exactly what constitutes fair use. Therefore, in lawsuits that involve fair use, the courts look at (1) the purpose of the use, (2) the nature of the work being used, (3) the amount used in relation to the size of the full work, and (4) the impact of use on the market for the content.

The development of higher-speed modems and computers with larger memories has created serious problems with copyright protection. The first assault on copyright protection occurred with the sharing of music online, which accelerated with Napster in 2000. By 2002, a survey found more than 17 percent of all adults who use the Internet had downloaded music.[22] The percentage of teenagers was probably considerably higher. Even though Napster ceased to exist in 2002 following lawsuits by the major music companies, a variety of music-sharing software continues to be used in violation of copyright law.

Online copying of music is just the beginning. As movies became digitized for DVDs, copying and distributing online and through CDs became easier. In 2002, Senator Ernest Hollings of South Carolina introduced the Consumer Broadband and Digital Television Act. It would require TV sets, computers, and DVD players to contain technology to stop digital copying of digital media. The bill is not likely to pass, but the issue of copyright infringement with digital copying will continue to be an important part of the copyright policy debate.[23]

Regulating Information after Distribution ✦ Regulating content before the fact

usually involves some conflict between the news media and the government. The government wants to keep something secret. Regulating content after distribution, such as through libel and privacy law, usually involves an individual or nongovernmental organization and the media. Regulating after publication or broadcast can take two forms. First, the media organization must pay the person or organization damages for the negative impact. These are *compensatory damages*. Second, the media organization might also be punished for its actions in an effort to discourage such actions in the future. These are *punitive damages*.

fair use: Use of a small portion of a copyrighted work by scholars, teachers, or reporters to further enlighten the public.

Libel and Slander. *Libel and slander* are probably the best-known types of regulation after distribution. Libel occurs when a person is defamed falsely in written form. Slander is spoken **defamation**. However, it is generally accepted that when a person is defamed through a broadcast, the defamation constitutes libel, not slander. Because broadcasting is not **limited speech**, as is person-to-person speech, it is considered to have the same impact as libel.[24] When libel or slander occurs, a person's reputation and character are damaged in some way. Comedian and actress Carol Burnett sued the *National Enquirer* in 1981 for running a story saying that she was drunk at a restaurant. She won. General William Westmoreland, the commander of U.S. troops in Vietnam, sued CBS for saying in 1982 that he deceived his superiors about enemy strength during the Vietnam War. The parties settled out of court after the trial started; CBS paid Westmoreland's legal expenses and agreed to apologize for errors in the report.

Libel cases often are perceived as the results of profit-hungry media organizations trying to build circulation or ratings by lying about someone. In reality, libel can result from mistakes, poor reporting skills, and arrogance when a news organization is asked to correct a mistake. The suits that get attention are not the average cases, and often the results of trials are changed by higher courts.

The difference between the initial jury awards and the eventual resolution during the appeal process reflects the complexity of libel laws. Just damaging a person's reputation is not enough to justify a judgment against a journalist. Several defenses can either absolve the journalist or reduce the impact of a judgment against the journalist.

Truth is a defense for libel. Reporting that someone is a convicted murderer constitutes defamation, but if that person was indeed convicted of murder, the report is not libelous. Even during the period of the Alien and Sedition Acts, truth was considered a defense for libel.

Qualified privilege is a second defense for libel. Privilege developed to make happenings in government proceedings available to citizens. Under qualified privilege, a journalist is protected while reporting statements from a public meeting as long as the report is accurate. However, the definition of what privileged information is varies from state to state. Usually, remarks made in a trial are privileged, but informal remarks made by a police officer during an investigation are not.

Fair comment and criticism defenses allow a journalist to express opinion in the most offensive ways without committing libel. The statement must be presented as opinion and not fact. This allows a no-holds-barred criticism of anything from political ideas to artistic performances. Perhaps the most famous case of fair comment and criticism was the review of the Cherry Sisters' vaudeville act at the turn of the twentieth century. The sisters sued when this critique ran in the *Des Moines Leader:*[25]

> Billy Hamilton, of the *Odebolt Chronicle*, gives the Cherry Sisters the following graphic write-up on their late appearance in his town: "Effie is an old jade of 50 summers, Jessie a frisky filly of 40, and Addie, the flower of the family, a capering monstrosity of 35. Their long skinny arms, equipped with talons at the extremities, swung mechanically, and anon waved frantically at the suffering audience. The mouths of their rancid features opened like caverns, and sounds like the wailing of damned souls issued therefrom. They pranced around the stage with a motion that suggested a cross between the danse du ventre and fox trot—strange creatures with painted faces and hideous mien. Effie is spavined, Addie is stringhalt, and Jessie, the only one who showed her stockings, has legs with calves as classic in their outline as the curves of a broom handle."[26]

This review is cruel, but according to the Iowa Supreme Court, it is not libelous. The review is fair comment and criticism.

Absence of actual malice, perhaps the strongest libel defense for journalists other than truth, reflects the legal status of the subject being covered. People who find themselves in the public eye have less libel protection than a private person does, and they must prove actual malice on the part of a reporter to win a libel suit. There are two types of public persons: public officials and public figures. A *public official* is someone who holds a position in government that affects public policy. A *public figure* is someone who places herself or himself before the public through the media or someone who is swept involuntarily into public controversy. Published comments about the second type of public figure can be protected only if they concern the controversy.

In 1964, a Supreme Court decision in the *New York Times v. Sullivan* case assured reporters that as long as they followed careful reporting procedures, random errors would not result in large libel judgments. The Supreme Court ruled that public officials—elected officials and individuals appointed to high offices—had to carry a heavier burden than did private individuals in libel judgments. The case arose from a *New York Times* advertisement titled "Heed Their Rising Voices," which appeared in March 1960, shortly after whites used violence at Alabama State College in Montgomery against black demonstrators who were protesting the segregation of public facilities. Alabama Police Commissioner L. B. Sullivan filed suit against the *Times*, which was considered a northern liberal newspaper, charging that he was libeled by the ad's general references to the police. The advertisement did contain errors. For example, it claimed that the students had sung "My Country, 'Tis of Thee," when in fact they had sung "The Star-Spangled Banner." Although the errors were minor, the implications of the suit were not. State libel laws were being used by southern states to attempt to control news coverage of civil rights demonstrations. The *Times* alone was facing eleven other libel suits in Alabama courts. When the case reached the Supreme Court on appeal, Justice William Brennan wrote that something far more crucial than an individual seeking to protect a reputation was at stake: the right to be able to discuss and to criticize government and government officials. The Supreme Court enacted the *rule of actual malice*, requiring that public officials had to prove that statements were made with actual malice, or "knowledge that information is false or with reckless disregard of whether it was false or not." Brennan argued that the case had to be considered "against the background of a profound national commitment to the principle that debate on public issues should be uninhibited, robust, and wide-open."

Since 1964 and the *Sullivan* ruling, the court has extended the actual malice rule to public figures. Michael Jordan and Madonna are public figures because they have voluntarily placed themselves before the public through the media. Because they have sought public attention, they must tolerate the comments and criticism that come with it. A private person can demonstrate libel merely by showing that a journalist was negligent in carrying out his or her work or that a journalist showed a lack of care in collecting information and writing stories.

Celebrities, such as the late John F. Kennedy, Jr., and his wife Carolyn Bessette, are often besieged by the press. Public figures have a limited legal right to privacy.

The difference between private and public people represents the concern Justice William Brennan voiced in the *Sullivan* case for a free and open marketplace of ideas. The need of a democratic society to explore as many ideas as possible, even despised ones, has led the courts to allow error on the side of open discussion. For this reason, people who are in the public spotlight are open for more criticism than those who are not. A sloppy journalist has some protection with public figures, though a malicious one does not.

A new type of libel law emerged during the 1990s. Thirteen states passed "veggie libel laws," which make it illegal to issue false statements that defame farming industries. Cattle rangers in Texas sued Oprah Winfrey in 1998 because she said on her television show that she would stop eating hamburgers. Following her show, beef prices dropped. She won the suit, but critics of the law are afraid other defendants will not have the $1 million she spent to defend herself. The U.S. Court of Appeals for the Fifth Circuit upheld the decision in 2000, and an effort to repeal the Texas veggie law failed in 1999.

Privacy. Privacy laws are similar to libel laws because they also involve protection of individuals from media abuse. Privacy laws address the right of a person to be left alone. People are entitled to keep parts of their lives

profile

Michael K. Powell

As chairman of the Federal Communications Commission, Michael K. Powell finds himself in the middle of a longstanding political debate about the role of government in people's lives. The most recent chapter, however, takes place against rapid technological change and growing economic concentration. His political orientation is clear, but how he reacts to changes in the media industries is less so.

Powell was appointed chair of the FCC in January 2001 by President George W. Bush. Before becoming chair, he served as one of the five FCC commissioners who determine FCC policy. However, FCC policy can be set only within the parameters of law. Courts can overrule it, and Congress can change the laws, as it did in the 1996 Telecommunications Act.

The debate about the future of the telecommunications industry seems more sharply focused because Powell follows former chairman William Kennard. Kennard, who was appointed chairman by former president Bill Clinton, believes the FCC should be much more active in promoting social goals. He argued for low-powered radio stations for community groups, to keep alcohol advertising off television, and for antidiscrimination guidelines for advertisers. Powell does not see the FCC as a tool for promoting social goals.

Powell, son of U.S. Secretary of State Colin Powell, came to the FCC with a history of government service. He served as chief of staff on the Antitrust Division of the Department of Justice and was appointed to the FCC in 1997. He served in the U.S. Army before retiring after a serious injury. He received his undergraduate degree from the College of William and Mary and his law degree from Georgetown University.

Although issues confronting the FCC are complex, they can be classified as either economic or social. The economic issues involve the regulation of media competition and concentration, and the social issues involve the impact of content and access on people who watch and listen to electronic media.

In his first appearance before Congress, in March 2001, Powell said, "We will harness competition and market forces to drive efficient change and resist the temptation, as regulators, to meld markets in our image or the image of any particular industry player." He followed with, "We will be skeptical of regulatory intervention absent evidence of persistent trends or clear abuse, but we will be vigilant in monitoring the evolution of the nascent markets."

His position that the FCC wants to promote competition but not overregulate may be a difficult one to maintain. Finding "clear abuse" and "persistent trends" is not always easy and often doesn't happen until after regulations are changed. At the heart of the debate is whether media markets, left unregulated, will tend to be competitive or to become more concentrated. After the 1996 Telecommunications Act, radio and television have become more concentrated. The question the FCC must answer under Powell is whether the concentration is damaging the public good.

Powell's critics see him as working primarily for commercial interest. He has spoken against the government helping reduce the "digital divide" between wealthier people who access the communication technology and poorer people who do not. However, some liberal critics also acknowledge Powell's position that government should not be involved in controlling content of electronic media.

The FCC is and always has been a politically charged body. The political orientation and philosophy has depended on the chair, and the president appoints the chair. The political nature of the position limits the FCC and its chairperson. As a result, Powell's ability to alter the telecommunication landscape remains unclear.

Sources: "Biography of Chairman Powell," Federal Communications Commission, www.fcc.gov/commissioners/powell, accessed in October 2002; William K. Powell, "FCC Chairman Michael K. Powell: Agenda and Plans for Reform of the FCC," Prepared witness testimony before the House Committee of Energy and Commerce, March 29, 2001, http:energycommerce.house.gov/107/hearings/03292001Hearing44/Powell216.htm; and Chuck 45, "Chairman Mike and the Digital Divide," theGully.com, January 2001, www.thegully.com/essays/US/politics_2001/010212powell_fcc.html.

away from public scrutiny. Although privacy is not written into the Constitution, it is derived from the Constitution's protection from unreasonable search and seizure and from self-incrimination. This area of law has become much more active as the number and type of national media outlets, both print and broadcast, have increased during the past thirty years.

Invasion of privacy can take several forms. Physically invading a person's solitude is classified as *intrusion*. A radio journalist cannot hide a microphone or camera in someone's room to collect information. Putting someone in a commercial without getting permission—*commercial appropriation*—also is an invasion of privacy. *Disclosing embarrassing facts* can invade privacy through the release of information a person would consider awkward. A television program cannot broadcast details of a private person's sexual behavior without permission. A person cannot be portrayed in a *false light* by media. Journalists cannot imply something about someone that is not true. For example, a camera crew cannot record video of people on the street and use the tape while talking about sexually transmitted diseases. However, victims who claim they have been portrayed in a false light must prove actual malice. The Hill family, who had been held hostage in their home for nineteen hours during a weekend in 1952, sued Time, Inc., for invasion of privacy when *Life* reported on a Broadway play that depicted the Hills as having heroically resisted brutish conduct by the invaders. In reality, the Hills' captors had treated them courteously. On appeal, the Supreme Court ruled that even private individuals must prove actual malice if they are involved in a newsworthy issue.

As with libel, laws regarding invasion of privacy are not equally applicable to all people. People who are part of newsworthy events can lose their right to privacy, but courts differ in their interpretations of newsworthiness. Although the purpose of these laws is to protect people who are forced into embarrassing situations, sometimes media cover such situations as newsworthy events. In 1929, for example, Mrs. Lillian Jones sued the *Louisville Herald-Post* for quoting her as saying she "would have killed" the people who stabbed her husband to death on a Louisville street. Mrs. Jones lost her case when the newspaper claimed it had simply covered a newsworthy event.

In a 1999 case that could affect the reality-based television programs, the Supreme Court ruled unanimously in *Wilson v. Layne* that reporters and camera crews entering a home during a "ride-along" violated the homeowners' rights. If law enforcement officers allow this entry, they can be subjected to civil law suits.

Regulating Advertising Content. Advertising falls under the heading of commercial speech, which is information aimed at promoting a commercial transaction. Until 1976, commercial speech was outside the protection of the First Amendment. That year, however, the Supreme Court ruled in the case of *Virginia State Board of Pharmacy v. Virginia Citizens Consumer Council*[27] that commercial speech that serves consumers with accurate and useful information deserves First Amendment protection. The Court did state that some forms of commercial speech should be subject to regulation.

The primary justification for advertising regulation is the protection of consumers from false claims that would mislead them. This justification dates to the late 1700s, when newspapers and other print media carried advertisements for patent medicines. Patent medicines were salves, ointments, and liquid concoctions that claimed to cure a wide range of illnesses and ailments. The following example ran in the *Pennsylvania Gazette* in 1777 for "Dr. RYAN'S incomparable WORM destroying SUGAR PLUMS, Necessary to be kept in all FAMILIES:"[28]

> The plum is a great diuretic, cleaning the veins of slime; it expels wind, and is a sovereign medicine in the cholic and griping of the guts. It allays and carries off vapours which occasion many disorders of the head. It opens all obstructions in the stomach, lungs, liver, veins, and bladder; causes a good appetite, and helps digestion.

The effects of patent medicines never lived up to the advertising claims, and in some cases the contents of the patent medicine could kill. The *New York Evening Post* temporarily stopped taking patent medicine ads in 1805 after a young girl died from using a patent medicine.[29]

Concerns about patent medicine advertising and other forms of consumer abuse led to the passage of the Pure Food and Drug Act in 1906 and the creation of the Federal Trade Commission (FTC) in 1914. The Pure Food and Drug Act gave the federal government regulatory powers over foods and medicines, and the FTC gave the government the power to control false advertising. Until 1934 the FTC was concerned with consumer protection only in the context of antitrust actions. That year the Supreme Court extended the FTC's authority to cover non-anti-trust cases, and in 1938, Congress made unfair and deceptive acts and practices in commerce illegal by passing the Wheeler–Lea Act.[30] In addition to enforcement specified by the act, the FTC also enforces several other consumer protection laws.

Unfair advertisements and practices are ones that cause substantial injury without offsetting benefits to consumers and businesses. The FTC uses its power to regulate businesses that mistreat consumers, although unfairness can also apply to advertising. For example, Orkin Exterminating Company was forced to cancel a rate increase for treating houses against termites. The company had signed a contract with homeowners at a lower price.

For the FTC to decide that an advertisement is deceptive, the ad must be misleading *and* it must cause the reasonable consumer to act in a way that results in real injury to the consumer. The FTC does not pursue cases that involve obviously inflated claims, such as "The Greatest Soda Ever Invented," because only an "unreasonable" person would believe such a claim. Real injury occurs when something is purchased; if the claim will not lead to a consumer's purchase, it is not likely to be regulated by the FTC.

If the FTC finds an advertisement deceptive, it can take a variety of actions. A consent agreement, for example, allows the company to stop the advertisement without admitting guilt. The FTC can also get a cease-and-desist order, which prohibits the practice in the future. It can even require corrective advertising, which attempts to correct false impressions created by past ads. For example, in 1975 the Warner–Lambert Company, which produces Listerine mouthwash, was required to include in Listerine ads a statement that the mouthwash does not prevent colds and sore throats. The corrective ads continued until $10 million was spent on Listerine ads.

The proliferation of cable channels, the Internet, and magazine titles has made regulating advertising more difficult. However, it appears that the FTC has become more aggressive. In early 2002, the FTC joined seven states in suing Access Resource Services (ARS) of Fort Lauderdale for misleading advertising. ARS runs the Ms. Cleo psychic network that was heavily advertised on television. In addition, a report about weight reduction advertising released by the FTC in September 2002 reported that 55 percent of the weight loss ads included false or misleading claims. The FTC reported that it had prosecuted ninety-three weight loss fraud cases between 1990 and 2002.[31]

Technology can help make it possible for people to control what they, or their children, can watch on their television sets. Parents in Omaha, Nebraska, can contract with Parental Guide, Inc., to block the reception of certain categories of objectionable television content through a coding system read by a V-chip inside their television set.

The Telecommunications Act and Content Regulation. The 1990s saw heated debates in Congress and elsewhere about regulation of television content. The decade began with the passage of the Children's Television Act in 1991, which forced broadcast stations to program for children and limited the number of commercial minutes in each hour of children's programming. This was followed up five years later by the passage of the Telecommunications Act of 1996.

Although most of the 1996 act concerns business activities, the most controversial portions cover content regulation. The act prohibits the transmission by means of computer of pornographic material to minors, requires television manufacturers to include a microchip (called a **V-chip**) in each set that allows electronic blocking of programs on the basis of a ratings system, increases fines from $10,000 to $100,000 for television and radio obscenity, and requires cable to scramble programs for subscribers who think the programs are unfit for children. After the act was passed, hundreds of World Wide Web sites changed their background screens to black and issued protest statements about the new regulations. At issue in the Internet-related cases is whether online communications will enjoy the broad protection given print media or the more narrow rights traditionally given broadcasting.

The regulation against indecent material on the Internet faced court challenges immediately after the act went into effect. The lawsuits involve arguments about the impact of the regulations on First Amendment rights. In June 1997, the Supreme Court ruled that the Computer Decency Act was unconstitutional. Justice John Paul Stevens wrote the majority opinion for the Supreme Court, noting that the Computer Decency Act cast a "shadow over free speech" and "threatens to torch a large segment

V-chip: An electronic device in a television set that blocks certain television programs.

of the Internet community." Stevens argued that an attempt to protect children from harmful materials "does not justify an unnecessarily broad suppression of speech addressed to adults."

The effort to regulate came about because most Americans were and remain concerned about TV violence. A study paid for by the National Cable Television Association found that in 1995, 57 percent of all TV programs contained violence. The researchers concluded that the biggest problem was not the violence itself but how it was treated. In 73 percent of the violent scenes, the perpetrator went unpunished, the negative consequences of violence often were not presented in these programs, and only 4 percent of the programs presented an antiviolent theme.[32]

In March 1996, the top executives in the television industry met with President Clinton and agreed to pursue a *voluntary rating system* similar to the one used by the motion picture industry. The system identifies six types of content with icons in the upper left corner of the TV screen during the first fifteen seconds of the program. The levels are age based and start with TV-Y for programs suitable for all children and end with TV-M, which is content not suitable for children under age seventeen. The ratings system allows the V-chip to filter out programs that parents deem unsuitable. All new TV sets manufactured after January 1, 2000, must contain the V-chip.

The effort to regulate content appears to have affected the level of violence on television. A study by the Center for Media and Public Affairs reported that the amount of sexual material on television dropped by 29 percent and the amount of serious violence dropped by 17 percent between 1999 and 2001.[33]

The Threat of Regulation

Regulations do not have to be enforced to change media content. The very threat of filing action under one of the regulatory laws affects what media organizations do. In some cases, this benefits people. The knowledge that they could be sued for intrusion keeps most media organizations from sending a reporter to a person's house with a hidden camera to record what happens. Not all such threats are beneficial, however. The threat of a costly libel suit can have a *chilling effect* on the work of journalists because the journalists will avoid covering a story or will change their writing because they fear a lawsuit.

Litigation can be expensive even if the newspaper wins the case. In addition, time spent on the case is time away from gathering news. People who appear in the news understand this and often file nuisance suits. Although the plaintiffs know that they will probably not win, they also know that the newspaper or other organization will have to spend money to defend itself. The plaintiff also may hope that the editors will be more reluctant to publish controversial articles in the future.

Measuring the impact of the chilling effect is difficult; it requires measuring what did not happen. Fear of adverse reactions leads to self-censorship. The process occurs in people's minds, often out of habit, and goes against the principles of open discussion of ideas and information in the marketplace of ideas.

Media organizations are not the only groups that can be chilled by lawsuits. Libel suits can be filed against anyone. Lawsuits called Strategic Lawsuits against Public Participation (SLAPPs) have been used against activist groups to discourage their activism. A public person who has been attacked can file such suits to discourage critics. Columnist Molly Ivins listed a number of SLAPP suits in one of her columns. These included suits against a Las Vegas doctor for saying a city hospital violated a state law, against members of a Baltimore community group for questioning the property-buying practices of a real estate developer, and against a West Virginia environmental activist for criticizing a coal mining company.[34] Such suits do not even

Driving toward Democracy on the Information Highway: The Internet and China

When the United States sought to release itself from an authoritarian regime during the 1700s, people used newspapers and pamphlets to share ideas and nudge the country toward freedom. Today, digital convergence has created an even more powerful tool—the Internet. Nowhere has the conflict between a government's desire to control information and a people's desire to share it become as noticeable as in China.

As the most populous country on Earth, China must develop an industrial- and information-based economy. This cannot happen without the free flow of information, but the free flow of information brings discussion and criticism of the Communist Party.

The Chinese government demonstrated its concern about the use of the Internet for political discourse in 2002, when it arrested Chen Shaowen for subversion. Chen had posted a series of essays on a U.S.-based web site calling for labor and farmers' unions and criticizing the Communist Party. One stated: "If the Chinese Communist Party continues to exist, there will be no 'New China' in the future." Chen was not the first activist to be arrested, nor would he be the last. People convicted for subversion have received sentences of up to thirteen years.

Jail is only one way of trying to stop political discussion online. In September 2002, the Chinese government blocked the U.S. search engines Google and AltaVista. The protest from the Chinese people was immediate, with many pointing out that English search engines were crucial for international business. One businessman said, "Without the English search engines, users in China are at a dead end." The government stopped blocking the search engines, but it replaced blatant censorship with a sophisticated system of allowing access to web sites while still blocking certain pages the government considered to be inappropriate.

Observers argue that the Chinese government is fighting a losing battle, just as the British did when they tried to stop printed publications before the American Revolution. Censorship perhaps represents the efforts of an aging political system. Duncan Clark, managing director of B.D.A., a telecommunications consulting firm in Beijing, said in a 2002 newspaper article, "It's about the feeling they can do something. But their leverage is diminished through the power of technology and the market."

Sources: Ching-Ching Ni, "China Searches for Internet Control," detnews.com, September 13, 2002, www.detnews.com; Martin Fackler, "China Turns to New, More Sophisticated Means to Control Internet," detnews.com, September 12, 2002, www.detnews.com; Joe McDonald, "Chinese Author Charged with Subversion for Internet Post," detnews.com, September 25, 2002, www.detnews.com.

need a chance of winning to be effective. The cost of litigation is often enough to keep the critics quiet.[35] Because the obvious purpose is the stifling of open discussion of matters that interest the public, SLAPP suits are being fought with countersuits. New York and California have passed laws against such lawsuits.[36]

GAINING ACCESS TO JOURNALISTS' INFORMATION

Most media laws deal with either content or business operations. Another area of law that concerns media and focuses specifically on newsgathering is called **evidentiary privilege.** Although this privilege is not universally granted to journalists, when it is, journalists who have promised a source anonymity do not have to identify that source in court. Such protection for confidentiality has long existed for lawyers and doctors; it has become an issue for journalists in the second half of the twentieth century.

Privilege involves three types of litigation: (1) the court seeking the identity of an anonymous source, (2) the court demanding materials such as notes and videotapes, and (3) the court asking journalists who witnessed an event to testify. When a court

evidentiary privilege: Rule of law allowing journalists to withhold the identification of confidential sources.

seeks information, it issues a subpoena that orders the journalists to provide information or testify in court. The journalist and news organization can ask the court to quash, or dismiss, the subpoena.

The U.S. Supreme Court has not accepted the concept of journalists' privilege based on the First Amendment. But as of 1996, twenty-nine states had *shield laws* protecting journalists from being forced to disclose information. Another seventeen states and the District of Columbia have recognized privilege under common law or state constitutions.

Government officials argue that journalists should have no more privilege than ordinary citizens because such privilege can hamper police and prosecutors' investigations. Journalists respond that the absence of such privilege would prevent sources from revealing information to them. They argue that privilege allows them to question people who are afraid to talk with police or other government officials. Many sources, such as government employees and crime witnesses, face retaliation if their identity is made public. As a result, a valuable source of information might be eliminated, and the public good might be harmed.

TRENDS

The extent and nature of regulation reflect changes in society. As the economy, culture, and politics of a country evolve, so does the regulation, or lack of regulation, necessary to maintain stability. Recent rapid changes in U.S. society are caused by a variety of regulatory trends.

Regulation and Access to Information

For the past twenty years, governments have become increasingly active in trying to withhold information from journalists and voters. In the summer of 2002, Governor James McGreevey of New Jersey used national security as an excuse to try to seal five-hundred categories of state documents. After public protest, journalists discovered that much of the information did not pertain to national security. A memo from Attorney General John Ashcroft encouraging federal department officials to be less cooperative with FOIA requests has led to withholding information. A person who works for the federal government told a journalist, "There was a dramatic, clearly visible change throughout theses agencies after Bush came in. Sometimes the Clinton people would be reluctant, but they would go ahead and obey the law. These guys have a meeting and try to figure ways to have FOIA requests delayed."[37] Similar events are happening in local government all over the United States.

The long-term trend toward withholding information explains the skepticism toward the Patriot Act of 2001. Few would argue that the U.S. government does not need the power to fight the continuing war on terrorism. However, the Patriot Act increased the power of the federal government to withhold and limit access to information, and the current government has shown a willingness to use this power. At a time when the public needs to trust its government, there are reasons not to.

Regulation and Media Content

Although broadcast television has begun to tone down the violence, media content found on television and radio has grown more sexually explicit. Driven by the need to gain the attention of viewers and listeners, some companies in the entertainment industry continue to push the envelope of what traditionally has been defined as good taste. Whether it is the language found in the *Osbournes*, the sexual images found increasingly on MTV, or the explicit lyrics of today's rock music, the public is experiencing increasing sexual content even as the V-chip has become a part of TV technology. The FCC has sent mixed messages, with Chairman Michael Powell saying government should not be involved with content regulation. However, lower-level FCC officials say the burden of proof in obscenity cases will be shifted to radio and television broadcasters. Congress has often joined this debate in the past and may do so again.

Digital Technology and Copyright

Convergence of content prompted by the digitization of media has enhanced the ability to steal copyrighted material. Naturally, holders of copyright want to see the laws enforced in order to protect both their profits and their intellectual property. However, enforcement has become increasingly difficult for two reasons. One, not all countries adhere to copyright laws and such countries often become homes for digital **piracy**. Second, individual Internet users download and share digitized music and video, bypassing the distributors and the cost of purchasing music.

The ease of pirating is forcing large corporations that control copyright to confront large corporations that control Internet distribution. The outcome of this battle has yet to be determined. Some critics are concerned that the outcome will dry up the free exchange of information. Copyright law has always tried to protect intellectual property but at the same time promote public discourse. In some cases, the development of profit-driven corporations has diminished the concern about public discourse, despite its importance to democracy.

Deregulation and Economic Concentration

One result of deregulation of the telecommunications industry has been the growth of larger corporations, which often means reduced competition within consumer and advertising markets. The FCC is currently reviewing rules that prevent newspapers from owning television stations in the same market, that limit the number of TV stations a company can own, and that limit the number of radio stations a company can own in a market. Elimination of these rules would certainly further the trend of increased size of media companies and less competition within markets.

In the current makeup of the FCC, three Republicans form a fragile alliance toward deregulation, and the lone Democrat, Michael J. Copps, has urged caution. (Law requires that no more than three members of the FCC can be from the same political party, and one seat remains unfilled.) The disagreement about deregulation also spills over into Congress, where both positions have allies.

The current debate is only the latest chapter in the long history of regulation. However, rapid changes since the 1996 Telecommunications Act and the digitalization of media make the current debate particularly significant. As Copps said, "There is the potential here to remake our entire media landscape, for better or for worse, for a long time to come."[38]

piracy: Using material without securing appropriate copyright authorization.

summary

- Regulation exists to mediate conflicts between the rights of two individuals or between a government or corporation and an individual.
- The Bill of Rights was created to limit government control of private affairs and to preserve individual liberties.
- Government imposes regulations (1) when people or organizations interfere with the workings of the economic market system, (2) when the use of a product or an industry or company's behavior has a negative impact on society as a whole, (3) when a product or behavior has a negative impact on individuals that outweighs its contribution to society as a whole, (4) during times of war, and (5) to preserve its own security and power.
- The First Amendment was designed to protect robust intellectual exchange within a democratic society.
- Governments regulate (1) the economic behavior of media companies in the consumer and advertising markets, (2) certain internal business activities of media companies, and (3) some content and information.
- Media regulation evolved not only from federal and state legislation, but also from court decisions.
- Economic regulations include antitrust laws and direct regulation by government agencies such as the FCC and FTC.
- Direct telecommunication regulation covers broader areas than print because in the early years government sought to avoid chaos in the airwaves, to allocate scarce resources (airwaves), and to force licensees to act in the public interest.
- Media companies are also subject to regulations that affect most businesses, such as labor laws.
- Content can be regulated before or after distribution. Regulation before distribution includes prior restraint, controlling government documents, and copyright law. Prior restraint includes laws relating to obscenity and government regulation of the press during wartime. Regulation after distribution includes libel laws and privacy laws.
- Open meetings laws, such as the federal Government-in-Sunshine Act, increase access of the public and journalists to the decisions of government bodies.
- *New York Times v. Sullivan* was a landmark decision because it assured reporters that random errors in covering the conduct of a public official would not result in huge libel judgments against them. The Supreme Court decision further ruled that government entities could not use libel suits as a way of silencing the press.
- Advertising is subject to all regulations affecting regular content and to additional controls that are intended to protect the consumer from misleading and dangerous claims.
- Although the Telecommunications Act of 1996 primarily affected business practices, it also initiated new content regulation.
- Often, the threat of regulation can have a chilling effect that not only curbs the excesses of media, but also sometimes curbs their desire to address controversial issues.
- State shield laws protect journalists from being forced to reveal information to courts and government agencies.

navigating the web | Regulation on the Web

Most web sites that cover media regulations are maintained by either universities or governments. They provide access to material about regulation and law, including full texts of some legal documents.

Communication Media Center at New York Law School
www.nyls.edu/mediacenter.php?ID=2
This law school site contains background about cases, statutes, and scholarly papers related to media law and regulation.

Libel Defense Resource Center, Inc.
www.ldrc.com
This site is a New York nonprofit clearinghouse for information about libel law in the United States.

Student Press Law Center
www.splc.org
This nonprofit center aims to promote freedom of the press in high schools and colleges. The site contains a variety of information, including reports and news articles about events relating to student press issues.

Silha Center for the Study of Media Ethics and Law
http://silha.umn.edu
This site of the University of Minnesota contains articles, news, and links related to issues of media law and regulation.

Telecommunications Act of 1996
www.fcc.gov/telecomm.html
This FCC site contains the full text of the 1996 Telecommunications Act, as well as material about the proceedings and various FCC activities after its passage.

questions for review

1. What are the five reasons government regulates media in the United States?
2. Why are broadcast media regulated to a greater degree than print media?
3. What are the three types of regulation of mass media in the United States?
4. What are the justifications for direct regulation of the telecommunications industry?

5. How do courts determine if media content is obscene?
6. What are the defenses against a libel suit?
7. What are the major types of regulation before publication?
8. What are the major types of regulation after publication?

issues to think about

1. Traditionally, broadcast media have been subject to more regulation than print media. In the computer age, broadcast and print blend. How would you apply traditional laws, such as those protecting copyright and restrictions against pornography, in the online world?
2. Do you think the public is adequately protected from invasion of privacy? How do you reconcile the right to privacy with the public's right to know?
3. Do you think competition among telephone and cable companies and other media corporations will enhance access to information?
4. Do you think the threat of regulation restricts reporters' desire to present full information about public behavior?

suggested readings

Carter, T. Barton, et al. *The First Amendment and the Fifth Estate: Regulation of Electronic Mass Media*, 5th ed. (New York: Foundation Press, 1999).

Clayton, Richard, and Hugh Tomlison. *Privacy and Freedom of Expression* (New York: Oxford University Press, 2002).

Middleton, Kent, Robert Trager, and Bill Chamberlin. *The Law of Public Communication*, 5th ed. (New York: Longman, 2000).

Overbeck, Wayne, and Bradford J. Hill. *Major Principles of Media Law* (Belmont, CA: Wadsworth, 2002).

Soley, Lawrence. *Censorship Inc.: The Corporate Threat to Free Speech in the United States* (New York: Monthly Review Press, 2002).

Mass Communication Research

From Content to Effects

Voters who went to bed early on the 2000 election night thought Al Gore had won the state of Florida. Those who went to bed late thought George W. Bush had won that state. Everyone woke up the next morning to find that no one knew who had won Florida or the presidential election. The confusion resulted from flaws in the way the Voter News Service conducted research for the state. The exit polls used to predict the winner contained bias because they did not include the more than 600,000 absentee ballots. Errors in counting votes contributed as well. The service had only miscalled one election in a dozen years, and trust in the research had become greater than it should have been.

Two years later in the midterm elections, the Voter News Service, a consortium paid for by television networks, refused to conduct exit polls because they felt their data might be misinterpreted. However, many newspapers paid for exit polls and continued using research to predict election winners. In 2003, Voter News Service closed.

Research for elections is just one type of research used by media. Research affects every aspect of every medium in ways most people do not realize. It helps determine the topics covered in newspapers and magazines, the endings of movies, and the content of advertisements. Its influence extends beyond media to all aspects of society. Research affects what automobiles look like, who runs for public office, and the taste of hamburgers sold in fast-food restaurants. Research influenced Congress to require the V-chip in television sets and to outlaw various chemicals from use in the environment. Research affects society and people because it helps us predict and explain human behavior, both of which are crucial in making decisions about the future.

Research is conducted by university scholars who build theories to explain the impact of media on individuals and society. Media companies and media consulting firms also conduct research. They use the results to design content, to sell content to individuals, and to track who uses what media and when.

This chapter helps explain how research contributes to the understanding of mass communication on both a practical and a theoretical level. The issues addressed include the following:

◆ How do media directly and indirectly affect individuals and groups?

◆ What forces shape media content?

◆ How do media affect individuals' knowledge of public issues and events?

◆ How do people use media?

◆ How do political and economic structures shape culture?

◆ How do media organizations use research?

◆ What is the relationship between research and government policy?

DEFINING MASS COMMUNICATION RESEARCH

Mass communication research involves the systematic study of media content, the forces that shape its creation, how and why people use media, and the impact of media content and media institutions on individuals and society. The reasons for conducting mass communication research vary with the researcher and the organization

Research *in Your Life*

What Do You Think? What Do You Know?

Often people think they know how mass media affect them. They make comments such as, "I never buy a product because it's advertised on television." Or, "I already know who I'm going to vote for. I don't care how candidates advertise themselves on television." Use the following questions to decide what you think the media's effects are on you. Then, as you read this chapter, consider whether the research you read about makes you change your mind about these effects. What you thought about media's effects on yourself may be correct—or you may discover that the media have a more powerful effect on you than you thought.

POSSIBLE EFFECT	YES	NO
Do advertising and public relations affect the brand of product that I buy?		
Does media coverage of a political candidate affect what I think of him or her?		
Does media coverage of issues cause me to think more about certain issues than others?		
Do I act in ways similar to those I admire on television and in movies?		

funding the research. ***Basic mass communication research*** is pursued primarily by academic researchers who want to develop theory that explains the relationship between people and media. For instance, one issue of interest in basic research is determining how violent programming affects children. Media organizations conduct ***practical research*** in an effort to understand what content and services their audiences want and need; the goal is to predict consumer behavior in order for media organizations to increase their audiences. The movie industry conducts research to determine the popularity of particular actors. Often the same research topic can be examined by basic and practical researchers. Determining how advertising affects voting can be considered basic research when it is done by political scientists or practical research when it is done by campaign consultants.

key concept

Basic and Practical Mass Communication Research Mass communication research involves practical and basic research. Practical research aims to help media organizations increase their audiences. Basic research aims to create a more theoretical understanding of human communication using mass media.

Approaches to Mass Communication Research

Mass communication research begins with a *paradigm*, which is a set of assumptions about the nature of human behavior. A variety of paradigms are available for scholars to use.[1] Each is based on previous scholarship. However, two paradigms dominate mass communication research. One uses a social science approach, and the other uses a critical approach. Of course, each of these can be broken down into many subdivisions.

The **social science approach** emphasizes the use of theory building and empirical measurement to learn about human behavior. The basic unit that is studied is the individual or small social group. The origins of this approach lie in an effort to adapt scientific methods to the study of human behavior. The social science approach involves studies such as experiments and surveys. Some experiments, for instance, have

social science approach: Research approach that emphasizes theory building and quantitative methods for testing theory.

exposed male college students to violent pornography and then measured their attitudes toward women. The purpose is to ascertain whether this type of pornography contributes to aggressiveness toward women.

The **critical approach** seeks an understanding of issues that are raised by the connections between media and society. Scholars studying these connections use a variety of techniques and have different economic and cultural perspectives. They may define themselves as qualitative studies scholars or as cultural or critical theorists. Here, we will use the terms interchangeably. Critical scholars have analyzed the narrative texts of television programs such as *Star Trek: The Next Generation* to understand its cultural message and to determine what the content reveals about today's society. They use historical analyses and interviews to investigate topics such as how the news media reinforce, or legitimate, the moral order. These topics illustrate the broad focus of critical studies.[2] **Cultural theorists** look at the symbolic meaning behind behavior.

Each approach is limited by its paradigm. No single method of inquiry is sufficiently comprehensive and free of bias to explain all human behavior adequately. Recently, some scholars have begun to try to combine the two approaches into better theories of mass communication creation and effects.[3]

Types of Research Methods

A number of research methods have developed as a result of both basic and practical research. They are classified as qualitative or quantitative. Scholar Ronald Taylor defines *qualitative research* as "any systematic investigation that attempts to understand the meaning that things have for individuals from their own perspective."[4] *Quantitative research* involves the use of statistical analysis with units of content or observations about individual behaviors or attitudes. The responses and content are assigned numbers. Both approaches have advantages and disadvantages and can be used for both practical and basic research.

In the world of academic research, both qualitative and quantitative research are used to understand human behavior. However, businesses and policymakers depend increasingly on quantitative methods. Statistics can analyze the responses from large numbers of people, and the quantitative approach includes a system for selecting a representative sample of individuals from a large group of people. Most of this chapter concentrates on the social science approach and quantitative methods rather than on cultural studies and qualitative research, which reflects the dominance of the social science approach in applied research rather than an ordering of importance. Critical studies and qualitative research methods serve a significant role in the quest to understand the relationship between humans and their media. Qualitative and quantitative supplement and complement each other in this quest.

Qualitative Research
✦ Qualitative research methods work well when researchers want to understand behavior in great depth. The methods are sometimes, but not always, associated with the critical studies approach. Qualitative research concentrates on real-life settings and content.[5] Examples of qualitative methods include participant observation, textual analysis, and in-depth interviewing. In **participant observation,** the researcher observes the subjects of the research in their everyday behavior. For instance, to study how editors make decisions, researchers would watch editors doing their job on a daily basis. In **textual analysis,** a researcher interprets text to find the symbolic form the communicator used to create meaning. For example, scholar John Pauly read hundreds of publications to determine the symbolic meaning that the Great Chicago Fire of 1871 had for Americans.[6] **In-depth interviewing** involves selecting subjects for study and conducting several detailed interviews at different times.

These participants in a focus group conducted by a snack food producer offer valuable information that will help the company market its product. However, the company must be careful not to generalize the opinions of these five participants to an entire population.

One qualitative method often used by practical researchers is the *focus group,* in which a researcher assembles people at a given location with a facilitator. The people in the group may have a wide range of backgrounds, in an attempt to replicate the individuals found in a community, or they may be individuals with similar characteristics, such as men more than fifty years old. The facilitator asks questions of the group and follows up answers with additional questions. Such an approach allows a researcher to collect in-depth information. Facilitators also may seek responses from participants who view videos or read magazine or newspaper articles. Focus groups can be used to test political ads, evaluate newspaper design changes, and test campaign strategies.

The main limitation of focus groups is that they are not large enough to accurately represent large social groups. When researchers mistakenly assume that focus group conclusions can be generalized, the goals of the research may not be achieved. For example, a group of suburban daily newspapers in the southwest that had covered only local news decided to shift to a combination of local and wire service coverage. The change resulted from a decision based on a series of focus groups. However, as local content declined, subscriptions did too. A survey using a random sample of readers of the local papers, which could have been generalized to the whole population, probably would have prevented the change. A year after adding wire service content, the dailies went back to all local coverage.

Quantitative Research ✦ Quantitative research involves turning observations into numbers in order to use statistical analysis. It helps researchers make general statements about large groups, such as all the voters in a state or all individuals who usually vote Republican. People who participate in quantitative studies are selected through random methods that then allow researchers to make generalizations from the data. However, although quantitative research allows for generalizations, it does not allow researchers to gain an in-depth understanding of individual behaviors and attitudes. If two voters support a particular candidate, their responses will seem equal in a computer, but that does not mean they both support the candidate to the same degree. This explains the great variation in support a candidate receives in political polls early in an election. Some voters who express support early in a campaign may change their minds. Those who changed their minds probably did not support the candidate to the same degree as those who did not change their minds, but in the earlier survey they were grouped together. For example, 50 percent of Democrats in November 2002 said they supported Al Gore as the Democratic candidate for the presidential election in 2004. The support probably indicates little more than name recognition.

profile

Wilbur Schramm

Internationally known communications researcher Wilbur Schramm wrote more than one hundred journal articles and books, including *Mass Communication,* which was one of the world's most widely used textbooks on communication.

Schramm graduated Phi Beta Kappa from Marietta College in his hometown, Marietta, Ohio, in 1928. He obtained a master's degree from Harvard University in 1930 and a doctorate from the University of Iowa in 1932.

Schramm worked his way through school. He worked as a waiter, was a reporter and editor at the *Marietta Daily Herald* and the *Boston Herald,* wrote for the Associated Press, and played semipro baseball with a farm club of the Pittsburgh Pirates for five dollars a game. Later he played flute with the Boston Pops symphony before a Harvard professor told him he had to choose between playing the flute and his studies at Harvard.

From 1934 to 1947, Schramm taught at the University of Iowa, starting as a part-time teacher of honors English and eventually becoming an associate professor and the first director of the nationally known Writers Workshop. When World War II broke out, he took a two-year leave to become director of the Office of Facts and Figures for the U.S. Office of War Information. One of his jobs was writing speeches for Roosevelt's "fireside chats."

Schramm returned to the University of Iowa in 1943 as a communications scholar and the director of the Iowa Journalism School. Five years later the department was granting the first doctorates of mass communication in the country. In 1947, Schramm transferred to the University of Illinois to start the Institute of Communications Research. By the time he left in 1955, he had also been a research professor, director of the University Press, and dean of the division of communications. At Stanford he was the founder and director of the Institute for Communication Research, a research professor, a fellow at the Center for Advanced Study in the Behavioral Sciences, and the Janet M. Peck professor of communication.

Schramm retired in 1973, only to join the East West Center in Honolulu as director of its Communication Institute and then its Distinguished Center Researcher. He also taught for two years at the Chinese University of Hong Kong as the Aw Boon Au professor in the Department of Communication. He conducted extensive research in many parts of the world, including Asia, Africa, El Salvador, Samoa, India, and Israel.

Schramm's last book, *The History of Communication,* was published a few days before he died at home in Honolulu on December 27, 1987, at eighty years of age.

Sources: "Stanford; Obit/Wilbur Schramm, Internationally Known Communications Researcher," *Business Wire* (January 12, 1988); "Wilbur Schramm Wrote Many Works on Communications," *The New York Times* (January 1, 1988), sec. 1, p. 64; Max MacElwain, "Meet Wilbur Schramm," *Saturday Evening Post* 257 (April 1985): 49.

---

experiments: A quantitative research method that involves the application and manipulation of a treatment given to groups of people, and then tests the result.

causation: The process by which one or more factors result in the occurrence of an event, behavior, or attitude. A variety of factors cause human behavior. For example, genetics, parental behavior, peer associations, media consumption, and other factors combine to create certain behaviors in children.

survey research: A quantitative research method that involves randomly selecting a small group of people, called a sample, from a larger group, called a population, and asking them questions from a questionnaire.

There are three primary methods in quantitative media research: experiments, surveys, and content analysis. **Experiments** involve the application and manipulation of a treatment given to groups. For instance, an experiment to test whether information graphics affect newspaper readers' interest in the front page of a paper might involve giving one group of readers a front page with information graphics and another group a front page with photographs. Then the members of the two groups would be asked to rate their interest in the front pages. Their responses would be compared to see which group found which front page more interesting. With experiments, researchers can control the nature of the treatment and the surroundings of the research, which helps establish **causation.** However, because most experiments occur in artificial settings, their results may not represent everyday behavior.

Survey research involves randomly selecting a small group of people, called a sample, from a larger group, called a population, and asking them questions. The people in the sample can be interviewed in person, over the telephone, through e-mail, or with a printed questionnaire through the regular mail. If the sample is randomly selected, surveys should result in accurate predictions of behaviors, such as voting, in the population. Nielsen ratings, for example, use a sample of households to infer what is being watched on television in all U.S. households. In addition, survey data can be used to break down such characteristics by demographic groups. For instance, Nielsen reports the TV viewing habits of men and women in various age groups.

When surveys are used in politics, they are called polls. Polls can represent accurate measures of how a group of people feels about issues, but it is difficult to phrase questions so that respondents understand them in similar ways. In addition, it cannot be assumed that responses about future behavior are accurate. How likely a respondent is to follow through with a stated intention can vary greatly. One of the best skills a pollster can have is the ability to carefully phrase questions to produce accurate and informative results.

Quantitative content analysis provides a systematic way of categorizing media content and using statistics to analyze patterns in the content. Content analysis uses a **protocol** to instruct coders how to assign numbers to diverse content. Coders can classify sentences, paragraphs, stories, photographs, characters in a movie, and actions in a video game. Before the numbers assigned to the content can be analyzed statistically, the reliability of the protocol must be established. A protocol is considered reliable when several coders use it to categorize the same content and agree on how the content should be categorized.

Just as with surveys, when researchers select samples of content randomly, they can draw conclusions about the larger population of content. If they are selected randomly, only fourteen editions of a daily newspaper are needed to describe accurately the content that appears in the paper for the year. Content analysis can describe a characteristic of content, such as the number of violent acts during an hour of television, and allow the characteristics to be compared and contrasted across media and organizations. Content analysis can answer questions such as: Do programs on cable contain more sex and violence than programs on networks? Do newspaper companies with high profit margins publish lower-quality news content than newspapers with low profit margins?

If a researcher is not careful, a protocol can result in coders counting events and losing context. For example, a coder could count the same number of violent acts in Shakespeare's *Macbeth* as in a network television program, but the context and meaning of the two would be very different.

The Role of Theory in Research

Media theory involves generalizing about the relationships between people and media and society and media. Theory goes beyond research findings that apply to limited groups of people to abstractions that apply to large numbers of people. A study of how news media coverage affected the issues that concerned voters in the 2000 presidential election would be a research project. The theory would be a set of statements explaining how news media coverage affects the issues that concern voters in all presidential elections. As with research, theory falls into social science and critical approaches.

Social science theory has adapted the scientific method used in the natural sciences. A social science theory is a set of related statements about people's behavior that (1) categorizes phenomena, (2) predicts the future, (3) explains past events, (4) gives a sense of understanding of why the behaviors occur, and (5) provides the potential for influencing future behavior.[7]

Building social science theory begins with empirical research, which is the systematic collection and analysis of data. From these data, researchers draw generalizations about social behavior and form theories. Creating a theory from research is only part of the process. The theory must be tested with further research and modified when necessary. Social science theories are based on **hypotheses**, which are statements of relationships between people and things. For example, the statement "the more violent television a child watches, the more aggressive acts the child will exhibit toward his or her playmates" is a hypothesis connecting violence on television with play behavior of children. Research tests these hypotheses. If the research results support the hypothesis, the theory that generated the hypothesis becomes stronger and more useful in explaining behavior. If the research does not support the theory, the theory must be modified to make it more consistent with reality, or it may

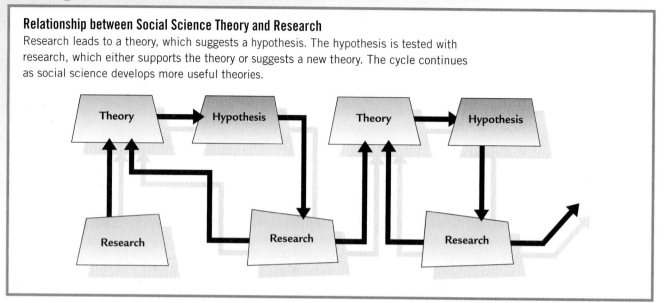

Relationship between Social Science Theory and Research
Research leads to a theory, which suggests a hypothesis. The hypothesis is tested with research, which either supports the theory or suggests a new theory. The cycle continues as social science develops more useful theories.

be discarded entirely. Figure 15.1 shows that the relationship between social science theory and research is dynamic and that new hypotheses constantly lead to more research and theory modification.

Over time, most social science theory gets modified for several reasons:

1. Behavior changes as societies and humans evolve.
2. The ability to measure social behavior improves, facilitating better tests.
3. The accumulation of research further facilitates better theory.

The critical approach also develops theoretical frameworks, but the methods used to develop them differ from social science methods. For example, ethnographic description may be a way to contextualize human experience in a given culture. Norman K. Denzin describes such interpretive research as "the studied commitment to actively enter the worlds of native people and to render those worlds understandable from the standpoint of a theory that is grounded in the behaviors, languages, definitions, attitudes, and feelings of those studied."[8]

The importance of developing theory can be illustrated by considering how children could benefit if the public wanted to reduce the impact on them of television violence. If a social science approach were used, a formal theory would categorize the TV violence and predict which types of violence would be most harmful to children. It would explain violent behavior of children in the past and future. More important, a useful theory would allow an informed public to influence policy and TV programmers to reduce the airing of harmful violence. Cultural theorists might develop a theory aimed at explaining the relationship between violent content on television and the nature of the economic structure or production process.

Research and Public Policy

Public policy makers use research about the impact on children of television violence to help shape mass media policy. The Report to the Surgeon General on Television Violence and Children in 1972 concluded that TV violence could promote aggression in children. This report was followed four years later by *cultivation theory*, which was developed by George Gerbner and colleagues at the University of Pennsylvania. Cultivation theory states that heavy television viewing influences people to adopt values, roles, and worldviews that are based on the television content they watch.[9] If television programs are violent, heavy viewers believe the real world is violent and scary.

Research and the War on Terrorism

It may be difficult to see how the war on terrorism that followed September 11, 2001, will affect communication research, but the potential exists. The expanded powers to obtain information and monitor communication that came with the Foreign Intelligence Surveillance Act certainly have had an impact on scientific research about biochemistry. For years the federal government has monitored research related to classified information, which is information that could affect national security. Now the federal government has created a new category of information called "unclassified but sensitive." Problems have resulted because the definition of "sensitive information" is vague and changing. Scientists could discuss their research with scientists from another country, which has always been common, and unknowingly violate the new law. This will likely put a damper on the exchange of scientific information, which is crucial for the scientific method to work properly.

For example, FBI agents visited a Pakistani-born scientist in 2002 after he bought several books on eBay. They asked if he planned to make weapons and engage in terrorism. He and his lawyer met with the FBI and explained that the books were for professional purposes. In another case, a graduate student at the University of Connecticut was charged under the Patriot Act because he had saved samples of anthrax bacteria while cleaning out an old refrigerator in the university labs. The sample had come from an infected cow thirty-five years earlier, and he was simply saving it in case it was needed for future study.

Obviously, the federal government has an interest in activities related to infectious bacteria and viruses, but why would they care about research related to communication? Communication researchers study cross-cultural communication that could include Muslim countries. Communication researchers study use of computers, which can be used for terrorist networking, and they study media treatment of the war on terrorism. The federal government now has far greater power to investigate than they did before, and the investigators have a lower level of evidence needed to arrest people. Barry Reingold, for instance, had two FBI agents come to his apartment in Oakland because he criticized U.S. policy toward terrorism. Someone called the FBI after hearing him voice the criticism while working out at a gym. Reingold is not alone. Since the power of federal law enforcement agencies has been increased, hundreds of citizens around the country have been questioned about their beliefs.

Communication researchers, particularly those with some connection to Muslim countries, may be monitored if they conduct research related to terrorism, religion, the war on terrorism, or any number of topics that the FBI might consider suspicious. This is certainly a disincentive to research such topics. Steven Aftergood, director of the Federation of American Scientists' Project on Government Secrecy, said of the federal government's expanded power: "There is a fundamental principle that any expansion of government authority should be matched by a corresponding expansion of oversight and accountability. And that, more than anything else, is the principle that I see being violated."

Sources: Seth Rosenfeld, "9–11–01: Looking Back, Looking Ahead: A Nation Remembers; Patriot Act's Scope, Secrecy Ensnare Innocent, Critics Say," San Francisco Chronicle (September 8, 2002): A1; Rosie Mestel, "A Chill in the Lab: Biological Attack: In a Post-9/11 World, the Scientists Who Study Anthrax and Other Infectious Microbes Are Feeling Hamstrung by New Laws, Heavy Scrutiny and the Threat of Criminal Charges," Edmonton Journal (September 15, 2002): D9; Diane Deitz, "University of Oregon Forum Examines Reach of Patriot Act," The Register Guard (October 25, 2002) via Lexis-Nexis.

The Surgeon General's report, cultivation theory, and subsequent research indicate that the impact of violent television is more pronounced on children than on adults.

This conclusion played an important role in Congress's inclusion of the TV program and V-chip regulations of the 1996 Telecommunications Act. These sections help shield children from violent content. In addition, the FCC moved to require television stations to broadcast three hours of educational children's programming each week. Despite strong opposition from the television industry, policy was thus changed because research convinced most of the public and public officials that children should be protected from violent TV content.

Today, the issue is not whether violence in movies and on television affects children's behavior but exactly how this effect occurs and what can be done to protect children. In the wake of school violence in Colorado, Arkansas, Kentucky, Georgia, and several other states, the U.S. Senate in May 1999 began investigating ways to reduce TV violence. Some ideas considered by the Senate included funding research about the effects of violent video games and music lyrics on children and the creation of a national commission to study what causes children to act violently.[10]

Research and Media Organizations

Media managers use research to understand what their audiences want, to decide what they should charge their advertisers, and to develop news and information. Determining what a media audience wants allows companies to produce media content that people will be likely to use and buy. Movie companies, for example, often present different endings to preview audiences to see which they prefer. The ending preferred by these preview audiences is used for general release. The increasing use of DVDs, which include these alternative endings, has made people aware of the long-running practice of alternative endings. Examples include blockbusters such as the 1987 movie *Fatal Attraction* and box-office bombs such as *Fierce Creatures* from 1997. In the original ending of *Fatal Attraction*, Alex Forrest (Glenn Close), who had been rejected after having an affair with a married man, Dan Gallagher (Michael Douglas), committed suicide. The knife she used had Gallagher's fingerprints on it, and the film ended with Gallagher being arrested. Preview audiences did not like this ending and wanted Alex to be punished. As a result, the movie's ending has Gallagher and his wife killing Alex after she has attacked his family. Alex got what the audience felt she deserved. With *Fierce Creatures*, test audiences did not like seeing the villain smashed by a rhinoceros. Although actor Kevin Kline was allowed to live, it didn't help ticket sales.

Television news departments also use research by gathering viewers and showing them videotapes of various anchors. The researchers collect and assess reactions and suggest which anchor should be hired. Not everyone believes such research is appropriate. Changing movies to meet audience demand takes away the creative control of directors and tends to produce mediocre movies. Allowing viewers to pick anchors or TV reporters based on videos emphasizes image, often at the price of journalistic ability.

Research also helps determine what advertisers will pay for space or time. The need for an independent organization to measure audience size arose during the 1800s when newspapers and magazines inflated their circulation numbers in order to draw advertisers away from other publications. The companies that bought advertisements rebelled against this practice and threatened not to buy advertising unless they could get independent confirmation of circulation. Today, the Audit Bureau of Circulation (ABC) conducts research to measure circulation for almost all U.S. daily newspapers and for some weekly newspapers. Nielsen Media Research estimates how many people watch particular television programs. These estimates become the basis for what stations and networks charge for advertising time or space. As use of the Web increases, companies demand accurate estimates of how many people visit sites before they will buy advertising on a particular site.

Research contributes to news coverage as well as business at media organizations. National and regional news organizations often contract for surveys to determine who is leading an election and what issues affect the race. These research results are used to develop election stories. Critics of polls argue that their use for determining who is winning treats the election like a horse race rather than a debate about important public policy issues. Polls might even influence voters and the election outcome.

In 1973, journalist Philip Meyer suggested using social science research methods, particularly surveys, as a way to generate news stories.[11] He called the practice **precision journalism.** Although some large newspapers have adopted precision journalism, more newspapers have moved toward computer-assisted reporting (CAR). This process can

precision journalism: The use of social science research methods to generate news stories that emphasize depth and social trends.

include precision journalism. But more often, CAR involves applying statistical procedures to existing databases, such as government budgets and records, rather than creating new databases. CAR allows journalists to see patterns in large databases that would be missed without the statistics. These patterns represent behaviors of and decisions by people. For example, a newspaper might statistically analyze sentencing by various judges in drug cases to see if some judges are stricter than others when administering the law.

MASS COMMUNICATION RESEARCH IN AMERICAN LIFE

Mass communication research started two decades into the twentieth century. During the 1920s and 1930s, researchers concluded that mass media had powerful effects on individual behavior. From the 1940s through the 1960s, researchers took the opposite tack and argued that the effects of mass media on people were limited. During this time, researchers also began to explore the factors that influence media content. After the 1970s, research into content influences grew enormously. Effects and uses research indicate that the impact of mass media on people and society is neither as powerful as once was thought nor as limited as researchers later claimed but that the impact of content depends on many factors. Critical studies scholars have pursued a variety of topics during recent years, with an emphasis on the commercialization of culture and the role of media in maintaining power structures.

Early Critical Studies Research in the United States

Two strains of critical studies developed in the United States during the first third of the twentieth century. In Chicago, Charles Cooley, Robert Park, and John Dewey, three midwesterners who had studied at Michigan and Minnesota, explored the positive possibilities of modern communication. They saw communication as the foundation for developing a sense of community in a postindustrial world. A second group of communication scholars came to the United States from Frankfurt, Germany. Theodor Adorno, Herbert Marcuse, and Max Horkheimer, theorists associated with the Institute for Social Research, which had been founded in Frankfurt in 1923, fled Hitler's fascist regime in 1933 and established themselves in New York with connections to Columbia University. The Frankfurt School's thought was more pessimistic than that of the Chicago School. Frankfurt theorists did not believe that modern media had the potential to improve society. Their theoretical approach was based on the economics of media organizations, and so they considered the specifics of professional practice to be irrelevant.

The Frankfurt School's theories developed out of traditional Marxist thought. Principles of Marxist thought include a belief that the economic basis of a society determines its social structure as a whole as well as the psychology of the people within it. Historical change was thought to have been a result of conflict between owners of property and workers, and class struggle is inevitable within a capitalist society. Marxist theorists believe that only revolution, not reform, can accomplish change; therefore, although labor unions might be useful training grounds for radicals, they only temporarily relieve the conditions of workers. Because reform creates only temporary relief, conditions will worsen until the workers' misery drives them to revolution. The government in capitalist societies is perceived to be the coercive instrument of property owners.

The young Marxist intellectual radicals who made up the Frankfurt School were disappointed that the 1917 Russian revolution had not spread throughout Europe. The dark years of fascism in Europe affected them deeply, and they were concerned that the postwar Western world appeared to be politically stable. Such stability, in their minds, meant an end of a conscious recognition of the need for radical change from within the working class. They saw the workers as suppressed by the culture industries—by the mass media. They viewed the Western press as being organized through rules and institutions.[12] The Frankfurt School theorists believed that within a capitalist society art could not be a revolutionary force. They argued that the media made art part of the established order, and although it might have made certain forms of high culture more accessible to the middle class, it did so at the expense of robbing high culture of its critical substance. Art thus became intertwined with official function. Herbert Marcuse, a founder of the Frankfurt Institute of Social Research, argued that language constantly imposed images, which worked against conceptual thinking. As a group, the Frankfurt School rejected the idea that theory could affect practice, and they retreated from allowing their research to lead them into a dialogue about modern media. Although there are now many strains within the cultural studies traditions, both in the United States and abroad, the traditions of the Frankfurt School had an enormous impact on the development of U.S. cultural theory.

Powerful Effects Research

Early research into the impact of mass communication developed from World War I propaganda. Governments, including that of the United States, supported mass communication efforts to mobilize their citizens in support of the war and to discourage the populations in enemy countries. Although some political and social groups in the United States opposed its entry into the war, the U.S. propaganda arm, the Committee on Public Information, flooded the country with leaflets, programs, and other materials that were designed to reduce media and citizen opposition to the war. Reflecting on these activities, Harold Lasswell published *Propaganda Techniques in the World War* in 1927.[13] The conclusions of Lasswell and others that media propaganda had been successful in generating support for the war led to the concept of universal, powerful media effects, which is known as the *magic bullet theory*. Scholars argued that the media worked like a bullet in their powerful persuasive impact on audiences.

Support for the *powerful effects theory* grew after the war with a series of studies between 1929 and 1932 that examined the impact of movies on children. In response to concern about the influence of movie sex and violence, the Payne Fund financed studies of adolescents that concluded that media—in the form of movies—did indeed have powerful effects.[14] For example, W. S. Dysinger and Christian A. Ruckmick used experiments in the early 1930s to study the emotional response of children to movies. They charted physiological responses, such as breathing, while the children watched the films and found that the children showed greater emotional arousal to films than did adults. They concluded that adults treated film as fantasy, but children did not.[15]

Scholars who developed the powerful effects approach conducted research at a time when social science methods were evolving. Often such research failed to control for influences that could have caused the effects the researchers found. Furthermore, the studies began with the simplistic assumptions that genetics determined all people's behavior and that all people are motivated in similar ways. Today, we know better.

Limited Effects Research

At the beginning of World War II, the U.S. government again used communication to develop support for the war effort. Carl Hovland and his colleagues used more sophisticated social science methods and found evidence

key concept

Magic Bullet Theory Propaganda efforts during World War I suggested that media were all-powerful. Propagandists believed that you could simply hit individuals with information, as though it were a bullet, and it would have powerful and immediate effects.

Posters distributed during World War I, such as this one encouraging people to grow vegetables to support the war effort, were considered to be highly effective propaganda pieces. This belief led to a supposition that mass media effects were exceedingly powerful and resulted in the "magic bullet theory" of media effects.

for a *limited effects model*. Although films and other forms of communication did motivate troops, their effects were specific and limited.[16] These results surprised communication scholars because they contradicted the powerful effects research of the previous two decades.

key concept

Limited Effects Model The media have limited effects on individuals—interpersonal impact is more important in influencing attitude and creating change. This approach recognizes that individuals interact with one another as well as respond to the media messages they receive.

However, the conclusion that mass media had limited effects on people found increasing support during the 1940s, particularly in studies of voting behavior. Researchers studied the voters in Erie County, Ohio, during the 1940 presidential election[17] and the voters in Elmira, New York, during the 1948 election.[18] They found that mass media converted only a small percentage of voters. Interpersonal communication played a greater role in influencing voting behavior than did media.

Early Content Studies

During the 1940s, people also began to study the forces that shape mass media content. Critics had always assumed that mass media content reflected the rational decisions of the people who created the content. If a story on government corruption appeared in a newspaper, it ran only because the editors wanted to achieve some specific goal, such as the punishment of crooked politicians. This approach seemed to explain media creation, but it failed to acknowledge that media workers face pressure as they create content. The pressure comes from advertisers, readers, sources of news, and even other journalists. Figure 15.2 indicates the complexity of creating media content and emphasizes that both external and internal forces are at work.

Gatekeeping ✦ The earliest content influence research involved gatekeeping studies. David Manning White in 1950 studied the decisions of a wire service editor as he selected material to put in the newspaper.[19] White asked the editor to explain why he excluded and included particular articles. The editor ran stories according to

figure 15.2

The Process of Creating Media Content
The creation of media content begins with observations and interviews with sources. The creator generates content that is edited by managers. The creation process is influenced by routines and social interaction within the media organization. In addition, economic, political, and social forces outside the organization help shape the process. Ultimately, the content is used by media consumers, and it affects them in a variety of ways.

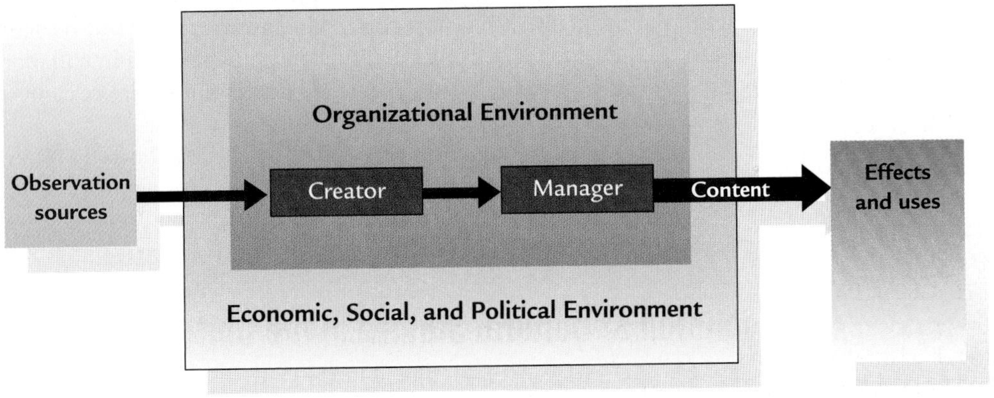

Rookies learn from veteran reporters the ways to sidestep informal policy constraints in newsrooms and get the stories that they believe are important published.

personal biases, his perceptions of what readers wanted, and the editorial policies of the newspaper. The editor was acting as a **gatekeeper** of information.

Since that time, numerous studies have found that a variety of factors influence the gatekeeper's decisions. For example, how often a particular type of article appears in the wire or other news services influences the gatekeepers' decisions more than do their shared news values.[20] If 25 percent of Associated Press stories are about other countries, about 25 percent of the newspaper's stories will be about other countries. Television gatekeepers are influenced by their biases, the visual impact of stories, and how attractive the stories will be to viewers.[21] One evening a house fire will get thirty seconds on the local TV news, and the next evening another house fire will get a one-minute story. The two stories are similar, but the station shot video of the second fire.

Social Influences ✦ Soon after the first gatekeeping study, researchers began studying the role of news organizations as social influences on news selection. Researcher Warren Breed interviewed 120 newspaper journalists during the early 1950s to determine how editors enforce newsroom policy.[22] He found that a **socialization process** taught reporters news policy without the editors having to explicitly tell them. Journalists learn what the paper's editors will accept as news from what was and was not printed in the newspaper, the way their stories were edited, and their knowledge of the editors' interests.

Reporting ✦ Another area of exploration involves the relationship between reporters and sources. In 1961, Walter Gieber and Walter Johnson published a study of reporters covering their local city hall and found that reporters often shared the values of their sources. The beat reporters and government officials depended on each other to do their jobs. Their informal relationships resulted in collaboration and cooperation in gathering and writing news.[23] Fairness and balance can become difficult when sources become more like friends than sources.

These early studies of gatekeepers and socialization showed that journalists were not autonomous individuals exercising their freedom of expression. Rather, journalists face a complex series of interactions with people who influence their actions in ways journalists do not even recognize.

Evolution of Cultural Studies in the United States

The work of Charles Horton Cooley, John Dewey, and Robert E. Park ushered in a new way of thinking about modern media. Theorizing from philosophical and sociological traditions, these **pluralist** social reformers believed that modern media could make possible a truly democratic community. Together, writes Daniel Czitrom in

gatekeeper: A person who controls the flow of information into and through the mass media.

socialization process: Reporters learn patterns of behavior by observing others and by learning to recognize the systems of rewards and punishments in a newsroom.

pluralism: A school of thought that espouses coexistence and cooperation among different elements of a power structure.

Media and the American Mind, they "construed modern communication essentially as an agent for restoring a broad moral and political consensus to America, a consensus they believed to have been threatened by the wrenching disruptions of the nineteenth century: industrialization, urbanization, and immigration."

Cooley tried to understand the interplay between modern media and social groups, such as the family, friends, play group, and peer group. He laid the foundation for later empirical research into how media effects are moderated and changed by interaction with other individuals and groups. Dewey and Park addressed the form and content of journalism, occasionally lamenting that it too often lined the pockets of the businessperson but also speculating about a newspaper that would carry no advertising and would appeal to the higher intellect. Unlike the Frankfurt theorists, these communication scholars of the **Progressive generation** had great hopes about the effect of media on modern society. Dewey wrote in 1915, in *Democracy and Education*, "There is more than a verbal tie between the words *common*, *community*, and *communication*. Men live in a community in virtue of the things they have in common; and communication is the way in which they come to possess things in common."

As the Progressive era gave way to the Great Depression of the 1930s, the emphasis on empirical research and social science approaches gained ascendancy. The daring hopes of the Progressives for a new form of community were dashed as the economy plummeted. Scholars turned to empirical methods to document media effects, and empiricism and social science approaches dominated in media studies, just as they dominated in other emerging fields such as political science. Through the 1960s, empirical research focused primarily on individual effects.

Current Research Topics: Moderate Effects Research

During the early 1970s, government and university interest in media research grew. Researchers shifted direction and began to label effects as "moderate," rather than "limited."[24] *Moderate effects research* found that media content had a greater impact on people's behavior than limited effects studies suggested, but the impact was not as great as was found by the powerful effects researchers.

Television Violence ✦ In 1972, the Report to the Surgeon General on TV Violence and Children concluded that a connection exists between TV violence and some children's antisocial behavior. Controversy followed the release of the forty research projects that were part of the report. The television industry argued that the research had not shown a causal relationship. Some researchers argued that the report's conclusions were weaker than the research warranted.

Progressive generation: Group of individuals in the early 1900s who championed political and social reform.

Media scholars are concerned about the effects of television on individuals, particularly children. Studies of violence and of heavy television watching indicate that media effects can be negative as well as positive. The critical question is whether media contribute to the development of a good society. Such a statement involves many assumptions and unanswered questions.

Knowledge gap research hypothesizes that those with the greatest amounts of information will more easily gather even more knowledge, increasing the gap between the information-poor and the information-rich. This cybercafé is an attempt to provide access to new forms of information to a wide variety of people.

Ten years later, in 1982, the National Institute for Mental Health (NIMH) issued a report analyzing the massive research effort that had followed the Surgeon General's report. The NIMH report covered a wider range of TV effects than violence, but violence got the bulk of media attention when the report was released. The report found a correlation between heavy viewing of violent television by children and aggressive behavior. It also found that television advertising affected children and that television could contribute to prosocial behavior as well as antisocial behavior.[25]

Knowledge Gap ✦ Other new ideas about media—especially about media and politics—emerged from massive research efforts during the 1970s. The *knowledge gap hypothesis* argued that people with more education and higher incomes would acquire knowledge of public issues more quickly than would those with less education and income.[26] Such a condition could dramatically affect democracy because the poor and less educated would be at a disadvantage when making political decisions. Knowledge gap research argued that a person who is uncomfortable reading or who cannot afford newspapers and magazines will be less likely than other people to participate politically and could be manipulated by politicians.

Research that followed the publication of the knowledge gap hypothesis supported its existence under some conditions.[27] However, the existence of the gap is influenced by more than socioeconomic background. The gap can narrow when people at lower socioeconomic levels have a strong interest in the topic and the information is accessible.

The growing use of the Internet to access knowledge has increased concerns about the existence and impact of the knowledge gap. Internet access requires an investment in a computer and some knowledge of technology, both of which are more readily available to people with high incomes and greater education. This problem will increase if companies decide to place information only on the Web. Using a computer in the library is not a solution, because the prices of computers limit the number of computers most libraries can afford.

News Gathering ✦ During the 1970s, many content influence studies concentrated on newsgathering. In 1978, sociologist Gaye Tuchman published a book that created a whole new research language.[28] She described the routines that are used to gather news as a *news net*. The net catches some types of events, which become news, and it allows others to pass through. Events that are prescheduled, such as city council meetings, or nonscheduled, such as earthquakes, may qualify as news. Problems and issues that are not connected to public events, such as unequal pay for women, do not become news.

Tuchman's criticism of the media grew out of her feminism and the failure of news organizations to adequately cover the women's and civil rights movements of

As the use of radio, television, and cable has fragmented and media have converged, it has become increasingly difficult to compare individual use across electronic media. Not only do people use the various electronic media differently, but also the methods of researching how people use media differ from one medium to another. Companies such as Nielsen for television and Arbitron for radio have used surveys, diaries, and people meters to measure use of media. Each, however, has limitations. Diaries and surveys can often underestimate those using a particular channel or stations because people forget to write down the viewing, or they forget to push the button that tells the people meter they are in the room.

Arbitron, with financial support from Nielsen, has been working on a portable people meter (PPM) for about a decade. The PPM is about the size of a pager and can be worn on a belt or carried in a purse. The PPM registers an inaudible code placed in radio transmission and in the audio of television and cable programs. This way, audience members don't have to record anything themselves. The PPM also has a motion detector, which allows Arbitron to monitor its use. At the end of a day, the PPM is placed in a home station that transmits back to Arbitron the information about what a person listened to and watched. Arbitron then analyzes the data.

PPMs are valuable because users do not have to actively record their media use. In addition, PPM can measure use of radio, broadcast TV, cable, and DBS, therefore allowing more accurate comparisons about use among these media. Because converged media use both audio and video, the PPM will likely be able to measure web use in the future.

Arbitron was testing the PPM in Philadelphia during 2002, and BBM Canada, which provides ratings data for Canadian radio and television, will adopt portable people meters for Montreal and Quebec in 2003.

However, not everyone is convinced that the PPM is better than traditional research methods. Although it allows the measurement of several types of media, it gives figures that are inconsistent with traditional research. In Philadelphia, comparisons of the PPM data and the Nielsen Station Index show that the PPM data averaged about 46 percent higher for stations than traditional measures. The PPM records the code when someone is within the "range of the audible signal." This may not be the same as watching or listening to content.

Whether the PPM becomes the new research method for measuring electronic media use in the United States has yet to be determined. The limitations of all methods suggest that using multiple methods to collect data might be best.

Sources: Erwin Ephron, "The Blunt Pencil: Measure for Measure," *Mediaweek* (November 4, 2002), via Lexis-Nexis; "BBM Canada Selects Arbitron's Portable People Meters to Measure Television Audiences in Montreal and Quebec," *Canadian Corporate News-wire* (September 23, 2002), via Lexis-Nexis; "Arbitron Updates Status of Portable People Meters," *Business Wire* (September 4, 2002), via Lexis-Nexis.

the 1960s and 1970s. It took some time, but many newspapers eventually discovered what she found: Using topical beats improves news coverage. Today, reporters cover the environment and civil rights beats as well as the city hall and school beats.

MASS MEDIA EFFECTS: CONTINUING ISSUES IN MEDIA EFFECTS

Two of the most volatile social issues are the relationship between media and politics and the impact of media on individuals. Not surprisingly, these issues have been the focus of continuing basic research. Unlike applied research, which is pursued as discrete research projects aimed at specific questions, basic research continues to

1880. Marx introduces survey techniques in a study of French workers.

1927. Lasswell publishes *Propaganda Techniques in the World War.*

1920s. Frankfurt School emerges.

1929–1932. Payne studies examine movies' impact on children.

1930s–1940s. Professional pollsters develop survey techniques.

1942–1945. Hovland studies attitude change for the U.S. Army.

1948. Lazarsfeld, Berelson, and Gaudet publish *The People's Choice.*

1400–1700	1800	1900	1920	1930	1940

1620. Pilgrims land at Plymouth Rock.

1690. *Publick Occurrences* is published in Boston.

1741. First magazine is published in America.

1776–1783. American Revolution

1830s. The penny press becomes the first truly mass medium in the United States.

1861–1865. American Civil War

1892. Thomas Edison's lab develops the kinetoscope.

1914–1918. World War I

1915. *The Birth of a Nation* marks the start of the modern movie industry.

1920. KDKA in Pittsburgh gets the first commercial radio license.

1930s. The Great Depression

1939. TV is demonstrated at the New York World's Fair.

1939–1945. World War II

1949. First commercial electronic computer is produced.

investigate the same topics with multiple projects for decades. These topics become the basis for theory, and theory evolves as new projects shed light on these topics.

Political Effects of Mass Media

Scholars and the public continue to be intrigued by the relationship between politics and mass media. The drafters of the Bill of Rights granted freedom of expression because they believed that public debate would guard against the imposition of arbitrary power by a repressive government and would create an informed populace that would be capable of governing itself. Especially with the advent of television, critics have become increasingly concerned that in politics the image has come to outweigh consideration of the issues. The prevalence of image advertising, spin doctors, and manipulation of the media agenda by skilled politicians remains a critical area for study.

key concept

Agenda-Setting Research Media research seeks to understand the relationship between readers' determination of important issues and politicians' and the press's treatment of them. The research focuses not on how media cover an issue, but on how they set an agenda for the issues they cover.

Agenda Setting ◆ *Agenda-setting research* contends
that the media influence the importance individuals place on public issues. The agenda-setting process involves placing an issue and ranking it by importance on the public

1950. White publishes the first gatekeeping study.
1954. Berelson, Lazarsfeld, and McPhee publish *Voting*.
1955. Breed publishes "Social Control in the Newsroom."
1959. Katz suggests the uses and gratification line of research.
1970. Tichenor, Donohue, and Olien publish knowledge gap research.
1971. Surgeon General issues a report on TV violence's impact.
1970s. Carey revives community orientation of U.S. cultural studies.
1972. McCombs and Shaw begin agenda-setting research.
1973. Noelle-Neumann hypothesizes the spiral of silence.
1970s. Gerbner and colleagues develop cultivation theory.
1976. Ball-Rokeach and DeFleur publish dependency theory.
1982. National Institutes of Health issue a report on television violence.
Late 1980s. Media economics research increases.
1991. Shoemaker and Reese publish *Mediating the Message*.
2000. On the basis of exit polls, TV networks mistakenly announce Al Gore wins Florida popular vote.

1950	1960	1970	1980	1990	2000

Early 1950s. Rock 'n' roll begins.
1969. First person lands on the moon.
1970s. VCR is developed.
1989–1991. Cold War ends and the USSR is dissolved.
Late 1980s. National Science Foundation creates the basis of the Internet.
1996. Telecommunications Act
2000. Presidential election nearly tied.
2001. Terrorist attacks on New York and Washington, D.C.

agenda. The original agenda-setting research by McCombs and Shaw questioned 100 undecided voters in Chapel Hill, North Carolina, during the 1968 presidential election.[29] The researchers analyzed the media content that the voters used and ranked the importance of issues on the basis of the amount of time and space the issue received. The voters then ranked the importance of the same issues. The ranking of coverage in the media and the ranking of issues by the voters came close to being an exact match. The conclusion from the study was that media can affect politics by influencing what the public considers important.

Audience characteristics affect individual agendas. How important an issue is to individuals, or its *salience*, affects the placement of an issue on the public agenda. For example, if unemployment is higher in the automobile industry than in other industries, unemployment will be a more salient issue to employees in the automobile industry. Salience interacts with media coverage. In Detroit, where the automobile industry is a major employer, unemployment has salience for many individuals. That salience reinforces the media's agenda-setting role. If media do not cover salient issues, their agenda-setting role is reduced.

Related to salience is the idea of obtrusiveness. An issue is *obtrusive* if an individual can experience something about it directly. An issue that is beyond direct personal experience is *unobtrusive*. If the price of a pound of hamburger goes up every

Proponents of agenda-setting theory argue that newscasters set the agenda—that is, they tell the public what to think about, not how to think about it.

week, most U.S. consumers have firsthand experience of inflation. Other issues, such as drought in Africa, are unobtrusive for most people in the United States because they have not experienced it directly. Media have more power when people do not have direct experience; this is why media play such a big role in international policy.

Research in agenda setting shows that mass media influence the public issues people discuss, and that, in turn, affects political behaviors. However, the importance of media in setting the agenda varies from person to person and from issue to issue. The goal of scholars in this area is to better explain contingencies and to explore the relationship among media, government officials, and the public in setting the public policy agenda.[30]

Spiral of Silence ✦ Shortly after the original agenda-setting study, Elisabeth Noelle-Neumann published a theory called "the spiral of silence."[31] This theory concerns the impact of mass media on public opinion. It states that three characteristics of mass media produce powerful effects on people: (1) *cumulation,* or the increasing effect of media across time; (2) *ubiquity,* or the experiencing of media messages almost all of the time; and (3) *consonance,* or the presentation of a consistent unified picture of the political world.

According to the spiral of silence, the unified, constant, and consistent picture of the world that the mass media present shapes people's perceptions of dominant political ideas. The majority of people do not share the ideas expressed by the media, the spiral of science theory argues, but media consumers think they do because of the power of media coverage. People in the majority assume they are in the minority, an assumption that makes them less likely to speak out about the issues. Over time, as the "silent majority" remains quiet, ideas that are held by a minority of people come to dominate the political discussion.

An example of the spiral of silence is media coverage of the National Rifle Association's support for the sale of assault weapons. If news media provide extensive coverage of the NRA's position, people may assume that a majority of U.S. citizens support the sale of assault weapons. As a result, each media consumer thinks that he or she is in the minority and avoids speaking out against the sale of these weapons. However, public opinion polls show that a majority of people in the United States support a ban on assault weapons. In this case, media have provided an incorrect image of public opinion. This incorrect image was reinforced because people failed to express their opposition to this issue.

A study of the spiral of silence in Austin, Texas, found that a person's perception of public opinion did influence outspokenness.[32] However, the person's perception was only one of several factors that had an influence. Gender, age, education, income, and political opinion also affected whether people would express their political opinions. The impact of this spiral of silence on people will likely decline as the fragmentation of audiences through convergence and interactivity reduces the consonance found in mass media.

Individual Effects Research

Research into media's effects on individuals examines what media do to people's cognitive processes, which determine how we learn and interact with others. Two notable areas, cultivation and dependency theory, are presented here as examples of this type of research. The two are related: Cultivation addresses television, and dependency theory covers a wider range of media.

Cultivation ✦ *Cultivation research* concerns the effect of television viewing on how people perceive the world. It states that heavy television viewers are more likely than light viewers to think that the world is actually like what is presented on television.

Cultivation research started with studies of violent television content by George Gerbner and his associates at the University of Pennsylvania during the early 1970s. They found that heavier viewers tended to perceive the real world as more violent, similar to television's world, than it really was. A person who watched television eight hours or more a day overestimated his or her chance of being a crime victim.

A steady viewing diet of *NYPD Blue, Cops,* and other graphically violent shows could easily create the impression of a scary, violent world. Just as important as what is watched is how much viewing takes place. Time spent watching television reduces exposure to reality. Without experience to counteract television, the TV world becomes reality. Dozens of studies have found a variety of limited cultivation effects in addition to violence. These include depression, changed political attitudes, sexism, and stereotyping.

Most scholars do not doubt that television affects people's perceptions of reality. However, just how much impact it has, and on how many people, remains an issue. Cultivation research has found a consistent but weak relationship between television viewing and some people's view of the world. This finding is weakened further by the question of how other factors come into play. These factors might reduce the impact of cultivation.[33]

Dependency Theory ✦ Sandra Ball-Rokeach and Melvin DeFleur tied together a variety of effects research with *dependency theory.*[34] Their theory explains why the impact of media varies from person to person and from situation to situation. It states that the system of media organizations controls information that people depend on to live. At the same time, people and groups in a society control scarce resources, such as information and money, that media companies need to survive. This mutual dependency between media and individuals contributes to the effects that each group has on the other.

The community newspaper illustrates this mutual dependency. Readers depend on the newspaper to help them know what has happened and what will happen in a community. People read the newspaper to learn about the decisions of the city council, the results of the high school football game, who is getting married, who died, and when local events will take place. The newspaper journalists in turn depend on the local citizens to tell them what is happening in the community. The newspaper company depends on the community to support the newspaper with advertising and subscriptions.

In addition to dependency between media organizations and individuals, dependency theory also states that social systems are interdependent. The political system

key concept

Cultivation Research Cultivation research looks at the effect that television viewing has on how people perceive the world. The theory states that heavy television viewers are more likely than light viewers to think that the world is as it is presented on television. Heavy viewers perceive the world as being more violent than it is.

key concept

Dependency Theory Dependency theory states that media organizations, individuals, and groups in society are mutually dependent on one another.

depends on media to help inform the electorate, and the media system depends on the political system to define its freedoms and to maintain a stable economic environment. The mutual dependency among social systems, groups, and individuals means that all these types of units affect one another.

Dependency theory suggests that media influences individuals in six ways:

1. *Self-understanding:* People depend on media to learn about themselves and to grow as individuals.
2. *Social understanding:* People depend on media to learn about the world and their community.
3. *Action orientation:* People depend on media to decide what to buy and how to act.
4. *Interaction orientation:* People depend on media to decide how to behave toward other people.
5. *Solitary play:* People depend on media to divert and entertain them when they are alone.
6. *Social play:* People depend on media to entertain them when they are with friends and family.

The importance of media in these six activities varies from person to person, across time, and from activity to activity. An introverted person may use media more for solitary play; an extrovert may use media to interact with others. People create their own mix of media information, and some people depend more on one type of media than on another.

The overall impact of media on a person depends on availability of nonmediated information, the individual's goals and interests, and the individual's background. The stereotypical "couch potato," for instance, depends greatly on television for play and social orientation. The couch potato's images of society and how people act reflect what he or she sees on television. However, if that couch potato gets tired of watching reruns on cable and joins in church activities, his or her ideas about how other people behave will be shaped also by the church members. Media content alone does not shape people's images of their surroundings.

Characterizing Effects Research

Ever since effects research began, the overriding question about media effects has been, How powerful an effect do mass media have on the public? Most answers to this question have concentrated on the number of people who are affected. Because of this focus, media effects have been characterized as powerful, moderate, or weak according to the number of people who exhibit the effects.[35]

However, effects research demonstrates that people are not all alike when it comes to media impact. In a 1993 movie titled *The Program,* about high school football, one scene showed an initiation ritual in which the players lay down on the center stripe of a road while cars whizzed past. Some teenagers who saw the film imitated the scene, and at least one death was reported. The movie distributor recalled the movie and cut the scene.[36] However, thousands of young people saw the movie and did not lie down on a highway.

On the whole, research indicates that media do not have powerful or weak effects; they have **contingent effects.** Media content's impact is dependent on many factors. Some involve the content, some reflect the situation surrounding media use, and some involve the background of the media consumer.

CULTURAL STUDIES TODAY

contingent effects: Effects that are caused by contingent, or indirect, variables rather than by the direct impact of media content.

James Carey, writing from the mid-1970s onward, revived the community orientation of U.S. cultural studies. Carey resisted the empiricists, who viewed communication as a transmission process. As you learned in Chapter 1, one model of communication includes a sender, a medium, and a receiver. Although interference of various kinds can affect the message, the task is to get the message intact from the sender to the receiver. Carey argued that the transmission model did not adequately represent communication; instead, communication should be viewed as a process through which a shared culture is created, modified, and transformed. Communication is not an extension of messages in space, but the maintenance of society across time. Carey further argued that communication was not the imparting of information or influence but the creation and transmission of shared beliefs. Carey has made an explicit effort to pursue cultural studies without reducing "culture to ideology, social conflict to class conflict, consent to compliance, action to reproduction, or communication to coercion." He writes convincingly that mass media should be viewed as a site, not a discipline or subject, on "which to engage the general question of social theory." Communication, writes Carey, "is a symbolic process whereby reality is produced, maintained, repaired, and transformed."[37]

Carey's work built on that of Raymond Williams and Stuart Hall, both of whom were actively arguing the concept of culture and communications in the 1970s when social science research was in ascendancy. Williams was then a fellow of Jesus College at Cambridge, and Stuart Hall was director of the Centre for the Study of Contemporary Culture at the University of Birmingham, which has become the center of Britain's cultural approach to communications. Williams and Hall both argued against using the term *mass communications research* because, expressed that way, it seemed to have little to do with culture. Also influential in the 1970s and beyond was Clifford Geertz, who, in his study of primitive cultures, attempted to explain the dilemma of describing the universality of human nature while acknowledging the importance of historical and cultural context.

During the 1980s and 1990s, Carey's optimistic views of community, communication, and culture were countered by scholars who were oriented toward the study of the influence of power. *Political economy* scholars, for example, (1) look at "how capitalists use their economic power with a commercial market system to ensure that the flow of public information is consonant with their interests" and (2) "attempt to understand how meaning is made and remade through the concrete activities of producers and consumers."[38]

Hermeneutics (an ancient technique of analyzing scriptural and literary texts), semiotics (the study of culture as a formal system of signs and what they signify), and ethnography (the anthropological tracing of cultures) remain significant tools for investigating the connection between communication and culture.

USES OF MEDIA

Research about how consumers use media falls under the heading of *uses and gratifications research,* which tries to identify why and how people use various media and what types of rewards they get from media content. Effects research examines what media *do to people;* uses and gratifications research examines what people *do with* media.

Early uses and gratifications research classified the reasons people decide to view, read, or listen to media. Research since the 1970s has consistently found four classifications for media uses: (1) surveillance of the environment, (2) social interaction, (3) entertainment, and (4) understanding and developing personal identity.[39] A more recent classification added the concept of using information for decision making.[40]

Using media for surveillance involves a person attending to events that may be important to him or her. Checking the baseball scores and reading about the stock market performance every day are forms of surveillance. Using media for social interaction occurs when people discuss what they watched on television or heard on radio. For instance, a group of people reacting to a situation that appeared on MTV's *The Real*

CBS's *Survivor* was one of the earliest and most popular reality shows. Some critics argue that these programs represent a commercial media system that emphasizes low-cost programming to attract young audiences for advertisers.

World allows members of the group to understand one another. Reacting favorably or unfavorably toward what the *Real World* characters do tells others something about the person reacting. Entertainment is a way people use media to escape their problems or even everyday activities. Watching *The Lord of the Rings: The Two Towers* allows viewers to lose themselves in the movie and forget reality for a while. In developing and understanding personal identity, people use media to analyze and come to terms with emotions, thoughts, and attitudes. For example, everyone has favorite songs that express how they feel about another person or life itself. Decision making with media information occurs when a person consults the Internet, newspapers, or magazines to help him or her solve a specific problem—buying a car, for example.

Uses and gratifications research has developed fairly consistent categories for the way people use media. However, this area of research has not produced an accepted theory that connects people's motivations with the use classifications. There is no doubt that people often use mass media for entertainment, but questions as to why people select media over other forms of entertainment have yet to be adequately explained. Equally important are questions about why individuals select specific media to meet their needs. For instance, why do young people more so than adults use popular music in their social interactions?

INFLUENCES ON CONTENT

Just as a variety of factors determine the uses and effects of media, several types of influences shape media content. The influences can be classified as individual, organizational, economic, and ideological factors. *Individual influences* include the psychological makeup of the people creating the content. *Organizational influences* involve the work routines, social interaction, and ownership goals found in media organizations and in the organizations covered by media. *Economic influences* involve the demand for media content and competition for media consumers. *Ideological influences* include the shared values and beliefs that are found in a social system.

These factors can work singly or together to influence media content. For example, a famous and successful novelist has more independence than does a beginning newspaper journalist. The famous novelist will be edited but ultimately has individual control over the book's content. The newspaper reporter depends on sources' statements to shape a story. This dependence reflects the organizational influence of work routines and professional ideology. Then an editor changes the story to fit available space on the basis of the news value of the story. The available space depends on the amount of advertising sold by the newspaper, which reflects economic influence.

Individual Factors

As was mentioned earlier, gatekeeping research examines the role of individual biases on the selection of news. As with all decisions, a journalist's perceptions affect the decisions to include one source instead of another, to emphasize a particular idea, and to pick a particular quotation. During the past twenty years, scholars have examined the impact of individual characteristics such as gender and professional beliefs on content creation. Much of the research has concentrated on journalists, but the results have implications for a broad range of communicators.

For example, the individual's perception of her or his journalistic role and acceptance of professional standards play a role in the creation of media content. Weaver and Wilhoit identified three roles journalists hold for themselves.[41] The *dissemination role* involves collecting information objectively and distributing it quickly to a large audience. The *interpretive role* requires journalists to investigate sources' claims and to analyze and explain complex issues to their audience. The *adversary role* assumes that journalists should act as antagonists to politicians and businesses. Adversarial journalists act as representatives for their audience to counterbalance powerful economic and political interests.

The interpretive role is supported by the highest percentage of journalists, followed by the dissemination and adversary roles. However, only a small fraction of journalists believe that journalists should be limited to a single role. All three serve news consumers in different ways at different times. Shoemaker and Reese concluded that organizational factors have more influence than individual factors on media content, but individual backgrounds can affect what is produced.[42] Of particular importance are ethics and professional attitudes.

Organizational Factors

Organizational factors take two forms. The first includes the socialization processes and work routines that are found within media organizations. The other involves the interaction between journalists and people from outside the organization. The study of organizational factors dates from the beginning of research on content influences.

Reporter–source relationships often affect the coverage of news during particular administrations. Here, Ari Fleischer, White House press secretary, fields questions from journalists early in the Bush administration.

Warren Breed's 1955 study of socialization in news organizations continues to be applicable today. Media organizations enforce policy more through social interaction than through formal policy.[43]

Research about the interaction of sources and journalists has continued along the lines started with Gieber and Johnson's work. A 1972 study of TV journalists found patterns of reporter–source relationships that were similar to those established by the two early researchers. The study concluded that journalists who do not assimilate the values of their sources are respected more by their sources than those who do.[44] A politician who can manipulate a journalist need not respect or fear that journalist.

One area that received extensive attention during the 1980s and 1990s involved the impact of company ownership on content. Scholars such as Ben Bagdikian[45] have argued that newspapers and television stations owned by a corporation with many media outlets perform differently than those that are owned by an individual or family. It is fairly easy to find examples of situations in which corporate managers have interfered with local newspaper editors or have reduced news budgets. However, it also is fairly easy to find corporate managers who have invested heavily in newsrooms to improve coverage.

Research results have been mixed, but the bulk of research about newspapers indicates only minor variations in content when group-owned and independent newspapers are compared.[46] The goals of a particular organization determine the impact of ownership on content. An independent newspaper company that wants a high profit will produce content that is similar to the content produced by a group-owned newspaper with high profit goals. Publicly held corporations, for example, that have retained much of the ownership control inside the organizations tend to have lower profit margins and higher newsroom budgets.[47] The corporation that owns the *New York Times* sells stock to the public, but the family that runs the newspaper retains almost all of the voting stock. That allows the *Times* to remain the best newspaper in the United States because the managers chose to reinvest some profits in quality rather than distribute all of it to shareholders.

Market Factors

Market factors include forces outside the organization, such as government regulations, economic competition, and consumer demand. Government regulations establish acceptable types of market behavior. Governments regulate some media more than others; television is the most regulated, followed by cable and radio.

An example of how regulations affect content can be found in the history of cable and direct broadcast satellite (DBS) transmission. As the FCC has removed regulatory barriers from the expansion of cable and DBS, the number and diversity of programming choices for viewers have boomed. The average amount of money spent to create network prime-time programs has increased as well. One can argue about whether the changes benefit viewers but not that regulation changes affect content.

Competition can have an impact on content depending on the type of competition and the intensity. Competition between newspapers can affect the amount of money that is available to the newsrooms and the amount of space that is available to readers. This is called the *financial commitment model*.[48] As competition increases, newspaper managers spend more money to make their newspaper different from the competition's paper. This differentiation tries to attract readers from the competition, but the news product must also remain similar enough to its competition to be considered a substitute.

Even though competition can improve news coverage, it also has a dark side. Some news organizations differentiate their newspapers and newscasts by using sensationalism. Two newscasts that have similar audience shares may each hire more reporters, but those reporters might end up covering more accidents and murders. Viewers may see more crime scenes than public affairs reporting. Just how competition translates into news content rests on the professionalism of the managers and the managers' perceptions of what the viewers want to see.

IDEOLOGY

How *ideology influences media content* has been studied more by critical theorists than by social scientists. Social scientist concentrate on microlevel factors, such as individuals, organizational factors, and market factors. Ideology is the collection of values, beliefs, and **symbolic meanings** that a group of people share. Ideology shapes that group's view of the way the world works. For example, capitalism is an ideology. People who support capitalism assume that capital, or money, is the most important factor affecting economic growth. Therefore, capital should receive a high rate of return (profit or interest) when it is invested.

k e y   c o n c e p t

Ideology Influences Media Content Ideology is the collection of values, beliefs, and symbolic meanings that a group of people share. Because ideology shapes that group's view of the way the world works, it influences the content created by members of the group.

Because ideology shapes the worldview of people who hold that ideology, it can affect the performance of people who create media content. Because the United States supports a capitalist ideology, the media system is a commercial one, in which most media organizations aim to make a profit. This goal affects the creation of content. The media system in a Marxist system would not aim to make a profit but to support the political power group that controlled the media system. Two systems with different ideologies produce different content. The capitalist system's content must attract consumers who will pay for it or who will view the advertisements. The Marxist system's content must motivate citizens of that system to support the efforts of the ruling party. Whether a person prefers one system over the other, of course, depends on the ideology that person accepts.

Shoemaker and Reese point out that ideology is not a conspiracy of powerful people. Reporters and movie directors do not think about their ideology as they go about their daily work. Ideology exists and evolves as an outgrowth of a social system.[49] It influences the way people think and work. Because of this, the relationship between ideology and mass media will continue to be a topic of basic research.

TRENDS

Both practical and basic mass communication social science research face challenges during the next decade. Practical research faces changes in media use that come with converging media, and basic research must aim toward synthesizing and integrating the accumulated knowledge from thousands of studies. As a result of these challenges, basic researchers will become more theoretical, and practical researchers will have to evaluate ways that they use research for examining media users.

Basic Research: Developing Integrated Social Science Theory

Mass communication basic research remains a young field of scholarly inquiry compared to other social sciences. As a result, many questions remain unanswered. In the years since the end of World War I, the field has changed from focusing almost entirely on individual and societal effects to include a study of factors that influence content creation.

Much of mass communication research has been aimed at developing empirical evidence. Studies have identified relationships among factors, such as how news routines affect issues and how events become news. There has been little effort to work these results into formal theories. Formal theories would specify the relationships among the factors far more exactly than summaries of empirical results. Formal theories explain how factors should be measured and which types of empirical results support theories.

Integrating the hundreds of research projects even within a narrow area of mass communication research will be difficult. However, two notable efforts developed during the last two decades. Shoemaker and Reese, in their book *Mediating the Message,* organized a hierarchy of factors influencing the creation of media content. In addition, they generated a list of hypotheses suggested from the existing literature. First published in 1991, the hypotheses are being tested currently by basic researchers.

symbolic meanings: Feelings, thoughts, attitudes, and images associated with symbols, such as words, constitute symbolic meaning. Members of social groups share these symbolic meanings. For example, a cross is a symbol of salvation for Christians.

The next step is to use these tests to adjust the model and then to develop a more formal theory that explains specifically how all of the factors interact.

A second example of integrating theory was published in 1998 by scholar Sandra Ball-Rokeach.[50] She integrates elements of dependency theory and uses and gratifications research into a formal, integrated theory. As an outgrowth of the theory, she predicts that the developing Internet is not likely to free individuals from their dependency on media. Instead media companies will develop ways to use the Internet to maintain consumers' dependency on them for the information they use in their daily lives.

The ability of surveys to influence public policy was demonstrated by the actions of President Bush following the attacks of 9/11. With his popularity ratings reaching an all-time high, he was able to successfully pass the Homeland Security Act and other legislation increasing the power of the executive branch of government. The polls showed that even though he barely won the presidency, more than 87 percent of the public approved of his performance by early 2002.

As government struggles with terrorism, public opinion polls will likely grow in importance. The political parties will use them to support their positions on legislation and enforcement. This increases the need for journalists who understand research methods. Otherwise, conclusions based on invalid data and spread by uninformed journalists might negatively affect public policy.

Impact of Technology on Research

The development of telephone technology is affecting the ability of researchers to collect information from truly representative samples. A representative sample of a population must contain people who have the same characteristics as the people in the population, and in the same proportion. This can happen only when the sample is large (usually more than one thousand) and random. Randomness requires that each person in the population has the same probability of being included in the sample. If each person does not have an equal chance, the sample is biased and can lead to inaccurate conclusions about the population.

Measuring Web Use

As advertisers and businesses have increased their use of the Web, they are requiring research to demonstrate how effective the Web is in reaching their goals. This research usually involves how many people visit web sites, who these people are, and how effectively the sites communicate their messages. Many companies, including Relevant Knowledge, Jupiterresearch, Media Metrix, and Nielsen/NetRating, conduct research about web use. However, the process of measuring web use is complicated by two factors. First, disagreement continues as to which data best measure web use. Second, people use the Internet for many purposes—from research for school papers to entertainment to e-mail. Unlike television and radio, which are used primarily for entertainment, researchers cannot assume anything about the purpose of a visit to a web site.

Sharon Machlis discussed the issues of appropriate Web measures in her 2002 article, "Measuring Web Site Traffic":

> In the beginning, there were hits. Today, hits are largely discredited as a measure of Web site traffic, since they count individual files served up. A single Web page can account for a dozen or more hits if it has a lot of photos, while a text-only page could generate just a single hit. These days, the Weberati talk about metrics such as page views, ad impressions and unique users. But don't be fooled by precise-sounding terminology and numbers. There are so many ways to define and count Web visits that traffic measurement is as much an art as it is a science.[51]

Of course, all measures related to people visiting web sites have the same drawback as TV and radio ratings. They can show someone visited, but they don't reveal how that individual used the information or even to what degree she or he paid attention to it.

The other problem in measuring the Web concerns its multiple uses. Initial efforts in measuring web site data were aimed at selling advertising. The data were suppose to demonstrate that the ads were being viewed. However, the many uses of the Web create needs for research beyond just the number of people's eyeballs looking at a page. Nielsen/NetRatings began an effort in 2002 to expand beyond measuring numbers of visits and page views. The company announced plans to issue a regular report called "Digital Media Universe." This will include numbers of people using instant messaging, web phones, media players, file sharing, online games, and even pages at the AOL and MSN portals.[52]

Even after research firms and research customers decide on appropriate measures and expand measurement to more types of web use, the same problems confronting all media research continue. Those include selecting who should be included in the samples for study and the methods (diaries, surveys, people meters, etc.) that would be most valid for collecting the data. Research is never perfect. Data always contain error. However, research also is essential for informed decisions. As the Internet grows in importance, so will research about its use.

summary

◆ Mass communication research plays an important role in public policy and solving practical problems for media organizations.

◆ Basic mass communication research takes two approaches. The social science approach examines the behavior of individuals and groups associated with mass communication, and the cultural approach (also called the critical approach) emphasizes the connections between media and society.

◆ Communication research is classified as qualitative and quantitative, which represent a variety of methods. Each of these methods has strengths and weaknesses.

◆ Early social science communication research concentrated on media effects.

◆ Critical studies developed from two major schools: the Frankfurt School in Germany and the Chicago School.

- Supporters of the Chicago School took a more positive approach toward the impact of communication in society than did scholars in the Frankfurt School.
- World War I propaganda led researchers to believe that media had an all-powerful (magic bullet) effect.
- By 1940, researchers began to shift their thinking to a limited effects model, which suggests that interpersonal influences were as great as media influences.
- An active area of political effects research is agenda setting, which deals with the impact of media on the political issues that are discussed by the public and addressed by government.
- Dependency theory holds great promise for individual effects research. It identifies the dependency relationships among people, media, and social systems and explains how these influence people and groups.
- Media uses research is an offshoot of effects studies. Uses research explores why and how people select media content.
- Research about factors that determine media content concentrates on several types of influences. Important among these are individual, organizational, economic, and ideological influences.
- Critical studies research involves the study of power and ideology. It can take the form of historical analysis, textual analysis, or the study of news production, as well as other investigations into media and society.
- Political polls are survey research tools that under some conditions can have a strong impact on public policy.

navigating the web

Mass Communication Research on the Web

Research resources are rich on the World Wide Web. Here are some sites that specialize in mass communication research.

The Media and Communications Studies Site
www.aber.ac.uk/media/Functions/welcome.html
This University of Wales, Aberystwyth, site has many links to communication studies and research sites throughout the world.

Penn State List of Mass Media Research Articles
http://psulias.psu.edu:1213/;&db=mm

The Penn State site lists most of the mass media research articles published in the United States from 1984 to the present.

Resources in Communications Economics
www.tukkk.fi/mediagroup/resources/default.htm
The Resources site contains bibliographies of academic research in a variety of media, lists of texts, and a few syllabi from courses. It also has links to several extensive lists of other useful links.

questions for review

1. What are the differences between quantitative and qualitative research methods?
2. How does the cultural studies approach to the study of mass media differ from the social science approach?
3. What is social science theory? What is it used for?
4. What is the difference between effects and uses research?
5. What is agenda setting?
6. What is the spiral of silence?

issues to think about

1. What are the possible effects of the gatekeeping process on news content?
2. Pick a current topic in the news and discuss the implications of the agenda-setting concept on how this issue became news.
3. Discuss dependency theory and its connection to media effects.
4. Explain the different theoretical perspectives in social science research and cultural studies approaches. What separate contribution does each approach make to understanding mass communication?
5. Discuss some possible organizational influences on content.
6. Discuss some possible individual influences on content.

suggested readings

DeFleur, M. L., and Sandra Ball-Rokeach. *Theories of Mass Communication*, 2nd ed. (New York: David McKay, 1982).

McQuail, Dennis. *McQuail's Mass Communication Theory: An Introduction*, 4th ed. (Thousand Oaks, CA: Sage, 2000).

Severin, Warner J., and James W. Tankard. *Communication Theories: Origins, Methods and Uses in the Mass Media*, 5th ed. (Boston: Addison-Wesley, 2002).

Wimmer, Roger D., and Joseph R. Dominick. *Mass Media Research: An Introduction*, 7th ed. (Belmont, CA: Wadsworth, 2002).

REFERENCES

Chapter 1

1. The Internet Public Library, www.ipl.org, accessed June 20, 2002.
2. C. Shannon and W. Weaver, *The Mathematical Theory of Communication* (Urbana: University of Illinois Press, 1949), p. 98.
3. "The Lower Case," *Columbia Journalism Review* (July/August 1986): 65.
4. Bruce H. Westley and Malcolm S. MacLean Jr., "A Conceptual Model for Communication Research," *Journalism Quarterly* 34 (1957): 31–38.
5. David Manning White, "The 'Gatekeeper': A Case Study in the Selection of News," *Journalism Quarterly* 27 (1950): 383–390.
6. S. H. Steinberg, *Five Hundred Years of Printing* (New York: Criterion Books, 1959), pp. 21–22.
7. For a detailed discussion of the impact of the printing revolution on Western society, see Elizabeth L. Eisenstein, *The Printing Revolution in Early Modern Europe* (Cambridge, England: Cambridge University Press, 1983). See also David Hall, "The World of Print and Collective Mentality," in John Higham and Paul K. Conkin, eds., *New Directions in American Intellectual History* (Baltimore: Johns Hopkins University Press, 1980), pp. 166–180. Eisenstein and Hall demonstrate the impact of technological change on society.
8. Richard Schwarzlose, *The Nation's Newsbrokers: The Formative Years from Pretelegraph to 1865*, vol. 1 (Evanston, IL: Northwestern University Press, 1989). Schwarzlose's volumes are the first complete history of the wire services.
9. Christopher Sterling and John Kittross, *Stay Tuned*, 2nd ed. (Belmont, CA: Wadsworth, 1990), pp. 52–55. This is a complete history of broadcast media.
10. "Internet: The Undiscovered Country," *PC Magazine* (March 15, 1994): 116–118.
11. John Markoff, "I Wonder What's on the PC Tonight," *The New York Times*, May 8, 1994, sec. 3, pp. 1, 8.
12. "Media Wars," *Media Studies Journal* 6:2 (Spring 1992): Preface.
13. Mark A. Thalhimer, "A National Information Service Background Paper," Freedom Forum Media Studies Center, December 1991; see also www.cnn.com/wires/US/02-01/telecom_glance/index.ap.html, February 1, 1996.
14. William B. Blankenburg and Gary W. Ozanich, "The Effects of Public Ownership on the Financial Performance of Newspaper Corporations," *Journalism Quarterly* 70 (1993): 68–75.
15. "Autonomy and Breadth Provide First Personalized Information 'Hubs' via Mobile Phone, Laptops, Personal Digital Assistants and Other Devices Across Europe," *Business Wire* (August 3, 1999), accessed via Lexis-Nexis.
16. Marshall McLuhan, *The Gutenberg Galaxy: The Making of Typographic Man* (Toronto: University of Toronto Press, 1962), pp. 272–273.
17. John Merrill and Everett Dennis, "Global Communication Dominance," in *Media Debates: Issues in Mass Communication* (New York: Longman, 1991), pp. 212–222.
18. Harold Lasswell, "The Structure and Function of Communication in Society," in Lyman Byron, ed., *The Communication of Ideas* (New York: Institute for Religious and Social Studies, 1948), pp. 37–51; Charles R. Wright, *Mass Communication: A Sociological Perspective*, 3rd ed. (New York: Random House, 1959), pp. 4–6. Together these scholars listed four functions of mass communication for society. Two of these, surveillance and entertainment, take place at the individual level and are considered individual uses here. Self-understanding as a use is taken from dependency theory. See Melvin DeFleur and Sandra Ball-Rokeach, *Theories of Mass Communication*, 5th ed. (New York: Longman, 1989), pp. 305–310.

Chapter 2

1. See Jeffery A. Smith, *Printers and Press Freedom* (New York: Oxford University Press, 1990), pp. 42–53.
2. Thomas Jefferson to Edward Carrington, January 16, 1787, in *The Papers of Thomas Jefferson*, Julian P. Boyd et al., eds. (Princeton, NJ: Princeton University Press, 1950), Vol. 11, p. 49
3. *1791–1991: The Bill of Rights and Beyond* (Washington, DC: Library of Congress, 1991), p. 18.
4. Stephen Botein, "'Meer Mechanics' and an Open Press: The Business and Political Strategies of Colonial American Printers," *Perspectives in American History* 9 (1975): 140–150.
5. Paul Finkelman, "The Zenger Case: Prototype of a Political Trial," in *American Political Trials*, Michael R. Belknap, ed. (Westport, CT: Greenwood Press, 1981); David Paul Nord, "The Authority of Truth: Religion and the John Peter Zenger Case," *Journalism Quarterly* 62 (Summer 1985): 227–235; James Alexander, *A Brief Narrative of the Case and Trial of John Peter Zenger*, 2nd ed. (Cambridge: Harvard University Press, 1971), p. 13. A narrative relates the text of the trial.
6. For a description for the times, see William E. Ames, *A History of the National Intelligencer* (Chapel Hill: University of North Carolina Press, 1972). The *National Intelligencer* was the prime political newspaper in early Washington, D.C. See also Richard B. Kielbowicz,

"The Press, Post Office, and Flow of News in the Early Republic," *Journal of the Early Republic* (Fall 1983), pp. 269–280. Kielbowicz connects the flow of news to congressional debates over postal policy.

7. Jeffery A. Smith, *Franklin and Bache: Envisioning the Enlightened Republic* (New York: Oxford University Press, 1990), pp. 147–148. Jeffery Smith, also the author of *Printers and Press Freedom*, explains the intellectual dimensions of the press in the early republic.

8. Jerilyn McIntyre, "Repositioning a Landmark: The Hutchins Commission and Freedom of the Press," *Critical Studies in Mass Communication* 4 (June 1987): 141; Commission on Freedom of the Press, *A Free and Responsible Press* (Chicago: University of Chicago Press, 1947), p. vi. See also Margaret Blanchard, "The Hutchins Commission, The Press and the Responsibility Concept," *Journalism Monographs* 49 (May 1977): 1–59, and D. L. Smith, *Zechariah Chafee, Jr.: Defender of Liberty and Law* (Cambridge: Harvard University Press, 1986).

9. Quotation is from McIntyre, "Repositioning a Landmark," p. 143.

10. McIntyre, "Repositioning a Landmark," p. 150.

11. John H. Colburn, "What Makes a Good Newspaper?" *Saturday Review* (June 9, 1952): 50, 52, cited in Ernest C. Hynds, *American Newspapers in the 1980s* (New York: Hastings House, 1980), p. 29.

12. Fred S. Siebert, Theodore Peterson, and Wilbur Schramm, *Four Theories of the Press* (Urbana: University of Illinois Press, 1956), p. 77; John C. Merrill and S. Jack Odell, *Philosophy and Journalism* (New York: Longman, 1983), pp. 162–163.

13. Agnew text, *New York Times* (November 14, 1969): 24, cited in William Donovan and Ray Scherer, *Unsilent Revolution: Television News and American Public Life* (Cambridge, MA: Woodrow Wilson Center for International Scholars and Cambridge University Press, 1922), pp. ix, x.

14. David Mindich, *Just the Facts: How 'Objectivity' Came to Define American Journalism* (New York: New York University Press, 1998).

15. Michael Robertson, *Stephen Crane, Journalism, and the Making of Modern American Literature* (New York: Columbia University Press, 1997).

16. Stephen Lacy and Hugh Martin, "Profits Up, Circulation Down for Thomson papers in 80s," *Newspaper Research Journal* 19:3 (1998): 63–76.

17. Alan Blanchard and Stephen Lacy, "The Impact of Public Ownership, Profits, Competition on Newsroom Employees and Starting Salaries in Mid-Sized Daily Newspapers," paper delivered to the Association for Education in Journalism and Mass Communication, Miami, Florida, August 2002.

18. P. J. Tichenor, G. A. Donohue, and C. N. Olien, "Mass Media Flow and Differential Growth in Knowledge," *Public Opinion Quarterly* 34 (1970): 159–170.

19. Alicia C. Shepard, "The Gospel of Public Journalism," *American Journalism Review* (September 1994): 29–30.

20. Shepard, p. 34.

21. Jennifer Harper, "Trouble for Ted Turner's CNN," *The Washington Times* online (June 21, 2002), www.washtimes.com/national/200220621-64430323.htm, accessed on July 13, 2002.

22. U.S. Census Bureau, "Voting and Registration in the Election of November, 2000," Document Number P20-542, pp. 1–4. www.census.gov/prod/2002pubs/p20-542.pdf, accessed June 17, 2002.

23. Television Bureau of Advertising, "Political Ad Spending," www.tvb.org/tvfacts/politics/index.html, accessed June 26, 2002.

24. Michael Kelly, "David Gergen, Master of the Game," *New York Times Magazine* (October 31, 1993): 62–71, 94, 97, 103.

25. Chip Brown, "Fear.Com," *American Journalism Review* (June 1999): 50–72.

26. David Noack, "Civic Journalism in Cyberspace," *Editor & Publisher* (November 1998): 26–28.

27. A. L. May, *The Virtual Trail* (Washington, DC: Institute for Politics, Democracy & the Internet, The Graduate School of Political Management, 2002).

Chapter 3

1. Edward L. Bernays, *Crysallizing Public Opinion* (New York: Boni and Liveright, 1923), p. 215.

2. This is a modified version of the definition from the United Kingdom Institute of Public Relations; see David W. Wragg, *The Public Relations Handbook* (Oxford, England: Blackwell, 1992), p. 3.

3. James E. Grunig and Todd Hunt, *Managing Public Relations* (New York: Holt, Rinehart and Winston, 1984), p. 8.

4. Scott Cutlip, "Public Relations and the American Revolution," *Public Relations Review* 2 (Winter 1976): 11–24.

5. David A. Haberman and Harry A. Dolphin, *Public Relations: The Necessary Art* (Ames: Iowa State University Press, 1988), pp. 14–15.

6. Neil Harris, *Humbug: The Art of P. T. Barnum* (Boston: Little, Brown, 1973), pp. 21–25.

7. Marvin N. Olasky, "The Development of Corporate Public Relations," *Journalism Monographs* 102 (April 1987): 2–15.

8. Ray Eldon Hiebert, *Courtier to the Crowd: The Story of Ivy Lee and the Development of Public Relations* (Ames: Iowa State University Press), pp. 99–100.

9. Hiebert, *Courtier to the Crowd*, pp. 298–299.

10. Edward L. Bernays, *Biography of an Idea: Memoirs of Public Relations Counsel Edward L. Bernays* (New York: Simon & Schuster, 1965), pp. 291–292.

11. Edward L. Bernays, *Crystallizing Public Opinion* (New York: Boni and Liveright, 1923), p. 215.

12. Elmer Davis, "Report to the President," in Ronald T. Farrar, ed., *Journalism Monographs* 7 (August 1968): 39.

13. William V. Ruch, *Corporate Communications: A Comparison of Japanese and American Practices* (Westport, CT: Quorum Books, 1984), p. 107.

14. Chester Barnard, *Functions of the Executive* (Cambridge: Harvard University Press, 1938).

15. Jane Whitney Gibson and Richard M. Hodgetts, *Organizational Communication* (New York: HarperCollins, 1991), pp. 219–220.

16. Haberman and Dolphin, *Public Relations*, pp. 19–20.

17. Lee W. Baker, *The Credibility Factor: Putting Ethics to Work in Public Relations* (Homewood, IL: Business One Irwin, 1993), pp. 54–59.

18. Clifton Brown, "Woods Says Each Side Must Bend on Augusta," *The New York Times*, October 17, 2002, www.nytimes.com.

19. Edward Bernays, "The Theory and Practice of Public Relations: A Resume," in *The Engineering of Consent*, Edward Bernays, ed. (Norman: University of Oklahoma Press, 1955), pp. 9–10.

20. Wragg, *The Public Relations Handbook*, pp. 87–89.

21. "Red Cross Unveils Plan for September 11 Funds," CNN.com, January 31, 2002, www.cnn.com/2002/US/01/31/rec.liberty.fund/index.html.

22. Stephanie Strom, "Red Cross Works to Renew Confidence among Donors," *The New York Times*, June 6, 2002, www.nytimes.com.

23. Randy Sumpter and James W. Tankard Jr., "The Spin Doctor: An Alternative Model for Public Relations," *Public Relation Review* 20:1 (1994): 19–27.

24. Ted Bridis, "Microsoft Pulls Ad 'Switch,'" *The Detroit News* (October 15, 2002), www.detnews.com.

25. Gibson and Hodgetts, *Organizational Communication*, pp. 212–230.

26. Daniel Katz and Robert Kahn, *The Social Psychology of Organizations* (New York: John Wiley & Sons, 1966), p. 239.

27. Gibson and Hodgetts, *Organizational Communication*, pp. 219–220.

28. S. Rosen, "More Than Postage Stamps Sends Messages at the Postal Service," *Communication World* (April/May 1998): 43.

29. J. Gerstner, "The Promise of Intranets: Expectations and Effectiveness," *Communication World* (1999): 1–13; and L. Platt, "Real People Doing Real Business," *Executive Excellence* (February 1999): 7–8.

30. "It's about Growth," O'Dwyerpr.com, June 19, 2001, wwww.odwyer.com.

31. NUA (October 19, 2002), www.nua.ie/surveys/how_many_online/n_america.html.

32. "Email Mailboxes to Increase to 1.2 Billion Worldwide by 2005," CNN.com, September 19, 2001, www.cnn.com/2001/TECH/internet/09/19/email.us.../index.htm.

33. Martha Stone, "The Online Pitch," pp. 26–28; and G. A. Marken, "PR E-Mail . . . Overused, Abused and Invaluable," *Public Relations Quarterly* (Winter 1997–98): 20–22.

34. "Press Releases Flunk. SEC Wants More," *O'Dwyer's PR Daily*, March 26, 2002, www.odwyerpr.com.

35. Patricia A. Curtin and Elizabeth M. Witherspoon, "Computer Skills Integration in Public Relations Curricula," *Journalism & Mass Communication Educator* 54 (Spring 1999): 1.

36. M. Fellman, "PR Professionals Seek Seat at the Strategy Meetings," *Marketing News* (December 7, 1998): 5.

37. J. Walker, "Getting Back to Basics," *O'Dwyer's PR Services Report* (March, 1999): 58–59.

38. Carole Howard and Wilma Mathews, *On Deadline: Managing Media Relations* (Prospect Heights, IL: Waveland Press, 1988), p. 191.

Chapter 4

1. "France's TFI Gets Kicked Around," CNN.com, June 11, 2002, www.cnn.com.

2. "Italian TV May Sue over Cup Exit," CNN.com, June 21, 2002, www.cnn.com.

3. "Total U.S. Advertising Volume," Newspaper Association of America, www.naa.org, accessed on July 12, 2002.

4. Philippe Schuwer, *History of Advertising* (London: Leisure Arts, 1966), pp. 9–10.

5. Blanche Elliot, *A History of English Advertising* (London: Business Publications, 1962), pp. 20–21.

6. Frank Presbrey, *The History and Development of Advertising* (Garden City, NY: Doubleday, Doran, 1929), p. 161.

7. Presbrey, *The History and Development of Advertising*, p. 160.

8. Presbrey, *The History and Development of Advertising*, pp. 180–181.

9. Presbrey, *The History and Development of Advertising*, p. 201.

10. James Wood Playsted, *The Story of Advertising* (New York: Ronald Press, 1958), p. 200.

11. G. Allen Foster, *Advertising: Ancient Market Place to Television* (New York: Criterion Books, 1967), pp. 120–121.

12. Foster, *Advertising: Ancient Market Place to Television*, pp. 156–157.

13. Presbrey, *The History and Development of Advertising*, p. 579.

14. Lawrence W. Lichty and Malachi C. Topping, *American Broadcasting: A Source Book on the History of Radio and Television* (New York: Hastings House, 1975), p. 522.

15. Joshua Cho, "Web Advertisers Undeterred by Clutter, Saturation," *Cable World*, www.cableworld.com/articles/news99/1999060717.htm; Christopher Saunders, "CMR: Web Ads Up from Last Year," August 28, 2002, www.internetnews.com/IAR/article.php/1453421, accessed in October 2002.

16. Joe McGinnis, *The Selling of the President, 1968* (New York: Trident Press, 1969).

17. Alan C. Miller and T. Christen Miller, "Election Was Decisive in Arena of Spending," December 8, 2000, www.latimes.com.

18. Ralph L. Lowenstein and John C. Merrill, *Macromedia: Mission, Message and Morality* (New York: Longman, 1990), p. 80.

19. Michael L. Rothschild, *Advertising: From Fundamentals to Strategies* (Lexington, MA: D.C. Heath, 1987), p. 755.

20. "Senate Opens Two-Week Debate on Campaign Finance," March 19, 2001, www.cnn.com.

21. "Darts and Laurels," *Columbia Journalism Review* (March–April 1995): 22.

22. Mike Ivey, "When Science Takes Its Place in the Dairy Case," *Capital Times* [Madison, WI], (March 23, 1999): 1C.

23. J. Paul Peter and Jerry C. Olson, *Consumer Behavior in Marketing Strategy*, 3rd ed. (Homewood, IL: Irwin, 1993), pp. 266–286.

24. Michael Shudson, *Advertising, the Uneasy Persuasion: Its Dubious Impact on American Society* (New York: Basic Books, 1984).

25. Leo Bogart, *Press and Public* (Hillsdale, NJ: Lawrence Erlbaum Associates, 1989), p. 166.

26. Stephen Lacy and Todd F. Simon, *The Economics and Regulation of United States Newspapers* (Norwood, NJ: Ablex, 1993), pp. 41–42.

27. *Veronis, Suhler & Associates Communication Industry Forecast* (New York: Veronis, Suhler & Associates, 1993).

28. Rothschild, *Advertising: From Fundamentals to Strategies*, p. 729.

29. David W. Nylen, *Advertising: Planning, Implementation & Control* (Cincinnati, OH: Southwestern Publishing), pp. 72–74.

30. "Total U.S. Advertising Volume," Newspaper Association of America, www.naa.org, accessed on July 12, 2002.

31. Abid Ali and Maryanna Dietz, "End of the Line for Free Web?" CNN.com, March 2, 2002, www.cnn.com.

32. John Yaukey, "End of Free," *Lansing State Journal* (April 16, 2002): 6C–10C.

33. "Yahoo! Breaks Losing Streak," CNN.com, July 11, 2002, www.cnn.com.

34. Cho, "Web Advertisers Undeterred by Clutter, Saturation."

35. "Publishers Sue over Pop-up Ads," CNN.com, July 1, 2002, www.cnn.com.

36. Eric N. Berkowitz, Roger A. Kerin, and William Rudelius, *Marketing*, 2nd ed. (Homewood, IL: Irwin, 1989), pp. 579–580.

37. Stuart Elliott, "The Media Business: Advertising, Research Finds Consumers Worldwide Belong to Six Basic Groups That Cross National Lines," *The New York Times* (June 25, 1998): D8.

38. Matt Bean, "Legal Troubles Escalate for Embattled Psychic Network," Court TV, February 22, 2002, www.cnn.com, accessed in October 2002.

39. Scarlet Pruitt, "Search Engines Sued over 'Pay-for-Placement,'" IDG News Service, February 4, 2002, www.cnn.com, accessed in October 2002.

40. Nancy Zuckerbrod, "Cigarette Makers Push Products in Stores," *Lansing State Journal* (May 28, 2002): 7C.

Chapter 5

1. Jonathan Karp, "Decline? What Decline?" *Media Studies Journal* 6:3 (Summer 1992): 45–53.

2. Elizabeth L. Eisenstein, *The Printing Revolution in Early Modern Europe* (Cambridge, England: Cambridge University Press, 1983); David Hall, "The World of Print and Collective Mentality," in *New Directions in American Intellectual History*, John Higham and Paul K. Conkin, eds. (Baltimore: Johns Hopkins University Press, 1980); Jeffery A. Smith, *Printers and Press Freedom: The Ideology of Early American Journalism* (New York: Oxford University Press, 1988).

3. Moira Davison Reynolds, *Uncle Tom's Cabin and Mid-Nineteenth Century United States: Pen and Conscience* (Jefferson, NC: McFarland & Company, 1985); and Thomas F. Gossett, *Uncle Tom's Cabin and American Culture* (Dallas, TX: Southern Methodist University Press, 1985).

4. J. Preston Dickson, *Young Frederick Douglass: The Maryland Years* (Baltimore: Johns Hopkins University Press, 1980).

5. Lewis A. Coser, Charles Kadushin, and Walter W. Powell, *Books: The Culture and Commerce of Publishing* (New York: Basic Books, 1982). This comprehensive volume thoroughly explores the relationship between economics and culture in book publishing.

6. Christine Bold, "Popular Forms I," in *Columbia History of the American Novel*, Emory Elliott, ed. (New York: Columbia University Press, 1991), p. 298. The *Columbia History* is particularly useful for studying genres historically and for understanding content in the context of history.

7. Association of American Publishers, www.publishers.org/industry/index.cfm, accessed March 23, 2003.

8. Bookwire, www.bookwire.com/bookwire/americanbookproduction.htm, accessed on July 18, 2002.

9. John F. Baker, "Reinventing the Book Business," *Publishers Weekly* (March 14, 1994): 36.

10. Don R. LeDuc, *Law of Mass Communications*, 7th ed. (Westbury, NY: Foundation Press, 1992), p. 695; see also John F. Baker, "Reinventing the Book Business."

11. "Paramount's Last Chapter—Not Quite," *U.S. News & World Report* (February 28, 1994); "Business Notes," *Maclean's* (February 28, 1994): 40; Mark Landler and Gail DeGeorge, "Sumner at the Summit," *Business Week* (February 28, 1994): 32; John Greenwald, "The Deal That Forced Diller to Fold," *Time* (February 28, 1994): 50; Don Jeffrey, "Industry Awaits Fallout of Paramount Deal; Victors in Takeover Battle Now Must Pay Down Debt," *Billboard* (February 26, 1994): 6.

12. "Titanic Tidings," July 12, 2002, www.publishersweekly.com/articles/19980914_70408.asp.

13. "O, No: Oprah Ditches Book Club," abcnews.com, http://more.abcnews.go.com/sections/us/dailynews/oprah020408.html, accessed July 19, 2002.

14. Trudi Rosenblum, "Audiobooks: Soaring Upward," *Publishers Weekly* (June 11, 2001): 38.

15. John F. Baker, "Reinventing the Book Business," *Publishers Weekly* (March 14, 1994): 36.

16. *Publishers Weekly* (May 3, 1999): 10.

17. "The Book Marketplace II," in *Reading in America: Literature and Social History*, Cathy Davidson, ed. (Baltimore: Johns Hopkins University Press, 1989), pp. 687–688.

18. http://weeklywire.com/disk$ebony/tw/www/ww/09–29–97/knox_feat.html, September 29, 1997.

19. "Amazon Finds Profits in Outsourcing," trendlines, October 15, 2002, www.cio.com/archive/101502/tl_ec.html, accessed on December 13, 2002.

20. Daisy Maryles, "Embraced by the List: Bestsellers 94," *Publishers Weekly* (January 2, 1995): 50+.
21. Jim Milliot, "It's All about Content," *Publishers Weekly* (June 24, 1996): 28–30.

Chapter 6

1. Guido H. Stempel III, "Where People Really Get Most of Their News," *Newspaper Research Journal* 12 (Fall 1991): 2–9.
2. Thomas C. Leonard, *The Power of the Press* (Oxford, England: Oxford University Press, 1986), p. 4.
3. U.S. Senate (May 1832), *Postage on Newspapers*, Report 147, 22, 1, cited in Richard Kielbowicz, "Modernization, Communication Policy, and the Geopolitics of News, 1820–1860," in *Media Voices: An Historical Perspective*, Jean Folkerts, ed. (New York: Macmillan, 1992), p. 130.
4. Richard Kielbowicz, *News in the Mail: The Press, Post Office and Public Information, 1700–1860* (Westport, CT: Greenwood Press, 1989).
5. *New York Sun* (September 3, 1833): 1.
6. Gerald Baldasty, *The Commercialization of News in the Nineteenth Century* (Madison: University of Wisconsin Press, 1992).
7. Stephen Lacy, "Understanding and Serving Newspaper Readers: The Problem of Fuzzy Market Structure," *Newspaper Research Journal* 14:2 (Spring 1993): 55–67.
8. Newpaper Association of America, "Readership Statistics," www.naa.org, accessed on October 1, 2002.
9. Newpaper Association of America, "Readership Statistics."
10. Adam Clymer, speech, George Washington University Graduate School of Political Management class, "Politics and the Media," 1994.
11. Tim Jones, "Alternative Press Faces Big Choices on Future," *Chicago Tribune* (November 15, 1998): sec. 5, pp. 1, 7.
12. William Blankenburg and Gary W. Ozanich, "The Effects of Public Ownership on the Financial Performance of Newspaper Corporations," *Journalism Quarterly* 70 (Spring 1993): 68–75; and Stephen Lacy, Mary Alice Shaver, and Charles St. Cyr, "The Effects of Public Ownership and Newspaper Competition on the Financial Performance of Newspaper Corporations: A Replication and Extension," *Journalism & Mass Communication Quarterly* 73 (Summer 1996): 332–341.
13. Stephen Lacy and Todd F. Simon, *The Economics and Regulation of United States Newspapers* (Norwood, NJ: Ablex, 1993).
14. Lacy and Simon, *Economics and Regulation of United States Newspapers*.
15. Joe Nicholson, "News Industry Anguish over Crumbling Credibility," *Editor & Publisher* (July 18, 1998): 8.
16. David Noack, "ASNE: How to Make Friends and Win Back Skeptical Readers," *Editor & Publisher* (December 19, 1998): 9; for 1999 ASNE follow-up story, see "National Time-Out for Diversity and Accuracy," www.asne.org, accessed on December 25, 2002.
17. Associated Press Managing Editors, www.apme.com/credibility02/right.html.
18. Stephen Lacy, James M. Stephens, and Stan Soffin, "The Future of the African-American Press: A Survey of African-American Newspaper Managers," *Newspaper Research Journal* 12:3 (Summer 1991): 8–19.
19. Barbara K. Henritze, *Bibliographic Checklist of African-American Newspapers* (Baltimore: Genealogical Publishing, 1994).
20. Tanya Gazdik, "Don Coleman Moving toward Full-Service Goal," *Adweek* (August 24, 1998): 5.
21. Walter H. Combs, "African-American Press Provided an Alternative View of Black Life," *The Buffalo News* (February 8, 1999): 11A.
22. Carolyn Foreman, *Oklahoma Imprints, 1835–1907: Printing before Statehood* (Norman: University of Oklahoma Press, 1936), cited in Sharon Murphy, "Neglected Pioneers: 19th Century Native American Newspapers," *Journalism History* 4:3 (Autumn 1977): 79.
23. James P. Danky and Maureen E. Hady, *Native American Periodicals and Newspapers, 1828–1982* (Westport, CT: Greenwood Press, 1984).
24. Richard LaCourse, "A Native Press Primer," *Columbia Journalism Review* (November/December 1998): 51.
25. Karen Lincoln Michel, "Repression on the Reservation," *Columbia Journalism Review* (November/December 1998): 48–50, 52.
26. Carlos E. Cortes, "The Mexican-American Press," in *The Ethnic Press in the United States: A Historical Analysis and Handbook*, Sally M. Miller, ed. (Westport, CT: Greenwood Press, 1987), pp. 247–260.
27. Herminio Rios and Guadalupe Castillo, "Toward a True Chicano Bibliography: Mexican-American Newspapers: 1848–1942," *El Grito: A Journal of Contemporary Mexican-American Thought* 3 (Summer 1970): 17–24.
28. Allied Media Corporation, www.allied-media.com/Publications/hispanic-publications.htm, accessed on December 25, 2002.
29. Felix Gutierrez, "Spanish Language Media in the U.S.," *Caminos* 5 (January 1984): 38–41, 65–66, cited in Cortes, "The Mexican-American Press."
30. "Darts and Laurels," *Columbia Journalism Review* (March/April 1998): 15.
31. Randal A. Beam, "What It Means to Be a Market-Oriented Newspaper," *Newspaper Research Journal* 19:3 (Summer 1998): 2–20.
32. John T. Russial, "Topic-Team Performance: A Content Study," *Newspaper Research Journal* 18:1–2 (Winter/Spring 1997): 126–144.
33. Leo Bogart, *Press and Public*, 2nd ed. (Hillsdale, NJ: Lawrence Erlbaum Associates, 1989), p. 196.
34. Bogart, *Press and Public*, p. 322.
35. "Credibility in Action," report of the Associated Press Managing Editors National Credibility Roundtables, 2002, www.2peme.com, accessed on December 25, 2002.
36. Matt Villano, "Teenage Wasteland?" *Editor & Publisher Interactive*, May 27, 1999, www.mediainfo.com.
37. Villano, "Teenage Wasteland?"
38. Howard Kurtz, "Slicing, Dicing News to Attract the Young," *The Washington Post* (January 6, 1991): A-1, 8.

39. David Noack, "Kansas Paper Bucks Free Content Trend," *Editor & Publisher Interactive,* June 1, 1999, www.mediainfo.com/ephome.

40. Steve Outing, "Web Community News Finds Its Way to Print," *Editor & Publisher Interactive,* April 26, 1999, www.mediainfo/ephome.

41. Quint Randle, Lucinda Davenport, and Howard Bossen, "Prepared for Crisis? Breaking Coverage of September 11th on Newspaper Web Sites," paper presented at the Association for Education in Journalism and Mass Communication annual meeting, August 7–10, 2002, Miami Beach, Florida.

42. These figures are taken from David H. Weaver and G. Cleveland Wilhoit, *The American Journalist in the 1990s* (Mahwah, NJ: Lawrence Erlbaum Associates, 1996) and "More Industry Facts 1998," National Newspaper Association, www.naa.org/info/facts/32html.

43. "Minorities in the Newsroom," *ASNE Bulletin* (September 1993): 26–29.

Chapter 7

1. Ellen Mazo, "The Look of 50: Modern Maturity Puts a New Face on Aging," *Pittsburgh Post-Gazette* (July 13, 1999): G-2 (via Lexis-Nexis).

2. Magazine Publishers of America, www.magazine.org, accessed on December 25, 2002

3. Richard Kielbowicz, *News in the Mail: The Press, Post Office, and Public Information, 1700–1860s* (New York: Greenwood Press, 1989), pp. 130–132.

4. Theodore Peterson, *Magazines in the Twentieth Century* (Urbana: University of Illinois Press, 1972), p. 60.

5. Peterson, *Magazines in the Twentieth Century,* p. 60.

6. Magazine Publishers of America, www.magazine.org/index.html, accessed in October 2002.

7. American Business Press, www.americanbusinesspress.com/resources/Facts.htm, accessed in October 2002.

8. Veronis, Suhler & Associates, "Communications Industry Forecast, Magazine Publishing," 1995, p. 275; Magazine Publishers of America, www.magazine.org/index.html, accessed in October 2002.

9. Veronis and Suhler, p. 276.

10. American Business Press, www.americanbusinesspress.com/resources/Facts.htm, accessed in October 2002.

11. Lorraine Calvacca, "Shared Approach: Similarities between Association and Commercial Publications," *Folio* (March 15, 1994): 5.

12. Samir Husni, "How Magazines Are Born," *Folio* (October 1, 1991): 54–55.

13. Bruce Sheiman, "From Start-up Idea to Magazine," *Folio* (January 15, 1994): 118.

14. Some examples of combination financing are from Gloria Steinem, "Sex, Lies & Advertising," *Ms.* (July/August 1990): 18–28; Michael Hoyt, "When the Walls Come Tumbling Down," *Columbia Journalism Review* (March/April 1990): 35–41.

15. Deirdre Carmody, *New York Times,* as it appeared in "Lear's Lived and Died on a Whim," *Houston Chronicle* (March 15, 1994), sec. Houston, p. 1.

16. Magazine Publishers Association, www.magazine.org/index.html and www.magazine.org/mpa/content/map.handbook/advertising/fcb_media_research.html.

17. Reed Phillips, "What We Learned from the Recession: Or Should Have," *Folio* (February 1, 1993): 61.

18. "$alaries in the City: What New Yorkers Make: A Survey up and down the Pay Ladder of 33 of the Town's Professions," www.newyorkmetro.com/nymetro/news/bizfinance/finance/features/4086/, accessed on September 17, 2002.

19. Bruce Sheiman, "Back to the Future of Magazines," *Folio* (October 15, 1995): 71–72.

20. American Demographers, Media Central, www.inside.com/default.asp?entity=AmericanDemo.

21. Loudon Wainwright, *Great American Magazines* (New York: Alfred A. Knopf, 1986).

22. *Folio,* September 5, 2002, http://foliomag.com/ar/marketing_glossies_unmagazines/index.htm, accessed on September 22, 2002.

23. Susan Thea Posnock, "New Kids on the Block," *Folio* (June 2002): 37–38.

24. Jillian S. Ambroz, "Integration and the Digital Duel," *Folio* (March 2002): 38–40.

25. Magazine Publishers Association, www.magazine.org/aboutMPA/membership/mpa_intl_fact_sheet.html, accessed in October 2002.

Chapter 8

1. Rick Lyman, "Job Openings in Hollywood: Heroes Wanted," *The New York Times,* August 4, 2002, www.nytimes.com.

2. Douglas Gomery, "Hollywood's Business," in *American Media,* Philip S. Cook, Douglas Gomery, and Lawrence W. Lickty, eds. (Washington, DC: Wilson Center Press, 1989), p. 94.

3. Bruno Bettelheim, Patricia Wise Lecture at the American Film Institute, Washington, DC, February 3, 1981, cited in *Hollywood: Legend and Reality,* Michael Webb, ed. (Boston: Little, Brown, in association with the Smithsonian Institution Traveling Exhibition Service, 1986), p. 17.

4. Louis Giannetti and Scott Eyman, *Flashback: A Brief History of Film* (Englewood Cliffs, NJ: Prentice-Hall, 1986), p. 15.

5. From an original transcript in the collection of Gordon Hendricks, New York, cited in *The American Film Industry,* rev. ed., Tino Balio, ed. (Madison: The University of Wisconsin Press, 1985), p. 45.

6. Russell Merritt, "Nickelodeon Theatres, 1905–1914: Building an Audience for the Movies," in Balio, *The American Film Industry,* p. 86.

7. Robert Anderson, "The Motion Picture Patents Company: A Reevaluation," in Balio, *The American Film Industry,* p. 134.

8. Douglas Gomery, "The Coming of Sound: Technological Change in the American Film Industry," in Balio, *The American Film Industry,* p. 230.

9. Giannetti and Eyman, *Flashback,* p. 372.

10. Clayton R. Koppes and Gregory D. Black, *Hollywood Goes to War: How Politics, Profits and Propaganda Shaped World War II Movies* (New York: Free Press, 1987).

11. Koppes and Black, "Blacks, Loyalty, and Motion-Picture Propaganda in World War II," *Journal of American History* (September, 1986): 394.

12. DeWayne Wickham, "Bassett Criticism Has Its Merits," *USA Today*, July 8, 2002, www.usatoday.com.

13. Jacquelyn Kilpatrick, *Celluloid Indians: Native American on Film* (Lincoln: University of Nebraska Press, 1999), pp. xv–xviii.

14. Joann Faung Jean Lee, *Asian American Actors: Oral Histories from Stage, Screen, and Television* (Jefferson, NC: McFarland & Sons, 2000).

15. Daniel J. Leab, *From Sambo to Superspade: The Black Experience in Motion Pictures* (Boston: Houghton Mifflin, 1975), pp. 70–72.

16. Leab, *From Sambo to Superspade*, pp. 173–174.

17. Gary D. Keller, *Hispanics and United States Films: An Overview and Handbook* (Tempe, AZ: Bilingual Press, 1994), pp. 195–196.

18. Mark A. Reid, *Redefining Black Film* (Berkeley: University of California Press, 1993).

19. Jacquie Jones, "The New Ghetto Aesthetic," in *Mediated Messages and African-American Culture: Contemporary Issues*, Venise T. Berry and Carmen L. Manning-Miller, eds. (Thousand Oaks, CA: Sage, 1996), pp. 40–51.

20. Gomery, "Hollywood's Business," p. 98.

21. Bruce Owen and Steve Wildman, *Video Economics* (Cambridge, MA: Harvard University Press, 1992).

22. David Germain, "Hollywood's 2001 Odyssey: Record Bucks, Big Franchises, Fallout from Terrorists Attacks," Associated Press (December 31, 2001), via Lexis-Nexis.

23. "Signs of a Slip at Box Office," *USA Today*, August 6, 2002, www.usatoday.com.

24. Fred Pampel, Dan Fost, and Sharon O'Malley, "Marketing the Movies," *American Demographics* (March 1994): 48.

25. Robert K. Elder, "The Teenager's Seal of Approval," *Chicago Tribune* (June 9, 2002): 7:12.

26. Adam Geller, "675 of Loew's Cineplex Movie Screens Going Dark," *Lansing State Journal* (January 24, 2001): 8C.

27. J. D. Reed, "Plugging Away in Hollywood," *Time* (January 2, 1989): 103, as cited in *International Journal of Advertising* (January, 1993): 1–3.

28. Reed, "Plugging Away in Hollywood" D.C. McGill, "Questions Raised on 'Product Placements,'" *New York Times* (April 13, 1989): D18; J. Schlosberg, "Film Flam Men," *Inside Media* (June 13, 1990): 34.

29. Josh Grossberg, "Minority Reports Product Placement," E! Online news, June 21, 2002, www.eonline.com/news/Items/Pf/0,1527,10138,00.html.

30. Gomery, "Hollywood's Business," p. 107.

31. Daniel Cerone, "'Jafar': New Journeys to Profitland?" *Los Angeles Times* (May 20, 1994): Home Edition, F1.

32. Bernard Weinraub, "Islamic Nations Move to Keep Out Schindler's List," *New York Times* (April 7, 1994): C15.

33. Robert Sklar, *Film: An International History of the Medium* (New York: Harry N. Abrams, 1993), pp. 502–506; and David A. Cook, *A History of Narrative Film*, 2nd ed. (New York: W. W. Norton, 1990), pp. 816–820.

34. Suniti Singh, "Devdas to Break Hollywood Records," *BBC News*, June 17, 2002, http://nes.bbc.co.bk.

35. Sklar, *Film: An International History of the Medium*, pp. 508–517.

36. "Movies on Demand to Be Coming Attraction for Broadband," *Tvinsite*, June 5, 2002, www.insite.com.

37. David Hayes, "Movie Theaters Slow to Adopt Digital Format," *Kansas City.com*, May 14, 2002, www.kansascity.com.

Chapter 9

1. Bill McConnell, "Rapper Sues FCC," *Broadcasting & Cable*, Febuary, 4, 2002, www.broadcastingcable.com.

2. Bill McConnell, "New Rules for Risqué Business," *Broadcasting & Cable*, March 4, 2002, www.broadcastingcable.com.

3. *Broadcasting & Cable Yearbook* (New Providence, NJ: Bowker Publications, 2001), p. D639, and more than 12,000 people work in commercial radio news; Vernon Stone, "News Operations at U.S. Radio Stations," August 3, 2002, www.missouri.edu/~jourvs/graops.html.

4. Thomas W. Hoffer, "Nathan B. Stubblefield and His Wireless Telephone," *Journal of Broadcasting* 15 (Summer 1971): 317–329.

5. Elliot N. Sivowitch, "A Technological Survey of Broadcasting's Prehistory, 1876–1920," *Journal of Broadcasting* 15 (Winter 1970–1971): 1–20.

6. George H. Gibson, *Public Broadcasting: The Role of the Federal Government, 1912–76* (New York: Praeger, 1977), pp. 2–3.

7. Federal Communication Commission, "Early History of Network Broadcasting (1923–1926) and the National Broadcasting Company," *Report on Chain Broadcasting* (Commission Order No. 37, Docket 5060, May 1941), pp. 5–20.

8. Lawrence W. Lichty and Malachi C. Topping, "Audiences," in *American Broadcasting: A Source Book on the History of Radio and Television*, Lawrence W. Lichty and Malachi C. Topping, eds. (New York: Hastings House, 1975), pp. 445–457.

9. John W. Spalding, "1928: Radio Becomes a Mass Advertising Medium," *Journal of Broadcasting* 8 (Winter 1963–1964): 31–44.

10. Gibson, *Public Broadcasting*, p. 21.

11. David H. Hosley, *As Good as Any: Foreign Correspondence on American Radio, 1930–1940* (Westport, CT: Greenwood Press, 1984), pp. 8–9. See also Jean Folkerts and Dwight Teeter, *Voices of a Nation*, 2nd ed. (New York: Macmillan, 1994), pp. 382–385.

12. Edwin Emery and Michael Emery, *The Press and America*, 4th ed. (Englewood Cliffs, NJ: Prentice Hall, 1978), p. 400.

13. "Total U.S. Advertising Volume," Newspaper Association of America, 2002, www.naa.org.

14. "Radio Listening Highest among Well-Educated, Upper Income Consumers According to Total Audience Data from Arbitron RADAR 73," Arbitron press release, June 6, 2002, www.arbitron.com/newsroom/archive?06_18_02.htm.

15. Bill McConnell, "Radio Giants Want More Turf," *Broadcasting & Cable*, March 8, 2002, www.broadcastingcable.com.

16. Bill McConnell, "FCC Tries, Tries Again," *Broadcasting & Cable*, July 15, 2002, www.broadcastingcable.com.

17. *Broadcasting & Cable Yearbook 2001* (New Providence, NJ: Bowker Publications, 2001), p. D639.

18. "Radio Listening Highest among Well-Educated, Upper Income Consumers According to Total Audience Data from Arbitron RADAR 73," Arbitron press release, June 6, 2002, www.arbitron.com/newsroom/archive?06_18_02.htm.

19. "Almost a Quarter of Americans Are Tuning into Talk Radio," Scarborough Research press release, July 14, 2002, www.scarborough.com.

20. Glen T. Cameron, Glen J. Nowak, and Dean M. Krugman, "The Competitive Position of Newspapers in the Local Retail Market," *Newspaper Research Journal* 14 (Summer–Fall 1993): 70–81.

21. Bruce Girard, "Introduction," in *A Passion for Radio,* Bruce Girard, ed. (Montreal: Black Rose Books, 1992), p. 6.

22. Bruce Porter, "Has Success Spoiled NPR?," *Columbia Journalism Review* (September–October 1990): 26–32.

23. *Frequently Asked Questions about Public Broadcasting 1997* (Washington, DC: Corporation for Public Broadcasting, 1997), p. 11.

24. *Frequently Asked Questions about Public Broadcasting,* p. 9.

25. Eric Boehlert, "Fund Cuts Could Hurt Artists, Labels: Public Radio under Attack in Congress," *Billboard* (March 18, 1995): 1, 85.

26. Vernon Stone, "News Operations at U.S. Radio Stations," August 3, 2002, www.missouri.edu/~jourvs/graops.html.

27. "Almost a Quarter of Americans Are Tuning in to Talk Radio," Scarborough Research press release, July 14, 2002, www.scarorough.com.

28. Steve Emmons, "Just What Do Talk Shows Listen For?" *Los Angeles Times,* Orange County edition (May 10, 1995): E1.

29. Emmons, "Just What Do Talk Shows Listen For?"

30. Peter Laufer, *Inside Talk Radio: America's Voice or Just Hot Air?* (Secaucus, NJ: Carol Publishing Group, 1995).

31. Donald R. Browne, *International Broadcasting: The Limits of a Limitless Medium* (New York: Praeger, 1982), p. 48.

32. George Wedell and Philip Crookes, *Radio 2000* (Manchester, England: The European Institute for the Media, 1991), p. 52.

33. *Australian Commercial Radio—A Study of Listener Attitudes* (Sydney: Federation of Australian Radio Broadcasters, 1979).

34. Michael Clancy, "Scrambled Signals: Deregulation Spells End of Era for Valley Radio," *The Arizona Republic* (August 15, 1999): E1.

35. Bill McConnell, "Radio Giants Want More Turf," *Broadcasting & Cable,* March 8, 2002, www.broadcastingcable.com.

36. Steve McClellan, "Clearly Unsettling," *Broadcasting & Cable,* July 29, 2002, www.broadcastingcable.com; and Bill McConnell, "Clear Channel Chiefs Sign Financial Affidavits," *Broadcasting & Cable,* August 2, 2002, www.broadcastingcable.com.

37. Dan Trigoboff, "That Dammed Streaming," *Broadcasting & Cable,* May 14, 2001, www.broadcastingcable.com.

38. Dan Trigoboff, "That Dammed Streaming."

39. Paige Albiniak, "Web Radio Rate Set," *Broadcasting & Cable,* February 25, 2002, www.broadcastingcable.com.

40. Albiniak, "Web Radio Rate Set."

41. Paige Albiniak, "Keeping the Streams Alive," *Broadcasting & Cable,* July 1, 2002, www.broadcastingcable.com.

42. Paige Albiniak, "Target: Radio Birds," *Broadcasting & Cable,* December 31, 2001, www.broadcastingcable.com.

43. *Broadcasting & Cable,* January 14, 2002, www.broadcastingcable.com.

44. Bill McConnell, "News Rules for Risqué Business," *Broadcasting & Cable,* March 4, 2002, www.broadcastingcable.com.

Chapter 10

1. Parents Television Council, "Harsh Reality: Unscripted TV Reality Shows Offensive to Families," *PTC Special Reports,* October 3, 2002, www.parentstv.org.

2. Christopher H. Sterling and John M. Kittross, *Stay Tuned: A Concise History of American Broadcasting,* 2nd ed. (Belmont, CA: Wadsworth, 1990), p. 576.

3. Lynn Spigel, *Make Room for TV* (Chicago: University of Chicago Press, 1992).

4. For a discussion of the early debate over technical standards, see Sterling and Kittross, *Stay Tuned,* pp. 526–527.

5. Sterling and Kittross, *Stay Tuned,* pp. 265, 267.

6. *Broadcasting-Telecasting* (December 21, 1953): 29, cited in James Scofield O'Rourke IV, "The Development of Color Television: A Study in the Freemarket Process," *Journalism History* 9:3–4 (Autumn–Winter 1982): 78–85, 106.

7. For a thorough discussion of legal issues from 1945 to 1952, see Chapter 7, "Era of Great Change," in Sterling and Kittross, *Stay Tuned.*

8. James L. Baughman, *The Republic of Mass Culture: Journalism, Filmmaking, and Broadcasting in America since 1941* (Baltimore: Johns Hopkins University Press, 1992), p. 54.

9. Sterling and Kittross, *Stay Tuned,* p. 278.

10. Melvin Patrick Ely, *The Adventures of Amos 'n' Andy* (New York: Free Press, 1991), pp. 1–10. The quote is cited in Ely from a resolution in Herbert L. Wright, letter to NAACP Youth Councils, College Chapters and State Youth Conferences, July 19, 1951, in National Association for the Advancement of Colored People Papers, II, A, 479, Manuscript Division, Library of Congress.

11. Stephen Fox, *The Mirror Makers* (New York: Random House, 1984), p. 212.

12. Walter Karp, "The Quiz-Show Scandal," *American Heritage* (May–June 1989): 77–88.

13. Fox, *The Mirror Makers,* p. 215.

14. Richard Morin and Claudia Deane, "Why the Florida Exit Polls Were Wrong," *washingtonpost.com,* November 8, 2000, www.washingtonpost.com.

15. Stuart Taylor Jr., "Witch-Hunt or Whitewash?" *The American Lawyer* (April 1995): 60.
16. "Fox and Murdoch Win a Big One," *U.S. News & World Report* (May 15, 1995): 17+.
17. Sydney W. Head and Christopher Sterling, *Broadcasting in America: A Survey of Electronic Media*, 2nd ed. (Boston: Houghton Mifflin, 1996), pp. 82–85.
18. "U.S. Advertising Expenditures—All Media," *Facts about Newspapers 2002*, Newspaper Association of America, www.naa.org, accessed in October 2002.
19. "Majority of Cable Subs Will Upgrade to Digital by 2004," PricewaterhouseCoopers, August 1, 2002, www.pwcglobal.com.
20. Stephanie McKinnon, "Looking Ahead for PBS," *Lansing State Journal* (January 19, 1995): B1, B5.
21. "PBS Discusses Advertising with FCC," CNN.com, July 10, 2002, www.cnn.com.
22. Marc Peyser, "Why the Sopranos Sing," *Newsweek* (April 2, 2001): 8–57.
23. Rebecca Pirito, "New Markets for Cable TV," *American Demographics* (June 1995): 40.
24. "FAQ-Research and Product Questions," Nielsen Media, October 26, 2002, www.nielsenmedia.com.
25. "Nielsen Media Research Top 20," *YahooTV*, October 26, 2002, tv.yahoo.com/nielsen/.
26. Clarence Page, "Networks Give Blacks Excuse to Nix TV," *Lansing State Journal* (July 21, 1999): 4A.
27. Tom Long, "Total Black Shows on TV—7," *Lansing State Journal* (May 11, 2002): 5D.
28. William B. Johnson, "The Coming Glut of Phone Lines," *Fortune* (January 7, 1988): 96–97.
29. "Majority of Cable Subs Will Upgrade to Digital by 2004," PricewaterhouseCoppers, August 1, 2002, www.pwcglobal.
30. Paige Albiniak, "Is DBS Competition in the Offing?" *Broadcasting & Cable*, April 29, 2002, www.tvinsite.com.
31. Marc Peyer, "Prime Time Crime," *Newsweek* (June 24, 2002): 82–83.
32. Bill Carter, "Mom, Dad and Kids Reclaim TV Perch," *The New York Times* (October, 15, 2002): C1, C5.
33. Gannett News Service, "TV's Family Ratings System Confusing, Draws Little Attention," *Tucson Citizen*, October 22, 2002, www.tucsoncitizen.com.
34. "MSU Expert Calls TV Ratings Confusing, Unreliable," Press release from Michigan State University Media Communications, June 18, 2001. www.msu.edu/media/releases/june01/tvratings.html.
35. Stuart Elliott, "Advertising," *The New York Times* (October 2, 2002): C9.
36. Ted Kulfan, "Marlboro Is Ordered to Butt Out," *The Detroit News* (June 7, 1995): 1B.
37. Martin Renzhofer, "Renzhofer: NBC Bans Hard-Liquor Ads but Soak in Beer's Riches," *The Salt Lake Tribune*, March 29, 2002, www.sltrib.com.
38. Rana Dogar, "Changing Channels," *Newsweek* (June 7, 1999): 64.
39. Jo Johnson, "Embattled French Film Empire Fights Back," *Financial Times* (May 18, 2002): 6.
40. Eric A. Taub, "The Big Picture on Digital TV: It's Still Fuzzy," *The New York Times* (September 12, 2002): G1.
41. Steve Smith, "Some Good HDTV Programming News," *TWICE* (September 16, 2002): 12.
42. Bill McConnell, "Critics: FCC Stacks Dereg Deck," *Broadcasting & Cable* (October 7, 2002): 10–11.
43. Long, "Total Black Shows on TV—7."

Chapter 11

1. H. Wiley Hitchcock, *Music in the United States: A Historical Introduction*, 3rd ed. (Englewood Cliffs, NJ: Prentice Hall, 1988), p. 96.
2. David Ewen, *Panorama of American Popular Music* (Englewood Cliffs, NJ: Prentice Hall, 1957), p. 58.
3. Ewen, *Panorama of American Popular Music*, p. 145.
4. John Rublowsky, *Popular Music* (New York: Basic Books, 1967), pp. 63–80.
5. Hitchcock, *Music in the United States*, p. 141.
6. Ronald L. Davis, *A History of Music in American Life: The Gilded Years, 1865–1920*, Vol. 2 (Huntington, NY: Robert Krieger, 1980), p. 63.
7. Hitchcock, *Music in the United States*, p. 276.
8. Hitchcock, *Music in the United States*, pp. 276–277.
9. Eric Berman, "The Godfathers of Rap," *Rolling Stone* (December 23, 1993): 137–142, 180.
10. Gale Research, Inc., "Paul Simon," *Newsmakers* (October 1992).
11. Hitchcock, *Music in the United States*, pp. 286–291.
12. John Lannert, "U.S. Latin Market Slows a Bit after Explosive Growth," *Billboard* (September 4, 1999), via Nexis-Lexis.
13. Brendan Kelly, "The New Latin Sound: An Infectious Innovation Is Shaking Up Dancefloors," *Montreal Gazette* (July 6, 2002): F1.
14. Joshua Kosman and Michael Dougan, "Classical Music: Tuning Up for the 21st Century," *San Francisco Chronicle* (July 15, 2002): D1.
15. John von Rhein, "It's Not Over, Beethoven," *Chicago Tribune* (January 10, 1997), sec. 7, pp. 1–13.
16. John von Rhein, "It's Not Over, Beethoven." p. 14.
17. David Lieberman, "Piracy or Fair Use?" *Lansing State Journal* (April 23, 2002): 6C, 7C.
18. *Veronis, Suhler & Associates Communication Industry Forecast*, 7th ed. (New York: Veronis, Suhler & Associates, 1993), pp. 23–24; and Robert Scally, "NARM Likely to Be Venue for Airing Digital Issues," *Discount Store News* (March 8, 1999): 4.
19. Geoffrey P. Hull, "The Structure of the Recorded Music Industry," in *The Media and the Entertainment Industries*, Albert N. Greco, ed. (Boston: Allyn and Bacon, 2000), p. 80.
20. Mike Hughes, "For the Record: Local Artists Are Making Music Their Way, the New Way," *Lansing State Journal* (November 17, 2002): 1D, 3D.
21. William Moylan, *The Art of Recording* (New York: Van Nostrand Reinhold, 1992), pp. 136–139.
22. Russell Sanjek, *From Print to Plastic: Publishing and Promoting America's Popular Music (1900–1980)* (New York: Brooklyn College of the City of New York, 1983), p. 54.
23. Keith Negus, *Producing Pop: Culture and Conflict in the Popular Music Industry* (London: Edward Arnold, 1992), p. 13.

24. "Rock and Roll Forever," *Newsweek* (July 5, 1994): 48.
25. Kerry Segrave, *Payola in the Music Business: A History from 1880–1991* (Jefferson, NC: McFarland, 1994), pp. 92–93.
26. Fredric Dannen, *Hit Men: Power Brokers and Fast Money inside the Music Business* (New York: Times Books, 1990).
27. Laura Randall, "MP3.com's Scheme to Let Artists Bid for Time Upsets Loyalists," *National Post* (October 19, 1999): C12.
28. Edna Gundersen, "Any Way You Spin It, the Music Biz Is in Trouble," *USA Today* (June 5, 2002): 1–2.
29. Joshua Klein, "Artists Taking Matters into Their Hands," *Chicago Tribune* (June 2, 2002): 7:9.
30. James Haskins, *One Nation under a Groove* (New York: Hyperion Books), pp. 65–86.
31. Haskins, *One Nation*, pp. 101–107.
32. Christopher John Farley, "Hip-Hop Nation," *Time* (February 8, 1999): 56.
33. Tony Mitchell, "Another Root—Hip Hop outside the USA," in *Global Noise: Rap and Hip-Hop outside the USA,* Tony Mitchell, ed. (Middletown CT: Wesleyan University Press), 1–2.
34. Jon Bream, "Lilith Will End Its Music on a High Note: In Its Three Years, the Fair of Female Musicians Has Changed Landscape for Music Business—and Women," *Star Tribune* (August 25, 1999): 1A.
35. Jim Farber, "Newcomers Redefining Gender Rap: Debuts by Eve and Sole Prove That Sexy's Back," *Daily News* [New York] (August 30, 1999): 42.

Chapter 12

1. Report of the Pew Foundation's Project on the Internet and American Life, "One Year Later: September 11 and the Internet," www.pewinternet.org/reports/reports.asp?Report=69&Section=ReportLevel1&Field=Level1ID&ID=304, accessed on November 13, 2002.
2. Vannevar Bush, "As We May Think," *Atlantic Monthly* (July 1945), via America Online, accessed in July 2000.
3. Larry Press, "Before the Altair: The History of Personal Computing," *Communications of the ACM* (September 1993): 27+, via Lexis-Nexis.
4. Press, "Before the Altair." See also D. C. Engelbart and W. K. English, "A Research Center for Augmenting Human Intellect," *Proceedings of the 1968 Fall Joint Computer Conference* (Washington, DC: Thompson Book Co.), pp. 395–410.
5. Eugene Marlow, "The Electrovisual Manager: Media and American Corporate Management," *Business Horizons* (March 1994): 61+, via Lexis-Nexis; see also a web site describing Atanasoff's contributions at www.lib.iastate.edu/arch/jva.html.
6. Cited in Denise W. Gurer, "Pioneering Women in Computer Science," *Communications of the Association for Computing Machinery* (January 1995): 58.
7. Gurer, "Pioneering Women," p. 50.
8. Michael Swaine, "The Programmer Paradigm," *Dr. Dobbs' Journal of Software Tools*, p. 109+, via Lexis-Nexis.
9. Robyn Greenspan, "Media Mixing for the Multicultural Market," http://cyberatlas.internet.com/big_picture/demographics/article/0,,5901_768141,00.html, accessed on January 12, 2003, compiled by Cyberatlas.
10. For a full discussion of the network, see "What Is the Internet?" in Ed Krol, *The Whole Internet User's Guide and Catalog* (Sebastopol, CA: O'Reilly & Associates, 1992).
11. Christine Frey, "Online Sales Rose Almost 20% in '01," *Lansing State Journal* (February 24, 2002).
12. "India to Roll Out Cheap, Handheld Computer," cnn.com/SCI-TECH, July 7, 2002, www.cnn.com/2002/TECH/ptech/07/05/india.simp.../index.htm, accessed on July 7, 2002.
13. Jim Stanton, "The Empire That's Easy Money," *Scotsman Publications Ltd. Evening News* [Edinburgh], (November 26, 2002): 4, accessed via Lexis-Nexis.
14. Greenspan, "Media Mixing for the Multicultural Market."
15. P. J. Tichenor, G. A. Donohue, and C. N. Olien, "Mass Media and Differential Growth in Knowledge," *Public Opinion Quarterly* 34 (1970): 159–170.
16. Veronis Suhler Stevenson, "2001 Report Highlights," www.veronissuhler.com/publications/report/highlights2001.html, accessed on January 3, 2003.
17. Jack Kitchner, "When No News Is Good News," *PC Magazine* (March 25, 1997): 30.
18. Saul Hansell, "Can AOL Keep Its Subscribers in a New World of Broadband?" *New York Times* (July 29, 2002): C1.
19. Peter H. Lewis, "Internet Hide and Seek," "Circuits," *New York Times* (April 8, 1999): E1.
20. For more information about electronic privacy and copyright, see Beth Haller, "Quoting in Cyberspace: Privacy and Copyright Issues in Journalistic Use of Computer Networks," Paper presented to the Communications Technology and Policy Division, Association for Education in Journalism and Mass Communication annual meeting, Washington, D.C., 2001.
21. Bob Kemper, "GI's Bosnia Weapons Seem Like a 'Star Wars' Takeoff," *Chicago Tribune* (December 13, 1995): 1.
22. Bill Gates, *The Road Ahead* (New York: Viking, 1995), p. 130.
23. David Astor, "Electronic Delivery of Comics Coming," *Editor & Publisher* (October 16, 1993): 36–37.
24. Wayne Robins, "Online News Consumption Is Flat," *Editor & Publisher*, www.mediainfo.com/editorandpublisher/headlines/articledisplay.jsp?vnucontentid=1532236, accessed in July 2002.
25. Michael Owen-Brown, "Keyring Camera, Video Phone. . . . James Bond Eat Your Heart Out," *The Advertiser* (November 30, 2002), accessed via Lexis-Nexis.
26. Christine Frey, "Online Sales Rose Almost 20% in '01," *Lansing State Journal* (February 24, 2002).
27. Scarlet Pruitt, "Online Casinos Hit Advertising Jackpot," cnn.com, accessed on July 13, 2002.

Chapter 13

1. Doug Brown, "How Much Is Too Much?" *American Journalism Review,* July/August 2002, www.ajr.org.
2. Brown, "How Much Is Too Much?"
3. Brown, "How Much Is Too Much?"
4. Hazel Dicken-Garcia, *Journalistic Standards in Nineteenth-Century America* (Madison: University of Wisconsin Press, 1989), p. 229.
5. See Jean Folkerts's review of Hazel Dicken-Garcia, *Journalistic Standards in Nineteenth-Century America* (Madison: University of Wisconsin Press, 1989) in *Journalism Quarterly* (Autumn 1990). Dicken-Garcia's book outlines the development of ethics within the context of the press as a social institution.
6. Marion Marzolf, *Civilizing Voices: American Press Criticism, 1880–1950* (New York: Longman, 1991), pp. 16–17.
7. Marzolf, *Civilizing Voices,* p. 106.
8. Clifford G. Christians, Kim B. Rotzoll, and Mark Fackler, *Media Ethics,* 2nd ed. (New York: Longman, 1987), pp. 9–17.
9. Cory Johnson, "CNN Goes Ahead with Thompson Hire," *The Industry Standard,* April 27, 2001, www.thestandard.com.
10. Bruce Bartlett, "Andrea Thompson: Actress Now CNN News Reader," National Center for Policy Analysis Idea House, May 9, 2001, www.ncpa.org/oped/bartlett/may0901.html.
11. Carol Guensburg, "When the Story Is about the Owner," *American Journalism Review* (December 1998), http://www.ajr.org, accessed in January 2003.
12. "Diana Zuckerman, "Hype in Health Reporting: 'Checkbook Science' Buys Distortions of Medical News," *Extra: Fairness & Accuracy in Reporting,* September/October 2002, www.fair.org/extra/0209/hype-health.html.
13. "Take 2," *American Journalism Review* (January–February 1996): 15.
14. John Giuffo, "Smoke Gets in Our Eyes: The Globalization Protests and the Befuddled Press," *Columbia Journalism Review,* May 2001, www.cjr.org/year/01/5/giuffo.asp.
15. Sharyn Vane, "Days of Rage," *American Journalism Review,* July/August 2002, www.ajr.org.
16. Paige Albiniak, "Dems Feel Dissed by Cable News Nets," *TVinsite,* March 22, 2002, www.tvinsite.com.
17. Jane Pauley, "Defending Dateline," *Quill* (November–December 1994): 63–69.
18. Kelly Heyboer, "Bad Play for a Great Photo," *American Journalism Review,* May 2002, www.ajr.org.
19. James Warren, "Paths of Janet Cooke and Marion Barry Cross," *Chicago Tribune* (July 4, 1996), Perspectives sec., p. 2.
20. Lori Robertson, "Romancing the Source," *American Journalism Review* (May 2002): 44.
21. Updated versions of these and other industry codes can be found in Conrad C. Fink, *Media Ethics* (Boston: Allyn and Bacon, 1995), or on request from the organizations themselves. Many organizations also publish their codes of ethics on their web sites.
22. Sissela Bok, *Lying: Moral Choice in Public and Private Life* (New York: Random House, 1989), pp. 111–112.
23. Jay Black and Deni Elliott, "Justification Models for Journalists Facing Ethical Dilemmas." Unpublished materials presented at a teaching ethics seminar by Jay Black, Philip Patterson, and Lee Wilkins, Association for Education in Journalism and Mass Communication annual meeting, Kansas City, MO, 1993.
24. Eugene Goodwin, *Groping for Ethics in Journalism,* 2nd ed. (Ames: Iowa State University Press, 1987), pp. 24–25. For additional suggestions on what an ethical journalist should do in various situations, refer to the last sections in each chapter in Gene Goodwin and Ron F. Smith, *Groping for Ethics in Journalism,* 3rd ed. (Ames: Iowa State University Press, 1994).
25. Clifford G. Christians, Mark Fackler, and Kim B. Rotzoll, *Media Ethics: Cases and Moral Reasoning,* 4th ed. (White Plains, NY: Longman, 1995), pp. 3–10.
26. The Potter Box has been adapted and edited many times since Ralph Potter presented it in his 1965 dissertation. This version appears in Black and Elliott, "Justification Models for Journalists Facing Ethical Dilemmas."
27. Myrna Oliver, "Harry Ashmore: Arkansas Editor Fought Segregation," *Los Angeles Times* (January 22, 1998): A20.
28. Richard Blow, "Gagging on 'Deep Throat,' " *TomPaine.common sense,* June 19, 2002, www.tompaine.com.
29. K. Tim Wulfemeyer, "How and Why Anonymous Attribution is Used by *Time* and *Newsweek,*" *Journalism Quarterly* 62 (Spring 1985): 81–86, 126.
30. Michael Doyle, "Opinion: Levy Coverage Rife with Anonymous Sources," *Modbee.com,* June 10, 2002, www.modbee.com.
31. From Paul Farhi, *Philadelphia Inquirer,* August 10, 2002, posted online under "Media/1999: ABC Paid Lawyer for Lewinsky Interview," at Signs of the Times, www.loper.org/~george/trends/2000/aug/93.html.
32. "ABC Just Can't Justify Paying Interviewee," *Chicago Headliner Club: Chicago Journalist,* August 1999, www.headlinerclub.org/journalist/1999/0899eth.html.
33. Stuart H. Loory, "Pursuit of Profit Hampers Journalistic Standards," *Kansas City Star* (May 8, 1999), Metropolitan sec., p. B6.
34. Fred Fedler, *Reporting for the Print Media,* 5th ed. (Fort Worth, TX: Harcourt Brace Jovanovich, 1993), p. 477.
35. Jennifer Harper, "Sensationalism Calls as 9/11 Anniversary Approaches," *Washington Times,* August 30, 2002, www.washtimes.com.
36. Lucinda D. Davenport, "News Quotes: Verbatim?" Paper presented to the annual meeting of the Association for Education in Journalism and Mass Communication, Portland, OR, 1988.
37. Alan A. Stone, "Political Football," *Boston Review,* April/May 2001, http://bostonreview.mit.edu/BR26.2/stone.html.

38. Tamar Vital, "Who Killed JFK?" *The Jerusalem Post* (January 31, 1992), Arts sec., p. 1.

Chapter 14

1. See Jill Rosen, "High School Confidential," *American Journalism Review,* June 2002, www.ajr.org, and "Editor Suspended from Duties for Advertising Web Site Following Dispute over Censored Article about Teacher Arrest," Student Press Law Center, September 27, 2002, www.splc.org.
2. Karen Miller, "Smoking Up a Storm: Public Relations and Advertising in the Construction of the Cigarette Problem, 1953–1954," *Journalism Monographs* 136, (December 1992).
3. Harold L. Nelson and Dwight L. Teeter Jr., *Law of Mass Communications: Freedom and Control of Print and Broadcast Media,* 4th ed. (Mineola, NY: Foundation Press, 1982), pp. 189–190.
4. Harold L. Nelson and Dwight L. Teeter Jr., *Law of Mass Communications: Freedom and Control of Print and Broadcast Media,* 2nd ed. (Mineola, NY: Foundation Press, 1973), pp. 26–27.
5. William Boot, "The Pool," *Columbia Journalism Review* (May/June 1991): 24–27; Chris Hedges, "The Unilaterals," *Columbia Journalism Review* (May/June 1991): 27–28.
6. Bruce M. Owen, *Economics and Freedom of Expression* (Cambridge, MA: Ballinger, 1975); Stephen Lacy and Todd F. Simon, *The Economics and Regulation of United States Newspapers* (Norwood, NJ: Ablex, 1993).
7. James W. Tankard Jr. and Kate Pierce, "Alcohol Advertising and Magazine Editorial Content," *Journalism Quarterly* 59 (Summer 1982): 302–305.
8. Lauren Kessler, "Women's Magazines' Coverage of Smoking Related Health Hazards," *Journalism Quarterly* 66 (Summer 1989): 316–322, 445.
9. Lacy and Simon, *The Economics and Regulation of United States Newspapers,* p. 106.
10. Bill McConnell, "Radio Giants Want More Turf," TVinsite, April 8, 2002, www.tvsite.com.
11. Kalpana Srinivasan, "Cable Rates Rise Despite Competition," detnews.com, January 15, 2002, www.detnews.com.
12. Laura Jett Krantz, "Cable Rates Rising for Second Time This Year," tylerpaper.com, September 28, 2002, www.tylerpaper.com.
13. Alicia C. Shepard, "High Anxiety," *American Journalism Review* (November 1993): 20; *Facts about Newspapers 1998* (Vienna, VA: Newspaper Association of America, 1998), p. 36.
14. Ted Pease, "Race, Gender and Job Satisfaction in Newspaper Newsrooms," in *Readings in Media Management,* Stephen Lacy, Ardyth B. Sohn, and Robert H. Giles, eds. (Columbia, SC: Association for Education in Journalism and Mass Communication, 1992), pp. 97–122.
15. Bob Worthington, "Personnel Management Concerns for Media Managers," in *Readings in Media Management,* Stephen Lacy, Ardyth B. Sohn, and Robert H. Giles, eds. (Columbia, SC: Association for Education in Journalism and Mass Communication, 1992), pp. 201–217.

16. *Near v. Minnesota,* 283 U.S. 697, 51 S.CT. 625, 75 L. ED. 1357 (1931).
17. Bill McConnell, "FCC's Top Enforcer Now Says It's Up to Stations to Disprove Complaints," TVinsite, March 4, 2002, www.tvinsite.com.
18. David B. Caruso, "U.S. Can't Force Libraries to Use Net Porn Filters," *Detroit Free Press* (June 1, 2002): 6A.
19. Jean Folkerts and Dwight L. Teeter Jr., *Voices of a Nation: A History of Media in the United States,* 4th ed. (Boston: Allyn and Bacon, 2002), p. 319.
20. Noelle Straub, "USA Patriot Act Powers Prompt Second Look," *The Hill,* May 1, 2002, www.hillnews.com.
21. Ruth Rosen, "The Day Ashcroft Censored Freedom of Information," *San Francisco Chronicle,* January 7, 2002, Common Dreams News Center, commondream.org.
22. David Lieberman, "Piracy or Fair Use?" *Lansing State Journal* (April 23, 2002): 6C, 7C.
23. Jube Shiver Jr., "Hollywood Lobbies for Stricter Copyright Rules," *Chicago Tribune* (March 22, 2002): 4:1 & 5.
24. Donald M. Gillmor, Jerome A. Barron, Todd F. Simon, and Herbert A. Terry, *Mass Communication Law: Cases and Comment,* 5th ed. (St. Paul, MN: West Publishing, 1990), p. 172.
25. Gillmor et al., *Mass Communication Law,* p. 173.
26. *Cherry v. Des Moines Leader,* 86 N. W. 323 (Iowa 1910).
27. *Virginia State Board of Pharmacy v. Virginia Citizens Consumer Council, Inc.,* 425 U.S. 748, 96 S. CT. 1817, 48 L. ED.2D. 346 (1976).
28. Nelson and Teeter, *Law of Mass Communications,* 2nd ed., p. 517.
29. Alfred McClung Lee, *The Daily Newspaper in America* (New York: Macmillan, 1937), pp. 314–316.
30. Gillmor et al., *Mass Communication Law,* pp. 525–526.
31. David Ho, "Most Weight-Loss Ads Deceptive, Study Finds," *Lansing State Journal* (September 18, 2002): 7C.
32. Michael Katz, "Pay Cable Tops Violence Ranking," *Broadcasting & Cable* (February 12, 1996): 22.
33. S. Robert Lichter, et al., "Hollywood Cleans Up Its Act," Center for Media and Public Affairs, March 2002, www.cmpa.com.
34. Molly Ivins, "Curbing Free Speech," NewsMax.com, January 18, 2000, www.newsmax.com.
35. Kent R. Middleton and Bill F. Chamberlin, *The Law of Public Communication,* 3rd. ed. (New York: Longman, 1994), p. 128.
36. Donald M. Gillmor, Jerome A. Barron, Todd F. Simon and Herbert A. Terry, *Fundamentals of Mass Communication Law* (Minneapolis/St. Paul, MN: West Publishing, 1996), p. 121.
37. Charles Layton, "The Information Squeeze," *American Journalism Review,* September 2002, www.ajr.org.
38. Stephen Labaton, "A Lone Voice for Regulation at the FCC," *The New York Times* (September 30, 2002): C1–C4.

Chapter 15

1. See Melvin L. DeFleur and Sandra Ball-Rokeach, *Theories of Mass Communication,* 5th ed. (New York: Longman, 1989), pp. 29–43.

2. Robert K. Avery and David Eason, *Critical Perspectives on Media and Society* (New York: Guilford Press, 1991), pp. 3–6.

3. Pamela J. Shoemaker and Stephen D. Reese, *Mediating the Message,* 2nd ed. (New York: Longman, 1996).

4. Ronald E. Taylor, "Qualitative Research," in *Mass Communication Research,* Michael Singletary, ed. (New York: Longman, 1994), pp. 265–279.

5. Robert S. Fortner and Clifford G. Christians, "Separating Wheat from Chaff in Qualitative Studies," in *Research Methods in Mass Communication,* 2nd ed., Guido H. Stempel III and Bruce H. Westley, eds. (Englewood Cliffs, NJ: Prentice Hall, 1989), p. 379.

6. This project is discussed in John J. Pauly, "A Beginner's Guide to Doing Qualitative Research in Mass Communication," *Journalism Monographs* 125 (February 1991): 16–21.

7. Earl Babbie, *The Practice of Social Research,* 6th ed. (Belmont, CA: Wadsworth, 1992), pp. 27–48; and Paul Davidson Reynolds, *A Primer in Theory Construction* (Indianapolis, IN: ITT Bobbs-Merrill Educational Publishing, 1971), pp. 3–11.

8. Norman K. Denzin, "The Logic of Naturalistic Inquiry," *Social Forces* 50 (December 1971): 166–182.

9. George Gerbner and L. P. Gross, "The Scary World of TV's Heavy Viewer," *Psychology Today* (April 1976): 41–45, 89; and Werner J. Severin and James W. Tankard Jr., *Communication Theories: Origins, Methods, and Uses in the Mass Media,* 3rd ed. (New York: Longman, 1992), pp. 249–250.

10. Paige Albiniak, "Washington Demands Answers," *Broadcasting & Cable* (May 17, 1999): 23.

11. Philip Meyer, *Precision Journalism: A Reporter's Introduction to Social Science Methods* (Bloomington: Indiana University Press, 1973).

12. James Curran, Michael Gurevitch, and Janet Woollacott, "The Study of the Media: Theoretical Approaches," in *Culture, Society and the Media,* Michael Gurevitch, Tony Bennett, James Curran, and Janet Woollacott, eds. (London: Methuen, 1982), pp. 11–29.

13. Harold D. Lasswell, *Propaganda Techniques the World War* (New York: Peter Smith, 1927).

14. Shearon A. Lowery and Melvin L. DeFleur, *Milestones in Mass Communication Research: Media Effects,* 5th ed. (New York: Longman, 1989), pp. 31–54.

15. W. S. Dysinger and Christian A. Ruckmick, *The Emotional Responses of Children to the Motion Picture Situation* (New York: Macmillan, 1933).

16. Carl I. Hovland, Arthur A. Lumsdaine, and Fred D. Sheffield, *Experiments on Mass Communication* (Princeton, NJ: Princeton University Press, 1949).

17. Paul F. Lazarsfeld, Bernard Berelson, and Hazel Gaudet, *The People's Choice* (New York: Columbia University Press, 1948).

18. Bernard Berelson, Paul F. Lazarsfeld, and William McPhee, *Voting: A Study of Opinion Formation in a Presidential Campaign* (Chicago: University of Chicago Press, 1954).

19. David Manning White, "The 'Gatekeeper': A Study in the Selection of News," *Journalism Quarterly* 27 (Winter 1950): 383–390.

20. D. Charles Whitney and Lee B. Becker, "'Keeping the Gates' for Gatekeepers: The Effects of Wire News," *Journalism Quarterly* 59 (Spring 1982): 60–65.

21. Dan Berkowitz, "Refining the Gatekeeping Metaphor for Local Television News," *Journal of Broadcasting & Electronic Media* 34 (1990): 55–68; and John H. McManus, *Market-Driven Journalism: Let the Citizen Beware?* (Thousand Oaks, CA: Sage, 1994).

22. Warren Breed, "Social Control in the Newsroom: A Functional Analysis," *Social Forces* 33 (May 1955): 326–335.

23. Walter Gieber and Walter Johnson, "The City Hall 'Beat': A Study of Reporter and Source Roles," *Journalism Quarterly* 38 (Summer 1961): 289–297.

24. Severin and Tankard, *Communication Theories,* p. 260.

25. National Institute of Mental Health, *Television and Behavior: Ten Years of Scientific Progress and Implications for the Eighties* (Rockville, MD: National Institute of Mental Health, 1982).

26. Philip J. Tichenor, George A. Donohue, and Clarice N. Olien, "Mass Media Flow and Differential Growth in Knowledge," *Public Opinion Quarterly* 34 (1970): 159–170.

27. Severin and Tankard, *Communication Theories,* pp. 230–246.

28. Gaye Tuchman, *Making News: A Study in the Construction of Reality* (New York: Free Press, 1978).

29. Maxwell E. McCombs and Donald L. Shaw, "The Agenda Setting Function of Mass Media," *Public Opinion Quarterly* 36 (1972): 176–187.

30. Wayne Wanta, *The Public and the National Agenda: How People Learn about Important Issues* (Mahwah, NJ: Lawrence Erlbaum Associates, 1997).

31. Elisabeth Noelle-Neumann, "Return to the Concept of Powerful Mass Media," in *Studies of Broadcasting: An International Annual of Broadcasting Science,* H. Eguchi and K. Sata, eds. (Tokyo: Nippon Hoso Kyokai, 1973), pp. 67–112.

32. Dominic L. Lasorsa, "Political Outspokenness: Factors Working against the Spiral of Silence," *Journalism Quarterly* 68 (Spring/Summer 1991): 131–140.

33. W. James Potter, "Cultivation Theory and Research," *Journalism Monographs* 147 (October 1994).

34. Sandra J. Ball-Rokeach and Melvin L. DeFleur, "A Dependency Model of Mass Media Effects," *Communication Research* 3 (1976): 3–21.

35. Severin and Tankard, *Communication Theories,* pp. 247–268.

36. William Grimes, "Life Imitates Movies? Yes, Experts Say," *International Herald Tribune* (December 1, 1995), via Lexis-Nexis.

37. James Carey, *Communication as Culture: Essays on Media and Society* (Boston: Unwin-Hyman, 1989), Chap. 1.

38. Peter Golding and Graham Murdock, "Culture, Communications, and Political Economy," in *Mass Media and Society,* James Curran and Michael Gurevitch, eds. (London: Edward Arnold, 1991), pp. 15–32.

39. Dennis McQuail, J. G. Blumler, and J. R. Brown, "The Television Audience: A Revised Perspective,"

in *Sociology of Mass Communications*, D. McQuail, ed. (Harmondsworth, England: Penguin, 1972).

40. Stephen Lacy and Todd F. Simon, *The Economics and Regulation of United States Newspapers* (Norwood, NJ: Ablex, 1993), p. 28

41. David H. Weaver and G. Cleveland Wilhoit, *The American Journalist* (Bloomington: University of Indiana Press, 1986), pp. 115–120.

42. Shoemaker and Reese, *Mediating the Message,* pp. 63–103.

43. Gieber and Johnson, "The City Hall Beat."

44. Dan Drew, "Roles and Decisions of Three Television Beat Reporters," *Journal of Broadcasting* 16 (1972): 165–173.

45. Ben Bagdikian, *The Media Monopoly,* 4th ed. (Boston: Beacon Press, 1992).

46. Lacy and Simon, *The Economics and Regulation of United States Newspapers*, pp. 131–157.

47. William Blankenburg and Gary Ozanich, "The Effects of Public Ownership on the Financial Performance of Newspaper Corporations," *Journalism Quarterly* 70 (Spring 1993): 68–75.

48. Barry R. Litman and Janet Bridges, "An Economic Analysis of Daily Newspaper Performance," *Newspaper Research Journal* 9 (Spring 1986): 9–26.

49. Shoemaker and Reese, *Mediating the Message,* p. 251.

50. Sandra J. Ball-Rokeach, "A Theory of Media Power and a Theory of Media Use: Different Stories, Questions, and Ways of Thinking," *Mass Communication & Society* 1 (Winter/Spring 1998): 5–40.

51. Sharon Machlis, "Measuring Web Site Traffic," *Computerworld,* June 17, 2002, www.computerworld.com.

52. "Measuring an Exploding Digital Media Universe," *Internet News,* September 30, 2002, www.internetnews.com.

GLOSSARY

3-D: Film technique designed to create a sense of depth. Viewers wore special glasses for viewing.

8-track tape: A plastic cartridge that holds a continuous recording tape. Invented primarily for automobile play during the 1960s, its eight tracks allowed high-quality stereo reproduction in an easy-to-handle cartridge.

35 millimeter: Photographic film that has a frame for exposure 35 millimeters in length. It is used for both still and moving pictures.

A and B pictures: *A* films are usually high-budget films that studios expect to be box-office hits. *B* films are low-budget films designed to make money.

absolute ethics: A code of ethics that allows no deviation from its rules.

accuracy: The reporting of information in context that allows people to understand and comprehend the truth.

Advertising Council: Formed to promote the civilian efforts in World War II, the Advertising Council is supported by advertising agencies and media companies. It conducts advertising campaigns in the public interest.

Alien and Sedition Acts: Federalist laws passed in 1798 to restrict freedom of information. They were used to quell political dissent.

AM: Amplitude modulation attaches sound to a carrier wave by varying the intensity, or amplitude, of the carrier wave.

analog and digital technologies: Analog technologies transform one form of energy into another to transport content. For example, analog broadcast TV changes the actions of actors into electronic impulses that can be carried by the energy waves of the electromagnetic spectrum. Broadcast digital technology transforms the actors' actions into a binary code of zeros and ones, the same code used for computers, that can be carried by energy waves. Digital technologies are more efficient and carry more content for the same amount of energy than analog technologies.

anthology: A favorite television format of the 1950s that consisted of stage plays produced for TV.

apartheid: Strict racial segregation. Usually associated with South Africa's political system that was overthrown in the early 1990s.

areas of dominant influence (ADI): Areas defined by the ratings company Arbitron for purposes of reporting listener data.

art theater: Outlet for films designed for their artistic quality rather than for their blockbuster audience appeal that usually are produced by independent companies rather than by the big studios.

association magazines: Magazines published by various associations to publicize their activities and communicate with their members.

audion: A three-electrode vacuum tube amplifier, which was the basis of the electronic revolution that permitted the development of radio.

bandwidth: A measure of capacity for carrying information.

beats: Beats are regularly covered topics of news such as police and science. Reporters contact sources on a beat regularly to check for events that might be newsworthy. Desks have one or more beats connected with them.

blacklist: A list of individuals compiled with the express purpose of forcing them out of their jobs. Blacklisting was used during the 1950s to label certain individuals as Communists and to force them out of the information and entertainment industries.

blind booking: Marketing strategy common in the 1930s and 1940s that required theaters to book movies before they were produced.

block booking: The practice of forcing a theater to book movies as a package, rather than individually. Declared illegal in the 1940s.

bop: Jazz that developed during the 1940s as a reaction to big band swing music. Usually performed by small groups with fast tempos and conflicting rhythms. Also called be-bop.

breakout boxes: Shorter pieces of information, often direct quotes, that are connected to the larger story being covered. They are used to emphasize specific points and for design relief.

broadband: Fiber-optic cable with the capacity to carry large amounts of information.

broadside: Handbill, also called broadsheet, that was printed only on one side of the paper.

cable modems: Devices used to connect computers to the Internet and other online services that operate through cable, rather than telephone, lines.

capital intensive: A production process that requires a large investment of money.

causation: The process by which one or more factors result in the occurrence of an event, behavior, or attitude. A variety of factors cause human behavior. For example, genetics, parental behavior, peer associations, media consumption, and other factors combine to create certain behaviors in children.

censorship: Restriction of access to information; deletion of information from a story; or refusal to let a correspondent mail, broadcast, or otherwise transmit a story.

channel: A way of transmitting a message from a person or group of people to a person or group of people, e.g., a telephone line or newspaper.

channel noise: Interference in a communication channel, e.g., static on a radio.

chapbooks: Cheaply printed paperback books produced during the 1700s.

checkbook journalism: Paying subjects or witnesses for information or interviews.

Cinerama: Trade name for process that produces widescreen images.

circulation: The number of copies sold by a newspaper during its production cycle (week or day).

coaxial cable: Cable that contains two conductors: a solid central core surrounded by a tubelike hollow one. Air or solid insulation separates the two. Electromagnetic energy, such as television transmission signals, travels between the two conductors.

computer language: An intermediate programming language designed for programmers' convenience that is converted into machine language.

conglomerate: A corporation formed by merging separate and diverse businesses.

contingency plans: Plans designed well in advance to accommodate situations in which the turn of events was unpredictable; such plans help organizations cope with possible undesirable outcomes.

contingent effects: Effects that are caused by contingent, or indirect, variables rather than by the direct impact of media content.

controlled circulation: Technique of sending magazines free to individuals within an industry to increase identification with an organization.

copyright: A law that protects authors, playwrights, composers, and others who construct original works and keeps others from reproducing their work without permission.

credibility: A measurement of how well a journalist or media organization is trusted. If a high percentage of the public perceives a journalist as truthful, that person has credibility.

crier: In ancient Greece and Rome, a person who walked through the streets crying out news to the people. Preceded printed news.

critical approach: Research approach that studies the connections between media and society and the impact of those connections on culture.

crossover artist: A top-selling musical artist in more than one music segment. Country and rhythm and blues often cross over with Top 40 music.

cultural theorists: Scholars who examine the symbolic meaning of media content for the audience.

cumulative weekly audience: The total number of people who listen to radio during a given week in a given market.

Dark Ages of journalism: Period when the republic was formed and reporters and editors were highly partisan in their efforts to build a new political system.

databases: Software for recording statistics. Data can be sorted into categories and reports printed in various forms. Used by businesses that need to sort customers by zip code, for example.

defamation: To misconstrue facts or misrepresent a person in such a way as to lower the individual in the estimation of others.

demographics: Characteristics of an audience for mass media based on age, gender, ethnic background, education, and income.

design: Visual elements, including headlines, photographs, and graphics, organized to make the newspaper interesting and easy to read.

desk: A newspaper department with an editor in charge. Most newspapers, for example, have a city desk and a sports desk.

desktop publishing: Writing, illustrating, and designing publications with a personal computer.

differentiating the product: The process of trying to get the consumer to perceive one product as being different in nature and quality than other products.

dime magazines: Magazines that cost ten cents and appealed to a broad class of readers. These magazines were less expensive than the quality monthlies that preceded them.

dime novel: Cheap, paperback fiction produced in the mid- nineteenth century.

distributors: Companies that help get magazines from the printer to the wholesalers; the people of the movie industry who arrange to engage movies in theaters, then on television.

documentaries: Film or video investigations. Based on the term documents—these accounts document the details of a historical or current event. Often used as a term that implies investigative reporting.

downlink: Transmitting an electronic signal from a satellite to a ground facility.

DSL: Telephone lines that foster extremely fast connections to the Internet and other online services.

e-commerce: The selling of goods and services online.

economies of scale: As the number of units produced at a plant increases, the average cost per unit decreases. This comes about because the company has to invest large amounts of money just to produce the first unit.

editing: The technique of joining pieces of film or of digitally manipulating images in a creative process.

electrotyping: A metal plate used in letterpress printing by coating a lead or plastic mold of the page to be printed.

evidentiary privilege: Rule of law allowing journalists to withhold the identification of confidential sources.

executive privilege: The president's right to withhold information if disclosure might harm the executive branch's functions and decision-making processes.

experiments: A quantitative research method that involves the application and manipulation of a treatment given to groups of people, and then tests the result.

external PR: Messages directed at publics external to the organization.

fair use: Use of a small portion of a copyrighted work by scholars, teachers, or reporters to further enlighten the public.

fakery: Posing that which is false to be true.

fast film: Generic term for the film that photographers use to stop fast action. Does not need long exposure to light to capture the photographic image.

features: Stories that emphasize activities of people instead of "hard news events" such as crime and disasters.

feedback: Signals sent in response to a message. These may be verbal or nonverbal.

fellow travelers: During the period of intense fear of Communism in the 1950s, people in the broadcast and entertainment industry who were unfairly accused of sympathizing with the beliefs of the Communist Party.

fiction factory: Late nineteenth-century publishing of formulaic books, in which publishers dictated story lines.

FM: Frequency modulation attaches sound to a carrier wave varying the frequency of the carrier wave.

focus groups: Groups of individuals representing different interests who are assembled to discuss a topic. A form of research used to get in-depth information, but not information that is representative of an entire audience.

full-power station: A station that reaches a large percentage of households in its market and that must broadcast a schedule of programs.

gatekeeper: A person who controls the flow of information into and through the mass media.

genre: A kind or style of movie.

graphical user interface (GUI): Arrangement on the screen that imitates a desktop.

high fidelity: Reproduction of sound with minimal distortion.

hoax: An act or story intended to deceive; a tall tale; a practical joke or serious fraud.

Horatio Alger story: This story began as a real account of how Horatio Alger worked his way up the social and economic ladder, but soon developed into a term to represent the glorification of individualism in American life.

household penetration: The number of households subscribing to a newspaper compared to the number of potential households in an area.

Hutchins Commission: Commission established in the 1940s to review press conduct. The commission argued that the press should provide intelligence that would enable the public to understand the issues of the day.

hypothesis: A theoretical statement of a relationship between a causing agent and a resulting action, behavior, or attitude.

in-depth interviewing: A researcher selects subjects for study and conducts several detailed interviews at different times.

infomercial: A media message that offers consumer information.

information model: Pattern of behavior for disseminating information as news; incorporates values such as objectivity over partisanship.

infotainment: A blend of information and entertainment. Critics believe such treatments masquerade as journalism and deceive the public.

interactive: Interactive systems involve two-way communication. The information receivers act as senders and vice versa.

interactive television: The ability of computers and TV sets to jointly send messages to and receive messages from the company that provides the television signals. Typically, viewers can access video-on-demand and interact with program hosts and audiences in studios.

internal PR: Communication within the various units and between individuals of the organization.

Internet: A linkage of thousands of academic, government, and commercial computer sites created when the U.S. government saw the need for an emergency communication system. Computers are tied together through special high-speed telephone lines.

investor relations: Communication with those who invest in the company, that is, those who buy stock.

joint operating agreement (JOA): An agreement that allows two newspapers in the same city to operate the business and production sides of a newspaper together in a fashion that normally would violate antitrust law.

joint product: Term economists use when one production process serves two markets. For instance, the process of printing magazines serves readers in the consumer market and companies in the advertising market.

journalistic balance: Providing equal or nearly equal coverage of various points of view in a controversy.

jump music: Small band music that merged swing and electric blues during the late 1940s. Jump developed into rhythm and blues music.

kilobyte: A measure of memory size equal to 1,024 bytes.

kinetoscope: A boxlike mechanism used to view short films during the late 1800s. The viewer looked into an opening and watched film move past a lightbulb.

limited speech: Speech that is not widely disseminated.

lobbying: Persuading legislators and other government officials to enact or support legislation favorable to one's cause.

market economy: An economy in which the interaction of supply and demand determines the prices of goods and services and the levels of production. In a nonmarket economy, government determines prices and production.

market niche: Portion of the audience a particular magazine gains as subscribers or buyers.

markets: Markets are geographic areas in which businesses and consumers exchange goods and services for money. *Major markets* include a metropolitan area and have many media choices; *outstate markets* are removed from metropolitan areas but are not rural and include some diversity in media choice; *isolated markets* include rural areas with limited media choices.

market segments: The target audience. The group of individuals a magazine selects to target for its readership.

mass advertising: Advertisements that aim to reach the largest number of people possible.

mass media: A form of communication (radio, newspapers, television, etc.) used to reach a large number of people.

media kit: A collection of information about a particular event or person, such as a recording release. The kit can include text, photographs, audiotapes, and even computer discs and CD-ROMs.

media mix: Consumers' use of a variety of media, such as newspapers, television, and the World Wide Web.

mercantile press: Early American newspapers that served businesses, shopkeepers, and tradespeople. These newspapers also contained political news.

microcomputer: A small computer using a microprocessor as its central processor.

minstrel: An entertainer, with blackened face, performing songs and music of African American origin.

model: A diagram or picture that attempts to represent how something works. In communication, models are used to try to explain what happens in the creation, sending, and receiving of a message.

modulator: Device that processes the carrier wave so that its amplitude or frequency varies. Amplitude modulation (AM) is constant in frequency and varies the intensity, or amplitude, of the carrier wave. Frequency modulation (FM) is constant in amplitude and varies the frequency of the carrier wave.

muckraking: Using the journalism of exposure. The term was given to the press by Theodore Roosevelt, who claimed the press "raked the muck" but refused to regard the "celestial crown." Often used as a term for reporting on business.

network: Computers that are connected by communications lines. The computers may be connected within a restricted geographic area, such as a laboratory in a mass communication program. This network is a local area network (LAN). The Internet networks millions of computers worldwide through telephone and fiber-optic lines.

new journalism: Used at different times in the history of journalism. In the 1890s, it defined sensationalism. In the 1960s, the term was used to describe experimentation in reporting strategies and writing styles.

news council: A committee that reviews potentially unethical activities of news organizations.

newsmagazines: Fifteen- to twenty-minute news segments put together to form hourlong electronic magazines such as *60 Minutes* or *Dateline*. These programs combine soft features with hard-hitting investigative reporting.

news service: Organizations that collect and distribute news and information to media outlets. Some professionals still use the term *wire services*.

niche publishers: Small publishing houses that serve very narrowly defined markets.

nickelodeon: Small storefront functioning as a theater; popular about 1910. These preceded the grand movie palaces.

objectivity: Reporting facts without bias or prejudice, including a deliberate attempt to avoid interpretation.

oligopoly: A business situation in which a few dominant companies control enough of the business that each one's actions will have a significant impact on the actions of the others.

ombudsman: A person within an organization who represents customers and investigates potentially unethical conduct of the organization and people within it.

on-air personalities: One of the attractions of radio has been listeners identifying with a personality they tune in to regularly on the radio. Whether the radio host reads the news or announces music, the on-air personality gives a station a singular identity.

open video system: A system that rents entire channels or time on channels to unaffiliated programmers without discrimination.

operating systems: Programs that tell the computer how to behave. DOS and Windows, produced by Microsoft, dominate the world market for operating systems. The Macintosh operating system is second,

used by about one-tenth as many machines as the Microsoft systems.

package deals: A series of media tie-ins.

Panavision: System of lenses used in filming that enabled a film shot in one wide-screen version (Cinemascope, for example) to be shown in theaters without the lenses for that type of projection.

participant observation: Researchers join activities so they can observe research subjects in everyday behavior.

pass-along rate: The total number of readers who read a magazine regularly, including those who read copies that were given, or passed along, to them.

patent medicines: Packaged drugs that can be obtained without a prescription. Before the Food and Drug Administration was created, these drugs often contained large amounts of alcohol and sometimes opium.

perk: Short for *perquisite,* or payment for something in addition to salary.

piracy: Using material without securing appropriate copyright authorization.

pluralism: A school of thought that espouses coexistence and cooperation among different elements of a power structure.

popular government: Government that is controlled by the citizenry rather than an elite cadre of officials.

precedent: A legal decision that sets a standard for how subsequent cases are decided.

precision journalism: The use of social science research methods to generate news stories that emphasize depth and social trends.

press pool: A small group of reporters selected to gather information and pass it on to the larger group of press people. Used when the number of reporters gathering in one spot is problematic.

press release: An announcement of some event, such as a recording release, sent to various news media outlets.

prior restraint: Restricting publication before the fact rather than banning material or punishing an individual after the material is already printed.

professional communicator: Person who selects information from sources and processes them for delivery to an audience.

profit margins: The difference between revenue and expenses.

Progressive generation: Group of individuals in the early 1900s who championed political and social reform.

promotion: Promotion involves the ways a company gains attention for its product or service, including advertising, public relations, packaging, and personal selling.

propaganda: The art of persuasion. Material disseminated by a group or cause to persuade another group of the validity of its own position.

protocol: Content analysis that contains instructions that researchers use to assign units of content to categories that in turn receive numbers. The instructions contain detailed steps every coder must follow.

pseudo-event: An event created solely for the purposes of public relations to gain favorable notice for an organization.

public investment: The buying of stock in a company by the general public.

publicity: The dissemination of information to attract public interest.

publics: The various groups to whom PR professionals address messages. They may be internal or external to the organization.

pundit: An expert on a particular topic; a person consulted because of his or her knowledge.

quantitative content analysis: A quantitative research method that provides a systematic way of categorizing media content and using statistics to analyze patterns in the content.

quiz show: Show on which contestants answer questions that show their knowledge of selected material.

radio frequency: An electromagnetic wave frequency used in radio transmission.

rational thinking abilities: The cognitive processing of information by considering options based on conscious comparison of influencing factors.

right of privacy: An ethical and legal area of decision making. The right to be protected from unwarranted intrusion by the government, media, or other institutions or individuals.

seditious libel: Criticism of the government. In colonial times, such criticism was considered libelous even if it was true.

semantic noise: An interference with communication because of misunderstandings about the meaning of words or symbols.

serialized book: A book printed in parts in a magazine or newspaper over a certain period of time.

socialization process: Reporters learn patterns of behavior by observing others and by learning to recog-

nize the systems of rewards and punishments in a newsroom.

social responsibility theory: As applied to freedom of the press, a philosophy that states that with freedom comes responsibility to the social good.

social science approach: Research approach that emphasizes theory building and quantitative methods for testing theory.

sound bites: A short quotation used on radio or television to express an idea.

specialized publishers: Publishing houses that produce a particular type of book, such as religious or children's books.

spin doctors: Public relations personnel, usually associated with political communication, who try to get journalists and other publics to believe a particular interpretation of an event or information.

spot news: News based on one-time events such as accidents or crimes.

spreadsheets: Software that allows for organization and tabulation of financial data; commonly used in planning budgets.

stand-up shot: Photographs of active people who appear to be news sources or reporters.

stereotyping: The use of a paper mat to make cylindrical molds for printing.

strategic planning: Planning that includes elements designed to work toward a goal.

stringers: Reporters, often at a location remote from the newspaper, who sell occasional pieces at "space rates," or by the column inch.

studio film rentals: Movies produced by studios to rent to distributors and/or theaters.

sunshine laws: Laws requiring that meetings of federal or state administrative agencies be open to the public.

superstation: A station that reaches hundreds of markets throughout the country by means of satellite distribution of a signal to cable systems.

survey research: A quantitative research method that involves randomly selecting a small group of people, called a sample, from a larger group, called a population, and asking them questions from a questionnaire.

swing: Big band music played with a jazz rhythm that was popular during the 1930s and early 1940s. Swing enjoyed a revival during the 1990s.

symbolic meanings: Feelings, thoughts, attitudes, and images associated with symbols, such as words, constitute symbolic meaning. Members of social groups share these symbolic meanings. For example, a cross is a symbol of salvation for Christians.

syncopated beat: The regular metrical accent shifts temporarily to stress a beat that is normally weak. Syncopation is important in African and African American musical traditions and is considered the root of most modern popular music.

syndicated material: Programs made available for sale directly to stations or cable channels rather than distributed by networks to affiliates. Examples are *Xena: Warrior Princess* and *The Oprah Winfrey Show.* Discontinued network shows that have had long successful runs, such as *Cheers,* are also candidates for syndication.

syndicated programming: Nationally produced programming that is supplied to stations through telephone lines and by satellite.

take: One effort to record a piece of music.

targeted advertising: Trying to sell a product or service to a particular group of people.

telecommunications industry: Organizations that are involved in electronic media such as broadcast television, cable, radio, and telephone, or the transmission of information over wires and with satellites.

television network: The radio network system became the model for developing television, and network-affiliated TV stations shared programs. The individual stations, which also produced local programs and sold local advertising, rebroadcast the programs to viewers in a geographic area.

textbooks: Books used for elementary school, middle school, high school, and college classroom work.

textual analysis: A researcher interprets text to find the symbolic form the communicator used to create meaning.

tie-ins: The connection made when a magazine runs a story about a product advertised in the magazine.

trade book: Most mass marketed books sold at bookstores or through book clubs. Excludes textbooks.

trade press: Periodicals that target a specific industry. *Broadcasting & Cable* magazine, for example, targets the broadcast and cable industry and is an example of a trade magazine.

traffic: Department that controls movement of programming through the day, logs what goes on the air, and supplies information for billing advertisers.

transistor: A small electronic device containing a semiconductor. A key component of an integrated circuit that paved the way for portability.

uplink: Transmitting an electronic signal to a satellite for storage or further distribution.

user-friendly: Software that is designed for use by individuals who are not familiar with complex computer languages.

V-chip: An electronic device in a television set that blocks certain television programs.

venture funding: Funding of an enterprise with cash from several investors who are interested in innovative enterprises that carry both risk and the potential for large profits.

vertical integration: A system in which a single corporation controls production (including obtaining the raw materials), distribution, and exhibition of movies. Declared illegal in the 1940s.

wave band: An electromagnetic wave within the range of radio frequencies.

wholesalers: Companies that deliver magazines from a warehouse to dealers, such as bookstores.

wire service: Organizations that collect and distribute news and information to media outlets. Referred to as "wire" because before computer transmission, these services relied on use of the telegraph wires.

world music: Generally used to refer to non-English-speaking musicians singing in their native language. Usually applied to music originating in developing countries. Often songs of protest.

WYSIWYG: Text on a computer screen that corresponds exactly to the printout: What you see is what you get.

zines: Inexpensive magazines produced using desktop publishing programs and usually distributed over the Internet.

zoning: Printing an edition of a newspaper for a specific geographic area (or zone) that has content aimed at that area, usually in a specific section of the paper.

INDEX

Women
    in the movies, 204–205, 216
    in music and recording industry, 310–311
Woodward, Bob, 351, 372
Working at Home, 179
Working Mother, 176
Working Woman, 176
WorldCom, 82
World music, 295–296
WorldSpace, 241
World Trade Center terrorist attacks (2001), 1–2, 6–7, 13,
    23, 326–327, 332, 336, 360, 363, 371, 407
World War I, 11, 384, 410, 425
    newspapers and, 141
    public relations and, 62
World War II, 11, 384
    book publishing after, 118, 119
    computers and, 319
    movies and, 197, 201
    newspapers and, 143

public relations and, 62–63
radio and, 39, 40, 41, 239
television and, 252
World Wide Web, 324, 328, 330, 391–392.
    See also Internet
Wozniak, Steve, 322
Writers Workshop, 404
WYSIWYG, 319–320

Xerox, 108
XM, 243–244

Yellow journalism, 143, 361
YM, 177
Young, Owen D., 11

Zenger, John Peter, 32, 33, 140
Zines, 164, 173–174, 184–185
Zoning, 150